TONY HANCOCK

TONY HANCOCK

The Definitive Biography

John Fisher

HARPER

HARPER

An Imprint of HarperCollins*Publishers*
77–85 Fulham Palace Road,
Hammersmith, London W6 8JB

www.harpercollins.co.uk

First published by HarperCollins*Publishers* 2008
This edition 2009

1 3 5 7 9 10 8 6 4 2

A CIP catalogue record for this book is
available from the British Library

ISBN-13 978-0 00-726678-4

Printed and bound in Great Britain by
Clays Ltd, St Ives plc

For Sue,
with love,
for always being there

The extracts taken from the following scripts are copyright of the writers Ray Galton and Alan Simpson: *Calling All Forces*, *Noah*, the Budgerigar sketch, the Crooner sketch, *The Rebel*, the Regent's Park sketch, *Star Bill*; and episodes of *Hancock's Half Hour* and *Hancock* including: *Ericson the Viking*, *Sunday Afternoon at Home*, *The Alpine Holiday*, *The Blood Donor*, *The Chef that Died of Shame*, *The Diary*, *The End of the Series*, *The Reunion Party*, *The Succession: Son and Heir*, *The Threatening Letters*, *Twelve Angry Men*

The extracts taken from *Educating Archie* and *The Tony Hancock Show* are the copyright of Eric Sykes

'The Dummy Speaks' poem by Roger Caldwell, from *This Being Eden*, Peterloo, 2001

'Judy Garland is Dead' poem by Gerald Locklin, from *Go West, Young Toad: Selected Writings*, Water Row Press, 1997

Hugh Stuckey and Michael Wale, scripts for 'Hancock Down Under'/*The Tony Hancock Special* for Australia's Channel 7, Jan 1972, The Seven Network, Australia

All photographs supplied courtesy of the Tony Hancock estate, with the exception of the following: ABPC/Ronald Grant Archive 14 (bottom left); Allstar Picture Library 13 (bottom left); Alpha Photo Press Agency Ltd 10 (top left), 11 (bottom left); Baron/Getty Images 7 (middle right and bottom right); BBC Photo Library 10 (bottom right), 12 (bottom); Bob Collins/National Portrait Gallery, London 12 (top); Don Smith/Topfoto 11 (bottom right); Edward Joffe 15 (bottom left); Graham McCarter 15 (top and bottom right); Harry Todd/Fox Photos/Getty Images 8 (top); Joan Williams/Rex Features 14 (bottom right); John Pratt/Keystone Features/Getty Images 10 (middle right); PA Photos 11 (top and middle left); Peter Isaac/Fleetway Publications Ltd 16; Popperfoto/Getty Images 6 (top left and bottom), 10 (top right); Ron Case/Keystone/Hulton Archive/Getty Images 7 (top); The Tony Hancock Archives 3 (top right), 3 (bottom), 4 (bottom left), 8 (bottom left), 14 (top right); Topfoto 12 (middle left), 13 (top and middle left)

While every effort has been made to trace the owners of copyright material reproduced herein and secure permissions, the publishers would like to apologise for any omissions and will be pleased to incorporate missing acknowledgements in any future edition of this book.

CONTENTS

Praise for Tony Hancock

Bob Monkhouse: 'His show emptied more pubs than the rise in the price of a pint.'

Denis Norden: 'If he did a show that wasn't up to scratch one week, people would say, "Oh, it wasn't so good this week, but it will be good next week." They believed in him, they trusted him, they had faith in him. They put their hopes in him.'

Dennis Main Wilson: 'He had this incredible presence on stage – you could stand at the back of the stalls looking down on thousands of people and literally see rows of shoulders rocking with laughter. I've never seen anything like it.'

Frankie Howerd: 'A great artist must have sensitivity. He must have some knowledge of suffering … Tony had it. It showed. He never did anything that wasn't real and true.'

Ray Galton: 'He was the most interesting and competent comedian that we've ever worked with, and the most fulfilling.'

Alan Simpson: 'He performed as if he admired what we'd done, which is a great feeling.'

Spike Milligan: 'I think his memorial is that he was a clown – a very great clown – and you can't say more than that of a man.'

Sid James: 'He was an absolute master.'

Praise for John Fisher

Roger Hancock: 'I want it to be the definitive book – as near as you can get to the truth – and you are the person to write it.'

LIST OF ILLUSTRATIONS

Section One

ACKNOWLEDGEMENTS

The writing of this book would not have been as rewarding without the support, encouragement and friendship of Roger Hancock, the surviving brother of its subject. His willingness to cooperate for the first time in such a venture, not least in sharing with me personal and at times painful memories and in placing at my disposal his family archives, cannot be conveyed in words. The warm hospitality provided by his wife Annie and the backing given by his son Tim also demand my gratitude. In addition, the story of Tony Hancock is inseparable from that of his two key writers, Ray Galton and Alan Simpson. I am especially indebted to them for their help and cooperation at all stages, a sentiment that extends to their dedicated manager Tessa Le Bars. I am equally grateful to our national comic treasure Eric Sykes, who played such an important part in formulating the Hancock persona during its early years, and his manager Norma Farnes for their friendship and generosity. Of key importance in defining many of our favourite memories of Hancock is his working relationship with the actor Sidney James. His widow Valerie was characteristically gracious in answering my questions and I extend my affectionate thanks to her also.

The incentive to write was further endorsed by the willingness of many people to share with me their memories and opinions of its subject over an extended period that embraced the profile of this great comedian in my earlier book *Funny Way to be a Hero* and editions of my *Heroes of Comedy* series for Channel Four, in which I celebrated not only Tony Hancock, but also Sidney James. Those to whom I owe a distinctive debt in this regard include Brad Ashton, Peter Brough, Paula Burdon, Ronald Chesney, Steve Coogan, David Croft, Barry Cryer, Russell Davies, Clive Dunn, Ronald Elgood, George Fairweather, Bruce Forsyth, Liz Fraser, Sir Peter Hall, Lady Doreen Harland, Sir Reginald Harland, Patricia Hayes, Damaris Hayman, Roy Hudd, Eddie Joffe, John Junkin, Miriam Karlin, Joan Le Mesurier, Moira Lister, Hugh Lloyd, Paul Merton, Sir Spike Milligan, Bob Monkhouse, John Muir, Denis Norden, Barry Norman, Philip Oakes, Phyllis Rounce, Derek Scott, Sir Harry Secombe, John Sessions, Graham Stark, Hugh Stuckey, Frank Thornton, Lyn Took, Beryl Vertue, Michael Wale, Dennis Main Wilson, June Whitfield and Duncan Wood.

Many others have enhanced my knowledge and understanding of my subject or have advanced the progress of this book in different ways. They include Ray Alan, Roger Allan, Joan Allum, Dame Julie Andrews, John Archer, Tom Atkinson, Hermione Baddeley, Michael Bailey, Kenneth Baily, Ronnie Barker, Jean Bartlett, John Beaver, Laurie Bellew, Alan Bennett, Eric Bentley, Michael Billington, Peter Black, Horatio Blood, Nancy Bratby, Bob Bray, Alec Bregonzi, John Bretton, Richard Briers, Lord Asa Briggs, Mel Brooks, Ivor Brown, Chris Bumstead, Anthony Burgess, Hugh Burnett, Max Bygraves, Gay Byrne, Roger Caldwell, Patrick Cargill, Dick Cavett, Jonathan Cecil, Soo Chapman, Simon Cherry, Levent Cimkentli, Russell Clark, Dr. William Cloverly, Sid Colin, Lee Conway, Alistair Cooke, Alan Coren, Len Costa, Sir Bill Cotton, Mark Cousins, Mat Coward, John A. Cunningham, Peter Dacre, Jim Dale, Stanley Dale, John Howard Davies, Clifford Davis, Dabber Davis, Michael Dean, Sarah Domellof, Ed Doolan, Roy Dotrice, Charlie Drake, David Drummond, Valentine Dyall, Jimmy Edwards, Richard Emanuel, Dick Emery, Martin Esslin, Richard Fawkes, Geoff Felix, Elizabeth Few, Dick Fiddy, Matthew Field, Bryan Forbes, Andy Foster, Eric Frankland, Stephen Frears, Alan A. Freeman, Catherine Freeman, John Freeman, Sir David Frost, Stephen Fry, Steve Furst, Eric Geen,

Larry Gelbart, Stan Gibbons, Denis Gifford, Brian Glanville, Peter Goddard, Peter Goodwright, Michael Grade, Barry Grantham, Gerry Gray, Hughie Green, Carl Gresham, Damon Hammonds, Jonathan Hammonds, Peter Harding, Andy Harries, Rolf Harris, Trish Hayes, Celia Helder, Peter Hennessy, Fay Hillier, Robina Hinton, Mary Hobley, Richard Hoggart, Bernard Hollowood, Frankie Howerd, Angela Ince, Virginia Ironside, Ken Irwin, Jack Jackson, Mary Jacobs, Hattie Jacques, Sidney James, Sue James, Derek Jameson, Brian Johnston, Philip Jones, Ted Kavanagh, Bill Kerr, Michael Kilgarriff, Nigel Knight, Johnny Ladd, John Lahr, John Le Mesurier, Bernard Levin, David Lewin, Henry Lewis, Mark Lewisohn, Gerald Locklin, Pamela W. Logan, Colin MacInnes, David Mamet, Marcel Marceau, Billy Marsh, Steve Martin, Freda Maud, John Maud, Roddy McDowall, Joe McGrath, Tony Medawar, Andy Merriman, Gerry Mill, David Mills, Warren Mitchell, Andrée Melly, John Moffatt, Joe Moran, Sally Mordant, Angela Morley, Harry Morris, John R. B. Moulsdale, Frank Muir, Brendan Mulholland, Barry Murray, Nan Musgrove, David Nathan, Patrick Newley, Fred Norris, David Nunn, Ray Nunn, Peter Oakes, Bryan Olive, John Osborne, Robert Ottaway, Elsa Page, Sir Michael Parkinson, Nicholas Parsons, Bertie Pearce, Gale Pedrick, Bill Pertwee, Roy Plomley, Michael Pointon, Gareth Powell, J. B. Priestley, Philip Purser, Jeff Randall, Peter Read, Ralph Reader, Nigel Rees, Dee Remmington, Charles Reynolds, Regina Reynolds, Wally Ridley, Ken Robins, David Robinson, Leonard Ross, Willie Rushton, Stephen Russell, Sidi Scott, Neil Shand, Nancy Banks Smith, Elsie Sparks, Janet Spearman, Larry Stephens, Jeremy Stevenson, John Styles, Sylvia Syms, Alan Tarrant, Jacques Tati, Weston Taylor, Terry-Thomas, David Thomson, John Timpson, Mike Tomkies, Barry Took, Al Tunis, Alwyn W. Turner, Joan Turner, Michael Turner, Kenneth Tynan, Raoul Vaneigem, John Wade, Ronnie Waldman, John Watt, Colin Webb, Fay Weldon, Vic Weldon, Len Whitcher, David Wilde, Kenneth Williams, Peter Wilson, Sir Norman Wisdom, Ronnie Wolfe,

Andrea Wonfor, David Wood, Chris Woodward, Francis Worsley, Graham Young and Donald Zec.

All writers owe some debt to those who have explored their territory before them. Hancock's stature within British comedy is confirmed by the fact that since his death no less than eight volumes have been dedicated to aspects of his life and career, excluding the many issues in book form of selected scripts written for him by Ray Galton and Alan Simpson. *Hancock* by Freddie Hancock and David Nathan (William Kimber, 1969) and the monograph by Philip Oakes on Tony Hancock in the series *The Entertainers* (Woburn Press, 1975) provided essential background information. At a more specialised level, Richard Webber's *Fifty Years of Hancock's Half Hour* (Century, 2004) gave a useful overview of the radio and television show from the perspective of the relevant files within the BBC Written Archives. At a more personal level, both Joan Le Mesurier and Eddie Joffe have written of Hancock's last few years from their individual viewpoints. *Lady Don't Fall Backwards* (Sidgwick & Jackson, 1988) and *Hancock's Last Stand* (Book Guild, 1998) respectively address his declining years with a combined candour and affection that will not surprise those who know them both. Above all, no work on Hancock can fail to acknowledge the detailed research carried out by Roger Wilmut in his *Tony Hancock – Artiste* (Eyre Methuen, 1978). As has become accepted practice, unless I have specified otherwise, I have in this work used the titles assigned by him to the individual episodes of Hancock's radio and television series. A less academic approach to the Hancock story can be found in the same author's *The Illustrated Hancock* (Macdonald, 1986). The last of the eight volumes, *When the Wind Changed* by Cliff Goodwin (Century, 1999), needs to be approached with circumspection. Nevertheless the timeline of Hancock's career at the end of the book – although itself not without inaccuracies – is useful as an initial point of reference.

A similar measure of Hancock's impact and ongoing importance may be measured by the devotion of his many present-day admirers.

From the inception of this project, the members and officers of the Tony Hancock Appreciation Society – details of which may be found at www.tonyhancock.org.uk – have been unstinting in their support. I should like to make special mention of the contribution made by Clare Burman, Andrew Clayden, Mike Roberts, Peggy Roberts, Cyrilla Rogers, Ray Rogers, Lesley Hidden and Elaine Schollar. The time and energy dedicated to the society by its long-standing President, Dan Peat, is prodigious, and I thank him for the personal kindness he has extended to my wife and myself on our visits to THAS functions. This is matched by the help and attention extended to me by the society archivist Keith Mason, whose energy and scholarship inspired me at some of the more torturous moments of my undertaking. Fellow member and Goon Show historian Mike Brown kindly shared with me his original research on the life of Hancock's early writing partner Larry Stephens.

No less rewarding was the input given to this volume by Jeff Hammonds and Malcolm Chapman. Their combined knowledge of the subject of Hancock is awe-inspiring, and the enthusiasm with which they applied themselves to aid my efforts at all stages of the writing process fills me with gratitude. At a more specific level, Malcolm's scrupulous research into Hancock's early life and school-days, and Jeff's kindness in providing me with obscure but important sound and video items from his collection, are both acknowledged with thanks. Individually they hold two of the most comprehensive archives of material on Tony Hancock extant, the resources of which are now being shared with a wider audience through their shared website, which may be found at www.tonyhancockarchives.org.uk.

Other resources and institutions that proved of major help to research were the Family Records Centre and the General Register Office of Great Britain; Bournemouth Reference Library; the BBC Written Archives Centre at Caversham Park, Reading; the British Film Institute; the Performing Arts Collection within the

Westminster Reference Library, St Martin's Street, WC2; the Newspapers Division within the British Library at Colindale, NW9. The service provided both by Janet Dolan at the Service Personnel and Veterans Agency, Thornton-Cleveleys, Lancashire, and by Martin Tomlinson of Officers' Records, RAF Disclosures, at RAF Cranwell was as meticulous as it was helpful. The film archivist and researcher Cy Young made special efforts to educate me in the more recondite aspects of Hancock's film career as well as guiding me around the intricate labyrinth provided by the television audience research processes that were in operation during his television years. Among other kindnesses, Colin and Pauline Burnett-Dick, the current guardians of Archie Andrews, made available to me Peter Brough's original script files of the radio series, *Educating Archie*. The celebrated broadcaster Alan Whicker shared with me his memories of Hancock's last in-depth interview in this country, filmed for his series *Whicker's World*, but for reasons explained in the text – where it is quoted with his permission – never used. Also valuable were other interviews with my subject from publications as diverse as the *Australian Woman's Weekly*, the *Birmingham Evening Mail*, *Chance* magazine, the *Daily Express*, the *Daily Mail*, *Films and Filming*, the *Glasgow Sunday Mail*, the *News of the World*, *Nova*, *Planet*, the *Radio Times*, the *Scottish Daily Mail*, the *Scottish Sunday Express*, the *Sunday Dispatch*, *Television Mirror*, *Television Weekly*, *Tit-Bits*, the *TV Times* and *Weekend*. A unique bonus was provided by the discovery of an unpublished typescript in Hancock's own words dating to 1962. It runs to ninety-four pages and it is impossible to tell whether it was intended for magazine publication or was envisaged as a preliminary draft for a more detailed autobiography to be expanded at a later date. It is quoted from in the foreword and extensively within my text, where it is often referred to in the latter context.

I'd like to extend my gratitude to all those who have kindly granted permission to reproduce the various extracts that appear in this book. While every effort has been made to trace the owners of copyright material produced herein, the publishers would like to apologise for any omissions and will be pleased to incorporate missing acknowledgements in any future editions provided that notification is made to them in writing.

I shall be forever grateful to Trevor Dolby for kick-starting this project and to Chris Smith of HarperCollins for subsequently taking up the baton. The subsequent editorial process has been made easier by the kindness and skills of my editor Natalie Jerome, as well as by managing editor Simon Gerratt, and all the team at Fulham Palace Road, including Colin Hall, Kay Carroll, Louise Connolly and Graham Holmes. Once again I owe an enormous debt to my agent Charles Armitage at Noel Gay Management. His advice, friendship and encouragement sustained my muse throughout this undertaking. I also thank his associate Di Evans for her contribution.

As my opening pages will show, Tony Hancock helped to define my childhood. The laughter he evoked then was shared with my parents James and Margaret Fisher and my sister Ann. My love for them is entwined in every line that follows, as is that for my wife Sue and my daughters Genevieve and Madeleine, whose care and understanding as I set about my task knew no bounds.

FOREWORD

Sid James used to claim that he learned his lines during the television commercials. That was always a sore point with me, a plodder who takes about three hours to learn one page. All the time I sweated over my own script, going through what I call my hair shirt routine, I imagined Sid looking up from a cornflakes advertisement and saying, 'Hmm … yes, I've got that,' and I could have killed him.

I shall always remember the day I went to Pinewood to watch him playing a part in Chaplin's picture *A King in New York*. He had a foolscap page and a half of dialogue to learn. He handed it to me and said, 'Give us a run through, will you?' I rehearsed it with him a couple of times and by then he was word perfect.

I was lucky to get on the set at all. Chaplin liked to work on his film behind locked doors and it was a long time before his production assistant would admit me into the fortress. All I wanted to do was to watch a genius at work, and seeing *A King in New York* come to life under that man's magic touch was an unforgettable experience. His vitality was astounding. He seemed to be everywhere at once, directing a scene here, playing in one there, and never sitting down for a moment.

Now *there* is a man who knew all along exactly where he wanted to go and got there. Without aspiring to be another Chaplin, I hope I shall be able to look back on my career and say the same.

Tony Hancock, 1962

Preface

'REMEMBERED LAUGHTER'

*'For a comedian to leave behind that kind of echo
of remembered laughter – it is hard to think of
his life as a complete tragedy.'* Denis Norden

He would have relished the fact that by Coronation Year his name
had been immortalised in a dirty joke. As a performer he renounced
smut at an early age, but years later my school playground rallied to
the cheeky charade of which his idol, Max Miller, would have been
proud. Four deft pats on their respective body parts posed the question – 'Who's this?' – and said it all. 'Toe – knee – han' – cock!' The
playground, then as now, knew no taboos. We all performed it out of
bravado. And it is reassuring to learn that while he never allowed his
professional funny side to stray into the *double entendre* terrain of
seaside comic postcards colonised by the great Maxie himself, nevertheless from an early age 'the lad himself' would have been at the
harmless vanguard of such fun.

I had the edge over the other members of my peer group in that
I had seen our eponymous hero with my own two eyes. Hancock first
became crystallised in the national consciousness by the radio comedy series, *Educating Archie*, starring ventriloquist Peter Brough
and his dummy Archie Andrews. No sooner had the programme tak-
en wing than Brough was touring the variety theatres with a stage
show capitalising on its success. In November 1951 the pair arrived

to spend a week at my local theatre, the Gaumont in Southampton. To a small child fast approaching seven years of age Archie was a real live boy, as genuine as any who would share that playground joke a year or so later. I prevailed upon my parents to take me to see my idol in the 'flesh'. The parade of acts that preceded Brough's ventriloquial turn stays etched in my memory to this day: Ossie Noble, a clown of antic finesse, able to fling an unruly deckchair across the stage in such a way that it stopped just short of the wings in perfect sitting position; Edward Victor, a hand shadow artist who secured the biggest applause of the evening with his *pièce de résistance*, a silhouette of Winston Churchill puffing at his cigar; Ronald Chesney, a virtuoso harmonica player with the uncanny knack of making his instrument talk; and a young girl singer hitting the high notes with, I now realise, a vocal control unusual for her years, Julie Andrews. The last two were regular members of the radio cast, as was the comedian on the bill, Tony Hancock.

It seems appropriate now that, on the show that introduced me to the delights and serendipity of variety, he should be there. Outside of the pantomime, he was the first comedian I saw perform on a theatre stage, and he set the standard thereafter. To those whose memory of Hancock is geared to his later *Hancock's Half Hour* success, this performance would have been a total surprise, a triumph of visual athleticism as he threw himself into a series of impersonations of the sportsmen who featured in the opening titles of the *Gaumont British Newsreel*, preceded by a display of miming skill as he jerked and contorted his hands and arms and legs into an impression of an increasingly rampant robot to illustrate the song he was singing. When a few years later the theatre critic Kenneth Tynan outlined his concept of high-definition performance, he might have had Hancock in mind, although at the time all I cared about as he created physical patterns that seemed to linger in the air was the pain of laughter in my side.

Personal experience tells me that our favourite funny men inspire a loyalty that other entertainers seldom achieve. As

Hancock's career gathered momentum and prestige, he came to define the era of his greatest success – my childhood and teen years – with almost Proustian exactness, while his comparative fall from critical grace during the 1960s seemed to make its own comment upon a harsher and more cynical world. Only something transcending mere nostalgia can account for the emotional tug of war that his staunchest fans experienced as we observed the highs and lows of his career. When the slide set in, comedy – however brilliant Howerd and Steptoe and Pete & Dud proved to be – never seemed the same again. One was always waiting for Hancock to dazzle in a way that would cap the achievements of his rivals, but it never truly came. When I heard the news of his death in the summer of 1968, the hollowness of the moment seemed to say that we, his public, had failed him, that he had never been repaid for the great years. This book is an attempt to redress that debt.

Of the volumes produced on the life and work of Tony Hancock in the years following his demise, none has possibly made the impact of the first, a memoir by his second wife, Freddie Ross Hancock, written in association with that astute journalist David Nathan and published a stark year after his death. Temporarily the book, a frank and honest account of the troubles that beset the comedian down the years as well as a wider biographical treatment, turned its subject into basest clay. Emerging from a sheltered childhood protected by the enduring love of my parents' marriage, I experienced the chill of disappointment to discover that the man I revered had been possessed by unconsidered demons. His apparent inconsiderateness and cruelty, awash in the dregs of an alcoholic despair, were nothing if not distressing to me at so impressionable an age. The book had been a gift from my parents and I recall wanting to keep it from them, so sensitive was I to the alienating aspects of its subject as he was depicted therein.

Maturity teaches that there exist the two clichéd sides to any story. In time I discovered that all star performers are marionettes whose strings are drawn upwards by the public's expectation of them, whether on stage or off. We tend to place a burden on the object of our admiration that at times places honesty off limits. But the candour of Nathan's text may have been self-defeating. In subsequent years the Hancock biographical record has not been helped by much that has been speculative and sensation-seeking. The doom and gloom of the final act of the story has always suggested a tragedy with few, if any, mitigating features, while in the years since his suicide in Australia in 1968 the myths have cohered and clung like barnacles to the hull of his reputation. It has therefore been rewarding to discover for much of the time a lighter, happier, even ordinary Hancock as the veils of my research have lifted; also a performer who managed to succeed for so long despite his innate insecurity, rather than someone who failed because of it. The alcoholic excess and its attendant troubles clouded only the last few years of a spectacular career, while, as Roger Wilmut, zealous chronicler of the Hancock career in all media, has pointed out, he was capable of giving fine stage performances far away in Melbourne as late as 1967. Forty years on he continues to stand tall as arguably the greatest British comedian of my lifetime. Certainly in terms of the broadcast media it is impossible to think of anyone who has subsequently surpassed his achievement. There was little that was funny about his insatiable desire for perfection and the self-doubt that came in its wake, but the sorrow at the end has to be balanced by the utter delight of a nation in his comic skills. As Denis Norden, the doyen of British comedy scriptwriters, has said, 'For a comedian to leave behind that kind of echo of remembered laughter – it is hard to think of his life as a complete tragedy.'

Few comedians have affected the lives of their public in the way Hancock did. Even today it is impossible for a member of his audience to realise they have forgotten to cancel the newspapers while on holiday, to endure the agonies of the common cold, to be bored senseless on a Sunday afternoon, to get stuck in a lift, to donate blood, without enjoying again the bonus of the laughter he created when he found himself in those circumstances. In these contexts Norden's phrase 'echo of remembered laughter' becomes especially relevant. Moreover even today the thought of what Hancock would have said or done in a particular situation provides a constant pick-me-up at moments of mounting frustration as bureaucracy and technology take more and more of a stranglehold on our lives. In this way he exercised – and continues to exercise – a strong emotional pull over his audience. It is the great paradox of his story that one to whom life became unbearable in its last few years should forty years after his death continue to make life bearable for others.

Chapter One

THE IMAGE OF HANCOCK

'I was always trying to make life a little less deadly than it really is.'

Seldom has a comic persona played a more tantalising tug-of-war with the character of the individual behind the mask than in the case of Hancock. It was Denis Norden again who voiced the opinion that rather than write a succession of scripts for Hancock, Ray Galton and Alan Simpson found themselves writing a novel, so fully rounded was the character they refined and defined while writing in excess of 160 radio and television *Half Hours* over a period of seven momentous years. Even had they set out to think this way – which they didn't – they could have had no idea they were inadvertently compiling a virtual biography of their colleague at the same time. Irrespective of the extent to which the world view, mind-set, spoken idiom of the Hancock character belonged to the performer in real life, it is remarkable to discover that so many of the pivotal aspects of the Hancock saga and mythology are foreshadowed in their words. While they obviously did not create the man with all his problems and complexities, many of which still had to reveal themselves after they parted company professionally, there was, as we shall discover, scarcely a twist or turn in Tony's corkscrew of a career that wasn't pre-empted with spectacular – albeit involuntary – prescience by Alan and Ray, and sometimes poignantly so.

All great comedians from Chaplin and Keaton to Cooper and Tati have understood the idea of personal branding. With Hancock the process evolved more gradually through his collaboration with two scriptwriters of brilliance, until the outer trappings of the character they created together proved too constricting to bear and he attempted to change direction, ultimately parting from them, having already revised his wardrobe and locale. Nevertheless their shared creation is how he is most fondly remembered, and his portrayal of it remains his greatest achievement. This is the Hancock of his BBC years, from the start of the classic series on radio in 1954 until the last modified episode on television in 1961. There was much else on the credit side, a dazzling amount, including his earlier radio work, two feature films, more television of variable but not entirely negative quality, and a stage repertoire upon the extent of which many a lesser talent has fashioned an entire career. But the BBC was where most would say he belonged. It has even been said that the institution has ended up more like him than its former self. 'The BBC is the corporate equivalent of Tony Hancock,' observed Jeff Randall, the financial journalist, in the *Daily Telegraph* recently. 'Full of talent but riddled with self-doubt.' In Hancock's day Auntie certainly seemed more assured of her identity, in spite of – even because of – the burgeoning competition from the commercial television sector. There was then a creative climate in which all associated with Hancock drew strength.

Half a century after his heyday there can be no disputing the earlier dominance of the individual whose dodgy initial aspirate could be seen as the template for the television aerial fast becoming attached to every rooftop in the nation, the technological icon of a new age. Comparisons with his contemporaries in the broadcast media are as irrelevant as applying the process to Chaplin's place in the history of the cinema. *Hancock's Half Hour* remains both pioneer and benchmark when the British situation comedy is discussed. Hancock represents the archetypal British telly comedy character, his single surname carrying the totemic resonance of that show business elite that includes not only the little tramp, but Garbo and Bogart and Sinatra too. To my knowledge no other performer has been featured as often as seven times on the front cover of the flagship listings magazine, the *Radio Times*, six times during his short career and once posthumously. A correspondent to the *New Statesman* a short while after his death said it all. Having mislaid his passport on his return from Geneva, the writer became ensnared in a dialogue with a testy immigration officer at Heathrow. 'Where do you live, sir?' asked the official. 'Cheam.' 'And what does the name Hancock mean to you?' 'But that's East Cheam,' countered the traveller. 'You can go through,' came the response. 'No one who knows that could be anything but British.' All was right with the world again.

It is sometimes difficult to accept that the character moulded by Galton and Simpson for Hancock had its origins in radio. It seems to have been tucked away in the visual folk memory of the nation, sharing space with intrinsically British icons like Mr Pickwick and John Bull, for far longer. And yet only in 1956, by which time as a radio show *Hancock's Half Hour* had been triumphant for three series, did it transfer to the television screen and the combined instinct of writers, producer, wardrobe mistress and star conjure up the grandiose Homburg hat and oppressive black coat with its astrakhan fur collar that defined the pretensions and pomposity of his character as securely as the frock coat, cigar and painted moustache had summed up Groucho's aspirations to upward mobility for another era. Already Hancock the man and Hancock the entertainer shared the physique that epitomised the sagging melancholy that contributed to his comic *tour de force*. 'I look like a bloody St Bernard up the mountain without a barrel' was a line that would creep into his act. The hunched shoulders, crumpled clothes, deflated stance – like a punctured Michelin Man recast as a sorry failure for a scarecrow – all made their morose contribution to one of the symbolic figures of the twentieth century. Within a short while the image had resonance for radio listeners as well. In an episode where Hancock is courted by Madame Tussaud's, the waxwork technician played by Warren Mitchell knows exactly the look he is after. With all good reason he sees the model in astrakhan collar and Homburg, spats and patent-leather shoes. Hancock protests that this is merely his 'walking out gear'. He envisages his look-alike in a more casual, homely pose: 'silk dressing gown, cigarette holder, Abyssinian slippers, Cossack pyjamas and a fez'. Curiously our preconception of the first makes the second image funnier, since everything you need to know about the man, the catalyst for the laughter, is contained in the basic brand.

If any physical aspect defined the man it was his feet. He had the exact measure of them. 'My feet don't seem to be with me,' Tony muttered to one interviewer. 'They're living a separate existence. They've been put on all wrong. They don't join the ankle properly. Sometimes they feel as if they're flapping like penguin flippers.' Poise was never on the agenda at the comic academy, but it irked him just the same. 'Let's face it,' he admitted to his friend Philip Oakes, 'I look odd.' When Oakes's basset hound produced puppies he refused the offer of one as a pet. Someone had pointed out the similarity between his own feet stuck at their quarter-to-three position and the splayed paws of the animal. 'Can you just see us trotting along together?' he queried. 'They'd be entering me for Cruft's next.' If his feet were something of an obsession with Hancock, Galton and Simpson were only too happy to latch on to the characteristic. In one episode, having failed the driving test for the seventy-third time, Hancock protests, 'Me feet are too big – that's the trouble. They overlap I put me foot on the brake, half of it goes on the accelerator as well and we're off again!' On another occasion Sid James surprises Tony with his nickname from the time he supposedly served in the Third East Cheam Light Horse, 'Kippers Hancock'. He is nonplussed that Sid could have known this, but as James explains, 'With your feet what else could they call you?' They were, in fact, a normal size 8½ and the man, not his writers, should be given the final word on the subject: 'I feel as though I've got the left one attached to my right leg and the right one attached to the left leg. Quite horrible. If you examined my feet closely, you would see they were only good for picking up nuts.'

Jacques Tati claimed that comedy begins with the feet up, and if so Hancock might appear to have had it made from day one. The fact remains, however, that his greatest physical asset was his face. What his body lacked in definition was compensated for by the quicksilver precision of his features, capable of conveying every single nuance of the human condition with ease. Boredom, frustration, worry, exasperation, misery, insomnia, complacency all became funny when Hancock registered them, not least because of the skill with which he could appear so effortlessly to pick them out of the ether. At odds with the sagging jowls and the baggy eyes, he could transmit the subtlest thought with a simple twirl of a lip, the merest quiver of a cheek. On occasions the eyes defied you to tell him what he was thinking. You knew and laughed and he didn't even have to speak. In many ways he was sited on a line equidistant between Chaplin and Buster Keaton, combining the chameleon flexibility of one and the abstract quality of the other. The unfortunately named 'stone face' of Keaton, upon which cinema-goers were able somehow miraculously to project their feelings, may have something to do with it. However, the comic effect he could achieve with the laugh that simmers, the frown that explodes, the word unspoken that came to the tip of his tongue to be swallowed almost instantly were totally Hancock's and Hancock's alone.

His facial prowess made him absolutely right for the emerging medium of television, but that fact only serves to underline that Hancock's initial claim to attention was as a radio presence. At all stages of his career it helped that he had a voice that sounded as he looked. As we shall discover, the Hancock of *Educating Archie* sounded totally different from that of the performer remembered today. His microphone voice became modified considerably over the years, but once it found its natural level, consistent with the naturalism he and his writers were anxious to cultivate in comedy, it was hard to imagine him speaking in any other way. Plump, rounded and listless, given to sudden explosions of protest or triumph, it conveyed everything about the look and the attitude of his complex character. The emphatic caution with which he pronounced the aspirates of the title of his show – 'H-H-H-H-Hancock's Half Hour' – dated from the very beginning of the radio show in 1954 and the device became a vocal calling card that firmly set the mood for each episode.

It is a paradox of the Hancock phenomenon that while he remained indisputably recognisable, understandably inimitable, he nevertheless proved well-nigh impossible to impersonate. The irony of the last radio script that Galton and Simpson wrote for him is that it revolved around the premise of someone who could do so successfully and in so doing take from the character profitable work in a television commercial that the lad deemed beneath his dignity. In this episode, the variety impressionist Peter Goodwright made a fair stab at the task and succeeded to a degree, but something was missing, even in sound alone. In later years Mike Yarwood would don the Homburg and astrakhan collar, but the impression always seemed stillborn, lacking the freedom and *joie de vivre* that he and others achieved with the likes of Cooper, Dodd, Morecambe, Howerd and all the other comic icons from and around the same period. The answer may reside partly in public perception. In Cooper and company we – and that means Yarwood on our behalf – saw uninhibited Masters of the Revels to whom in a Saturnalian moment we all wished to aspire: who hasn't waved an imaginary tickling stick, or donned a makeshift fez and, arms outstretched, fumbled his way through a cursory attempt at 'jus' like that'? On the other hand, in Hancock we saw our basic selves and perhaps thought best to leave well alone. The subtler, lower register of the Hancock voice did not help either, nor did the depth of the character as portrayed by the writers who shifted the personality of the man they knew up a gear or two to bring about their marvellous shared creation. It is ironic that one of the weaknesses of that character should be an irresistible urge to drop into impersonation at the drop of a hat, in his case the Chevaliers, Laughtons and Newtons of a bygone Hollywood age.

For all Hancock would cling to exhibitionist tendencies fashioned in another era, no comedy show caught more astutely the social history and culture of its own day, as its hero came to terms with the new prosperity to emerge from the post-war gloom, the new consumerism, the new media consciousness. Its only contender to any sort of crown in this regard was radio's *The Goon Show*, the anarchic comic explosion that sounded like a verbal hybrid of freak show and firework display played out in celebration of our accumulated imperial past. But for all its energy, invention and a three and a half year start, it was less accessible than *Hancock's Half Hour* and, in spite of varying attempts, had the disadvantage of being impossible to translate to television. It needed to be heard. Its four original chief protagonists – Michael Bentine, Spike Milligan, Harry Secombe and Peter Sellers – had recently, like Hancock, been catapulted out of the armed forces into performing careers that would have seemed impossible when hostilities began. All knew each other socially. If one concedes to Milligan the creative advantage, it is feasible that had the comedy pack been shuffled in a different way Hancock could have ended up in the first show in lieu of one of the other three performers. Both programmes shared the same producer, the wiry and dynamic Dennis Main Wilson, and Milligan's co-writer in the early days, Larry Stephens, was an even closer friend of Tony and the author of the bulk of Hancock's stage material. Moreover, Hancock had still properly to formulate his views on naturalism in comedy, a quality that amounted to anathema in the parallel universe of the Goons. Both shows in their contrasting ways drew regular comic inspiration from the folk memory of a conflict that now seems so distant and yet in those bleaker times loomed like an unwelcome ghost in people's lives.

Hancock the man had served in the RAF. Hancock the character, being all things to all men, had, albeit in tall-story-dom, served on all fronts. In the episode where he gets stuck in a lift he describes himself as an old submarine man, to whom the confined space of the moment is a mere bagatelle. When the vicar, played by Noël Howlett, retorts that he thought he had just said he had been in the army, Hancock, resourceful as ever, claims that he was actually attached to a Commando unit being transported by submarines to blow up the heavy-water plants in Norway: 'Very tricky stuff, heavy water, very tricky. Have you ever handled it?' For another episode he had spent the hostilities punishing the Hun high in the clouds: 'Did me victory roll over Hendon airport picking up packages off the tarmac with me wing tips. Nerves of steel – 144 missions and never turned a hair!' Most memorably, when asked at the blood donor clinic whether he has given before, his imagination spiralled into new levels of derring-do: 'Given, no. Spilt, yes. Yes, there's a good few drops lying about on the battlefields of Europe. Are you familiar with the Ardennes? I well remember von Rundstedt's last push. Tiger Harrison and myself, being in a forward position, were cut off behind the enemy line. "Captain Harrison," I said. "Yes sir," he said. "Jerry's overlooked us," I said. "Where shall we head for?" "Berlin," he said. "Right," I said, "and the last one in the Reichstag's a sissy!"' However outrageous, such reminiscences not only provided the perfect platform for the overblown conceit of the character; they also resonated with an audience to whom much of his swagger touched upon reality.

The Hancock character has been rightly described as 1950s man, a Charlie Chaplin for the Welfare State. For all he might rattle on about his vainglorious past, the present provided the real challenge. Long before the character reached television, the public could visualise perfectly the world he inhabited. Rationing may at long last have been heading for the 'exit', but we should not be deluded by nostalgia. Britain was still a pretty grim place, and his writers' evocation of Hancock's home base, the seedy side of sprawling suburbia epitomised by East Cheam, only served to make it even grimmer. Not for nothing did the philosopher Henri Bergson chide that to understand laughter we must put it back into its natural environment, 'which is society'. Hancock's specific address at 23, Railway Cuttings signified grime and austerity. One could never quite imagine the sun shining through the soot that persisted in the damp, dank air; never envisage the streets entirely free of potholes and puddles. Hancock's disaffection was perfectly captured in the depiction of a National Health Service that for all its promise was rapidly becoming overstretched: when he goes to the doctor to cure his cold, only to find the medic can't even help his own, he pontificates, 'I don't pay ten and threepence a week to cure you!' Not that he was without a chippy optimism, born of the patriotism that was his life's blood. Even Hancock expected things to get better, that he would arrive, in the words of one fan, the film director Stephen Frears, at a sunlit upland where he would be treated with the right degree of respect and have a comfortable life. He certainly knew his priorities, ever ready with a Churchillian swagger 'to strike a blow for the country that gave us our birthright, our freedom, our parliamentary democracy and our two channelled television set'.

Hancock had the full measure of the new ITV – 'Just like the BBC, but with advertisements instead of breakdowns!' – just as Galton and Simpson had their grip on the consumer revolution that would provide the rose-tinted panacea for the times. The recognition sparked and enlivened the comedy. Their scripts soon became a repository of marketing lore for subsequent generations. Hancock proved a sucker for the 'individual fruit flan', 'the drink on a stick', 'the flavour of the month'. Only hours before his shows members of the audience would have been purchasing such commodities, the thought of laughter far from their minds. But on the next trip to the supermarket, the next treat at the cinema, the product would register and produce a second laughter response, 'remembered laughter' on a shorter time scale. When he goes to the movies himself, the lad is more anxious to see the advert where the toffees wrap themselves up and jump into their cardboard box than the main feature. At times his aspirations seem defined by the process. When his character shows ambitions to be a chef, it is to enable him to have his picture on the buses holding up a packet of salt; when leading man parts fail to come his way, he remains hopeful that the actor playing the old retainer who holds the barley water can't last forever; his cricketing dream has less to do with playing for England than taking Denis Compton's place on the hair cream ads. One of the most brilliant sequences ever enacted by Hancock was the running commentary on London at night as he sits side by side with Sid on a bus ride to the big city. The posters, the shops, the neon signs come to life as he peers through the window provided by the television screen and explodes with enthusiasm at the two scruffy kids sniffing gravy, the sea lion pinching the zookeeper's Guinness and the animation provided by a myriad of light bulbs that announces the arrival of Piccadilly Circus. This has long had him puzzled: 'I always thought there was a little bloke behind with a big bag of shillings belting up and down working a load of switches!'

In his engrossing survey of such matters, *Queuing for Beginners*, social historian Joe Moran has shown how the cheap free gift in the cereal packet became the symbol of the tacky promises of consumerism. An episode where Hancock fights a by-election as a Liberal candidate is made doubly funny by a subplot featuring his obsession with finding the elusive trumpet player to complement a full band of plastic guardsmen given away with cornflakes. Another ruse entailed sending in a requisite number of packet-tops for a supposedly free gift. In a parallel scenario – well before 'salvage' was made fashionable in the green interest as 'recycling' – Hancock bemoans his absence once again from the New Year's Honours List and resolves that never again will he put his country first by sacrificing his cereal packets to the paper cause: 'Never again! They can whistle for their salvage in future. I'm gonna stock myself up with

Davy Crockett hats and bus conductor sets and assorted scenes from *Noddy in Toyland*. We'll see who's the loser in the long run.' But a social tide had turned and it was all about winning. The relatively cheap accessibility of foreign travel and entertainment, the easy automation of household tasks, the national obsession with football pools and newspaper competitions were all symbolic of a new acquisitiveness. Sometimes the character became confused along the way. Who can forget him in the launderette transfixed by the swirling display through the window of the washing machine and then sneaking a look over his neighbour's shoulder: 'I'm not interested in your washing – just thought you were getting a better picture on yours, that's all.' Nothing escaped the Hancock experience. Not for nothing was 'you never had it so good' – a phrase we shall come back to – described as the 'token' phrase of the new era.

Coping with the new shallow affluence was only one aspect of people's lives that attracted Galton and Simpson. There was little in keeping with the times that bypassed them, even if they claimed years later that they were too busy working to notice the parade as it passed by their office window. They could almost have had a hotline to Mass Observation, the organisation that during the middle years of the century set out to record everyday life in Britain through a formal programme of observation and research. The later television show set in the bedsitter in which Hancock tediously, from his point of view, edges himself through another humdrum day might pass as a parody of one of the movement's completed questionnaires – or 'day surveys' as they were called – if it were not so true. Nothing was not noted down, however mundane it might seem. One can imagine Hancock's log: lay down, smoked cigarette, tried to blow smoke rings, did exercises, burnt lip, looked for ointment, applied butter instead, did impersonation of Maurice Chevalier, and on and on. One atypically appreciative newspaper article described the process as 'a searchlight on living' and it was taken seriously in many quarters. In recent years the archive has illuminated the era, but one questions whether it has done so more effectively than the accumulated observation of two brilliant scriptwriters and their unparalleled interpreter.

The Belgian philosopher Raoul Vaneigem might have had the measure of the phenomenon when he commented, 'There are more truths in twenty-four hours of a man's life than in all the philosophies.' Hancock's character would have devoured the remark. His eager quest for easy knowledge was a doff of the Homburg to the *Reader's Digest* cum *Teach Yourself* culture of the day. This reached comic heights as he struggled between Bertrand Russell and the dictionary in that same bedsit episode, before concentration plummeted and he took refuge in a whodunnit, *Lady, Don't Fall Backwards*. The lad's conversation is peppered with tortured quotes and gaffes of schoolboy-howler horror. When John Le Mesurier's plastic surgeon describes a potential model for Tony's new nose as 'aquiline', Hancock's response is, 'That means you can use it under water, doesn't it?' But there is no consistency: '"This is a far, far better thing I do now than I have ever done" – Rembrandt!' is compounded at a later date by the double sting in the tail of 'Did Rembrandt look like a musician? Of course she didn't!' Often the character displayed an ornate use of language totally out of sync with the times, but entirely in keeping with the holy grail of self-education. As he prepares to get ready for a night on the town, he declares, 'Time the peacock showed his feathers, I fancy.' But then in no time at all we are brought down to earth by the uncouth slang of 'ratbag', 'bonkers', 'stone me!' and 'a punch up the bracket'.

The turgid posturing is not the stuff of youth culture, and it is so easy to forget how young they all were. When *Hancock's Half Hour* first went on air, its star was only thirty – albeit it has been said he was born middle-aged – and its two writers a mere twenty-four. The point is that at certain levels the show tapped into the preoccupations of the young in an amazing way. Young people had at last discovered that they had the money that had always been denied them, to use now at the time of their greatest energy and vigour. In one early radio show Hancock found himself in a dance hall of the time, the sequence now as secure an evocation of its era as it is possible to imagine. Characteristically our hero is unimpressed. When Bill asks him what he thinks of the Palais, he replies he feels 'like Marty standing here', a reference to the eternal wallflower portrayed in Ernest Borgnine's current film hit. It is never the intention that Hancock should fit in: 'I'm fed up with this chewing gum – I nearly swallowed it three times – swinging this perishing key chain's getting on me nerves.' In an impressive cameo Bill Kerr later departs from his usual characterisation to play a convincing version of the Marlon Brando streetwise hoodlum who sends panic through the dance hall. 'I've never seen a hokey cokey break up so quickly in me life,' observes Tony. But at other times he was more than content to frequent the frothy coffee outlets, the protest marches, the beatnik milieu.

Many have commented that the decade of *Hancock's Half Hour* was also that of *Look Back in Anger*, that Hancock corresponded to a comic version of Osborne's Jimmy Porter, an angry – or at least frustrated – young man in a *faux* middle-aged shell. In one of the less typical radio episodes, *The East Cheam Drama Festival*, a third of the show is dedicated to a pastiche entitled *Look Back in Hunger* by John Eastbourne. As an exercise it is superficially funny, but in many ways redundant. Galton and Simpson through Hancock, their mouthpiece, were the comic complement to everything Osborne and his contemporaries represented. Porter was the first to rail at the excessive boredom of the British Sabbath – 'God, how I hate Sundays! It's always so depressing, always the same.' Galton and Simpson took the disaffection and made it into arguably their most successful radio half hour. But there was never a sense that they were parodying the earlier work, nor were they consciously doing so. Even their most accomplished television script for the comedian, *The Blood Donor*, was pre-empted by Porter's query, 'Have you ever had a letter, and on it is franked, "Please Give Your Blood

Generously"?' When Porter, in an attempt to explain his supposed non-patriotism, declaims, 'We get our cooking from Paris, our politics from Moscow and our morals from Port Said,' we can almost hear the voice of Hancock and it becomes funny – or funnier – when we do. If one sets aside the emotional undertow of the play, there are passages – not least the more verbose monologues – that would become hilarious if Hancock were enacting them, in the same way that long swathes of Galton and Simpson dialogue would lose much comic lustre if performed by straight actors with no thought of comedy on their agenda. It is all in the perception.

While Hancock may share Porter's feisty indignation, for all his bluster he lacks his overriding self-confidence. Jimmy always knows he is right. Hancock is never too sure. He may rail at the petit-bourgeois whim for having plaster ducks on the wall, while knowing full well he has them on his own. As the television critic Peter Black pointed out, 'A deeper aspect of this was that he perfectly well knew it: the best part of the Hancock creation was his stoical acceptance of himself. He knew in his heart he was doomed.' We certainly never knew which way he would turn. Conned by the consumer giveaway culture in one episode, in the next he can be talking like an ombudsman: 'Ten packets of that muck! Do less damage taking your shirts down to the river and bashing them with a lump of rock.' He is punctilious as he sets out his stance to the vicar at the tea table: 'I'm no snob. It's just that I think that if people expect to sit down at high-class tables, they can at least take the trouble to learn how to conduct themselves in a proper and mannerly fashion.' Then, after a pause, 'If you're not having any more tea, can I pour my grouts in your cup?' One of nature's committed aristocrats one moment – his rare blood group is enough to convince him of that – the shabby keeping up of appearances becomes his very life force the next. Forced by circumstances to a menu of bread and dripping for Sunday lunch, he hastens to draw the curtains lest the neighbours should see a man of his calibre (always with the stress on the middle syllable) reduced to such means. As a comic icon he was and remains classless, and not merely because he succeeded in cutting across all demographic barriers. If one could have cloned Hancock a couple of times, only his size would have held him back from enacting all three parts in that classic sketch that featured John Cleese, Ronnie Barker and Ronnie Corbett. The conceit, like the idea of living in a classless society, is, of course, an illusion, one Hancock and his writers understood only too well.

Once entrusted with their task by producer Dennis Main Wilson and script editor Gale Pedrick, Galton and Simpson proved themselves magicians of the deftest skill in the way in which week in, week out they rang the changes on the character and his circumstances. Sometimes he was affluent; sometimes he had only one shirt to his name. Sometimes he was a failed theatrical, sometimes the successful star of a radio or television comedy series. Sometimes he was a law-abiding member of the community, sometimes an army deserter who had lain low in a cave on the Yorkshire Moors for six years. Sometimes the continuity might appear suspect, but the almost dreamlike flexibility never stood in the way of the naturalism in comedy which all three set out to achieve at the start. As Alan Simpson has commented, 'He was what we wanted him to be at any given time. That was the great freedom one had in those days. On one show we had him as a barrister. Nobody commented on the fact that you need seven years training, you need diplomas. Nobody cared.' Anyone asked in an over-the-top television quiz to name a top racing driver who in his spare time was a purveyor of quack medicines, who had served in the Foreign Legion and whose grandfather had been a member of 'The Three Tarzans' music-hall act, could do worse than hazard a guess at the personage of Anthony Aloysius St John Hancock, to give the character its full monicker. The question might as easily have been to nominate the derring-do test pilot who was stolen from his cradle by the gypsies, went on to inherit his great-uncle's newspaper empire and ended up living as a hermit on

Clapham Common. They both tick all the boxes. The Hancock invention was its own Pandora's Box of possibilities.

Even later when he discarded the Homburg and fur collar the inner man somehow remained constant. Simpson uses the attitude to food and France to show how the character could paradoxically live within his own contradictions: 'One week he would say, "I can't stand that foreign muck. I want sausage, egg and chips." And the next week he'd be *haute cuisine*: "I don't eat that rubbish. Bring on the sea bass." If he met an intellectual he might try to keep up with him or dismiss him with "what a load of old rubbish!" Never throw away a good joke – it all relies on what you think of.' The approach gave them full rein to present Hancock as Everyman for the twentieth century. In time he was acclaimed 'a massive caricature of mid-century man'. According to Philip Oakes, the comedian rather fancied the title. Every possible foible, every potential flaw was refracted though the persona. No comic has succeeded more admirably in making us laugh at our own fears, failures and insecurities. While Bob Hope majored on cowardice, Jack Benny on meanness and vanity, John Cleese on a manic paranoia, Tony Hancock was all our sins personified. Long ago Galton and Simpson described the character as 'a shrewd, cunning, high-powered mug'. Roger Wilmut was more comprehensive in his cataloguing: 'pretentious, gullible, bombastic, occasionally kindly, superstitious, avaricious, petulant, over-imaginative, semi-educated, gourmandising, incompetent, cunning, obstinate, self-opinionated, impolite, pompous, lecherous, lonely and likeable fall-guy'. Only a few redeeming qualities there, but then the funniest traits will always be the weaknesses.

That said, Hancock wasn't just likeable – he was loved. His neuroses, grumbles and hang-ups were endemic in the larger proportion of his potential audience. As Philip Oakes has said, 'He was truly representative and so he could be excused,' right down, it would appear, to the murderer that lurks in us all. When he needs the cash to match a bet that he cannot go one better than Phineas Fogg and travel around the world in less than eighty days, he shows his shady resolve: 'I'll get the money. I've just remembered I've got a great grandfather up in Leeds – of a very nervous disposition. I think a good strong paper bag popped behind him should see me all right.' He isn't joking. On one occasion his attitude to Bill Kerr, humbled into carrying out some repair work underneath Hancock's motor car, is positively sadistic: 'I've a good mind to jump on his ankles. I'd love to see him spring up and hit his head on the big end.' His disposition to petty larceny pales by comparison: when Richard Wattis checks his card at a hotel reception desk he soon discovers an outstanding issue from last time, 'a little matter of four towels, a tea service and an ashtray'. The cleverness of the casting and character of Sid James as the great swindler rampant in Hancock's life was that Tony himself was just as questionable in the honesty stakes. It was totally in character that he should be less successful at iniquity, although in one episode, *The Scandal Magazine*, he *is* revealed as being more corrupt than Sid. James is the editor who has the Chief Constable and the Director of Public Prosecutions in his pocket. After Hancock clears his name and wins a king's ransom in damages, it soon emerges that the initial exposé on his sordid dalliance with a cigarette girl was not without foundation.

That may have been an extreme case. As Dennis Main Wilson explained, 'The beauty of it was that you could identify him not with yourself, but with your Uncle Fred or your next-door neighbour. Johnny Speight gave the objectionable characteristics to Alf Garnett, but much more harshly, much more cruelly, in a much later, crueller world. We did the Hancock shows in a much happier world.' At least they appeared to become happier as the new prosperity took hold. The analogy with Alf Garnett, as immortalised by actor Warren Mitchell, is significant, reminding one that much about Hancock would now be considered sexist, racist and politically incorrect. Much of his sexist disgruntlement was directed at the buxom and bounteous Hattie Jacques, in her radio role as the mountainous secretary Miss

Griselda Pugh. When she is too busy to take a letter because she is knitting herself a jumper, Hancock acknowledges the fact: 'Of course. I saw the lorry bringing the wool in this morning.' When she is conscripted into service as a teacher at the school Sid has coaxed him into opening, she suggests adding 'Cantab' after her name, to which Tony responds, 'No. I think Oxon would be better for you.' In the music-hall era his comments would have been labelled 'fat' jokes. Here they serve the comedy of characterisation and produce some of his biggest laughs. When the similarly endowed Peggy Ann Clifford boards a crowded bus, he refuses to offer her his seat: 'You wanted emancipation. You got it. Stand there and enjoy it.' In the last television show Galton and Simpson wrote for him, he curtly dismisses one of the candidates for his hand in matrimony: 'I can't imagine her staying at home all day mangling.'

When Tony wishes to show solidarity with Sid he slaps him on the back with a triumphant, 'Sid, you're a White Man. When they made you, they threw away the mould.' In the blood donor clinic the question of his nationality brings out a primitive nationalism: 'Ah, you've got nothing to worry about there ... British. Undiluted for twelve generations. One hundred per cent Anglo-Saxon with perhaps a dash of Viking, but nothing else has crept in ... You want to watch who you're giving it to. It's like motor oil. It doesn't mix, if you get my meaning ...' As Ray and Alan have observed, in those days no one batted an eyelid at material that would today be considered squirm-inducing: there were other things to worry about, not least 'the threat of annihilation by a nuclear holocaust'. It was also a time when ordinary decent people were unconsciously fed the prejudices that emanated simply from feeling different from what they were not. And who is to say that the expression of such a difference could not then be channelled in the direction of comedy?

Hancock, as a gauge for the human condition and the worst excesses of its folly and aspirations, remains timeless. However, now – or in a hundred years' time – it is conceivable that anyone from another time or place wanting an inkling of what it was like to live in the Britain of the 1950s could do worse than listen to *Hancock's Half Hour*. It is certainly significant that as the man for his day he should reflect the three key prime ministers of the decade as colourfully as he did. We have already seen he was capable of a sly impression of Churchill when the mood took him. The bulldog image fitted all his own delusions of political grandeur, although these were not given full rein until May 1955 when in one episode Galton and Simpson exchanged No. 23 for No. 10, at least in Hancock's dreams, by which time another Anthony, namely Eden, had been in office for two months. His espousal of the Homburg as his favourite headgear first reached television screens in July 1956, the month that Eden, with whom the style had long been associated, was confounded by Nasser's nationalisation of the Suez Canal Company. Hancock later claimed, 'Homburg hats have always struck me as the acme of self-importance.' Most significantly Hancock's peak period coincided with the period of office of the politician dubbed by Enoch Powell as the last of the old actor-managers, Harold Macmillan. If Galton and Simpson have a fondness for one facet of the Hancock characterisation, it is for the faded thespian reduced to dragging his threadbare cultural offerings to the far reaches of the kingdom. That tedious train journey to the Giggleswick Shakespeare Festival readily comes to mind. Later when Hancock finds himself reduced to appearing in a commercial for pilchards he sighs for the past: 'Oh for the days of the actor-manager, me own theatre and that [the thumb goes to the nose] to all of them.'

Away from the political arena Denis Norden's notion of the 'Hancock' canon as a novel sends one scurrying for literary parallels. The naïve, pompous, lower-middle-class Pooter from the George and Weedon Grossmith comedy classic, *The Diary of a Nobody*, is an obvious link. Significantly it began life as a *Punch* column, a device not a million miles away from the half-hour situation comedy device of sixty years later. Here the house in suburbia again backs onto a railway line, the curate calls, albeit not played by Kenneth Williams, and social aspiration dictates the life of the chief resident. A more complex character is Kenneth Widmerpool from Anthony Powell's *A Dance to the Music of Time*. Military man and politician in a way that Hancock could only pretend to be, he is revealed by turns through a twelve-volume cycle as villain and victim, manipulator and fool in a way that chiefly serves to remind us of Hancock through the sympathy Powell manages to engage on his behalf, from his very first appearance at school wearing 'the wrong kind of overcoat'. At times pompous to the point of ridicule, he gets by like Hancock, blustering against fate, cushioned by speeches of windy verbosity. A more light-hearted literary character has an equal claim to be considered Tony's alter ego. In formulating the Hancock character Galton and Simpson found themselves reversing the anthropomorphism of Kenneth Grahame's enduring creation from Toad Hall. In a television interview, Bill Kerr catalogued the similarities: 'The bluster, the pomp, the dignity, the frailty.' But more than that he looked like Toad. Once in a while television companies raid the current stock of familiar comic faces to cast the classic afresh. It is a tragedy that nobody gave Hancock the chance. Bubbling over with his own self-importance, all airs and graces, he would have made it impossible for another actor to follow in his amphibious tracks. To hear Toad rhapsodising on the prospects of motor travel, one might well be travelling with Hancock, tooting along on the open road to the Monte Carlo rally in one of his early radio shows: 'The poetry of motion! The *real* way to travel! The *only* way to travel! Here today – in next week tomorrow! … O poop-poop!' They could have changed places. The thought of 'Toad's Half Hour' and a dressing room with his name on the door would have puffed up the creature's ego even more.

Of course, Hancock had the advantage over any fictional character in that on television he could look you in the eyes. As Duncan Wood, his principal television producer, said, 'He looked like a beaten-up spaniel – even if the dog bites you, you still pat it on the head again.' Alan Simpson risked stating the obvious on the matter: 'He was a very sympathetic performer. Certain people on television – irrespective of how good they are – if they don't like the look of you, you're dead. The character of Hancock was such a terrible failure at everything he did, everybody felt sorry for him, even though he was very arrogant, very pompous.' But there was another quality. For all he may have played a 'mug', and an often unpleasant one at that, there always bubbled beneath the surface of his BBC portrayal a level of charm, intelligence, not to mention enjoyment in the task at hand. Intuitively an audience picks up on such qualities and subconsciously enters a sharing game with the performer. It was partly in the words, but it was entirely in the playing. Dennis Main Wilson, who knew the man as well as anybody professionally, once said that 'to be a great clown you have to have vulnerability and indeed humility and if you ain't got them as a clown, you ain't gonna be a star – no way!' In its inner self the great British public sensed this in spades.

In time this book will address how much of the Hancock image was rooted in reality, how much the fictitious accretion for laughter's sake alone. For the moment it is enough to know that Hancock himself had the full measure of what was going on. As was so often the case, it seemed to come back to the feet. He told a reporter on the *Coventry Evening Telegraph*, 'You can't get away from it – underneath the hand-made crocodile shoes, there are still the toes.' He saw the pretensions with which people clothed themselves as the key to his humour, his role being to puncture them. Six years later that was still his credo. In an interview in *Planet* magazine he explained, 'What I portray is what I find pretentious in myself and others. I play up pretensions, pomposity and stupidity in order – I hope – to destroy them. Who first decides about the position of the little finger when you're drinking a cup of tea? Or who first decided the correct way to hold your soup bowl? Let's say we did a comic skit where two people had a great barney about the right way to hold a soup bowl, showing up the stupidity of the whole thing. After the show the audience might go somewhere for a meal and remember the skit when they started on the soup. The impression might not last very long, but it would be there.' It is reassuring to know that he and presumably Alan and Ray were ahead of Denis Norden on that one. But he was always at pains to point out the one thing he was not. As he emphasised to Russell Clark on Australian television a few months before he died: 'I wasn't a little man fighting against bureaucracy. This is nonsense. I was always trying to make life a little less deadly than it really is, and a lot of it was extremely belligerent comedy.' As Philip Oakes noted, 'Hancock, far from being the classic figure of the clown (that is, he who gets slapped) was the first to slap back.' But there was always the suggestion of uncertainty in the aggressiveness. It was inevitable in the case of a character that wanted the whole world and yet had no means of achieving it except on the cheap.

Chapter Two

'YOU'LL GO FAR, MY SON'

'A double feature, half a bar of Palm toffee,
and three and a half hours in the dark –
that was my idea of fun.'

He always claimed that his earliest recollection was of an egg timer. Later in life he went on record as being able to boil 'a very good three-and-a-half-minute egg without having to glance at my watch once'. Eggs, with the attendant 'soldiers' to dip into their soft-boiled interiors, would provide a comfort factor – and at one point a professional windfall – in a life that began as Anthony John Hancock at 41 Southam Road, Hall Green, Small Heath, Birmingham, on 12 May 1924. The more grandiose middle names met in the previous chapter were the stuff of comic fiction. The house with its bay windows and turreted chimneys was the sturdy type of semi-detached that helped to define the identity of the British lower middle class between the wars and beyond. The 'lower' may be misleading in that the Hancocks were able to afford a nanny and a cook, whom Tony remembered as 'a painfully thin woman who, no matter how much food she consumed, never put on a single pound'. The Hancocks were the original residents of the dwelling purchased new for the sum of £400 shortly after the arrival of their first son, Colin, in March 1918. By the time of Tony's birth his father, John Hancock, had progressed in status to branch manager for the Houlder Brothers steamship line, which he had joined as a messenger boy in 1900, although his heart beat faster when he applied himself to his avocation as a small-time entertainer with a welcome entrée into the round of clubs, smoking concerts and masonics that thrived throughout the city. It is appropriate that in heraldic circles the name of Hancock did originally mean 'son of John', 'Han' being a Flemish form of John, 'cock' an affectionate term sometimes used to mean 'son of'.

Hancock was what might be called a deadline baby, in that his father left it forty-two days before registering the birth of his second son at Kings Norton register office, the maximum period allowed by law. When the child was three years old, the family, prompted by medical advice in the matter of his father's bronchial troubles, relocated to the purer air and more temperate, more genteel climes of Bournemouth. In later times Hancock would recall the event with typical deadpan insouciance: 'What a brave band we were, striking south that summer morning. Every hamlet, every village, every town we passed through accorded us a truly remarkable lack of attention, exceeded only by the complete anonymity of our arrival in Bournemouth itself.' By all accounts his father was a thrifty soul, refusing to buy enough petrol to take them beyond Bath, where they had to refuel for the final leg of the momentous journey. He had an automatic refrain when questioned why he didn't fill the tank up completely, the same words of morbid circumspection he used when his wife constantly queried his purchase of one Alcazar razor blade at a time, rather than a packet of six: 'You never know.' The move was made viable by the monetary support of Tony's maternal grandfather, Harry Samuel Thomas, an enterprising printer and lithographer whose success provided him with the financial cushion to serve for twenty-one years as a director of Birmingham City Football Club. His photograph is contained in the handbook published to mark the opening of the St Andrew's ground in 1906. It was said of him by Harry Morris, a chairman of the club in the 1960s, that 'he was always a very good judge of a footballer'. His daughter, Lucie Lilian, had married her husband eighteen days after the outbreak of the World War on 22 August 1914 at the parish church of St Oswald's, Bordesley. On the marriage certificate she is recorded as two years younger than her partner, the son of William Hancock, a foreman builder. The Hancocks originally hailed from a family of stonemasons in the West Country. John, or Jack as he became known, was born in the Bedminster district of Bristol on 14 December 1887 to William, a carpenter and joiner, and his wife, Elizabeth. The family subsequently relocated to Sutton Coldfield. Tony's mother entered the world on 4 September 1890 at 323 Cooksey Road, Small Heath, the child of Harry and his bride, Clara Hannah *née* Williams.

The search by Tony's parents for a combined work and investment opportunity – subsidised in part by a £950 profit on the previous sale and in part by Thomas, who also fancied the idea of Bournemouth as a retirement prospect for himself – resulted in the purchase of an unlikely business in the northern hinterland of the resort. The Mayo Hygienic Laundry was situated on the south side of Strouden Road at Nos 144 and 146, washroom and shop respectively, with living accommodation over the latter, in the district of Winton. Hancock found himself genuflecting to this aspect of his heritage only once in his comedy career. As he settles down on his flight to an alpine vacation where the yodelling Kenneth Williams will prove particularly irksome, he stresses, 'I needed this holiday – it's been hard work in the laundry lately.' In spite of the enthusiasm Lily expressly put into what had been an ailing business – a secondary outlet to receive and redistribute washing in the centre of Bournemouth being a decided asset in this regard – there was scant likelihood that the genial Jack would flourish in an environment which presented so little opportunity for the *bonhomie* of the social world. When, at the turn of the new decade, Strong & Co., the Romsey-based brewery, presented him with a chance to become the licensee of a central hostelry, little time was wasted. It may seem a big leap from running a laundry to managing a public house, but both were service industries and both left a pungent reminder on the olfactory sense of the future comedian: bleach and hops would provide him with a mental trigger *à la recherche du temps perdu* to the end of his days.

A valuable eye-witness to these times was the aforesaid nanny, Elsie Sparks, who joined the family at the age of seventeen on a salary of £1 10s. a week. More than sixty years later in an interview for the *Bournemouth Evening Echo* she recalled Tony as 'a lovely chubby little chap' who wouldn't let her out of his sight, although 'you could always tell when he'd been naughty or done something he shouldn't have done because he'd hide under the table. And if you ever took him to the park and there were other boys around, he'd run off and bring their caps back to you!' Tony, like herself, was not too happy with his first impressions of the holiday town: 'He couldn't understand the accent, and the sea frightened him.' It was through Sparks that Hancock had been christened Anthony: long before he was born she could not stop talking about the previous charge she had left in order to attend initially to his brother, Colin. Lily was convinced her second child would be a boy and made a promise that if correct she would call him by the same name to keep her happy. As his brother surged ahead of him, Anthony *redivivus* became her sole charge. On nature walks in the lanes and fields that encroached upon the new home, she soon observed an introspection and lack of confidence that she sensed was set off by the move south: 'He disliked meeting anyone new, trying anything new ... he couldn't wait to get home. In fact, the only place he was really happy and relaxed was in the small, fenced-in back garden.'

By Christmas the unhappiness and heavy heart had been joined by a physical setback. The doctor soon diagnosed the swelling around his wrists and leg joints as rickets. Not funny at the time, the disorder left him with that hollow-chested, hunched-shoulder look that became part of his comic vocabulary throughout his adult life. An attempt in childhood to straighten himself out led to exercises that involved hanging from a bar until his arms gave way. The procedure came to an abrupt end the day he caught sight of his shadow: 'I looked like a bloody great bat,' he grumbled. It is also the consensus of opinion that he grew into an untidy child, a fact with which Hancock concurred: 'Mother would take us out on a shopping spree and set us up in smart new suits, but so far as I was concerned she was wasting her time. Colin and Roger would arrive home looking as spruce as you could wish, but I always let the side down. My suits had a way of looking old and ill fitting the moment I got into them.' The uneasy feeling with clothes persisted through the years of his greatest success.

In retrospect the move to Bournemouth with its bustling entertainment industry both in and out of season provided Hancock senior with the ideal milieu in which to vent his frustrated skills as an entertainer. He would soon be caught up again in the whirl of concerts, ladies' nights and private bookings that had made life in Birmingham more bearable, culminating in November and December 1923 in two broadcasts, billed first as a 'humorist' and then as an 'entertainer', on the radio station 5IT that broadcast from the city between 1922 and 1927. Now as the landlord of the Railway Hotel at 119 Holdenhurst Road, near to Bournemouth's town centre, he had discovered the perfect environment in which to combine business, the entertainment of others and the ability to socialise with the colourful parade of theatricals that frequented the venue, both as occasional drinkers and overnight guests. The hostelry epitomised the racy side that between the wars bristled alongside the more respectable image the resort has always seemed anxious to cultivate. In many respects it may be no different from other South Coast seaside towns with their palm court and putting green aspirations to genteelness, but where else but Bournemouth do you discover illuminations that still shun neon-lit vulgarity in favour of a flickering wonderland of candles each lit by hand in its coloured glass jar?

Remembered from his Birmingham days as great company – 'he always had three words to your one,' recalled Harry Morris –

Jack Hancock, in the few photographs that survive, is revealed as a worldly cross between the music-hall *lion comique* tradition of 'Champagne Charlie' and his fellow coves, and the debonair, dapper precision of a Jack Buchanan. One picture shows him in the convivial company of that definitive boulevardier from the halls, Charles Coborn no less, immortalised in song as 'The Man that Broke the Bank at Monte Carlo'. Another image, posed as a publicity shot, reveals a slim, sharp-eyed alertness as he looks into the camera. His black bow tie and white wing collar stand to attention, and one can almost hear the overture playing. Everything is right about him. One line in his act is still lodged with affection in the comic lexicon of his youngest son, Roger, who was only four when he died. He would swagger on stage with a folded copy of *The Times*, then acknowledge an invisible presence in the wings: 'Put the Rolls in the garage, George. I'll butter them later.' The act then segued into a succession of stories and topical comments that he would read from the newspaper – a device not dissimilar to that used in the breakfast-oriented openings to his son's radio series – in addition to monologues and impressions.

George Fairweather, his friend and fellow semi-professional, recounted his first impression of the tall, handsome figure in top hat and tails, with white scarf and silver-topped cane to complete the image: 'he was over-dressed even for a formal night out, but within seconds the audience identified with him … he may have been dressed as a toff, but there were no class barriers … he joked about the same things and poked fun at the same people as they did.' This in part confirms his middle son's recollection of him as 'a dude entertainer' with an upper-crust stage voice. According to George, there was more than a touch of the Terry-Thomas about him, right down to the elegant holder from which he would chain-smoke the Du Maurier cigarettes he kept in their gold case. Tony himself identified show business as 'undoubtedly the real love' of his father's life: 'He enjoyed nothing better than making people laugh … Mother used to accompany him at the piano. I am told that she laughed so much at his gags, however often she heard them, that she could hardly play a note. That must have been a great comfort to him on the odd occasions when things weren't going so well with the audience.' The act often included a monologue about a lonely old man and a little dog. It would reduce his wife to hysteria with tears irrigating her cheeks. When in later years she recalled it for her famous son, it produced an equally convulsive effect. Their marriage was strengthened by his gift for comedy. 'She could never stay cross with Dad for long,' remembered Tony. 'He would pull a funny face, or use a silly voice, and that was that.'

When she was not wiping her eyes from laughter, the hotel gave his mother a new sense of purpose. She soon revealed herself as her father's daughter as she set about capitalising on its unique situation. Only a hop, skip and a jump from the main railway terminus, it quickly became a magnet for the business customer out of season as much as for the holiday-maker and day-tripper within. In the spring of 1931 press advertisements announced the opening of the New Palm Lounge within the hotel: 'The ideal rendezvous for ladies and gentlemen, and the most up-to-date retreat in central Bournemouth.' The tag that followed was a product of Jack's own sense of humour: 'It is said that trams stop by request – others by desire!' He was himself an integral part of the attraction. Peter Harding, a Bournemouth journalist who included the hotel in his regular round, was himself reported as saying that you never saw Hancock's dad working behind the bar. He always had his regular place at one end where he held court, occasionally leaving it to greet someone he knew, but only to bring them back to his corner: 'By the end of the night he would be surrounded by a group of laughing men and women and always with a household name among them.' The presence of the theatrical profession only emphasised the overall ambience of the place, the spiritual ancestry of which would have suggested the cheery backchat and cheeky banter of the music halls.

The family were domiciled in the claustrophobic attic flat at the top of the building. Tony and his brother Roger, who was actually born there on 9 June 1931, have both admitted that a business with an often chaotic twenty-four-hour claim on the attention of its owners did not provide the environment most conducive to a traditional family life style. His mother once explained in an interview: 'Tony once asked why he couldn't have a home life like the other boys. But it was impossible – I was busy with the customers all the time.' For Hancock the answer to the impersonal, though unintentional, disregard by his parents was to raid the petty cash and find escape in the silver screen: 'Will Hay was my favourite. A double feature, half a bar of Palm toffee, and three and a half hours in the dark – that was my idea of fun.' At a later time and in different circumstances Roger would cope with a similar situation in the same way, claiming that the constant exposure to the cinema taught him everything he knew about judgement and material, the grounding for his successful career as a literary and theatrical agent.

If Hancock took his theatrical flair from his father, his energy and strong-mindedness must have come from his mum. Known to all as Lily – and, to the annoyance of her family, to her husband as 'Billy' – she had denounced Lucie almost as soon as she could talk. Lily survived her son and therefore came within the acquaintance of many of those who figured in his career. To the writer Philip Oakes she was funny and racy, with a warm practicality that cut to the quick of her son's excesses: when on one visit to the Oakes' home Tony's boozy obsession for conversation and music showed little respect for the midnight hour, she finally drew herself up and turned to Philip's wife: 'I'll put my gloves on … it always worked with his father.' It usually worked with Hancock too. His agent Beryl Vertue first met her on a Mediterranean holiday and was immediately impressed: 'You could almost see where he got some of his mannerisms from in terms of delivery and everything … she would strut across the beach, full of funny anecdotes and with a kind of feigned vagueness about how to tackle any particular problem.' As her son ribbed her about her food foibles they became like a double act together. Lily's friend, the theatrical hairdresser Mary Hobley, recalled for Jeff Hammonds the suddenness with which she would go from being jolly and bright to being serious: 'She'd talk about life and all that – she seemed a bit mixed up in some way, but she was fun ... Tony was like her in a way – he was very bright, but underneath there was this sadness.'

Their close relationship even spilled over into a mutual love of sport. He talked about her to the journalist Gareth Powell, in one of the last interviews he gave in Australia: 'My mother is seventy-seven and a bit of a card. I telephoned her when I was sailing on the *Andes*. I said, "I think I'm going to play a bit of cricket with the Australians." And she said immediately – and I'm talking to her on a boat, on the *Andes* – "Now I would suggest three slips, one gully, two short legs ...!" and she went through the card on this bloody thing. And she's got no right to do this. A very funny woman indeed. Seventy-seven years and fighting as she goes.' Even sex was not off limits in their conversation. When, in an echo of Les Dawson's hypochondriac travesty of a Northern housewife, she delicately referred in company to having something wrong 'down below' Tony couldn't help himself. 'Get your legs round a good man,' he would guffaw. 'That'll put you right.' Modesty dictated she would not be drawn further, although it is tempting to imagine the spirit of Tony's friend Dick Emery, another fine comic transvestite, intruding on her behalf: 'Ooh, you are awful!' Indeed, looking at pictures of her in later life one surely gets some idea of how Tony would have looked in drag. The popping eyes and chubby cheeks are there, although school friend Ronald Elgood remembers the very domineering, almost Wagnerian presence of the lady who would collect her son at term's end. Their love was unquestionable and she remained supportive of him until the end of his life, although others have referred to a negative side in their relationship. 'She never let me grow up,' he once said to Joan Le Mesurier. 'Once we were out on a drive and she said to me,

"Look at the choo-choo puff-puff."' When Joan queried what was wrong with that, he replied, 'I was thirty-two at the time.' Arrested childhood development would provide Galton and Simpson with another common trait in the years to come: finger games, matchstick men drawn on windows and the announcement of the sight of 'Cows!' as if they were Martians all dominate that wearisome television train journey to the North.

Roger was well aware of the closeness between Tony and his mother, and assesses his own standing in the triangle between them with honesty: 'There was a sort of fixation there between the two of them and I was not part of that. It doesn't worry me. I don't feel any lack of affection. I think I've come out of this very well, actually. I could have been a screwed-up mess, but I'm not because I think I accepted the special relationship between them. It really was.' Not that everything was always well between them. Lyn Took, Tony's secretary at the height of his fame, found it hard to discern a maternal presence at all. His friend, the actress Damaris Hayman, thought she exerted a rather unhealthy hold on him: 'He used to say that she was very fond of "my son, the celebrity" and she sort of dined out on it, to use the phrase.' Roger is prepared to admit that she aggravated her son at times: 'I can understand that, because she'd go off on cruises and she'd always sit at the captain's table and she'd come home and say, "I don't know why I'm sitting at the captain's table." And I'd say, "It's because you're always telling everyone who you are and dishing out signed photographs of Tony into the bargain. Why else do you think you are?" She was the cruise queen. He paid for them. He was wonderful to her and rightly so because she had been so wonderful to him. From my point of view it was totally understandable.' Hancock became resigned to the humour in the situation: 'One day I caught her in a pub distributing signed portraits of me all around the bar all in one quick, deft movement as if she were dealing cards at Las Vegas. There they were drinking their beer and playing shove-halfpenny and suddenly before I could do anything about it, they found a Hancock picture in their hands.' More importantly, on his *Face to Face* interview with John Freeman, Tony described as his most vivid memory of his mother 'the encouragement she gave me to do what I wanted to do, though I showed no sign at all of being able to do it initially'. Roger is not prepared to admit that his mother may have seen more of the father – and the vicarious realisation of his father's theatrical dreams – in her middle son. Tony, in the same interview, acknowledged the lead his father gave: 'I think in many ways it was a deep thing with me to try and justify it. Because I believe he was pretty good.'

Roger scarcely knew his father. His only memory is a poignant one: 'He was going upstairs and he paused half way up on his way to the top floor. I sort of indicated that I wanted to come up with him and he said, "No, don't – don't come up." By that time he was dying, but I didn't know. Why would I know?' Jack Hancock died of peritonitis aggravated by both lung and liver cancer at the Royal Victoria Hospital, Boscombe, on 11 August 1935. He was forty-seven and had been ill for nearly a year, the last month in the hospital. By that time the family, spurred on by the resentment shown by the brewery to Jack's extracurricular activities as an entertainer and promoter of his own shows around the district, had moved from the Railway Hotel to their own independent venture. By August 1933 they were installed at the Swanmore Hotel and Lodge at 3 Gervis Road East, a select but neglected property within easier reach of the sands huddled beneath the East Cliff. According to his youngest son, a piece of advice handed down in the family by his father over the years had been, 'Whatever you do, it's your face that matters, not your arse!' The posher new address with its wide pavements and leafy feeling away from a bustling main road met the criterion. To make it sound even more exclusive it was rechristened the Durlston Court Hotel after the preparatory school in Swanage where the eldest son, Colin, was a boarder.

Designated by its proprietors as an 'Ultra Modern Private Hotel', the new venue boasted forty bedrooms. Private suites could be had for 12 guineas a week and 'Residents' were deemed a 'Speciality'. The ambience now had less to do with the music hall and the saloon bar and was more, as Hancock pointed out, in keeping with a Terence Rattigan *Separate Tables* type of existence endorsed by 'a solid core of elderly gentlefolk who have come to the coast to see out their days on their modest means'. But the theatricals, who continued to keep their allegiance to his father, were still welcomed. This was a world where *Country Life* and *Tatler*, in which his mother advertised assiduously, jostled side by side with *TitBits* and the *Stage*. The clash between the refined respectability of one outlook and the rorty raffishness of the other would inform Hancock's comic outlook for the rest of his life. On 7 August 1935, sadly only four days before Jack's death, a feature article on the recently reopened and refurbished premises appeared in the *Bournemouth Daily Echo* and singled out its 'unrivalled advantage of a natural environment of extreme beauty without art.ificiality', adding that 'the tender green of the lawns contrasts pleasantly with the strong white surface of the building'. The article was accompanied by an advertising feature in which all who had been involved in the renovation work displayed their calling cards. Tucked away in the bottom right-hand corner of the page was a box that read, 'The whole of the Electrical Installations for the above by R.G. Walker.' It gave his address as 37 Palmerston Road, Boscombe. He would soon move back to the hotel in another capacity.

Tony was eleven at the time of his father's death and his memories were more concrete. He confided in Philip Oakes the image he cherished of his father in the back of a taxi putting himself together in readiness for his act. It is easy to see why it appealed to him. To a man who was congenitally dishevelled like Hancock the idea that somebody could reassemble himself in the back of a cab as a paragon of wedding-cake elegance was heroic. When in 1967 David Frost asked him who had most influenced him as a comedian, Tony used the question to reminisce fondly about the one occasion his father managed to top the bill: 'It was at St Peter's Hall (in Bournemouth). In those days a semi-professional entertainer used to wear one of those collapsible top hats and a monocle, always! There was one entrance to the hall – through the front. And he was refused admission, in spite of his gear, because he hadn't got a ticket! He explained that he was top of the bill, and they said, "Sorry, no ticket, no entry." So he was out. In the end, he climbed through the lavatory window. The show must go on, you know. But it didn't go on with him again. He never got a return date.' On another occasion Hancock added, 'If that had happened to me, I would have gone straight home and to hell with them! But I hope he brought the house down for his pains.'

Jack Hancock was a practical joker too. A story was passed down in the family concerning another car journey. Jack suddenly turned to his friend and fellow publican, Peter Read, and with reference to a prop basket on the floor of the car shouted out, 'It's gone again … quick, get the flute and play it, otherwise we'll never get it back in the basket!' The driver, increasingly agitated, pulled up on the verge: 'Either you get that snake back in the basket or we don't budge another inch.' Other memories were more sombre. He proved a trooper to the end and even in the last stages of his illness, when he was severely emaciated, Tony remembered him wrapping a sheet around his jaundiced shoulders and regaling the patrons with an impression of Gandhi. As Eric Morecambe would have said, 'There's no answer to that!' His last performance had been given at a midnight matinée at Bournemouth's Regent Theatre the previous Christmas, when he shared a bill with radio favourite Ronald Frankau and his old friend George Fairweather and tore the place down with his impersonation of Stanley Holloway delivering the monologue, 'Albert and the Lion'.

When asked by the journalist Ray Nunn in the summer of 1962 whether he thought his father's death had had a lasting effect on his personality, he replied, 'I prefer not to answer that.' With respect for the response, Nunn moved swiftly on to his next question, 'What do you hate most of all?' 'Any form of cruelty,' said Hancock. Osborne's Jimmy Porter had been ten years old when his father had died: 'For twelve months I watched my father dying ... he would talk to me for hours, pouring out all that was left of his life to one lonely, bewildered little boy, who could barely understand half of what he said ... you see, I learnt at an early age what it was to be angry – angry and helpless.' It would be wrong to read such intimacy into Hancock's situation, but Damaris Hayman, who sensed the love Tony had for him, recalled an emotional moment when he told her his father reminded him of the stag in *Bambi*, the moment when the young fawn acknowledges him as his sire and his mother explains, 'Everyone respects him ... he's very brave and very wise. That's why he's known as the Great Prince of the forest.' 'Obviously,' says Damaris, 'his father was an almost god-like figure to him.'

On that same appearance with David Frost, Hancock reminisced about one of the songs his father used as a closing number. He couldn't remember the words, but a member of the viewing public later obliged and he was invited back on the following evening's show to interpret them. The song was called 'First Long Trousers' and it took the son some emotional effort to get to the end:

Say, young fellow, just a minute,
These are your first long trousers, eh?
Your little grubby knee breeches
Are for ever put away ...
... Gee, you look well in them, sonny!
I can't believe my eyes.
It doesn't seem a year ago
When you were just – this size!
A little pink cheeked youngster,
Why, you toddled more than ran
Every night to meet your daddy –
Now you've got long trousers on.

Oh, I don't know how to tell you,
But I want to, yes I do,
That your mummy and your daddy both
Are mighty proud of you.
And we're going to miss the baby
That from us this day has gone.
But that baby we'll remember
Though he has long trousers on.

By that time there wasn't a dry eye in the house.

It was only after his father's death that Tony was sent away from home to school. He had spent the autumn term of 1929 at Summerbee Infants School, now the Queen's Park Infants School, at Charminster, about half a mile from the family laundry. A conversation between Hancock archivist Malcolm Chapman and a fellow pupil revealed that he turned up in a smart brown suit, which was most unusual at a time when most parents in the area could not afford that kind of apparel. When the family moved into the hotel trade, his education climbed a notch up the social scale. Saugeen Preparatory School, founded in 1873, announced itself to prospective parents as 'a preparatory school for boys for the Public Schools and the Navy'. It could boast of John Galsworthy as an old boy and had links with Robert Louis Stevenson (Lloyd Osbourne, the stepson for whom he wrote *Treasure Island*, had gone there as well). Coincidentally, the building in Derby Road is now occupied by another hotel, the Majestic. Coincidentally again, *Treasure Island* provided a leitmotif that would resonate in Hancock's stage act down the years. The young Tony was now obliged to adopt a school uniform that comprised Eton collar, short jacket and black pinstripe trousers. The establishment provided the choristers, the young Hancock among them, for St Swithun's Church only a few hundred yards away both from his parents' second hotel venture and the school itself. In the spring of 1935 Saugeen School relocated to nearby Wimborne.

Events moved quickly in Hancock's life after his father died. On 1 January the following year his mother remarried. A few days later he followed in the footsteps of his elder brother, Colin, and was enrolled as a pupil at Durlston Court School in Swanage. That he made the move halfway through the academic year suggests his mother may have needed to regroup and give herself the additional space to manage the business and her new life. It may merely signify that Saugeen School – had he continued to attend its new Wimborne location – closed down or was about to close down around this time. In his will Jack Hancock left the gross value of his whole estate of £13,961 to 'Billy' for 'her unstintable [*sic*] and loving kindnesses during my life'. The remarriage so relatively soon after her first husband's demise caused some consternation among many of the family's friends. George Fairweather had little time for Robert Gordon Walker, twelve years his wife's junior, the electrical contractor involved in the renovation of Durlston Court Hotel. A man of athletic appearance, he had played for Boscombe football club as a semi-professional for ten years. Within six months of the marriage he had sold his electrical company and was registered as a joint director of the hotel.

According to Roger, however, there was little question of his becoming a major presence in the lives of the three brothers: 'My mother always said, "You mustn't have anything to do with him. You're my son and I'm the one who makes all the decisions. You're not to take any decisions from him." She rather put him down.' When years later Roger himself married, he took his bride down to Bournemouth to meet his stepfather: 'I'd always been put off him by my mother. When Annie met him for the first time, she said, "I think he's lovely." And for the first time in my life I realised he actually was a very nice person, but I'd always been talked out of it by my mother.' It is understandable to imagine that any guilt or embarrassment Lily felt in the circumstances may have been channelled into brainwashing her children in this way. In her lifetime she married three times, but as Roger stresses, 'Never for money! Never for money! Except the last one, who dropped down dead at her feet. He was a multi-millionaire. They were about to be married. There was going to be a fourth.' One thing he will never take away from her is the intensity with which she threw herself into running the business: 'She worked so bloody hard. Twenty-four hours a day.' If she was not in the office, she was in the kitchen. Not that she was without back-up staff. Her youngest son recalls the Swiss chef who used to chase everyone around the kitchen with a knife when his anger was roused. Colin was by now managing the accounts, when, that is, he was not indulging his passion for tap-dancing. When questioned about the social contradiction in how a relatively modest family could afford to process three offspring through private education, Roger can only point to her industry: 'I wish I had known my mother better. She was so supportive. She paid all the school fees. But children don't think of that at the time. It wasn't as if they were well off. She grafted so hard.'

Tony Hancock remained at Durlston Court School in Swanage until the summer of 1938. When he joined, there were around sixty-five boys on the register. Converted in 1903 from a large mid-Victorian private house, it occupied a commanding position overlooking the bay and the resort's monumental Great Globe, 40 ornamental tons of the Portland limestone that characterised the area. Between 1928 and 1965 it could boast the redoubtable Pat Cox as headmaster, immortalised later by another Durlstonian, the scriptwriter and producer David Croft, as the part-inspiration for Captain Mainwaring from *Dad's Army*. 'It's not that he was a pompous man,' David recalls, 'more that he represented all the best characteristics of being British, loyalty, and the old school.' Cox had been a junior officer in the Durham Light Infantry during the Great War at the age of seventeen. 'It's not *if* we win the war, it's *when* we win the war,' he would pontificate during the later conflict. Croft arrived just after Hancock left. He recalls that the mistress in charge of the junior school had with some foresight told Hancock that if he didn't sit up straight and hold his head erect he would grow into a round-shouldered old man. Sadly he did not need to reach old age to fulfil the prophecy. According to Roger, himself an old boy, the school's motto, engraved on its crest beneath the imperial Roman eagle, was *'Erectus Non Elatus'*. This quickly translated into 'Upright, not boastful'. Hancock might have preferred the line from the old George Formby song: 'I'm not stuck up or proud – I'm just one of the crowd – a good turn I'll do when I can!'

It was inevitable that he would apply himself to the drama life of the school. He made his first public appearance cast as the 'celebrated, underrated nobleman, the Duke of Plaza-Toro' in an end-of-term production of *The Gondoliers*. This required him to lead a train of noblemen on stage and announce with great dignity, 'My Lords … the Duke!' On opening night, the nobility was assembled, the audience was expectant, and his moment came. Hancock raised his hand in an impressive gesture, his lips parted, but the only sound that emerged was a strangled gargle. The voice of a master from the prompt side urged him to go off and come on again. The crocodile traipsed back into the wings. At the second attempt things were even worse. Tony recalled, 'My jaws worked hard – like a gramophone without a record on it. Not one other sound could I raise but for a mouse-like squeak. "All right, Hancock," said the teacher, "you've had your moment of clowning."' The school magazine reported, 'The part of the Duke had to be played silently in mime!' He progressed sufficiently to be offered a part in the next production, *The Pirates of Penzance*. Tragically, between auditions and casting his voice broke, 'which was just as well considering what little I had done with it in its intact state,' wrote Hancock. 'I sounded like a cross between Lily Pons and Paul Robeson.' The master, knowing full well that parents were paying large sums for small boys to flaunt their exhibitionist tendencies in this manner, clutched at a particular straw: 'What I really want is a good stage manager.' But Hancock's determination knew no bounds. By making a nuisance of himself he was allowed to join the chorus on strict instructions: 'Remember, Hancock, you can whack your thigh. But you must *not* sing.' Eventually he was reduced to demanding roles like falling out of cupboards and wardrobes: 'I can claim to have died the death in more ways than one at Durlston Court. The odd thing was that the more I failed as a child actor the more I determined to succeed as an adult ... setbacks and adversity in general have always stiffened my resolution and it was so maddening to lie there on the stage being stepped over and prodded for heart beats when I felt I had it in me to make people laugh.' There was little doubt about that. Many years later his mother told an Australian newspaper that he had been a 'funny little lad' since the age of three: 'He used to do such funny little things that had everyone laughing and always had a funny saying at the tip of his tongue.'

For the moment he was markedly more successful on the playing field. The school records reveal that as a victim of measles in his first term he got off to a slow start both academically – coming twelfth out of twelve in his class – and athletically. He rallied sufficiently to win the school's welterweight boxing final 'by a narrow margin – he is quick and hits very hard and showed that he can take as well as give punishment'. He went on that year to excel on the cricket field, taking thirty-five wickets with an average of 6.3 including seven for six against Old Malthouse School. At soccer he scored twenty-two goals in fourteen matches. The following year saw cricket figures of seventy wickets in thirteen games, including one return of eight for twelve. A member of the school shooting team, he was awarded his First Class marksmanship badge in his final year, and on sports day 1938 the Victor Ludorum Cup. His final cricket season revealed figures of fifty-seven wickets at an average of 4.3. The headmaster wrote, 'In Hancock, A. J. we have one of the best bowlers Durlston has ever had.' He had been more specific at an earlier date: 'He always bowls a good length with plenty of nip off the pitch and swings in from the leg rather late.' As for lessons, he managed to win the prizes for English and French in his final year and to achieve 76 per cent in the Common Entrance Algebra exam to secure his place at public school.

He moved on to the long-established Bradfield College, near Reading, in the autumn of 1938. It might appear he was set securely on the educational ladder to British middle-class success. He stuck it for little more than three terms. His housemaster, J.R.B. Moulsdale, confirmed his aptitude for sport, but as for academia: 'he was not academically very bright – no qualifications at all – and it is *rumoured* that his housemaster once wrote a report that said, "this boy thinks that he can make a living by being funny"'. As if to substantiate the pupil's opinion, Moulsdale added as an aside on another occasion, 'He was much, much better at imitating his masters. His mother told Joan Le Mesurier of how one visiting day she had gone to the Dean's office to discuss his academic progress. The news was not encouraging. As she left he told her that she would find her son leaving the hall with the rest of the school. She expressed her concern how she was going to pick him out of the crowd. "It's simple," replied the Dean with a twinkle. "He'll be the only one with his mortarboard stuffed under his arm and his gown trailing on the ground."' The impression of a *Just William* caricature has been endorsed by Richard Emanuel, for whom Hancock acted as fag: 'He was permanently untidy. His clothes never appeared to fit, his tie veered towards the back of his neck and his collar had a life of its own. He invariably had inky hands and not infrequently ink on his face. His hair was generally in keeping with his collar and tie.' Whatever his natural propensity for untidiness, Hancock was registering a protest: he hated the place. Soon after the beginning of his fourth term he literally, in his brother's words, 'threw the mortarboard and gown away under a bush and jacked it in in disgust'. Fortunately his decision to quit the system, without any apparent opposition from his family, forestalled the prospect of being haunted by a public-school accent for the rest of his life. It is always feasible that family economics were the reason for his departure and that Hancock was at last putting on a good acting performance. The prospect of war could not have had a settling influence either. According to Ronald Elgood, when in the early 1950s Tony found himself playing the Palace Theatre, Reading, ten miles away, Moulsdale invited him back to the *alma mater* for old times' sake. He refused point blank, saying how much he loathed Bradfield. Moulsdale appeared somewhat surprised, as though he had not realised his old pupil had this particular chip on his shoulder.

Elgood was a contemporary of Hancock at both Durlston Court and Bradfield. His abiding memory, aside from the fact that there was nothing lugubrious about him – 'that came later' – is of a sense of mischief: 'He was fairly streetwise. I don't know if he came from a state school. I well recall a game of football with Tony at centre forward. We were naïve little gents and he tapped the ball with his hand when the referee wasn't looking. We were amazed.' His tone suggests that they also secretly admired his cheek. He is certainly remembered 'as a good-natured boy, a nice guy'. To Pat Cox's wife he was 'just an ordinary likeable schoolboy'. To Peter Wilson at Bradfield he was 'a cheerful soul – full of jokes and the joys of spring'. There is no evidence to suggest that he suffered adversely from the notion that it helps to build the character of children by the enforced separation from their loved ones in a repressive, potentially alienating environment, although his brother does point out that he was a shy child. Another Bradfield contemporary, Nigel Knight, observed a 'complete and utter silence, uncommunicativeness (markedly towards groups)'. Tony admitted to John Freeman being an extrovert till the age of about fourteen, 'and then it sort of packed up'. He had no idea why. Roger puts it down to public school: 'You were kept away from the punters. Later I cracked it. I went to a party, at the House of Commons of all places, and I thought nobody knows anybody at this party. I'm no worse off than anybody else. So I started going up to people. But Tony was not particularly gregarious. He was shy. If he did crack it later, it was with the drink, but not without. But it was a wonderful education, particularly in the business my parents were in when you really had no home life. So you were going back to school and seeing your friends, which is really the reverse of what you would expect.'

Preparatory and public school, albeit minor, provided an unlikely background for a professional comedian who would go on to achieve mass appeal. On radio and television the Hancock character often goes to great pains to recover his imaginary past – scholastic, military, ancestral, professional – by asserting a status he apparently never had. Had his true educational history been common knowledge, the radio episode *The Old School Reunion*, in which Tony regales Sid, Bill and Hattie with his boyhood triumphs at 'Greystones' – 'seven of the happiest years of my life: started off as a fag and worked my way up to head cigar' – might not have been as funny, even if the *dénouement* does insist that he turned out to be the worst school porter they ever had. Galton and Simpson also indulged his passion for sport in many an episode. It is comforting that their grandiose *Roy of the Rovers* soliloquising on his behalf was rooted in a certain schoolboy truth: 'Picture the scene – Wembley Stadium 1939 ... the ball was cleared high in the air – I caught it on my forehead – balanced it there – tilted my head back and with my nose holding it in position I was off. Past one man, past two men, forty-five yards, the ball never left my head. I was holding the lace in my mouth ...' But his soccer skills were nothing to his cricketing ability. He claims he is known in cricketing circles as 'Googly Hancock', and not as Bill Kerr suggests because of the way he walks: 'Perishing Australians! What do they know about cricket, anyway?' snorts Hancock with disgust.

Cricket became something of an obsession, a passion that lingered until the end of his life. He developed into a fine medium-pace seam bowler, and one of his proudest moments came at a charity match in 1958 when with little dispute he bowled out Ian Craig, the

Australian captain, lbw with only his second ball; unfortunately the umpire, acknowledging the crowd had come to see the touring side, gave 'not out'. His mother recalled that as a boy, 'He used to go round the hotel swinging his arms. He was always bowling at something.' It also provided the defining bond between the two brothers, in spite of the age gap between them. 'I suppose,' says Roger, 'that between seven and ten I got to know him better because we played a lot of cricket in the yard at the back of the hotel.' His real-life athletic prowess would have especially pleased his father, who had engrained the love of sport in his son. Among his other accomplishments Jack had been an extremely good billiards player, a superb golfer and a boxing expert. He had coached boxing on an *ad hoc* basis at Durlston Court School and boasted a certain notoriety as a licensed boxing referee officiating at tournaments at the Winter Gardens, the Stokewood Road Baths, and elsewhere locally. His youngest son claims that he was 'the most unpopular referee in Hampshire – as soon as he was announced, he was booed'. Tony had his own memories: 'Regularly we trotted along to his fights, sat ourselves down in free ring-side seats and promptly stood up and booed every decision he gave. Very popular we were, I don't mind telling you.'

In his *Face to Face* interview Tony made it quite clear why he left Bradfield: 'I wanted to get into the theatre ... I felt I could do it somehow ... I don't know why really.' He emphasised to John Freeman that he had wanted to be a comic for as long as he could remember. Ever disparaging of his appearance, he added, 'perhaps looking like this it was perhaps the only thing I could do'. He would not be the first comedian to turn such a deficiency into a workable option. At another level, however, one needs to jump back to when he was around six or seven years old to discover the emotional heart of the matter. There would have been no single moment of annunciation. Whatever the schools he attended, the most engaging, most enduring part of his education occurred as he fell under the continual spell of the variety artists who clustered around his father in the hotel bar in the early 1930s. In later life he revealed that he had the measure of them exactly: 'They fascinated me. Those old pros were so much more extrovert than people in the business today. It seemed as if they would go into an act at the drop of a hat. They were different from any other kind of people I had ever met in my life. They seemed to get so much more out of life simply by being alive.' In later years he would parody the world of 'no business like show business', but he never lost his respect for the professionalism of the variety trade that catered for a million eventualities in the tireless round from one venue to another.

It was a significant time in the development of British entertainment. A new breed of performer was breaking through in variety, a more sophisticated type whose talent, often nurtured in concert parties, had been lifted to success in the radio studios of the day. In comedy a more sophisticated approach underpinned humour that still somehow managed to remain accessible to a wider audience, as the Oxbridge satirical movement would thirty years later. How could a boy of impressionable years not be impressed by both Pavilion favourites and Hancock hotel patrons like Norman Long, billed as 'A Song, a Smile and a Piano', the Western Brothers, listed as 'The Singing Songwriters' with their admonition, 'Play the game, you cads,' and Gillie Potter, 'The Squire of Hogsnorton', with his erudite ramblings about his mythical but oh-so-real village? Their billing matter beckoned as Tony gravitated towards his destiny. The week commencing 3 October 1933 was a red-letter one. Placarded on the posters around town as 'England's Premier Radio Stars in Person' were the 'In a Spot of Bother' double act Clapham and Dwyer, Tommy Handley of later 'ITMA' renown, and Elsie and Doris Waters all wrapped up in one bumper fun parcel. The last two were especially significant with their portrayal of 'Gert and Daisy, the Radio Flappers', comedy where the accent was less on jokes, more on characterisation as the public seemingly eavesdropped on a conversation driven by the minutiae of existence, the tedium of bus queues, shop queues, cinema queues, in short the sluggish inertia of suburbia writ large. No comedian would come to embrace those aspects more effectively than the adult Hancock.

Looking back from the vantage point of his own success Hancock would single out the occasional act. The select members of his extended dream family included 'Stainless' Stephen, billed proudly as 'The British Broadcasting Comedian', a Sheffield-based performer who knew Jack Hancock extremely well. His speciality was a form of 'punctuated patter', articulating the symbols that add meaning to the words in a way that predated Victor Borge's splendid verbal games for a later generation: 'Somebody once said inverted commas comedians are born comma not made. Well ... slight pause to heighten egotistical effect comma ... let me tell my dense public (innuendo) that I was born of honest but disappointed parents in anno Domini eighteen ninety something ... end of first paragraph and a fresh line.' A sometime schoolmaster whose real name was Arthur Clifford Baines, he heightened the effect on stage by wearing a costume that embraced a stainless-steel waistcoat and a bowler hat with steel rim to match. Hancock later acknowledged that by listening to Clifford he first learned the importance of timing in lifting a relatively trite script to a more exalted level. Moreover, according to Tony, it was 'Stainless' Stephen who 'gave me my first whiff of greasepaint by taking me behind the scenes at the Bournemouth Pavilion Theatre. That was a magic night for me and thereafter I made a beeline backstage at every opportunity.' Recently completed in 1929, the Pavilion Theatre on Bournemouth's Westover Road rose majestically in its commanding position like a red-brick Taj Mahal. His school uniform soon became as familiar a sight in the wings as the stage manager's pullover. One incident there loomed large in the notes he made in 1962:

One night the Houston Sisters were on, Renée and Billie. Renée looked so sweet and attractive that I stood there entranced. Then she came off and said a few sharp things to the man who was handling the lights. She really gave him the works and I was twenty-five before I knew what all the words meant. It was a shock for a lad of eight wearing his school cap, imagining he was in some wonderful fairyland until – whoosh! That lovely creature came bursting into the wings and shattered all his illusions. Renée was right, though. That man *was* making a pretty fair hash of the lighting.

Few performers made a greater impression on him than the traditional double act Clapham and Dwyer, who claimed a complete paragraph in his jottings:

It may sound strange now when my own line of comedy is so remote from anything they ever did, but nevertheless that pair taught me the rudiments of the job. Charlie Clapham – in topper and monocle, again – was the funny one, a spry, scatterbrained whippet and quite a dog in every way. Billy Dwyer was the mastiff of the act, but in his solid fashion he was great fun. In fact, he bore out what I have always felt about these comedy partnerships; that the straight man is invariably much funnier than he is credited with being. In a way the Clapham and Dwyer relationship reminded me of Laurel and Hardy's. I have always thought that Hardy was as funny as Laurel and Billy Dwyer used to amuse me enormously. I followed their act all over the place and often stayed with the Dwyer family. They may not always have wanted me but they got me just the same. Bill had an odd quirk of humour. When I arrived at his home he would say, 'Goodbye!' and tell me, 'There's a good train back at 6.30 tonight.' Sometime I wonder whether he actually meant it, but I prefer to think it was one of his little jokes.

And then there was Sydney Howard, who was a movie star as well. If back then a cross between a soothsayer and a casting agent had been looking to replicate the Hancock of the future, they need have searched no further. His rotund build, his equally rotund speech, his 'googly' gait, his sense of comic mournfulness were all spot on. He too epitomised pomposity in the context of a frayed, shabby gentility. To watch him today in one of his most successful low-budget comedies, *Fame*, is a revelation. He plays the floorwalker in a department store. When a boy insults him, he goes to swipe him with his hand before thinking better of it and quickly converts the movement into an insincere pat on the head: one can almost hear a muted 'Flippin' kids!' – the catchphrase that defined Hancock's early radio success. At another point he asks a customer what kind of jumper she requires. Her answer is enough to send Howard off into the patriotic travesty of a bargain-basement Richard II: 'A Fair Isle – this fair isle – this sceptred isle, this earth of majesty, this seat of Mars, this Eden, demi-paradise, this fortress built by nature for herself against infection and the hand of war, this happy breed of men, this little world, this precious stone set in the silver sea …' and so on until the drapery department curtains come crashing around his head. Later Hancock would make his own comic capital out of the speech. There is no evidence that he saw the film, although it is exceedingly unlikely that he did not. But, crucially, any similarity is in the attitude.

On one of Howard's visits to his parents' hotel, Tony plucked up the courage to tell the great star he was keen to go on the stage: 'He told me I would be crazy if I did. "Keep away from it, lad," he said. "I wouldn't let a dog of mine go into show business!" Then a pause, and Sydney said in his wonderful Yorkshire way, "But if you *do* get into it, let me tell you one or two things." And he took me into a corner and showed me all sorts of tricks of timing and hand movements.' It may have been the most important 'lesson' of his life. They met on at least one other occasion. When Tony was about ten years old the Hancocks and the Howards found themselves holidaying by chance at the same hotel in the South of France. The comedian and his wife made a fuss of the young Hancock, incongruously cocooned in his prep-school uniform as the Riviera sun streamed down. One day Sydney spotted a loose thread on the Eton jacket. He went to remove the offending strand. As he pulled it away, it just kept coming. The other end, far away, was on a spool secretly threaded through from Tony's pocket. Hancock may well have picked up the gag from Chaplin's *City Lights*, a film that had a life-long impact upon him, although its origins are probably enshrined in the annals of the practical joke. 'You'll go far, my son,' said the astonished comedian with a gleam of surprise in his eye.

One mealtime during this holiday Tony was served a whole fish, complete from head to scaly tail. According to his mother he took one look at the lifeless eyes of the forlorn creature staring up from his plate and declared, 'I'll stick to good old bread and *fromage*, thank you.' It is good to know that his father was able to witness his son's slowly emerging comic style. To Tony, his father shared something of the vitality and example of his famous friends and provided that last zing of incentive for him to pursue his chosen path. Ultimately he needed no other justification. When he was nine, his dad pulled strings to secure him a film test, although nothing came of it. Years later in his dressing room at the Adelphi Theatre he read out the letter of invitation to appear in the 1952 Royal Variety Performance to their mutual friend, George Fairweather. He burst into tears as he explained, 'If only Dad could have been here.' 'He will be,' assured Fairweather. 'I wish I could be as sure,' added Tony, extracting a promise that George would attend the gala evening in his father's place.

To her credit his mother ensured that after his father's death laughter continued to ring through the rooms of the family apartment at Durlston Court Hotel. The extent of the family's capacity for letting its hair down has been conveyed in her memoir by Joan Le Mesurier, with Lily at the forefront of the hilarity: 'When the family was all together they were always laughing. His brother Roger would try to climb up the wall. Tony would roll on his back and wave his legs in the air, and Colin would kneel on all fours, banging his fists on the ground, all of them fighting for breath.' Roger recalls the roles somewhat reversed: 'Tony literally climbed up the wall if he was hysterical, and we were hysterical a lot of the time.' It extended into young adulthood when the brothers would send their impromptu parody of the popular panel game *Twenty Questions* spiralling into Rabelaisian heights – or depths. 'What is mineral with an animal connection?' 'Could it be the spade up the dromedary's arse?' responded Tony with Isobel Barnett primness. According to his brother, he would become literally helpless with laughter at such sessions. A photograph survives from an earlier time showing Tony in the company of his mother, stepfather and two brothers. He is mugging self-assuredly at the camera without a care in the world.

In time he came to translate his conventional boyhood fantasies into his first comic material. As a very young boy he nursed an ambition to become the Wyatt Earp of a make-believe town he referred to as Toenail City. The upper precincts of the Railway Hotel rattled to the ricochet of toy-town gunfire. One Christmas he received the gift of a sheriff's outfit from his parents. Later he complained about the pains in his legs. His mother admitted that only then did they discover that he had strained the muscles from walking around all day bow-legged. Roger recalls that with time he gave the fantasy the comic treatment in an early recitation entitled 'The Sheriff of Toenail City'.

> *I've come here to give you a story*
> *Of the rip-roaring wild woolly west,*
> *Where the Indians chew nails and drink liquor*
> *While the men grow sweet peas on their chest.*
> *In the township of Toenail City*
> *Lived the Sheriff, a man of good class,*

But he drank like a fish did the Sheriff,
Till his breath burned a hole through the glass.
But the pride of his life was his moustache –
It was famous as Niagara Falls
And his missus when washing on Fridays
Used the moustache to hang out the smalls.
His moustache was so long and whippy
People spoke of it under their breath
And the old-timers said that the Sheriff once sneezed
And it practically flogged him to death.
But whenever the Sheriff was shaving,
You could see him all covered in gore.
His whiskers just blunted the razor,
So he hammered them back in his jaw.
'Twas with Hortense, the bartender's daughter
That he finally found his romance
Till one day she sat down beside him
She got one of his spurs in the pants.
She walloped him hard in the pants,
Her temper was starting to foment,
But the Sheriff's false teeth just flew out with a pop
And bit her on the spur of the moment.
Then Hortense turned round on the Sheriff
And kicked him real hard on the jaw
And hearing the cowboys applauding
Pulled the hair off his chest for encore.
But the Sheriff at last found his false teeth
And shoved them in reverse in his head,
So that when he attempted to talk to Hortense,
He chewed lumps off his back stud instead.
Then up rode Hortense's fiancé,
It was all he could do to keep standing.
He was so thin his landlady had to take care,

Lest the cat got him out on the landing.
The gorgeous beast jumped from his mustang,
And said to the Sheriff, 'Desist!
'Unhand this poor innocent maiden,
'Or I'll come and slap you on the wrist.'
The Sheriff just drove him so deep in the ground,
His face turned quite yellow with terror.
He went so deep that coalminers lunching below
Chewed the soles of his gumboots in error.
'Twas a shame for Hortense's fiancé,
He was only just out of his teens.
He was too full of holes to be buried,
So they used him to strain out the greens.

The first reality to confront him upon leaving Bradfield was far removed from the 1930s' variety stage, although it had everything to do with the comedy he would make his own in later years. He soon became involved in life at the hotel and brought all his powers of observation to bear upon a different world: 'It was the kind of place which attracted little old ladies. They used to set out for the dining room at 11.30 and get there just in time for the gong at one.' The intake seemed to be dominated by 'several dowagers who used to sweep in like galleons under full sail, with their frigates of female companions, bouncing along nervously in their wake. What those companions put up with for the sake of a winter at Bournemouth!' Christmas provided an exceptional opportunity to observe the idiosyncrasies of the British at play. Lily poured her heart into making sure all had a good time, but not all went to plan. As her son remembered, they had to drop a game dubbed 'Woolworth's Tea': 'The idea was that everybody came to tea wearing something they had got from Woolworth's which, in those days, meant it had cost not more than sixpence. Then your partner had to find out what it was. Fine, until somebody nominated a lady's priceless family heirloom. End of

Woolworth's teas!' The Christmas fancy head-dress party proved more popular: 'There was the man who came as a Christmas pudding … he wore the plate round his neck and on his shoulders like a ruff and encased his head in a *papier-mâché* pudding complete with sprigs of holly on the top. And he refused to take it off. He sat throughout dinner feeding himself through a visorish trap door in the front. We tapped on the side between courses to make sure he was all right. It must have been very hot in there … pity, because he didn't even win a prize.' One of his jobs was to write out the daily menus: 'The soup was the same every day – it sort of accumulated over the years. We used to do it geographically. I used to call it *Potage Strasbourg*, *Potage Cherbourg*. Then we got into the West Country and called it *Potage Budleigh Salterton* and *Potage Shepton Mallet*. It all tasted exactly the same and was repulsive.'

The hotel business gave him the opportunity of learning all he needed to know about *petit-bourgeois* gentility: how fierce, precarious and destructive it could be, while always open to comic interpretation. Nothing escaped Hancock as he turned over in his mind the potential for characterisation in comedy. He even observed that the old ladies marked the levels of their marmalade jars. Lily was well aware of her son's comic perspective: 'It wasn't the way he told jokes. It was the way Tony saw the world. The way he never forgot anything.'

He was now fifteen, his only distraction from such matters provided by his decision to enrol for a commercial skills course in shorthand and touch-typing at the Bournemouth Municipal College. Records state that he signed up for the course the day after war was declared at the beginning of September, so he did not waste time. It was while, in his own words, he was 'fondly beating out the old a-s-d-f-y-;-l-k-j-h to music' that he decided to announce to the world what he had known for a long time, that he wanted to spend his lifetime making people laugh. This in spite of the fact that he soon acquired speeds of 120 wpm for shorthand and 140 wpm for typing!

Chapter Three

'REMEMBER GIBRALTAR?'

'It took me ten years to go on a stage without a
hat on! It was some sort of protection.
Like a clown's mask.'

The kaleidoscopic skill with which Galton and Simpson rang the changes on the life and times of their radio and television creation was reflected in the diversity of occupations the real-life Hancock held down – sometimes it seems for little longer than a broadcasting half hour – once he decided against continuing his academic career. Any hopes that he might have sauntered straight onto one of Bournemouth's several stages had been felled in the summer of 1939 when he petitioned the local impresario and entertainer Willie Cave. Cave was not only responsible for the concert party that strutted its stuff on the Bournemouth sands. He had also been one of his father's closest friends and, at Jack's suggestion, had given their mutual pal George Fairweather his big break, when they managed to persuade him that he'd be better off on £4 a week than on the 37s. 6d. he was earning as a postman who had to be up by four in the morning to sort his mail. Throughout his childhood Tony had been captivated by the makeshift auditorium on the sands that precariously housed 'Willie Cave's Revels'. With a stage constructed from canvas and girders, it could seat a deck-chaired audience of 500: when a strong wind blew, the cast would brave the possibility of collapse and turn their skills from song and dance to tent maintenance. Cave, not prepared to be won over by the sentiment of past friendships, was straightforward with the eager teenager, telling him he was far too young and inexperienced to be treading his boards.

His formal education over, Tony ventured into his first job as a tailor's apprentice at the local branch of Hector Powe. Visions of upholding the sartorial elegance of the local gentry were soon dispelled. When he held out his hand for a tape measure, he found a kettle in its place. He lasted four hours: 'The first chore they gave me when I arrived at nine was to sweep out the cupboards. At ten they set me brushing down the stairs. At ten thirty I had to brew the tea. And at eleven I handed in my notice.' After a short while he progressed to the equally unlikely post of Temporary (Unestablished) Assistant Clerk, Grade 3, for the Board of Trade. Having purchased an umbrella to look the part, he found himself stamping clothes rationing forms in the incongruous setting of the newly requisitioned but still elegant Carlton Hotel. The work lasted two weeks, but only because he had to give two weeks' notice. He may have said this jokingly, since at other times he seems to suggest the work continued into 1941. 'Nothing worse outside a Siberian salt mine,' was Hancock's final judgement on this period of his life. But the experience did pay dividends of a kind. Before undertaking the role he had asked of its prospects, only to receive the reply: 'Surely, Mr Hancock, it is not necessary for me to outline the *prospects*. This is the Civil Service.' As he later admitted, anyone who caught his programmes would know that that voice haunted him for years to come. The whole experience left an indelible mark on his psyche, informing his portrayal of bureaucracy's underdog with depth and precision. One can imagine John Le Mesurier as the resigned administrative officer: 'Very well. I think you'll fit our requirements. We can arrange for you to start in about a week.' One can equally imagine Hancock's measured pause before responding, 'I won't decide right at this moment, if you don't mind ... there are several other irons in the fire ... I'll drop you a line in a day or so.' As Tony said, 'Nothing like this had happened to the Civil Service since tea went on the ration.'

The other irons were, of course, non-existent. For a while he expressed a flurry of interest in journalism, something that in subsequent years reared its head in many interviews, not least to win him the allegiance of yet another painstaking provincial reporter. Heartened by his proficiency in touch-typing and shorthand, he returned to the city of his birth to explore the possibility of a job on the *Birmingham Evening Despatch*. 'I had two ambitions,' explained Hancock. 'One was to be a newspaperman. The other was to go on the stage. I saw myself first as the *Despatch*'s chief reporter and then, a fortnight later, as one of the leading lights of Fleet Street.' The editor could not subscribe to this agenda, and Tony was politely asked to leave. The only other work to come his way not directly connected with show business was through the kindness of his father's friend Peter Read, now running the Pembroke Bar and Silver Grill in Poole Hill, Bournemouth. He remembered Tony as 'a quiet boy, but very observant ... he always knew what he wanted to do. He wanted to be a comedian, and not only that, he wanted to be a star comedian.' When Read explained to Lily that he could offer her son the post of potman, she sensed the title might not flatter his more elevated ideas for himself. Read was resourceful. 'All right,' he said, 'we'll call him something else.' And so the new dogsbody was installed as the hotel's 'domestic manager'. In nostalgic interviews later in life Hancock would cling possessively to the title. Read's recall of his new employee was vivid: 'One day I remember giving him a job in the store room, putting empty port bottles back in their crates. I completely forgot about him until, about half an hour later, I heard some weird noise ... eventually I found him hidden behind the crates and bottles reciting Shakespeare and completely overcome by the fumes ... port can do that to you.' Hancock claimed he was rehearsing, imagining the rows of crates and barrels to be 'a wildly applauding audience'. It sounds like a scene from a Sydney Howard movie. On another occasion he was discovered insensible from using primitive siphoning methods to decant the port. He swallowed so much of the stuff he had to be poured helpless into a taxi, never to return. But he did survive for around six weeks and could later admit that for much of that time 'at least I was happy'. The only other employment he undertook outside of show business came when his mother and step-father were temporary wardens of a girl's hostel at Swynnerton, near Stone in Staffordshire, later in the war. For about a month he was employed in an armaments factory as an 'electrician's improver', a title Hancock looked back upon with disbelief: 'It was great ... they said, "Put on your spurs and get up the telegraph pole." What? Not me, mate!' 'Electrician's mate' would have been a more apt designation for the task in hand.

Throughout these diversions Hancock's show business ambitions did not lie dormant. One summer afternoon in 1940 in the restaurant at Beales, one of Bournemouth's fashionable department stores, George Fairweather had just finished his regular teatime stint as a vocalist with the resident Blue Orpheans band, when he was approached by Tony's mother. He had not seen her since the year of her first husband's death, the resentment at her remarriage so soon after the demise placing a barrier between her and Jack's inner-most circle of friends. He never forgot her exact words: 'I don't want to hold a pistol to your head, but Jack, my husband, was very good to you when you first started, wasn't he?' George nodded and Lily continued, 'I wonder if you would return the compliment, because young Tony's got his father's talents and is dying to get started, and since you're running troop shows, could you do anything for him?' George committed himself to his protégé's future progress at that moment. He was by then in charge of the Bournemouth War Services Organisation, which put on two shows a week for the forces at the local Theatre Royal and toured the nearby army camps and ack-ack sites under the sobriquet of the 'Black Dominoes' concert party: 'There was no money in it and everybody worked for nothing, so that is how he got his first break.' George had last seen Tony when he was a boy, first at his father's hotel and then hanging around the 'Revels': 'He used to stand at the back with all the kids watching the show for nothing. And he was always very intrigued because in those days there weren't the coloured lights there are now. We used dead white light and when you were on stage you had to have a full make-up, which in the daylight was hideous. It was a brown-red make-up with blue eyelids, lovely maroon lips and mascara on the eyes. But when you finished the show, so that you wouldn't lose the audience who were watching for nothing, you had to dive down out in the open air and go through with the box, which they used to call "the bottle". Tony used to kill himself laughing seeing me coming in this awful make-up with all the local yobbos going "bloody 'ell".'

Now reacquainted, Fairweather remembered Hancock as 'not gloomy in those days – bright as a button – terribly conceited – knew everything like we all did when we were young'. More importantly George discerned the awakening of a talent, even if he felt he was using it in the wrong way. By his own admission Hancock had already been accumulating material, much of which he was far too young to understand: 'from stage acts, from jokes that other people got laughs with in pubs. All was grist to the mill. If it got a laugh, into the act it went.' With a certain logic he clung most tenaciously to the gags that raised the biggest reaction, which were invariably the most risqué. Suddenly his shorthand skills were serving a use he may not have anticipated as his hand skedaddled across the page of his notebook to record the latest comic gem. In the spring of 1940 through friends of his father he was booked for a smoking concert at the Avon Road Labour Hall. For what was almost certainly his first professional engagement he was paid a fee of 10s. 6d. Precociously billed as 'Anthony Hancock – the Man Who Put the Blue in Blue Pencil!' he sashayed on stage like a juvenile Max Miller, the comic icon of the day, whose outrageous motley of technicolour patterned suit with plus fours, jaunty white trilby and corespondent shoes he attempted to replicate with a check jacket, top hat and a pair of the aforesaid two-tone shoes that cost him a complete week's Civil Service salary of £2 10s. Hancock had not reckoned with the beer served throughout his act. The clinking of glasses and the rowdyism of the crowd made it difficult for him to be heard by the few who were prepared to listen.

In later years Miller and Hancock could be seen as cultural counterpoints: 'The Cheeky Chappie' who took the art of communication with a live audience to a zenith never repeated with greater panache and personal assurance, and 'The Lad Himself', pioneer and unsurpassed exponent of the more distant and paradoxically more intimate medium of television. Tony never lost his affection for the man John Osborne celebrated as 'a saloon bar Priapus'. He was totally outrageous, but never really blue, at least in a mucky sense. If the colour applied at all, it was more in keeping with the defining sparkle of his laser-beam eyes. The pair have come to epitomise the cavalier and the roundhead of British comedy, and not just in a visual sense. The day would come soon when Hancock – by now styling himself 'The Confidential Comic' in outright homage to his idol – would renounce vulgarity, however honest, however clever, however exhilarating, for ever.

Fairweather agreed to give Tony a try-out in one of his shows at the Theatre Royal. It may be hard to imagine that you could play to army audiences of the day without being suggestive, but George was adamant this was not the style he required. 'But the troops laughed,' protested the younger man. 'Of course they laughed,' said his father's friend. 'Put four or five hundred soldiers in a hall and they'd laugh if you came on and said "arseholes". But it's not artistry.' For all Fairweather's advice, he had still to learn his major lesson. Fuelled by misguided zeal, he accepted an independent booking at the Roman Catholic Sacred Heart Church Hall on Richmond Hill. Fairweather was incredulous when he was told. When he queried whether he intended to use his old material, Tony replied, 'Why not?

They're troops.' George explained there would also be Sunday school teachers and church officials serving the refreshments, but he had made up his mind. When the older man next saw him Tony was in tears, blubbering, 'If only I'd listened to you.' In time the detail came out. No sooner had he leaned across the footlights to tell the joke about the commercial traveller and the blonde than three old ladies got up to catch an early bus. When he gave them the one about the sergeant major and the ATS officer, silence hung in the air: even the troops were stunned into embarrassment. The one involving the land girl and the farm labourer might have worked had it been heard above the sound of the general exodus that was now taking place. Fairweather adjudged it the dirtiest act he had heard. The words of the priest as he reluctantly paid off the comedian remained with him forever, like the stain of some mortal sin: 'Hancock, I know your parents well, and I'm sure if they had been here they would have been as disgusted as I am.' As he dragged himself off the platform, the lady who had booked him told him not to return for his scheduled second spot, adding, 'We want to fumigate the stage.' He told Philip Oakes that he subsequently burned his script and in time disposed of the hat and the shoes. Although he was far from a puritan in his private life, in the years to come he would as a performer treat risqué humour with the obsessive contempt of someone with a compulsive cleanliness disorder. He even went as far as questioning a classic line in *The Blood Donor*. Alan Simpson explains: 'It wasn't his line. It was Patrick Cargill's, when he says, "You won't have an empty arm, or an empty anything!" "Do we need the 'empty anything'?" queried Tony. Patrick said, "I like it." Since it was his line, Tony let it stay.'

The experience strengthened his respect for George Fairweather, who was thirteen years his senior. In return, the relative old stager, impressed by his promise never again to use smut on stage and seeing the conceit knocked out of him as a result of the church hall incident, became all the more inclined to help him, even if in the young Hancock he saw the total opposite of his father.

Whereas Jack both on and off stage had represented the epitome of elegance, immaculate down to his fingernails – 'the reason he used a cigarette holder was because he couldn't stand nicotine on his fingers' – Fairweather would refer to his son as 'the unmade bed': 'He had no idea about clothes – just threw them on to keep him warm.' Soon an emotional bond built up between the two. The younger man never stopped plying his mentor with questions about his father: 'It was as if going over things again and again somehow brought Jack back to life. He never really got over his father's death.' Hancock began to adapt his act with George's advice, instructing him to learn by watching others, without actually copying their material. Early inspiration was provided by the newly popular radio comedian Cyril Fletcher, whose plummy voice imported a comic solemnity to his famous 'Odd Odes', a phrase that entered the language. Hancock's original instinct had been to spice them up for the troops; Fairweather made sure he removed anything that might be considered off-colour.

In time he broadened his writing efforts to embrace the surrealist travesty approach of the music-hall comedian Billy Bennett, whose billing 'Almost a Gentleman' summed up the social inadequacy he projected on stage in shrunken dress suit, curling dickey and chunky hob-nailed army boots. The eulogy to the Sheriff of Toenail City dates from this period, together with rhymes like these, which he happily shared with his friend, the actor Jim Dale, in later years:

He came from the mud flats of Putney,
His tongue hanging out like a tie.
From the tip of his toes to the top of his head,
He must have been fourteen stone high.

That was just the first verse. There were twenty-five more, of which Dale also recalls:

The force of the bang was horrific,
Every man was blown out of his shoes,
And a block of tall flats by the side of the road
Caught the blast and was turned into mews.

The assumption is that he did write them himself. Without access to Bennett's complete canon there is no way of checking, but neither is there any reason to suppose that his relish for sharing them with Dale was fed by anything other than nostalgic pride for the minor achievements of his youth.

Hancock also admired the style of the monologist Reggie Purdell, who became better known as the voice of the magician in the famous BBC children's radio series *Toytown*. To the accompaniment of 'descriptive' piano music he recited short comic fables, one of which had something to do with a deer coming down to drink at a forest pool. When Purdell died in 1953, Hancock acquired all his material in manuscript form, but by the early 1950s, when his true style was fast emerging, it represented an anachronism. According to Philip Oakes, Tony also admitted to an early fascination with the comic alphabet that defines letters in an ersatz cockney accent. Probably first brought to wider recognition in the 1930s by Clapham and Dwyer, who dubbed it their 'Surrealist Alphabet', it also surfaced in the Purdell repertoire. Part of the fun was in the number of variations that could be rung on the basic theme: 'A for 'orses, B for mutton, C for yourself, D for 'ential, E for Adam, F for vescence,' all the way to a rousing finale of 'X for breakfast, Y for God's sake, and Z for breezes.' It needs to be read aloud to make full sense.

Hancock continued to ply the loop of small-time club bookings and trudge around the service camps gaining experience with Fairweather and his hard-working gang. In the spring of 1941 encouragement came when he attended an audition in the café of Bobby's department store in Bournemouth for the BBC Bristol-based producer Leslie Bridgmont. Bridgmont would eventually become a stalwart of the medium with shows like *Much-Binding-in-the-Marsh*, *Waterlogged Spa*, *Stand Easy* and, for the aforementioned Cyril, *Fletcher's Fare*, as well as playing a modest role in Hancock's later career as a radio star. For the occasion Tony performed a monologue entitled 'The Night the Opera Caught Fire' and won a booking. Bridgmont never forgot him: 'He was dressed in his best dark grey suit. My goodness, he was nervous – absolutely gibbering with fright. He had a script that he had written himself and it was absolutely terrible … still, I could see the boy had an individual style that was quite out of the ordinary, so I gave him a chance.' His contract stipulated he submit his material in typescript. In the excitement Tony got carried away. He explained, 'Being raw in the business, I took this to mean having this set up by a printer and so at great expense I arranged with a local firm to do it that way. They made a handsome job of it, but I have never been able to convince Leslie Bridgmont that it was not a gag.' The producer never forgot his surprise upon receiving the copy of Hancock's words laid out in heavy Gothic type elaborately bound in thick paper. Bridgmont later recalled not only his suspicion that this was an illuminated address that had been torn out of a book, but also his concern that had it not been original with Hancock it would be of no use for the show. When Tony met up with the producer, Leslie explained, 'A typewritten copy would have done.' One can picture Hancock's expression. The job had cost him £3. He later joked, 'It was cheap at the price: only ninety per cent of my fee.' A month later at 11 a.m. on 6 June 1941, billed in the *Radio Times* as Tony J. Hancock, he made his first broadcast on a programme entitled *A la Carte*, described as 'a mixed menu of light fare'. Transmitted from Bristol on the Forces station, the forerunner of the Light Programme, it was not an amateur talent show as has been surmised. The others appearing were all established broadcasters including Jack Watson, the comedian son of veteran Nosmo King as 'Hubert' and Al Durrant's Swing Quintet.

Hancock may not have known at the time that the person he had most reason to thank for the broadcast was the actor and variety artist Jack Warner, later to become legendary as the evergreen copper 'Dixon of Dock Green' of television fame and in those early days of the war basking in the radio success of his show *Garrison Theatre*. Indeed the phrase 'blue pencil!' – as in 'not blue pencil likely' and adapted by Tony in his early billing matter – had, alongside 'Mind my bike!' and 'Little gel', been one of several catchphrases that Warner had used to boost morale in those times. In his autobiography, *Jack of All Trades*, Warner recounts the occasion his mother and his wife Mollie were staying at the Durlston Court Hotel when the proprietress confided she had a son who was desperate to enter show business and asked whether Jack might be able to help. This led to Warner watching a performance by the young Hancock, presumably when he was appearing at the Pavilion Theatre for the week of 14 April 1941 in the stage version of his *Garrison Theatre* hit. Making all the allowances in the world for his inexperience, Jack 'knew at once that he had a great future before him. He was truly Chaplinesque in the way that he could make pathos and comedy come together.' Warner arranged an introduction or two, as a result of which the invitation to audition for the producer transpired a month later. Bridgmont had given Jack one of his own big breaks in radio only a few years before. As Tony continued to struggle for recognition, he wrote to Mollie Warner, possibly out of gratitude, although it is not that aspect that impressed her husband when he recalled the letter: 'It was almost entirely devoted to self-criticism, and written in a mood of desperate melancholia.' When it was possible the star returned to see his act again and offered all the encouragement he could muster, but, mused the kind-hearted maestro in later life, 'just how do you convince a very funny man that he is a great comic when he is convinced that he isn't?' The doubt, like the talent, was always there.

With one broadcast to his name there was no rush by the BBC to provide Hancock with a repeat booking, but his confidence received another lift that summer when George Fairweather at last invited him formally to join his 'Black Dominoes' concert party. The timing was propitious. In the autumn Fairweather would enter the army and it was convenient for George, as well as a natural progression for Tony, now a veteran of the Dorchester–Wareham–Blandford–Ringwood troop circuit for him to take over as head of the Bournemouth War Services Organisation. He was paid £2 a week for chartering buses and organising the tour rota in addition to his own activities as a performer. He once stood for over thirty minutes in driving rain at the head of a battalion of tired and patient entertainers waiting for the charabanc that would take them home from Dorchester, until it occurred that he had forgotten to book it. The experience would have resonated in his mind many years later in an exchange of radio dialogue when together with Sid James and Bill Kerr he finds himself soaked to the skin waiting for the last bus home. Bill notes that the rain has stopped, only to be corrected by Tony: 'No it hasn't. The wind's blowing so hard it can't land, that's all.'

It is no surprise that he did not remain in the job for long. It is surprising to find that he was still persisting with the 'Confidential Comic' approach, although Fairweather's absence may explain this. At one camp by default he did secure a *bona fide* belly laugh. As he crouched forward over the edge of the temporary stage with all the complicity of Max Miller at his intimate best, he trod on a loose plank and fell over the footlights into the lap of the Commanding Officer seated in the front row. He later explained, 'This piece of unrehearsed knockabout, followed by my struggle to clamber back on stage over the feet of the top brass sitting in the front row, bang up against the rails, proved more hilarious than any of my carefully rehearsed gags.' Once when he was acting as compère for the 'Black Dominoes' at the Boscombe Hippodrome, his entrance was greeted with zero applause and his nerve failed him so completely that he retreated to the wings and continued to announce all the acts from an off-stage microphone. In 1967 Hancock attempted to summarise the experience of his early comedy apprenticeship for David Frost: 'It took me ten years to go on a stage without a hat on! It was some sort of protection. Like a clown's mask. You know, when you've got the mask on, then you can have the funnel down the trousers and the water poured down, and it's not you. While I had this hat on, it wasn't really me doing it. Then gradually as you go along, you shed these things until you are confident enough to be yourself.'

In handing over the reins to his friend, George deputed more to the young Hancock than responsibility. Perhaps not realising that a duodenal ulcer would be responsible for invaliding him out of the army in a very short while, he also around this time entrusted to him much comic business from his own repertoire, items that had already reduced Tony himself to fits of laughter. One routine focused on a comic with catarrh and a predilection for taking snuff. It is almost impossible to transcribe as George described it, but for the record went something like this, with the sniffing and snuffling best left to the imagination: 'This fellow was walking along the street the other day and – *sneeze* – excuse me – and a fellow came up to him and said, "Do you know where so and so's place is?" – *sneeze* – "No, it's just across the road, I think" – *sneeze* – "Ask the taxi driver." "Yes, I will" – *sneeze* – … ' The sequence builds in crescendo fashion until the inconsequential finish of the biggest sneeze you could ever expect. To understand how funny this would have been as performed by Hancock, one has only to recall the television episode where he suffers a cold and his stoic attempts to hold back a sneeze in the face of Sid brandishing an aerosol germ spray – 'that crop sprayer', as Hancock dismisses it – give way to the final explosion. The ticklish anticipation of the moment takes full possession of his face and provided television with some of its funniest close-ups.

More enduring, not least because it planted the seed of a comic attitude that would stay with Hancock for life, was the 'Pick a card' routine. George would play the magician to Tony's hapless stooge coaxed out of the audience to participate, his gormlessness accentuated by flat cap, inseparable carrier bag and shabby umbrella. A catalogue of misunderstanding and ineptitude as the stooge fails to keep pace with the conjuror's instructions, the skit culminated in the total disgruntlement of the put-upon prestidigitator, his self-esteem in shreds: 'If you don't look at it, how are you going to know what the card is? There's not much point in me being here is there? ... Five hundred people in the audience and I've got to pick you. Listen, mush. Take a card, for God's sake ... Isn't it marvellous!' Years later when asked by a guest in a Southampton dressing room where his character came from, Hancock had only to point to the man at his side: 'Go on, George; tell them about the card trick sketch.' Fairweather's natural courtesy always conceded a modest 'I can't see it myself,' but he knew perfectly well the part he had played in influencing the Hancock persona and in sharpening his friend's understanding of comic timing.

In time Fairweather, with an eye on Hancock's aspiration to become involved in services entertainment when he entered the forces, gave him *carte blanche* to access his regular act. His forte was impressions. In the days before tape recorders George used to spend every available moment in the cinema listening to the voices, watching the mannerisms of the stars of the moment. His repertoire included Maurice Chevalier, Jimmy Durante, the radio comedian Robb Wilton, Charles Laughton as Captain Bligh of the *Bounty*, the flat-profiled George Arliss as Disraeli. Tony had started to develop his own flair for impressions at Bradfield College. His friend Michael Turner recalled, 'He was a great admirer of W.C. Fields and James Cagney and could give a very fair impersonation of both. He was also fascinated by Damon Runyon and the New York Brooklyn accent, remarking after one divinity class taken by the headmaster, "I like dis guy Whitworth wit da neon dome."' So far this enthusiasm had yet to find a place in Tony's act. Whereas Fairweather was a straight impressionist, his advice to Hancock was to approach things from an original angle: 'You have a flair for burlesque – do my act as an amateur would do it and burlesque it.' Hancock must have thought this a good idea. He continued to do so in his stage act until the end of his life. Laughton's Quasimodo from *The Hunchback of Notre Dame* was always a *tour de force*: 'You're so beautiful and I'm so ugly. I'm deaf, you know. It's the bells. It's the bells. Sanctuary! Sanctuary!' Then suddenly, dropping the histrionics, he would announce 'Sanctuary much!' and lurch off stage. The last bit was Hancock's, the rest Fairweather's, in spite of claims Tony made later in life that the impression had been inspired by Peter Sellers's spine-tingling version of Jekyll and Hyde, with which he would terrify impressionable young WAAFs when they were in charge of the RAF Light Entertainment wardrobe department together at the end of the war. Most probably Sellers's influence enhanced the grotesquery.

Whatever the vicissitudes that beset Tony's early working life, he had so far enjoyed a not uncomfortable war. Although the lights had gone out over Bournemouth and the tourist industry was in recession, his mother and stepfather persisted with Durlston Court Hotel, ensuring their son a strong, albeit erratic, domestic base, until it was requisitioned and they set out on a round of pub and hotel management that took them, according to Roger Hancock, all over the country to no fewer than thirty-two different establishments during the hostilities. Both the industry and the illusory calm of their various lives were shattered at the beginning of September 1942 when the news came through that Colin William Hancock, Pilot Officer 132998, 269 Squadron, Royal Air Force Volunteer Reserve, was 'missing presumed dead'. Married in November 1939, he had joined the service on 22 April 1940; the following day he was recommended for training as 'Wireless Operator/Air Gunner'. He was eventually stationed at the RAF airbase at Kaldadarnes, thirty miles south east of Reykjavik in Iceland. He went missing on 1 September 1942 somewhere over the North Atlantic. The squadron annals record the incident as follows: 'Hudson of No. 269 Squadron sighted U-boat. Attacked when submerged. Some oil seen. At 18.53 hours strike aircraft Hudson M despatched (Pilot Officer Prescott, Sergeants Smith, Hancock and Harris) but failed to return.' The following day three further Hudson aircraft searched for the missing plane. Again one of the three failed to return. On board was Eric Ravilious, the Official War Artist, today regarded as an artist and illustrator of considerable standing, who had arrived at the airfield only the day before. Today Colin's name, one of over 20,000 Allied airmen with no known grave who were lost in the conflict during operations from bases in Britain and Europe, is commemorated on Panel 69 of the Air Forces Memorial at Runnymede in Surrey. Records reveal that he had been awarded his commission as Pilot Officer as recently as 4 August 1942, information that does not appear to have been known within No. 269 Squadron at the time he went missing and which became known to his family only after his death.

In recent years Colin's business skills in helping to run Durlston Court had reassured his parents that the venture would continue to succeed for another generation in his hands. According to Roger, that is why his mother refused to return at the war's end, 'selling the property for a terribly low price in the region of £26,000, when two years later she could well have achieved close to £100,000 for it'. The family was looking after the hostel in Staffordshire the day the news arrived. Even today Roger, disoriented by the thirteen-year gap between his elder brother and himself, wrestles with the poignancy of the moment and the absence of any great surge of personal grief: 'I remember being in that corridor and she came down and told me. It didn't mean anything to me. That was the terrible thing. It was somebody removed. But the awful thing is I didn't even think for *her*. I remember saying, "You know there's a letter in from him this morning." I mean, how long had that taken to come? It was later that I realised what she'd gone through. She was absolutely torn apart, and that turned her into a spiritualist. And she got a lot of comfort from it, she really did. But unfortunately she started to believe it all too much, over-compensating. But you can totally understand why.'

In the years to come on tour Hancock would sit up into the early hours with his agent Stanley Dale, affectionately known as 'Scruffy', and beg him to recount his own wartime experiences as a navigator in bombing raids on Germany. Dale recalled, 'He would get out my flying log and go through it with a fine-tooth comb, making me give all the gory details – how my companions were killed, how I got shot up, how I won the DFC. He worshipped that log book. One of his favourite subjects was war and how futile it was.' It is impossible not to suppose that he was somehow projecting his brother's memory onto Dale's achievements. That memory worked in other ways too. In the late 1950s Cyril Fletcher approached Hancock with the request that he appear in one of the fund-raising concerts he and his wife, Betty Astell, organised for the 'Guinea Pig' Club formed by patients of Sir Archibald McIndoe, the pioneering plastic surgeon, who during and since the war had worked for the Royal Air Force on the treatment and rehabilitation of badly burned air crews. Jimmy Edwards, shot down at Arnhem, was arguably their most famous member. While major stars dropped everything to support the cause, Hancock could not be persuaded. Fletcher never forgave the younger comedian for his refusal, but maybe Hancock had personal reasons for not wishing to meet and perform before the badly scarred and disfigured victims in McIndoe's care. Fletcher certainly had no idea of how close Hancock had come to the brutal reality of war. Even today some of Tony's closest friends like Graham Stark, Damaris Hayman, Ray Galton and Alan Simpson react with surprise at the news of Colin's very existence. However, at the end of his life in Australia, Hancock did share his deep affection for his brother with Eddie Joffe, the producer of his last uncompleted television series. To Eddie he came over as 'a tall, slim, charming and charismatic young man ... Tony claimed that Colin's spectre regularly appeared to him in dreams, swathed in seaweed.'

Our most painful memories are those compounded by our worst imaginings. There is no way Hancock could have said 'Yes' to Fletcher without seeing in the faces, the eyes and the minds of those damaged heroes the elemental horror his brother had failed to survive.

That last letter Colin addressed to his mother was dated 26 April 1942. It had taken four months to arrive. In it he expressed genuine concern for Tony's immediate future and what his impending enlistment might entail:

> Please tell him he is to do *nothing* until I come home. I'll brain him if he does!! Because I know just what will happen. He will join some branch or other and then be sorry he did. Naturally I can help him no end and can advise what to try for. As for a full time job on the entertaining side, this is of course out of the question. I have not received his letter yet, so expect he will mention it. Anyhow please tell him not to do anything until I have seen him. I can't write about it very well. I shall never finish.

There is no evidence that the brothers met again, nor any reason why no more letters appear to have come through after being sent at three-weekly intervals until then. Tony had to find his own way of dealing with the tragedy, and his immediate enlistment on 7 September 1942, within days of the announcement, provided bittersweet distraction. He also volunteered for air crew, but was failed on his eyesight. Tony liked to joke his way around the fact by claiming that his arms were too short to reach the controls. From the beginning he had a friend by his side, Slim Miller, another comedy hopeful who had been with him in Fairweather's concert party. Their shared ambition eased the journey from Bournemouth Central Station. 'By the time we reached Romsey, just beyond Southampton, we'd written half a show,' Miller recalled later. For the moment, though, they 'wanted to get a crack at the fun'. The earthbound reality proved otherwise. Initially they were posted to Locking, near Weston-super-Mare, for fourteen weeks' basic training with the RAF Regiment, the body entrusted with the duty of defending air bases against ground attack. Hancock did not take kindly to the new disciplines. One night, as he burned the midnight oil writing letters home, he was disturbed by a caped figure that put its head round the door and bawled, 'Put out those lights.' 'All right, cock – just a minute,' replied Hancock engagingly, at which the NCO tore off his cape and angrily shoved three stripes under his nose. From that point on he saluted everybody. When the flight sergeant on parade told him to stick his chest out, he answered, 'What chest?' The officer, unaware of his earlier struggle with rickets, failed to appreciate the joke. When he was confronted with bayonet practice and the need to shout like a savage during the exercise, he protested, 'I'm not doing this. It's bloody barbaric.' According to George Fairweather, he was put on a charge for that one.

Having persuaded the entertainments officer that he would be of greatest use to the unit by reprising his skills as an entertainer, he was let off the weekly route march to rehearse for the show that evening and given a signed chit to that effect. 'By a happy coincidence,' Tony recalled, 'he forgot to date it, so while the others were struggling on their marches I would produce this thing and hop off to Bournemouth to collect props or make excuses about needing make-up.' The marches were of an escalating nature, the ground covered being increased by a mile each week. By the time the regiment was up to fourteen miles Tony was told the shows had been cancelled: 'So on went the kicking strap, the canister, the kitchen sink, the lot, and off I set ... I really don't remember the last few miles. It was agonising. My feet were practically aflame and I had to be helped in by a couple of mates.' From that point Aircraftman Second Class (General Duty) Hancock was rumbled, marked down as an individualist and a rebel. One senses he revelled in the reputation.

Before long the RAF Regiment decided that both he and Miller were surplus to requirements and soon after Christmas reassigned them both to a Canadian unit that fortuitously happened to be stationed at Bournemouth, where their duties included guarding the offices and laboratories of a small photographic intelligence unit. He never forgot the first roll call:

'Sikersky.'
'Check, Lootenant.'
'McLaren.'
'Yeah, Red.'
'Anderson.'
'Here, Buster.'
'Hancock.'
'Present and correct, sir.'

'So we've got a damn limey who's trying to be funny, eh?' spluttered the officer. It seems that only Hancock could get one step nearer to a court martial by calling an officer 'sir'. 'It was fatigues again,' he admitted, although the opportunity the posting gave him to swan around his old haunts in uniform and to socialise with old buddies including Fairweather, now back in the resort and flourishing even more as an entertainer in professional shows at the Pavilion, was more than compensation. He and Miller were billeted at the swish Metropole Hotel. After less than two months they were redirected to a transit office in Blackpool, where they parted company. Hancock was given the opportunity to train as a wireless operator. He failed on four words a minute – 'which takes some doing,' he said – and was posted to Stranraer in Scotland. A week later a bomb fell on the Metropole.

At RAF Wig Bay, five miles north of Stranraer on the west shore of Loch Ryan, Hancock was assigned to the Marine Craft Section. His principal duties appear to have been the custody of a heap of coal and a boiler house. In a cunning echo of his earlier designation as a 'domestic manager' he made the decision to endow himself with the title of 'fuel controller' and hung a sign stencilled by himself to that effect on the door of his hut. He explained, 'It gave my mother something to be proud of when I wrote home and told her my title. It also boosted my own morale and took some of the ache out of the job to read those words every time I trudged back to bed.' In addition he was responsible for the lighting of fires in the Nissen huts, a process he soon had down to a fine, if dangerous, art. Not for Hancock the fuss and bother with wood and paper and getting the right draught. All he needed was a bit of rag, well soaked in paraffin. Having left the door of the hut well open behind him, he tossed this among the coal, followed quickly by a lighted match, and departed like lightning: 'They used to go like a bomb. The only thing was the black stains on the ceilings. That seemed to bother them a bit.' Throughout this time he must have looked like a refugee from a minstrel show, his face and hands begrimed with coal dust and soot. The image of Hancock slogging around with his wheelbarrow of coal is one of drudgery personified. In time he would stamp his own comic seal on such situations; for the moment one notes the gradual emergence of a sardonic sense of humour he would make his own.

He was characteristically disparaging about life on the desolate edge of the west Scottish coast. He dubbed Stranraer 'the Paris of the North – you can't see a sign of life after five o'clock in the afternoon' and would joke of a typical Scottish evening out: 'Chuck a caber about, have a quick dance over the swords, cut your feet to rhythms, and away you go.' When he felt so disposed he would make amusement for himself by sending up his Commanding Officer without mercy. On one occasion he was attempting to resurface a path when the officer approached: 'No, no, no. That's not the way to do it at all.' As Hancock tugged away at his cap in apology, he continued, 'No. Look. This is how it should be done.' Hancock explained that without so much as a by-your-leave he then took his shovel and started throwing stones and pebbles around like a man who had lived in a glass house all his life. When the officer triumphantly asked, 'Now do you see what I mean, Hancock?' the latter seized his opportunity: 'Well I think so, sir, but I wonder whether you would mind just showing me that bit where you flick your wrist again.' This was the cue for the jacket to come off, the tie to be loosened. The gravel flew like fury, but Hancock continued to act dumb: 'I still don't quite see it, sir. Sorry if I seem a bit dim.' Inspired by those last few words the officer became even more possessed, but as Hancock later said, 'I must say that to this day I have not seen a path better resurfaced than by that CO.'

Al Tunis, a Canadian radar technician based at RAF North Cairn, the nearby radar station, retained a vivid memory from those times. Shaving one morning in the washroom, he heard splashing and shuffling followed by the gush of a flushing toilet: 'Through the mirror I could see the figure of an airman emerge, carrying a bucket, only to disappear into the next stall. He was clad in fatigues with a wedge cap on his head at a careless angle. When he came into view again I inspected a thin, stoop-shouldered figure, topped off by a sallow, sad face with heavy-lidded eyes. He grunted a greeting and carried on with his work.' In time a friendship developed and out of a mutual enthusiasm for all things theatrical the idea of a concert party servicing the local camps emerged. In the weeks leading up to the performance Hancock kept himself largely to himself. Tunis was puzzled that he did not appear to rehearse: 'I had visions of him going through his paces down at the shore, against the backdrop of the bee-hive-shaped Ailsa Craig looming to the north, shouting his lines over the turbulent waves.' He need not have worried. For all his nerves during the day, come the night all went well: 'The spotlight was clearly intended for a slight, stooped young man with sad eyes who stepped on stage to assume the identity and the manner of the born comedian ... he delivered a performance with the deadpan expression of a Keaton.' The era of 'The Confidential Comic' was over.

Encouraged by his reception, by the end of 1943 he had applied and been accepted for an ENSA audition. When he stepped onto the stage of the Theatre Royal, Drury Lane, he could have been back at school playing the leading nobleman in *The Gondoliers*. His whole body quivering with nerves, he could barely utter 'Ladies and gentlemen' before the words froze in his mouth. Angry and depressed, he made the long train journey back to Scotland. There was little consolation to receive from ENSA a few days later a formal card that read: 'Dear Sir/Madam, we have much pleasure in informing you that we liked your act at audition, and will let you know in due course if we require your services ...' So much, Hancock must have thought, for the personal touch.

While cross with himself on the one hand, he also knew that show business could provide the only escape from the icy hell of RAF Wig Bay in wintertime, where it was so cold the men literally slept in their uniforms. 'Everyone shaved fully dressed,' he remembered. 'You stood in the ablutions at seven thirty in the morning singing "The Whiffenpoof Song" in the boots you had been wearing in bed.' By January he was attending a second ENSA audition, having this time applied under the name of Fred Brown, 'just so the officials wouldn't be prejudiced'. He recalled, 'When they saw me on the stage they said, "Haven't we seen you somewhere before?" but I pretended not to hear and just went on with the audition. At least I tried to, but the same thing happened as before. A complete dry-up!' However, the big break was not far away. Ralph Reader, who had successfully translated his pre-war Gang Show success with the Boy Scout Movement into entertainment for the RAF – initially as a ploy to cover his work as an intelligence officer – did show an interest, after Tony had won an amateur talent competition in Dundee. Later Reader reminisced, 'I asked him if he had any comedy material and he rolled off about a dozen jokes. Apart from one, I hadn't heard any of them before. They were not real jokes but mostly service situations. This was fine because we wanted people who could play in sketches.' He was speedily assigned to the No. 9 Gang Show unit posted at Abingdon and in the summer of 1944 discovered himself aboard the *Edinburgh Castle*, a troopship converted from a Royal Mail steamer, bound for Algiers at the start of a twelve-month tour of duty that would travel throughout North Africa, Italy, Yugoslavia, Sicily, Malta, Crete, Greece, Gibraltar and the Azores.

His fellow Gang Show trouper John Beaver has shared his memories of being on tour with Tony at that time: 'He was completely unable to look after himself. He had tropical shorts – known later as Bermuda shorts – and his came down to the ankle. We were in Athens on VE Day and I remember him going out that night and coming back with an "Out of Bounds" sign.' One token concession to comfort for each Gang Show member was the regulation issue of a collapsible bed. Hancock never forgot his: 'We used to call it the pterodactyl. The thing was it had got bent and lying on it was rather like being stretched out on a rack … your feet and head were on one level and the middle of you was about a foot higher, which can be very painful.' Beaver remembered the time they spent on an empty rail cattle truck somewhere in central Italy. By now the 'pterodactyl' was in an even greater state of disrepair: 'The back part supporting his head was tied together with a piece of string. As we trundled through the countryside the string broke, but I was next to him and he slept all through the night. All the time his head was going bump, bump, bump, but he didn't wake up at all, except with a thick head in the morning!' Years later Galton and Simpson portrayed a restless Hancock attempting to get some sleep on a train journey. He nods off with his head against the window, but the jolting of the train causes him to keep banging against it. Eventually he rubs his head and gives up the effort. Perhaps he recalled the earlier journey.

Ralph Reader was a slick and appealing performer of rise-and-shine ebullience with a background in musical theatre both on Broadway – where he had worked with Al Jolson – and in the West End. A prolific producer and choreographer, he continued to be active at all levels of the entertainment business long after scouting took his career in an additional direction. Thanks to George Fairweather, Hancock was already familiar with the standards he set. Although the shows played exclusively to service personnel, dubious material was *verboten* and woe betide anyone who caused the pace and spirit of the show to flag. As Graham Stark remembered, no one was ever allowed to take a bow: 'You finished and got off – the standard of entertainment in the services was pretty low and we were dynamite.' Every single performance on every single battle front opened and closed with the song of Reader's own composition that remains his abiding trademark, 'Riding Along on the Crest of a Wave', the accompanying hand movements to which were as obligatory as the words. Hancock could not possibly have relished the waving-pointing-wriggling-clapping ritual, but Reader only remembered the obliging professional. 'In those days he didn't worry. He was a joy to be with and was one of the favourites of the unit. He used to take everything in his stride ... sometimes when we called very early rehearsals [and] had to work three shows a day and probably travel forty miles afterwards in an open lorry, he was one of the gay sparks of the crowd ... I was very fond of Tony and I watched his career. When one gets successful obviously one is going to be crowded and I don't think Tony ever liked crowds. What he did like was friends.'

When he began to compile notes for a possible autobiography, Hancock was anxious to pay his tribute to Reader and those days. His words reveal that they somehow understood each other:

> We were an extraordinarily mixed bunch – an impossible assortment, you would have thought, of professionals and 'boy scouts'. Yet somehow Reader's organising flair managed to weld us together into a smooth running team. He used to infuriate me by telling me what to do when I didn't want to be told, but I had to admire his gift for controlling crowds. I have seen him walk in that breezy, boyish way of his into a draughty great hangar, take command of about

seven hundred bored, belligerent fellows and in no time have them working like one man. I often thought then and still think now what a wonderful film director he would make, if he would only apply to directing individuals his skill for directing masses. Brilliantly though he did it, I always felt that he underestimated his ability and had no idea of his own talent for close individual direction.

Throughout his lifetime few friends were closer to Hancock than Graham Stark. When No. 9 unit was amalgamated with No. 4, Stark's old outfit, in July 1945 Graham was despatched to Abingdon to supervise. Hancock immediately impressed him: 'this strange little shuffling airman with extraordinary feet and bizarre sort of hair stuck apparently at random on the top of his head – a bit portly – but Christ, he was funny!' Graham recalls that when it was time for him to allocate the sketches, Robert Moreton, 'a very nice man, but a bit waspish,' looked at him in a sort of twisted way and asked, 'Have you two met before?' 'I've never set eyes on him,' said Stark. 'Then why is he getting all the material?' Even today Graham takes great delight in reliving the moment: 'I always remember I leaned forward quite calmly and simply said, "Because he's funny." Tony always reminded me of that down the years.' There was another moment that ricocheted back from the past when they were high-flying on radio together in the early 1950s. As the Garrick Theatre resounded with laughter during a recording of *Star Bill*, all Tony had to whisper to his friend was, 'Remember Gibraltar?'

The highlight of the European tour for the new amalgamated unit under Stark's control was the performance presented in a 2,000-seat theatre converted from a cave in the colony. All the services were represented in the audience as Hancock and Stark performed a sketch in which they played two old officers looking back over their lives, with so many medals between them they trailed all the way down their backs. The routine must have been reminiscent of the act

Morris and Cowley did as two Chelsea Pensioners on the music halls for many years. On the night in question the laughter was such as they had never heard before. 'This wall of noise came and was so phenomenal,' says Stark, 'we got the scent of victory half way through that sketch and we looked at each other and said that this is the night we shall always remember.' And they always did, always grateful for the justification why they were prepared to commit themselves so fully to an occupation so scarifying, so precarious and so unsocial. Brian Glanville, in his evocative novel *The Comic*, inspired by aspects of the Hancock story, summed up the elation: 'Each fresh laugh was like a charge, giving you power, making you want to go on and on, surpass yourself, excel yourself, till they were laughing so hard that they were right out of control, and you couldn't hope to make yourself heard.'

Vic Weldon, another Gang Show veteran, has recalled Hancock's extremely idiosyncratic approach as a solo comic. In one of his 'gags' he would point to the front row and, thinking of the proverbial lilies in the field, remark, 'Look at this lot in their finery. All that gold braid. It makes you go religious and think of the text, "They reap not, nor do they sow, yet Solomon in all his glory could not outshine one of these."' In one sketch entitled 'Rumours' Tony found himself in a skirt alongside John Beaver and Fred Stone, the leader of that unit, as three charladies caught up in an air-raid, coping with life to their hearts' content (or discontent) until the arrival of a Duchess played by Robert Moreton. Another sketch featured Tony Melody and 'Hank' Hancock in 'Candle to You': the presence of two Tonies in the unit necessitated the adjustment in Hancock's billing, something that would linger into early civilian life. Presumably one of them was in drag. Melody would sing adoringly to Hancock, 'No one can hold a candle to you,' in distant anticipation of Morrissey's success with a similar title, but different song, many years later. One of the lines sung by the pop star may have had relevance: 'Or am I Frankenstein?' In his comprehensive survey of forces entertainment, *Fighting for a Laugh*, Richard Fawkes mentions that Hancock also specialised in one act as a green-faced ghoul.

Melody went on to achieve a solid career playing recurring policemen and as a comedy support in radio and television. Fred Stone's most memorable moment came in the original London production of Sandy Wilson's *The Boy Friend*. Hancock always held him in high regard: 'He was a very strong personality who managed to keep eleven men who were living as closely as we were in reasonable shape. No matter what he felt personally about anything, it couldn't interfere with a performance. I was only twenty or so at the time, but it was a great example to me.' Tony attempted to cling to the philosophy to the end of his career and, for all the distractions and aggravations of his troubled times, for the greater part succeeded. Arthur Tolcher, the harmonica player who achieved notoriety on *The Morecambe and Wise Show* with his consistent failure to get a note in edgeways, was also arour.d at times, as was the renowned circus clown Jacko Fossett, who must in later life have looked with sympathy upon the man who turned down the Beatles. When Tony asked Jack for advice, his reply was succinct: 'Go home and work for your mother – you'll be better off.' Most notable for subsequent achievement was Rex Jameson, who as the 'weak-willed and easily led' Mrs Shufflewick provided the definitive portrayal of a gin-swilling gossip whom Hogarth knew only too well, as the authentic music hall spluttered its last gasp. Most poignantly, Robert Moreton, the bumbling comedian of later *Bumper Fun Book* fame, who would pave the way for Tony as the tutor on *Educating Archie*, took his own life when his career appeared to disintegrate in 1957.

Hancock came to see the time he spent under Reader's influence as crucial to his development as a professional. In an episode of a radio series entitled *The Laughtermakers* in 1956, he admitted, '[So far] I hadn't found any really satisfactory sort of approach, but those years gave me what I badly needed – confidence and experience. There just isn't time to get nerves, or think deeply about art, when you're doing shows in caves, in ships, from the backs of lorries in the desert.' He could have added, on every single day, in conditions ranging from sub-zero temperatures to desert heat so intense that the sand and the flies competed to cause the greater discomfort, and with little regard for how near the front line they might have been, although in a moment of honesty he once declared that this was never nearer than three miles away. He expounded on the matter for John Freeman: 'There were only eleven men in the company ... you made about fourteen appearances in a show and although you did a lot of things that you weren't really suited to do, it somehow opened us up a little more and you saw possibilities of expanding in a way that you hadn't thought of before.' He failed to add that the RAF stations were the saddest places to play. The comedy actor Kenneth Connor recalled for Fawkes that one end of the mess where the performers would be entertained before or after the show would always be banked high with wreaths and floral tributes for those who had gone missing in action. Throughout a performance it was customary to hear the Tannoy going, 'Crash crew, stand by,' while planes would come limping in from raids and those who were lucky enough to emerge from them would come hobbling in to see the end of the show. He doubtless dreamt of Colin on those nights.

But life was not without humour. Hancock loved to tell the tale of how as they unpacked three decks below water level on that first voyage to Algiers, Robert Moreton unwrapped a white dinner jacket from his kitbag, 'in case there's a dance on board'. Nor was he unprepared to tell a story against himself. Having decided to respect naval tradition by smoking a pipe for the first time in his life, with all 'eyes on the distant horizon' – to quote from the Gang Show anthem – Hancock leaned over the railing in best *In Which We Serve* fashion and took his first puff. The bowl fell off and plopped into the briny, and Hancock never smoked a pipe again. He shared with George Fairweather another incident, this time recalled from one of Ralph

Reader's auditions. His friend re-enacted it for me: 'A broad Brummie got up on stage and Ralph said, "What do you do?" He said, "I jump." He said, "No. What's your act?" He said, "That's my act. I jump." He said, "What do you mean, you jump?" He said, "Well, I jump and get higher and higher. That's what I do." He then stood to attention and he jumped and he jumped and he got so high. It became a standing joke between the two of us. If I phoned him and he asked, "Who's that?" I would always say, "I jump." He always knew who it was then, and we were away.' The adenoidal naivety of the poor *sauteur* never failed to add to the merriment.

Reader was fond enough of Tony to write a song especially for him, although it is not clear whether this happened during the war or when a later expanded version of the Gang Show went on a conventional theatre tour after the hostilities. The number capitalised on his appearance as an 'erk', the service slang – for an aircraftman on the first tier of duty – that captured so brilliantly the forlorn, shambling demeanour of so many who were plunged indiscriminately into the conflict. Both Tunis and Stark had spotted his ability to project the type with comic effect from the stage. As Reader said, 'I must admit it seemed to come terribly naturally to him.' The song was called, 'I'm a Hero to My Mum', and he sang it straight as a ballad. It took him until 1 June 1946 – 'a record that was beaten only once, I believe' – to achieve promotion from Aircraftman Second Class to Acting Sergeant, by which time the war was over. 'I doubt,' recalled Hancock, 'whether I would ever have risen to Acting Sergeant if they hadn't been so short of NCOs by then and found there was nobody else to produce the Ralph Reader shows. We called them variety shows, but the first one I put on consisted of twelve singers and two comics. So much for variety!' Hancock would not be demobbed until 7 November 1946. The challenge of turning himself into the star comedian of his dreams awaited him. A letter he wrote to his brother, Roger, from Italy in June 1945 is significant:

Spaghetti is eaten by everybody, though there are several different approaches to it. Some believe in getting one end into the mouth and giving a long hard suck until the spaghetti unravels and vanishes into your mouth with a 'plop', while others use the mid-air method which consists of lifting the spaghetti off the plate in a lump between a knife and fork and juggling with it, making frequent determined lunges at it with the teeth. But as it looks as if you're knitting a balaclava helmet, this can be a bit embarrassing.

His gift for observational humour was already developing. The promise was there.

Chapter Four

'IT'S NOT EASY, IS IT?'

'I'm Anthony Hancock, comedian.
I wonder if you've got anything?'

Hancock was catapulted out of the forces on 6 November 1946, although any immediate exhilaration must have drained away when the dreariness of the life ahead of him sank in. In retrospect the influx of new comedians onto the British show business scene after the war appears like a tidal wave, but the process was far more gradual. At the beginning the whole glorious parade of them – Hancock, Howerd, Wisdom, Secombe, Sellers, Milligan, Bentine, Cooper and many more – had yet to be prised from an indiscriminate blur of desperate hopefuls, from which the fittest – or funniest – would survive in an eerie parallel to the struggle from which they had just emerged. Gang Show veterans like Hancock were also at a disadvantage; not released from the service until after more established ENSA members, they consequently found themselves in an already overcrowded market for entertainers.

Tony recalled that he flew through the demob centre at Wembley 'like a typhoon', making a grab for his £60 gratuity and the first clothes he could put his hands on whether they fitted or not. Hancock admitted, 'I thought the battle was over when they sent me out into the world in one of those stiff, hairy suits and hard pale blue trilbies that no one would have dared to wear in public except for the sheer joy of getting out of uniform. But it had only just begun.' For two weeks he installed himself in a room at the British Lion Club in Ebury Street, before moving to the Union Jack Club for veterans just across the way from Waterloo Station. His room resembled a cell, but provided a paradise: 'It meant that for the first time for four years you didn't have to be with other people if you didn't want to. It was luxury unimagined.' The downside was provided by the regular visits from the police, 'who came from time to time to see if there were any deserters'. Like customs officers, they must have cast the shadow of ersatz guilt upon him. The threat of the redcaps became a recurring comic motif in the radio version of *Hancock's Half Hour* almost ten years later, as Hancock the poseur made spectacular claims to a derring-do war career he never had.

At Ebury Street he was reunited with his old chum, Graham Stark. Graham recalls that they survived on a diet of coffee and doughnuts – Hancock used to joke that he ended up with a hole in his stomach – and spent much of their time together in the Nuffield Centre, the club for service personnel then situated in Coventry Street, where it embraced the restructured remains of the bombed-out Café de Paris next door. They spent their time wondering when someone was going to offer one of them a 'walk-on' part at the very least. Stark remembers, 'It was almost a relief when the weekends came, the agents' offices were closed, and nobody could give us the brush-off.' They whiled away the time with the *Daily Telegraph* crossword puzzle, turning the solving of it into an exhibitionist ritual designed to command attention. As Graham wielded the pencil, Tony would extemporise: 'Oh, here's one, right – let's think now – C – blank – T – four-legged animal – feline – it's not easy, is it?' Sitting there in their demob suits, they received free coffee and sandwiches and nobody asked any questions. Crosswords never lost their allure for Hancock, and his fascination with words – the magic of holding them up to the light and teasing out their innermost meaning – was brilliantly caught by Galton and Simpson in the bedsitter episode, as he stared into the mirror and pondered his teeth: 'I wonder which one's the bicuspid. It's a funny word that, isn't it? B*icus*pid. Bicus*pid*. *Bi*cuspid … yes, that's probably from the Latin. Bi meaning two, one on each side. Cus, cus meaning to swear. Pid meaning pid. Greek probably, pid. Yes, Greek for teeth. So bicuspid – two swearing teeth.'

When Stark was offered a spell in repertory in Kidderminster, Hancock took the first step in the direction of some form of self-sufficiency by moving into a one-room flat with two beds at the end of a bombed terrace at Edith Road, Barons Court, with another Gang Show pal, John Beaver. Here they shared a washbasin with no running water and a bucket underneath to catch the water when you pulled out the plug. Hancock was always forgetting to empty the water, and this played havoc with the landlady's ceiling underneath. Here also Hancock endured the freezing winter of 1947, keeping warm by clinging to the bed covers – 'I just gave up looking for work and took to my bed' – and subsisting on a distinctive brand of sausage: 'It tasted like hell, but you ate it and if you had a couple of glasses of water each day for about three days following, you felt full.' Beaver recalled a slightly more varied menu: 'Tony was afraid of getting scurvy and insisted on a diet of green stuffs.' They used to go shopping for Brussels sprouts, potatoes and the infamous sausage, but because his pride did not allow him to be seen carrying a shopping bag, Hancock insisted on using an old cardboard attaché case. In those days, when it was not easy to come by new kitchen utensils, they were restricted to a single knife, fork and spoon each, a frying pan and a saucepan. Everything was cooked over a gas ring. The spirit that pervaded the ménage is shown by a mock-diploma that some friends, the actor David Lodge among them, presented to Beaver: 'Know by all men by these presents [*sic*] that this Golden Spoon, to be known hereafter as the "Culinary Trophy" was presented to Johnathon Beaver, Esq., of the Beaver-Hancock household as a token of esteem and regard of the Gastronomical Triumphs over the

Sausage.' Beaver was keen to emphasise that it was all in good fun, describing his roommate as 'somebody who was always in a good mood, in a good temper – you could always get on with him – no big-time attitude about him – he would always give and take'.

As poverty competed with the rationing culture of the day, the exigencies of the kitchen were matched by those of the wardrobe. In addition to 'the railings', the name Hancock gave to his pinstripe grey demob suit, he admitted to two shirts and a change of under-wear. Celluloid collars came in useful. Uncomfortable as hell, they could at least be washed clean under a running tap. The Fleet Street veteran Derek Jameson recalls meeting Tony by chance at the old Lyons Corner House in Leicester Square some time around this peri-od. As the young journalist sat there with a cup of tea and his pile of newspapers, an easy target for anyone wanting a chat, he was approached by the aspirant young comedian:'He wanted a gander at my *Daily Mirror*. What he said made little impression on me at the time. What he wore stayed in my mind forever. It was his tie. A per-fectly normal, rather dull neckpiece. Only he had no shirt under it. Just a crumpled sports jacket.' The memory would have come as no surprise to Tony's close friend, the comedian Dick Emery, who bumped into him in a similar state of half-dress in nearby Lisle Street soon after. Tony was carrying a parcel wrapped in newspaper. When Dick asked where he was going, he confessed that he was try-ing to find someone to lend him the money for his laundry, namely the shirt tied up with string under his arm!

When Beaver went into pantomime at the end of 1946, John Herod, another Gang Show chum who later became prominent in Australian show business as Johnny Ladd, moved in. Elsa Page was a mutual friend with an RAF background who remembers them as a typical 'Odd Couple': 'They were not compatible as roommates. John was very precise with everything very clean, in its place, and well organised. Hank (as he was still affectionately known during these times) was untidy and left pans about, so John was cross and Hank would go home to Mum.' Hancock could not have survived thus far without the support of his mother. When she came up to town, tea at the Regent Palace Hotel was *de rigueur*. Often Graham Stark saw her slide a ten bob note to her son under the table to save him the embarrassment of not being able to pay. The ritual was one that family friend Mary Hobley also observed. Tony always acknowledged the encouragement his mother gave at this time: 'For years she had every right to tell me to turn it in, but she never did.' In another interview he went further: 'She thought that everything I did was great. It was only when I was settling down that she started to become critical. She was clearly very successful at hiding her doubts.'

According to Elsa, it was Herod who bullied Hancock into pursuing work. Each day he would take the tube from Barons Court to Charing Cross Road, where the variety agents had their offices *en masse*. Tony had a special mantra that helped him on his way. 'You will call on every agent in London,' he would recite to himself over and over as the train rattled on its way. When he emerged into the daylight his resolution disintegrated and, seduced by the smell of coffee beans roasting, he would allow himself to be drawn into the womb of the Express Dairy or a rival establishment for the newspapers, then lunch, followed by the decision-making process of what film to see that afternoon. One day hunger conquered fear and he forced himself up a dingy staircase into an agent's office: 'Heart thumping, eyes fixed and rather glazed, I burst in and announced, "I'm Anthony Hancock, comedian. I wonder if you've got anything?"' As he extended his hand in greeting, he misplaced his foot and slipped on the rug. His feet went forward as he went backwards, half out of the door. The thunderstruck look on that agent's face stayed with him forever. According to Beaver, Tony eventually went to great lengths to have an acetate recording made of his act to tout around the agents, but his lack of confidence in himself was not helped by his own assessment of his material. He sensed – perhaps correctly – that what had worked three miles from the front line was not what was required outside the theatre of war. The fear turned out to be academic. He had not been forgotten by Ralph Reader, who in the spring of 1947 offered him an audition for a very special new theatrical venture that would provide Tony Hancock with his first genuine professional engagement. Presented by Reader on behalf of the Air Council, the show attempted to tell the 'epic story' of the RAF in twenty-seven scenes of pageantry, comedy and song with a cast of around 300. The majority were still serving as airmen and women attached to the RAF Theatre Pageant Unit, who were supplemented by a small core of professionals, or 'civvies' – for civilians – as they became known. Hancock qualified as one of the latter.

His appearance in *Wings* provided Lily Hancock with her proudest moment from her son's career. Without his knowledge she travelled to Blackpool in April 1947 for the opening at the Opera House, the largest theatre in the land. As she remembered things, she had reached the interval with no obvious sign of Tony in the first half of the show, when suddenly the curtain went up again. All her anxieties were dispelled as he sidled on in his definitive 'erk' characterisation and sang the sentimental appeal that Reader had written especially for him:

Intelligence is not the thing I'm famed for.
I may not be a personality.
Everything that happens I get blamed for,
But on one thing all agree:
I'm just a nuisance to the Sergeant,
I don't get any break at all,
I'm just the feller what peels the spuds,
I'm at everybody's beck and call.
I'm just the guy who takes the can back;
They all think I'm dumb.
But I don't care tuppence,
'Cos I know darn well I'm a hero to my mum.

As Lily emphasised, 'It really was the biggest moment of my life.' Fellow cast member Bryan Olive recalled how the last line would bring the house down: 'He used to deliver it perfectly and it always brought laughter and applause.' But it was also a moment that in later life Tony wanted to forget. Philip Oakes claimed that a production still of the act showing 'a phenomenally lean Hancock' with broom in hand singing robustly into the spotlight was 'a weapon which could always be used to silence him in arguments about artistic integrity in later years'. Who does relish being reminded of one's apprentice years? For the moment, though, the taste was sweet. He could put the bad times behind him – little realising they would return even worse – and relax into the relative security of a five-month run of the largest theatres in the land at the unheard-of salary of £10 per week.

Reader proved to be in his element as his production traced the birth, progress and achievement of the RAF with all his customary flair for the spectacular. Wherever the Gang Show had played during the war, however precarious the conditions, he had insisted upon full make-up, full costume and his trademark backcloth, a light blue curtain emblazoned with the words 'Gang Show'. Now he was spoiled for choice. The local Blackpool press gave a rousing send-off to 'these fine-looking lads and lasses who put all they knew into this heart-warming pageant of memory in which times, trumpets, tears and triumph are all served up in laughter and light and spiced with the wine of youth'. In truth the spectacle and ebullience had the edge over the comedy. The sketches were perceived as 'a little long and a little futile, although the audience mostly liked them'. A scene on a troopship was described surprisingly – in the light of Reader's standards – as 'tiresome ... with some risky "jokes" at which the young people were supposed to laugh and applaud ... there is no excuse for questionable "humour" in a show as good as this'. Within a decade Hancock would go on to epitomise the humour of a new generation, and there was one single moment when the show provided a glimpse of what was in store. As he interrupted a gymnastic display set on

Blackpool sands by shambling across the stage in a hopelessly ill-fit-ting uniform, an apoplectic Drill Sergeant yelled, 'Where do you think you are? Just look at your trousers. Look at your jacket. You are a disgrace to the service. How long have you been in the Air Force?' The shaking Hancock looked up, paused and, literally shrugging the words off his chest, replied resignedly, 'All bloody day!'

The show boasted no stars as such, but semi-recognisable names in the company included John Forbes-Robertson, the grand-son of the famous actor-manager; Brian Nissen, who had appeared in films for J. Arthur Rank and, like John, was still serving as an Aircraftman First Class; and Edward Evans, who would become famous as Mr Grove in the pioneer television soap opera *The Grove Family*. Ten motor coaches and many trucks were needed to trans-port cast and scenery from town to town. Among his comrades Hancock made a distinct impression. Bryan Olive, still technically a pilot within the service at the time, recalls that a vote was taken among a group of them as to who would achieve the greatest success in future life: 'There was a first, a second and a third. He must have had a noticeable something even then, because he came first! And I'm not really certain we ever told him ...' In spite of playing to packed houses for most of the eighteen-week run, the show lost a staggering £32,000, losses met by the Air Council with the assis-tance of the Treasury in the cause of propaganda and the further recruitment drive for the service. The tour culminated in a special enhanced staging at the Royal Albert Hall on 14 September for a Battle of Britain remembrance show, when for one night only Richard Attenborough paid a personal tribute to those who fought the Battle of Britain, John Mills recited Tennyson's 'Loxley Hall' and the evergreen George Robey with Violet Loraine reprised the tear-jerker that defined an earlier conflict, 'If You Were the Only Girl in the World'.

One looks to his comrades for some insight into Hancock's approach to his work and his aspirations during those days. His artistic integrity stood out. John and Freda Maud, who met on the show, remembered him as a 'forthright and honest character' who, even though he seemed to prefer the company of the amateurs to that of his fellow civvies, 'stood out as a professional – he couldn't perform something if it wasn't right'. Olive noted that while not without a sense of humour, Hancock came over at times, although mainly with hindsight, as melancholy for one so young: 'I think it was obvious that in a subtle way, even then, he had designs on becoming a big international star and also strangely I think he had a touch of snobbery in him, again in a somewhat subtle way.' This did not prevent him coming over to one and all 'as a friendly sort of guy', although one who sensed his limitations. When an opportunity arose for some of the company to hold an informal concert of their own, Bryan distinctly recalled overhearing one of the lads urging Tony to do something, but he would not comply: 'I can't without a script.' He could be, added Olive, 'a bit mysterious and/or complicated'. Elsa Page might have understood: 'There was a depth to Hank, a more serious side to our pal than just a clown … mind you, in the old Nuffield centre days, we WAAF and WREN mates had to buy him a few pints before we could get him up to dance with us!'

The pomp of the Royal Albert Hall extravaganza could only have heightened the sense of letdown that the tour was over. For a while he shared a house, or part of it, with Edward Evans in Grey Close, Hampstead Garden Suburb. It was back to straitened circumstances until a more conventional booking came his way, the part of an Ugly Sister in pantomime at the Oxford Playhouse. But before then an epiphany had occurred in his life that would have a major effect on his comedy outlook. Throughout 1947 the current comedy idol of the West End held sway in the revue *Piccadilly Hayride* at the Prince of Wales Theatre, right across the road from the Nuffield Centre. There was no escaping the fact that Sid Field was the man to be seen. Hancock and Stark went together, and to this day Graham can enact the experience: 'We were kicking the seats in front of us – it was so funny – he was magic – we'd never laughed so much.' He recounts the moment in a Shakespearian burlesque from the show in which Sid played King John and a young Terry-Thomas his cook, Simnel. Taking one look at the man-at-arms standing nearby in full suit of armour, Field commented, 'You wanna get a fourteen pound hammer and put a crease in them.' That was the moment a convulsed Hancock turned to his friend and whispered his allegiance: 'He's the one. He's the one for me.' The ability to give an inconsequential line comic depth was only one attribute that would in due course find an echo in Hancock's work. It helped that Sid had also been born in Birmingham.

Field was a revue comic who shone in situations provided by sketches as distinct from a stand-up comic with a direct line of attack to his audience. In this respect he was multi-faceted, ringing the changes on a succession of comic types that included the wide boy, the effete photographer, the apprentice golfer, the moonstruck musician and more. While Hancock, by contrast, evolved into a single-character man, the comic projection of himself, he nevertheless found a way of absorbing many aspects of Field into his central persona, although he did sidestep the camp quality of much of his idol's work. It was osmosis born of hero-worship, rather than conscious copying. In one sketch Sid played a landscape painter pestered by the attentions of an irksome schoolgirl. One can hear Hancock delivering the response: 'Why don't you go and play a nice game on the railway lines – with your back to the oncoming engines?' And then, after he has pacified her by producing a bottle of lemonade, 'Get the bottle well down your throat.' Throughout Hancock's career comedy aficionados with sharp ears could detect the influence of Field in his own delivery. When Sid James attempts to correct Tony during a boxing lesson, Hancock becomes aggrieved: 'There is no need to shout. I didn't know. I wish I hadn't come.' We could be listening to Field the golfer on the first tee with his instructor, Jerry Desmonde. When Hancock gets into an altercation in the cinema, the breathy belligerence gives him

away: 'What's the matter with you? Hold me coat. You picked a right
boy here. I'll knock him back in the three and nines. A quick left and
he won't know what's hit him.' It could be Field's boisterous cockney
spiv, Slasher Green, remonstrating. When the emigration officer
explains that all potential immigrants must be vetted and document-
ed, Hancock sighs, 'What a palaver!' It must have been difficult to
resist switching it for Sid's catchphrase. 'What a per*form*ance!' the
older man would seethe, as his dignity was destroyed, his patience
unravelled. Even the arch preening of Field's society photographer, if
not the camp sexual ambivalence, was caught in the television
episode where Tony applies his hand to the camera and prepares to
take Sid James's portrait. All Sid expects is a 'snap'; Tony, all aflutter
in large floppy velvet bow tie and smoking jacket, is intent on creating a 'symphony in emulsion'.

In his appearance on *The Frost Programme* in January 1967,
Hancock brilliantly conjured up the magic of his hero for a whole new
audience:

> And Jerry Desmonde would come on and say, 'Now ladies and gen-
> tlemen, with great pleasure I would like to introduce England's
> leading exponent of the tubular bells, Mr Eustace Bollinger.' And
> Sid would come on with two mallets, and a terrible wasp waistcoat
> and bicycle clips – which have always seemed to me to be funny
> anyway. He used to say to the musical director, 'What do you think
> I should play?' and he'd say, 'Why don't you play Beethoven's 15th
> Movement of the 7th Symphony in E flat minor with the modulat-
> ed key change to G flat major?' and Sid had a good long look at him,
> and then he got hold of one of these mallets and said, 'Yes, I thought
> you'd suggest something like that,' and tried to belt him with this
> stick. Then the orchestra all rose up and tried to clout him with
> their violins, so nobody was in any doubt as to what the relation-
> ship was for a start! Then a voice from the box said, 'Maestro,' but
> Sid knows it's not true. That was the beauty of it. Anybody calling

him 'Maestro', he knew the man was a fool. And on a table by the
side he'd got a Ludo set, a toy fire engine, a toy poodle – by the side
of these tubular bells – and this bloke in the box says, 'Maestro,
what's all the junk on the table?' 'Junk?' 'Yes, what is all that junk
on the table?' 'That's not junk,' says Sid. 'That's prizes!' That para-
lysed me. You could just imagine him sort of cycling up from Sidcup
or somewhere, with his clips on and all this gear on his bike. Most
of it is in your imagination. Like any great comic, Sid relied a great
deal on the imagination and warmth of his audience.

In Field's work Hancock saw the comedy of exasperation, as taught
to him by George Fairweather in the magician sketch, raised to its
highest level so far. Hancock's world of 'stone me!' moroseness, of
'how dare you!' indignation was partly derived from his own character and background, partly the product of his writers' creation; but a
small corner of it – one forever Birmingham – will always remain a
legacy from Sid Field. This blissful, benign comedy god died from a
heart attack on 3 February 1950 at the sadly premature age of forty-
five, with, as Tynan observed, alcohol and self-criticism his pall-
bearers. The whole world of theatre mourned: according to Phyllis
Rounce, Tony's agent at the time, 'It was the only time I ever saw him
in tears.' He was so besotted by him he christened his first two cars
accordingly, one 'Sid' and the other 'Harvey', after the invisible rabbit of the play of the same name in which he was playing at the time
of his death. Not discovered on the West End stage until March 1943
after years of provincial touring, Field had packed the cream of his
achievement into seven years. The same time span reverberates in
any assessment of Hancock's own greatest success, the darker
echoes of alcoholism, anxiety and self-doubt providing their own disturbing postscript to his own story.

No one can say how much of Field's ambience rubbed off on the
young Hancock as he trod the boards of the Oxford Playhouse that
Christmas. Frank Shelley, the artistic director of the Playhouse, had

offered him the part of the Ugly Sister after being impressed by his performance in *Wings* at Oxford's New Theatre the previous August. In one scene he had to sit on his sibling's shoulders as they lurched down a flight of stairs together. In a fit of mischief on the third night Hancock had the funnier idea of throwing his skirt over his partner's head. Unable to see a thing, the latter staggered across the stage and then tried to steady himself above the footlights before losing all equilibrium and landing them both in the orchestra pit. From that moment Hancock decided to play things by the script, in which he was billed as the Hon. Sarah Blotto. His counterpart, the Hon. Euphrosyne Blotto, was played by the actor John Moffatt, who much later would become familiar to television viewers as Coméliau, the prickly superior judge to Michael Gambon's Maigret in the Granada series based on the stories by Georges Simenon. What most impressed Moffatt was Hancock's 'great good taste – he couldn't bear any kind of vulgarity on stage. I played the haughty, pretentious sister and Tony played the draggle-tail who was always letting me down, so he had great opportunities to be vulgar, but he never was.' The *Oxford Mail* praised their clowning as 'slapstick of a very high order'. Hancock, with a nod to the dreaming spires, joked that it was a very intellectual panto: 'Three minutes of Latin in the wood scene – which had to go – and people chatting about Nietzsche during the ballroom scene. Lots of philosophical chat. Extremely successful for Oxford.'

To economise he bypassed the standard theatrical digs and rented a gypsy caravan for £1 a week in a field outside the city. It sounded a good idea until the first morning a herd of cows gave him their version of an alarm call when they vigorously started butting the sides. The farmer had his explanation, one it is difficult not to imagine Hancock himself delivering in that rortiest of rustic voices he reserved for the part of Joshua Merryweather in Galton and Simpson's travesty of *The Archers*, *The Bowmans*: 'Them cows allus go round that there 'van first thing in the morning. Allus have done.

They sharpens their 'orns on it.' The last night arrived and in best theatrical tradition the ladies in the cast were plied across the footlights with chocolates and flowers. Then, unannounced, two youths bounded out of the audience and regaled Sarah and Euphrosyne with bouquets fashioned from onions, carrots, cabbages and bottles of stout. It was not until many years later that Moffatt discovered that one of those lads was an enthusiastic young theatre buff named Ronnie Barker, whose own career received a substantial boost shortly after when he joined the Playhouse's repertory company under Shelley.

In 1993 Barker dedicated his autobiography to the director, one of 'the three wise man who directed my career; without men like these, there would be no theatre'. Hancock could not have disagreed. By the end of April he was back at the Playhouse, although Moffatt admits he cannot vouch for the story that Shelley offered him the job when he bumped into Tony picking up a penny from the pavement in Charing Cross Road, saying, 'Well, if you're as hard up as all that, I can use you in this large-cast play we're doing.' The piece was Noël Coward's *Peace in Our Time*. He had three small parts and re-enacted them with relish in the years to come: 'The first role – it said "A man" and I had to say "Goodnight, Mrs Shattuck."That's all. I walked straight into the juvenile lead, who said to me, "Get out of my bloody way, you bastard." Every night I used to say "*Good*night, Mrs Shattuck," "Good*night*, Mrs Shattuck," "Goodnight, *Mrs* Shattuck." It all meant something. Nothing! Then I played a German civil servant with a pork pie hat on. And the producer said, "Will you keep an undercurrent of German throughout the scene." And I had bifocals on and I couldn't even find my drink and I was fumbling under the table to find my glass and keeping up an undercurrent of German. "Auch was ist *ummm* Bahnhof *ummm* ich habe nien *ummm* Düsseldorf." Then I finally appeared as a drunken, brutal Nazi soldier. I had the lot on. The jackboots, the gun, the swastika armband. And for this character Coward had written the worst line he had ever written without any question. I said, "Bitte." "The bitter's off but we've got some old and mild," the landlord replied. And I thought when I was playing it even then, "Jesus, what is this man doing?"' He returned to London and the pursuit of comedy – intentional comedy, that is.

There had been a second agenda for visiting the Prince of Wales Theatre those several months ago. Another old RAF colleague, Derek Scott, was in gainful employment there as the accompanist to Terry-Thomas in his impressionist act, *Technical Hitch*, a remarkable display of virtuosity in which the rising star played both a frantic disc-jockey and the voices – Paul Robeson, Ezio Pinza, Richard Tauber and Hutch were a few – on the records that he had mislaid, or, if the budget of the show allowed, broken. Scott, who had a profitable career ahead of him as a musical director and consultant in commercial television, would become a life-long friend of Hancock. One night at a party Tony, against type, found himself improvising an act with Derek, on the keyboard, acting as feed. It was a great success and at Scott's suggestion they set about polishing it with a view to offering it to Vivian Van Damm, the legendary impresario of the Windmill Theatre, the venue where, as Denis Norden has remarked, 'young ladies were barely paraded and comedians were barely tolerated'. In later years Derek recalled one of the gags that surfaced in their efforts: 'Shall we walk down to the pub and have a pint, or shall we take a bus and have half a pint?' Roger Hancock remembered another, something about a stag's head on display in a pub: 'He must have been going at a hell of a lick to get through that wall.' Tony, who will never be celebrated as a joke teller as such, clung to the latter until the end of his life.

More relevant was the main thrust of the routine, which owed a little to Terry-Thomas and no doubt far more to George Fairweather. The theme was an impromptu concert party with, as Hancock put it, a lot of 'dashing on and off, and putting on funny hats and things'. It was reprised for his second radio broadcast, when he made his début on the Sunday night hit show *Variety Bandbox* on 9 January 1949. The script he used for the occasion survives. One has no difficulty guessing where he obtained the inspiration for the opening:

> I want you to imagine that it's cold and wet. The scene is a seaside town in the middle of summer. You're sitting on the sand, the umbrella raised as the rain beats softly down. You're patiently waiting for the commencement of the local concert party, probably the world's worst concert party, complete with ancient jokes and aspiring tenor and so on. The curtain jerks slowly back and the Tatty Follies are about to begin – so on with the show.

A few lines into the opening song, we are introduced to some of the cast:

> *I'm Bertie Higginbottom and I'll make you smile*
> *And I will serenade you for a little while.*
> *I'm the brightest young soubrette that you have ever seen,*
> *And I'll impersonate for you the stars of stage and screen.*

A rousing burst of 'Colonel Bogey' then takes us straight into the comic's act:

> By gow, it's grand to be back here at Tatty-on-Sea. I've got a couple of funny stories here for you. I think they'll make you laugh. I were coming along to the theatre the other day. A fella came up to me. He says, 'Joe.' He says, 'D'you know why the chicken crossed the road?' He says, 'Well, I'll tell you. It's for some foul reason.' Aye, well, we'll not bother with that one. I've got a bit of poetry for you. There was a young lady from Ryde, who ate some green apples and died. The apples fermented inside the lamented, and made cider inside 'er inside. By gow, yon were a hot 'un.

The chicken joke was vintage Max Miller; the limerick doubtless Hancock's own; the idiom that of variety's broad Lancastrian rapscallion Frank Randle. He goes on to introduce Sinclair Farquhar, the show's tenor, who gives us a burst of Ivor Novello's 'Shine through My Dreams' before cueing 'Knightsbridge March', the signature tune for *In Town Tonight*, the popular radio interview programme of the day. This was a device that had also been used by Terry-Thomas in a second spot on *Piccadilly Hayride*, also accompanied by Scott. The two comedians remained close throughout their lives, so obviously they had an amicable understanding on the matter. Even then Hancock was deliberately milking the outdatedness of his material: 'My first impression is, I believe, entirely original. I think I am right in saying it has never been presented on any stage before, at any time, in any country. Ladies and gentlemen, I give you, Charles Laughton in *Mutiny on the Bounty*.'

No one ever bellowed 'Mis-tah Chris-tian ... I'll have you hung from the highest yardarm in the Navy' to the imaginary Clark Gable with greater disdain or to funnier effect than Hancock. This was obviously the point in the concert party routine where he could expand or contract accordingly, limited only by the scope of Fairweather's own repertoire and anything he had the nerve to add. For the radio broadcast he fell back upon Quasimodo, with its echo of Laughton again, although the contorted freakishness of the character would have been lost on the home audience, together with a visual gag, for which Hancock needed to keep his hair at a special length, in which he discovers he cannot see the audience and then with a deft flick of his head rights the matter, often the cue for applause.

> And now, ladies and gentleman, I feel that up to now we've had a certain amount of levity, jocularity, laughter and gaiety and I do feel that the time has come to strike a rather more serious note in the programme. So put the children under the seats, while I pull my hair over my face to get right into the character of the Hunchback

of Notre Dame ... where are they? ... Oh, there you are. I'm terribly
sorry ... got the hair in my eyes and couldn't see!

Derek would then join Tony to evoke the upper-class cadences of
Kenneth and George, the Western Brothers, with words that this
time around amounted to so much gibberish:

Scapa on the haybox with scanson on the skay
Forlip with the cranston on the line
Jayboy in the chipmunk and the omi on the tray
Forlip with the cranston on the line
Scarfan is the skipmark with a scarpment in the plee
Nante with the bullcut and the trampot at the gee
But scara scara scara and a flagnap on the ree
Forlip with the cranston on the line

Or something like that, before a brief burst of double talk, a reprise
of the nonsense verse and a parody of a rousing chorus song to finish.
'A Song to Forget' may have been penned specifically for *Variety
Bandbox*, since it was credited to two rising names, musician and
scriptwriter Sid Colin and musician and broadcaster Steve Race.

Everybody shout it,
Sing a song about it,
If you ever doubt it you'll be blue.
Oh the drums are drumming,
'Cos a great day's coming,
And about time too.

Hancock later claimed that Derek hated uttering a single word during the whole proceedings and that when he had to open his mouth
'he would curl up into embarrassment at the sound of his own voice'.
Interestingly, a small part of the act brought back family memories:

'He did a grand job at the piano and boosted my morale no end, as my mother once boosted my father's, by laughing all through the act. I had no need to turn round; I could hear him spluttering away behind my back. More often than not it was because something had gone wrong – that man went delirious over disaster – but no matter. It was heartening to know that he was enjoying himself, however firmly those blocks of stone out front might sit on their hands.'

The *Variety Bandbox* broadcast was still in the future when Scott and Hancock, billed as 'Derek Scott and Hank', played the Windmill Theatre for six weeks from 12 July 1948. It was the most encouraging sign yet to the young comedian that his career was on track, although why he had reverted to using his wartime Gang Show appellation is a mystery. To audiences on the *Wings* tour and in Oxford he had used his birth name, and there would appear to have been no rival 'Tony' in the new cast. The additional comedy support on a bill dominated by musical sequences and the so-called 'scenas' that featured bare expanses of the statuesque female form for which the theatre was famous was provided by a comedy ventriloquist with a dithering style who would one day drop his dummy, figuratively speaking, and a rather rough conventional double act. Van Damn really could afford only two of the three acts, but took them all on trial on the understanding that he could let one of the double acts go at the end of the first week. Harry Worth was safe, and Morecambe and Wise – they had recently changed *their* billing from their actual names, Bartholomew and Wiseman – fell by the wayside. No one needs telling that their talent and resilience were such that it did not matter. One wonders if Hancock, with or without his partner, would have bounced back from such early rejection.

What may well have been Hancock's first mention in the national press appeared in a review in the *Daily Herald* the day after the Windmill opening, stating how 'young comedian makes a hit' performing his 'brilliant thumbnail impressions of a "dud" concert party among the nimble youthful feminine pulchritude' of what was the

214th edition of *Revudeville*, the revue in miniature with its coy intimation of nudity in its title, at the theatrical institution that could proudly boast of its wartime record, 'We never closed,' only for some wag to echo, 'We never clothed!' At a much later date Barry Cryer recalled his surprise at discovering that between shows, which were otherwise more or less continuous, a voice would boom over a loudspeaker with a request that patrons not climb over the seats to get nearer to the front for the next show, an announcement that was usually drowned out by the very sound of men clambering over the seats to get nearer to the first row. Jimmy Edwards, one of the most successful comedians to make his initial impact there, christened the ritual 'The Grand National'. Every morning the theatre handyman had to tighten the bolts to ensure the seats were secure. The initial slogan, incidentally, referred specifically to the period between 16 September and 12 October 1940 at the height of the Blitz when the Windmill was the only theatre to remain open in London, and not the two weeks at the outbreak of war when all such venues were closed by Act of Parliament.

Later Hancock remarked that his season at the theatre just around the corner from Piccadilly Circus coincided with the London Olympics, and that the front six rows of the stalls were full of Mongolian discus-throwers and non-English-speaking Ethiopians. He was a little less flippant when John Freeman asked him about the experience: 'It's a marvellous place to run in an act. We did six shows a day, six days a week, and you learnt to die like a swan, you know, gracefully. The show used to start at 12.15. I used to go on at 12.19 to three rows of gentlemen reading newspapers, and nothing, you see, absolutely nothing, but you'd learn to die with a smile on your face and walk off. Then you came back again at two o'clock to see the same people, and you died again. But it was a great experience. I didn't enjoy it at the time, but it's been a great benefit afterwards … but I'll tell you what was the best thing. The drunks used to come in about twenty past three, when the pubs were closed, and they were quite lively, so it made the day go.' On a later radio interview, he added, 'Windmill? Call it the Treadmill … either you're a comedian after that or you're out.' Hancock boasted of arriving at the theatre with four minutes to spare before his first entrance, a situation helped by the decision, forced upon him by necessity, to wear his street clothes, the hardy pinstripe demob suit. 'I wanted to appear casual,' he would explain by way of excuse.

For all the pressure to succeed, these were obviously happy times with a close-knit family atmosphere backstage. Phyllis Rounce remembered how the girls would fall about with laughter backstage, unable to go on properly, as Tony mimicked the way they walked, his own penguin gait not entirely conducive to their elegant high-heeled demeanour. What he could never bring himself to do was to refer to Van Damm as V.D. in the way everyone else did. From the beginning he settled for 'Sir' or as he once admitted, 'Mr – er – um – V – er – um – Mr Van – Damm'. His reticence had no effect on the success of his audition and continued until the end of their association. Also on the bill was a magician, Francis Watts, with whom Hancock shared a dressing room: 'He had just time between shows to grab a cup of tea, then start putting the strings up his sleeves, folding the trick silk flags, putting the rabbits back in the hat … and he was on! Just time to get on stage. Perpetual motion.' On one occasion the schedule did not go to plan. Someone knocked over a tray of drinks that were an integral part of the act. Hancock and Scott gallantly came to his aid, helping to load the various accoutrements into his bulging dress suit. Unfortunately not everything went into the right place, leaving the conjuror on stage more bewildered than his audience and Hancock helpless with laughter again at the side of the stage. Derek recalled that the big finish to the act was a paper-tearing trick that revealed a torn-out representation of a clock showing the time of the moment accompanied by the grand pronouncement, 'As the time is now … whatever it was … I shall say good afternoon,' or whatever was appropriate. The pressure of six shows a day, six days a week eventually got the better of Watts, and Tony would lose control as the magician found himself saying, 'As the time is now nine thirty ...' when the paper clock told the world it was not yet teatime. As Derek added, the real tragedy was that no one noticed, which made the situation all the more appealing to Hancock. With their U-boat Commander binoculars around their necks, those out front had not come for miracles, let alone laughter, only for the nudes, or as Tony, perhaps ungraciously, once referred to them, 'these little scrubbers with small tits like dartboards'.

They were paid £30 a week. Hancock worked this out as the equivalent of about 4s. an hour. 'At these rates,' he added, 'no wonder they never closed!' It was, however, a small venue with a limited capacity of just over 300 and, at the time Hancock played there, entertainment tax to pay of £50,000 a year. But it was never just about the money. There was curiously the glory as well, or what would one day be perceived as such. It may be a myth that Van Damm had the skill of Nostradamus when it came to spotting comedy talent. The law of averages dictated that most of the acts that passed the Windmill audition were forgotten, while among those who failed Van Damm's scrutiny were Spike Milligan, Benny Hill and Roy Castle. But ahead of Hancock, as the roll call of honour installed in the front of the theatre would show, were Jimmy Edwards, Harry Secombe, Alfred Marks, Michael Bentine, Peter Sellers, Arthur English and, noticeably, Bill Kerr. There became a sense of almost military pride in which those who survived the six-week campaign could vaunt their achievement. Galton and Simpson picked up on this in the radio episode where Hancock contemplated his old school reunion. Sid points out that the rest of his contemporaries may well be big-business tycoons and cabinet ministers by now, but Tony reminds him that he too has made his mark in his chosen profession. 'You got your name up on the board outside the Windmill,' Sid replies cynically. 'What weight's that gonna carry?' Hancock is not impressed.

It can be recorded that Hancock's first visit to the Windmill occurred before the war. He claimed that one afternoon on a trip to London with her son to purchase his school uniform, his mother, desperate for a respite from the pressures of shopping in the big city, suggested they pop in for an hour to a theatre advertising the convenience of non-stop entertainment that she had spotted up a side street not far from the statue of Eros. 'When she saw the girls, she began pushing me under the seat,' he added. The comment may have been his invention. He claimed he was seven years old at the time, but if the girls had caused an embarrassment he must have been older, since the idea of nudes had not been introduced into the *Revudeville* concept of continuous variety until much later in the 1930s. Whatever his age, whatever part the show played in his sexual enlightenment, the tale provides an amusing preface to his later association with the theatre.

No one became a star overnight through Windmill recognition, but its stage provided one of the key shop windows where agents and producers could spot emerging talent. Hancock and Scott were by now registered with an agent. Not much is known of Vivienne Black, outside of her early connection with Hancock, but while he was at the theatre his talents came to the attention of another representative, Phyllis Rounce, a founder of International Artistes. Hancock described her 'as a charming thing who dropped in and said she was pleasantly surprised to hear people laughing at the Windmill and that indeed I was a funny man', to which he responded, 'Well, that lot only come to see Gladys starkers. It's the hardest job in the world getting a laugh out of tired men who've been queuing in the rain since 10.30 with newspapers over their heads.' 'And that,' explained Rounce, 'is why I want to talk to you about a contract ...' Hancock, impressed by the fact that she was brave enough to sit, a lone female, in a front row full of men, felt flattered he had been *discovered*. At this time the quick route to fame lay in broadcasting. Names like Jimmy Edwards, Frankie Howerd, Derek Roy and Jon Pertwee were quickly becoming established favourites in radio comedy, while the newly reopened television service was slowly gaining a toehold. Not least with this in mind, Scott encouraged Hancock that they should enter the act in its embryonic form for a BBC audition. During the Windmill run Hancock had moved in with Derek Scott and his wife at their house in Wood Green. He remembered, 'They had not long been married and hardly collected any furniture together. My bed-room had no curtains and the only way I could dress in the mornings was by lying flat on the floor.' The roof over his head may have helped his decision to go along with his friend's suggestion. When the call from the BBC came, Hancock was persevering with a week's solitary cabaret booking at the Grand Hotel, Grange-over-Sands, overlook-ing Morecambe Bay. After some dithering, at the eleventh hour he accepted the invitation, and less than a month after they finished at the Windmill, on 14 September 1948, they were auditioning for BBC television at the Star Sound Studios in Rodmarton Mews, just off Baker Street.

With the express instruction that their performance should not exceed ten minutes, they registered reasonably well. The card index record made out after the event described 'two pleasant young men in lounge suits' providing 7¼ minutes of a 'concert party burlesque' that embraced 'Yorkshire comic tenor, impressionist cameo, ama-teur talent competition winner, Western Brothers'. The recorded ver-dict was that they were 'not untalented and perform with verve. Should prove suitable TeleVariety or Revue.' Things moved quickly. A cryptic figure '8' at the bottom of the card indicated that they would either be given a camera test or recommended direct to a producer. No record exists of a camera test. On 1 November at three in the afternoon Hancock made his television début with Scott on a pro-gramme called *New to You* for pioneer producer Richard Afton for a meagre 14 guineas, but not before a significant change had been made in the running of his business affairs. The venture provided the opportunity to break away from Vivienne Black, who disapproved of the audition and in doing so had revealed her distrust of the new medium, a view not uncommon among agents who still clung desperately to the old variety traditions. On 19 October 1948 Hancock signed an exclusive five-year contract with Phyllis Rounce. She was convinced his future prosperity resided in television.

Rounce, a one-time BBC secretary, had a background in Army Welfare Services – Entertainment, another area of forces show business. Resembling a more robust version of the actress Peggy Ashcroft, when peace was declared she went into partnership with her War Office boss, Colonel Bill Alexander, to form the grandly titled International Artistes Representation, not only on the premise that they already knew most of the acts that had entertained the troops, but also to manage young performers emerging from the war as fully fledged entertainers looking for the chance to break into professional show business. From beginnings in a bomb-shattered office – described by her as 'a converted tarts' parlour' – in the remains of a brothel in Irving Street off Leicester Square, she would in time, with the Colonel, steer the careers of, most notably, Terry-Thomas, slapstick star Charlie Drake, television hocus-pocus man David Nixon and the Australian jack-of-all-talents Rolf Harris. For the first, born Terry Thomas Hoar-Stevens, she suggested the snappier name and inserted the hyphen: 'I thought of it after looking at the gap between his two front teeth.' As testimony to their success, International Artistes continues to flourish today, responsible for comedic talents as diverse as Paul Merton, Joe Pasquale and Alan Davies under the astute but genial stewardship of Alexander and Rounce's protégé, Laurie Mansfield.

There would be no further call on Hancock's services by television until February 1950 when he appeared in a variation of Fairweather's old conjuror routine in *Flotsam's Follies*. The new service was extremely limited, with only one channel on air for only a few hours a day. More crucial to his career at this stage was a second BBC audition, this time specifically for Bryan Sears, the producer of the successful radio show *Variety Bandbox*, in December 1948. The audition took the form of an actual warm-up for the show, in which Hancock and Scott resorted to their Western Brothers parody, 'without', as Tony liked to boast, 'an intelligible word being spoken'. On 9 January he made his début on the show billed as 'Tony Hancock', but accompanied by Scott with, as we have seen, a reworking of the concert party sketch. It would be the first of fourteen appearances on the programme, alongside ten outings on other traditional variety offerings like *First House – Look Who's Here*, *Workers' Playtime* and *Variety Ahoy*, over a period of three years. The last two series, broadcast on behalf of national morale from factory canteens and naval bases throughout Britain, saw him performing from the Sterling Metals works in Coventry, HMS *Woolwich* off Harwich, HMS *Indefatigable* off Portland, the Royal Naval Hospital at Gosport, and within one week in 1951 three factories distributed through County Antrim and County Down. One imagines that his new agent had to coax her client gently into the seeming drudgery of such bookings, but as long as she was prepared to battle on his behalf he could hardly refuse.

According to Roger Hancock, his brother couldn't stand Colonel Alexander, joking that the only commission he ever secured was from his artists. Phyllis was a different matter. If she impressed Tony with her vision, he also admired her pluck. In the wake of his growing success on *Variety Bandbox*, she wrote in November 1950 to Pat Newman, the BBC Variety Booking Manager, to draw his attention to the anomaly that while her client was now receiving 12 guineas a show, on his last outing his script had cost him 10 guineas – by special arrangement with the writer who usually charged more – and his band parts had amounted to 4. Declaring this to be an uneconomic proposition, she requested an increase to 18 guineas for his next broadcast, to which Newman agreed. The economics still seem a little shaky, but Hancock was the first to acknowledge the value of the exposure as well as the need to keep material fresh. It had not taken him long to discover the insatiable appetite of broadcasting for new material. In his interview for *The Laughtermakers* in 1956 he observed: 'I wrote a lot of the material myself, and very bad it was. The audience reaction was often terrific, but from the radio point of view it was a waste of time. The trouble was that I liked doing visual work and it was very, very hard to adapt myself to the other thing … I gradually got the feel of the medium, [but] I was never very happy about the single act. At the back of my mind I knew I could do better with the sketch, the comic situation.' However, any aspirations he had to become the new Sid Field – who never made an impact in radio – did not prevent him from becoming a semi-resident on the programme. But Hancock was philosophical: 'I welcomed that because I realised that before I could do the thing I wanted to do, I should have to make some sort of a name even if my heart wasn't in the means I had to employ.'

To Hancock, Rounce proved more than an agent. 'Nursemaid' is one word that comes to mind. Grooming him was a constant challenge. Shortly before her death at the age of 89 in 2001 she reminisced: 'It was an absolute nightmare to get him kitted out in anything. He'd say, "I'm not going to put that on," and you'd say, "Well, it's an audience out there, darling. You can't go out in that ghastly, filthy suit. Take the thing off!" It was all that all the time, but it kept me on my toes … I was forever having to haul him out of wherever he was and drag him along. And the moment he was in the studio he was magic. But it was very tiring as well. I'm surprised I'm still alive to tell the tale!' Shoes presented a special challenge. Well aware of the comic importance of his feet, he became paranoid that the laughs would not come when an old pair wore out: 'He was awful, absolute hell, because we had to get him new ones and get somebody else to run them in before he would put them on. I'd put them there for him in the dressing room and he'd hide the new ones – on the ledge outside the window, in the toilet cistern – and put on his old ones and then the management would come to me.' Matters came to a head

when he began to play the prestigious Moss Empire circuit. Cissie
Williams, who booked the chain, was a disciplinarian who did everything by the book. She argued, 'If he comes in those shoes, Miss
Rounce, he will not be allowed on the stage.' 'Coming from her,' said
Phyl, 'that meant that he would not be allowed on the stage.'
Eventually, halfway through the week, when Rounce made the point
that the shoes were integral to his character, Williams conceded, as
long as he polished them. Rounce also knew in her innermost heart
that they represented his security blanket too: 'Without those old
shoes he was a dead duck. He fumbled and mumbled and nearly blew
the whole thing. It was quite extraordinary.'

In her unpredictable life it was nothing for his agent to receive
a phone call at four o'clock in the morning begging her to come round
on her bicycle to see him. There was no sexual agenda; he just needed someone with whom he could share his anxieties, be they professional, psychological or philosophical. Rounce became used to him
invading her office at all hours of the day, sinking himself into her
largest armchair in his 'grey bear coat' while she carried on with the
business of running a talent agency. Sometimes no words would
pass between them at all. Several hours later he would suddenly
shock himself out of this haven and announce, 'Well, I suppose I had
better be going then.' On less frequent occasions he could be bright,
talkative and playful, reminding her of a chatty sea lion. Phyl was
never less than understanding: 'I think most people on the edge of
being a genius are like that ... he never got a big head because he
was so frightened and that's what made audiences adore him ... he
was marvellous, impossible, lovable and hurtful – all rolled into
one.'

Shortly after Tony's début on *Variety Bandbox*, Hancock and
Scott went their separate professional ways, Derek's family ties
keeping him in London while his partner remained on call to the last
gasp of the variety tradition that could spirit him away to any part of
the country at a moment's notice. Rounce secured for her client what

appears to have been his first conventional variety booking for the week commencing 11 April 1949 at Feldman's Theatre, later the Queen's, in Blackpool. Also in a lowly 'wines and spirits' spot on a bill topped by the magician, Raoul, was another soul mate, Harry Secombe. The roly-poly Goon, who would one day deputise for his friend in the most bizarre fashion on his radio series, never forgot celebrating with Hancock the birth that week of his first daughter with fish and chips and Tizer – the pubs had shut by the time they left the stage door. Afterwards these two young clowns, high on sentiment and bursting with ambition, strolled down to the promenade together. Harry remained nostalgic for the moment they leaned against the railings and discussed their futures together peering out across the Irish Sea: 'We had the same kind of feeling about things. We were both ex-servicemen, tadpoles in a big pond hoping to become frogs ... we shared the same dreams of success and we argued about what we would do with the world now that we had fought to save it, looking into the dark sea and seeing only brightness.' In those days Harry found his chum 'gentle and self-mocking'. Hancock was, in fact, not scoring particularly well, and Robina Hinton, who was on the same bill appearing with her husband as 'The Hintonis' in their hand-balancing act, has described the struggle endured by Hancock – no longer cocooned by the solidarity and propaganda of the *Wings* tour – in order to adapt to the Blackpool crowd. Noisy and restless, one night the audience even resorted to throwing things on the stage:'He was in a painful state and in tears at one point. My husband, who had started his act in the twenties and had survived far worse, spent a long time with Tony, trying to give him some confidence.' Hancock, of course, knew better than most that a seaside resort out of season can be dull and dispiriting. It might have cheered him to know that within a couple of months he had a conventional summer season ahead of him much nearer to home. On 13 June 1949 he opened in *Flotsam's Follies* at the Esplanade Concert Hall, Bognor Regis, for £27 10s. a week.

Flotsam, alias B. C. Hilliam, had been one half of the famous 'Flotsam and Jetsam' songs-at-the-piano double act that had registered in radio as early as 1926. Hilliam was the high-voiced one: 'The songs sung by Jetsam are written by Flotsam.' Malcolm McEachern was the one with low voice: 'I sing the low notes – you'd wonder how he gets 'em.' Their most famous number conjured up the magic and romance of the early days of wireless:

Little Miss Bouncer loves her announcer
Down at the BBC.
She doesn't know his name,
But how she rejoices,
When she hears that voice of voices.

Following his partner's death in 1945, Hilliam, the droll, piano-playing half of the team, found considerable success with his own radio show under the *Flotsam's Follies* banner for several years, a 'weekly musical, lyrical and topical half-hour' produced by Tom Ronald, who would, come 1958, be responsible for the radio production of *Hancock's Half Hour*. The Bognor season was presented by another notable name in the history of radio comedy, Ted Kavanagh, the legendary script-writer of Tommy Handley's long-running radio success, *ITMA*, unquestionably the top show of the time.

Hancock always gave full credit to Hilliam for helping to turn him into a really professional act. In doing so Flotsam complemented the work already done by Fairweather and Reader, and had at his disposal the device of the traditional seaside summer show – ironically guyed for so long by Hancock – before it became superficially slicker, 'streamlined' by impresarios like Bernard Delfont and Harold Fielding into lavish resident revues with no changes of programme during the season. Hilliam expected his young comedian to provide five separate acts to ring the changes required from June through late September. Tony provided four and Flotsam let him off the fifth. To complement the concert party parody and the comedy impressions he found himself drawn towards visual and prop comedy. He later joked, 'I found that to get an act on stage I needed fifteen flying ballet dancers, seventy-eight trumpeting elephants and anything else a scrounging stage manager could lay his hands on.' The *Stage* reported that 'a new and original comedian, Tony Hancock, has registered strongly and his travesties of human life are a feature of every programme'. At the end of the season he combined what he considered the highlights of the four different spots into a single act, and this served as the foundation of his immediate stage work. More importantly the show enabled him to appear in sketches, provided by the production, with other members of the cast.

Meanwhile Rounce refused to take her foot off the pedal when it came to driving along Hancock's broadcasting ambitions. On 11 August the Bognor season delivered one bonus in the form of a radio transmission of an extract from the show, in which Tony was featured. As has been noted, Flotsam gave him a second break on television early the following year. It is tempting to suppose that the person who would exert the greatest influence on his radio career made several forays to the South Coast to watch him during the summer. On 22 February 1949 Rounce had written to BBC television at Alexandra Palace requesting they take note of a performance her client was due to give at the Nuffield Centre the following Friday evening. Now relocated to premises within the old Gatti's restaurant in Adelaide Street in the back of St Martin-in-the Fields, just off the Strand, the forces club had become an unofficial testing ground where aspiring performers with a service background could get up and entertain in a free-and-easy atmosphere on Tuesday and Friday evenings. There was no pay, just the compensation of copious coffee and sandwiches afterwards. It soon became a favourite haunt of agents and producers. Hancock had needed persuasion from Phyl to go on at all, but looking back on those days he pinpointed the difference between the Nuffield Centre, 'where the audience laughs at anything', and the Windmill, 'where nobody laughs at anything, because they haven't come to laugh'.

A copy of Rounce's letter, with its recommendation that here was 'an ideal intimate act for television as there is a lot of excellent facial expression and miming', was forwarded to the desk of radio's unofficial head of auditions. Dennis Main Wilson – he inserted the 'Main' to avoid confusion with the musician of the same name – was a recently demobbed Armoured Cavalry officer who after the war, while still in uniform, had ended up 'liberating' the German radio station in Hamburg, replacing Nazi-style broadcasting with his own brand of humour under the remit of the Control Commission for Germany. At the age of twenty-three he had subsequently joined the staff of the BBC radio variety department, where his first assignment was to find new talent. He was never less than conscientious, and it is unlikely he would have needed prompting to have been there on any evening newcomers were scheduled to do their stuff. He was already a familiar face to the likes of Bentine, Hill, Secombe, Monkhouse and all the other comics who had appeared at the venue. 'I was the only one on a regular salary,' he recalled. 'Guess who bought the drinks?' In the notes he made for an autobiography Hancock recalled his first encounter with the man: 'Not that anyone would ever have taken him for a BBC producer at sight. He could not have looked less like the part. He was dressed very formally with a bowler hat and rolled umbrella, but he was only a junior producer at the time. He has got over that phase since then. He was always a man of wild enthusiasm. He never stayed still for a moment and would sit up all night thrashing out an idea for a show. Nothing was impossible to him.'

That Friday night was important for both of them, not least for Dennis, whose eventual production of *Hancock's Half Hour* on radio more than five years later provided this eager, bespectacled man with a credit that would one day stand alongside shows for both radio and television that included *The Goon Show*, *Till Death Us Do Part*,

Citizen Smith, Marty, The Rag Trade, Barry Humphries' Scandals
and many more. His enthusiasm and nervous energy were prodigious, while his instinct and insight as a talent-spotter were capable
of seeing the potential of a performer several leagues down the line
from the moment of discovery. If you were a member of ex-service
personnel it was not difficult to obtain a BBC audition at this time,
and during one six-month period it was estimated that in excess of
6,000 hopefuls were put to the test. Many of these would have come
under Main Wilson's appraisal. He recollected that the quality left a
lot to be desired: 'Most were no better than village hall turns. You
were as kind as you could be and told them to go home.' When it came
to comedy, Dennis was probably at his most ruthless. As he said, 'You
can pretend to be serious, but you can't pretend to be funny.' At the
Nuffield Hancock delivered a variation of his concert party act.
Dennis was not too impressed by the material, but noted that 'the
characterisations were fabulous ... he did the stand-up comedian,
the juvenile lead in a ham play, the tenor, the impressionist ... you
sensed there was a tremendous latent talent there'. In that respect
he considered he stood out from all the other ex-service comedy
types. He also noted that 'he had no body language from the shoulders down. He would slouch on stage. His entire comedy was from his
face and his facial expressions.' Perhaps at that early stage even
Main Wilson would have expected Hancock to have made his major
impact on the small screen.

By the end of 1949 writer Larry Stephens had replaced accompanist Derek Scott as Hancock's best male chum and working partner. Stephens is recollected by Graham Stark as a red-complexioned
ex-commando captain who was 'possibly too genteel for this profession'. When Rounce referred to the accommodating scriptwriter in
her 1950 letter to the BBC, she almost certainly meant Larry, whom
she had introduced to Tony in the autumn of 1949. Larry wrote much
of the material that would continue to complement Fairweather's
original routine and the concert party take-off in Hancock's stage act

until the end of his days. He would be best remembered for his collaboration with Spike Milligan in the early period of *The Goon Show* and subsequently for his contributions to the *The Army Game*, commercial television's early standout comedy success from Granada, prior to his premature death at the age of thirty-five from a cerebral haemorrhage in 1959. Spike's affinity with them both became a *fait accompli* from the moment he eavesdropped on the pair improvising a fictional family seat for Hancock's ancestors: 'In 1883 they built a west wing, the following year they added an east wing, and the year afterwards … it flew away!'

It may have been through Hancock that Spike met Stephens. As the less gifted members of the post-war comic surge drifted away to more mundane roles, so a camaraderie – strengthened by their combined ambition – built up among the survivors, often centred on the pub in Archer Street opposite the Windmill or, more especially, the Grafton Arms, the tavern run by Jimmy Grafton at Strutton Ground, Victoria, where the plans for *The Goon Show* appear to have been hatched with all the complicity of a second Gunpowder Plot. Grafton, an ex-major, would ostensibly go on to manage Secombe's career and become himself a serviceable scriptwriter; in truth he acted as champion, catalyst, confessor in varying degrees not only to the Goons, but to Eric Sykes, Max Bygraves, Tommy Cooper, Jimmy Edwards, Alfred Marks, Benny Hill, Stephens and Hancock. For those few post-war years when pennies were scarce, work constituted a luxury and dreaming was everything, his hostelry represented arguably the most exciting enclave in the history of British comedy. Among this select breed, an unofficial cooperative system good-naturedly fell into place. Hancock never lost his affection for those days: 'There was a very special atmosphere. We all seemed to know each other. Anyone who was working helped the others.' Dick Emery was a member of the club. He once visited Hancock backstage at the Windmill. He was nearly destitute and Tony insisted on tucking a note into his top pocket. When Dick protested, his benefactor insisted, 'It's only money.' A few months later, when Dick was doing well at the same theatre and Hancock – wandering around with that laundry under his arm – was out of work, Dick came to the rescue. 'It's only money,' Emery shouted as his friend went on his way back down Lisle Street.

For a while Hancock and Milligan were particularly close. For extended spells Spike would sleep under Jimmy Grafton's grand piano, feeding Hancock's theory that the Milligan comic genius derived from the brain damage he suffered by constantly knocking his head on the bottom of the instrument when he woke up. Tony struck Milligan as 'always generous to people worse off than himself'. Spike recalled the occasion he had been in a psychiatric ward: 'He sent me a letter through Larry saying that he wanted a script as they seemed to have dried up. I wrote what I thought was a very funny one about Father Christmas and Tony paid me a fiver for it. Later I asked him if he ever used it and he said "no".' He never needed it in the first place. Spike was also struck by the bond between Larry and Tony: 'They were like brothers ... they seemed to have come from nowhere. They both liked to laugh at the human race and they'd have hysterical laughing bouts. Sometimes they didn't go to bed at night and I'd come in in the morning as I was writing a script with Larry and there would be this hysterical laughter and it was hurting their heads to laugh.'

At the end of 1949 Hancock and Stephens were sharing a flat in a derelict book and magazine warehouse in St Martin's Court, the theatre alley off Charing Cross Road. It was the first of several residences scattered across London where they could be found during the next six months, all the way from Bayswater via Primrose Hill to Covent Garden. In order to keep abreast of his debts, Hancock turned his attention to making some pin money bookmaking. This was illegal and dangerous and, as Spike Milligan confided to David Nathan, resulted in him having to change address 'very quickly – and very quietly'. Nevertheless, it was the flat at St Martin's Court that acquired the greatest mystique. To gain access you had to pass down a long, narrow corridor that was still the worse for war damage and then lower yourself precariously through a trap door. Phyllis Rounce was never allowed past that point and remembered having to get down on her hands and knees in order to have a conversation through the opened flap. Dick Emery did succeed in penetrating the inner sanctum to discover no furniture whatsoever. As he explained to his partner Fay Hillier: 'There was just a sink, a gas cooker, and a loo down a gloomy passage. There wasn't even a mirror. He shaved in front of a polished copper geyser.' When Dick asked Tony where he slept, he pointed to a pile of newspapers in the corner, explaining: 'Fresh sheets every day, matey! And I put a coat over myself for warmth.' What little food he could afford he would eat standing up at the mantelpiece.

All the while Rounce wore her fingers to the bone attempting to fill the long gaps that yawned in her client's calendar between the occasional broadcasts and the seasonal shows. In this regard pantomime proved a godsend, even if her client regarded the format with the nausea of a spoilt child being forced to swallow its medicine. No sooner had Phyl taken over his career than Hancock was reprising his role as an Ugly Sister in Frank Shelley's version of *Cinderella* at the Dolphin Theatre, Brighton, for the Christmas of 1948. The season ran for a mere two weeks. At the same time Sid Field was playing in his out-of-town tour of *Harvey* at the resort's more prestigious Theatre Royal. He might have drawn some consolation from the fact that from an early stage Field too had hated the festive genre, the perfectionist within him complaining that he was constantly distracted by the hum and murmur of the children in the audience. In 1962 Tony noted that the nearest he came to meeting his hero was when he found himself sitting near him one day in the pub behind the Theatre Royal, Brighton: 'But even if my name had meant anything to him I wouldn't have had the heart to introduce myself. He looked too miserable. I remember he wore a jockey cap, a ghastly black and white affair. I can't think why unless he needed something to cheer him up. He was just breaking in "Harvey" and the strain of wondering whether the public would accept the transition after those years on the halls was written all over his face.'

At the end of 1949 *Cinderella* beckoned again, but this time in a new production with Hancock as the comedy lead, Buttons, at the Royal Artillery Theatre, Woolwich. He would never don skirts, which he abhorred, for the Christmas institution again. The review in the *Stage* was impressive: 'Tony Hancock shows himself the master of subtly differing styles of humour and his affection for Cinderella carries a conviction comparatively rare in pantomime.' The words must have settled on his stomach like cold Christmas pudding. Dennis Main Wilson, fast becoming a friend Hancock could trust, mustered together a bunch of mates to provide him with moral support. Actress Miriam Karlin and comedian Leslie Randall were two who dragged themselves along with him to the eastern extremities of the capital to cheer Tony on his way. The nadir for Hancock came when he had to coax an audience of children into singing from a song-sheet 'Chick-chick-chick-chick-chicken, lay a little egg for me.' At this performance, the voice of his friends drowned out the juvenile chorus. By the end of the exercise, Main Wilson and his cohorts had been asked to leave the theatre.

The following Christmas he was able to venture into other areas of the story book, cast as Jolly Jenkins, the silly-billy, well-meaning page to the Baron in the tale of *Red Riding Hood*, with a young Julie Andrews in the title role at the Theatre Royal, Nottingham. This engagement showed a considerable advance in status within the profession, the venue being one of the country's prime provincial dates. The show also carried the prestige of being a Tom Arnold production: Arnold had arguably the foremost reputation as a producer of spectacular entertainment for the provinces at this time. Tony owed everything to the power of the radio exposure Rounce had been building for him, principally through his bookings on *Variety*

Bandbox. The run of the panto extended from 23 December until 10 March 1951 and must have seemed like a prison sentence. Hancock endured personal degradation every time he had to sing 'Every little piggy has a curly tail ...'. He recalled, 'There followed five minutes of mutual dislike. Every night I felt like walking up to the footlights and having it out with them: "You don't like it and neither do I, believe me. It's too long anyway. Why don't we call it off and go home?"' Dame Julie recalls, 'I knew him a little and liked him ... In his hilarious sketches life was always tough and he would stand, gazing out at the audience with thick-fingered, "wet fish" hands at his side, trying to understand the trials and tribulations that befell him.'

Hancock would play pantomime only once more, when he returned to Nottingham for Tom Arnold as Buttons for Christmas 1953. By this time he was a recognisable name with full-blown star billing. During the run he received a letter from Pat Newman from the BBC, who with tongue in cheek drew to Tony's attention a criticism from an acquaintance who lived there, namely that he was acting in the manner that a Nottingham panto was beneath him. Newman quickly removed the sting by adding that he would almost certainly prefer his performance if this were the case. Tony replied, 'Regarding the remarks from the young lady from Nottingham, I found them a little hard to take after casting fourteen stone of exhausted Hancock twice a day to the ground solely for the pleasure of the children ... best wishes, head down, left arm stiff, foot pointing to the sky, Tony.' Hancock was not necessarily speaking metaphorically. He made his entrance in the ballroom scene by sliding down a flight of stairs from the wings to the centre of the stage on his heels, pausing at an intermediate landing, and then sliding down another flight to arrive at the front of the stage. Main Wilson paid him a visit during the season and was immediately impressed by the feat, whereupon Hancock promised to take the flights at a single run the following night. On the first part of his descent, however, he slipped, fell the rest of the way and brought the house down, together – literally – with part of the scenery and two chandeliers. 'The incident provoked gales of laughter from the audience,' said Dennis, 'but Tony worried about it.' During this visit Main Wilson had his realisation that Hancock could raise laughs merely with a look confirmed. George Bolton, a raucous variety comic of the old school, played the Baroness. One night, when Dennis was in the wings, he overheard Bolton say to Hancock just before the kitchen scene, 'We'll do the teapots.' He was referring to an old piece of pantomime business of which the uninitiated Hancock had never heard. But there was no time to learn now and for the next few minutes Bolton was forced to go through a solo version of the routine, while Buttons stood by with a look of bewilderment and resignation that gained most of the laughs.

A sense of Hancock in pantomime can be gained from a radio episode where Galton and Simpson, prompted no doubt by their star's anguished memories of his experiences, decided to parody *Cinderella*. This time Tony himself, prevented by Bill and Sid from attending the National Film Board Ball, is forced to stay behind in the kitchen coping with the drudgery of housework: 'Here I am, a pathetic-looking figure – huddled round an empty grate – no friends – no one to care for me – miserable and lonely – the sort of thing Norman Wisdom dreams about!' At other times the nostalgia is more specific. As he is driven around Moravia in an open-top car in a not dissimilar pastiche of *The Student Prince*, he rhapsodises, 'Ah, this is the life – I never got treated like this when I played Buttons at Woolwich.' On a television episode, possibly with the *Stage* review for Woolwich in mind, he chides Sid for not taking his talents seriously: 'You never did see me in pantomime, did you? My rendition of Buttons had a depth of meaning that astounded everybody who saw it … the whole performance in the best tradition of the Russian theatre and Stanislavski.' When Sid suggests he didn't get any giggles, Hancock adds, 'I didn't try to get any giggles. I saw the part as a tragedy.' He was able to get his own back on what he saw as the whole demeaning tradition when towards the end of 1957 he was invited to participate in *Pantomania*, a Christmas Night television spectacular with a high 'works outing' element attached, as the likes of Eamonn Andrews, Huw Wheldon, Cliff Michelmore and Sylvia Peters stepped out of their presenting roles to let their hair down in a burlesque romp loosely based on *Babes in the Wood*. All goes well until Hancock as Aladdin wanders into Sherwood Forest and the deconstruction – helped by Sid as a disobliging genie – begins.

Returning to his earlier career, one finds Hancock's slow climb to the top characterised by sporadic dates that came to bear the doomed hallmark of his emerging comic persona. There was the cabaret booking at the Victoria Hotel, Sidmouth, in November 1949, when he arrived a full week early. With two pennies and a halfpenny in his pocket – enough for a life-saving cup of tea at Micheldever Station and no more – he returned to London on the slow train, only to have to go back a week later: 'I think I made a net loss of about five quid on the deal.' There was the cabaret for the Election Night Ball at Claridge's on 23 February the following year. As Hancock proceeded with his act, the toastmaster, who had not endeared himself by introducing him as 'Mr Hitchcock', would hold up his hand for Tony to freeze mid-impression while the next result was announced. Only after each seat was declared was he allowed to continue stop-start fashion until the act was through. Tucked away in a corner of the room as he was, he felt he needn't have bothered. It was a Tory function and he always claimed that at that point he became a committed socialist. The summer of 1950 saw him spend three months at Clacton as principal comedian for impresario Richard Stone – later to mastermind the career of Benny Hill – in the *Ocean Revue*, initially at the Jolly Roger Theatre on the Pier, and then at the Ocean Theatre at the pier entrance. He neither forgot nor forgave the fierce competition he encountered from the scenic railway known as 'Steel Stella': 'It always seemed as though she reserved her loudest clang and her passengers' loudest screams for the moment I came to the end of a joke. Every performance it was always a running fight between her, them and me.' He then added, 'While I was playing at Clacton I got married.'

He had supposedly been engaged before. While he was appearing in *Cinderella* at Brighton for the 1948 Christmas season, the local press carried a news story heralding the forthcoming marriage between the Ugly Sister and Prince Charming, played by the actress Joan Allum. The article announced that they had met at rehearsals only a fortnight before and had become engaged on Christmas Eve. It went on to give a boost for Tony's début on *Variety Bandbox* the following Sunday, and added bizarrely that at midnight, during the New Year's Eve Ball attended by the Duke of Edinburgh at Earl's Court, Allum had been chosen as 'Miss 1949'. It would be flippant to dismiss the whirlwind fairy-tale romance as a publicist's ploy, since the pantomime had only days to run. But although the wedding was mooted for March, Miss Allum does not appear to have featured again in Hancock's life. There had been an earlier pantomime romance with another actress, Celia Helder, in Oxford the previous year. She had played the unexplained part of Lady Llanfachlfechlfychl. On Hancock's death she looked back on their liaison: 'Tony had great, big haunted eyes, but he was as slender as a reed and an extremely attractive person. He was very sweet and gentle, the kind of boy of whom any girl would say, "He's a dependable chap."'

He had been introduced to Cicely Romanis by Larry Stephens, whose girlfriend, Diana Forster, worked with her as a model. The occasion was a skating party held by Cicely to celebrate her twentieth birthday at the Bayswater ice rink on 3 April 1950. According to Phyllis Rounce, on the day after the party he wandered into her office and announced, 'I've just met the woman I want to marry.' The Hancock–Stephens ménage had relocated to Covent Garden by now. Forster had become inured to the shabby, Spartan conditions in which they lived just around the corner from the noisy fruit and vegetable market, a fact that may have eased the way for Cicely's own acceptance. It was long before *My Fair Lady* would romanticise the environment; *Pygmalion* never quite had. For a long period of their courtship his fiancée found herself commuting between Clacton, where Tony had moved out of digs and into a one-bedroom flat to set up home with her, and wherever the fashion world demanded her presence. In the more strait-laced moral climate of the day, the arrangement would have caused some consternation with her parents.

Cicely was born Cicely Janet Elizabeth to William Hugh Cowie and Dorothy Romanis at home at 120 Harley Street on 3 April 1930. Her father was a senior surgeon at St Thomas's Hospital, who in the late 1920s had written with Philip H. Mitchener *The Science and Practice of Surgery*, a book that remains one of the definitive handbooks on surgical procedure. With her Dinah Sheridan looks, she was already successful in her profession as a mannequin, being one of the first British models to tread the catwalk for Lanvin in Paris. She had stunning auburn hair and a zest for life to match. With an athletic background and nothing if not strong-willed, by the time she met Hancock she had taken a course in judo to protect herself from unwelcome suitors, an occupational hazard of her profession, and revealed an aptitude for motoring at the wheel of a sports car of which her future husband would become envious. Both activities would affect their life together in what – in those early, innocent days – were unexpected ways. They presented an incongruous couple, the elegant fashion plate and the slumped shaggy figure of a man enveloped in the duffel coat he wore for all seasons. His secretary Lyn Took, however, takes pains to insist that she was never ostentatious: 'She always looked groomed, always wore lipstick, and had a penchant for straight, close-fitting trousers and simple tops when they were the fashion.' It is said that Fred gave Ginger class, while Ginger gave Fred sex appeal. Cicely had the class already. Whatever frisson connected Tony and Cicely, the attraction between them was not diminished by the fact that she laughed at most of what he said.

They were married at Christ Church, Kensington, on 18 September 1950. Hancock had fun recalling the honeymoon: 'I had to dash to Clacton for the show. She had a fashion parade. She arrived at Clacton at 6.45. I was onstage at seven. And she had to leave at six the next morning for another engagement.' It scarcely needs adding that he only just made the church in time and had to rely on his best man for sartorial help: 'In my rush to catch the train to London I just dived into the wardrobe and snatched together what I mistook for a complete suit. It turned out in the unpacking to be the jacket of one striped suit and the trousers of another. So there I was gaping at myself in the mirror in a ridiculous ensemble of blue above the waist and grey below. Larry lent me a pair of trousers to match the jacket. I felt it would be churlish to complain about the cigarette burn just below the knee and so I covered it up as best I could!' It appears that at the last moment the Clacton season had been extended by a week, a situation that would explain the raggedness of the arrangements. Cicely's elder sister, Doreen Harland, recalls the unpredictability that surrounded the occasion, notably the moment ahead of the service when the best man dropped the gold wedding ring down a grating in the church floor. Expediency demanded that he borrow Doreen's platinum ring 'temporarily'. No one was more surprised than Cicely when later her betrothed put the differently coloured ring on her finger. It would be six months before Tony bought her another and Doreen had her ring returned. The original was never recovered from the grating.

Two days later the Hancocks were both back in London to officiate as witnesses at Stephens's marriage to Diana. For a few months they kept on the Clacton flat, an arrangement of greater inconvenience to the bride than the groom, with her frenetic modelling schedule and the metropolitan life style that accompanied it. However, it is significant that while Hancock gave his own profession as 'actor' on the marriage certificate, Cicely left that space blank. After the first of his Nottingham pantomimes, heartened by her faith in him – she admitted later, 'I knew he was going to be a big star' – she essentially gave up her career to look after her husband. In time, they moved in with Cicely's parents, now relocated to Cornwall Gardens, Kensington, before acquiring their own apartment at 20 Queen's Gate Place in Knightsbridge during the summer of 1952. It happened to be on the fifth floor of a Victorian mansion block without a lift. 'We knew who our friends were in those days,' Hancock would joke. 'They *had* to be friends to climb up all those stairs.' The climb kept Cicely's figure in even finer trim, while Hancock was often known to be breathless upon arrival at his own front door.

Meanwhile any pretence at domestic routine would be disrupted by the growing demand for Tony's services in provincial variety. In February and March 1950 he achieved four weeks at mainly minor syndicate halls; by October he was booked into a four-week run of the mighty Moss Empires. With his increasing radio popularity, 1951 saw fourteen weeks of varied work on the halls between pantomime and the end of the year. Initially he was billed in succession as 'The Modern Clown', 'The New-Style Humorist', and then with a semi-catchphrase that had been surfacing in his radio work, 'Isn't it sickening?' For Phyllis Rounce a kind of breakthrough came when he was invited to support Nat King Cole for a couple of dates – Birmingham and Liverpool – on his 1950 British tour. Even today Graham Stark relives the excitement: 'There he was at one of the lowly London halls – first house on the Thursday night – dying like a dog – he always tried to do a clever act, but nothing …! The next day he received the call from his agent to tell him he was going out with Nat King Cole, which was like saying you'd won a million pounds. Cole was a great star and whoever went out with him got to play only the best dates. Tony couldn't believe it. He said, "What happened?" "Well," explained Phyl, "Val Parnell – the Moss Empires chief – happened to be in on Thursday first house and saw your work." But Tony said, "I died the death." "Ah," she said, "he realised that and the audience were terrible, but he said to me, 'I've never seen a comic work so hard to try to get an audience as he did. He didn't get them, but that isn't the point – he did work'," and that's why Parnell gave him the break.' So far Hancock had been a supporting act to the comedians Dave and Joe O'Gorman and radio name Carroll Levis with his Discoveries, solid but unspectacular attractions that enabled variety to hang in there with fortitude during its last dying years. But there were not too many stars of Cole's international stature who were prepared to slog their way around the British hinterland, and Tony was soon back adding his weight to bills topped by staunch veterans like the comedy band Dr Crock and his Crackpots, Murray the Escapologist and the close-harmony singing brothers from Ted Ray's radio show, Bob and Alf Pearson.

1951 was also the year when television began to show a more constructive interest in his talents. Breaking up the dreary grind of provincial weeks was a run of five appearances between May and June in a fortnightly series called *Kaleidoscope*, an entertainment magazine in which Hancock played a character called George Knight, 'a would-be rescuer of damsels in distress', in a segment entitled 'Fools Rush In' written by Godfrey Harrison, who later achieved fame with the delightful *A Life of Bliss* in both radio and television. The short sketches represent Hancock's first foray into situation comedy. Roger Wilmut describes one in which 'he rashly takes over the job of a hotel receptionist so that she can go and meet her boyfriend, and gets himself into a state of total confusion with the telephone switchboard, an irate colonel and a confused foreigner'. On 1 August 1951 he was also featured in the first episode of another Harrison television project, *The Lighter Side – a humorous slant on current affairs*. The subject of the first programme was food, and Hancock was cast as a civil servant, the bureaucratic *bête noire* against whom before long he would himself have some of his most memorable encounters in the medium.

That August represented a *mensis mirabilis*. It should not be forgotten that sound broadcasting was still the dominant entertainment medium in the country. What might have been construed as a potential setback to Hancock's radio career had occurred in June 1951 when the decision was taken at the pilot stage of a new comedy series entitled *Dear Me*, written by Ted Kavanagh for the laconic Michael Howard, to drop him from a supporting role in the project. Hancock and the producer, Jacques Brown, appear to have been in accord that there was a similarity between the vocal intonation of the star and his own. He seemed far from perturbed. He may already have been aware of other irons in the fire. Over 2 and 3 August his career in radio would take two enormous leaps with his first resident appearances in two series featuring other established wireless stars. One would make him a household name; the other, while less successful, brought him into proper working contact with the man who never lost faith in him, Dennis Main Wilson, and in the process effect the meeting with the two men who would take his comedy to heights of hilarity and credibility that have arguably never been attained in the broadcasting medium since.

Chapter Five

RADIO WAVES

'Did you write that? ... Very good!'

Without warning of any kind the landscape of radio comedy changed dramatically on 9 January 1949. This had nothing to do with Tony Hancock's début on *Variety Bandbox*, radio's top Sunday evening showcase for variety talent. With a precision bordering on poignancy, it had everything to do with the colossus of the medium who shared his initials and had dominated the genre for the past decade. At 5.30 that Sunday the 310th edition of *ITMA* enjoyed its customary weekend repeat. At the end of the broadcast there was a pause before the reader of the six o'clock news stunned a nation into silence with these words: 'The BBC regrets to announce the death of Mr Tommy Handley, the comedian.' Only hours before he had been struck down with a massive cerebral haemorrhage. Although long regarded as a senior figure of the broadcasting establishment, Handley was only eight days short of fifty-seven when he died. Hancock recalled the moment: 'We were in the middle of the recording when someone came in with the news that the most revered of radio comedians had suddenly died while bending to pick up his collar stud. The whole studio went cold with the shock of it.' Tony failed to mention if he had completed his contribution. The show's star

Frankie Howerd, whistler Ronnie Ronalde and comedienne Avril Angers were more established artists whose professionalism would have been tested in the circumstances. Not that Hancock needed or should have expected excuses. According to Phyllis Rounce, his performance was lacklustre in the extreme: 'Tony was petrified and the broadcast was a shambles. The producer said, "Never bring that man near me again."' Mercifully Rounce was able to persuade Bryan Sears to give Hancock a second break on the show eleven weeks later, and his broadcasting career gradually acquired impetus from that point. In the heat of the moment Sears would have given no second thought to his words to Phyl, but they contained an uncanny echo of those behind the acronym of the Handley show – 'It's That Man Again.'

No broadcaster had come to epitomise the age more tellingly than Handley. It is an indication of a performer's stature when in the aftermath of death the media go into overdrive in an attempt to nominate that person's successor, a futile exercise akin to making a superlative of the word 'unique'. In his favoured medium Handley was the King. A product of concert party and revue, he had a snappy delivery with a razor's edge timing that crackled over the airwaves, together with a warmth and homeliness that identified him as a friend to the British people without resorting to sentiment. The phrase 'It's That Man Again' first connected with the public through Hitler-inspired headlines whenever the Führer called for '*Lebensraum*'; indeed Churchill himself often referred to the Nazi ogre as 'that man'. In his tribute to Handley, Sir William Haley, the BBC's Director General, wrote: 'How typically English it is that an epithet at first devised for something threatening and hateful should have been transferred to one of the most welcome, most lovable of men.' The show was a mad hatter's tea party of eccentric voices and musical interludes, lightning puns and recurring catchphrases stopped just this side of insanity by the brisk, cheerful presence of its star. In the dark days of the war it became a weekly rallying post for civilians and service personnel alike. When peace was declared the comedian, with help from his writer Ted Kavanagh and producer Francis Worsley, cannily reinvented the concept by relocating his activities to Tomtopia, the never-never-island where he reigned as governor over an environment as outlandish as wartime Britain had ever been.

The innate surrealism of *ITMA*, its creative use of sound effects and its stream of preposterous characters pointed forward in the development of radio comedy to programmes like *Ray's a Laugh*, *Educating Archie*, *The Goon Show* and *Round the Horne*. In this respect *Hancock's Half Hour* was an outsider. But if Handley had a true successor as a comedian, both in the magic of his microphone skill and in the ability to project himself as the type of person we all acknowledge ourselves in our innermost hearts to be, he was there in embryo that sad Sunday evening trying his best as a nation mourned. Hancock's moody dreamer would reveal himself to be as perfectly attuned to the Cold War era as Handley's jack-in-the box opportunist ever was to real war and the Pyrrhic peace that followed. As his career progressed the younger comedian – in the cause of originality and his own sanity – would denounce many of the devices that Handley and his team had developed to the level of art. There is no reason to suppose that had their roles been reversed the affable Liverpudlian would not have done the same.

As 1951 advanced it became apparent to the puppet masters manipulating the strings within the walls of Broadcasting House and its ornate variety outpost, the Aeolian Hall in Bond Street, that Hancock was coming to the conclusion of some form of radio apprenticeship. His accumulated appearances on shows like *Variety Bandbox* and *Workers' Playtime* represented an early stage in some form of established *cursus honorum* for performers of his age and experience. He would, by now, have been hoping for a regular part in a long-running series. Dismissive of the letdown of the Michael Howard project, he was suddenly offered not one, but two parts that might bring with them both temporary security and the satisfaction of another hurdle overcome. In a round-up of radio reviews on 6 August 1951 the *Daily Mirror* reported on the two shows side by side. Of *Happy-Go-Lucky*, first transmitted on the Light Programme on 2 August, it said, 'Cuts in the recording made this lavish, hour-long Thursday night offering an uneven, ragged business. As the star, Derek Roy was lost in a *mêlée* of overlong and unfunny contributions from others.' Of *Educating Archie*, which aired in a half-hour slot the following day at 20.45 on the same station, it stated, 'Tony "Flippin' kids" Hancock shoots to star billing in his first outing with the "A" team. This man is funny. A slick script and smooth production make this a winter's winner as usual.' The mark of a successful catch-phrase was such that it could identify itself that quickly. Already Hancock was marked with the two words that would now haunt him for several years.

An intriguing sidelight to the two reviews, not deemed worthy of mention to *Mirror* readers, is that both shows were produced by the same man, Roy Speer. While this was ludicrously too large a burden for one individual, Speer would have been the first to concede that the established show, which had already completed one award-winning series, had something more than an 'A' team at its disposal, not least – in Eric Sykes – a co-writer of inspiration and – in Peter Brough – a star with class, enterprise and his own finger on the pulse of aspiring talent. Unfortunate is the ventriloquist whose name begins with 'B', but, when his dummy spoke, Brough was never 'Grough' by name, and certainly never gruff by nature. All three saw the potential of Hancock when they watched him together in a London music hall earlier in the year, but he may not have been the first choice. A press release to herald the second series at the beginning of June 1951 announced Harry Secombe as the new tutor to Archie, while an internal BBC memo ahead of the very first series also suggested Harry as a potential member of the original cast. Secombe would not get his opportunity to educate Archie until the third run of the show, when he took over from Hancock, who was anxious not to outstay his welcome and be typecast as a schoolmaster comedian, at the same time as Brough and Speer were anxious to keep the basic format refreshed with continual cast changes.

It is feasible that without Ted Kavanagh, the influential creator of *ITMA*, *Educating Archie* would not have come into being at all. He certainly provided the final piece of the jigsaw for Brough's success. Peter was a struggling ventriloquist on the variety circuit when one night in 1942 he was advised by the music publisher and record producer Wally Ridley either to invent a new character for his doll or to get out of the business completely. In devising 'Archie Andrews' Brough displayed all the skills of a producer himself, accessing the best individual talents to contribute to the completed whole. Len Insull, now a legend in ventriloquial circles, crafted the puppet to coincide with Peter's creative vision. On an unrelated business trip to Brora in the Highlands, Brough and Ridley took long walks together on the beach as the ventriloquist tried to find the voice required, until, as Peter recollected, 'out of the empty sea, sky and shore one voice suddenly seemed to click – the thin, cheeky treble of a boy of fourteen or so!' However, the personality was not complete until Peter revealed the doll to Kavanagh in a dressing room at Lime Grove film studios, where Ted was working with Handley on a film. A name was required and without hesitation the burly, witty writer responded, 'His name, Peter, is Archie Andrews.' Duly christened, in Brough's eyes his new wooden partner became a real person from that moment, and in due course, with his elegant guardian, a variety attraction on a level with Max Miller, Tommy Trinder and Gracie Fields.

As Archie's tutor, Hancock came on board the second series of *Educating Archie* in the role played initially by his ex-colleague from the Gang Show, the daffy Robert Moreton. The premise was that Archie – a magnet for trouble when not instigating it himself – could only be taught at home: no school would take him. Tony joined an established cast that included Max Bygraves as the cheery odd-job man, youthful *ITMA* stalwart Hattie Jacques as Miss Dinglebody – 'Call me, Agatha' – who has eyes for Tony, and Julie Andrews as Archie's girlfriend. Hancock's duties in the show extended beyond the tutorial role. The opening cross-talk segment between the ventriloquist and his dummy defined the relationship of Brough as the moralistic father figure and Archie as the cheekily nonchalant Pinocchio within his care, before segueing into an encounter with an unnamed Hancock in whatever job happened to fit the situation, whether dentist, car salesman, zoo keeper, estate agent, train driver or gym instructor. Whatever the occupation, a seedy obsequiousness was his calling card, waiting to be worn dog-eared by the precocious schoolboy. In their very first encounter Brough takes Archie to the barber.

TONY: Just kneel on the chair, will you, sonny? There we are then! Now where are my scissors? Scissors, scissors …

ARCHIE: These what you're looking for?

TONY: Ah yes, thanks – ahahaha. That was a jolly good idea, dipping the handles into the brilliantine, wasn't it?

ARCHIE: I thought it wasn't bad.

PETER: Archie, you shouldn't have done that.

TONY: That's all right, sir. All in good fun. I love children. Especially boys and girls. Now let's get started … where's he gone to?

ARCHIE: I'm over here.

TONY: Ah yes there … what are you doing with that razor?

ARCHIE: Just sharpening my pencil.

TONY: Just sharpening … give me that! Now kneel up on the chair, laddie. Ahahaha. Flippin' kids!

No matter what job Hancock held down, Archie would be there to plague him. Only following a musical interlude did Hancock don mortarboard and gown for the middle section of the show that began by focusing on Archie's schoolroom activities. As far as the listener at home was concerned, Brough had now left the scene and the emphasis was set securely upon teacher and pupil:

ARCHIE: Good morning, Dr Hancock, sir.

TONY: Good morning, Andrews. I fervently hope – admitted with a certain amount of trepidation – that our relationship will be fruitful and none the less amiable, for the fact that I may impose a discipline you may not have encountered hitherto? Do you follow me?

ARCHIE: Well, I got as far as 'Good morning, Andrews.'

Much of the humour was schoolboy-howler based, with Archie always one step ahead of his mentor:

TONY: Why did Boadicea build the Suez Canal? Steady, Andrews. It's a catch question.

ARCHIE: Well the catch answer is 'Boadicea did *not* build the Suez Canal.'

TONY: Exactly – the catch being that you don't build canals – you dig them – simple, isn't it?

ARCHIE: Not half as simple as you are.

TONY: Ahahaha – saucy scholar …

The sketch would then expand to include Hattie, Max and the occasional guest star who was allowed to wander in and out of the format. After Julie Andrews's song the third segment spiralled off into a fantasy dimension not unworthy of *The Goon Show*, with Archie often identifying himself in his imagination with an iconic figure from history, literature or legend, abetted by Hancock, Max and Hattie in appropriate roles. In Hancock's time, Alexander Graham Bell, Hannibal, King Arthur and Christian of the *Bounty* all received the Archie treatment. Because of these constant shifts of focus, the show never became boring. Once Peter, figuratively speaking, had left the microphone to leave Archie centre stage, the role of comic foil zigzagged back and forth between the schoolboy hero and the eccentric members of Brough's household.

The conventional opening dialogue between Brough and Archie originated from the pen of Sid Colin; when the action opened up to include the others, Eric Sykes took over the writing reins for the lion's share of the half hour. According to Eric, not only did Tony's presence lift the show considerably, they also shared an instant rapport. In one of the closing sketches Hancock found himself showing a miscreant Archie around Hell, where he is working as a guard. 'It was at the time the Russians were vetoing everything,' recalls Sykes, 'and there was this sound of marching feet and the cry of "Niet, niet, niet, niet" as they trudged past, and as they went by Tony had to say, "They're from Russia." And he said to me, "How would you say this, Eric?" And I said, "When you are saying it, imagine that you have a cigarette in your hand and you are tapping the ash off it." He said, "I've got it, I've got it." And he did it and it got a marvellous laugh. And he said to me afterwards, "What impressed me all the more was that you didn't *tell* me how to say it, you *showed* me how it should be delivered." From then on we were lifelong friends.' They became so close that when Eric got married in early 1952 Tony and Cicely arranged for him and his bride, Edith, to hold their wedding reception in the apartment that belonged to Cicely's parents. Hancock also made secret arrangements for a brass band – in effect, the brass section of the BBC Variety Orchestra – to play them off from the tarmac as they flew to Jersey on their honeymoon, only to have to cancel the plans when the day coincided with the funeral of King George VI. Eric concedes that the farewell strains of 'Wish Me Luck as You Wave Me Goodbye' would have been in very bad taste.

The part played by Sykes in helping to formulate the essential Hancock persona can never be underestimated. He had cut his teeth writing for Frankie Howerd, attracted by the scope the comedian's hesitations and interjections gave for defining his character. In a similar way he latched onto something in Hancock's inner psyche and from it developed the seedy grandiloquence and supercilious air that spelled out what his later audience would have taken for granted, that being teacher to a doll was beneath him. Eric insists, 'In real life he was a very likeable man, but there was a great dignity about Tony. When you talked to him you realised this man was not a bank manager, he was not someone in the City, he was not in the Civil Service, and he didn't sweep the roads. You had this man who looked like an actor-manager when he was young enough to play juvenile leads.' The rough, crude prototype of what Galton and Simpson would go on to polish soon fell into place. Lee Conway, writing mid-series in the *New Musical Express*, acknowledged, 'He is always the essence of outraged dignity. The rich fruity voice, the cultured speech with the aspirants omitted are his stock in trade, not the gag book. Give Hancock a situation and instantly you have him creating belly laughs.' Dennis Main Wilson noted that Sykes had given him more than this, namely 'an attitude to performing'.

Who first coined the 'Flippin' kids!' catchphrase that contributed to Hancock's early fame has always been a matter of conjecture. Although Eric Sykes surely deserves some credit for placing it in a comedy context, Tony's mother traced its origins to Durlston Court Hotel days: 'He remembered the saying from an old porter we used to have at the hotel. In the summertime when all the children used to come in from the beach, there used to be sand everywhere. So all summer you would hear the old man say, "Those flippin' kids!"' Her friend Mary Hobley recalled that 'flippin'!' was a constant epithet in Tony's vocabulary when a young man. It is hard to believe now that more than fifty years later 'kids' is sometimes considered politically incorrect, while, according to the lexicographer Nigel Rees 'flipping', its shared cue for laughter in this family-oriented show, has been the most common euphemism for a stronger participle beginning with the same letter since the 1920s. Significantly the catchphrase was used during the first of Hancock's three appearances, sometimes as much as three times, and not in the main scholastic sketch. In the latter he was referred to by name as Dr Hancock. He did little if anything to vary his voice between the two characters, which only added to the surrealism of the whole affair. It might be difficult for an outsider to connect the softer, lower register – more akin to his natural delivery – which matured into being with *Hancock's Half Hour* with the strangulated, high-pitched tones that characterised Hancock during the early 1950s. It may be summed up as highfalutin with ignorant undertones, with a touch of Cyril Fletcher's haughtiness alongside a dash of Sid Field's preciousness. Scrutiny of the scripts suggests that Sykes tried at times to inject an additional pattern into the tutor's speech. For some passages of nervous exasperation Hancock's words are peppered with *mm*s. That is according to the script; when heard the interjection presents a transcription challenge, with Hancock managing to pronounce it *ñah*. Eric may have had the *oohs, aah*s and *er*s of Frankie Howerd in mind, all originally scripted by himself. The effect is of Hancock chewing his words:

TONY: Now Andrews A. ... mm ... er in a few weeks' time ... mm ... it will be ... mm ... end of term ... ahahaha ... before you put a match to your desk ... listen.

ARCHIE: All right then, I'll hold my fire.

TONY: Before ... mm ... end of term, there will be the examinations ... mm ... dealing with ... mm ... lessons contained in parts II and III ... mm ... of the school curriculum ... mm ... come in 'A' for Archie.

At times it sounds like a voice destined for advertising allergy cures, on the threshold of a sneeze that never comes. It never caught on.

Hancock never forgot his introduction to Brough's co-star. No sooner had Peter ushered him into the dressing-room and picked up the little fellow than Archie was away: 'It's good to meet you. I want to welcome you to the show. I hope you'll be happy working with us.' One imagines Tony was lost for words. Something within him was never entirely comfortable with the idea of working with an inanimate object, however great Brough's skill as a puppeteer in bringing it to life. Ten years later he wrote:

> It was uncanny working with a dummy like Archie. He became so human to us that we would ask, 'Is Archie going to rehearse today?' as if he could think and feel and talk like a real person. The public obviously shared this conviction. Over the air he became a lovable human being to millions of children and I have known them cry bitterly when they discovered he was only a dummy and not a real boy. This made it all the more macabre to see him hanging unceremoniously from a hook or sitting in a chair with his head lolling over the side.

Hancock, ever susceptible to maleficent forces, could not bring himself to walk in alone for fear of Archie's accusing slack-jawed gaze following him around the room. He claimed it gave him nightmares. For all of Archie's pert charm, it is not difficult to comprehend his feelings. The sinister undertones exerted by a ventriloquial *doppelgänger* had sent a collective shiver down the spine of the nation in Cavalcanti's 1945 film, *Dead of Night*, as a dummy took over the mind and personality of actor Michael Redgrave playing the ventriloquist. Maybe Hancock was aware that Peter's father, Arthur Brough, a pro from the music halls, had acted as technical consultant to the movie and provided the doll. To those suggestible enough, the frozen eyes and grotesque features of the standard dummy, with their mockery of childhood and mad insight into the relationship with the manipulator upon whose reality it depends, must prove as unnerving as the Day-Glo tackiness, the sadistic *schadenfreude* of the circus clown to a sensitive child. Brough ensured that Archie was an aristocrat among dolls, but there was always part of Tony that never grew up, distrusted wood and wires over flesh and bone. And then there was the uneasy truth hinted at in Roger Caldwell's poem, 'The Dummy Speaks'.

I speak through him – he does not speak through me.
He's my automaton, invention, and his life
is not worth living that's not also mine.
Check-suited fool, death's entertainer,
does he think, when he's alone, I am no better
than the wire-pulled god he made in his own image?

Hancock tried to qualify his disdain: 'I really hated that dummy – only during the shows, I mean – but you've got to get the mood … I had to hate Archie, and I did, and so it was funny.' Peter noted jokingly that Tony's hatred did surface at times outside of the act: 'He used to growl, "Your grandfather was a gate-legged table," and as Archie I would have to reply, "And your grandfather drank his way under my grandfather."' Whatever his feelings, they did not stand in the way of his performance. His demand for naturalism led Hancock to insist that Brough work with the doll at rehearsals and not merely for the studio broadcast. 'I cannot make the script live unless he's here,' he would plead to Peter. The ventriloquist understood the need, while resenting the sacrifice of having to stand like a stork for longer than necessary. At the time Brough was agonising over varicose veins, but the comedian would insist, 'I can't make it work unless I work to him … now come on, let's do it properly.' Tony himself admitted that Archie seemed to bring out the best in everyone. 'I'm not going to let a wooden doll get away with this scene' summed up the pervading attitude. And at last he had a regular opportunity to flex his muscles in the comedy of situation, even if it was not tagged 'situation comedy' at that stage.

Whatever his superstitions, the exposure, which extended over a run of twenty-six weeks, caused Tony no setback. Indeed, the various repeats helped him to achieve his largest audience to date, often in excess of 20 million listeners in those heady radio days, a pre-Muppet phenomenon on a Commonwealth scale. The show with its resignedly bouncy signature tune

We'll be educating Archie;
Oh what a job for anyone!
He's no good at spelling – he hasn't a clue;
He tells us three sevens still make twenty-two.
It's a problem you can see
To be educating Archie.

acquired the reputation of a lucky talisman for those who appeared on it, the majority either achieving breakthrough fame or consolidating what may until then have been only passing success. In addition to the names already mentioned, they included Dick Emery, Beryl Reid, Ronald Shiner, Graham Stark, Benny Hill, Bernard Miles, James Robertson Justice, Ken Platt, Bernard Bresslaw, Gladys Morgan, Warren Mitchell and Bruce Forsyth. When the programme reached its last series in 1959 Sid James became Archie's final tutor, but not before one last attempt has been made to see if Hancock wants his old job back. Brough and his ward make the pilgrimage to East Cheam, only for Sid to answer the door. Hancock is not at home, and Sid, with the sniff of money in his nostrils, senses an employment opportunity. Archie is sceptical, but James rises to the occasion: 'No, look – Hancock was your tutor, wasn't he? – Well, who do you think tutored Hancock? Me! I was your tutor's tutor and you can't do better than a tutor's tutor.' The series was running down, but James gave a special fillip to the last few episodes, not least with the vicarious presence of Hancock that he somehow evoked.

Hancock's tenure with the radio programme amounted to one of the busiest periods of his life. No sooner was he established as a regular member of its cast than he was attached by Brough as principal comedian to the stage show that took Archie to all the top variety theatres in the land. Hancock remembered, 'The show packed them in wherever it went. If we saw two vacant places in the standing room, we wondered what had gone wrong.' This kept him occupied most weeks between October 1951 and March 1952, with a four-week sabbatical at Christmas at the Prince of Wales Theatre in the West End where *Archie Andrews's Christmas Party* occupied the venue with sell-out matinées during the mornings and afternoons. The *Daily Express* made the analogy of 'a Children's Crazy Gang show' while Peter Brough, in his autobiography, singled out the running feud between Archie and his long-suffering 'Sir' as the principal attraction for the parents: 'As insult fell upon insult, and Tony writhed from sweet reason to acid invective, the audience roared the more. Maybe we're all repressed infants deep down and reap most joy from the sight of a schoolmaster being put through the hoop.' Val Parnell, running the show with Brough, also booked Hancock for the self-contained revue, *Peep Show*, playing twice-nightly at the same theatre. This amounted to four weeks of four performances in one day in two shows on one stage. Sundays were reserved for recording the radio show. Maybe it came easy after the Windmill. 'Do you know any good nightclub that wants a good cabaret act?' he joked wearily to Brough one day. 'And I could do with a few Sunday concerts as well. I'm wasting my time, you know – I actually have some moments when I've nothing to do but sleep!' One extra performance was squeezed in when Peter Brough, who for many years organised and starred in the entertainment for the Royal Household Christmas Party at Windsor Castle, added Tony to a company that included Peter Sellers, Kitty Bluett and Hattie Jacques. Brough recalled later that Hancock was unquestionably the success of the night: 'He made Princess Margaret laugh so much that she was in danger of ruining her make-up.' One wonders which engagement made him more nervous, his first performance before the royal family or the four-week run on the stage which Sid Field had colonised as his own for the last seven years of his life.

One aspect of *Educating Archie* that must have appealed to Hancock was the association it gave him by proxy with another of his idols, W.C. Fields. Peter Brough never hid the fact that his big break with the BBC came about through the original success on American radio achieved by ventriloquist Edgar Bergen and his principal dummy, Charlie McCarthy, in the 1930s. Fields also had cause to be grateful to Bergen. When his career sunk into a trough of ill-health, despair and alcoholism, it was the Bergen radio show, initially christened *The Chase and Sanborn Hour* in deference to its sponsor, that provided him with a new lease of professional life, the series developing a feud between the comedian and McCarthy that was extended to the cinema screen with *You Can't Cheat an Honest Man* in 1939. Hancock shared with Fields that intense vulnerability that managed to put the shutters up on pathos. Otherwise all human weakness was there, and although a hatred for children as abrasive as that practised by Fields was never allowed to develop in Hancock, of all the comedians who braved the enemy fire of ink pellets in front of Archie's blackboard he was the one who came closest to the spirit of the American. While Moreton, Secombe, Shiner, Forsyth and the others projected something approaching friendship in the role, the frequency with which Archie gained the upper hand over his wheedling superior and the indignation he showed in return cast Hancock snugly in the Fields mould. He could not have failed to notice the parallel. Philip Oakes recalled Hancock's relish at the story of Fields lacing the orange juice of his real-life child co-star Baby LeRoy with over-proof gin. 'Calls himself a trouper!' rasped the curmudgeon as the child passed out. 'Marvellous!' said Hancock. 'What a man!'

In later years Hancock admitted to the importance of Archie Andrews in his career and, at the risk of incurring further nightmares, went out of his way to refer to him in his act. In his soulsearching solo performance alone in his bedsitter, Galton and Simpson allowed time for their star to turn back the years. Clenching his teeth before the mirror he ponders his own ventriloquial ability: '"Hello Brough." "Hello Archie." "You're going gack in the gox," "I'm not going gack in the gox."' Swivelling his head back and forth, he might have had Brough's arm up his back as he rattled through the alphabet in time-honoured fashion. Only the glass of water is missing. It is a touching moment in a moving show, but, with deference to Fields, never pathetic in the sense of evoking pathos.

Pathetic in a different way had been *Happy-Go-Lucky*, the series that débuted the day before *Educating Archie* returned with Hancock for its second series. It was the sort of show – pushed through by someone high up in the BBC chain of command, who had dreamt up the title and should have known better – that according to Dennis Main Wilson should never have gone on air: 'You know that the moment you call a show "happy" it's going to go down the drain ... also there was a rule that anything that came down from above was doomed. It was far better if ideas came from the floor up.' Derek Roy, its main star, came with a large following brought from *Variety Bandbox*, where he had struck up an effective feud with Frankie Howerd – for a time they alternated weekly as the show's resident star comedian. In retrospect, Roy appears a sad cipher against the much-loved maestro of *Up Pompeii* and so much more besides. Howerd was arguably Max Miller's true heir in the originality he brought to the basic approach of the stand-up comedian, cajoling or chiding the theatre audience into submission as he traded gossip over the footlights like a fishwife in the bread queue. Roy's lasting claim to immortality may reside in the classic words he used to open what was only the second programme to air on commercial television, when it was launched in this country in 1955: 'Hello deserters.' For a while he billed himself on the halls as 'The Fun Doctor', but not even his medicine bag could effect the cure required to save this ailing show. He was, according to Bob Monkhouse, a kind man, punctilious to the point of embarrassment in paying a writer for every joke used every time it was used, but his career tailed off into relative obscurity as the 1950s progressed.

Happy-Go-Lucky was constructed to a magazine format that included early reality radio – each week a couple celebrating a wedding anniversary became involved with Roy at the microphone – as well as musical interludes and a resident comedy sketch centred around the activities of a boy scout patrol called the 'Eager Beavers'. Hancock was contracted to play Mr Ponsonby, the head of the recalcitrant troop, that also included Graham Stark as Bottrell, Peter Butterworth as Creep, and, for the first three shows only, Bill Kerr as Dilberry. Indeed, it is a mark of Hancock's early influence on Roy Speer that he recommended Stark for the job. Graham recollects Tony visiting him in a sorry state of health and sustenance in a damp-infested basement flat in Holland Park and leaving with the words, 'Christ, I've got to get you out of here – you'll die in this bloody room.' A few weeks later Tony returned: 'I want you to ring up a fellow called Roy Speer.' 'That started my whole career in radio,' says Stark gratefully. The scripts were transparently bad. Years later Kerr was gracious enough to comment that the only one of them to shine through the morass was Hancock. The most that might be said of the writing was that it allowed him to display a sub-Will Hay kind of desperation. The scoutmaster motif had been worked much more funnily on radio in the 1930s by John Tilley, a comedian of the old school and coincidentally an old boy of Durlston Court at Swanage. There is, too, a limit to the humour that can be derived from woggles, 'Be prepared' and outdoor activities of a restricted nature. On the thirteenth and penultimate episode the end-of-pier banality of it all depressed Hancock and Stark so much that they begged for their sketch to be dropped that week. The show was running over by six minutes and the producer did not need persuading. Memos circulated within the BBC that the artists were still to be paid accordingly, in Hancock's case his 18 guineas fee, as distinct from the 20 guineas basic – that is, separate from repeats – which he commanded for *Educating Archie*. It was not the last time he and the producer would work harmoniously together, but that producer was no longer Roy Speer.

During the recording of the eleventh show, Speer collapsed with a nervous breakdown or, in Ray Galton's words, 'a diplomatic illness'. In time he was allowed to concentrate on *Educating Archie*, while the baton of *Happy-Go-Lucky* was handed to Dennis Main Wilson.

Dennis described his predecessor as a true English gentleman. That may be a euphemism for his lack of resilience when confronted by the kind of fiasco into which the Derek Roy show had degenerated. Main Wilson, a 'fun doctor' if ever there was one, had no qualms about what medicine was required. With the ruthlessness of Genghis Khan he sacked all the writers at a stroke, although this had no effect on Hancock's contribution: the scout sketches had been bought up front from a pair of Australians named Ralph Peterson and E.K. Smith, and presumably contractual and budgetary constraints meant they had to be used. Many years later Dennis confessed that he deliberately caused the penultimate show to overrun by six minutes so that something would *have* to be cut from the show. That week the 'Eager Beavers' sketch had degenerated into a tasteless tirade on the subject of seasickness with lines like, 'I've just thought of a little something I should have brought up a long time ago,' and 'If I don't keep this down, I'll never live it down.' The sketch was happily consigned overboard.

Fortuitously around this time two young men who had met in a TB sanatorium at Milford in Surrey, where they whiled away their time by writing comedy scripts for the in-house hospital radio service, had made an impression on the BBC script editor Gale Pedrick. This had led to an informal arrangement between themselves and Derek Roy whereby they found themselves writing jokes for him at 5s. a time. They never forgot the first one he used on air: 'Jane Russell pontoon? It's the same as ordinary pontoon, but you need thirty-eight to bust.' Originally they were beholden only to Roy, not to the BBC. Their names were Ray Galton and Alan Simpson. The former was once described as 'a cross between Svengali and a polar explorer'; the latter had to make do with 'clean shaven, dark and chubby', although intermittently he has been known to sport a beard too. Ray has also been given as 'a bit of a worrier', with Alan as 'confident and expansive', two phrases conveniently indicative of the yin and the yang of the Hancock persona.

Graham Stark never forgot being in Dennis's office when things were at their most critical: 'We've got no writers and a show on Sunday! What are we going to do? A fellow called Gale Pedrick put his head round the door: "I hear you've got trouble with the writers." Dennis said, "We haven't got trouble with the writers – we haven't got any writers!"' There were no writers on contract available to step into the breach, but Pedrick went on to introduce the producer to his two new protégés. 'Shall I bring them in?' he asked. 'There's no alternative,' said Dennis. On the Tuesday two tall, shambling young men came into the office. Alan, who recalls the production meeting happening at Derek Roy's house, recollects the turning point in their careers: 'Ray and I were twenty-one and he [Dennis] said, "Are you two writers?" We were standing at the back of the room. And we said, "Well … yeah." And he said, "Right, you write the next three shows." And we looked at each other and we thought, "No way." We'd no experience, but we thought we'd better say nothing. Fortunately, it was by then a fortnightly show, so we said, "All right, yes, of course we can, yes." And it was frightening. But of course it was the best thing we could have done. It threw us in at the deep end. And it was pretty lousy stuff we were writing, but it was better than what had gone before.' According to Stark it was more than better: 'From the moment Dennis gave us the script, we knew. The difference was like the parting of the Red Sea – miraculous.'

It also meant a considerable advance from 5s. a gag to 40 guineas a show. They bought their first typewriter with their first fee. At the time Alan was working as a lowly-paid clerk in a shipping office; Ray – a pen-pusher for the Transport and General Workers' Union when he was taken ill – was on National Assistance. They had been inspired by the success of Frank Muir and Denis Norden, whose witty scripts for *Take It From Here* had raised the bar when it came to giving the listening audience credit for any sort of intelligence as far as comedy was concerned. It also helped that, as a result of three years of hospitalisation each, they were steeped in the great tradition of North

American humorous writing epitomised by the likes of Stephen Leacock, James Thurber, Robert Benchley and – their entrée to the genre – the underrated Topper novels of Thorne Smith, with their sharp ear for the witty cut and thrust born out of character. They have admitted that when they first started few people fully understood what scriptwriters were. When they went to open a bank account, the manager asked, 'Well, what do you do?' When they told him, he thought they did sign-writing on windows. When they explained that they wrote scripts, he said, 'Yes, but what do you do during the day?' Ahead of them lay a joint career as Britain's most successful comedy writing partnership.

The irony of their *Happy-Go-Lucky* commission was that since Hancock's participation in the show was self-contained within the 'Eager Beavers' episode, they would have to wait some time before they wrote for him. Few words passed between them during the last few weeks of the *Happy-Go-Lucky* experience, but those that did have become immortalised in comedy lore. The date was Sunday, 11 November 1951. According to Ray and Alan, Tony was a hunched-up figure in the stalls of the Paris Cinema, where the show was record-ed, as they walked past him following the rehearsal of a particularly successful sketch. 'Did you write that?' he murmured. They nodded. 'Very good,' replied Hancock with all the savour of a connoisseur. A few inches taller, they continued to walk down the aisle with Main Wilson. The sketch that impressed was based upon a children's tea party, featuring Roy, Stark and an inexperienced Benny Hill, who had been brought in to deputise for Butterworth. To read the ma-terial today is to be struck instantly by its emphasis on character at the expense of jokes, even if the ages of those participating have been scaled down to the level of the premise. Benny played an impertinent American child, Stark an introspective one, Roy the gushing party boy: in the space of a few minutes something approaching a chem-istry emerged between them. A few months after the demise of *Happy-Go-Lucky* in December 1951 Hancock spoke to Galton and

Simpson again, this time by telephone. He had another broadcast pending on *Workers' Playtime* at the beginning of April and needed a new five-minute spot. When he asked them their rates, they hadn't a clue. He immediately offered to pay them half his own fee. Alan remembers the commission: 'We said "Fine" – so we got 25 guineas. Fantastic! That tells you how much he was getting and, besides, 25 guineas was three times what we were getting for writing similar spots for Derek Roy. Usually comedians are extremely mean with fees for writers, but Tony wasn't.' Alan may have his figures wrong, since BBC files reveal that Hancock was paid only 25 guineas for the show. Nor was a separate contract issued to the writers. It is not impossible that Hancock, grateful for the exposure, donated his entire fee to Ray and Alan and never let on.

Another portmanteau format thrust by the BBC on Light Programme listeners was *Calling All Forces*, devised by the General Overseas Service for personnel serving at home and overseas:

Calling All Forces, hello!
This is your radio show.
Tune in the set, then sit beside it.
Tell us what you want and we'll provide it.

After hosting the more-or-less weekly show since its inception on 3 December 1950, Ted Ray stepped aside for the unlikely pairing of Hancock and Charlie Chester to assume the role of co-host together on 14 April 1952, by which point the programme had moved from Sunday to Monday evening. It might have made sense for the show to have been passed to one or the other, but not necessarily to them both. Chester had been relatively dispossessed on the airwaves since his knockabout *Stand Easy* show had drawn to a natural close the previous year. Hancock, with *Happy-Go-Lucky* happily-and-luckily behind him and the decision to move on from *Educating Archie* having been taken, was obviously in line for a new vehicle that would underline his growing star status: on the same day as pre-recording the first episode, 12 April, he opened as co-star to Jimmy Edwards and Vera Lynn in a major theatrical production at London's Adelphi Theatre. As the jolly jester and the despairing droll, Chester and Hancock might on paper have complemented each other like the sun and the moon, but in reality Hancock always ran the risk of appearing in the literal shadow of Chester, who regardless of the fact that he was the poor man's Max Miller had seven sterling years of radio fame behind him. Tony had already made a couple of solo guest appearances on the show, which since it began had been written by Bob Monkhouse and Denis Goodwin and co-produced by an echo from Tony's young past, Leslie Bridgmont. When the replacements for Ted Ray came along, the producers changed too. Bob and Denis hung in for another ten episodes, before a combination of exhaustion and frustration led to their departure. In his autobiography Monkhouse graphically and excrementally describes the use to which Hancock put what he regarded as the worst of the material they wrote for him. In literally clearing the air, the new producers, Jacques Brown and John Hooper, deserve their share of the credit for inviting Galton and Simpson, now on the BBC's accredited list of writers who could handle a series, to take over for the last six weeks. But equal credit must be extended to Phyllis Rounce. Well aware of the potential one-sided nature of the partnership in Chester's favour and her client's reservation that Monkhouse and Goodwin did not connect with his character in the way that Eric Sykes had done on *Educating Archie*, she wrote to the BBC hierarchy: 'He feels that, generally speaking, his participation in the programme has been under-written … and would like to express himself (and know that others have the opportunity to do likewise) before all concerned in the hope that some mutual benefit can be established.' It always peeved Ray and Alan that with three episodes to go Chester asserted his own independence by insisting that he write his own monologue, and insisted that their fee be docked the 10 guineas he expected for writing his own jokes.

The first exchange Ray and Alan wrote for them has a knowingly ghoulish quality. Chester has been talking about the miracle of television:

CHARLIE: Just think, I've only got to stand in front of a camera and I'll
   suddenly appear in a little wooden box.
TONY: (*Shouting off mike*) And do you want it with or without brass handles?

Temperamentally off-camera Chester and Hancock were never meant to be Barker and Corbett. The compulsive quipster mellowed into a friendly broadcaster over the years, but towards the end of his life could recall Tony only as 'a very insular person ... I had the feeling he was very insecure.' He went on to confide to Jeff Hammonds, 'He got very depressed if he felt you had more jokes than he did ... he would count the jokes in the script and insist on having an equal number of laughs.' This appears a harsh judgement on a man who mostly detested jokes *per se* and not least for the lack of subtlety with which someone as basic in his humour as Chester would deliver them. Perhaps the self-styled 'Cheerful' Charlie sensed that his microphone partner felt this form of humour was beneath him. It is not difficult to imagine Hancock sighing at the boisterous excesses that to many, this writer included, pushed the 'Cheerful' over into 'Cheerless'. A contrasting picture emerges from Alan Simpson's memory of a *Calling All Forces* rehearsal, where Tony took exception to the jokes that had been written for him and handed them over to Chester: 'In the end he had only a few pages left, while his colleague had practically the whole book. We had to write an entirely new script for him.' It was not that the jokes were necessarily unfunny. Presumably they had to be more character-driven.

The structure of the show was formulaic. Hancock and Chester – in the manner of 'The Two Ronnies' – would both perform solo material and work together, in addition to appearing in a sketch with that week's star guest and interacting with other principal performers on the show. One innovation Tony did tolerate from Monkhouse and Goodwin was his portrayal of an indignant female character, although he later claimed some credit for the device. In an interview he gave just before Ray and Alan took over he came clean: 'I got the idea for that from my wife, Cicely. She did not know at first. But she does now. She thinks it's very funny. But exaggerated, of course!' Of their shared material, Monkhouse commented on another anomaly, whereby 'he was a conman conning Charlie Chester – entirely the wrong way round – but comedians would make these demands of the script'. Certainly Ray and Alan continued this theme, often portraying him as a petty crook, albeit on a fantasy scale. It was enough for Tony to have just returned from a party for Chester to sense he had been up to no good:

CHARLIE: How did you manage to smuggle that huge grandfather clock out of the house without being seen?

TONY: Well, I must admit it was a bit tricky, Charles. After all it's not easy carrying a grandfather clock under one arm.

CHARLIE: One arm! Why didn't you use the other one?

TONY: What, and drop the piano?

One no sooner begins to think how much funnier – because much more in character – this exchange would read with the roles reversed and Sid James substituted for Chester, than a few lines later the tables are turned. Chester has returned to the subject of television and is attempting to sell a model to Hancock:

CHARLIE: This is the most modern set money can buy. A 1952 model with all the refinements present day science can provide. I'll just give the handle a few turns.

TONY: Handle? What's the handle for?

CHARLIE: You want the pictures to move, don't you? Believe me, Tony; this set is worth every penny of £350.

TONY: How much do you want for it?

CHARLIE: (*Tentatively*) Would fifty-eight and six be asking too much? What
do you say? Is it a deal? You've got the makers' guarantee, you know?
Look! Ginsberg, Goldstein and Levy.

TONY: Oh yes. The well-known Irish firm.

These lines – with James in lieu of Chester, of course – could have
come straight out of an early episode of *Hancock's Half Hour*. Galton
and Simpson are feeling their way towards new horizons. Petty criminality, in fact, was always a mark of Tony's early *Hancock's Half
Hour* character, but rendered 'acceptable' in a shifty moralistic way
by the less venial waywardness of Sid James. Moreover, in Hancock's
universe, Sid was the gatekeeper to a loose form of comic credibility,
a role of which the bland Chester was incapable.

It was in the final episode of *Calling All Forces* on 28 July 1952
that the public was introduced to the more grandiose name to which
Hancock's evolving character aspired, in a sketch that featured the
two stars as window cleaners:

CHARLIE: We've got to clean the outside of the windows now, and as we're on
the ninth floor, that means that we've got to climb out on to the ledge –
haven't you?

TONY: Yes we have, haven't I? … Oh no. Oh no, no, no, no … you're not going
to catch Anthony Aloysius St John Hancock the Second putting his
plates outside that window.

CHARLIE: Come on, Tony. Stop playing about. Get out on to that ledge. It's
quite safe. You've got nothing to worry about. You'll be perfectly
alright. You know I wouldn't send you if there was any danger. (*Pause*)
Here, sign this.

TONY: What is it?

CHARLIE: A life insurance policy.

How much funnier it would have been if Sid had been around at the time!

The perceived wisdom has long been that when *Calling All Forces* came off the air at the end of July 1952, the format was almost immediately rebranded as *Forces All-Star Bill* with Hancock as the sole compère. In fact for the new series the master of ceremonies was changed weekly, a role which Hancock fulfilled for the seventh show in the run transmitted on 15 September. Significantly the broadcast united him with Graham Stark and producer Dennis Main Wilson, although the script was now in the hands of two other friends, Spike Milligan and Larry Stephens. To historians of radio comedy and BBC schedulers alike, he was now about to enter the most confusing period of his radio career. It resembles an outrageous game of musical chairs. It was all down to titles. Hancock used to joke that they must have employed a crossword expert just to dream them up. There would be only one more edition of *Forces All-Star Bill* before it was curtailed to *All-Star Bill*, although to add to the confusion the shorter title had already been used by another producer for eight weeks in 1951. Hancock returned to present the third edition of the new strand for 13 October 1952. Stark, in a resident capacity, and Main Wilson remained attached to the programme, with Ray and Alan now back in the writers' chair. The abbreviated title endured for thirteen episodes, until there was an about-turn and *Forces All-Star Bill* was reinstated on 6 January 1953, although no longer on a Monday night at nine o'clock, but on Tuesday at eight where it had to alternate weekly with *The Forces Show* featuring Richard Murdoch, Kenneth Horne and Sam Costa. The run was scheduled for eleven weeks of which Main Wilson produced the first six, although Galton and Simpson were there for the duration. With little sense of pattern the show veered between guest compères like Ted Ray, Michael Howard, Bonar Colleano and no compère at all, other than the contribution made by a continuity announcer. Hancock was featured throughout the run as the resident comedy lead in a threesome that also featured Graham Stark and Joan Heal, although she was replaced by Geraldine McEwan when Alistair Scott-Johnston replaced Dennis Main Wilson. Although Tony insisted in newspaper interviews, 'The *show* is the star,' there is no doubt that Hancock was perceived as the star of the show both by the public and by the BBC, as reflected in his 35 guinea fee, a figure established when he became the co-star of *Calling All Forces* with Chester. However, whatever his status, he took no part in the third and fourth recordings, dates that coincided with his absence from the ongoing stage success at the Adelphi Theatre.

The run was successful enough from Hancock's point of view to tempt the administrators at Aeolian Hall into another title change – once again downplaying the services connection – and a rethink on scheduling. On 7 June 1953, with the nation at the height of Coronation fervour, *Star Bill*, subtitled 'The Best in Britain's Show Business', moved into the coveted nine o'clock Sunday evening slot on the Light Programme. Scott-Johnston continued as producer, Ray and Alan still providing the words. This marked a return to weekly transmissions, with the additional change that the new series was broadcast live. So far most of his important work for radio had been pre-recorded. Still accompanied by Stark and McEwan, he saw his fee rise to £50 as compensation and now was able to welcome the likes of Ted Ray, Charlie Chester and Derek Roy on board as *his* guests. The series ran for twenty-one weeks, although Hancock left amicably after the ninth show on 2 August to be replaced by Alfred Marks. This again initially coincided with a temporary absence from the Adelphi show, a continuing source of anxiety to him, as we shall discover in detail later. An insightful article in the *Television Mirror* for 6 March 1954, to coincide with the start of a shorter second series of *Star Bill*, stated that it was against Hancock's wishes and professional instinct to find himself a star at the age of thirty. This was not out of false modesty: 'He is a worrier. He worries about his performance if things don't seem to be going too well in the theatre some nights. He worries when he has the audience convulsed with laughter. He worries as much over a box-office "sell-out" as when the auditorium is only partially full. And he worries himself sick over every broadcast he does ...' Doctors had now advised him not to combine broadcasting with theatre commitments. This, together with a genuine desire not to overstay his welcome with the listener, as expressed by Pat Newman, the Variety Booking Manager, in a memo of 20 May 1953, meant that he was off the air in a regular vehicle for seven months. The second series of only ten shows beginning on 28 February 1954 would easily allow him to accommodate a new stage show scheduled for the Blackpool summer season in June.

For this second series Dennis Main Wilson returned as producer and Moira Lister replaced McEwan to complement Tony and Graham in the resident team. Galton and Simpson, who had missed a few early episodes of the previous run to be replaced by permutations of Sykes, Milligan and Larry Stephens, were also on hand for all the shows. Alan explained their earlier absence thus: 'By now we'd established a complete working rapport with Hancock. But we were still very young and that's why they wouldn't entrust us with all of the first series. And also from Tony's point of view – he was the star and he'd been working with Larry for a long time, and it served as a kind of insurance policy for him.' In a 1963 interview Hancock testified to that same rapport: 'We remained very close and the tendency was for them to ask me if they were doing a show and vice versa. From this closeness *Hancock's Half Hour* was born.' Main Wilson's presence must have been promising for writers and star. As early as May 1953 he had been campaigning behind the scenes for the type of show they all most wanted to do, a character-led half hour away from the itty-bitty distractions of sketch-driven vaudeville.

Throughout the various configurations of title, writers, cast and producer, Galton and Simpson were gradually edging towards their idealised perception of Hancock as a fully rounded comic character with its shabby gentility, put-upon petulance and unpredictable moodiness. Although there was still something of the fly boy about him, by the time of *Star Bill* the failed fantasist was also bubbling to the surface:

TONY: Any sign of that lifeboat yet? Poor blighters out in this weather. The waves are like mountains. (*Raising his voice*) Have a message from the flagship – eleven U-boats in the area. Look! There's one surfacing. My heavens, I don't think he's spotted us. Full steam ahead. Action stations. Starboard to helm. Stand by the depth charges. Stand by the forward guns. Fire!

GRAHAM: Tony, how much longer you gonna be in that bath?

All Hancock's future Walter Mitty-style dreams are encapsulated in such a moment, in the same way that his tendency to dejected soliloquy was foreshadowed in this birthday plea from the heart in the same series:

TONY: Forgotten. Unwanted. No presents for the lad. No little fire engines to push around the floor on a wet Saturday afternoon. And I was looking forward to a new bus conductor's set. And me little lead soldiers – standing on guard outside me fort with no heads on. And I wanted a new golly ... to hug. If I'd known this was to be my lot I ... I would have asked the stork not to have brought me in the first place.

A verbal economy with its matching rhythm was also establishing itself in the confluence between comedian and writers:

TONY: Hello. Where are you two going?

MOIRA: Graham's taking me for a ride in his car.

GRAHAM: Yes – mine's the yellow drophead parked next to the scrap heap.

TONY: Yours is the scrap heap parked next to the yellow drophead.

Stark himself soon picked up on the emphasis Ray and Alan were beginning to place on reaction in the non-visual medium: 'I would say, "'Ere, you're good on motor bikes, aren't you?" And Tony would say of course he was. Then I'd say, "Simple – the wall of death – dead easy." And when I had talked him into doing it and just as he was about to roar off, I'd say, "But don't look behind you. The lion doesn't like it." Now that may not be very funny in itself, but it was Hancock's "Cor, stone me!" that got the laugh.'

Anyone perusing back issues of the *Radio Times* from the fifth show of the second *Star Bill* series may be puzzled by the inclusion in the billing of the name 'Higgins'. This was a character who never spoke and whose name would surface from time to time in *Hancock's Half Hour*. He provided Hancock with an invisible straight man, a device at its most effective when he was able to engage with him in exasperated one-sided dialogue, as in this segment where Tony is conducting guests to their room in a seedy seaside boarding house:

TONY: That's it, right. Now we'll be up there in no time. I'll just get it
started. I have to shout up the lift shaft to the engineer. Pardon me.
(*Shouts off*) Higgins! Second floor! That's right – ready – pull. Good
lad. Heave, Higgins. Oh, well done. We made five foot on that one ...
yeah, I know we're dropping. Dig your heels in Higgins, lad. That's it.
Well done. Another two foot, Higgins. That'll do it ... you fool ... don't
let go! We haven't got out yet – hah – hold it – there! (*To microphone*)
Swipe me. I'll have that cable round his neck before the day is out.

In later editions of *Hancock's Half Hour* this ability to hold imaginary conversations with people enabled the paranoia within his persona to parade itself to dazzling comic effect.

These were exhilarating and enlightening times for the two young writers. As Simpson has observed, 'We were writing for virtually every comedian in the country. Each show had guest comics, guest actors and singers, and we had to adapt our writing for their different styles. This is how we learnt our craft. It was an invaluable apprenticeship.' The most surprising of those guests must have been Gene Autry, the singing cowboy, appearing in London with his rodeo show at the Empress Hall. Stark recalls that he was hopeless in sketches, but his presence did lead to some telling topicality – on the back of an atrocious pun – in the show that was broadcast on 26 July 1953. When Autry explains that there are no Red Indians in America now, Tony enquires, 'Since when?'

GENE: Since McCarthy took over …

TONY: Oh yes, McCarthy … that's where we have one over on America here.
I can lean out of the window and tell everyone I'm a Communist and nobody would bother … free speech and all that …

GENE: You don't say.

TONY: Yes, watch this. I'll open the window …

(Effects: *Window opens*)

TONY: (*Shouts*) I'm a Communist … you see …

GENE: Why, that's pretty good.

TONY: Yes, nobody bothers … after all everybody is entitled to …

(Effects: *Terrific explosion – debris – the lot*)

TONY: It was an old building anyway.

It does not quite have the ring of authentic Hancock. A great deal is explained when one discovers that Autry's visit coincided with one of the weeks Ray and Alan made way for Sykes and Milligan.

I would hazard that the most memorable encounter for the star of the show was working alongside the legendary music-hall comedian Jimmy James. Long before Hancock, James had discovered the ability to make ordinary speech funny. In his iconic relationship with his two stooges – one gormless, one bumptious, both as moonstruck as he was – he also majored in the art of comic suspicion that Hancock took to even higher levels with the members of his East Cheam household. The night the veteran shared the stage of the

Garrick Theatre with Hancock for his *Star Bill* broadcast he was, as Galton and Simpson admit, understandably nervous about a script in which he did not have full confidence. Dennis Main Wilson had vivid recall of the occasion. Between the dressing room and the stage – all of 30 yards – James somehow lost his copy. Hancock was not an ad-libber, and the show was live. James looked at Hancock and, after a heartbeat pause, asked, 'Are you the chap?' Tony went, 'Eh?' 'I thought it would be more of a military gentleman,' said the guest. The senior droll caused a white-faced Hancock to ad-lib for several minutes before they managed to get back on track, namely the sur-realist musings of James on the missing salt in the packet of crisps he'd bought at the station on the way down: 'There can't be a short-age of salt. They're going full blast in Siberia ... somebody's knocked me salt off. Do you realise at this very minute there's a bloke walk-ing around Stockton-on-Tees with a couple of packets of salt in one packet of crisps. I'll call in the police station when I get back to see if he's handed one packet in.' Meanwhile Main Wilson was frantically telephoning Broadcasting House to apologise for the overrun. 'Who cares?' was the response. As inconsequentially as a breeze, James spun magic from the framework Galton and Simpson had provided for him and afterwards had the courtesy to thank them for so doing. There are moments when one considers the *oeuvre* they wrote for Hancock – with its precision of language and grasp of a realism that borders on the absurd – and ponders who else in the comic firma-ment they might have served as well. One always comes back to Jimmy James. Once asked by a BBC producer exactly what he did on stage, James replied, 'I'm glad you brought that up; it's been worry-ing me for years.' Hancock would have hugged him, had he been there.

The fifteen-minute sketch format favoured on the music halls by James, and colleagues like Sid Field, Robb Wilton and pioneer Harry Tate, was the forerunner of situation comedy as it has become known in more recent times. The tendency of both radio and television to mimic the broken format of variety stymied for a long time the lateral thought that might have led sooner to the development on air of the extended sketch into a half-hour story line without musical interludes. In retrospect it is hard to realise how innovative the concept must have seemed in the early 1950s. Technically *Hancock's Half Hour* could not claim to be the first of the genre that would dominate comedy for the greater part of half a century, although it certainly established a new benchmark. The exception had been on the family/domestic front. *Life with the Lyons*, first broadcast in 1950, and *Meet the Huggetts* and *A Life of Bliss*, both in 1953, all prefigured the Hancock project, although wheels were turning within the BBC for something along these lines to materialise for Hancock as early as July 1952, at which point Dennis Main Wilson was not the prime mover. Even then *Life with the Lyons* favoured the formulaic joke-driven American style, and was not truly character-driven. All three shows had about them the air of cosy domesticity that the quirky arrangements of 23 Railway Cuttings would travesty.

On 8 July 1952, with Hancock uncomfortably cocooned with Chester in his *Calling All Forces* residency, producer Peter Eton submitted to Michael Standing, the Head of Variety, a proposal that had come to him from the comedian and Larry Stephens. In this Hancock would play the part of an 'unimaginative, unenterprising, charming idiot', juggling his life as an estate agent, town councillor and bachelor in a small South Coast resort. He lives with his aged aunt in a ghastly semi-detached villa. She spends her time attempting to marry him above his station into the 'county set', in spite and because of his predilection for the local girls. Additional grit in the oyster is provided by a crooked garage proprietor with a raucous laugh and flair for gauche bonhomie. Already there was a potential part for Sid James! Each half hour would be dedicated to a complete narrative with no interruptions, no studio audience and no set formula, although the internal memo does stress that, while pompous and blundering, his character would remain likeable. The memo also contained a footnote which stated that upon recently taking part in a sketch in a Saturday morning children's radio programme called *Hullo There* Hancock had been advised that his forte was non-audience comedy, somewhat uncertain advice to a talent honed in the 'live' cut-and-thrust of variety and concert party. Stephens was given the green light to produce a pilot script and Eton took the star – perhaps unnecessarily in light of the disproportionate amount of time he had already spent in seaside towns – on an atmospheric recce to Seaford in Sussex, a resort that he felt fitted the script to the letter. *Welcome to Whelkham* emerged as a somewhat limiting title, but since Hancock was a Variety property and Eton still at that point a Drama producer – he would later switch over and take over *The Goon Show* from Main Wilson – Tony was sidelined from the project. It was eventually recorded as a vehicle for the actor Brian Reece, of *PC 49* fame, with Dorothy Summers, 'Mrs Mopp' from *ITMA*, in the role of the aunt. The response from listeners was that the show was 'feeble, forced, hackneyed, and not at all funny'. This is not to say that Hancock would not have made it hilarious, although in retrospect it does appear that he enjoyed a lucky escape.

In October, John Hooper, one of Tony's producers on *Calling All Forces*, went in to bat with another suggestion. In his memo to Pat Hillyard, the Deputy Head of Variety, Hooper refers to Hancock as being 'in wide demand' and is well aware 'that there are, indeed, other programme suggestions incorporating him in [the] process of being worked out'. The comedian was obviously making waves as a major star of the future. In the new idea he was cast as the multi-purpose fixer and bodyguard proprietor of ''Ancock, 'Ancock, 'Ancock and 'Ancock'. Co-starring would be the glamorous Yolande Donlan as a rich American with more money than brains, intent on doing and seeing everything on a visit to the capital in Coronation Year. Hancock is hired by her father to see that her plans go accordingly and no harm comes her way. Inevitably the comedy hinges on the opposite outcome. Max Wall was suggested as the third addition to a trio of stars in the *Take It From Here* tradition, appearing in a variety of guises as the smooth operator intent on separating Donlan from her cash. A script by Laurie Wyman and Len Fincham was submitted and the powers-that-be saw the possibilities, while expressing the concern that 'the three-handed dialogue, which the writers seem to have taken great pains to formulate, tends to reduce the "punch" of Hancock at times'. It was also suggested that the timbre and delivery of Hancock and Wall might possibly be too similar. The project coasted along until the much-respected Peter Eton was allowed to pass his judgement. He saw nothing but 'just another very dull, uninspired, three-spot comedy show completely lacking in the one thing Tony needs – *situation comedy*'. The 'three-spot' reference would have been the main obstacle to narrative credibility. The presence of the Hedley Ward Trio to chop up the thirty minutes into three parts was an obvious step backwards, even if a plot did run through the scripted material on either side of the music. No more was heard of the proposed project, but Eton's memo, dated 31 March 1953, may be significant. It is the first use of the phrase, italicised on the previous page, that I have been able to find in BBC files. It is impossible to know whether it was coined by him. Had he or someone else not done so, Dennis Main Wilson would have.

In view of Hancock's input into the 'Whelkham' idea, it was inevitable that he would have discussed similar projects with Galton, Simpson and his old champion from the Nuffield Centre days. On 1 May 1953 Dennis addressed his own memo to his boss, the Head of Variety. Main Wilson's proposal had the advantage of being less specific than the other two, but cut to the quick of the matter in his brisk, no-nonsense style. He explained he was anxious for Hancock to have a half-hour series of his own 'based on reality and truth rather than jokes, merry quips, wheezes, breaks for crooners who've got no reason to be in the show in the first place anyway'. As far as Dennis was concerned, the old mould of 'first sketch, singer, second sketch, band number, last sketch' could be assigned to oblivion. A pragmatist adrift in a in a fantasy world, he may have been overreacting against the madness of *The Goon Show*, the success of which owed much to his creative energy. At a time when *ITMA* was still regarded as the Holy Grail in the upper echelons of the BBC, the bare bones of the concept must have appeared revolutionary. But, as Graham Stark points out, Dennis was one of life's masochists: 'the more difficult the task, the more he would enjoy it'. It took several months before he achieved a breakthrough, with Ray and Alan – carried away by idealism and preoccupied anyhow with the scripts they were writing at the time – not discovering until after Main Wilson's death in 1997 that it had not been an easy task.

Aside from the tried and trusted nature of his relationship with Tony and his writers, if one quality allowed Main Wilson's suggestion to win out over rival bids, it was his ability as a producer to empathise with a project as vividly as those performing and writing it. Production was not a formal process where something just emerged at the end of a conveyor belt. The BBC came to recognise this gift within him and, as his career advanced, would probably place greater hope in a three-line suggestion on the back of an envelope from Dennis than in a more detailed synopsis from somebody else. Not that he was incapable of the long memo to fight his and his colleagues' corner when it was required. By 12 February 1954 all was in place for Tony Hancock to star in a new series the following October, and Dennis wrote to C.F. Meehan, the Assistant Head of Variety Programmes, by way of confirmation. He referred back to his communication of 1 May and, to preclude confusion, spelled out the bullet points again, whereby the comedy style would be 'purely situation', in which the central character would be built up as a real-life person in corresponding surroundings. Anything at all reminiscent of *The Goon Show* would be *verboten*. However, he did allow his writers some latitude when he stated that the construction of the show would have as loose a formula as possible. In other words, listeners would be as likely to hear three different narratives on three different themes as they would a complete half-hour storyline. It seldom worked out this way, although some of the most memorable single moments from the series can be pinpointed to these triple-decker episodes. It would take a long time for all their objectives to be achieved, not least as a result of Main Wilson casting at the eleventh hour arguably the funniest purveyor of funny voices in the business. However, this and the air of outrageous unreality that clings to many of the early shows might have softened the blow for those on high who still needed convincing.

It should be stressed that in breaking away from many of the established conventions of radio comedy Hancock was anxious to prove his own man. His own comic idealism, doubtless bolstered by just a touch of that subtle snobbery that his old *Wings* colleague, Bryan Olive, had once discerned, enabled him to rise above the devices favoured by others, but it should never be allowed to cast a shadow over the quality and excellence that managed to exist in the areas he shunned. For two successive generations *ITMA* and *The Goon Show* raised the catchphrase to a level of social acceptability that forged, in the phrase of the radio historian Peter Black, 'a kind of national togetherness', establishing in their short-hand reference a common ground between strangers at critical points in our history. They were originally voiced, for the main part, by various characters with distorted voices, but there still remains something complete and memorable about Colonel Chinstrap and Mrs Mopp, Bluebottle and Eccles that deserves a place in the folk memory of humour as securely as the more bizarre denizens of Lewis Carroll's Wonderland. One can hear Hancock declaiming, 'Nonsense!' Exactly! They were as valid to the British way of letting off steam as pantomime, Derby Day and Guy Fawkes Night. And thanks to *Hancock's Half Hour* he and Sid would win their own special place in that nostalgic hinterland too.

Chapter Six

HANCOCK'S RADIO *HALF HOUR*

*'I would work at an inflection as if I were writing
a sonnet. I worried about every word.'*

The first episode of Dennis Main Wilson's dream project was aired on
the BBC Light Programme at nine thirty in the evening on Tuesday
2 November 1954, having been pre-recorded the previous Saturday.
The working title of *The Tony Hancock Show* had been discarded as
too mundane at an internal Corporation meeting six weeks earlier.
The storyline of the first edition was based upon the Pirandellian
premise of Hancock under dubious circumstances giving a party for
the BBC hierarchy and the press to celebrate the first edition of his
new radio series. To condition listeners ahead of the event, a note of
shady criminality was sounded by the qualification in the announcement in the *Radio Times* that the programmes were 'based on the life
of the lad 'imself from the files of the *Police Gazette*', although that
was contradicted somewhat by the reference three lines later that the
show had been written and adapted by Galton and Simpson from *The
Junior Goldfish Keepers' Weekly*. In the years ahead flexibility would
be their key, and from day one the temptation was resisted to cement
the star character into a set pattern of status or employment. Main
Wilson, knowing full well that there were only so many jokes you
could make, say, about an estate agent and town councillor living on

the South Coast of England, recalled this rationale later in life: 'I did seven series of *Till Death Us Do Part*, and to this day you don't know what Alf Garnett did for a living.' On radio, *Hancock's Half Hour* ran for 103 episodes and six series until the end of 1959, the lack of restrictive detail in the early stages contributing considerably to the long run. However, while the writers were encouraged by the capacity of the medium to give full scope to fancy and imagination, irrespective of the apparent contradictions this presented along the way, this did not stop them from taking pains to define the precise living environment for their hero.

There is a myth that Cheam was chosen as a suitable destination on the basis that Phyllis Rounce's mother lived there and that Hancock found the idea irresistibly funny. More than fifty years after the event Galton and Simpson deny this had any bearing upon the issue and, if they ever knew of the nostalgic detail, profess to have forgotten it along the way. It is unlikely that their memory is playing tricks, and both claim that the reason they used East Cheam in particular was purely for themselves. Ray lived not far away in Morden and as a youngster had helped deliver the milk to the area for United Dairies at weekends: he thought it was the poshest place he had ever seen. Alan lived in nearby Mitcham and played Saturday morning soccer games on the Sutton Grammar School ground: Sutton and Cheam were inseparable as the exclusive preserve for a certain kind of South London swank. By adding 'East' to the name, in effect fictionalising the location since, unlike North Cheam, the place exists only as a compass bearing and not as a recognised district, they subtly emphasised the gap between Hancock's aspirations to gentility and the reality. The more specific setting of Railway Cuttings evoked the faded grandeur of a Victorian past and provided the giveaway clue that he lived where the coal yards were, in an inescapably grimy tumbledown terrace down a siding somewhere. One can just see the broken milk bottles in the gutter, the parked cars with their forlorn abandoned air, and the groundsel suffused in cat piss poking through cracks in the tarmac wherever one treads. Alan recalled, 'We toyed with other names like Gasworks Lane before we decided on Railway Cuttings. Once we'd done it, then it lives with you. Hancock was always at 23 – as if 22 and 24 were much inferior addresses – it's actually funnier, like cucumbers are funnier than apples and oranges.' In time it became as familiar to the British public as 10 Downing Street. Quite blatantly, the writers were cocking a snook at the posh environment to which as young men they too could only have aspired. In the imagination of Galton and Simpson, by every measure of civilisation – health, crime, employment, lifestyle – East Cheam is the comic pits.

Although the ambience was there from the beginning, the exact topography did not fall into place at once. The 'East' prefix was the last piece of the jigsaw to tumble out of the box, not really coming into its own until television added itself to the equation in the summer of 1956. The first radio episode referred to the Hancock lodging as 'Tony's flat in the English quarter of London's West End'. It was not until the second episode of the third series, when he deigned to give his address to the salesman in a car showroom as 'Hancock Castle, 23 Railway Cuttings, Cheam', that we know for certain that his shabby milieu has been transported to the extremities of South London. Nineteen shows later, for some strange reason, the number of the house changes for one show only. When Hancock returns from holiday to find Kenneth Williams illegally installed by Sid as a tenant, his address is given as number 7. But artistically Galton and Simpson, as we have seen, never intended consistency to be their guiding star and may have been trying to confirm for themselves that 23 was a funnier number. The basis of Hancock's occupancy would vary from week to week as unpredictably as his means of employment or his status in the entertainment profession. At various times he is a council tenant, a private rent payer and the property owner, although the last tended to dominate in the later shows. For one memorable episode where Sid's scheming demands that his grounds are taken over to make way for a greyhound track, we find him installed in a country mansion. As Bill Kerr is heard to comment, 'It's more than a retreat – it's a mass surrender.' When the plot and his delusions of grandeur dictate, No. 23 is even allowed a garden: 'I am not ruining my glads and daffs for anybody – it's taken me three years to get these bulbs right. You wait till they come up. I've got me coat of arms in one bed, and the number of the house in another, and then there's me face in the centre.'

A well-defined fictive universe grew up around the residence. The house was given claim to historical significance: Hancock was proud of the fact that it had been the finishing line of the Cheam pancake race for centuries. From more recent history, the ravages of the war were never far distant. On one occasion an unexploded bomb is found in the cellar and blows the edifice sky high. Of course, within a week the magic of radio allowed the residence to continue as a private educational establishment under Hancock's tutelage, as if 'doodlebug' had been no more than a squiggle on Hitler's scratch pad. When the local council threatens Fred's Pie Stall in the market square with closure, Hancock displays the campaigning zeal of a Betjeman to rescue a tradition that has helped to feed the local community for sixty years. No episode provided a clearer bird's eye view of the area than the one in which Tony found himself acting as a guide to a coach-load of Americans on one of Sid's Mystery Tours: 'Over the bridge across the picturesque polluted river, down which float impressive mountains of detergent foam ...' One link with reality was provided by the local, the Hand and Racquet: this was based on a pub at the corner of Orange and Whitcomb Streets, just off London's Haymarket, where cast and writers would sometimes gather between rehearsals and recording when the show was taped at the Paris Cinema studio in Lower Regent Street.

Long before the location was transplanted to television, listeners could picture the interior of Hancock's home in detail, showing kinship with the small girl who, when asked why she preferred radio to television, replied that she thought the scenery was nicer. Not that there was much that was nice about the inside of No. 23. You could smell the soot in the fireplace, the mildew in the kitchen, the dampness of distemper that had never been allowed to dry. In time decorative detail that did not become apparent until television cameras entered the abode also crept into the radio scripts. When Hancock is persuaded at last to take out an insurance policy on his furnishings and fittings, the inventory comes readily to mind: 'You mean me stuffed eagle, and me brass bedstead, and me camel saddle television chair?' To which he might have added his potted palm, his painting of Queen Victoria, the glass dome with the piece of his mother's wedding cake beneath it, not to mention the harmonium and the Winston Churchill toby jug. The seedy antiquated living space was further enhanced by the regular members of the team that inhabited the dwelling. It is the responsibility of the producer to cast a show, and Dennis Main Wilson surpassed himself, even if he was dependent, one assumes, on his star's approval and for one historical suggestion on the inspired instinct of the writers.

Moira Lister moved gracefully across from the *Star Bill* format as the star comedian's token girlfriend, a device carried over from American comedy shows of the period. In retrospect her husky voice and no-nonsense approach would have provided the perfect contrast for the softer, more laid-back delivery that Hancock later achieved, but for now the more artificial style that lingered from his *Educating Archie* days did not sit easily with her more refined approach and she proved the least effective member of the new team. At the end of the first series Lister would be the first to leave the curious commune, but the show's four male stalwarts would stay together until the beginning of the sixth. One recalls Paul McCartney's astonishment that the Beatles ever came into being: 'What are the odds that those four guys would find each other?' Graham Stark was not one of them, a decision that appears to have been taken jointly by Hancock and Main Wilson. Instead Bill Kerr filled the role of Tony's chirpy best friend, worst adviser and indolent drain on his resources. Once billed as a child star as 'Wee Willie Kerr – the Jackie Coogan of Australian vaudeville', he already had a big following on *Variety Bandbox* and similar shows as the lugubrious fugitive – 'I've only got four minutes' – from Wagga Wagga (pronounced *Wogga Wogga*). Kerr with his Australian accent provided greater vocal contrast with Hancock than Stark would have done. They had all worked together in the early 'Eager Beavers' sketches in *Happy-Go-Lucky*. Much was made in later years of Graham's displeasure at this turn of events, but he is keen to emphasise that, while disappointed, he never regarded this as a personal slight by Hancock. There *had* been a hiccup when a hint was dropped that Hancock did not want him to continue during the last six shows of the *Star Bill* run, but Main Wilson forced the issue in his favour. Today he sounds sincere when he stresses, 'I don't remember wanting to be in *Hancock's Half Hour* at the time.' He had no need to. That November, with his old officer character from Gang Show days reborn as the upper-class twit Nigel Bowser-Smythe, he moved into his own long-running radio association with Peter Brough and Archie Andrews.

In spite of Kerr's Australian parentage, both Bill and Moira were South African by birth: Bill's parents had been touring the Union in vaudeville at the time of his arrival in 1924. It must surely have been against all McCartney-style odds that the third member of the supporting team to be cast would also hail from that country, even more so that he might have been born – from cockney-Jewish ancestry – in *Hancock* Street, Johannesburg, on 8 May 1913 and had already worked with a fifteen-year-old Moira Lister in children's broadcasting in the colony. Unaware of this, Galton and Simpson knew instinctively the character they wanted to represent the rogue element in the series. He had scored heavily as the crook Lackery Wood in the 1951 Ealing comedy success, *The Lavender Hill Mob*; they had to catch up with the movie again at a flea pit in Putney and sit through the film a second time to check the credits to find out his name. That name was Sidney James. No actor in the world could have captured more effectively the get-rich-quick mentality they needed to highlight the gullibility of the character they were developing, someone of whom Hancock could say, 'He can hear a pound note rustling down wind two miles away.' It would have been so much easier for them to have targeted a radio comedy stereotype of the day in the con man mould of Sam Costa or Harold Berens. James was a total newcomer to broadcast comedy, although his face, if not his name, was already one of the most recognisable in the land. It is not easy to think of him as a shrinking violet, but as an actor who had always relied on gesture and expression he did need persuading to work in a medium where the home audience would not see him. To show how far in advance they were working, Main Wilson arranged for Sid to visit a broadcast of *Star Bill* at the Garrick Theatre during the early part of 1954. This coincided with the period when Hancock and James were both working at Beaconsfield on the film *Orders are Orders*. Sid agreed with some reluctance to tackle the project on a one-show-at-a-time basis.

When at last he stood before the microphone on 30 October 1954, he did so with a Harry Lime furtiveness, his trilby pulled down to shadow his face so that he could not be recognised. Apparently, the script in his hand shook so much that the rustling threatened to disrupt the recording. But, according to Alan Simpson, within a few weeks the old pro – now grandiosely styled Sidney Balmoral James by the writers – took over and he was holding the pages steady in front of him, hat off, playing to the gallery without a care in the world. Film critic Barry Norman paid him a special compliment when he said, 'To act without appearing to be acting is an enormous skill.' In the astute words of fellow pro Bruce Forsyth, 'He was a natural at being natural,' while Beryl Vertue recalled that by the time she came on the scene he had all the confidence in the world, 'with the aftershave to match'. As the series progressed and broadened its scope into television so Sid, with a face like tangerine peel and a laugh like scraped toast, would change from portraying an out-and-out crook to a latter-day Sancho Panza representing the 'gorblimey' voice of bluntness at Hancock's side: 'If you ain't got it, get it. When you've got it, spend it. Eat, drink, be merry – for tomorrow we snuff it.' His personal popularity, both in and out of the business, did much to strengthen the success of the series on radio and television over seven years, prompting Galton and Simpson to say in unison together, 'He was one of the most likeable people who ever existed in the theatrical world.' His craggy voice had a 'lived-in' feel that connected immediately with audiences. He was born to vaudevillian parents as Sidney Joel Cohen and legend has it that he made his first stage appearance when only a few months old. During his early years in South Africa he diversified as a coal heaver, skating instructor, diamond polisher, hairdresser and professional boxer before acting claimed his full attention. He used to joke, 'I guess you could call me a character actor – and it's taken a lot of hard work to get that character.' Like Hancock, he too had been inspired by Max Miller, when the legendary comedian made his only overseas tour in South Africa in 1932. Sid arrived in the reverse direction in 1946 and quickly became known in the business as 'One Take James', soon commanding one of the highest daily film rates in the business for a character actor. At times the recording schedule of the Hancock show would be moved around to take into account his busy work pattern. His contribution to the Hancock legend is inestimable.

In the best traditions of radio, another actor – a 'voice man' – was required to play all the other individuals destined to throw obstacles in the path of Hancock's paranoia and pretentiousness. In *The Uses of Literacy* in 1957, the cultural historian Richard Hoggart expertly caught the measure of their kind in a single word: '"Them" includes the policemen and those civil servants or local authority employees whom the working-classes meet – teachers, the school attendance man, "the Corporation", the local bench. Once the Means Test Official, the man from "the (Board of) Guardians" and the

Employment Exchange officer were notable figures here. To the very poor, especially, they compose a shadowy but numerous and powerful group affecting their lives at almost every point: the world is divided into "Them" and "Us".' With a tip-off from an agent friend, Dennis Main Wilson found the enduring comedy voice of 'Them' in unlikely circumstances. So far he had been falling behind in the semi-pledge he had made to his superiors in his memo of 12 February 1954 to 'find a few really *new* names to put into the show'. Neither Lister nor Kerr would have fallen into that category, although Sid represented a scoop. Dennis was about three weeks away from the first recording. He then made a discovery that instantly threw to the wind some of the best intentions of writers, producer and star, someone who in his stylised way would make as indelible a contribution to British comedy as Hancock and James. He found Kenneth Williams in the most unlikely of circumstances, playing the part of the Dauphin in a revival of Shaw's *Saint Joan* at the Arts Theatre Club. Main Wilson was impressed by the way in which the elfin-like actor switched vocally between humour, sadness and malevolence in the role. New to radio comedy, Williams would perform in all but four of the first series and then seventy-two further radio episodes, before leaving early in the final run in 1959. Two years before his departure Hancock had explained in a newspaper interview that the Williams part was specifically 'written so that he can irritate me'. To those in the know, the words could be interpreted at two levels. For the time being a comment by Ray Galton will suffice: 'After the first week with Ken in the show, bang went our idea of no funny voices and no catch-phrases.'

In the first episode Williams would be given the most memorable line, although it had no bearing on the catchphrases that would emerge later. As Lord Bayswater, the dyspeptic ancient who through Sid's duplicity has unknowingly lent Hancock his Park Lane apartment for his first-night party, he returns to find the place in ruins. Distraught, he turns to the comedian and – with a yearning that walks a tightrope between genuine emotion and burlesque – asks, 'Who threw jelly over the Rembrandt?' Hancock, oblivious of who he is, responds with a chuckle, 'I suppose it was the same bloke who slashed the Goyas.' Not for the last time would the star be upstaged by the newcomer. Equally prophetic was the opening sequence that daringly held back on words in favour of pauses, here interwoven with the clacking sound effect of Bill tediously typing party invitations with one finger. When Tony hassles him, he begs not to be rushed. Hancock reminds him that it might help if he took his gloves off. The ball is now back in Bill's court: 'my hands are cold – (seven keys struck slowly) – anyway, what's wrong with typing in gloves? – (six keys struck) – I *like* typing in gloves – (five keys struck) – lots of people type in gloves'. Four more keys are struck and then, after the merest hesitation of a pause, Hancock goes in for the kill: 'Not in boxing gloves.'

Two devices in the first episode would not pass the test of time. They included the character of 'Coatsleeve Charlie', played by Gerald Campion, who from 1952 had already made an impact with his portrayal of Billy Bunter on television. The decision to include such an obvious throwback to a more gimmicky style of radio comedy appears surprising. Charlie was intended as a crony of Sid who couldn't manage to get two words out without wiping his nose on his sleeve and interjecting a couple of tell-tale sniffs. As Hancock himself wrote, 'It may sound an essentially visual gag, but it came over all too horribly in sound. It was a ghastly idea and I cannot imagine how we ever thought it would be acceptable, let alone funny. We must have been mad to try it at all.' The character disappeared up its own coat sleeve after a single episode. Less reprehensible was the decision to include Alan Simpson in a cursory speaking role as the anonymous monosyllabic foil in a regular free-association monologue by Hancock. Simpson's character might be a customs officer, a pavement artist or just a face in the crowd, but always capable of distracting Hancock into a rambling discourse that began something like,

'D'you think I look like Jack Hawkins?' – 'No' – 'Just thought I'd ask.'
or 'Of course, I'm an artist myself – you can tell by the way I use my
shirt as a paint rag.' All Simpson had to do was interject a soft-voiced
'Yes', 'No', 'Really', 'Oh, dear' or 'Get away!' as appropriate. It pleased
Hancock to find someone in constant agreement. As he says to
Simpson on one occasion, 'Cheerio then – I'll see you next week … it's
been delightful. You're the only one that understands me.' In this
way the sequences point forward to the platitudinous chats in which
he would later engage with Hugh Lloyd in television. They were
phased out during the course of the second series, as they started to
impede plot development and Kenneth Williams's versatility came
more to the fore. Heard now, they carry considerable charm. They
were also important in helping to encourage the lower register of
Hancock's voice and his ongoing development as a more natural performer.

In a magazine article in 1963 Hancock commented, 'That first
show was received fairly poorly, but we survived.' Twelve per cent of
the adult population listened to the programme. By the end of the
first series the last five programmes were averaging audiences of
nearly 6.3 million, an increase of one and a half million. Producers
soon learn to distrust the exhibitionist comments of the distorted
few who are given voice in audience research surveys, and it would
be futile for this volume to give credence to too many of them here.
Amid contradictory praise for the cast and disappointment with the
writers, a Methodist minister on the listening panel did remark,
'This has been the funniest thing on radio recently. All good fun and
no crooners and jazz. No rowdiness.' Main Wilson would have been
pleased with the penultimate sentence. The programme never went
back on its oath to maximise the laughter potential of the seven or
eight minutes that other such shows deemed irrelevant to comedy.
However, it is remarkable how little they adhered to some of the other principles they had set down for themselves, namely that all
humour would emanate from natural situations with no jokes, no

catchphrases, no funny voices and no flights of fantasy. Carried along on the tide of laughter they created, they soon discovered that the comedy of character they were aiming for could work within what they might have regarded as constraints and without disconcerting the audience at all. In fact, the pressures of the weekly turnaround dictated their own agenda and a compromise emerged, although one day experience and circumstances would lead both writers and star to a cherished Utopia where realism reigned.

It was once said of Hancock's American hero, Jack Benny, that he uttered the word 'joke' as though he were afraid the gods of comedy were going to wash out his mouth with soap and water. There are moments within the first series of *Hancock's Half Hour* when the strongest of detergents might have been called for. A nadir was reached when Hancock announced he was going to sail the eight great rivers of England. Bill points out there are only two, the Severn and the Thames. Tony ripostes, 'Seven and one?' 'Eight.' 'Correct!' There are times, however, when the bad joke can illuminate character in a distinctive way, as in the exchange between Kenneth as the upper-crust car salesman – 'We don't sell Rolls to people in lounge suits' – and Tony as a pretender to membership of his clientele:

KENNETH: Dry sherry?
TONY: No. If it's all the same to you I'd rather have a wet one.
KENNETH: Oh, his lordship jokes!

It is seldom in the history of the show that a joke *per se* achieves the status of an unforgettable Hancock moment, although this did occur in the 1957 episode where Tony is displeased that yet again he has been overlooked for a knighthood. Bill suggests this has been nagging away at him ever since he found out that he was an OBE. Hancock questions this. 'Yeh,' confirms his friend, 'Order of the British Empire.' The response is timed with signature precision: 'Bill – you were ordered *out* of the British Empire.' The memory is not complete without the echo of the spontaneous cheer that erupts from the audience at this point. It should be stressed, however, that – good or bad – the jokes never dominated the comedy, and they faded away as the years rolled on.

On the other hand, the fantasy element that featured in many of the plots never entirely disappeared from the radio show. The dreamer in Hancock's character often excused this, both within the context of an actual dream and in the hyperbole of his affectation, particularly in the multifarious versions of his war exploits. The writers were soon confronting a reality of their own. As Alan Simpson has admitted: 'Radio allows you to be a little more fantastic ... you have to remember, when you're writing a twenty-week radio series, you're grateful to come up with any ideas, so if they turn out a bit over the top, then so be it. You haven't got time to worry about that.' The surrealism of some detail could have come straight out of *The Goon Show*, as in the scene at Stonehenge, where Kenneth Williams portrays the policeman on duty who guards the stones by taking them home on his bike each evening. Then there is the affair of the puppy that forces Hancock to live in the garage: 'The dog is a freak – he's already two inches taller than me and he's still only eight weeks old.' The fantastical reached its apotheosis in the episode where in response to the national rail strike of June 1955 Sid and Hancock decide to run their own train service with Stephenson's original *Rocket*, which has mysteriously disappeared from the Science Museum, for locomotive. Once they have addressed the matter of carriages, Bill is lost in admiration: 'What a train this is – a pram, two bath tubs, a wheelchair, a four-poster bed and a pie stall.' In time a violent storm derails the vehicle *en route* to the coast, but they manage to keep it running along the road until miraculously it is diverted onto the roller-coaster at Battersea Fun Fair. Radio sucked them into a comedy world closer to the madcap slapstick ethos of Will Hay and Norman Wisdom than they could ever have predicted; television would not allow that freedom and tightened the rein on realism to which they aspired. Only in radio could Sid have got away with the premise of converting a derelict army camp on an artillery practice range into a substitute for Butlin's; of selling Hancock Lord's cricket ground for development as a farm, throwing in Hyde Park as a tea plantation on the side; of conning his upwardly mobile friend into buying a refitted stolen police car minus the insignia and the flashing light. When Hancock is allowed the redress of a replacement car for this last transaction, he acquires a fire engine with a similar history: 'Red open sports car! He told me that the ladder was for seeing over the top of buses!'

A paradox exists in the casting of the key female character in the series. This only became truly successful – and credible – when a caricature in the form of Hancock's gargantuan secretary Miss Pugh came on board. In many ways, no one could have been more realistic than Moira Lister. Listening to her contribution to the first series, one senses she could have been cast in the image of Tony's real-life partner, Cicely. She brought to acting the style, pedigree and sparkling intelligence that characterised the first Mrs Hancock and would go on to consolidate her fame in sophisticated comedy on both stage and, by way of *The Very Merry Widow*, television. She lost Hancock's allegiance before the end of the series when she asked his permission for leave of absence for one week to attend a film festival to which she had been invited in Rio de Janeiro. He flatly refused, saying they had built up a situation in the show that would be destroyed if she left. In recalling the incident she admitted he was right: 'A show has to come before any personal considerations.' It was perhaps naïve of her to ask, and one questions whether Main Wilson had also been approached, since the ultimate decision would have been his, but in the light of Hancock's forthcoming absence from his own series the request and the refusal both carry a particular irony. By early 1955 Moira had discovered she was pregnant. She announced her departure at the end of the series in February, but there is nothing to indicate that Hancock had forced her to go.

Indeed, the eleventh-hour decision by the BBC to renew the show gave Dennis only eight weeks to find a replacement before the next run began and expediency might have preferred that she stayed, even if that did mean working with Harry Secombe initially. Anyway, by the time the second series had started, the happy mother had embarked on a European tour of *King Lear* with John Gielgud! More importantly, the relationship between the lad and Lister had not gelled in the context of the stronger comedy demands of the new show. By their own admission, writing for women has never been Ray and Alan's strongest suit, the ladies reduced to little more than talking signposts with lines like 'Hello, Tony,' 'What happened then, Tony?', 'What are you doing, Tony?' and 'Where are you going, Tony?'

They fared little better with the casting of Andrée Melly, the sister of jazz legend George Melly, for the second and third series, although when she was allowed to drop the sub-Bardot French accent with which she was saddled in her first series she did begin to radiate a warmer presence than Lister. The misplaced accent, which they regretted ever after, arose from the writers' avowedly mistaken belief that 'French equals sexy' and an attempt to enliven the girlfriend character. However, either way it was impossible to take seriously the idea of a genuine romantic link between any girl and Hancock. Tony was aware of the problem: 'Women don't fall in love with buffoons ... that's why I'd oppose any script that arranged a romance between myself and a normal young girl. The sort of girl who'd go for 'Ancock would have to be a beatnik!' Nor was his character under any delusions about his appeal to the opposite sex: '[It's] just that I can't be choosy, a man of my build. I fancy Anita Ekberg the same as everybody else, but I'm realistic about it – if one can't have the butterfly, one is forced to have a bash at the moth.' Scrubbers and bluestockings were his forte. Later in the radio run and subsequently on television Patricia Hayes and Liz Fraser respectively would flutter in and out of his love life, setting the perfect antagonistic tone for comedy. Seduction always led to bathos, although he always hedged his bets by spending not too much on the chocolate and flowers and never became maudlin when the woman made it clear she did not fancy him. 'I've had better nights,' complains Fraser in one television show. 'You've seen better days, too,' retorts Hancock. At the end of the third radio series Melly would leave the cast and Ray and Alan fell on their feet when Hattie Jacques was cast not as the romantic interest, but as the fearsome, gluttonous secretary Miss Griselda Pugh.

The writers now had no uncertainties regarding the way forward, and Jacques, with her standing in radio comedy already established through *ITMA* and *Educating Archie*, was professional enough not to be phased by the psychology of their approach. Alan Simpson has admitted that they wrote for her as if she were a man – not literally, but in such a way that they could get over that element of reserve and embarrassment in the British character that forbade all but grotesques to be held up as figures of fun when women were concerned. There was nothing grotesque at all about the sexy, exquisite, vivacious Hattie, unless one considered her size. In real life her personality provided the misdirection that rendered this insignificant. In the comic imagination of two writers working at a time before political correctness forbade you to dwell on the wonderful diversity of the human race, her bulk provided the key to some of Hancock's most memorable asides. From the moment she walked through the door of 23 Railway Cuttings during the fifth show of the new series in 1956, the tenor of the programme went up a notch. It could now be claimed without question that the whole was greater than the sum of its parts. The show would stay that way for thirty-seven glorious episodes, for as long as Hattie was in the team. As Hancock is badgered by Bill into hiring someone to organise his correspondence, one can discern a real-life echo of Dennis Main Wilson in Blackpool a few years earlier persuading him to do just that, when Freddie Ross entered his employ and found herself wading through the unopened mail overflowing from suitcases in his dressing room. However,

Hattie is found to be less competent at keeping the paperwork under control than her boss, and it soon becomes clear that the roles of employer and employee will be reversed:

TONY: Miss Pugh, Come here. I need you.
HATTIE: I can't – I'm busy. I'm doing some filing.
TONY: Well, finish it later.
HATTIE: I can't. I've only done four fingers.

Hattie made much of a tutti-frutti voice that could turn to one of stentorian authority at the flick of a switchblade, but as the series advanced her character mellowed from aggressive virago to one capable of occasional matronly concern. Nor was she unsusceptible to dreams of romance, either where Sid was concerned or when the American forces hit town:

HATTIE: Oh, Mr Hancock, guess what? I'm getting married.
TONY: Stone me! They've only been here two hours.
HATTIE: It was love at first sight. He swept me off my feet.
TONY: What was he driving? A bulldozer?

Size jokes never had such a field day. The battle lines are drawn in her first episode, although it helped that she was fully aware of her own predicament. As Hattie admitted in one interview, 'They all make nasty cracks about lack of office space and lifts only carrying six people. I usually have to finish up by resorting to violence. I clout them with my umbrella.' 'Well, you won't find me hard to get along with,' yields Hancock on first meeting. It more than helped the comedy that she should live in. Thus Hancock complained that her appetite kept him in penury, although her residency meant that she could double as cook: 'I'm ready for my bacon and pease pudding now, Miss Pugh. If there's any left. Look at her plate piled up there. You can't see her, just her arms coming round the sides. Are you there?'

The camaraderie among the cast at the microphone, even before Hattie arrived, was unquestionable and can be sensed on the shows that survive. If Tony could be persuaded to do his impression of a lighthouse during the warm-up session, the atmosphere would be even jollier. For this he closed his eyes and rotated slowly, opening his eyes and mouth each time he confronted the crowd. By the time he had completed three revolutions, both cast and audience were in hysterics. Very seldom did Hancock see the script before the day – he feared it would curdle on him if he did – and it was the greatest reward for the writers to see him helpless with laughter at the initial read-through of their week's work. According to Galton and Simpson, there were times when he would literally fall out of his seat onto the floor with the giggles, pulling the rug from under any reputation he had for being morose and downcast. If he became introspective at times – the overriding impression of Moira Lister, for example – it would be out of concentration and concern for the show. Ray and Alan remember no backbiting amongst the team. Hancock would often graciously defer a funny line to one of the others and Main Wilson would happily oblige. 'He will be able to do it better than I can,' he would add. When Dennis expressed to his star an early concern that Kenneth Williams was doing *too* well, Hancock's response was, 'The show's getting the laughs, isn't it?' When he looked back on his radio series at the time he contemplated his autobiography, there is no reason to doubt that he was speaking from the heart:

> We had a happy team in *Hancock's Half Hour*, not because I am particularly easy to work with, but because I happened to surround myself with unselfish people. We never jostled for laughs. If it was Sid's or Kenneth Williams's turn to be funny, I never tried to cramp his style and no one ever tried to cramp mine. I have no time for selfish actors, anyway. Selfishness invariably means unintelligence and I find that kind of aggressive stupidity a bore. Some people

seem to revel in it – the kind of people who love working in an
atmosphere of intrigue and friction – but I can only work with
artists I like and admire.

In his published diaries, Williams created a picture of personal discontent that did not accord with his outward demeanour: 'Not a very
good script, my part was negligible' – 'the script was terrible' – 'this
team is so dreary to me now'. But, although he would come to be dissatisfied with his continuing involvement, his outpourings may perhaps – for the moment – be regarded as the wayward recalcitrance
of the perpetual adolescent. In a happier mood Williams used to revel in the memory of the time early in the first series when the recording channel went down between the studio at Camden and
Broadcasting House. Hancock's theatrical instincts quickly took
over and he marshalled his troops. While he stood centre stage reciting a monologue, 'It's a funny old world we live in,' the rest had to run
on with crossover gags. Bill entered and said, 'I've got a pound of
meat for only a shilling,' at which Tony asked, 'Was it mutton?' 'No,
rotten.' Sid followed with 'What's got four legs and flies?' for Tony to
declare, 'I don't know. What's got four legs and flies?' 'The corporation
dustcart.' Then it was Kenneth's turn: 'I had to come on prancing
round the stage pretending I was throwing dust. Tony asked me
what I was doing. I had to tell him I was sprinkling woofle dust to kill
the wild elephants. When he protested that there were no wild elephants, my line was, "No, and this isn't real woofle dust."' Hancock
just stood and stared at Williams's antics nonplussed. Eventually
Kenneth sidled up to the star to tell him to ask him what he was.
'Don't worry,' replied Hancock, 'we all know what you are,' securing,
Williams had the grace to acknowledge, the biggest laugh of the
evening.

Although both Hancock and Sid were disciplined script-bound
men, when fluffs did occur they seemed to enjoy them. Much of Tony's
corpsing survives on the recordings, revealing a more flexible

performer than many have supposed. In an early show he has to deliver the line 'This place gives me the willies – it's winter and the wet weather's with us and well …' Here he corpses gently and mutters, 'Better cut one of those *w*s, I'm sure.' In the 1956 episode where he contests his income tax demand, Tony seeks advice from a chartered accountant. Sid turns out to be the manager of the firm and admits to his sceptical client that he learned the trade in prison: 'Well, I told Fothergill Witherspoon was fiddling; then I told Witherspoon Fotherg – *here we go! Hah hah hah! Make 'em Jones and Brown!* – well I told Fothergill Witherspoon was fiddling, then I told Witherspoon Fothergill was spiddling …' There are laughs and applause all round. Neither Hancock nor James can contain themselves. Tony urges Sid to 'have a run at it', which he does successfully. 'I made it,' he gasps to spontaneous cheers from cast, crew and audience alike. When in a scene at sea Sid mangled 'bring the boat alongside and get the stuff aboard' into 'bring the boat alongside and stuff the broad' Hancock could not continue for ten minutes. When Bill had to deliver, 'Many's the time I've been punting down the Cam with a bird in a boat,' and found the Reverend Spooner tying knots in his tongue, Hancock spluttered in front of the stunned audience before restoring order with an admonitory 'William, I think you ought to read that line again.' At times they're like kids who can't keep a secret, hardly able to restrain their laughter at the outrageousness of the material they're delivering, whether the obvious transparency of Sid's latest scheme or inconsistencies in the plot where realism has been truly shot to pieces. That Hancock was relaxed most of the time can be judged from the way he would – against type – banter with the audience. Hot on the heels of the OBE joke he looks up from his script and says, 'Don't go mad. We've got twenty-five minutes to go yet – save it!' When a woman lets out an especially loud shriek of laughter in a courtroom scene in the income tax episode, he expostulates, 'Madam! Clear the court!' – only for the laughter to build. It might be the same woman cackling away when, in the grip of Bolshoi fever, he attempts to practise his ballet steps: 'Leave the hall, madam, please. I've had enough from him [Bill] without you chipping in all over the place.' It may well have been Kenneth Williams's mum, a frequent champion in the crowd. Williams and Kerr themselves are often discernible off mike laughing along with the audience. According to Bill, there were times when Main Wilson had to stop the tape because they – the cast – were laughing so much.

All his colleagues adjudged Hancock the greatest reader of a script ever, capable of giving at first sight an almost perfect rendition in accordance with his writers' wishes, every nuance, every pause, every beat and every sigh on target. Hattie Jacques once admitted that she was sometimes late for her own entrances because she was carried away by the brilliance of his technique. The ability to project to the microphone only so far and not beyond to the live audience is itself an often overlooked skill. Moreover, Hancock the performer had a way of imparting vitality to ordinary speech, adding a pumped-up cock-sparrow dimension to the words that lifted the work of Galton and Simpson off the page to a higher level. As with poetry the sound was part of the strength and the power, but it never sounded like reading. He enjoyed the gift of emphasis that could impart sarcasm or cynicism or despair without effort, his powers of inflection able to make a seemingly inert line sound funny. Lines like – to Hattie – 'I'm not mending your bed again' and – as he peeps through the net curtains – ''Allo, over the road's going out,' not to mention, 'Ah, that spider's still up there … I'll get the vacuum over him tomorrow,' become hilariously funny when Hancock says them, irrespective of the context of the plot in which they are delivered. The delivery informed the persona and vice versa, just as the voice came to match the man, plump and rotund: not for nothing did he acquire the nickname 'Tub' from Bill as the series progressed. Not that he was ever fatter than 'well fed': 'Are you insinuating that I'm portly?' he would protest. In many ways quotation is futile, unless one can hear the exact delivery of the man, but at times his run at the words and the speed he builds is breathtaking, as in the sequence where he was rhapsodising about his beloved cricket: 'they were referring to me speciality ball – the one that comes out the back of me hand – moves away from me arm – pitches just outside the left stump – turns in, rises, hovers in mid-air, looks around, nips in between his legs – they have to climb the gasometer to get the middle stump back'. But speed for speed's sake was never the imperative. More importantly he raised hesitancy to the level of a science.

Dennis Main Wilson once described silence on radio as like bringing down the curtain during the course of an act. The proven master of the technique was the supreme American funny man, Jack Benny. In many ways Benny stood as the pioneer of what Hancock was about, the prime mover in the 1930s of character-driven comedy in radio, who had challenged the jokey vaudeville conventions of the day and would in both radio and television lay the foundations of what became situation comedy. He tolerated musical interludes in his show, but never at the expense of the situation. Any singers there were became absorbed in the gang of disparate characters who peopled *his* household. They were there to assassinate his character; he was there to react with his signature stare, one capable of registering bland resignation, pained confusion and revengeful indignation all at the same time. In Tynan's telling phrase, 'He is the duck's back; they pour the water.' Motivated by mammon more than any man on earth, he made radio history when asked by a gangster, 'Your money or your life?' It scarcely matters how long it took to answer, 'I'm thinking it over.' The longer Benny stayed silent, the louder the laughs came, fuelled by the universal understanding of his weakest trait. Harold Pinter once told the drama critic Michael Billington that he first became attuned to the power of the pause when he saw Jack Benny at the London Palladium in 1952.

As with Benny, Hancock's skill with a pause was gravity-defying. The device of reading a newspaper at breakfast time gave him a useful springboard for this talent. Galton and Simpson might indicate where they wanted the silence to intervene, but only Hancock could judge when to let go and when to come back in again. It was not merely a matter of not speaking. He had to allow the laughter to run its natural course as well.

Hullo, hullo. They're at it again. You can't trust 'em, can you? (*Pause*) Man denies weekend in caravan. (*Pause*) Mmm, she's nice. (*Pause*) Seventeen-year-old model from Gateshead. (*Pause*) No ring on her finger. (*Pause*) Record crop of rice in Tibet this year. (*Pause*) Vicar punches driving instructor. (*Pause*) She doesn't look seventeen, does she? (*Pause*) Oh, look at this kitten sitting in the Wellington boot, isn't it lovely? (*Pause*) She's got a nice figure, hasn't she? (*Pause*) Hello, I see Mr X has been had up again. He's in every week; he'll overdo it one day. (Pause) Seventeen years old, eh? Well I don't know. (*Pause*) I say, there's a good film south of the river this week. 'I was a Teenage Rock and Roll Vampire' and 'Kiss the Blood off my Washboard.' Marvellous. (*Pause*) Have to get there early, before the schools come out. (*Pause*) I bet she's nearly eighteen.

Another device was the skill with which Hancock could use the briefest of pauses to change comic direction, swerving with the *élan* of a matador. In one episode he has acquired some new publicity photographs, only to notice that the insides of his legs are straight. Bill comments that the photographer appears to have taken one of his legs, split it down the middle and moved it over. 'He hasn't,' disputes Hancock, before after a split second's delay he concedes, 'He has, you know. You're dead right, he has. Look, I've only got two and a half toes on each foot.' You could almost see his puzzled face over the radio. The same technique was employed in an exchange on a television episode where he is trying to impress a new girlfriend played by Annabelle Lee. 'Ooh, I love cider, don't you?' says the girl sipping at her bubbly. 'Cider, what d'you mean, cider?' replies Hancock. 'It's the finest vintage champagne – (*Pause*) – how did you know it was cider?' He was the master of the sudden shift. When he ventured forth to run a railway, he fantasised about his train packed with foreign ambassadors dining with exotic female spies with split skirts and long cigarette holders, then suddenly shifted his voice to a lower register to add 'hanging onto the pie stall counter for dear life!'

Sid James was lost in awe at his timing skills and, while recognising the cliché of the word, could find no other way of conveying what Hancock did so well. For a radio profile of the star in 1971, he admitted, 'There isn't a better expression for it. Tony had absolutely instinctive perfect timing for radio, which is one thing, then on stage, and then in television … it's like timing in golf, timing in boxing. Your weight's in the right place and you're throwing the punch or hitting the ball … he was an absolute master.' The previous year he had confessed in a television interview how much he learned from his colleague: 'I find myself pinching his timing very often – you learn every time you work with somebody … he was tremendous. Just about the greatest there ever was.' Late in his life, Hancock attempted to explain his trade to the journalist, Robert Ottaway: 'I would work at an inflection as if I were writing a sonnet. I worried about every word.' However much he might attempt to hone it to perfection, it was, nevertheless, a natural gift. Had he gone to a doctor to have it removed, he would have been shown the door.

Few episodes saw the skills of writers, producer and performer coming together more effectively than that of *The Threatening Letters*, in which silence, sound effects and the spoken word were all called into service in the most dazzling display of radio as a dramatic medium. Here Hancock's facility for holding imaginary conversations with others came into its own. The recent recipient of hate mail, he has barricaded himself into his home. Footsteps sound up the path. They crunch to a halt. Hancock decides to bluff the intruder.

All right, men. Aim the machine gun on the door. You fifteen men
   get ready to pounce on him. Have you got the hand grenades
   ready, sergeant?

Yes, sir.

Corporal?

Sir.

Tear gas ready?

Yes, sir.

He's walking into a trap. He doesn't know it. Machine-gun crew,
   you all ready?

Yes, sir.

Ah, sir.

Yes, sir.

Ah.

Yes.

Ah.

Right men, he can't get away. If he's got any sense, he'll go back to
   Durham while he's still got the chance. Have the battalion of
   paratroopers arrived yet, sergeant?

They're hidden in the garden.

Stand by and the minute he comes in let him have it with all the
   *guns. (*Knocking at door*) I give in – don't come near me – don't*
   touch me!

The speed and constant vocal fluctuation make the sequence, which
is much longer in the original, wholly convincing. One wonders if
Hancock's knowledge that W.C. Fields had a life-long habit of conducting loud conversations with imaginary bodyguards from his bed
at night to warn off the kidnappers he constantly feared had any
bearing on its realism. In the storyline there immediately follows a
news announcement to the effect that the police have detained a
man accused of sending poison-pen letters to public figures through
the mail, while Mr Anthony Hancock has been detained at East

Cheam police station, having gone berserk and violently attacked a vacuum-cleaner salesman.

Like Jack Benny before him, Hancock proved to be the impossibility of the mime artist who could work on radio, particularly after his transfer to television in the summer of 1956 fixed his famous look in the minds of the nation, making his pauses even more meaningful. For someone who so far had essentially been a visual comedian, radio had presented a challenge. When the radio series was behind him, he admitted to Philip Purser in the *Sunday Telegraph* how difficult it had been: 'I still feel like a visual comic ... When I finally got into radio properly I really had to work harder than in any other medium. When we changed to television it was [with] a sigh of relief.' Part of the strength of Galton and Simpson was the way in which they channelled their verbal descriptive skills in a way that Hancock could exploit in the visual imagination of the listener. It is difficult to imagine comedy in dance working on the wireless, but between them they managed it: 'Delicacy of movement is the secret of this lark – the symbolic movement of me arms and legs in time with the music, the subtlety of the slight twists and turns of the body and the hands. Note the position of the head as I *entrechat* and the poetry in motion as I do me *pas de* ... *(clattering FX)* ... and the deft twist of the torso as I clamber out of the coal bucket.' In the episode from the second series where he aspires to being a celebrity chef, he finds himself coerced into providing a demonstration of how to make flaky pastry. The result was far funnier than any kitchen scene he ever attempted in the dark days of pantomime. He gets to the stage where he has a large sticky lump of dough at his mercy:

> We pick it up and place it on the rolling board. Now ... gently removing our left hand ... our left hand ... so as not to ... gently removing our left hand ... our left hand ... gently removing our *right* hand ... ha ha ... our right hand ... holding it down with our ... we gradually ... placing our foot on it we pull ... ha ha ... scraping it off our foot

we then … we then … *sitting* on it, we roll over … wedging it in the
door … we push with our feet … bringing our left hand from behind
our right leg … we then … scraping it from out of our hair we … putting our right … our left … pulling the … tugging at the … stretch-
ing the … we then … *Spaghetti!*

When Galton and Simpson wrote these words they could have had
little idea of the life he would inject into them, a triumph of emphasis and repetition. No comedian in any medium proved a more hapless victim of viscosity and gunge in the service of the culinary arts.
With Hancock even a physically frustrating task like attempting to
tie a bow tie arguably became funnier in the medium of sound alone:
'It's doing it in front of the mirror that confuses me, 'cos when you
think your hands are going forwards and left, they're going backwards and right. Daft, idiotic things, mirrors … ooh, I do hate dressing up!' Hancock had a repertory of 'oohs' and 'ahs' and 'grunts' that
registered pain and discomfort as no other comedian could. At every
level of experience from stepping on cold lino to being assaulted from
afar by voodoo pins, you could both feel and *see* his agony: 'It's alright
for you – ooh – aah – aah – my word! I say – what's that? Watch it
there – ooh – by Jove – there's some dart players in the crowd. Ooh –
hello, double nineteen!'

Public enthusiasm for *Hancock's Half Hour* built quickly after
the start of the twelve-programme second series in April 1955, the
year in which the country became truly conscious of the Hancock
phenomenon, with a third series of twenty episodes being commissioned to start in October. Tuesday was traditionally Hancock day –
or evening – although for some reason Wednesday laid claim to the
third series. Valuable Sunday daytime repeats became a regular
part of the transmission pattern from the second series, even if with
a similar inconsistency they were unaccountably shifted to
Thursday evenings for the fifth series. In terms of audience figures –
an inexact science at the best and worst of times – the series peaked

towards the end of the third series when three episodes, *How Hancock Won the War*, *The Greyhound Track* and *The Conjuror*, all achieved 7.14 million listeners on their first transmission. If there was disappointment at a general downturn from that moment – the average audience for the fourth season that ran from October 1956 to February 1957 being, at 4.19 million, approximately 2 million less per episode than for its predecessor – this has to be attributed to the waning power of radio as television became the dominant medium, as well as the fact of life that many who relied on the cathode-ray tube to hear *and* see their hero fell out of the habit of merely listening. The penultimate series of twenty shows broadcast between January and June in 1958 rallied somewhat, although the sixth and last series, mainly bereft of the talents of Hattie and Kenneth, slumped to 3.36 million, even though it contained some of Hancock's best radio work. On balance the episodes in the first three series go through at a faster pace with more complicated plots. Only as the series became established did the team move closer to their original goal of greater naturalism and the more relaxed tempo this encouraged. However, the unwritten adage that the number of laughs per episode of any sitcom drops in relative proportion to the number of series it runs falls by the wayside as far as Hancock is concerned.

If one show typified what they set out to achieve at the outset of the project in 1954 it was the one that aired on 22 April 1958. *Sunday Afternoon at Home* is the show where time crawls like a wounded tortoise and nothing happens at all. Here Galton and Simpson proved they had no need of plots as such, capable of extracting comedy from the dreary minutiae of humdrum existence. Hancock was possibly never seen or heard to greater effect than when he was simply doodling, verbally, facially, manually, to relieve the tension of life's banality. And his writers were clever enough to understand that the challenge of making boredom funny was to keep it this side of being boring itself; indeed they knew implicitly that Hancock's constant complaint that life is boring itself bears witness to a refusal to be bored. The episode in which the East Cheam household plods its weary way through a barren suburban Sabbath is regarded by most aficionados as the summit of his radio career. The mood is set from the beginning when Hancock's control of silence reached the apogee of its effectiveness and his achievement. On the page the opening looks bereft of laughs, until one hears his adventurous magic:

TONY: (*Yawns*) Oh dear! Oh dear, oh dear. Cor dear me. Stone me, what a
    life. What's the time?

BILL: Two o'clock.

TONY: Is that all? Cor dear, oh dear, oh dear me. I don't know. (*Yawns*) Oh,
    I'm fed up.

SID : Oi!

TONY : What?

SID : Why don't you shut up moaning and let me get on with the paper?

TONY : Well, I'm fed up.

SID: So you just said.

TONY: Well so I am.

SID: Look, so am I fed up, and so is Bill fed up. We're all fed up, so shut up
    moaning and make the best of it.

TONY: (*Yawns*) Are you sure it's only two o'clock?

In that entire sequence, the first four lines alone take up forty-eight seconds. Only Hancock could make the mere exhalation of breath funny, pushing the pauses and sighs to the limit for maximum effect.

    This is the episode where the jadedness of a million lunchtime palates is summed up in response to Miss Pugh's culinary efforts: 'I thought my mother was a bad cook, but at least her gravy used to move about. Yours sort of lies there and sets.' As afternoon draws on, the comedian begins to imagine pictures on the wallpaper: 'There's an old man with a pipe ... screw your eyes up, now stare hard, squint a bit, that's it, now concentrate on that bit by the serving hatch.' On television Hancock mined the same principle in *The Train Journey*, a man in his mid-thirties reduced by aimless tedium to drawing matchstick men on steamy train windows and greeting the first sight of cows out of London with the ecstatic delirium that might be reserved for the eighth wonder of the world. Other devices – the hospital stay, the breakfast table, the sleepless night, the bus queue, the broken television set and the broken-down lift – would trigger essentially the same premise in both media down the years. Curiously, the Sunday idea would not work in the same way today, but in the 1950s there were no shops open, no sport to speak of, and entertainment and drinking hours were severely curtailed. The episode contained an inner irony: as part of the fifth series, it never received a Sunday repeat, one thing that at other times made Sunday worth looking forward to. In the wake of the show the Director General of the BBC received a complaint from an aggrieved viewer in Bristol that the programme was 'nothing more than a subtle attack on the day of rest and worship'. Doubtless with a twinkle in his eye, the producer was happy to reply that the focus had been on the *afternoon*, implying that Hancock may well have attended church in the morning. Be that as it may, it is possible that Galton and Simpson themselves never came closer to being in the presence of the angels than when they wrote this masterpiece, identifying with the eternity of heaven and the boredom that the angels, ever expectant, must know for themselves.

That doyen of comedy, Mel Brooks, once pontificated, 'Comedy writing is all about rhythm, about turning out jokes and lines of dialogue that have a distinctive beat to them, just as a drummer beats out musical rhythms with his drumsticks.' Hancock at the peak of his career was fortunate to have two writers who understood this implicitly, able to interpret the rhythms of everyday conversation in pursuit of the comic Grail. They shared with Harold Pinter the ability to pick up on the complexity of ordinary speech in all its incoherent and repetitive disarray and on the small talk behind which people hide their everyday anxieties. According to Ray and Alan, when Hancock went to see the original production of Pinter's first major success with the public, *The Caretaker*, in 1960, he had to be dragged out of the Arts Theatre Club because he was laughing so much. His first words to them the next day were, 'You've been doing that for years.' Michael Billington has pointed to the connection – both subversive and eccentric – between what was happening in comedy and what was happening in the theatre at the time. Pinter had been a writer of revue sketches, and it is not difficult to see all three as part of the same movement, although the suggestion that has been aired that Galton and Simpson picked up on his achievement seems unfair and lopsided as well as historically unsound. It would not be the last time comedy is dismissed as a mere sideshow in the assessment of all things theatrical.

The influence of Osborne, as we have seen, and indeed of Beckett may be more significant. *Waiting for Godot* opened at the same London theatre in August 1955. The understanding of the idea of waiting as an inextricable part of the human condition and of dead time as a meaningful part of life itself links the Irish playwright and the two 'boys' from South London as cohesively as Laurel and Hardy. In his radio play *Embers*, first broadcast on the Third Programme in June 1959, Beckett gives his central character, Henry, a line that yearns for Hancock. Struggling with the boredom of existence and in the process pinpointing the futility of so doing, he ends the play by saying, 'Saturday ... nothing. Sunday ... Sunday ... nothing all day. *(Pause)* Nothing, all day nothing. *(Pause)* All day all night nothing. *(Pause)* Not a sound.' What Hancock might have achieved in the straight theatre is sadly a matter of conjecture. Another comedian, Max Wall, Beckett's favourite interpreter of his work, is the measure of what might have been. We know that as Hancock's voice glided up and down the scale, he brought to the work of Galton and Simpson a musicality that underlines what scriptwriter Barry Took had in mind when he said, 'They wrote the character – Hancock interpreted it. It was chamber music of the mind.' As his performing voice became more natural, the more melodious it sounded. By the end of the third series he had attained the confidence not to need the stilted accent with its clipped speech to convey pretension and vainglory. Galton and Simpson followed the lead of the rhythm as all three adapted alongside each other, aware that one too many syllables in a line can render it unfunny. The writers always quote an instance from the classic television episode, *The Blood Donor*, to make their point – the moment the doctor insist that he needs a pint rather than a smear and Hancock says, 'A pint – why, that's very nearly an armful!' Alan remembers that it took about a quarter of an hour to get that right, deciding whether it was going to be 'that's nearly an armful' or 'that's just about an armful' or what they eventually agreed. The precision defined the comedy.

On radio other modifications took place in time, with Sid claiming second billing from Bill Kerr at the start of the fourth series. As – at the expense of James the schemer – he gradually became more prominent as Tony's down-to-earth best mate, so Bill was happy to become less the smart-alec figure and principal foil to Tony, and to hover on the periphery in a role that became characterised by a Stan Laurel-style daftness. 'If we'd have been meant to fly, they'd have given us wings,' he says at one point, to which Hancock retorts, 'If you'd have been meant to think, you'd have been given a brain.' As they prepare a picnic together, Hancock reached the end of his tether: 'Oh, for crying out loud ... when I said take the shells off the eggs, I meant the ones we've boiled. Look at the mess on the floor.' Kerr also provided a useful buffer in the constant war that raged between householder and secretary. Bill's appetite became even less discriminating than Hattie's, leading Hancock to reject him accordingly: 'The old waste bucket here! I'm sure if you trod on his foot, the top of his head would fly open.' It was part of Kerr's strength in the role that he never became tiresome or unsympathetic. Sometimes his naïve innocence allowed Hancock to appear smarter than he actually was; at other times there was little to choose between the two. No sooner has he bemoaned the fact that Bill is retarded for still believing in Father Christmas – 'He's known the other facts of life for years … how this one got overlooked, I do not know!' – than Sid chides Hancock for being the first one out there with a conker on a string when autumn comes around. At times like these we accept that a part of Hancock never grew up: 'I've still got a 62-er from last year. It's in the vinegar bottle. It should be like a lump of concrete by next year.'

It became a standard joke with Galton and Simpson that whenever they were lost for an idea they went to the cinema for inspiration. It is surprising therefore that they resorted to obvious parody of this kind on only four occasions. *Around the World in Eighty Days*, *The Blackboard Jungle*, *The Student Prince* and *Anna and the King of Siam* (the title of the novel that inspired *The King and I*) all took the team away from the environs of East Cheam with hilarious results, but the writers understood intuitively that the basic human predicament was funnier and less formulaic than the genre take-off could ever be, even if the idea of a Hancock as Yul Brynner was irresistible: 'You mean they don't believe that I haven't got ten arms and the strength of a regiment and that I can turn myself into a crocodile?' The other device that paid dividends at uninspired moments was the triptych episode, often an excuse for pulling together three undeveloped ideas they could not take further. In the first series, *The Hancock Festival*, with a nod to Somerset Maugham, presented three short plays from the pen of A. Staffordshire Hancock, with Tony self-cast as a painter in the South Seas, a gambler in Monte Carlo and an officer on the North West Frontier. More successful was the occasion of *The East Cheam Drama Festival* during the fifth series when direct from the stage of the Scout Hall, Cheam, the East Cheam Repertory Company was pressed into service to perform three further playlets. For the melodrama 'Jack's Return Home' Hancock announces that the name part will be played by 'Mr William Kerr, the great Australian outdoor player', while the parents will be played by his good self and – significantly – 'Miss Hattie Jacques, who is best known for her sterling performance in *Moby Dick*'. It is the only time in the series when she is referred to by name and not as the aggravating secretary, Miss Pugh. 'Mr Sidney James,' continues Hancock, 'will be seen as the villainous, unscrupulous, money-grabbing landlord – a role which requires no acting ability on his part whatsoever.' The second skit, 'Look Back in Hunger', gave Bill a chance to score as a creditable Jimmy Porter in a diatribe on tea – one savours the phrase, 'the whole rotten system stained in a tea of apathy' – while the musical travesty, 'The Life of Ludwig van Beethoven and the Songs that Made Him Famous', ended with the company singing the Liechtenstein Polka: 'Well, you try to sing his Ninth Symphony, mate. Right lads, quick as we can, the pubs are open ...'

The most engaging of these fringe shows aired on 30 December 1956. Called simply *The Diary*, it did not admit to its inspiration until the very end of the programme when Hancock's last diary entry for the year refers to the prospect of being sued by the man who wrote *The Secret Life of Walter Mitty*. James Thurber's short story had been made into a less than inspired film starring Danny Kaye in 1947, but had become known to millions even without the intervention of the cinema since it was first published in the *New Yorker* on 18 March 1939. It was reprinted around the world, most notably in *Reader's Digest*, while a learned article in the British medical journal, the *Lancet*, ascribed the title 'Walter Mitty syndrome' to persistent day-dreaming. It is reputed to have made its author more money per word than any other story in the history of literature and would have been ideal for Hancock as a radio vehicle. Thurber's fellow humorist, Robert Benchley, had performed it to perfection in an adaptation for American radio in 1944. In their version, sequences by Galton and Simpson in which Hancock fantasises about being a surgeon and a lion tamer are rapidly overshadowed by the final part of the trilogy in which Hancock has his most notable encounter with Kenneth Williams at his most irritating, in the character that became known

to cast and crew as 'Snide'. Tony is playing a test pilot when he hears
a peculiar knocking sound on the windscreen. He slides back the
cockpit cover to be greeted by, 'Good evening. It ain't half cold out
here. Can I come in?' It transpires he's the mechanic who was still
working on the tail on take-off. Having inveigled his way in, he
becomes intrigued by the controls:

KENNETH: What's this one?

TONY: Don't touch it.

(Ejector seat going off)

KENNETH: Oooh, it's the ejector seat. Come back. Where are you?

TONY: I'm out here sitting on the tail.

KENNETH: No, stop messin' about! Come back in. It's no use sitting out there
sulking. I can't drive the thing.

TONY: Well go into a dive, so I can slide down.

KENNETH: All right. I'll try this lever.

(Ejector seat again)

KENNETH: Hallo!

For those involved, the sequence produced unexpected returns similar to those achieved by the original short story, being made into a
successful gramophone record and played many times over outside
the context of the original programme. However, the laughs in this
show were not monopolised by Hancock and Williams. One advantage of these peripheral episodes was the opportunity they gave the
members of the resident team to appear out of character and therefore funny in a way that cut against the grain of our expectations of
them. Many would regard the line uttered by Flight Sergeant Sid
James, as he adoringly contemplates Hancock's venture into the
pale blue yonder, as worth the price of admission: 'Oh, that I had his
moral fibre!' The dream device stood the writers in good stead
throughout the history of the radio show, allowing them to launch
Hancock into reveries as Prime Minister, Father Christmas, the

winner of the Monte Carlo Rally and England cricket captain. But if the plots were fantastical, the writers always remained true to Hancock's character within them.

The diversity of the series makes it impossible to pinpoint any one episode as typical. A recent poll among aficionados within the Tony Hancock Appreciation Society accounted *Sunday Afternoon at Home* as the most popular episode by far. The episode from the last series known as *The Poetry Society*, which we shall address in the context of Hancock's first main feature film, came second, while *The Wild Man in the Woods* was third. In this Hancock, having decided there is no happiness in the world for a man of his intellect, cuts himself adrift from society to seek refuge as a hermit first on Clapham Common, and then on a plot of forest rented from Sid who has fast latched on to the voyeuristic potential such a spectacle might offer the coach trip trade. Of the top twelve rated episodes, nine – including *Sunday Afternoon at Home* – emanate from the last two series in 1958 and 1959 and were produced not by Dennis Main Wilson, who had moved on to television, but by Tom Ronald. The remaining three fall within the last five shows produced by Dennis for the fourth series. While a considerable number of the early shows do not survive, nevertheless the vote certainly appears to favour the more naturalistic course the series came to adopt. It seems unfair that Main Wilson's name is attached to only three of the dozen, but his spirit and his objective are as inseparable from the shows that do not bear his closing credit as if they were watermarks on paper.

A ringmaster in tweed jacket and horn-rims, Main Wilson had been the pioneer, the evangelist for something corresponding to truth in comedy, who went out on a limb to battle with the immovable forces that have always seemed to comprise the BBC. As the original producer, he also set the creative agenda in many ways not immediately apparent to the listener. While he resisted the inclusion of musical interludes, he ensured that the incidental music that drove the narrative of *Hancock's Half Hour* was of the highest quality yet achieved by a radio comedy programme. His original instinct was to commission the Hancock theme from the respected light music composer Stanley Black. When at the last moment – he *is* listed as the composer in the very first *Radio Times* billing – Black had to pull back from the project, Main Wilson approached his associate, Wally Stott, for the task. Stott, who has now redefined himself in life as Angela Morley, recalls vividly how she wrote the familiar, jaunty signature tune – 'dum-diddy-dum-dee-dum' – without once meeting Hancock or hearing or seeing him perform. She recalls, 'The producer came over and did an impression of his voice and style – I based it on Dennis Main Wilson really!' In the process she composed the equivalent of Laurel and Hardy's 'Dance of the Cuckoos' for a modern age. It is scored for tuba, because, she reasoned, if Hancock had been a musical instrument, that is what he would have been. Morley's genius literally set the comedian to music, but did not stop there.

Following a briefing from Dennis and the writers, for the initial music pre-recording session on 29 October 1954, the day before the recording of the first show, she wrote in the region of twenty-eight musical links based in some way on the original theme to correspond with every possible mood and situation they could suggest. None of them was tailored to fit a specific script as such. The intention was to build up a library for every occasion. Each piece carried a title for easy reference behind the scenes. Together they represent a vivid evocation of the series: 'Hethereal Hancock', 'Time and Movement through Town', 'Hancock Covers the Waterfront', 'Back to Tony's – Sad', 'Back to Tony's – Happy', 'Painted Hancock', 'All Going Wrong', 'Going Downstairs', 'Going Upstairs', 'Falling Downstairs', 'Hancock's Doing Fine', 'Hancock Rumbled – All Scarper', 'Hancock's a Busy Bee', 'Persecution Complex', 'Casanova Hancock', 'Comfy Domestic Hancock', 'Genevieve Hancock', 'Haunted Housecock', 'All Going Well', 'Helgar Hancock', 'Palm Hancock', 'Mal-de-Mercock', 'Hancock in Spring', 'Tony Goes to Paris, Middle East, Latin America,

China', 'Hancock in Space', 'King Tony the One', 'Scarface Hancock' and 'Sergeant Hancock'. The cinematic references in this roll call provide their own clue to the quality of light music they were seeking. Listening to *Hancock's Half Hour* had the lush feel of going to the cinema for half an hour every week. All Hancockian life was set to music, and in an interview in 1956 he made a point of crediting Dennis's ingenuity in this regard: 'You'd be amazed what a difference it makes when you add music like that to a scene. When you're a ham, basically, like I am, it gives you a great lift.' The library continued to expand with a supplementary recording session on 12 October 1955 in time for the third series.

However, the situation came under threat between the third and fourth series when the Musicians' Union raised the matter of recorded music. Until then the recording of signature tunes and incidental music had operated on an 'all rights', or once-for-all, payment basis. Now incidental music could be purchased for use on the first programme alone and attracted a 50 per cent repeat fee for each subsequent use. Such an arrangement would play havoc with any producer's programme budget. But Main Wilson was determined to resist the recommendation from his superiors that he use 'funny links' from the much cheaper stereotyped mood-music library that bore no relevance to the Hancock theme. With less than three weeks to go before the new series began he went into battle with a tersely worded five-page memo in which he argued that the music was as much a part of the show as Hancock himself, that much of it provided an atmospheric background to inspire the star, and that to replace something of high order with a bad substitute would be stupid; moreover *Hancock's Half Hour* did not use 'funny links' and the loyalty of the star was at stake. Nor, at the back of his mind, did he wish to lose the cooperation of Hancock in putting his own finishing touch to the show's opening. Resistant to gimmicks of all kinds, Tony originally resisted Main Wilson's suggestion of crowning the signature tune with the hesitant title line, 'H-H-H-Hancock's … Half Hour'. 'I asked

him to trust me,' recalled the producer. The device stayed throughout Hancock's BBC career on both radio and television. Main Wilson
also won his case musically and with some nimble programme
accounting settled for a compromise whereby Morley was commissioned to rewrite the links for a smaller orchestra, down from thirty-
five members to twenty-five. Even that sounds extravagant by
today's standards, although the financial constraints within which
he had to work also seem unreal today. That fourth series had a budget allocation of only £285 per show, which embraced a rise of £25 a
show from the first series and of which 65 guineas went on the star's
fee, which had begun at 50 guineas for the first series and would double by the end. It should also be mentioned that throughout these
years Morley – or Stott – did not conduct the BBC Augmented Revue
Orchestra assigned to the show. That task was entrusted to Harry
Rabinowitz, yet another South African welcomed on board by
Hancock. Rabinowitz wielded the baton for the first three series,
Stott for the final three.

The musical battle was not the only crusade Main Wilson waged
on behalf of the programme. In the first series the BBC's Head of
Variety came down on the use of guest stars. By the third series the
producer's protest that they should be endorsed if they added reality to a show bore fruit in the final episode, where Hancock is allowed
his dream as captain of England. Main Wilson defiantly played his
four aces by booking Colin Cowdrey, Frank Tyson and Godfrey Evans
from the national team *and* the BBC's own voice of the sport, John
Arlott. Broadcasting historian Roger Wilmut has identified one of
the less desirable traits of the BBC Variety Department around this
time as its tendency to eat its young: 'Having given a new show every
sort of encouragement, including the best technical and production
staff, the hierarchy would then start sniping, particularly at any
manifestations of "controversy" or "bad taste".' Main Wilson, also
responsible for *The Goon Show*, understood this syndrome to the letter. When in November 1955 the programme was criticised by

remote areas of the press and public alike for not taking the subject of juvenile delinquency seriously in its parody of *The Blackboard Jungle*, Main Wilson dismissed the complainants as 'cranks' and 'neurotics' and justified the approach by arguing that the aim of *Hancock's Half Hour* was to present a satire on contemporary life: 'We must be controversial – that is our job ... far sooner this than choose "milk and water" subjects and be just another radio series.' He was determined that this would never happen, and before he left the programme Galton and Simpson had provided their take on Anglo-Russian relations and the effects of the Suez crisis. *The Blackboard Jungle* was the first film to feature rock music and Dennis went out of his way to obtain permission to use the original theme music, Bill Haley's 'Rock Around the Clock'. It is almost certain that the first airing in the British media for this rallying call for the new rock-and-roll movement was within *Hancock's Half Hour* on 23 November 1955. Earlier, in the episode inspired by the rail strike of June that year, the producer even interrupted the conventional signature tune at the start of the show with the sound of a steam train thundering by and the comment from Hancock, 'Just thought you'd like to hear one again.' Sometimes, though, topicality can work in a disconcertingly reverse way. On 16 June 1955 the British submarine, HMS *Sidon*, was destroyed with much loss of life in an explosion while on a training exercise in Portland Harbour. Five days later the series featured an unusual episode called *The Three Sons*, in which Hancock played four roles, ageing Ebadiah Hancock and the three offspring he is anxious to see before he dies. One of them happens to be an incompetent naval captain whose ship is blown up after he engages on a collision course with a mine. The BBC switchboard was besieged with complaints of bad taste and it was left to Dennis to pick up the pieces when protocol dictated that the scheduled Sunday repeat did not go ahead. In its place he decided to rebroadcast the earlier episode from the same series in which Hancock dreamt of becoming Prime Minister.

Complaints were also made about the over-enthusiastic nature of the studio audiences. Main Wilson admitted that this was the first series where he had to ask his Studio Manager to hold the audience laughter down. The problem was not new. According to the BBC Year Book for 1930, roars of laughter ruined Will Hay's act, when it was broadcast from the London Palladium in 1929, by 'overwhelming the microphone'. Technically that was a long time ago. Matters would not have been helped in Hancock's case by the fact that he was so fashionable. The producer adjusted the position of the audience microphone, tried to ensure that 'hysterical looking bobby-soxers' were kept to the rear of the auditorium and begged audiences not to clap at funny lines. He would have agreed with the stricture of the novelist George Meredith, who, when discussing the nature of laughter, said that 'to laugh at everything is to have no appreciation of the comic of comedy'. Main Wilson's sensitivity on such matters also kept him attuned to the need to find the best recording venues. Often *Take It From Here* seemed to have first claim on the Paris Cinema; the Camden Theatre – also in use as a BBC studio – seemed to produce an audience of housewives. When he opted for a late-evening recording time at the Paris, all their show business chums came along – at his suggestion – and he brought upon himself the overenthusiastic crowd that at other times he fought against. For the third series, heedful of the part the Garrick Theatre had played in the success of *Star Bill*, he was able to persuade the BBC to allow him to use the Fortune Theatre, a congenial house for comedy as Flanders and Swann and the magical foursome of *Beyond the Fringe* would soon discover.

Few problems are more horrendous to a producer than a star who goes absent without leave. When this happened with Hancock, Main Wilson addressed the challenge with his customary determination. Some time during the week before the first recording of the second radio series he arrived at the Adelphi Theatre, where Hancock was appearing in the revue, *The Talk of the Town*, intending to give him the script for the following Sunday's programme. The producer was greeted by 'Old toothless Fred', the stage door keeper, with the news, 'If you're looking for the boy, sir, he's gone.' The first house was still in full flow. Frantic calls to Tony's wife, Cicely, and his agent failed to reveal his movements, and Dennis and co-star Jimmy Edwards began to weave a weary labyrinth among every night club and watering hole ever patronised by Hancock in the West End without finding him. In the early hours of the morning a tired and agitated Main Wilson received a surprise call at home from Chief Superintendent 'Ginger' Rose of Scotland Yard's Special Branch, an old acquaintance of the producer who had a few days before given him some tickets for the impending studio recording. The question he put to Dennis was fraught with intrigue: 'What's the bloke we're gonna see on Sunday doing catching the last plane to Rome? D'you want him followed?' Following an overnight stay in Rome, the star was traced unofficially by Interpol to a cheap *pensione* in Positano on the Neapolitan Riviera. No one had any jurisdiction to bring him home. Various accounts give the date of Hancock's departure as Friday 15 April 1955, but this could not have been so since internal memos about the problems left in its wake were circulating within the BBC by the 14th and, according to Kenneth Williams's diary entry, Harry Secombe was standing by to take his place from the 15th.

The writers assumed the show would have to be cancelled, but the producer, acting under instructions from above and perhaps hoping to call his star's bluff, was adamant that it would go ahead, if only with a replacement. After gentle persuasion, agent Jimmy Grafton gave his blessing for his client to juggle a *Goon Show* recording with a *Hancock* session on the same day. Having the complete confidence of Secombe from their *Goon Show* association, Main Wilson saw the Welsh clown rise to the occasion, fizzing like sherbet through the first episode. According to Galton and Simpson Harry soon adjusted from the madcap frenzy of the Goons to the more leisurely pace of the Hancock style, with only slight adjustments needed to the scripts to

account for his presence. The producer's verdict on his guest's performance over the first three episodes of the series tallied: 'The first
one was like a *Goon Show*. The second one, Harry got the hang of it.
And by the third he showed, potentially, what a fabulous comic actor
he was.' Main Wilson would not have been surprised. For all the surface discrepancies in the two comedians, he was well aware of the
underlying intelligence beneath Secombe's clownish exterior and
the subtle vocal cadences of which he was capable at the microphone.
And in those early days there was much in Hancock's delivery that
now seems reminiscent of Harry. The self-mocking strangulated
reach for a higher pitch, together with the laugh that gives way to
despondency with a thump – 'hah hah hah – ugh!' – when he realises his argument has no substance, were both comic traits also
firmly established in the Goon's comic arsenal.

In his keenness to serve the star and the show, Main Wilson was
inexhaustible. Alan Simpson has said, 'He was very manic. For a 100
per cent result he put in 120 per cent effort. Sometimes he would
overwork, become over-enthusiastic, but that's better than being
under-enthusiastic.' That enthusiasm led him to commission a special prologue to the very first *Hancock's Half Hour* in which the distinguished actor Robert Donat introduced the key members of the
cast. It is not known whether it was used. No recording survives and
no relevant contract exists for Donat in the BBC archives. However,
it underlines the commitment of a producer whom the writer
Richard Webber summed up as follows: 'Whenever he believed in a
project he went about his duties with gusto, doing his utmost to
ensure the show was given its chance to prosper.' The same applied
to Hancock's career generally. On 5 November 1952 he had ventured
bravely in mounting a one-off special, *The Guy Fawkes Show*, 'a
musical-comedy travesty of history' by Jimmy Grafton, starring
Tony as 'Hancock, the butler and his ancestor, Guy Hancock-
Fawkes'. The inclusion of Jimmy Edwards, Max Bygraves and
Graham Stark in the credits confirms that this was traditional light

entertainment fare. More adventurous was Main Wilson's ninety-minute production for New Year's Eve, 1956 of *The Man Who Could Work Miracles*, an adaptation of H.G. Wells's 1936 screenplay from his own short story, for the Home Service. Hancock was cast as George McWhirter Fotheringay, an ordinary mortal who discovers he possesses the ability to make miracles happen. In one scene he commands all the world's rulers and heads of state into his presence. In order to create a distancing effect in a pre-stereo age, Main Wilson positioned Hancock on one side of the studio facing a vast phalanx of experienced acting talent that included Harry Fowler, Deryck Guyler, Howard Marion Crawford, Charles Lloyd Pack and Alfie Bass on the other. At this point the star became less than comfortable and took Dennis aside, saying, 'Look, don't think I'm being awkward, but I find this terribly embarrassing – all these marvellous actors facing me and there's me, rubbish, looking at them and making an ass of myself.' When Hancock arrived at rehearsals the next morning he discovered that his obliging and quick-witted producer had repositioned the microphone so that he could play the scene with the rest of the cast *behind* him. It would be Hancock's first departure into straight acting, although the impact was sadly weakened by the use of the *Hancock's Half Hour* signature tune for incidental music. Neither this nor the fireworks spectacular survive in recordings. We have to rely on a comment from Kenneth Williams's diary for a clue to Tony's performance: 'He failed to come up at the end, and I know it was because he didn't believe in what he was saying. If he is philosophically opposed to a script-idea, he doesn't seem to be able to perform it.' Williams played the appropriately named Rev. Silas Maydig in the production.

On 21 February 1957 Dennis Main Wilson recorded his last *Hancock's Half Hour*. He claimed that he never met Hancock again. Less surprising is the comedian's concern at his departure for the new medium of television. He made an issue with the BBC management when Pat Dixon was assigned to the next series without his

The first photograph.

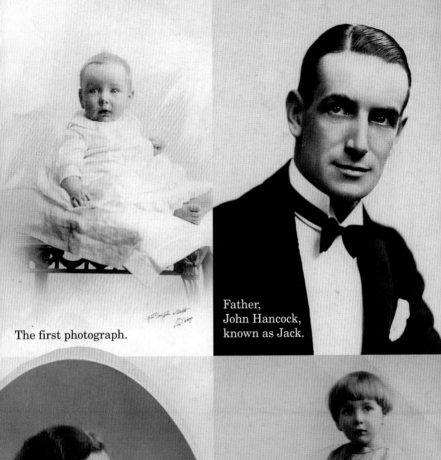

Father,
John Hancock,
known as Jack.

Mother, Lucie Lilian Hancock,
known as Lily.

Toddler Tony.

Jack Hancock with the music hall veteran Charles Coborn.

Playing to the camera at an early age: (from left to right) Colin, Tony, Roger, Lily, grandmother Clara Thomas and stepfather Robert Walker.

Tony with his father and grandmother Elizabeth Hancock.

The boy cricketer.

In the chorus of *The Pirates of Penzance*, between the two policemen.

Captain at last.

In later life with Bournemouth chums, Slim Miller (left) and mentor George Fairweather.

'I'm a hero to my mum.'

Brother Colin's marriage to Pauline Mansfield, November 1939.

In the RAF Gang Show with Tony Melody.

Matinée idol Hancock: an early publicity pose.

Three early faces of professional Hancock.

Tony and Cicely: a couple for their time.

Wedding Day, September 1950: (from left to right) William Hugh Romanis, Robert Walker, Lily, Larry Stephens, Tony, Cicely and Dorothy Romanis.

Tony and Cicely: messing about in boats.

London Laughs: with Vera Lynn and Jimmy Edwards.

Tony as
The Crooner.

Pleased about something.

Educating Archie: with Peter Brough and Archie Andrews.

Star Bill: with Moira Lister and Graham Stark.

Backstage with Cicely.

consultation. With only one show recorded in the fifth series, Tom Ronald, a veteran with shows as varied as *Old Mother Riley, Hi Gang!* and *Life with the Lyons* to his name, was quickly brought in to chaperone the remaining nineteen instalments and then the final series to their successful conclusion. No one could have appreciated more than Hancock the contribution that Main Wilson's drive and resolve made to his success. And to all intents and purposes they seldom disagreed. Towards the end of the fourth series, however, the producer was summoned by the star who complained that Galton and Simpson were tending 'to write him down'. In the first episode Hancock had ended up in a doss house; before the series was two thirds through he had been thrown into gaol by the end of no less than four episodes. Moreover, the shadow of the labour exchange also hung over East Cheam like a pall. Hancock had spotted something that had bypassed Main Wilson, who conceded in retrospect that Galton and Simpson had gradually been allowing things to get sleazier and sleazier. He recalled that Hancock trying to be angry was 'quite a giggle', because he didn't do it very well: 'I want to be up – they must write me up – because the higher up I am, the further I have to fall, which comically is useful. If the boys can't do it, I'm gonna get Eric Sykes – he knows how to write me up.' It never happened, but the message got through, although at the beginning of the sixth series he ended the first episode of *The Smugglers* back in gaol again. Legend has it that Hancock had admitted himself into the London Clinic to lose weight and that his summit meeting with Main Wilson took place there; the circumstances would certainly account for his irritability, but the timing may be suspect. According to Kenneth Williams's diary, he was certainly a patient there during the New Year period of 1956, during which period he was let out on Sundays to record the show, but the nature of the complaint was unfounded then. It was not until October 1956 that Hancock and Bill have to repair to the doss house when they return from holiday to discover that Sid has rented out their home in their absence.

On one occasion Hancock did refuse to perform a radio script, which, as Ray and Alan recall, can only have come about because for some forgotten reason they were ahead of themselves in their writing schedule. Only that would have allowed him the luxury of pre-judgement. They have forgotten precisely why it was rejected, although when they are reminded that Hancock again ended the show in prison, in unison they exclaim, 'Ah!' Known as *The Counterfeiter*, the episode revolves around Hancock and Bill getting caught up in a counterfeiting racket run by Sid. It moves between labour exchange, Sid's hideaway, courtroom and gaol with a shady, snaky grace, somewhat reminiscent of the mood of *The Lavender Hill Mob*, which, of course, was James's passport to the series. Galton and Simpson did Sid proud. Dennis Main Wilson was right in saying that around this time the writers were gravitating more towards the lowly social realism that would characterise *Steptoe and Son*. He might have added that they were also displaying their implicit understanding of dishonesty as a motivating force in comedy. Few put it more persuasively than the drama critic Eric Bentley in his *The Life of the Drama*: 'In how many comic plots there is theft or the intention of theft! If men did not wish to break the tenth commandment, comic plotting, as we know it, could never have come into being.' Both Ray and Alan, and Hancock too, admitted to being greatly influenced by an earlier comedian who personified the larcenous ideal, the snivelling conniver of some of the most impressive British film comedies ever made, Will Hay. Together both Hancock and Sid were spiritual heirs to the schoolmaster comedian, who somehow managed to scrape along by opportune cribbing from his own pupils and used the type of slang they used in the 1950s back in the 1930s. The relationship between Hancock and James became the most dominant – and fondly remembered – motif of the series, with Sid majoring in the duplicity and Hancock in the pretension and indignation that Hay used as a smokescreen to hide his basic ignorance. In an episode from 1955 entitled *The Red Planet* Galton and

Simpson turned their attention to astronomy, when Hancock discovers a new planet which he thinks is on a crash course with the earth. In fact Sid has decided to play a trick on his crony by painting on the lens of his telescope a red spot that he makes bigger every day. Away from the bright lights of show business the older comedian had been a respected astronomer, who is claimed to have found a white spot on Saturn. Hay, who died in 1949, would have loved the programme, endorsing as it did his two great loves of laughter and learning. Likewise, Hancock would have embraced the idea of the episode as a tribute, however unintentional, to him.

Sid's smile was the most disarming in the history of sharp practice. An encyclopaedia could be compiled of the scams, schemes and swindles that he threw across Hancock's path. In the opening show of the fifth series Tony was in reminiscent mood: 'I remember what you were doing when I took you under my wing. You were crawling through my bedroom window with a striped jersey on, a black mask and a large sack on your back marked "swag". And what did you say when I turned the lights on? "Come quickly, doctor, me mother's ill." I was halfway down the stairs looking for me little black bag before I cottoned on!' But like the most dazzling three-card monte operator in the business, the more Sid charmed, the more his victim stayed at a loss. In one instalment Hancock was tricked into taking out a policy which proves so costly he has to work all the harder just to pay the premiums: 'So in a nutshell my ten pound a week wages are all gone on the insurance policy – so I've got to get a better job so I'll have enough money to pay the increased premium which entitles me to more compensation which I need because I haven't got enough to live on after paying the ordinary policy without the compensation in the first place?' Sid goes to great lengths to stress that he represents a 'friendly society' operating in the public interest. 'I suppose I'm doing the right thing,' muses Hancock.

The ruses perpetrated by Sidney James Enterprises were always at their most entertaining when they embraced a twisted logic. Lewis Carroll could well have been hovering over the Simpson typewriter – he, not Galton, did all the typing – in the early instalment where Sid gets to build Hancock a new home on the land he's just sold him on condition he gets the building concession for the land. He proposes to build a house on the beach underneath the cliff to take advantage of the shelter, but this will have to be supplemented by another house on the cliff to take into account the fact that the tide comes in at eight o'clock every night. Sid claims to have Hancock's interests at heart: 'I mean, you don't want to stay in that one on the beach all night and drown, do you?' When Tony protests that he cannot afford two lots of furniture, Sid puts him at ease. He simply takes it with him when he goes. If he begins to move the furniture at four o'clock in the afternoon, by the time the tide has come in at eight he'll just have time to pop back down and lock all the doors.

TONY: Why?
SID: To stop the sea getting in.
TONY: Well, if the sea can't get in, why can't I stay down there?
SID: What? And leave all the furniture out on the cliff top all night?
TONY: Of course! I hadn't thought of that.

Moira cannot see why they can't make do with just one house on the cliff top, leaving Tony curious about who's going to live in the one on the beach: 'You expect me to leave it down there empty, after all the money I've paid for it?' Sid then explains that if the weather gets rough and the sea erodes the cliff, the house on top might collapse. That is why he is going to build him yet another house two miles inland. By now Tony is totally on Sid's side, proclaiming him the saviour who has saved his life. By the end of the discussion the suburban shyster has included in the plans an elevator connecting the first and second houses and a railway between the second and third. Meanwhile the cost has rocketed to £144,000.

James's rasping voice banged the drum of each new enterprise with unscrupulous abandon. In the 1956 episode where Hancock dreams about his cricketing triumphs, Sid, as the Chairman of the MCC, has the media in the palm of his hand in a sequence that has not dated to this day: 'I've got to ring up the ITA and kid 'em that the BBC have offered me ten thousand nicker for the Test Match rights. Then I've got to ring up the BBC and kid 'em that the ITA have offered me eleven thousand.' 'Have they really?' queries Colin Cowdrey. 'No,' replies Sid, 'but somebody's got to make the first move, haven't they?' Sid's wildest schemes did not necessarily have to be plot devices. The gold mines in Epping Forest, for example, were mentioned by Hancock merely *en passant*: 'Two hundred pounds an acre for the mining rites. I was up there for three weeks with me frying pan and not a smell of it.' The only gold Hancock found was the filling that fell out when his pick flew up and struck him in the face. Somehow it never mattered how many times Sid was caught: 'He's a twister – do you know, last week he sold me two tickets to see a West End show … it wasn't till I got inside and bought me programme I found out it was the one I'm in.' When Sid fails to give Hancock the correct change in one transaction, he talks his way out of it by drawing attention to the decline in purchasing power: if the pound was worth sixty shillings in 1927, a half-crown with that date has to be worth seven and six. A short while later the lad is taking a bus ride with Alan Simpson playing the conductor:

ALAN: Fares please.

TONY: Three fourpennies please.

ALAN: Three fourpennies. (*Ticket machine FX*) One shilling please.

TONY: Here's a 1914 sixpence.

What Bentley describes as the 'itch to own the material world' is not confined to James alone. The venial Hancock is not beyond trying to put one over on Sid, who at one point demands ten pounds he is owed.

Tony counts out ten crisp new ones. Sid goes to check them: 'One, two, three, four, five …?' 'Oh well,' moans Hancock, 'if you're gonna unfold 'em!'

If Hancock protested to Main Wilson about being written down the social scale, he came to make even greater noises over the anomaly that hung over the spirit of their project from the moment Main Wilson first succumbed to the talents of Kenneth Williams. The funny voice syndrome had been one of the driving forces in radio comedy from the beginning of the device of the regular half-hour show. The ever-changing procession of impossible zanies through the door of *ITMA* and lesser programmes kept the public's interest alert when limited resources forbade other avenues of renewal and revitalisation, while old favourites like 'Colonel Chinstrap' and 'Mrs Mopp' inspired individual loyalties on a par with that accorded the star himself. On *Educating Archie* not only Hancock, but even Max Bygraves, Benny Hill, Alfred Marks and Dick Emery were all welcomed on board initially with a funny voice that had little bearing on their actual speech, while in *Ray's a Laugh* and *The Goon Show* Peter Sellers raised the formula to the vividness of an art form: it could be said that nobody knew how he spoke at all. The device enabled laughter to take on a Pavlovian aspect as each week each character cropped up yet again like a jack-in-the-box with his or her catchphrase. The trick was to ensure that no one outstayed their welcome, like party guests who persist with a trick when the novelty has become stale, although capable of growing funny again after the passage of time. Of all the voices Kenneth Williams brought to *Hancock's Half Hour*, only one had a recognisable name to the general public, the occasional minor character of 'Edwardian Fred', a sinister member of Sid's gang whose voice seemed to betray not only his years but a constant state of constipation. Otherwise Williams rang the changes as the plot dictated on an assortment of visiting foreigners, geriatrics, clergymen, policemen, judges and other members of Richard Hoggart's 'Them'. To their credit, Ray and Alan always wrote within the character of each voice; but, in a strange paradoxical way, although the actor gave to each a totally distinctive sound, they all bore the inescapable, unmistakable stamp of Kenneth Williams. It had something to do with those braying nasal tones. If Peter Sellers was the chameleon of the genre, Williams could never claim anonymity, whatever background the script placed him against. And of all his characters, there was one that was marked out for extinction from the moment its insinuating nasal whine was unleashed on the world.

According to Alan Simpson, Kenneth came up with the voice for the character of a jockey in the episode where, during Hancock's indisposition, Bill and Harry get entangled by Sid in the seamier side of horse racing. The appearance was brief. Secombe and Kerr are looking for Sid when they approach the character:

BILL: Hey, little boy. Here's a sweet. Where can we find Mr Sidney James?
KENNETH: You know what you can do with your sweets, don't you?
BILL: Oh, I'm sorry.
ANDRÉE: Who was that?
BILL: Charlie Smirke.

In real life Smirke was a racing legend of the day: Hancock would have seen the irony in the character that became known as 'Snide' being born out of a basic gag. The voice was deliberately written into the script of the next episode, in which Hancock gallantly takes a trip to Swansea to thank Secombe for standing in for him. Here the voice direction *'Precious'* is marked against Kenneth's role as the clerk who delays Hancock in conversation at the railway ticket office. Already the pattern was falling into place, that of the irksome one-sided chatterbox with no respect for the other man's time until, in Hancock's case, he too gets carried away on a trivial tangent of his own or even sweet-talked into thinking what a nice man he is. Williams recalled in an interview with radio host Ed

Doolan that he received the instruction from Ray and Alan that they wanted the character to sound like 'someone who creeps up on you'. The word 'Snide' was not given as a direction in the script until the sixth programme of the series, where Hancock is cast as a celebrity chef whose success becomes compromised by fame, alcohol and loose living.

TONY: Hey you, same again.

KENNETH: (*Snide*) You haven't bought anything yet.

TONY: Oh. Well give me two and make the second one the same as the first one.

KENNETH: Yes, but what shall I make the first one?

TONY: You're a bit nosy for a barman, aren't you?

KENNETH: I'm not a barman … this is a chemist's shop.

He truly comes into his own in the next show, *Prime Minister Hancock*. Hancock is canvassing votes for parliament when a door opens:

KENNETH: (*Snide*) Yes?

TONY: Good evening. I'm Anthony Hancock, your local candidate. Can I count on your vote?

KENNETH: Er, no … I don't think so. I'm very sorry …

At this point Andrée is sent inside to use her feminine wiles to win him round. When she hasn't emerged after three hours, Hancock has to admit, 'Perhaps she's having trouble persuading him.' Not until the next episode, *The Rail Strike*, would the character be given any prominence, when he makes a nuisance of himself first to Andrée at Clapham Junction – 'I'm a bit of a devil when I get going!' – and then to Tony – 'She fancies me!' – *en route* to Brighton. In the next episode Snide, now a neighbour, gatecrashes 23 Railway Cuttings wanting milk and any bits of fish going for his cat – 'He's not fussy … cod fillet, bit of plaice, anything like that' – at the very moment Hancock is set-tling down to watch a play on his newly acquired television set. Before long Snide too has joined the family circle:

KENNETH: Where's the sandwiches?

TONY: Where's the what?

KENNETH: Where's the sandwiches? Every time I go into people's homes to watch television they always offer me sandwiches.

TONY: We haven't got any sandwiches.

KENNETH: Ah, but I'm hungry. It won't take you long. Cut some bread … open a tin of meat … make some cocoa … a few cakes. I only want a mouthful of something.

Before the end of the evening this nerdish know-all has attempted to repair the television set, the house has burned down to the ground as a result and Hancock has been rendered destitute. Nothing in his universe will be predictable again. 'He only came in for some milk for his cat,' he sighs.

Within a few episodes even a catchphrase had evolved against the writers' best intentions. 'No, stop messin' about!' and, to a lesser extent, 'No, don't be like that!' would, with Ray and Alan's blessing, accompany Kenneth for the rest of his career. The character of Snide was tedious enough to make anyone squirm, but would in time be greeted with instant applause in almost every episode, emphasising the way it stood apart from the show as a whole. Galton and Simpson were grateful for the big finish it tended to provide: most of Snide's appearances came in the last six or seven minutes of the programme. But in his diary entry for 10 June 1957 Williams noted that Hancock felt increasingly that '"set" characters make a rut in story routine'. The character did not return for the fifth series in January 1958. Simpson has admitted, 'It was restrictive in the development and construction of the show … you had to write toward what Snide was going to do this week'; while Galton adds, 'the temptation was overwhelming ... [but I] don't think Tony was jealous of him, just thought it was becoming too much of a cliché.'

When they did sneak the instruction '*(Snide)*' into the script for the fourth show of the new run, Williams wrote, on 10 February 1958, 'When Tony arrived he said he was angry about it, and that it should go. He really believes that it is "cartoon" ... every time he asks me if I mind, I have to say *no* because after all this fuss I'd feel *awful* doing the damned voice! And every single time, he says, in front of everyone, *and me*! – "It's no good – it's a gimmick voice, and untrue to life" ... Oh well – I suppose it's a compliment, in a way.' However, Galton and Simpson insist that Tony could be teased on the whole issue, as can be seen in some illuminating moments from the show themselves. In Alan's words, 'We did tease him and gave him certain things to do and he'd say, "Oh yeah, oh yeah!" but he did them and to his credit he would see the funny side of it ... he'd say, "You bastards!" and do it and make it funny.' One such moment occurred during the penultimate show of the fourth series, when the writers allowed the character to make his own comment on the situation. In the episode called *The Emigrant* Snide, as the pilot of a plane taking Hancock out of the country, acknowledges who he is:

KENNETH: I listen to your radio show every week.

TONY: Oh – ho – ho! Do you like it?

KENNETH: No! I think it's rotten. All except that bloke with the funny voice. He's a scream, isn't he? Oh, he has me in stitches. You know, there are actually people like that?

TONY: (*None too pleased*) Get away!

KENNETH: No, no. There are – honest. I've met some – you want to hang on to him.

In the next and last show of the series, *The Last of the McHancocks*, Snide receives his comeuppance at a Highland Games event when the rocket-powered hammer thrown by Bonnie Prince Sidney fells him. Hancock goes to survey the death scene to hear a last-gasp version of the infamous catchphrase, before being heard to rejoice: 'He's copped it at last! I've been waiting weeks for something like this to happen. I die a happy man. Lead on Macduff!' To those in the know, the programme was beginning to resemble a looking-glass world, with art reflecting life and vice versa. The fun picked up again at the start of series five in January 1958 with an episode appropriately known as *The New Radio Series*. Sid and Bill have been summoned to a conference with Hancock. According to Miss Pugh his recent television success has gone to his head, a point confirmed when he insists on being addressed as 'Mr Hancock' or 'Your Grace' and announces his decision to step down from the airwaves out of respect for his public: 'For their sake I can't risk destroying the legend that is Hancock.' It is all bluff, of course, but things go wrong when the BBC, which has other plans, takes him at his word and gives Bill his series instead. Hancock goes down on one knee to his old friend: 'You'll want somebody in it with you – supporting cast – you can fit me in there, can't you, Bill? Very experienced – funny voices – character parts – old men – heh heh heh ... and I'm cheap.' The teasing becomes even more pointed by the end of the episode when he is discovered by a BBC interviewer amid 'the human driftwood of London' underneath the arches at Charing Cross. Any hope of a comeback is short-lived, as the broadcaster brushes him aside in trusty travelogue style: 'And as the last of the older school of radio comics sinks slowly in the west, we return you to the studio.'

Valerie James, who attended many of the recordings in support of her husband, shared with Sid the sense that for all the outward magnanimity he expressed to Main Wilson, Tony came to be frightened by Kenneth 'because he became too strong'. However, after Snide's departure Hancock was happy enough for Williams to remain with the show. In his last complete series Kenneth did contribute the occasional characterisation that departed from his usual stereotypes, most notably as a vet masquerading as a doctor in *The*

Insurance Policy and as the photographer Hilary Sinclair in *The Publicity Photograph*, a characterisation that more than lived up to Tynan's description of Williams as 'the *petit-maître* of contemporary camp'. But he felt more and more that there was less for him to do and after the second show of the sixth and final series he asked his agent Peter Eade to extricate him from the remainder: 'I think that I am quite superfluous now.'

Williams may have had a fragile ego, but in the early stages of their working relationship there can be no doubting the rapport that existed between him and Hancock. At the microphone a joyful vibrancy existed between them, with Tony often entering into the true spirit of Kenneth's style, mimicking his accents and manner, not least of Snide. And no one on the team was better equipped intellectually to understand Hancock's quest in comedy. On 4 January 1956, halfway through the third series, Williams sets out to summarise his thoughts on art and his own 'worth as an Artist' in his diary: 'I see that in Art is man's striving for the truth – for the order – for the sense, which has evaded him in the stupidity of existence. Only in the recognition of this Truth in Art can my respect be commanded. Here is where my duty as an Actor lies. I must be the perceptive eye.' Pretentious it may sound, but I will not be the first commentator to point out that if you replace the word 'art' with 'comedy', it could easily be Hancock arguing his cause in the high court of laughter, or, for that matter, telling Main Wilson and the writers that Snide has to go When he came to rationalise Hancock's apparent isolationism in a tribute after his death, Williams was both forgiving and astute: 'It's not to do with the fact that [people] were dropped because of their playing, or the fact that they were getting extra laughs – [it was] to do with the fact that the whole was not coming together in his eyes as a truthful view of a comic facet of life which he wanted explored … now that isn't stupidity and it isn't vanity – it's a genuine desire to pursue an idea. And that is fine in life as long as you're pursuing it, making compromises on the way, because if you don't bend with the wind, you crack.' When Hancock looked back on this period in 1962, he used less tortuous language to say approximately the same thing before giving Williams his due:

> There were changes in our team from time to time, but that was no reflection on the performers; nor did it mean that I had fallen out with them. It was simply that a series like *Hancock's Half Hour* needs to keep fluid over the years. Once this kind of comedy sets into a rigid pattern I feel it is doomed. When characters become too strongly identified, cliché situations begin to creep in and that is fatal. [As for] Kenneth Williams, we used to sit up half the night debating his future, hammering out his problems. He was always worried about his capacity for carrying a show on his own. He felt he could never advance beyond the 'supporting actor' stage. Had he stayed with my series and had it gone on and on until it just died from exhaustion, a supporting actor is all he might have remained. Instead he branched out into revue and the straight theatre and became a star in his own right. And who would doubt his box-office pull today? It was the same with Hattie Jacques. She has done better for herself as the sister in Eric Sykes' television series than she ever had a chance of doing on radio in *Hancock's Half Hour.*

In his 1985 autobiography, *Just Williams*, Kenneth provided another view of those late-night discussions at Tony's flat at Queen's Gate Place: 'Tony always returned to the same themes – "What is the purpose of human existence?" and "Is there a discernible pattern in human progress?" Again and again he held that such imponderables were unanswerable and when I ventured to suggest that only faith would explain apparent meaninglessness, he rejected that on the grounds that it was unprovable. "Our reason must be answered by reason," he would say. "Men want a rational answer, not mystery and magic." ' By now Cicely would have retired upstairs, leaving the two of them to continue the discussion into the early hours amid the debris of empty wine bottles and overflowing ashtrays. On 20 January 1957 Kenneth writes in his diary, 'Tony has given me a book called *The Suez War* – very good of him.' It is hard to picture him making a gift of such a volume to Sid or to Bill. But within his secret journals Hancock the professional would never be exempt from the vitriol of Williams's two-sided pen.

Upon his death in 1968 Hancock was dismissed by Williams as 'an indifferent performer saved by two of the most brilliant scriptwriters of the decade'. The previous year Williams had been listening to some early *Hancock's Half Hour* recordings and targeted 'the absence of real professional expertise and technical cleverness'. When in 1975 a chance meeting with Harry Secombe causes him to reminisce about the time the Goon came to the rescue in the star's absence, his praise for the one is tainted by his contempt for the other: 'What a lift he gave to that series! And how much better he was than the absentee!' However one might theorise about such behaviour, one assumes these introverted schizoid outpourings helped him in some way to deal with the world. As has been discovered since his death from an overdose of barbiturates on 15 April 1988, his personal relationships were not straightforward. He could be gregarious and reclusive at the toss of a coin, and his confused sexuality did not help. If hypocrisy were a clinical condition, then Williams might be a test case. Dennis Main Wilson made the point that Hancock did not want Kenneth Williams to be fired, and both his diaries and BBC records confirm that he left the set-up entirely of his own accord. There would be no reconciliation between them. When Hancock attended a performance of the Peter Shaffer double bill, *The Private Ear* and *The Public Eye*, at the Globe Theatre in June 1962, he was upset that Hancock gave precedence to visiting Williams's co-star, Maggie Smith, backstage and that they only met accidentally when he called in to see her. Four years later Tony *would* come knocking on Williams's door, only to discover it firmly shut.

That Hattie Jacques did not return for the final series was obviously part and parcel of the move to reality that Hancock sought and the desire to break away to an extent from the domestic environment of Railway Cuttings. The story goes that at the end of the fifth series she surprised her colleagues by announcing that she was going to have a baby. It was actually due the following week, but no one had noticed any appreciable increase in her size. It is fatuous to suppose, as many accounts claim, that her pregnancy led to her departure from the show. There was a one-year gap between the recording of the fifth and sixth series, and besides she did return for a one-off Christmas special in December 1958. In an echo of Graham Stark's feelings from a few years before, she may have been disappointed not to be invited back for the final run, but from a professional point of view she was certainly not perturbed. The ephemeral business of show business never offers a job for life: the true professional never makes the assumption of automatic renewal as far as contracts are concerned. Certainly no one raised an eyebrow when in order to keep the format fresh a show like *Educating Archie* underwent major cast changes from series to series. Hattie, like Hancock, had come and gone in that epic too. Like Kenneth she had worked alongside Tony in early versions of the televised *Half Hours*, and would do so again, but not before – as Hancock was keen to stress – her long and affectionate partnership with Eric Sykes began for the television cameras in March 1959.

With Jacques and Williams gone, less familiar actors were brought in to play support roles, adding to the realism of many of the shows. Warren Mitchell, Patricia Hayes, Fenella Fielding, Liz Fraser and Harry Towb – all less known then than they were to become – were among their number. Significantly five of the episodes in the aforesaid top twelve, *The Poetry Society*, *The Last Bus Home*, *Fred's Pie Stall*, *Sid's Mystery Tours* and *Hancock in Hospital* came from this last short series of fourteen, which Hancock, now well established on television, was reluctant to do. It is claimed that he only committed himself because he thought Ray and Alan 'needed the money'. The recording pattern also worried him. To forestall a clash with the fifth television series due to be recorded from September 1959, the shows were all pre-recorded at odd dates during a three-week period in June with the writers forced to write at double speed at the rate of two episodes a week once the fourth television series had ended in the spring. Hancock worried about the effect this would have on standards, but obviously need not have worried. And in radio terms he was well recompensed, to the tune of 100 guineas a show, an increase of 25 from the previous run. Moreover two episodes endorsed his inescapable celebrity. The first acknowledged that in April 1959 Madame Tussaud's decided to add his effigy to their exhibition. For the sake of the radio series Sid has a better idea, to create their own museum – Madame James's – and make their own waxwork of the star. It is eventually sold off to a cinema owner to promote a movie, *I Married a Monster from Outer Space.*

When Galton and Simpson sat down to write the last radio show, broadcast on 29 December 1959, they did not know for certain that it would be the final one, however much Hancock's and their own increasing involvement in television predicated that fact. *The Impersonator* was based on a true incident in which the voice of the actor Alastair Sim was used in a commercial without his blessing. That he thought it beneath his dignity and the fact that he wasn't getting any money from it either seemed to have 'Hancock' written all over the situation. There was a certain inevitability in the way that his impersonator, played by Peter Goodwright, would so impress the BBC that he would inherit Hancock's series, ensuring that this would be the last episode and that Hancock would then have to lower his sights to advertise the offending brand, Harper's cornflakes, himself. The wheel turns full circle when he resorts to brushing up his old stage act for the purpose: 'Mis-tah Chris-tian, bring me some Harper's or I'll have you strung up from the highest yardarm of the British navy – no? – Robert Newton – ah, Jim lad –

here's your cornflakes, lad – ah hahh hahh hahh (*segue into closing music*).' In this episode Sid fulfilled his occasional responsibility as Hancock's agent. Inevitably he leaves his older client to represent the new pretender, leaving the lad stranded on the shore of isolation that would, once he himself had in reality parted from Sid, come to characterise some of his most memorable television work. And yet with or without television, his reputation was secure in sound alone. In time the radio programmes were broadcast in around twenty countries, including Australia, New Zealand and South Africa. They continue to be transmitted over the air, while the recordings receive a new lease of life with every subsequent change in technology. It is indicative that, although the outrageous glory of *Round the Horne* had yet to appear, there has been no advance in radio comedy since those halcyon Hancock days. And as Dennis Main Wilson once poignantly reminded me, 'We were all so young at the time.'

Before we examine the transition of *Hancock's Half Hour* from radio to television, it should not be overlooked that throughout the intensive period of radio activity that began in August 1951 with *Educating Archie* and *Happy-Go-Lucky* and followed through to the first transmission of *Hancock's Half Hour* on 2 November 1954, Hancock was engaged – apart from periods of stress and indisposition and the three-month spell solely devoted to his second *Star Bill* series – almost exclusively in the theatre on a nightly basis. Routine variety work, his 1953 Christmas pantomime and two revues alongside Jimmy Edwards, namely *London Laughs* and *The Talk of the Town*, poised either side of the panto, occupied him, in fact, until he left the second Adelphi show at the end of October 1955, by which time he had the first two radio series of *Hancock's Half Hour* under his belt, evidence that he had soon disregarded the earlier medical advice not to combine radio and stage work. It is now timely to consider his activity and standing as a theatrical performer.

Chapter Seven

'GOING THROUGH THE CARD'

*'If you ask me why I go on with it, the answer is
that I like to suffer. Possibly it is the masochist in
me, but I find the very strain of it stimulating, a
challenge to keep me on my toes.'*

In the years following his death the theatrical chapter of Hancock's
career has been crowded into a corner by the less ephemeral nature
of the best of his broadcasting achievement. Those looking to dispar-
age the total accomplishment of his life will take refuge in the criticism that he was nowhere near as effective on stage as he allowed
himself to be in the confines of a broadcasting studio. It is admittedly hard to think of a British comedian who for a limited period shone
as brilliantly once the 'On Air' light flashed, whether for sound or
vision; but comparisons between the two disciplines are misleading
and cruel. Any passport to the medium of broadcasting was won on
the back of live performance, that turnstile through which comedians in all disciplines have first to pass, be they Charlie Chaplin or
Jack Benny, Woody Allen or Jacques Tati. Hancock may not have
been cosy with the cheeky chatter of his early 'Confidential Comic'
approach, one taken to its zenith by the flashy banter of Max Miller,
but there are other styles, other skills. In a manner befitting
his intelligence he conscientiously developed a way forward
that allowed the well-honed perfection of his act to shine – albeit
intermittently – when his broadcasting career tailed off into

disappointment and disaster. When in the summer of 1966 the title of one of his early stage successes, *London Laughs*, was revived at the London Palladium, one reviewer commenting on the relatively sorry affair wrote that what was needed was 'a real twenty-two carat star – a Dietrich, a Borge, a Hancock, a Gracie Fields'. That's pretty good company to be keeping.

Duncan Wood, the producer of his best work for television, once passed harsh judgement on his star: 'Situation is the only medium for Hancock and without it he becomes a mediocre performer.' The iniquity of that remark has to be measured against his visceral ability, witnessed by this writer on three occasions, to dominate an audience in the largest of theatres. In *Grace, Beauty and Banjos*, his encyclopaedic retrospective of variety performers, the music-hall historian Michael Kilgarriff testified to his 'massive presence and large features which so clearly registered from the farthest seats'. As a visual comedian he excelled, a quality that makes his success in radio all the more unlikely. On reflection, however, one realises that, regardless of whether the audience could see him or not, the situational device needed his visual reactive skills and vice versa to make him work as well as he did in both sound and vision. The radio producer Leslie Bridgmont noted that a comedian who is ideal on sound usually loses something when he appears on stage and the other way around. Tommy Handley was never as winning on a theatre stage; Tommy Cooper steered clear of the radio microphone entirely. As Bridgmont added, 'That's where Hancock scores. He keeps his individuality either way.'

In the radio episode where, innocent of Sid's crooked plot to divert him into the clutches of the Foreign Legion, he subjects himself to an audition to entertain the forces in Malta, Hancock – or Galton and Simpson on his behalf – made comic capital of his understanding that he would never be Max Miller's heir apparent, while nevertheless hinting at the standard he might attain to by less cheerful means: 'You can't expect me to give a performance in an office – it's on the stage where you should see me. That's where my magic shows itself. Magnetic is the word – from the minute the lights go down. I come on with my bow tie going round and my three foot long boots flapping and the stem of my buttonhole getting longer and longer … I come on and say, "'Ow do, Portsmouth?" – or wherever I happen to be. And they all shout back, "'Ow do, Tony?"' Kenneth Williams, at his most superciliously catarrhal, snaps back that somehow he thinks the troops will respond with something entirely different. Whatever risks that may have entailed, in real life Hancock did not entirely bypass the direct conversational approach of the traditional stand-up comic. If he accepted that the Bob Hope-inspired monologue delivered to the audience machine-gun fashion was not for him, he also avoided for the most part its polar opposite, namely the sketch format and occasional double-act mode favoured by his idol, Sid Field.

His act had no real sense of progression, a weird and wonderful catch-all of funny moments and set routines each of which revealed a different level of observational or physical virtuosity. At length it would vary between a traditional twelve minutes on a variety bill to a fully expanded hour, although that was probably pushing it a bit. Damaris Hayman explained that, for all his admiration for the early Danny Kaye, Tony shared with many of his breed the resentment that, following the American's Palladium success, before long they were all expected to perform for close on thirty minutes when they were topping the bill, a state of affairs that edged the need for material to the limit. On other occasions, however, the chance for Hancock of performing added time did nothing but feed delusions of grandeur Sammy Davis Junior-style, a situation that got out of hand at a critical point later in his career in 1966 when for one night only he appeared at London's Royal Festival Hall. But what came to distinguish Hancock from unlikely-sounding rivals like Bruce Forsyth, Roy Castle and Dickie Henderson, who had no qualms about following in the preening, toe-tapping steps of either American, was the attitude he embodied. Early in his career he established a mood with his audience that stared show business in the face with the full disparaging glare of insecurity and disillusion. It was – in effect – another situation, one that the worthy Duncan Wood, locked into the discipline of his television world, overlooked.

The seed had been planted with his concert party routine, if not even earlier with George Fairweather's gift of his own repertoire coupled with the licence to burlesque it. Upon close inspection neither shows great promise as the cornerstone of a stage act that would service a top funny man for his entire career. However, long before he became famous and the concept of the imaginary Pierrot troupe was jettisoned, the novelist J.B. Priestley claimed to have found the measure of the stage Hancock. His assessment would hold true until the end of the comedian's life. What most impressed the writer was the psychological distance the comic placed between himself and his material: 'He was not a routine comedian doing an act, but another kind of comedian despairing of an act ... he was being funny on another deeper level.' If the early material had started out as a direct satire of the sadder side of show business, by transposing the material directly upon himself Hancock was able to shift the comic focus. No longer the commentator, he became the clown in his determined efforts to entertain us with an act that was transparently beneath him in the increasingly exalted venues he found himself playing. Here was the difference on the one hand between a slick but conventional entertainer like Dickie Henderson announcing with his transatlantic twang, 'Have you ever wondered how the average Joe would attempt an impression of x, y or z?' and on the other the spotlight falling on someone approaching the average Joe himself. When Dickie presented his pastiche of Sinatra, he was in effect providing a demonstration; when Hancock encroached upon such territory, it was with the comic hubris that he was more than a match for the original. Henderson would never have thought of adapting his equally loose-structured variety act into a vehicle for

sending himself up. For all his undoubted skill, he was never funny
per se. But Hancock *was* funny, hilariously so against all the odds, a
great clown let loose in a hostile environment, but not one defined
by the dictates of a specific sketch. The act was the joke; the joke was
the act. The obvious analogy is that of Tommy Cooper's conjuring
travesty, but for all Cooper's hidden technique subtlety is not the
quality one associates with the great fez-capped zany as he fumbled
his way amidst the gaudy debris of his misbegotten miracles.
Hancock's impersonations were the equivalent of Cooper's tricks,
but whereas the borderline between success and failure in a magician's routine is easily apparent, that in an impressionist's act is
gradated upon a more subtle scale of familiarity and freshness,
quite as much as upon accuracy.

It actually helped Hancock's purpose that several of the
Hollywood notables who fell under his scrutiny were either dead or
going out of fashion as his career took flight, not least George Arliss,
filmdom's monocled Disraeli prototype, introduced with mock indif-
ference by Hancock as 'And now here's one for the teenagers.' Arliss
– himself ironically famous for his interpretation of historical characters Wellington, Voltaire and Richelieu, alongside Disraeli – died
in 1946, but remained in Hancock's act until the end. The knack with
which side-on to the audience he spontaneously contorted his profile
to correspond to the inflated features of the original was usually
worth a round of applause even to those with no point of reference.
The indignation shown by the star if nobody clapped provided an
even more sublime moment, the makeshift monocle achieved by left
forefinger and thumb doubling as a sign of contempt where a thumb
to the nose would have been out of place. From countless supporting
roles in musicals and screwball comedies, there was Edward Everett
Horton of the fussy manner and disapproving gaze – something
Hancock had no difficulty with at all: 'Oh dear, oh really, oh really,
hmm ...' Charles Laughton could be evoked on the *Bounty* quarter-
deck with two words alone – 'Mis-tah Chris-tian' – as well as

alongside Lon Chaney in their Hunchback of Notre Dame personae, their two portrayals sixteen years apart and straddling the advent of sound in the cinema. Comedy deriving from deformity *per se* would have been an undesirable exercise if the two originals had not existed. The philosopher Henri Bergson addressed the issue in his treatise on *Laughter* and without benefit of the hindsight provided by movie stereotypes came to the conclusion that 'a deformity that may become comic is a deformity that a normally built person could successfully imitate'. He was writing in 1900 and public attitudes have undergone a transformation since then, but even today his words provide their own imprimatur on Hancock's performance as he buckled his legs and shifted his bulk out of kilter to suggest a hump on his shoulder: 'So, ladies and gentlemen, put the children under the seats – I give you my spine-chilling impression of the Hunchback of Notre Dame!'

Roger Wilmut caught the exact measure of his vocal take-off on Laughton: 'If you can imagine an upper-class English voice, dropped half an octave in pitch and slowed accordingly, and spoken with one half of the mouth glued together with Sellotape, you will begin to have some idea of Hancock's delivery.' 'I'm so ugly,' he would protest. 'I'm so ugly ... shocking weather for humps!' The sequence taught Hancock that his face at its eye-rolling wildest could score as much laughter as anything written for him. He had a disconcerting talent for being able to propel his left pupil into the corner of his eye and whirl it around like a penny in a pudding basin. On a talk show in London a few months before his final departure for Australia, Jimmy Edwards reminded him of one of the basic rules of thumb that had underpinned Hancock's career as a comedian, namely that if ever in doubt about an audience Tony could be heard to murmur, 'I'll give 'em the eye; that's what I'll do. That'll fix 'em!' However, when it came to eye-rolling, it is difficult to think that any of the impressions gave him more relish than that of Robert Newton in his scene-stealing Long John Silver guise. This was the newest of the batch, the Disney production of *Treasure Island* dating back to only 1950. In time Hancock's impersonation became more famous than the original, a point highlighted by the opening line of Newton's entry in David Thomson's *New Biographical Dictionary of Film*, where the comedian is mentioned ahead of the actor, although the writer continues to credit the 'eye-rolling exaggeration of villainy [that] would have delighted Stevenson' where it was due. Hancock would hobble about one-legged on an imaginary crutch with the microphone for occasional support, his head tilted to one side to accommodate an imaginary parrot on his shoulder: 'How these storks keep this up all day, I'll never know.' Peter Brough would have sympathised. Plagued by the invisible bird, he attempts a conversation with another shipmate: 'Ah hah, there you are then, young Jim lad, hahh hahh ho ho … get off there, Polly … I cannot abide that boid … most boids I can abide, but that boid I cannot abide … look here, Jim lad, I'm going ashore … don't drink all the brandy and if anybody comes aboard, fire the cannon … hahhh hahhh ho ho … ho hahhh hahhh hahhh ho … cor, it doesn't half do your throat in, this one!' It is quite surprising his eyes did not burst.

Whenever they had the opportunity, Galton and Simpson were more than happy to let him wear his capacity for impressions, and for Newton in particular, like a badge of honour in the world of East Cheam. In the television episode where his set breaks down, it is not long before he is projecting his own fantasy version of an episode of Newton's subsequent television series as the pirate onto the blank screen: 'He's been on for ten minutes – what would he be doing now? Yes, he'll be on the poop deck waving his crutches. There he is – I can see him. Avast there, me hearties. Ah hahh hahh hahh, we'll be in Portobello on the noon tide … Where's young Jim? … We'll have our pockets lined with gold by tonight.' He is in his element until Sid creeps up behind: 'No, don't switch off – you carry on!' In another half-hour where, in order to place himself in line for a knighthood, he turns his thoughts to the legitimate stage, he mistakes *Treasure*

Island for a work of Shakespeare and ends up interpreting the role of Hamlet and much else besides with a parrot on his shoulder and a crutch. Newton even came back to haunt him in the episode where he portrayed a tiresome yokel in the daily soap opera, *The Bowmans*. While Hancock protests that he has spent six months on a cider farm in Somerset perfecting his accent, the producer, played by Patrick Cargill, is precise in his complaint: 'It's never the same two perform-ances running. Sometimes it's Somerset, sometimes it's Suffolk, a bit of Welsh, Birmingham, and last week I could swear we had a bit of Robert Newton in there.' In this way his stage act obliquely fed his broadcasting work and vice versa. Perhaps that is why one of his most memorable stage creations was the invention of Galton and Simpson.

The Crooner, originally based on Johnnie 'Cry' Ray and the mass hysteria surrounding his London Palladium success in the early 1950s, was written by Ray and Alan for the second of the stage shows co-starring Hancock with Jimmy Edwards. The pale blue 'zoot' suit with an enormous jacket almost down to the knees, string tie and thick brothel-creepers – 'Ooh, these crepe soles don't half draw your feet!' – that were originally worn for the portrayal later fell by the wayside, but the merciless way in which he guyed the irksome, insin-cere style of the earlier period became reinvented when much of the material was transferred effortlessly to his Sinatra parody. Years later, Ray Galton, who found exactly the right crepe shoes the sketch required, claims he is still owed 8 guineas from his estate. Originally introduced as 'Mr Rhythm, himself', Hancock would go into his spiel in a hybrid accent to which neither Birmingham nor Los Angeles would wish to lay claim: 'Now, I'd like to sing you a little toon, a toon which we recorded over there and would like to bring over here from over there to over here, our latest record which didn't sell so many back in the States – because they forgot to drill a hole in the middle of it ...' This was the cue for the band to launch into a fast tempo ver-sion of 'Knees Up, Mother Brown'. At an appropriate point he had to introduce his pianist: 'Now I'd like to introduce my pianist, arranger, composer and brother-in-law – Sam.' Sam would enter in an identical suit. The badinage that ensued between them demanded that he stamp Hancock quite viciously on the foot. One night he came down so hard Hancock had to go to hospital. When the poor nurse asked what had happened, the comedian explained 'A feller stamps on it twice nightly.' He told Murray Graham, the perpetrator, 'If there is no pain, they don't laugh.'

Hancock's talent for mime was put to effective use in a running gag where one of his crepe soles kept getting stuck to the boards: 'I've been looking for that piece of Wrigley's all night.' There was much strutting around the stage and twitching of the lip and suffering of cramp. Only eventually did he get to rend to pieces one of Ray's signature numbers, 'The Little White Cloud that Cried'. In the original revue the sequence ended with Hancock besieged by a posse of berserk teenagers, who came running down the aisle of the theatre to claw the clothes of the moment – press-studded together in a pre-Velcro age – off his back. Ray Galton remains in awe at the energy he invested in the routine: 'He would jump in the air and bring his feet together scissors-fashion – he was very physical and quite athletic for a man of his build – but he never worked out to be fit.' 'Although everyone thought of him as fat,' added Simpson, 'he wasn't that fat – at that time he was quite slight in many respects.' The words they wrote summed it all up for him: 'Oh, it's ridiculous. A man of my build and calibre, leaping about like a porpoise, spending half me life three feet off the ground. I think I'll get myself a violin and a few jokes.' At an earlier stage he had broken away from the American idiom to deliver what many still nominate as the quintessential Hancock line: 'How they do an hour and a half at the Palladium in shoes like these, I'll never know … I've got toes like globe artichokes.' As we have seen, with Hancock dignity always ended at the ankles.

Over the years other impressions rounded out the repertoire, not least Nat King Cole, Noël Coward and Maurice Chevalier. None were all that good, but neither were they meant to be. While Cooper's comedy came out of his dysfunctional approach to his speciality, Hancock needed only to be seen poised somewhere between mediocre and average. Those who towards the end of his career found his act to be jaded and out of date appear to have been out of step with the essential Hancock characterisation built up by radio and television. Because he never appeared on a theatre stage in a set depicting his East Cheam milieu and only very seldom wearing the trademark Homburg and astrakhan, many seemed unable to accept his stage performances within the context of his on-air persona. And yet when one did so – something for which his loyal fans needed no prodding – everything fell into place. Indeed, it would have been a mistake to have updated the ancient repertoire of impersonations that became associated with him through the years, let alone to have insisted on accuracy in their portrayal. Likewise, it would have been a discrepancy for him to have continued singing 'There's no business like show business' when convinced that he can't go on with 'this load of rubbish'. Or not to have dropped to bathos when detailing his credentials to membership of the Hollywood Clan that he looked up to so reverently: 'Yes, there's me, Frank Sinatra, Shirley MacLaine, Elsie and Doris Waters, Sandy MacPherson – we're out every night playing Monopoly – swigging down brown ale – don't get to bed till nine.' On stage 'the lad himself stood revealed', frustrated pretender and buffoon, stubbornly afloat in his own incompetence, impervious to the gaps in his own talent: 'Tonight you are getting the lot. You'll be getting Terpsichore – dancing, sword-swallowing – painful but lucrative, impressions, Shakespeare. I shall be going through the card – because you are looking at Mr Show Business himself!' It was only a short step from the star-struck hopeful of one radio episode: 'I've seen 'em – Basil Rathbone, George Raft, Tom Mix – all my contemporaries! I know what's going on. I've got my finger on the pulse of the nation, don't you worry.' As the broadcasting persona gelled, so his act became funnier.

Hancock once confided to Joan Le Mesurier that the longest walk in the world was from the wings to the microphone. There are probably few comics who disagree, although Alan Simpson has pointed out the disadvantage under which Hancock originally worked, not being a stand-up comedian in the conventional sense: 'When Frankie Howerd walked out he was Frankie Howerd. He'd walk to the centre of the stage and he'd start his act. Hancock was nobody until he got to centre stage – the most embarrassing part of the act was his walk across – but once he got to the microphone and then went into character, then he was home and dry.' Max Bygraves, invited by his old radio colleague to his first night at the London Palladium as late as 1963, picked up on the same observation. On the big night Hancock entered at breakneck speed, anxious to get to the microphone and into his act as quickly as possible. When asked by his friend after the show if there was anything he could put right, Max suggested he should enter more slowly, stopping halfway to the microphone to look back into the wings as if in despair at some invisible enemy: 'As the welcoming applause subsided, I said, he should look off stage again and then murmur to himself so that the audience could hear, "Flippin' stage managers!"' Bygraves also advised against the immaculate tuxedo, suggesting an ill-fitting suit or the astrakhan-collared coat. Whether Hancock followed the second piece of advice I cannot recall. One memory of him in that show is of a slouched figure descending upon the microphone in an oversized sweater, which would equally have fitted Max's criterion. The late record of his stage act that survives from the 1966 concert at the Royal Festival Hall shows Hancock in a suit that couldn't be more tight-fitting, the trousers just too short for comfort, but one fears this may have been the fashion of the day. Nevertheless, Tony remained grateful to Bygraves for his advice and a few days before he died wrote to Max, 'I will always appreciate the time you advised me to slow down my entrance at the Palladium.'

As I have indicated elsewhere, my earliest memories of Hancock as a live performer extend back to 1951 and are dominated by two routines, one of which certainly survived in his act until the close, by which time he was happy to acknowledge its antiquity as 'a piece of material I wrote just after the First World War – ladies and gentlemen, I give you the *Gaumont British News*'. The newsreel was a fixture of British cinema until early 1959 and so the sequence, in fairness, retained a semi-topicality. As late as 1967 he admitted to this as one of his two favourite routines, the other being his burlesque Shakespearean cameo. 'I'm a real ham,' he admitted with relish. 'Sometimes I get carried away. It's agony in the dressing room afterwards.' His all-round sporting prowess at school would have stood him in good stead for what must remain one of the most strenuous routines ever attempted in the name of comedy, although it was never easy to equate Hancock with the high energy level required to bring off this and much else in his act. Beginning with his take on the bulbous town-crier bellowing 'Oyez' as he swung his bell up and down in the centre of the cinema picture, he then flung himself into an impressionistic one-man montage of the kaleidoscopic images of the sporting world that appeared in the four corners of the screen around him. Rowing, throwing, boxing, bowling, riding, driving, kicking, leaping, Hancock hurled himself around the stage in a physical maelstrom of activity, finishing with four well-orchestrated dives to the floor press-up fashion. He claimed it kept him in the pink of condition. Apart from wondering how he never came to harm himself, one has tried many times to get inside the psyche essential for pulling off so demanding a piece of business night after night, the equivalent, I imagine, of facing the diving-board or the penalty shoot-out, and not the mind-set of precision parody. In the early days he did wear padding to protect himself, but when this proved insufficient he engaged a trained acrobat to teach him how to fall without hurting. As the years progressed, the routine did become shorter, the dives to the ground fewer, but it must never lose its place in the highest echelon of Hancock moments and the temptation to use it as a torturous metaphor for his own personal Armageddon should be resisted. It is a sequence which unconsciously embodied the *jeu d'esprit* of one of his great idols, Jacques Tati. The great French com-edi-an began in the music halls performing an act of 'sporting mimes'. Colette observed his skill at being at a single moment 'both the foot-ball and the goalkeeper, the boxer and the opponent, the bicycle and its rider … he plays on your imagination with the talent of a great artist … when Tati imitates horse and rider, Paris sees a psychologi-cal creature come to life, the centaur'. Colette would have been impressed by Hancock too, and he would have appreciated the Gallic endorsement.

The other memory of my early years also conjures up an image of Hancock as an instrument of nearly inhuman energy, more akin perhaps to manic Danny Kaye than the subtler approach of the mime artist. Because he never clung to the routine as possessively as he did the newsreel act, one's recall is far sketchier, although helped by the lyric of the song he sang to accompany his actions. It was called 'The Mechanical Man' and began with an echo of Hancock's earlier life in the Civil Service:

> *I had a peaceful job at the Food Office,*
> *Tea drinking and answering phones*
> *And helping poor gorms*
> *To fill up forms*
> *And with laughter drowning their groans;*
> *But the Government proved refractory*
> *And I was sent to a factory.*

Bergson again propounded a theory that 'the attitudes, gestures and movements of the human body are laughable in exact proportion as that body reminds us of a mere machine'. One need look no further than Chaplin and *Modern Times*, but Hancock with this routine pro-vided a worthy, if cruder equivalent in true vaudeville vein while maintaining a hangdog seriousness throughout:

I clocked in in the morning, feeling more dead than alive,
And the foreman said, 'Now, Spurgeon, you must help the export
    drive.
You'll operate this here machine from six o'clock till five.
Get cracking – no slacking – or I'll know the reason why.'
So I started – bing – bang – bong – bing …
This went on to ten o'clock when we had a break for tea.
Bing – bang – bong – bing …
On again till four o'clock and then we had a change and went
Bang – bong – bing – bang …

Each time he returns to the workplace he is assigned to a different, more demanding machine. Each time the jerky movements that accompany the spoken sound effects become even more frantic, spreading from hand to arm to leg to the point where his whole body is in spasmodic overdrive. Eventually he can take no more.

They took me away on the Thursday
Shaking in all of my joints,
But I'm sure once again,
Except when on a train
*It goes rattling over the joints and I go … (*FX and actions*)*
So if when you're travelling you happen to see
*… (*More FX and actions*) … it'll be me.*

As he put words to the pictures for a radio audience in May 1952, commentator Brian Johnston made the observation that the result of all his stiff and jerky movements was to resemble 'a wound-up clockwork toy'.

Sadly no recording of Hancock's 'Mechanical Man' appears to exist in any medium, and to appreciate his gift for mime one has to turn for recourse to those special moments in the television shows when Galton and Simpson acknowledged that he possessed visual skills that transcended even his basic body language and talent for facial expression. Duncan Wood's earlier strictures become harder to understand in light of the fact that mime is a theatrical skill that seldom works on television. The classic sequence takes place in a library where the enforced silence dictates that Hancock has to mime the entire plot, playing all the characters of a detective novel for the benefit of Sid James. The *tour de force* conjures up the passion between buxom girl and broad-shouldered guy; the sudden intrusion of her husband; the ensuing struggle; the firing of the bullet that kills the lover; the death scene; the sadistic pleasure of the killer; the pleading of the girl; a further struggle; another death scene as the girl is killed by accident; the remorse of the husband; his attempt to revive her; the interception of the police; the submission to handcuffs; the judge in session; the donning of the black cap; and the final macabre touch as Hancock grabs the back of his collar to signify the gallows. At this moment he is spotted by the librarian, played by Hugh Lloyd, and his own embarrassment brings the curtain down on the scenario. The sudden mercurial changes he effects between each stage of the narrative are dazzling to observe. In variety's heyday an expanded version of just one such routine would have kept an old-fashioned trouper on the boards for years.

Hancock's body had a stunning capacity for going limp in the cause of humour. When in the knighthood episode he does find employment at the Old Vic, it is in the prompt box, which he wilfully transforms into an impromptu Punch and Judy show, flopping over the edge of the miniature proscenium, sliding himself along the board, all the time displaying a reckless head-bashing abandon. In the half-hour dedicated to the common cold, he tries to stand up, but – 'Hallo, the aches have set in' – dizziness takes over and he flops to pieces like a rag doll. With his flair for portraying cowardice and his robotic mime skills, anyone casting Hancock in a stage production of *The Wizard of Oz* would have been hard pressed to decide for which of the trio of lion, tin man and scarecrow he would have been best suited. At other moments his gift for bringing words to life with gesture and signal takes on the nature of charade and comic crusade simultaneously. In *The Cold* again he gets on his high horse in defence of patent medicines: 'I've seen them all on television – in the adverts. Miracles worked every night. The diagram of the sore throat, the tonsils throbbing away there, arrows pointing towards them, white rings coming out of them – doing! doing! doing!' In the script the only stage instruction Galton and Simpson needed to provide was '*does it*'. This kind of business was instinctive with him and needed no further direction. The actions could also illuminate the most humdrum minutiae of life. 'Have you ever,' he asks Sid, 'tried getting a [collar] stiffener in, once you've got your tie on – eh? It can be very nasty. I nearly strangled myself once. I got this bent stiffener – I was up like that and suddenly I got a bit of cramp and ...' His actions suit the words and have every male in the audience who has ever suffered the experience reaching for the wintergreen.

The earliest recording of a Hancock theatre performance to survive, in sound only, is that of his appearance on the Royal Variety Performance on 3 November 1952. In third spot on the bill, sandwiched between the harmonica revels of the Three Monarchs and Billy Cotton and his Band, Hancock performed three set pieces written by or in collaboration with Larry Stephens. The newsreel and mechanical man routines predated his friendship with Stephens: Tony always claimed originality for the former and may well have been responsible for the latter, in which Flotsam may also have had a hand. Certainly the earliest record I can find for the item is during the season he spent with the entertainer the summer before he met Larry. For the royal occasion he continued to parody the cinema with a spoof version of another staple of the silver screen, the James FitzPatrick travelogue; went into naval mode with possible regard to the presence of Prince Philip in the Royal Box; and then delivered an impassioned curtain speech on behalf of the British working man. If he performed other material that night at the London Palladium, as he may well have done, it was edited out for sound transmission.

Scriptwriter Brad Ashton recalls Hancock's continual reliance on the travelogue send-up. When he could be coerced into providing a warm-up before the recording of his television show, it was an easy piece of material to dust down: 'The front row of the audience often resembled a writers' outing and we'd all join in in unison.' FitzPatrick was an American documentary maker whose patronising, self-righteous style provided an easy target for humour, his *Traveltalks* comprising an integral part of the programme at news cinemas throughout the country in a pre-television age. More familiarly around this time, Frank Muir and Denis Norden provided Peter Sellers with his own similarly inspired overblown observations on the London suburb of Balham, 'Gateway to the South'. In traditional 'as-the-sun-sinks-slowly-in-the-West' mode, Hancock set his sights, perhaps inevitably, on a seaside town, 'lovely, lovely Margate, city of love and laughter'. Imagine the arch American voice of the newsreel commentator given a pronounced West Country burr:

> As far as the eye can see stretches the azure blue of the sky as the sea slowly laps over the great jagged rocks that form the beach. Sitting on the beaches are the natives, wearing the national headgear of a white handkerchief knotted at each corner. Let us pause for a moment and listen to the merry chatter of the natives on the beaches … 'Edie (*shouts*) … Edie (*louder*) … put that shark down – you don't know where it's been!' On we go through the leafy lanes of England, when suddenly we hear a familiar sound (*whistles*) and we ask ourselves what is Ronnie Ronalde doing up that tree.

Even in the countryside Hancock could not resist a show business reference: Ronalde was the hit parade *siffleur* of the day. The words and directions tell only half the story. For the shark business his demeanour and accent shifts into that of the dowdiest of housewives, while a substantial part of the routine had to be edited from the broadcast because it was so visual. Pontificating that 'even in this community we find the maternal spirit is just as strong as we see a mother carefully tending the seven small children in her charge with the love that only a mother can give', he turns himself into the commonest of slatterns: 'Come 'ere, 'Arry – I'll bash your 'ead in!' Grabbing the invisible child, he does just that, lambasting him to kingdom come before kicking him into the air and then sagging under his weight as unexpectedly he catches him in his arms: 'You've come here to enjoy yourself and enjoy yourself you're going to!' At which point he administers another wallop more brutal than any that have gone before.

Regaining composure as the narrator, he goes on to explain that they could not leave England without a visit to the British Navy. Looking out to sea, he draws the audience's attention to the submarine under the command of Lieutenant Commander Humphrey Pumfret Pumfret, Royal Navy.

He speaks to his men in his rough sailor-like fashion: 'Careful there, Johnson. Don't bang yourself on that torpedo there. Come away, Jones. Jones, come away – you'll get your hands covered in grease.'

The voice is far from rough, rather 'ever so awfully' refined, accompanied by a flurry of effete saluting from both hands that comes from all directions like a shoal of fish with no sense of destination. Again the sequence needed to be seen. The funniest moment – the first of several lost on the radio audience – came as he shouted, 'Up periscope,' and staggered backwards, as the hand that was miming the same periscope caught him off-guard under the chin. Then there is trouble with the crew:

Put me down, Hathaway. No grog for you. Well, it's half past four. I think we'll pull up for tea. As you will. Yes, yes, put the kettle on, Harmsworth. What's that? Oh, you've put the kettle on. Yes, I see you have. Yes, I think it suits you, too.

That this joke should garner laughter and applause suggests either that it must have been new at the time or gained added impetus in an unfamiliar context. The time Hancock takes to get to the punch line suggests the former.

All right, men. Prepare to submerge – whoop – whoop – whoop – whoop – whoop – whoop …

Having finished his impersonation of the warning siren, he shouts the command, 'Submerge!' Panic takes control of his features. 'Well let me get in!' he yells, stamping his foot on the fast-descending sardine can. It is too late. 'Fools!' he screams, as through the medium of mime he swims his way towards the footlights, all the while gallantly saluting or at least attempting to do so. The critic in *The Times* pointed out that his naval posturing had all the qualities of a figure by Fougasse, the legendary cartoonist of 'Careless Talk Costs Lives' fame. Through different media the comedian and the artist both concerned themselves with deflating our various pretensions; the analogy was privileged recognition for Hancock's command of visual technique.

He then slid back into travelogue mode to return to the shore, where they find 'the natives of England enjoying their favourite recreation, that of watching workmen digging up the road'. Adopting a working-class accent he launches into a superbly theatrical farewell speech given by the foreman once the task is complete:

Well, ladies and gentlemen, on behalf of the whole company, I'd like to thank you for the support you've given us this week. If you've enjoyed watching us as much as we've enjoyed watching you, then it's all been worthwhile. Next week we shall be appearing at the corner of Corporation Road and High Street in a little thing entitled 'Getting the Drains Up'. And we shall be featuring Harry Trubshawe on the steam roller (*cheer from the band*). We shall also be featuring a special solo on the pneumatic drill by Charlie Perkins (*another cheer*). I think if we can persuade Mr Perkins (*final cheer*) to put down his drill for a few moments, he'll be good enough to say a few words.

With a touch of bathos Hancock stutters out a single line of thanks, before reverting to narrative mode with a crowning touch of burlesque: 'And so it is with regret, as the sun pulls away from the shore and our ship sinks slowly in the West, we say farewell to England, lovely, lovely England.'

Hancock's inclusion in the royal show was acknowledgement of his enhanced stature in the theatre following his inclusion in the revue *London Laughs* with Jimmy Edwards and D-day diva Vera Lynn at the Adelphi Theatre in April of that year. Hancock had been added to the cast two weeks before opening when Dick Bentley, Edwards's radio co-star on *Take It From Here*, backed down after a supposed dispute over billing, although he would flatly deny that his departure had anything to do with money or billing. The short notice may have helped Phyllis Rounce secure her demand for a weekly salary of £500 for her client. 'I knew Tony was worth it,' she later recalled. 'I just wasn't sure Jack Hylton was willing to pay that much.' After a pause for reflection, without ceremony the star bandleader-turned-impresario replied, 'All right,' and replaced the telephone. Bargaining did not come into it. Intended to capitalise on the light-hearted celebratory mood occasioned by the imminent Coronation, the show ran for 1,113 performances over a twenty-two month period, although Hancock would have several periods of absence and was replaced for the last two months by Tommy Cooper. The show was nominally presented by Hylton, who controlled the theatre, and George and Alfred Black, Sid Field's old producers, a fact that would not have been lost on Hancock. No one described Hylton more vividly than Frank Muir, who now also found himself employed by him to write material for the new show with his partner Denis Norden: 'Shrewd, dictatorial, coarse-textured, given to eating fish and chips in the back of his Rolls, followed by a pound or so of grapes, the skins and pips of which he spat in the direction of an ashtray. But with all that he was a remarkably good judge of popular taste.'

Hancock was assigned two solo spots on the programme, one for his basic act, billed – almost as a warning – as 'Interruption!' and the other for his mechanical man routine, billed as 'Machine Age'. His other appearances were in production scenas, including an Al Jolson finale that required him to sing 'Toot-Toot-Tootsie', and in comedy sketches with Edwards. 'A Seat in the Circle', one of the Muir and Norden contributions, was based upon a popular radio feature in which a commentator, often the aforesaid Brian Johnston, would in subdued tones explain what was happening where necessary during a relay from a current West End film or stage show. Here Edwards played a selfish, discontented cinema-goer who arrives late and proceeds to cause havoc to the despair of Hancock as the BBC commentator, clinging to his microphone with Reithian determination until the circle itself practically collapses. There could have been no sharper contrast between Hancock and the bluff, burly Falstaffian whose billing on the posters appeared in equal-sized lettering, but in the more favourable left-hand-side position. Both on paper and on stage Edwards had a certain edge over Hancock. In spite of his university background, a distinguished service career and his burgeoning acceptance as a member of the landed gentry, he had in the short time since being shot down over Arnhem in 1944 – for which he won the DFC – proved himself to be an old-stager in the fullest variety tradition, capable of improvising on a theme, tailoring each moment to the unique demands of the individual audience. Hancock, on the

collective panic when a drunken fan, poised precariously on the edge of the circle, threatened to launch himself into space. An usher restrained him and the police led him away. Hancock proved more than the master of the situation, easing the crowd back into a feeling of security, but topping everything he had done with his standard curtain speech. He had recited it a thousand times and would continue to do so for several years more: 'I want to thank Abdullah for the fags, Kayser Bondor for the socks, Frank Sinatra for the boots that are killing me ... and are going back ... and I want to thank the police for controlling the crowds ... *inside the theatre.*' He had displayed the authority equal to any emergency, and as the Liverpudlian crowd cheered him to the rafters Edwards would have been proud. It is indicative that when during a live recording he had to cover some technical *longueur* or other he resorted to the Edwards manner. In one television episode a piece of scenery fell just as he was about to say, 'Imagination, sir, that is what the theatre lacks.' The laughter acknowledges the freakish serendipity of the moment, while his eyes roll from his fellow actor to the audience in acknowledgement: 'Watch it over there – the star's talking!' He had obviously learned something at the academy of 'Professor' Jimmy Edwards.

The Professor was one of the first to testify to Hancock's overpowering feelings of insecurity as a performer. During a party to celebrate the run of their second show together Hancock confessed to his friend, 'Jim, for me every night is like a first night.' 'In other words,' explained Edwards, 'he got himself tightened up inside every night.' The longer the run, the more self-perpetuating the tension was. Few performances went by on stage or television where he was not overtaken by dry heaving, if not actual vomiting, in his dressing room before the show. Jimmy recalled how with ten minutes to curtain on a sunny evening he would be outside the stage door in Maiden Lane passing the time of day with the stage crew when Hancock would come around the corner with a dejected look: 'As he went through he just sighed – like a man going to the gallows – every night. It's got to tell on your nerves in the end.' According to Jimmy, Hancock had three nervous breakdowns during their time together at the Adelphi: 'Once he stopped in the middle of his act. He just stopped and said, "I can't go on" and walked off stage … in the theatre there was total panic … and people were sent flying up and down Maiden Lane into the pubs saying, "Tony's off! Tony's off!" and we all scrambled back as fast as we could and gradually there was an orchestra and then there was a chorus and we got the show going. The audience didn't notice. Audiences don't notice a lot if you're careful about it, but by the time I got into the theatre he was already at the stage door waiting for a taxi and he just shook his head at me and said, "I'm sorry." His head was going up and down in shock – literally. That was the first time I'd ever seen anybody in shock and it was a very damaging sight. And he went to a hospital – one of the clinics in London – and just lay in bed under sedation, until they got him right. That was tension and alcohol.'

Not that the Dutch courage provided by drink was really the problem at this time. In the early days he was principally a beer drinker, but growing affluence is the alchemical factor that transmutes pale ale to wine to spirits. In that regard success is its own worst enemy. Galton and Simpson claim he never drank before a performance, but there were exceptions to the routine. Sharing a dressing room with Hancock alongside Ted Ray and Jerry Desmonde on the occasion of the 1952 Royal Variety Performance was Norman Wisdom. Disturbed by the speed with which Hancock was consuming a bottle of brandy, he plucked up the courage to suggest enough was enough. Hancock just muttered something and carried on drinking. When his time came to go out on stage, he switched off the Tannoy in the room and left. Inevitably his three colleagues switched it back on again, apprehensive that his act would be a disaster, but the result was a triumph. Sir Norman remembers that Tony's delivery and timing were superb; something borne out by the BBC recording that survives to this day. Returning to the room, completely unimpressed by his own success, he finished the brandy before retiring to the nearest hostelry until it was time to come back on in the final scene.

Eric Sykes was a frequent visitor backstage at the Adelphi in the early 1950s and always remembers Tony as someone who 'used to drink a bit'. One night he turned to Eric in the dressing room and said, 'I've given it up, you know.' 'Well, that's a funny thing you should say that,' replied Sykes, 'because so have I.' Eric had, in fact, done so and admitted he was feeling the better for it. Tony continued, 'So do I. I can taste my food now.' There was a long pause before he added, 'Of course, I haven't given it up altogether.' He bent down and took out a bottle of wine from under the dressing table and asked Eric whether he'd like a glass. He said 'Yes' and his memory tells him that by the time they left the dressing room together later that night they had downed three bottles between them. According to Eric, at the time it all seemed so innocent. He had no understanding of the essential difference between him and Hancock, namely that he could wake up with a hangover and say never again and stay abstinent for three weeks at a time and have no worries: 'But Tony was dependent in a different way. I came to pity Tony as it gradually took a hold on him. The alcoholism and the soul-searching together – he was driving himself up a wall and killing his frustration with drink.'

Dennis Main Wilson also experienced Hancock's paranoia with the Tannoy, disregarding his host's wishes as soon as he was left alone in the dressing room. Listening to the act over the loudspeaker system he recalled that the laughs never came in the same place twice. 'He would get huge laughs on lines that were supposed to be straight,' the producer added, but when Dennis tried to pump him later for what he had done to achieve this he was met by a blank stare. Main Wilson considered him an intuitive rather than a cerebral performer: 'He had tremendous projection. In the theatre he could dominate and not know that he was dominating … it could well have been some woman sitting in Row G who giggled and he gave her a jolly good staring-at and that's it – wallop! – the audience would just explode.' He remembered the long auditorium of the Adelphi with its very narrow sight lines. Standing against the rail at the back of the stalls, the producer would look out ahead of him upon row upon row of shoulders literally rocking with laughter. He would stress that, with the possible exception of the veteran Jimmy James, he had never heard such 'warm pit-of-the-stomach laughter' of the kind that Hancock raised. He would also have recognised that no comedian experienced greater 'pit-of-the-stomach' anxiety to achieve this.

No market research is needed in the business of being funny. Solo comedy especially is arguably the hardest of theatrical techniques, instantly and inextricably judged by the automatic indicator of success or failure provided by the audience's laughter, or lack of it. On the theatre stage mediocre purveyors of other skills can always muddle through, protected by the cushion of polite, albeit lethargic, applause. The stage comedian has no such escape. No one understood the process better than Hancock, who had a conspiracy theory about those who paid to see him perform: 'I think an audience assembles in Hyde Park and decides what sort of an audience it's going to be. When they've all decided, they go to the theatre.' He wore his memories of those early weeks struggling in the provinces like a row of medals. In Glasgow he claimed they threw rivets at him: 'I hated the place. I couldn't wait to get out … the next week I was playing in Peterborough, where they come to the theatre in tractors. I got the bird there, but it was rural and quiet and peaceful.' At Bristol he claimed he had 7½d. thrown at him: 'I picked it up carefully off the stage, went over the road and bought half a pint of bitter.'

Part of Hancock's problem was not being able to recognise success when it occurred. His Gang Show colleague Rex Jameson, alias 'Mrs Shufflewick', confided to journalist Patrick Newley, 'I once caught his act from the side of the stage and he went down a bomb. The audience adored him, but he came off stage and looked at me and was shaking and said, "I've been a failure, Rex – it's all a disaster."'

The total lack of confidence seemed at odds with the rewards of performance which he conceded in a radio interview in 1956: 'It's only in that moment when you go on the stage and do your stuff that you feel completely yourself. Then you drop back to normal, pack up and go home. You can't get away from it – there is something tremendously morose about this comic lark.' But even the sense of liberation that performing provided was not enough to undermine his fear of the stage. He attempted to explain the paradox when John Freeman tackled him on the matter in his *Face to Face* interview:

> It's a bit of hell just before it starts. There's a lot of champing around and trying to get the right edge so that you are relaxed but also have a kick, so that you're going to be alive and also relaxed. It means a great deal of concentration and hold upon yourself to do this ... it's very challenging. It is enjoyable as a whole. [But] there's too much immediate concentration to really say, 'Oh well, we can have a bit of a ball,' you know.

Almost five years later, in a radio broadcast in December 1964, he claimed, 'In the last analysis, when you walk on a stage, there is nothing anybody can do, which is a strange, fascinating feeling, which is something I love and hate at the same time.' He was even more honest when in 1962 he wrote, 'If you ask me why I go on with it, the answer is that I *like* to suffer. Possibly it is the masochist in me, but I find the very strain of it stimulating, a challenge to keep me on my toes.'

It is hard to accept that Hancock – masochist or no – was not of the persuasion of the American comedian Steve Martin, who in his incisive autobiography, *Born Standing Up*, has admitted to finding scarce pleasure in the live performance of comedy, equating enjoyment with 'an indulgent loss of focus that comedy cannot afford'. To those of lesser mettle who question the why and wherefore of braving all to perform comedy alone in this manner, akin possibly to walking the high wire over the lion's cage, the answer may be found

in Martin's description of the feat as 'the ego's last stand'. If Hancock
was a born worrier, he had somehow found the ideal profession in
which anxiety and the conceit of social approval went hand in hand.
Coughs and sneezes may spread diseases, but they are also up there
on the list of distractions that can murder one's timing or throw the
mood of a routine alongside latecomers, hecklers, other noises off, a
faulty sound system, lighting from the dark ages and more. What he
would have made of mobile phones is anybody's guess. The moment
of performance passes, only to be replaced by the gaping prospect of
an infinity of similar trials in the career ahead and, at those times
when success tastes sweetest, the realisation that no one can remain
at a peak for ever. It can never be enough just to go down well; the law
of averages provides the trigger of doubt that success may be a random matter until one has the unlikely assurance that one can score
every single night. The actress Miriam Karlin worked with Hancock
in the theatre at an early stage of his career and recalled, 'There'd be
a post-mortem after every performance as to why he might have lost
a laugh – an obsessive if ever I saw one.'

The phrase 'post-mortem' is appropriate. That comedy is a serious business can be detected in the language and imagery of death
that surrounds it. Fred Karno, a comic impresario from an earlier
age, talked of that awful moment 'when everything goes quiet and
cold … and there are bloody big holes where the laughs ought to be'.
At the funeral of Jay Marshall, one of American vaudeville's most
respected magicians and comedians, a message on his coffin read,
'Not the first time I've died.' To a comedian failure is death, but the
process is not one-sided. When comics succeed with the audience,
they talk of slaying them, murdering them, laying them in the aisles.
To pretend that a contest is not taking place – every thrust and par-
ry as potentially vicious as a bullfight – would be wrong. Let the bull,
like the enemy in battle, know you are scared and death comes one
step closer. To subject oneself to the procedure night after night in
the vocational cause of laughter may, to many, seem like madness

and renders the simple phrase 'stage fright' somewhat deficient. The drama critic John Lahr has referred to 'stage fright' as a misnomer, fright implying a shock for which one is unprepared, whereas professional performers are here confronted only by 'the very thing they're trained to do'. Certainly Hancock's fear was at total odds with the fact that once on stage performing came completely naturally to him. Lahr's reasoning, however, does not fully take into account the total unpredictability of the comedian's role, even if it does explain Hancock's preference for the security of a script and a characterisation to hide behind. As Jimmy Edwards said, 'When he did his act as the crooner, for example, he never changed a single movement or word or action in it the whole of the two years he did it in the show we were in. He was not an embroiderer.'

All performers have their personal method of psyching themselves up for the show to come. Hancock's came to border on selfloathing. He would not have been the first to discover that physical pain can trump psychological fear. The singer-songwriter Carly Simon who has resorted to jabbing her hand with clutched safety pins before going on stage, confessed to Lahr, 'If you have something that's hurting you physically, the pain is the hierarchy.' His last television producer, Eddie Joffe, saw the comedian apply the excruciating Chinese burn technique to himself on many occasions, encircling his forearm within the circle of the extended thumb and forefinger of the other hand and wrenching it to the point of skin-tearing. In 1966 Hancock explained to the journalist Robert Ottaway that he would stand in the wings before he went on shouting to himself, 'Get on with it, you idiot! What the hell do you think you're doing! Pull your finger out, you nit!' In an interview for television the following year Alan Whicker raised a similar point:

WHICKER: A friend of mine was on a show with you and told me before you
    appeared, you were wandering around back-stage and muttering,
    'Professional idiot, that's what I am – a professional idiot.'

TONY: I give myself a bit of a coating before I go on. Sort of helps makes my
    shoulders drop when I start. Takes about half an hour of abuse. Self-
    abuse. Some people think it's intended for them, which is a pity.

To Ottaway he had explained the exercise as 'my way of getting up
steam, reaching the right pitch of self-confidence to face the audience'. More happily, while he pandered to his low self-esteem, he also
subscribed to a more traditional professionalism. Phyllis Rounce
recalled, 'He was very meticulous about the stage, that everything
was spot on … he knew exactly what he had to do and he was very
anxious to get it right for those who had paid to see him.' He
explained to the Australian interviewer Russell Clark that he would
always try to arrive at a theatre some time before he was due on
stage: 'Not necessarily to hear the reaction to the other artists, but
there's a sort of sniff about a theatre. You think – hmmm, it seems a
little strange tonight – and I'll probably adopt a different tempo to
try to fit the audience.' He needed little time to work himself up into
his state of tension in the wings, pacing up and down and going over
his lines again and again as if his life depended upon it, which, in the
morbid phraseology of his trade, it did.

    Hancock's health led, in January and August of 1953, to two
periods of absence of four weeks' duration from the long run of
London Laughs before he left the show for good the following
December. The situation might have been worse if the management
had not had the sense to recognise the pressure of their twice-nightly steamroller of a show by granting the entire hard-working cast
three individual weeks' holiday at carefully spaced intervals. The
success of the Edwards–Hancock combination quickly led to a sequel
for the same management. Co-starring the comedy impressionist
Joan Turner in lieu of Vera Lynn, *The Talk of the Town* – not to be confused with the West End night club of the same name that Hancock
would play in later life – opened for a long pre-London summer season at the largest theatre in the land, the Opera House, Blackpool,

on 5 June 1954, seven years after he had stepped onto the same stage with Ralph Reader's *Wings* tour in vastly different circumstances. After a week on the road at Oxford's New Theatre it came to the West End on 17 November. The bonhomie that existed between the two male stars was caught in the moment when spontaneous applause broke out at the appearance of a figure arrayed in academic cap and gown sporting a handlebar moustache and blowing his trademark trombone. Seconds later Edwards himself appeared to retrieve his instrument from Hancock, who had been decked out as his look-alike for the gag. This was the show in which, with Galton and Simpson, he originated the crooner sketch: Johnnie Ray, as well as Al Martino and the original 'Mr Rhythm', Frankie Laine, had made their huge impact at the London Palladium during the preceding year. The other comic highlight was a shared routine developed by Frank Muir and Denis Norden from an idea of Michael Bentine.

In 'Send the Relief!' Edwards played the creaking old salt of a lighthouse keeper who attends to his responsibilities with the aid of a shilling-in-the-slot meter. Tony took the role of his loyal but shattered mate. Relief has not arrived for ninety days and Hancock has reached the point of hysteria, which Edwards tries gallantly to keep in check by attending to business as usual: 'We can't have any hysteria 'eria!' was vintage Muir and Norden wordplay. Some distraction for the keeper is provided by the upkeep of the log, but every time Hancock is sent to the porthole to check the weather, the state of the tide or whatever, he receives a bucketful of water and fish in the face. All the while his superior's heroic sense of duty is being hammered deafeningly in his ears: 'Don't just stand there, you lily-livered, chicken-hearted, low-living landlubber!' Eventually Tony is lowered on a rope to bring in the milk; he re-emerges with an octopus on his head, using one of its tentacles to strike a salute. The light itself is treated with the reverence accorded some mysterious sacred flame: whenever it is mentioned, which is often, both stand dutifully to attention as the first four bars of 'Rule Britannia' are played briskly.

Eventually there is a knock at the door. 'It must be the relief,' shouts Hancock. He opens the door and two pretty girls in bikinis and sailor's hats come in. They too salute:

TONY: Our relief has arrived – what do we do now?
JIMMY: Shut that door, and turn that flaming light out!

In the hot summer months the bucketfuls of water thrown at him provided their own kind of relief; at colder times he was more than happy to endure the icy discomfort in the service of his art, although he was happier when the stage hands took the chill off by adding a hot kettle or two. The blatant slapstick does not immediately suggest Hancock's style, but his facial reactions made the piece. And never far away would have been the memory of W.C. Fields enduring agonies of another kind: 'It ain't a fit night out for man or beast!'

In the autobiographical notes he compiled in 1962, Hancock revealed particularly vivid memories of working with Edwards in this sketch, at the same time giving an interesting insight into their respective attitudes to comedy and audiences:

Jim is the only comedian I know who will play all the longer to a bad audience. Most of us, when things are getting sticky, try to finish the job as quickly as we can and then get off. But not Jim! He would never give up. The harder they resisted him, the harder he dug his heels in. When we were playing our lighthouse sketch, he would utter as he passed me, 'Bloody awful audience tonight!' I would mutter back, 'Then let's wrap it up and get off.' But no. Jim would say, 'I'll give 'em a funny little walk.' At the end of it, I'd ask him, 'Was that a funny little walk, then? Strange. I heard no laughter.' (You developed quite a ventriloquial knack of carrying on lone conversations like this without moving your lips or conveying a sound to the audience.) Jim would say, 'Never mind. I'll give 'em another one on the way back.' But still no response whatsoever and the audience grew so restless that I'd plead with him, 'Let's get to the water in the face and clear off. We know they like the water bit.' But by that time Jim was sitting at the table laughing hopelessly – the only one in the whole theatre who *was* – and saying, 'I'll get 'em. I'll get 'em.' I almost got to the point of stepping forward and saying, 'Ladies and gentlemen, we know this is a waste of time from every viewpoint. You're bored and we're bored, so let's pack it in.' But Jim would never despair.

For one moment during the advance Blackpool run it looked as if Hancock might not make it back to the West End. Despite glowing press notices and appreciative crowds, after three weeks his old anxieties returned and he consulted a psychiatrist in Bolton, the nearby industrial town. A medical certificate was issued to the effect that if the comedian continued in the production his health would be seriously affected. Hylton was unimpressed and shouted his opinion at Hancock's management: 'I was born in bloody Bolton and you know what I'd give for a bloody Bolton psychiatrist.' Hylton threatened to send up an independent doctor and to sue for breach of contract should what he regarded as the shenanigans continue. In a show of support from Hancock's management, a second opinion was sought from a Harley Street psychiatrist, but the consultant refused to travel to Blackpool. At this point the scriptwriter Denis Norden found himself cast as an unusual intermediary between psychiatrist and patient, undergoing a strange kind of vicarious analysis whereby he lay on the couch and spouted out somebody else's problems. Denis later recollected to David Nathan, 'The most interesting thing we discovered was that Tony owned three cars, but couldn't drive. This was right up the psychiatrist's alley. "Obviously there is some sort of problem here," he said.' But both the comedian and the shrink continued to dig in their heels when it came to travelling to see each other, while Hylton was not a man with whom to become entangled in the law courts. Hancock reluctantly carried on with the twice-nightly routine. A few years later Tony's brother Roger found himself working in stage management at the Adelphi for another co-production between Hylton and George and Alfred Black. On opening night the musical director misread a cue and jumped the gun at the start of the second half. Suddenly, as the *entr'acte* played to a half-empty house, Hylton appeared out of nowhere backstage bellowing, 'Where's that fucking Roger Hancock?' The brother owned up. 'I hope you're not going to haunt me like your fucking brother,' came the reply. The show, starring Al Read, was appropriately called *Such is Life*.

Tony did have genuine problems and Hylton, however reluctantly, would have to concede as much in time. He had, in fairness, already given Hancock leave of absence to recharge his energies in the South of France during one of his absences from *London Laughs*. The decisive moment came when Hancock went missing in the spring of 1955. The disappearance, as we have seen, coincided with the first episode of the second radio series of *Hancock's Half Hour*, due to be recorded on 17 April. The reason for Hancock's behaviour is understood to have been the general nervous strain attached to the stage show and not any misgivings he had regarding his new radio venture. In many ways radio was his easiest medium and he may feasibly have been happy to come back to the microphone sooner, had Hylton – and George Black Limited, to which he was technically contracted – not insisted that if he was unwell for the theatre he could not be fit for broadcasting either. In the end he was absent from the stage show for ten weeks, but back at the microphone on 8 May, the impresarios, whose permission Hancock needed to broadcast, having graciously backed down from their view that audiences at the Adelphi would be upset if he was heard on the air while deemed unfit to tread the boards of their theatre. During his absence he was replaced by the actor and comedian Bonar Colleano, and then by rising television comic Dave King.

The disappearing act bears eerie parallels with the defection forty years later of the actor Stephen Fry from the London run of the Simon Gray play, *Cell Mates*. Both carry echoes of an earlier vanishing in November 1951 when the sinister-voiced radio actor Valentine Dyall, who had found recent fame on the back of his success as radio's *The Man in Black*, conjured himself away invisibly to France. The comments he made in a newspaper interview upon his return could almost apply to the other two: 'I felt ill, tired and depressed, the sort of feeling when one is keyed up. Elastic can be stretched too far ... I felt I had to get away from it all before I went round the bend ... when you have a nervous breakdown you do not have to climb the curtains, have trembling hands or make funny faces. I didn't.' Phyllis Rounce remembered having discussed the case with Tony and recalled the empathy he shared with Dyall. Although no longer his representative, perhaps of all those who knew him best she was now the least surprised by his behaviour. Eventually Hancock too returned. Dennis Main Wilson said he resembled 'a little dog with his tail between his legs – he did not give any explanations and I didn't think I was entitled to ask for any'. Technically Hancock had broken his contract, but the BBC commendably showed a compassion linked to an understanding of the complexities that lurk behind a great talent and allowed both him and itself to move on.

Hancock's state of mind was not helped by the unyielding routine of having to repeat the same material night after night, trapped in a psychological cage which had no fears for looser, more flexible talents like Edwards and Secombe, who were able to invest every show with a feeling of spontaneity that came second nature to them. In 1962 he wrote:

After a while I found my performance falling flatter and flatter until I felt I had squeezed every last drop of comedy out of every situation. I began to bore myself so much that I could hardly help boring the audience. Being paid, like me, for boredom was bad

> enough, but *paying* for it was even worse and I would lie awake at
> night wondering what I could do to put some new life into the
> laughs. I eventually worked myself up into such a state that my
> health broke down.

He came to regard long theatre runs, if not like prison, at least like
house arrest. Nor did his own sense of perfectionism make life easier when the walls crowded in on him. This is where Hancock found
the ever-changing challenge of radio and television so invigorating.
After lobbying Hylton to be released from his contract without success, in August 1955 he collapsed on stage with an abnormally high
temperature. This time in the face of medical advice he was given
their blessing by Hylton and the Blacks to spend four days under
sedation in a London nursing home. Upon his return he would perform in *The Talk of the Town* until the end of October when he was
replaced till the end of the run in December by Dave King again.
With and without Hancock the revue achieved an impressive run of
656 performances.

Jack Hylton, as a founding father of the new commercial television channel, had stolen a march on the BBC in considering Hancock
as potential television material. In those early days it was not an
automatic consideration that a radio series, however successful,
should automatically transfer to the new medium. Although
Hancock had left the second Adelphi show at the end of October
1955, by which time he was just starting a third series of *Hancock's
Half Hour*, he remained tied to Hylton not only for stage appearances, but also, as far as the impresario was concerned, under the
exclusive nature of his contract for everything else. By the end of
January 1956 the BBC had made Hancock the offer of a contract to
appear in an initial six-episode television version of his radio show.
At the same time it suited Hylton – and Hancock – to give the comedian a television series on his own network rather than another
stage show, something that, according to Galton and Simpson in

internal BBC memos of the period, had been on the cards since the summer of the year before and almost certainly contributed to Hylton agreeing to release Tony early from *The Talk of the Town*. In an interview in the *Sunday Graphic* on 5 February that year, Hylton, questioned about his lacklustre start as a television producer, was honest about the potential conflict between his stage and television interests: 'Maybe I began too soon – at a time when the people I would have liked to put on television were tied down in the theatre. I am changing that. I've had to wait for Arthur Askey, for example. Al Read is another … I won't book them into the theatre again until I get them on television.'

After much legal wrangling and in a seemingly fair spirit of compromise Hylton allowed the BBC to proceed with its plans for its own television series based on the radio show as well as a fourth series of twenty radio episodes that had also been under threat, provided that he had access to the star for not one, but two series of his own show to be scheduled either side of the BBC television series. The second series for commercial television came about after some nifty footwork on Hylton's part, in which he threatened to take up an option in his contract with the artist for a new long-running stage show to open later that year. This could have delayed the date when Hancock became available again to the BBC for either sound or vision until well into 1957. Hancock was only too happy to effect a swap for another sentence of panic and tedium. It is ironic that Hylton had laid the groundwork for his career as a theatre producer by buying the stage rights to early radio comedy successes like *Band Waggon* and *ITMA* right up to *Take It From Here*. That he did not have the rights to *Hancock's Half Hour* was underlined by his inability to secure the services of Galton and Simpson as writers, under exclusive contract as they were to the BBC. Eric Sykes was the automatic, and possibly better, second choice for the sketch format the first series followed. The intention had been for other writers from the Associated London Scripts cooperative co-founded by

Eric to provide the second run. Eventually he did write the first two shows for this second series, before it went into limbo for two episodes with Tony relying in one episode at least upon material from his stage act. In early 1957 Ray and Alan were given leave of absence temporarily from the BBC to switch channels in the spirit that it was in the interest of all parties that the quality of Hancock's work be sustained and on the understanding that they be uncredited by Hylton. In an ideal world they would have arrived on the scene two weeks earlier.

The first series of *The Tony Hancock Show* ran weekly on the commercial station from 27 April 1956; the second fortnightly from 16 November into the following year. All the shows went out live and came under the banner of Associated-Rediffusion Limited, the company licensed to provide commercial programming during weekdays in the London area. The first series was directed by Kenneth Carter, who went on to produce some of Benny Hill's best work in a similar vein. Heading the supporting cast in the opening run were June Whitfield and Clive Dunn. June remembers the début programme beginning with Hancock kneeling in front of a giant photo of Hylton and swearing on oath that he will keep the show clean and not reveal his salary; the dispute between Hylton and the BBC had been sufficiently well publicised for the few viewers that commercial television had in those days to get the joke. The shows – tailored as they were to a revue format – fit conveniently into an appraisal of Hancock's stage work, revealing him to be a far more multi-faceted entertainer than situation comedy allowed. Talking about those times today, Clive Dunn gives the impression of a small boy cast back in time wanting to go out to play again with his best pal: 'There was so much more to Tony than the later public ever saw.' Suffused with the fun of it all he chuckles contentedly, 'I had the best of Hancock, because I had him when he was youngish and a bit happy-go-lucky and going for it like we all were ... if he had wanted, he could have been the greatest revue artist ever.' That is high praise coming from someone who was disconcerted when a few years earlier at the Nuffield Centre, Phyllis Rounce had introduced his future friend to him as 'the new Sid Field'. The praise is justified by the evidence of the first series that, thanks to the medium of tele-recording, has survived within the Jack Hylton Archive, now cared for lovingly by NFTVA, the National Film and Television Archive. The second series, which for the first four shows adopted a single storyline approach, was not so lucky.

From cod-operetta to pastiche-Agatha Christie, Hancock tenses his muscles in all departments, revealing unlikely talents burlesque-style as an Apache dancer, a flamenco dancer, a Balinese dancer, a magician – 'and now a little trick that Channing Pollock stole from me, the appearing pigeons' – and a dead ringer for Marlon Brando in a sketch based on *A Streetcar Named Desire*. In the latter, after June Whitfield in the Vivien Leigh role has delivered about a page of what she has described as passionate Southern Belle nonsense, Tony looks at her as only he could and mutters, 'You've built that up a bit!' In a sketch in a restaurant the priggish John Vere gives his order to Hancock's waiter: 'I'll have scampi with mayonnaise, a bottle of Burgundy '48, a rare steak, stewed onions, and a sprinkling of asparagus.' 'Good luck,' responds the comedian with two glorious syllables dripping with disdain that seem to sum up the futility of the whole human condition. Throughout the series Whitfield persisted as the voice of realism, anxious that the audience does not take what it is watching too seriously. When Hancock welcomes viewers to 'my show', she pushes him aside and insists, 'His show? It's not his show at all.' One moment Hancock is Matt Dillon in a *Gun Law* sketch; the next he is bemoaning, 'She's done it again! We're trying to build up an atmosphere.' The device becomes especially poignant when he masquerades as an orchestral conductor and her revelation that he is not what he seems leads to a suicide attempt on London's Embankment: 'It's no good – I've made my mind up – I'm gonna end it all ... here I am trying to be a symphony conductor and impress the intelligentsia and all the people viewing are saying he wasn't at the Albert Hall at all … I'm gonna jump!'

The series was not deemed a runaway success, but how that could be fairly assessed in those experimental times is hard to grasp. Television comedy was still in its infancy. Scene and costume changes had to be plotted laboriously to account for the live transmission, with compromise often setting the final agenda. The commercial station had been introduced in the London area only the previous September. As June Whitfield says, those were the days when you judged success on whether the scenery fell down or not, and if a stage-hand appeared at the back of shot in a sketch set in the Far East it was scarcely thought worthy of comment. At one moment during the first show Hancock is heard to joke, 'I hope it isn't as bad as this at the BBC,' but he was the first to admit they may have been overambitious at times: 'The first sketch – I suggested it myself – was about a coffee bar with the plants gradually strangling all the guests, the espresso machine sinking through the floor. It is pretty difficult to get plants to strangle people. It needs about six months preparation really … the results were weird and hilarious but in the wrong sort of way.' The nylon threads animating the rampant vegetation soon gave the game away. Appropriately the coffee bar was called the Bar Depresso. Hancock was fast discovering, as the Goons had before him, that this sort of thing was much easier to achieve in radio. Nevertheless, from what little documentation survives, his efforts would appear to have been rewarded in terms of viewing figures, the first series – restricted to audiences in the London area, the Midlands and the North West – being seen in approximately 776,000 households, around 55 per cent of those capable of receiving both channels, and in the week for which more accurate figures do exist beating soon-to-be-standard ITV fare like *Take Your Pick* and *Sunday Night at the London Palladium* into top position.

Throughout the shows that survive Sykes ensured that Hancock's comic grandiosity flowed on effortlessly from where he had left the case on *Educating Archie*. This was helped by the fact that Tony's voice was becoming less strained in a highfalutin way. There are also many moments and situations where the series seems to point the way forward for the future of *Hancock's Half Hour* on television. In one sequence the whole premise of the exaggerated actor-manager is caught in broad brushstrokes as he sits at a dressing table on opening night guardedly spraying his tonsils: 'I expect you're pretty excited, eh? Of course, it's not much to me after writing the words and the music and doing the dances and making the costumes – well, you feel pretty sure, you know. Actually this is the seventh long-running musical I've put on in this theatre in the last four weeks.' Not that Eric found it easy to write for Hancock now that he was the star of the show: 'One programme we did, I said, "Tony, you know when you say *good night*, make it *good evening*." And he said, "No, it says *good night*." I said, "I know – I don't care what it says – it's better the way it flows – *good evening*." And he said, "This should have been in before I got the script." I said, "Scriptwriting for television is not set in stone. It's got to be fluid, it's got to be rhythmic and it's got to be natural." He insisted and I said, "Well, I'm going to leave you now." He said, "I suppose you'll be going off to the golf course." I said, "If I can get a game, yes." And I left.' Soon after, Hancock persuaded Eric to take his wife, Edith, to Paris for the weekend: 'He said, "You need a rest. You've been working too hard." So I said, "That's not a bad idea." He told us of a little hotel where he stayed. So on the Saturday morning we came down to reception and in walked Tony and Cicely. Of course, my wife looked at me as if I'd arranged all this and Tony pretended to be surprised at seeing us and said, "There's a café very near here that serves the best *crevettes* in Paris." Straightaway we're off. We get there and after a bottle of red wine and the prawns he announces, "No this isn't the place," and we're off to another place and from then on to another – by mid-afternoon our wives delivered us back to the hotel in no fit state and they were free to explore the museums by themselves.' The bonding exercise at

Hancock's initiative enriched the friendship, but Sykes never wrote for Hancock again after the Hylton experience. It is a pity that some of his better material for Tony never received a wider audience, if only within the confines of a stage revue, but that would have played Hancock back into the clutches of the long-running demon he was most keen to escape.

It is a paradox that while he clawed at the claustrophobia of a long run in a single venue, the idea of a conventional tour of variety theatres held far less fear for him. After the two seasons at the Adelphi, he appeared in the West End only twice again, in seasons at the London Palladium and, in cabaret, at the Hippodrome, reconstituted as the other Talk of the Town. At varying moments in his career, either on the back of phenomenal success in television or to take up the slack of his life when things became more difficult, he ventured forth on forays to what survived of the old outposts that had made up the prolific Moss and Stoll circuits. There is a story that when contemplating an early tour he stuck coloured pins into a map of the country, each corresponding to a fan letter received. The resultant pattern was intended to indicate where he might expect a good reception, although, whether he followed the plan or not, he still ended up for the most part playing the biggest venues in the more important towns.

While he resented the persistent repetition demanded by a long stage run, Hancock seemed less phased by the continual performance of his standard stuff within the confines of his own variety act. Moreover, while he would appear to be reluctant to try out new material, nevertheless for a succession of dates between 1957 and 1962 he did allow Galton and Simpson to repackage some old wine into new bottles. Interleaved with foot jugglers, aerialists and novelty musicians, Hancock would appear in a succession of sketches, including a reworking of the crooner routine, before closing the show with his conventional top-of-the-bill spot. For a short while Hugh Lloyd helped him in a Dickens sketch, which had enjoyed an early outing in the second Adelphi show and suggests a kinship with Tommy

Cooper's memorable 'Hats' routine. The success of the actor Emlyn Williams in his portrayal of the author at this time gave the sketch added piquancy. Hugh recalls, 'He used to do readings from Charles Dickens, changing wigs and hats and everything with a screen on stage. I was the footman that stood behind and helped him. Of course, he ended up with all the wrong hats at the wrong time – wonderful, hysterical stuff.' One memorable moment occurred when Hancock, evoking the memory of Scrooge and Tiny Tim, had to repeat ''Tis Christmas Day' four times, his voice raised louder and louder until at last the footman threw a pathetic handful of paper snow over the aggrieved thespian. Less successful was a sketch set in a tailor's shop, where he contrived to have a customer lie down on a piece of cloth with arms and legs outstretched, drew an ominous chalk line around him and then shouted offstage: 'Cut two of these out and sew 'em together.' The fault may have been that the sequence would have been no less funny in the hands of any one of a number of other comedians, although it should be noted that this was one of the sketches written by Ray and Alan for the last two television shows for Jack Hylton. It was also the one item in this expanded stage repertoire that did not play upon his theatrical aspirations. Alan Simpson stresses that the agenda behind most of the sketches was that they provided continued evidence of his delusions of grandeur as an entertainer: 'The idea was that all his acts were done inefficiently – it was all "tat" – that was *his* speciality.' The same applied to an opening sequence that started with his entrance in Homburg hat and astrakhan collar and led to an altercation with the orchestra leader for playing his music at the wrong tempo. Getting to the theatre had not been easy: 'I wore out four pairs of shoes. Terrible time I had, sticking me hand out at passing cars. Didn't get a single lift and I had four pairs of gloves whipped.' Taking off his coat, he then segued into a comedy juggling routine in which he would be partnered by grotesques like that whine-on-legs Johnny Vyvyan and the shadily aristocratic Mario Fabrizi, both intentionally cast as if he had just picked them up at the labour exchange. Standing in for the act that has not arrived, he insists that the idea of Hancock in a bright satin frilly shirt and tight trousers is one not to be laughed at: 'The real stuff, this – made out of me mother's old wedding dress.' The lines and the looks were far funnier than all the dropped clubs and balls put together.

Arguably the most successful of these later sketches was that set in the open-air theatre at London's Regent's Park where Galton and Simpson gave Hancock, in blond wig, baggy tights and billowing open-necked shirt, full rein to indulge his love of Shakespearian burlesque in a whistle-stop tour of the Bard, long before the Reduced Shakespeare Company made the approach fashionable. Hancock's attempts to deliver the speech of Henry V before Harfleur are compromised somewhat by the intrusion of a tramp who enters and lies down on the bench beside him:

TONY: Once more into the breach, dear friends, once more ...

TRAMP: Want a bite of me sandwich?

TONY: No I do not ... or close the wall up with our English ... what are they?

TRAMP: Cheese and tomato.

TONY: Oh, thank you. One does get a bit peckish during a heavy performance. Quite a nice bit of bunghole you got here.

When he gets to declaim the Shylock speech – 'His need was greater than mine' – he finds himself working on two levels, distracted by an orator who sets his soapbox only a few feet away:

SPEAKER: Our record speaks for itself. What did we say in 1919?

TONY: What if my house be troubled with a ... alright, what did you say in 1919? Go on, what did you say?

SPEAKER: We said it should never have happened.

TONY: But it did though, didn't it ... am I pleased to give ten thousand ducats ... Lloyd George had your lot weighed up.

SPEAKER: And we said it again in 1927.

TONY: Rubbish ... homes fit for heroes to live in, you said. Look what he's got. (*Points to tramp*) You won't get my vote ... some men there are love not a gaping pig ... when are you going to repeal the Corn Laws?

SPEAKER: That has nothing to do with it.

TONY: I've met your type, matey ... to be or not to be, that is the question ... what about old age pensions?

The nominal climax of the piece comes when he enacts the death scene from *Julius Caesar*, pulling a sheet around him and stabbing himself with a rubber dagger. Sinking onto the bench – 'I die, I die' – he is intercepted by a policeman on a charge of vagrancy. One longs for all the other parts to have been played by Kenneth Williams, as in a radio version they would have been.

Sometimes in a simpler version of the Shakespearian device he simply essayed a cockeyed impersonation of Olivier. Johnny Vyvyan would roll on stage and fix him with his complaining eye, 'Sir Laurence doesn't do it like that.' 'I know,' replied Hancock, 'but we can't all make a fortune out of fags' – a reference to a brand to which the knight had allowed his name to be attached. It couldn't happen nowadays. 'I shall kick off with Richard the Third and go straight through the book,' Hancock would rant, '... all four thousand pages ... Richard the Third ... who, as you know, was a hunchback ... fortunately for me ...!' With hardly a moment to spare for 'the winter of his discontent made glorious summer' he would head straight for Henry V. With a hop, skip and a jump to the microphone, nothing could stop him: 'In peace there's nothing so becomes a man as modest stillness and humility. Stillness or humility or not to be? *That* ... is the question. Whether 'tis nobler in the mind to suffer the slings (*he mimes a sling*) and arrows (*and fires an invisible arrow*) of outraaageous (*with outrageous stress on the middle syllable*) fortune or to take arms (*he spreads his arms*) against a sea (*he dances a hornpipe*) of troubles (*he breaks into giggles*) ... it's a game, innit?' The

'outrageous' line was one of the very few times he hit a note of camp-
ness in his performance – it lasted no longer than the syllable itself.
He could, it seems, mangle Shakespeare *ad infinitum* and may have
done more to put back Shakespearian studies than anyone since
Leon Cortez, a 1940s radio comedian of cockney bent, who made a
particular speciality of explicating the plots of the Bard:'So 'e gets up
the ladder just in time to 'ear 'er say, "Romeo, Romeo, wherefore art
thou Romeo?" So 'e whips out 'is ukulele and serenades 'er and
'alfway through the second chorus she opens the winder and empties
the goldfish bowl over 'im.'

One other sketch for the stage must claim our attention,
although it was originally devised for television following an invitation to participate in January 1957 in *A–Z*, a variety-cum-magazine
programme in which the host, the urbane Alan Melville, contrived
an entertainment around a different letter of the alphabet each
week. Perhaps no other device but the letter 'H' could have found
Hancock and Jack Hylton herded together not only on the same
show, but also on the BBC. For an original contribution, the comedian educated Galton and Simpson to an idea he had first entertained
in the pre-war days at his mother's hotel, where she kept a rather
bumptious budgie in a cage. As Hancock saw things, when the bird
became peeved, it would hide its head under its bell, peeking out
occasionally to see if the coast was clear. 'Look at that stupid bird,'
Hancock told his mum. 'One day I'll do an act about that.' It was successful enough first time around for Hancock to wish to make it his
offering for his second appearance on a Royal Variety Performance
in November 1958. However, since it presented a staging challenge
for the theatre, it was considered sensible to ease the item in on the
road during the short tour he made that year. Hancock played the
budgerigar, complaining about its treatment by its owner, played
first by Irene Handl – conveniently another 'H' – for Alan Melville,
but by Hattie Jacques for the royal show. For the tour the actor Alec
Bregonzi played the vicar engaged in conversation with the bird's

owner – first Tottie Truman Taylor, and then Evelyn Lund – and remembered the staging problems, all down to size, which could be cheated so easily in television:'They did it by having me and the own-er in the spotlight with a normal-sized cage covered over. When I asked her, "How's your little budgie?" she took the cloth off, the spot-light went off us and the tabs parted to reveal Tony in the giant cage. We then did all our other lines off stage.' Hancock appears to have become bored with the premise on the tour and it was dropped dur-ing the run. Only at the eleventh hour, the week before in Hanley, did he change his mind again for its inclusion on the special show, for which Bregonzi's part was changed to that of a scoutmaster for fear of upsetting the Church!

At the London Coliseum, the royal venue that year, he was the hit of rehearsals, in spite of the initial consternation of producer Robert Nesbitt. Hancock recalled, 'I was wheeled in and he said, "What are you supposed to be?" I said, "I'm a budgerigar in a cage." He said, "Jesus, this is all I need!"' Soon the rest of the cast were in hysterics and Nesbitt himself was seen to suppress a chuckle or two.

WOMAN: What a naughty mummy, being away so long at that naughty, naughty whist drive.

TONY: Naughty, naughty whist drive! More like the naughty, naughty Bricklayers' Arms. It's not good enough. Stuck here all day with nothing to eat. Haven't had a decent piece of millet since last Thursday. How can I stop me feathers falling out if I don't get me proper nourishment? I'm not the bird I was. If I had Peter Scott's telephone number, I'd have him round here straightaway ... she's only got to leave that cage door open once and I shall be off. Sparrows or no sparrows, I'll take me chance!

However, Hancock did less well on the night. His nervousness showed, and besides he had already won the plaudits of his peers. Maybe his inner psyche told him that was enough. He remembered the experience well: 'Afterwards I was introduced to the Queen and she said, "All those feathers!" So we passed that by! Prince Philip with his hands behind his back said, "Are you going to do any more radio?" and I said, "No." End of conversation.' The costume was in fact hysterical, with hideous claws replacing shoes in what must have resembled one of Phyllis Rounce's worst nightmares. A recording survives from the inclusion of the sketch in the BBC's *Christmas Night with the Stars* from later that same year. Hancock is irresistible, evoking echoes of Chaplin's chicken in *The Gold Rush*, strutting up and down the cage, his mime technique perfectly capturing the natural movements of the bird, as he preens himself in the mirror, jabs the bell with his beak, all the while his head bobbing this way and that. All of Hancock's sensitivities are projected onto the bird:

WOMAN: I don't think beauty's getting enough iron. How would you like a rusty nail in your water?

TONY: How would you like a rusty nail …! Ah well, I'm fed up with this. I wish I was a cat. Just come in, have your dinner and go straight out again …

VICAR: He's getting old now, isn't he?

TONY: What d'you mean, old? How dare you? I'm in my prime. There's nothing wrong with me that a decent helping of birdseed wouldn't put right …

WOMAN: If he doesn't improve, vicar, I'm thinking of selling him.

TONY: Oh, so that's the way things are shaping, is it? Having given her the best years of me life, I'm to be flogged for a parrot.

Soon it is cabaret time:

TONY: Recite something for the vicar? It will be a pleasure. This will be my swansong. I shall go out in a blaze of glory here. There was a young lady named Nellie, who had a tattoo …

WOMAN: Oh, vicar!

The routine ended in pure vaudeville nostalgia as Hancock skilfully evoked the bird-warbling acts of a bygone age with, of course, further genuflection to the king of whistlers, Ronnie Ronalde.

Nervous performer he may have been, but it is a fair conclusion to draw that he never lost his love and fascination for the true spirit of variety that had been instilled in him as a boy. He relished the survival instinct, if not the desperation implicit in the billing of a vaude-villian like Kardomah, who 'fills the stage with flags'. One week Spike Milligan took an advertisement in the trade paper used by the magician: he had just shot himself in the hand on stage. The ad read 'fills the stage with blood'. In Hancock's estimation they would have been interchangeable. A great favourite was another magic man, 'The Great Claude', who used to throw a bouquet over his shoulder and then announce, 'Tonight a star is born,' as if seeing the flowers for the first time. As he performed, he delivered a disembodied commentary on his own act. He would tag his version of the egg and the bag trick, which could be bought in any novelty store, with the line, 'The man must be in league with the devil, a follower of the left-hand path.' According to Denis Norden, Tony couldn't think of that act without breaking out into a huge watermelon smile. Much of variety may have been small time, but at whatever level you hovered on the bill the camaraderie was there to be shared by all. When in the early years of Hancock's success George Fairweather introduced him to the legendary but not over-publicised Jack Wilson, one half of the male quotient of the eccentric dance team Wilson, Keppel and Betty, he could have been meeting Noël Coward: 'Tony was so excited to be in the presence of these people. He appreciated the theatrical tradition and this was like shaking hands with the Gods.' Coward and Wilson alike would have appreciated an anecdote he treasured from his mother. It involved two old music-hall pros who had struggled around the halls with the same act for years. They would amble on stage in moth-eaten fur coats, then for no apparent reason lie on their stomachs to deliver their lines. One hot, sultry afternoon in some tired theatrical backwater there was barely a handful of people in the audience. After going through their usual routine to the significant absence of any applause at all, they got up and one of them addressed the few: 'Ladies and gentlemen, my partner and I wish to thank you for your overwhelming ovation. So if you will kindly remain seated we will pass among you and beat the shit out of you with a baseball bat.' He told it many times over the years.

Hancock never became that desperate, even if he did perform the same basic act for years. There was no disputing his pulling power at any time. Throughout his BBC heyday, virtually every seat was sold out in advance. By 1957 he was commanding 60 per cent of the gross receipts of theatres like the Manchester Palace, the Bristol Hippodrome, the Birmingham Hippodrome and the Finsbury Park Empire, out of which he would be expected to pay the supporting company. By 1961 the figure had risen to 65 per cent against a guarantee of £2,000. The following year the figures spiralled higher still to 70 per cent. In 1962 an average night at the cavernous Liverpool Empire was capable of grossing over £1,500, which it did. Of his visit to the theatre in August 1958, the *Liverpool Echo* reported, 'If Tony Hancock could split himself into fifty Tony Hancocks of equal wit and bubbling folly, there would be no moaning in the bars of our theatres. Mr Hancock must have sent so many people home determined to buy a television set just to see him again.' Four years later he returned to the same theatre no less triumphant. He had by now succumbed to the suggestion of his brother Roger that he drop the conventional variety approach of a string of varied acts and target a more up-to-date image by appearing with the orchestra ranked behind him on stage. He performed the entire second half of the show, while the vocalist Matt Monro provided the first. In October 1962 the same newspaper was ecstatic all over again: 'If anyone had any doubts that this man is a major entertainer, this evening will have tossed them into the side aisles and into the wings as he mutters and mumbles and slides into an impersonation which just stops short of the

real thing … he holds the stage by the sheer bulk of his personality.'
The managers' report cards that were filed at central office for use by
the directorate of Moss Empires are replete with phrases like
'extremely well received', 'excellent reception', 'wonderful comedy'
and 'great ovation'.

By now the variety era had almost come to a close. When
Hancock addressed the possibility of an autobiography, he recorded
his thoughts on a subject that quite obviously both agitated him and
moved him greatly:

It is sad to think that most of the theatres where I used to die have
since died themselves. The obvious thing is to blame television, but
I think the trouble with variety goes deeper than that. There is a
strain of suicide in the murder. Whenever I go back to the halls, I
am appalled by the defeatist spirit among the managements, the
deadly take-it-or-leave-it approach to artists and audience alike. I
have known them turn the auditorium into a kind of Turkish bath
by switching the heating full on so that by the interval the audience
was parched and panting and the refreshment girls did a roaring
trade with ices and drinks-on-sticks. To go to the other extreme an
acrobat came to see me one night and said, 'Do you think you could
get them to do something about the heating? They've turned it off
and I can't loosen my limbs.' How can you imagine anything more
dangerous than that? The acrobat was lucky to be alive to complain. At the end of a week like that the manager comes round and
says, 'We look forward to seeing you back again,' and you tell him,
'Why do you think I should come back when all you can offer is a
cracked mirror in the dressing room and not even a decent basin
with a drop of hot water?' I have also played in theatres where the
lead trumpet worked in the bar across the road – and played like it,
too. I have been to band calls where the first trumpet has gone home
to lunch in the middle of it and left the rest of us to fend for ourselves. For all that I still go back. I know I shall look around that

dreary No. 1 dressing room and shudder to think what Nos 13 and
14 must be like. But there's still a magnetism about the music hall
– what's left of it – that I cannot resist.

When it came to his theatrical work Hancock had his own critics,
who complained that he clung to certain elements of his stage routine for too long, although that suggestion is made nowhere in the
aforementioned reports. It has always seemed an unfair stricture for
a performer who was operating in an area where his colleagues and
contemporaries were chastised when they did *not* deliver the familiar routine everyone was expecting. Throughout careers that often
extended far longer than Hancock's tragically short professional life,
his rivals were, on the criterion by which he was judged, allowed to
get away with murder. To think merely of Les Dawson and Jimmy
James, Max Wall and Frankie Howerd, Dickie Henderson and
Richard Hearne, Tommy Cooper and Sandy Powell, not to mention
Morecambe and Wise, is to conjure up a nostalgic montage of eccentric dances, funny walks, lunatic piano recitals, hackneyed recita-
tions, absurdist fantasies and ventriloquial travesties guaranteed to
keep the British laughing for several lifetimes. Polished through
constant performance, these routines were allowed to shine like
gems long after variety was officially seen to be recognised. Often the
audience knew the lines, but the recognition factor was part of the
appeal. Hancock had only to think of Sid Field constantly improving
his cherished routines as he footslogged around the provinces for
justification. One radio half hour from February 1956 played with
the issue, but long before it became a matter of critical concern. When
his East Cheam household gangs up on him because his act has
become old-fashioned, he responds, 'Old fashioned! Change me act?
The public would never allow it. That's half the attraction, the fact
that they know it off by heart. You don't ask Sir Laurence Olivier to
change *Hamlet* because you've heard it before.' It seems unfair that
many came to hold Hancock exempt from such consideration, but it

was, one feels, the price to pay for being associated with a persona developed to such an extreme degree in other media where almost impossible standards of freshness have been set and met week in, week out. Hancock was not surprisingly frightened of new material. He shared that distinction with every comic with a tried and tested routine. And he was never a joke-teller in the Bob Monkhouse mould where constant revitalisation is essential in the cause of topicality. It is to Hancock's credit that right up until the end of his life he was capable of delivering a brilliant performance when sober. Sound and video recordings of some of the last performances of his stage act in Australia show that no nuance of look or expression suffered, even if by then he could manage only a couple of dives to the ground for the *Gaumont British News*.

Before we move on to a detailed appraisal of his television triumphs in *Hancock's Half Hour*, it must be recorded that there was one major change and one significant new entry in the cast list of his life as he pursued his earlier theatrical and radio endeavours. On 19 October 1953, during the run of *London Laughs*, five years after he signed his contract with International Artistes, Phyllis Rounce arrived at the Adelphi to be told by the stage door keeper that he had been given instructions not to allow her admittance to Hancock's dressing room. Only later did the significance of the date hit her. Rounce was distraught: 'I was sad, very sad. We had been, and still were, very close and Tony had given me no indication something was wrong ... I thought we'd just go on.' The following evening she insisted on seeing him: 'I was asking for an explanation and he just sat there like a great woolly bear and said nothing at all.' As she upped to leave with a brisk, 'Oh well, cheerio,' she saw he had 'great wells of tears in his eyes'. Hancock may have been within his rights to terminate their agreement, but scared of confrontation – and not for the last time – he sadly lacked the courage that social courtesy required in order to end the professional relationship without unpleasantness. Perhaps it had been remiss of the agency amid the euphoria of his growing success not to have grasped the nettle sooner. Hancock had obviously been ticking off the days. He transferred his business affairs to Phyllis Parnell of the Archie Parnell Agency, which also looked after Sidney James, although it is wrong to assume that, intoxicated by the thought of a career in pictures, he had been persuaded to do so by Sid. Hancock did not meet the actor until the spring of the following year, most probably at Beaconsfield Studios, while filming a low-budget comedy called *Orders are Orders*. They hardly knew each other at the time and their work on the film together was sparse. They would not cement their special bond until they came together on radio in October 1954. More indicative may be the fact that the Parnell office had looked after the career of Sid Field. Whatever the attraction, it did not last long. On 30 December Hancock wrote from his pantomime dressing room in Nottingham announcing his new allegiance to Kavanagh Productions, the organisation founded by *ITMA* creator Ted Kavanagh, and of which Frank Muir and Denis Norden were leading lights. Jimmy Edwards was also a client. The elegant Jack Adams would be in charge of his affairs. At one point in the radio series Galton and Simpson show Hancock striking a blow for artistic independence by detaching himself from his fictional agent, played for the sake of the episode by Sid himself: 'The gravy train has just hit the buffers. You are now on your own. I do not need you any more.' When Sid mentions the matter of a contract, he digs his heels in: 'Contract? You've been holding that thing over me head for five years now!' One wonders if Hancock felt a sense of *déjà vu* at that point.

The following summer at Blackpool a chance encounter along the promenade between Dennis Main Wilson and the publicist Freddie Ross would have consequences upon Hancock's life that were incalculable at the time. In the resort to organise the public relations for a forthcoming tour by Ted Heath and his band, she was persuaded by Dennis to look in on rehearsals for the new show at the Opera House. Hancock was rehearsing the 'Crooner' sketch when they arrived. She recalled, 'His hair was longer than it should have been and he looked as if he was carrying all the troubles of the world on his shoulders.' When introduced to the comedian she did not hold back. 'If I had a talent like yours, I'd be proud, not worried' were words that would haunt him in later years. Freda Ross was born in 1930 to conventional, caring London Jewish middle-class parents who had supported her ambitions to make the grade in the public relations industry. In Main Wilson's words she came over as 'dynamic, driving and a bit daunting ... a bustling cookie ... a go, go, go lady'. At a meal with the Hancocks and the producer after the show she let slip the nature of her profession. Hancock – perhaps ironically – went immediately on the warpath, contemptuous of the worst excesses of a ruthless industry that traded talent as a commodity like soapflakes. Of that encounter, Ross recalled, 'We argued. We never really stopped arguing, ever ... he had a lasting effect on me from that moment.' At Dennis's insistence he took her into his employ and within three weeks she 'had answered about two years' back fanmail and Tony had got six new suits and a haircut'. His wife Cicely had no qualms about the situation, although she may not have been – or did not want to be – as perceptive as the producer: 'Freddie was clearly in love with him. I knew it would never work.' The arrangement continued intermittently until in 1959 she became his mistress.

Phyllis Rounce always claimed that Freddie had ordered the portcullis to be dropped upon her. This cannot be true, since the future lovers did not meet until the summer after her dismissal. However, it is not difficult to imagine Rounce's feelings becoming displaced and distorted once another woman had exerted an influence in his professional life. He loved and revered Cicely, but had known Phyllis longer. Until Freddie appeared on the scene, only Phyllis had been allowed to come near him in the wings of a theatre. She most probably knew his professional temperament better than his wife and perfectly understood the rationale behind the worst excesses of his behaviour: 'He had this tremendous warmth when he wasn't being hateful. He did do terrible things to people – he did terrible things to me – but I took it all because in my job I understand how desperately hyped up and how frightened they are. And Tony, of all the people I knew, was frightened … you always had to push him on a stage … but he was only worried he was going to let his audience down, petrified he wouldn't be able to make them laugh.' His fear became a metaphor for commitment, and for that a professional like Rounce would forgive anything. She never married. She must often have cherished a wistful sense of what-might-have-been as their lives continued on their contrasting paths.

Chapter Eight

HANCOCK'S TELEVISION HALF HOUR

*'Fat men look enormous on television,
so I narrowed myself for the little box.'*

In 1954 television was on the way to finding a presence in every home, the Coronation of Queen Elizabeth II the previous year having sent sales of the appliance on a fast upward curve. The growing prominence of the medium within the cultural life of the country was highlighted by the many references to it that contributed to the laughter during the radio series of *Hancock's Half Hour*. The first episode contained an indirect allusion to *What's My Line*, the major panel game success, when Kenneth Williams as the dispossessed Lord Bayswater asked Hancock whether he realised who he was, to receive the reply, 'I'm afraid your mime wasn't very helpful. Would you mind doing it again?' By the ninth show of the second sound series it was time for Galton and Simpson to exploit the social stigma of not having a set at all. Hancock bemoans the fact that he can't walk down the street with his head held high without the neighbours pointing at him and sniggering, in spite of the wooden aerial he's put up on the roof to disguise his shame. One of the panellists on *What's My Line* becomes his Achilles' heel as they set out to rumble him: 'They ask me what I thought of Barbara Kelly's earrings last night and I say "very nice" and they say, "That's funny – she wasn't on."'

However natural the progression from sound to vision may appear, the move was far from a foregone conclusion. For performers of the school of Jimmy Edwards, Frankie Howerd and Hancock, whose initial success had been secured on radio, television was perceived as the more inconvenient of the two, necessitating extensive rehearsal time and prohibiting the widespread theatre work that made their initial radio success with its relatively modest fees pay. A radio broadcast took a day or less, television most probably a full working week, and in those early days recording was out of the question. If you were due to appear mid-evening on the West End stage, there was no way you could be in front of the cameras in a BBC television studio at the same time. As a guide to the economics involved, the total budget for the opening show at the newly acquired Lime Grove studios in 1950 was a mere £300, at a time when Max Miller could command £1,000 a week in variety. However, as listening figures shrank, the television audience grew. The demand for some form of comedy was a *sine qua non*.

In 1951 Ronnie Waldman was appointed Head of Light Entertainment for the television service. In a *Radio Times* article for 23 February he stressed the need for formats in comedy and entertainment 'that had never existed before the invention of television', well realising that material that played admirably for a collective theatre audience would not necessarily win the approval of the family circle watching at home. He admitted that this would not happen overnight, adding that it took sound broadcasting about fifteen years to reach the first 'real and pure' radio comedy programme, *Band Waggon*, starring Arthur Askey in 1938. He would not have to wait that long. In the early 1950s television created comedy stars of its own, namely Terry-Thomas and Norman Wisdom, but, as it did so, priced them out of its own market. The former had been paving the way with his imaginative *How Do You View?* as early as 1949, but it was Askey again who in 1952 would with characteristic intrepidity provide the first big hit of the Waldman era with the sketch-driven

Before Your Very Eyes! In this the big-breasted model Sabrina proved to be the most eye-catching of foils, eliciting from the big-hearted little man the nickname of 'The Hunchfront of Lime Grove'. Askey brought a zest and *joie de vivre* to the sterile electronic vacuum of the television studio that has never been properly acknowledged.

Possibly the first to succeed in this country with something close to situation comedy proper was the unlikely figure of Bob Monkhouse in 1954. Now remembered with affection as one of the finest stand-up comics of his generation, during two series of *Fast and Loose* he revealed alongside his writing partner Denis Goodwin a true understanding of how to develop comic situation through character. Although this again was a revue-style show, the lucky advantage of a duration of forty-five minutes allowed for the lengthier sketches which made this possible. Most notable was his character of 'Osbert the Suitor', a dim-witted, accident-prone soul, whose courtship of June Whitfield was compromised by the calamity he brought down upon the heads of his prospective in-laws. The show was short-lived when Monkhouse came near to teetering over the brink of overwork, leaving the field clear for Hancock and his colleagues. *Hancock's Half Hour* would not only go on to dominate the medium artistically for six series between 1956 and 1960; it would also prove responsible for laying the ground rules, stylistically and technically, that would underpin the genre of the sitcom for a considerable time to come.

The transfer of *Hancock's Half Hour* occurred in the summer of 1956, between the third and fourth radio seasons. Hancock came to BBC screens with the experience of the practice run provided by the first of his series for Jack Hylton on the new commercial network. Waldman, his confidence no longer bolstered from a position of monopoly, could not have been happy with a situation whereby a BBC name was prevented from making his début as a television star on the parent network, any more than he was in 1956 when Hylton spirited the Askey show across to ITV. However, *The Tony Hancock*

Show did enable the comedian to work out of his system any need to perform within a sketch-driven format, which Terry-Thomas and Askey had established as the norm. It should be remembered that until the Hylton project in April 1956 Hancock had been virtually absent from television screens for almost five years, successfully cocooned in his radio and stage careers. The transition was not made easier by the rivalry that bristled between the two disciplines of sound and vision within the BBC itself. In 1954 the Canadian broadcaster Bernard Braden had been prevented from making a television series for Waldman when BBC radio held him to a clause in his contract that now limited him to sound broadcasting exclusively, in spite of his earlier success in the visual medium with the show *An Evening at Home* in 1951. The Controller of the Light Programme now gave his permission for the title of Hancock's show and its inseparable signature tune to be used, on condition that it was made transparently clear in all publicity that the television version was not a rehash of the radio show, a point, one would have imagined, more in television's favour than his own. There was a chill in the air as the guidelines were established and the formalities observed.

Throughout Hancock's double life in radio and television at the BBC, an uneasy truce existed between his two paymasters. Although they were both funded by the same source and were in a time-honoured way on the same side, there were times when tensions became strained. When in the latter part of 1956 Pat Hillyard, radio's Head of Variety, attempted to instigate contractual negotiations for a fifth series of radio shows to begin traditionally in the autumn of 1957, it was to discover that Hancock had already committed himself to two further television series – the second and third – to commence in the spring and autumn respectively of that year. This necessitated pushing back the start of the fifth radio season to January 1958. We have already seen how the final sixth series, conceded by Hancock out of loyalty to his writers, was concertinaed into three weeks of recordings in June 1959 to accommodate a simultaneous start for both the radio series and the fifth television series in September of that year, the only time the two ventures overlapped. Although the last radio series came off the air in a blaze of glory, it must have been a calculated risk for producer, performers and writers to address it in this compromised fashion. Throughout his career Hancock resisted a joint radio and television contract with the BBC. Such a phrase would have been no more than semantics for the star, although it would have ensured that radio and television were fully informed of each other's intentions. Since he had separate companies for his radio and television interests, a joint contract was not feasible anyway. Besides, Hancock was never less than his own master. As early as October 1956 he had told Waldman that he wanted to rest the radio series for a year in order to concentrate on the television version. In recent years shows like *Knowing Me, Knowing You, The League of Gentlemen* and *Little Britain* have all enjoyed early exposure on radio before moving across to television. Today whatever friction does or does not exist between the two creative camps, radio has become acknowledged as a proper and inexpensive sounding board for viability in comedy and not necessarily the Cinderella figure that Hillyard, perhaps with some justification, envisaged it becoming.

The move across from radio can be perceived either as an inevitable career progression or an impetuous leap in the dark. It is difficult to assess whether it was more daunting for Hancock or his writers. The comedian had the visual advantage of looking as he had sounded. While the full-blooded exuberance of people like Askey and Edwards could not help but be diminished by the confining dimensions of the 'box', Hancock seemed unaffected in this regard. Master as he was of the comic close-up and the sardonic shrug, no British comedian brought the contained discipline of Jack Benny to British television comedy more effectively. He zealously did his homework before entering the new medium. In a promotional interview for the new series, he explained away that sojourn in the London Clinic at the beginning of the year: 'Fat men look enormous on television, so I narrowed myself for the little box.' A strict diet and a fortnight in bed knocked 20 lb. off his 14 st. 9 lb. At the same time he intensified his study of television techniques: 'I turned into a mad viewer. For six months I watched regularly, never had time to read a book.'

In those early live television days Galton and Simpson soon discovered that what they could achieve with four or five people in thirty minutes on a radio show would take forty-five minutes to do on television. By their own admission, they were never 'gang show' writers of the *Dad's Army* kind. By necessity the transfer to the more literal medium slowed the pace and reduced the core cast so that greater emphasis could be placed on the relationship of the two principal characters, Hancock and James. It should be stressed that the larger team was still working together in radio during this process. Bill Kerr, Kenneth Williams and Andrée Melly – still to be replaced by Hattie Jacques – were all excluded from the first series of six fortnightly shows, and may have been happy not to be taking the risk. Alan's verdict on the cast changes is that no one was too perturbed by their omission: 'I think they all accepted it ... Bill, who was always filming or on stage, accepted the fact that life goes on.' However, when the series returned to the screen for another similar run in April 1957, Sid's filming commitments on *Campbell's Kingdom* in Italy precluded his taking part in the first two episodes. This time around Kenneth did appear in each of the six new shows, with Hattie – fresh from her success in the radio show – featured in all but the first. In an episode called *The New Neighbour* she was cast as Hancock's secretary with Williams as a policeman. This may have come as close as any of the television shows to the radio vehicle. In others Jacques pursued a familiar line in dotty aristocratic eccentrics. Only one show survives from these first twelve episodes, *The Alpine Holiday*, in a tele-recording made for technical purposes so that the programme's makers could watch their efforts since all television went out live. The first of the second series, it is most notable for Hancock's obstreperous mood as he flies to his destination: 'Slight pong of garlic here, if I'm not mistaken. Shall we have a window down ... are these winder-downers, slider-backers or pusher-outers?' Williams as Snide is cast as the yodelling champion from East Dulwich with whom Hancock is forced to share a hotel room. When to Tony's bemusement the character starts to display framed photographs on the furniture, the writers may have edged closer to Williams's true psyche than any psychiatrist, catching the extreme narcissism made obvious by his diaries later:

TONY: But they're all of you!

KENNETH: Yes – I haven't got anybody else.

TONY: How sad.

KENNETH: I know – nobody likes me. I don't know what it is. I seem to get on people's nerves. They think I'm daft.

TONY: I can't understand that.

KENNETH: I mean well.

TONY: I'm sure you do.

As a 'turn', Snide is less effective in the flesh. There is a disturbing quality to his forced-smile innocence, not helped by the short-trousered fashion of the Alpine uniform they both have to wear in this context. Hancock picked up on the sexual ambivalence, if Williams did not. In his autobiography, Kenneth quotes a conversation about the Tyrolean sequence that does not appear to be recorded in his published diaries. 'Yes,' said Tony, 'it went very well on the whole, but there were complaints from some people; they thought it was a bit poofy.' The 'two men in a room' device was basic Laurel and Hardy, but at one moment Snide extends his hand to Hancock with the little finger sticking out. Hancock coyly folds it back into Williams's hand. Kenneth was full of disbelief. 'But little fingers is a children's formula for *pax*,' he protested to his colleague. 'Yes, but they read these things into it, two blokes holding hands, you know,' explained Tony. Although strangely, whenever they are on screen together, the camera shots appear to favour Williams, you hardly ever take your eyes off Hancock. Nevertheless it was at the end of this series for television that the comedian expressed his misgivings to the actor about comic stereotypes, leading him to record in his diary on 10 June 1957 the comment about 'set' characters causing 'a rut in story routine'. Although, as we saw in an earlier chapter, they would continue to work together for a while on radio without Snide, they did not come together again for the visual medium. Hattie re-emerged as late as the fifth television series in the episode entitled *The Cruise*, where she played an overbearing, over-amorous fellow passenger:

HATTIE: I've seen you looking at me – too shy to make the first move – I'm a widow you know.

TONY: I'm not surprised – poor bloke – I should think he was well out of it.

As he observes before burying himself back in his book, 'What a farce! Two hundred birds on the boat and she has to be the one that goes berserk.'

As they found their way in the medium, Galton and Simpson bravely resisted much of the advice that came their way. Ray went on the record in this regard: 'Everybody told us that we must change, because television *is* visual, and actors had to be seen to be moving about … But most of our scripts were dialogue anyway, so instead of saying "pick up that bucket", we'd say "pick that up". That was our concession to television.' Although not referred to by name, Eric Sykes was a leading spokesman for the visual movement. In an interview for *The Times* in March 1959 the writers agreed that their opinion had been finally confirmed when they wrote a scene of moody domesticity which consisted entirely of Tony and Sid sitting in chairs talking to each other, presented simply in cross-cut close-up. It ran for nine minutes, but no one noticed the duration, only that it was the funniest part of the show. They might have guessed that a major contribution to its success would be provided by Hancock's skill at facial expression. The decision to keep Sid as his sparring partner for the series paid less predictable, although in retrospect obvious, visual dividends. He brought to the shows all his experience of the film industry, and as we shall discover understood implicitly how to use the camera to greatest effect.

The responsibility for stage-managing the journey of *Hancock's Half Hour* to television was assigned to the producer Duncan Wood. He had worked with the star before, as a junior radio producer in the BBC West Region, where he featured him as an act first on *Variety Ahoy* in July 1951 and then on a similar series, *Variety Cavalcade*, in May 1953. Wood would become revered in the industry for his instinctive understanding of whether a comedy script would play. In later life, in testimony to this, his credits embraced *Steptoe and Son* for the BBC and *Rising Damp* for Yorkshire Television. As soon as they met this burly ex-member of the Royal Tank Corps, Galton and Simpson knew they were in safe hands. Alan Simpson recalls, 'He was a very confident, decisive director … he was so efficient [with rehearsals] that we normally ended up with around an hour to spare before the show, which gave the cast plenty of time to relax.' Luckily trust was also established from the outset between Wood and Hancock. He devised for the comedian a template for reaction shots in the show, taking away from him the worry of having to address this issue constantly as the script progressed. Duncan reckoned to script an average of 250 camera shots per programme. In an interview for *Omnibus* he explained, 'I'd say to him, "I don't think you should concern yourself with 220 shots of the 250. What I'm really shooting there is the natural action. What I would like to do" – we always did this on the last day of rehearsal – "is to mark a little 'x' in the script against the other 30 shots, because they come between words, and those are specific reaction shots, which you'll never know I'm taking unless I tell you, because you're not speaking, not doing anything. So you learn those 30 and leave the other 220 to me." And that's how we worked.' The year after he worked with the producer for the last time, Hancock recorded his own thoughts on his colleague:

> Duncan Wood was a very determined man, but he kept his feelings well under control. He reminded me of those cartoon characters whose faces gradually fill up with red when they grow angry. Whenever we saw that happening with him we sensed trouble and curbed our tongues. He had a nerve-racking job. He was responsible for the casting, the scenery, and the music as well as for all the production problems and if ever a face was justified in filling up with red in moments of crisis it was his. One sure way of exasperating him was for the scriptwriters to blow into rehearsal towards the end of a trying day and say just as he was wrestling with some complex shot, 'Do you think we could change this line?' Duncan would clutch his head and say, 'Please! Not now. Leave me alone.' Because I tried to act as a peacemaker, Alan and Ray used to think I was taking sides against them, but I knew their suggestions were meant for the best – just part of their enthusiasm for the job – but they were just ill-timed, that's all.

Wood's discerning eye for casting became legendary. A major ploy made from time to time in the publicity for the show was that on behalf of realism regular or 'straight' actors were to be used in lieu of the comic regulars of the radio series. No one could question the inclusion of guests of the calibre of Jack Hawkins, John Gregson and André Morell, but their celebrity status tended to work against the desired aim, reducing the proceedings to the 'let's have a party' mood of the plays 'what' Ernie Wise 'wrote'. 'Jack Hawkins?' questioned Hancock. 'Never get anywhere in the theatre with a name like that. Sounds like a scrap metal merchant.' Other important figures made more than a single appearance, including that Mrs Malaprop for the

1950s, Irene Handl; the snooty owl of countless comedy films, Richard Wattis; and the prim authoritarian Raymond Huntley, whose pedigree went back to the Will Hay movies. On two more occasions in Hancock's television career the drum would be beaten to a similar tune on behalf of the 'straight' actor. No one could dispute the quality of the cast that supported Hancock in his final television series for the BBC without Sid James, or his subsequent 1963 series for ATV, but it should be emphasised that he never had greater genuine acting talent supporting him than when James, Jacques, Kerr and Williams were in close proximity. If a tendency had developed for them to be regarded as 'comic' actors, it was in large measure due to their success in playing against Hancock. During the course of the life of *Hancock's Half Hour* on television many of the names cast by Wood would acquire the same connotation.

The likes of Robert Dorning, Peggy Ann Clifford, John Vere, Dennis Chinnery, Anne Marryott, Ivor Raymonde, Evelyn Lund, Alec Bregonzi and others would come to be known as the Duncan Wood Repertory Company. Among their number the gruff-voiced cockney Arthur Mullard, the master of blank-faced monotony Hugh Lloyd and, most notably, the insouciant John Le Mesurier would go on to achieve distinctive niches of their own in British comedy. It must also have been galling for Kenneth Williams to observe obvious comic grotesques with little acting skill coming on board, principally the pint-sized, skew-eyed Johnny Vyvyan and the shifty, moustachioed Mario Fabrizi. The former had first become known to Hancock and the writers in their early radio days as Derek Roy's real-life secretary; the latter had been a band boy with the Vic Lewis orchestra who, according to Ray and Alan, claimed to be descended from a Vatican Count. Hancock would nudge his producer, 'They're hysterical – bring them back.' They would not have been booked by Wood if they had not brought a distinctive comic flavour to the enterprise, but it is easy to see them also as part of that *demi-monde* of hangers-on that stars tend to attract. Le Mesurier was also part of a Hancock inner circle, although his performances never conveyed that he was there on anything but merit. All these names played different roles from time to time in a way that would not work in a drama or comedy series today: the possibility of encountering the same highly recognisable actor from one show to the next would be merely confusing.

The most triumphant piece of new casting was the decision to give the occasional role of Hancock's ghastly charwoman to Patricia Hayes. Wood went about the task in an almost reverential way, addressing the actress like an archbishop bestowing alms: 'A great honour is going to be bestowed upon you, Miss Hayes. You are going to play Mrs Crevatte. She has only ever been mentioned before – nobody has ever set eyes on her – you will create this person.' According to Alan Simpson, Tony himself came up with the name: 'Where he got it from, I don't know. It could well have been the name of a landlady he came across once.' In later life Hayes recalled visits in childhood to see the doyenne of low comedy Nellie Wallace in music hall. A little of her brassy vulgarity must have rubbed off on the characterisation, but essentially her prime motivation was the bad grace with which she set about the no-nonsense task of administering to the household needs of Hancock and James. It seems impossible to accept that she appeared as the termagant in only four episodes of the television show, a statistic distorted by her inclusion in three other minor parts before then and the magnificent revival of her partnership with Hancock as the charlady in the long series of egg commercials several years later. With her coarse cockney accent and air of utter contempt, she provided the perfect counterbalance to Hancock's aspirations to a more elegant lifestyle. When he admonishes Sid for upsetting her, because of the difficulty of getting the staff for 'below stairs', she snaps back like a whip, 'Don't you call me "staff". One hour a week I come in here. And you have enough trouble finding the three-and-six for that.' Her most memorable moment came when she resorted to voodoo to cure Hancock of his infamous cold, gesticulating with her arms and chanting all the while: 'Fever, fever, hear me shout. Ague, ague, come on out.' At first he feels he is getting better, until the coughing starts and she grabs an aerosol spray to disinfect the air: 'Get out! You fraud! … You don't even believe it yourself … you're a charlatan, madam.'

The radio series had been so effective that, as the novelist Anthony Burgess observed, part of its power was that you imagined you had seen what you had heard. The designer, Roy Oxley, ensured that the living room of 23 Railway Cuttings materialised in all its dismal shabbiness. You were never entirely sure whether it was on the first or ground floor, in which specific direction this door or that door led, or whether the house itself was semi-detached or part of a terrace. As far as Galton and Simpson were concerned consistency was no more important in television than it had been on radio. Described by its incumbent in one episode as 'that wallpapered damp rabbit hutch', the residence came nearest to monumental status when, after some stealthy behind-the-scenes scribbling on the walls by Sid, Hancock becomes convinced that Lord Byron was a past occupant. No sooner has he presented his case for a grant for repairs to the National Trust than his imagination takes flight in the decorative direction he truly craves: 'I think Rococo with a slight Byzantine influence – veering towards the classic Georgian style with half a dozen flying ducks on the wall.' Frequently episodes would take place away from Railway Cuttings, but, as with the radio series, the abode would gradually become the hub of his world, the focal point of both his aspirations and his disappointments.

Hancock's Half Hour arrived on television on the Friday evening of 6 July 1956. The second and third series would be scheduled on Monday evenings, but otherwise Friday night remained traditionally Hancock night throughout his BBC career. The first episode, of which only the script survives, shows the writers trying to be more visual than, as they eventually learned, they needed to be. Ironically, it might have worked better in radio. In *The First TV Show* Galton and Simpson created their own version of a hall of mirrors again, beginning with a couple settling down to watch the show in their living room. They switch on the set and the announcer in vision introduces the first show of the new series. When Hancock appears the couple begin to criticise the star, who can hear them. In an attempt to ingratiate himself he launches into impressions of Arthur Askey, Norman Wisdom and Terry-Thomas as the couple start to compare him with each of them in turn. As Hancock's anger increases, we are educated to the cost of a television licence in those days:

HUSBAND: Not my cup of tea at all – we pay three guineas a year for that.
WIFE: I can't understand it. I heard he was alright on the radio.

Tony can take no more. He stalks out of shot, bursts into the room and smashes the set. He is next seen in hospital with his leg in plaster. He had no idea the husband was a heavyweight wrestler. However, Sid insists that the show must go on and the television cameras are brought to Hancock's bedside. The mere idea of Hancock taking part against his wishes in a sketch about Lord Nelson complete with hat, eye-patch and full scenic effects from his hospital bed seems visually strained. The transmission within a transmission is brought to a halt by the intrusion of the nurse, played by Irene Handl, who insists that visiting time is over. Hancock is given a sleeping pill, only to wake up hours later under delusions that he is still playing Nelson.

It was an ambitious undertaking for a first live show, with Sid cleverly deployed in conversation with the announcer and through the screen with the actual viewer to cover the interludes needed to get Hancock from one side of the studio to the other. The BBC Audience Research Department estimated that the programme was watched by approximately 6 million viewers, namely 16 per cent of the adult population of the country, equivalent to 36 per cent of the potential television audience at the time. Reaction was divided, the most astute comment on the viewing panel coming from an anonymous clerk who declared, 'Not a very impressive start, but given time to settle down – and rather better material – Tony Hancock and his gang should improve. I should say this looks distinctly promising.' A less insightful viewer wrote, 'Adult mentality is surely above this sort of rubbish. Senseless bilge from beginning to end.' One can almost hear the voice of Snide.

In spite of the keenness of the radio establishment that the writers should not resort to adapting radio scripts or plotlines for television, the guideline had to be relaxed at the end of the first series when the Suez crisis rendered a script entitled *The Diplomat* too sensitive for transmission. In this Hancock, plying the trade of a window cleaner for the sake of the plot, becomes privy to the secrets of a foreign embassy. Galton and Simpson had already left on a well-earned holiday and Duncan Wood called upon Johnny Speight, later to become synonymous with *Till Death Us Do Part*, to go through the radio scripts and rework something that was appropriate. In this way the episode known as *The Chef that Died of Shame* achieved a visual outing. Possibly no one had noticed that two shows earlier, the episode known as *The Bequest*, in which Hancock is left a fortune by his uncle on condition he finds a bride, had been a revamp of a radio episode from the year before. The floodgates were open, and many devices would subsequently recur. In the radio show *The Sheikh*, Hancock, fixated on the idea of a film career, signed up to make a film with Sid as director, only to discover that he was shooting with a baby box camera. When he queried the use of separate photographs, Sid explained, 'Yes – then we stick 'em all together, punch little holes along the edges and Bob's your uncle!' Almost five years later the same device was used in the opening television show of the fourth series, *Ericson the Viking*. Sid has persuaded Hancock to enter the prolific area of historical adventure films, but his shooting technique has not advanced at all, although viewers did have the advantage of seeing Hancock put through the hilarious paces of stop-frame animation technique. 'Good boy,' directs Sid. 'Next shot – left arm down a bit, right leg up a bit, hold it – shoot it – got it?' Plots based on emigration, poison-pen letters and returning home from holidays were also worked in different ways in each medium. The seed for the television show *The Cold* must have been planted by the festive misery of Hancock's attack of the flu at the end of the 1958 radio Christmas special. The radio show where Tony and Sid accredit spurious historical detail to their house and furniture to impress the influx of American forces in town – 'that spring's been sticking out of that chair since Oliver Cromwell sat in it with his armour on' – contains the first inkling of *Lord Byron Lived Here*. Sometimes a radio theme provided double service in this regard. On radio when Hancock is first excluded from the New Year's Honours List he enrols with 'Sid James, Gent Maker' for lessons in social etiquette; on television the same letdown leads him to pursue a career as a serious thespian, while the device of social self-improvement is saved for a second episode which turns upon his complete lack of success with the opposite sex. According to Galton and Simpson conscious self-plagiarism was not the issue here. As Ray has explained, for the first time in their career they were having to accommodate the demands of other departments: 'We were writing to strict deadlines to allow time for such things as scenery to be built, so we may have been running behind … it was only ever a last resort.'

For all concerned the learning curve of the new medium was a steep one. The early standard was inconsistent. One episode that survives from the third series, entitled *How to Win Money and Influence People*, has Hancock winning a newspaper competition, the prize of which is a date with Jayne Mansfield. The ending smacks of desperation when the sex symbol can't turn up and Sid – 'Well, you wanted a film star and you got one!' – is hired as a replacement at the last moment. There are other shows that Hancock would probably have best forgotten for technical reasons. The catastrophe that befell the live transmission of *There's an Airfield at the Bottom of My Garden* towards the end of the third series has passed into television folklore. Perhaps the most glaring inconsistency in the matter of Hancock's East Cheam address was that suddenly it found itself at the end of the main runway of a major airport. The writers took their inspiration from the fact that at the time Hancock's brother, Roger, lived in close proximity to Heathrow. As Roger remembers, 'Latterly when Concorde started it used to go one hundred feet above the house and all the windows rattled. You had no choice but to get used to the noise and apparently visitors told us that when a plane came over we used to stop speaking and when it had gone we started talking again, but we didn't hear it. We just blocked the noise out.' Philip Oakes recalled how Hancock, when describing a fraternal visit, would gleefully mime the family at the dinner table, all hands making a grab for the plates and cutlery that ran the risk of being swept away in the slipstream as a plane took off. To carry exaggeration even further Galton and Simpson sat down and wrote a script in which Hancock's house – in effect a new purchase from Sid – would fall apart at a climactic moment. For four disastrous minutes Hancock had all his professional reserves tested as the scenery disintegrated several pages ahead of requirements. A mantelpiece falls apart from the wall and a table collapses. When Hancock sets the table upright, he anchors himself to it to prevent it falling again. When the time comes for it to collapse in accord with the script, Hancock has to kick it before it will budge. When it does so, to tell from the expression on his face, it hurts his foot. Meanwhile Duncan Wood has abandoned his camera script and is shooting the show on a wing and a prayer. In the years to come the comedian would relish describing the chain of events, capping his tale with the line, 'and as I stood there, my braces broke – that was another little novelty'. For all the good humour and professionalism Hancock displayed throughout the incident, ad-libbing in a controlled way and restraining his hysteria as much as he could, the episode proved nerve-racking enough to point the way forward for both producer and star.

On 31 December 1957 the producer addressed a memo to his superiors reflecting on the strengths and weaknesses of the recently concluded third series, in which he drew attention to an attack of Asian flu suffered by Hancock during the run, when an episode had been postponed to be replaced by a repeat broadcast of the telerecording of *The Alpine Holiday*. At this early stage in his career the disease was not a euphemism for a drinking cure, although wrapped up in it were the elements of depression on the part of the star brought about by the constant strain of the television project, aggravated by the need to learn a new script weekly, a discipline not required in radio. Wood's words concede that his star is 'a highly nervous and, to a degree, temperamental artist' and voice the opinion that without the enforced week's break, which he regarded as a 'blessing in disguise', the later shows in the series would have suffered. The producer was able to use the situation to secure a tentative move towards recording four shows in advance, which could then be slotted into the next run of thirteen shows at four-weekly intervals and provide them with a stand-by show into the bargain. The pattern would not eradicate the uncertainty that befell the *Airfield* episode, but would provide a step in a more secure direction and presumably enable them to stage technically more adventurous shows during the advance period. Wood won the full go-ahead to implement his four-show advance plan for the fourth series, which would begin transmission on 26 December 1958, although his suggested transmission pattern went by the wayside when all four were transmitted at the start of the series, allowing Hancock a three-week Christmas/New Year gap before commencing rehearsals for the remaining nine recordings. The switch from telerecording – at its most basic the filming onto celluloid of a television screen – to video recording onto magnetic tape had occurred during 1958. It is indicative of Hancock's standing and Wood's persuasive powers that a mere entertainment programme should be granted this revolutionary new facility in November 1958, when the first

Ampex machine had been installed in Lime Grove only the month before.

Although picture quality had improved with the new system, the shows were still recorded in real time with no editing possible. If something catastrophic occurred, the decision had quite simply to be made whether to start again. This did not ease the pressure of fluffing lines, which had always been Hancock's worst nightmare. In one episode 'Who's been messing about with me concrete toadstools?' came out as 'Who's been messing about with me cardboard nutmegs?' This was highly entertaining for the audience, but grossly offensive to Hancock's professional pride. Although the Ampex process was akin to recording sound onto magnetic tape, technical reasons – something to do with the incompatibility between cuts and synchronising pulses – had led to the assumption that unlike sound tape video tape could not be satisfactorily edited. Wood challenged the notion by rolling up his sleeves and spending a day in an editing suite cutting the dance sequences out of a Stanley Baxter sketch show so that the Scotsman's humour was able to flow continuously during a much-shortened programme. In this way he proved his point that *Hancock's Half Hour* could be recorded in segments of between five and eight minutes' duration, allowing for lighting adjustments, scenery shifts, costume changes and camera moves that did not hold up the action and obviating the need for cardboard captions, tedious bridging dialogue and extraneous library film to cover delays. Moreover, in the event of a *faux pas*, only the individual segment would need to be re-recorded. He was supported in his endeavours by Hancock, who threatened not to sign a contract for a new series if the new process were not given a chance. By the time the fifth series of ten shows began in September 1959, Hancock and Wood had not only won the battle for all their shows to be pre-recorded, but in the discontinuous fashion that allowed greater opportunity for retakes. It was perhaps ironic that the first programme to be edited in such a fashion was called *The Economy Drive*: the cost of the process would have been prohibitive for a lesser show, with tapes costing £100 a time and, at a time when one tape would be used several times over, unable to be used again once cut. Within a few years the basic technique established by Wood and Hancock was commonplace in television comedy and remains viable for recording such a show to this day. It all seems so obvious now, but back in that pioneering age it must have felt like making a telephone call for the Victorians.

The investment had been sound. *The Economy Drive* marked a turning point in the quality of the show and enabled Hancock and Wood to feel they had vindicated themselves following an earlier internal BBC memo addressed jointly to the Controller of Programmes and the Head of Light Entertainment from Cecil McGivern, the Deputy Director of Television Broadcasting. This was all the more surprising in the light of the show's undoubted success. It was dated 1 April 1959, but was not a joke, and contained all the edgy concern of an executive in fear of his job. Having grumbled about the rising costs of the star and his writers, he added, 'In my opinion, the production (as opposed to the content) is far too slow … this production must be quickened up and the writers should be told this.' It continued, 'Live television need not be *so* far behind the speed of Bilko.' It is unlikely that McGivern would have understood where the solution lay. There can be no question that the fight for standards – both technical and artistic – by Hancock, his producer and his writers was relentless. Maybe the schoolroom climate kept them on their toes.

It could be said that Hancock, fully aware of what Wood was achieving on his behalf, had pre-empted any criticisms in the article, 'Problems of a Funny Man', which he contributed to the *Television Annual* for 1958, an Odhams Press Publication edited by the journalist Kenneth Baily. In this he wrote:

> If the programme does not click on the night, though it may have been effective at rehearsal, well – the opportunity to go back and make it click has gone for ever. For this reason I favour the

pre-filming of comedy shows. Immediately one says this, one raises that criticism of television using 'canned' shows as though these were somehow second-hand. Given that filmed vision and film-recorded sound are technically as good as live vision and sound, I think only one element is lost in a pre-filmed show. This is the sense the viewer feels that the thing is actually happening, there and then at that moment. I don't think we have really found out if this is so valuable an element as to outweigh the advantages of pre-filming. The main advantage to the comedy show is that the players are not dependent on the single moment of performance on the night. If a strived-for effect does not come off properly in filming, you can re-shoot. You can also revise by editing – taking bits out or putting second thoughts in. So take me 'canned'. I think you will get a better return for your viewing time and licence money!

Hancock would not win all his struggles. What he really wanted was the facility that came even closer to film technique, whereby he could record a show in even shorter takes – almost one shot at a time – without an audience; the laughter would be added when the assembled whole was played back to an audience at a later date. He saw this as the only way he could hope to be 100 per cent word perfect. As Roger Wilmut has pointed out, had he achieved this the programmes would have lost the spontaneity they derived from the more natural delivery that came from not being entirely script-bound. Duncan Wood, apart from seeing the downside from the point of view of facilities and finance, also knew the ambition was flawed artistically: 'If you play something in front of an audience it gives you a kick, and it lifts you, and your timing goes along – and I always thought Tony was better at timing in front of an audience than without one.' Hancock even called his own meeting with Equity where he proposed they give the BBC special dispensation in the matter, but the actors' union was no happier than the BBC with a plan that necessitated eight hours to record one episode instead of the usual ninety minutes maximum. A month before the start of recording for the sixth series, Hancock was mollified by Tom Sloan, the Assistant Head of Light Entertainment, who explained the complications as far as facilities and, inevitably, the Musicians' Union were concerned. The star accepted these points and expressed the wish that negotiations should continue with Equity, while agreeing that any agreement costed at film rates would be out of the question. Sloan listened and was happy to provide lip service on the matter.

In the early days the rocky road of technical progress may have contributed to a myth that Hancock was not as good on the box as on the wireless. In fact, his visual skills were made for television. Another advantage of the technical changes meant that with increased camera mobility more cameras could be used to cover a scene, allowing greater scope for close-ups and further opportunities for the comedian to exploit facially. Sid James, with his cinematic background and a constant eye on the monitors, spurred Tony on in this regard, nudging him when to suggest a close-up here or there. The part Sid played in the dealing of the reaction shot as the trump card in Hancock's hand can never be underestimated. He also understood how mannerisms had to be brought down for television, rather than exaggerated as for the stage. In a sequence in *Twelve Angry Men* Galton and Simpson parodied the relationship between them, with Sid prodding Tony as foreman of the jury when the judge's patience is beginning to snap at Hancock's frivolity and lack of decorum:

SID: You're not going to take that, are you? He shouldn't make you look a
    Charlie in front of everybody. Go on, tell him.
TONY: Melud, I would remind you I am the foreman of this jury and as such
    you shouldn't make me look a Charlie in front of everybody.
JUDGE: Mr Foreman, I would remind you I am the judge in this courtroom
    and as such I can replace you with somebody I regard as more
    competent.

SID: Tell him he can't talk to you like that.

TONY: My friend says you can't talk to me like that.

The director soon cottoned on to what was happening. 'Sid's at it again down there,' he'd chuckle up in the gallery, but was more than happy to indulge his star, even if it did appreciably increase the number of camera shots in the script. According to the producer, 'suddenly you had to work at twice the capacity on camera routines, and this put pressure on the crews, and on everyone'. Wood recognised the insight into human behaviour that Hancock could convey with the tightening of a single facial muscle, the most fleeting of glances, the slightest glimmer of a grin: 'When you went into a close-up on camera, you could see his mind working before he uttered the next sentence ... the laugh would frequently come on the close-up before he said the line. You could see it running through his mind – "This man's a bloody idiot and I'm gonna tell him so" – it's a marvellous ability to have.' Wood and the writers came to realise that when they could leave matters of plot initiation to Sid or the other characters, enabling Tony to react accordingly, they were doubling his appeal. Hancock later admitted to Philip Oakes that 'the biggest battle I ever won was to do comedy in close-up'. On the occasion of his awkward encounter with Kenneth Williams in Maggie Smith's dressing room several years later he was still fighting the cause: 'Just keep a camera on a man's face for ten minutes if necessary, because that's what life is.'

Nowhere was Hancock's ability to register thought, to convey laughter telepathically, seen to greater effect than in the episode called *The Reunion Party*, in which none of his old service colleagues live up to his recollection of them. At one moment he tries unsuccessfully to remember someone's name. For something like forty-five seconds the expressions ebb across his face like waves as his thoughts shift between confusion, disappointment, embarrassment, concern, inspiration, failure, apology, tip-of-the-tongue frustration and finger-clicking self-prompting. Such a sequence could not be written for him. The only instruction carried by the script was, 'Tony spends some time trying to remember the man's name, hitting his head with his hand, etc. Several times he seems to have it just on the tip of his tongue, only to lose it again. Finally he gives up.' The process was instinctive. This did not render the facial versatility needed to achieve it any the less staggering. In a television interview with Michael Dean as late as 1965 he explained the difficulty he had when photographers asked him to 'do the face': 'I honestly don't know what they mean … you should be so immersed in the scene, you don't know about faces, you don't pull faces. It either happens or it doesn't happen … it's as simple as that and as difficult as that.' Another virtuoso display occurred in the show where Sid bashfully admits to his chum that he is in love. Hancock's initial straight face – he has promised not to laugh – slowly disintegrates. First the eyebrows quiver, then the throat gulps. The lips are taut with difficulty, at odds with the smile that his eyes say is anxious to break through. Gradually his whole expression explodes into one of mirthful incredulity, and a mixture of ridicule and glee take over. Full-throated, open-mouthed laughter is the only outlet for his incredulity, '*You* in *love*? Oh dear!' Every show has a similar highlight, even if merely the 'How dare you?' glower to a sensitive question – 'Have you any physical peculiarities?' – or the moment of 'Stone me!' desperation when his world crumbles around him.

The writers and star soon discovered that television with its more matter-of-fact, self-explanatory approach helped the move to realism in comedy to which they aspired. The bizarre plots that radio handled so effortlessly – *vide*, perversely, the Lord Nelson escapade of the first television show – fell by the wayside. The new naturalism came to the fore as the fourth series progressed, significantly in the wake of the success on radio of *Sunday Afternoon at Home*. A common chord of observational humour united the national audience as many of the plots became identifiable with people's lives. The titles of episodes like *The Set That Failed, The New Nose, The Economy Drive, The Train Journey, Football Pools, The Big Night, The Cold* and *The Missing Page* told their own story. Jokes were discouraged even more stringently than on radio unless they underlined character, as at that moment on *The Train Journey* when Hancock's obstreperousness could not restrain him from passing comment on the general, the doctor and the vicar sharing the carriage with him: 'Well, we've got the lot in now. One kills them, one cures them and one buries them!' Paradoxically, conversation for its own sake seemed ideal for the new medium. Talking heads were used to convey the banality of ordinary, but credible speech, especially in the exchanges Hancock struck up with Hugh Lloyd, as at *The Reunion Party*:

TONY: Well, it's been a long time.

HUGH: Yes. Certainly has.

TONY: Yes, it certainly has. Been a long time. Fifteen years. Yes, that's a long time all right.

HUGH: Yes, a long time.

TONY: Yes.

One might have supposed that the comedy of boredom would not work as well on television as on radio. In fact, by the time of Hancock's last series for the BBC without Sid James, it had become a sustaining motif.

Wood ran a happy ship, but the demands of television meant that he had a more exacting task than Dennis Main Wilson, who came into working contact with his cast on Sundays alone. Alan Simpson painted the distinction vividly: 'For radio an overcoated gentleman – that's Tony – sits in the front row of stalls at a theatre. There are two half-hearted script-readings before a rehearsal on the mike, where the producer "whips up" things for the sake of timing. Then a "quick one" before the show, which is always the best reading of the lot. But at a television rehearsal you can't be so haphazard, and whereas a radio rehearsal takes about two hours, for television we want five days!' Hancock was always anxious to emphasise that the show was a matter of teamwork: 'No one person has the final word. Even our producer Duncan Wood does not force a point if he feels that others on the team do not agree.' Wood was able to compare the working methods of his two stars. Whereas Hancock – admittedly with the bigger part – needed all those five days to master his script, Sid was on top of his performance in two. In the words of Hugh Lloyd, 'Sid was the street-wise realist, while Tony was the dreamer,' and not just on screen. Their favoured rehearsal room at the Sulgrave Boys' Club in Goldhawk Road, West London, came replete with snooker and ping-pong tables. Sid described a typical day that began with coffee at 10.30, followed by a quick game of snooker and then two hours of rehearsals. A lunch break of a couple of hours would be followed by a round of table tennis and then another couple of hours of rehearsal. 'By this time,' said James, 'the boys of the youth club were starting to gather. He'd say, "Can we go over that one again, Sid?" and I'd say, "It's time to go home," and Duncan would look up to God [as if] to say, "Oh, for heaven's sake, when are we gonna get rid of this fellow?"' The show *would* fall into place, but not before a nervous Hancock would express the view, 'I get the feeling we haven't rehearsed this this week.' Hancock's delaying tactics were an inescapable part of his psychological drive and it fell upon James to play the tower of strength that rallied round, however nervous Sid might have been feeling himself – inside.

However, according to Beryl Vertue, his representative from those days, Hancock's dedication and concentration were colossal: 'On the day when he was doing a show, you didn't really speak to him. There was almost like a little cocoon around him.' During the course of a television series he would cut himself off from all social life and all other potential working engagements. Once Sid, reminded by his wife Valerie, went up to Tony at rehearsals to wish him a happy birthday. Hancock looked blank. He had no idea of the day. He was alert, however, to the performances of others and found time to give credit when it was due. Alec Bregonzi recalled the moment when he approached him with the suggestion of how to play a line: 'He said if you pause here, you won't get a laugh, but you might get a giggle. He was all for you, whereas so many comics just won't let anybody else in.' Warren Mitchell encountered a similar generosity on only the second live television show when Hancock dried in his presence. Mitchell, playing an art dealer in one of his speciality foreign accents, took the initiative and said, 'Mister Hancock, a word in your ear.' 'What?' exclaimed Hancock. 'A word in your ear,' he repeated. Warren fed him his cue and the rest was plain sailing. 'You're in, mate,' exclaimed the star afterwards. 'Anyone who can prompt me live!' He expressed his gratitude by ensuring that Mitchell, still to become a star himself, continued to appear at regular intervals in those early days. The actor recalled that he would make many suggestions to Hancock, not all of which he liked: 'But he loved you to add anything of value to the show. He wasn't the least bit selfish. He wanted the show to be a success.'

The pressure continued regardless. The first two series were transmitted live on a fortnightly basis, but from the start of the third, a run of twelve shows, the weekly schedule kicked in. Days off were mostly spent learning lines, before the inexorable cycle started turning again. Alcohol offered some relaxation, and fortunately throughout his BBC career Tony reserved his drinking for after hours. Sheer physical fatigue, however, resulted, to this writer's knowledge, in two further breaks in the recording routine during the last three series of *Hancock's Half Hour* on television. During February 1959 the ninth programme of the fourth series due to be transmitted live had to be postponed and replaced with a repeat, courtesy of the Ampex recording, of *The Set That Failed*. During October 1959 the recording of *The Cruise* halfway through the fifth series was pushed back by a week, although viewers would have been oblivious of a hiccup since there were now sufficient shows pre-recorded to cover the gap. Upon his return from the nursing home on the second occasion he entertained the journalist Elizabeth Few at his home: 'I was doing my nut. Got a bit strained. Couldn't remember my lines. So I thought, "Hancock's going into bed for a week while the going's good." I was doped. Had a marvellous sleep. Like a comatose toad, you know.' The interview ended on a morbid note: 'Half an hour after it was decided I should go into the nursing home someone rang up to say they had heard I was dead. Me? Dead!' For the moment, nervous strain or no, he was indestructible.

The series went from one high to another, a jewel in the BBC's television crown. Although only six episodes survive from the twenty-four shows that comprise the first three series, all thirty-three episodes of the last three seasons are now digitally secure for posterity. The gradual improvement they reveal in terms of quality, both artistically and technically, is outstanding. This was matched in audience terms. From an average 6.1 million viewers for the first series in 1956, the audience, with one slight blip, achieved an upward graph of 6.8, 8.2, 7.9, 9.9 and 10.9 million viewers on average per episode through the next five seasons. At the end of the fifth series Hancock was garlanded with plaudits like some emperor triumphant. In a memo to Tom Sloan dated 24 November 1959, Eric Maschwitz, the new Head of Light Entertainment, emphasised to his deputy, 'We must not at any cost let Hancock go.' Had it not been part of the strategy to retain his services, it might have seemed rash for Kenneth Adam, the Controller of Programmes, to enthuse, 'We all think that this was without doubt the finest you have done, and though we know the standard you are setting is very high indeed, we are confident that the next one will be even better.' With episodes of the standard of *The Cold*, *The Missing Page* and *Sid in Love* still ahead of them, the team delivered. Hancock was well rewarded for his day. With help from Wood, Hancock had broken the technical barrier; he now broke the financial barrier too, becoming the first entertainer to be paid the Utopian target figure of £1,000 a show on a regular basis. This amount, which represented his remuneration for each of the twenty shows that comprised the last two series, entailed an increase of 100 per cent over his fee for the first series. The latter had climbed slightly to £550 for the second and then leapt to £750 for the two interim series. Repeat fees calculated at 50 per cent of his basic fee and, thanks again to the Ampex process, the income from overseas sales – most notably to Commonwealth territories with their large expatriate population – boosted his earnings still further. However, in spite of all the persuasive techniques the BBC had at its disposal, throughout the period of his greatest success Hancock resisted the blandishment of a long-term contract. With his eye on cinematic success, he wanted to keep his options open, although – without necessarily putting his hand on his heart – he assured Sloan and his colleagues that he had no intention of working in independent television.

The audience figures in the previous paragraph are based on the findings of the BBC's own Audience Research Department. It has been estimated that by the time of the last television transmission of *Hancock's Half Hour* in May 1960 around 80 per cent of the population had television in their homes. Obviously the potential audience for Hancock had been growing as the medium came to dominate the nation's social habits. As this happened, competition for the BBC increased with the gradual spread of the federal system of commercial television across the country. Having opened in the London area in the autumn of 1955, the second channel would take until September 1962 to be accessible throughout the nation. In May 1960 South West England, the Border regions, the Isle of Man, North East Scotland, the Channel Islands and North and West Wales were all still denied the commercial coverage on technical and administrative grounds. However, in the more densely populated other parts of the country, ITV, as it would become known, had already established a lead in popular entertainment programming. It was often said of Hancock that when he was on air on Friday nights the pubs and streets would be empty. This may well have been the case, but the situation had as much to do with what was 'on the other side' as with the lad himself.

At first the BBC and Hancock would have lost out only in the few regions where commercial television was available, but by 1960 the mathematics were such that the discrepancy was enough to cause concern among executives who had to concede the bizarre situation whereby at the height of its popularity the funniest show produced in this country was losing out in the overall ratings to lesser comic opposition. The BBC might have been dismissive of the TAM (Television Audience Measurement) figures compiled on behalf of its new upstart rival – only in 1964 with the establishment of JICTAR (Joint Industry Committee for Television Advertising Research) did the squabbling begin to subside – but when their own findings showed similar results there was inevitable consternation. The methods of measuring audience sizes have always been somewhat arcane. Although both broadcasters used test samples based upon a form of arbitrary selection, matters were not helped by the commercial habit of estimating figures in terms of households and not individuals. The Deputy Director of Television Broadcasting sounded a warning note in that memo of 1 April 1959 when he said, 'for the amount we are now paying [Hancock and his writers], we must extract the maximum in content, in placing and in size of audience figures'. A few weeks into the sixth series on 4 April 1960, Eric Maschwitz fired off a salvo in the direction of the Head of Programme Planning that Hancock was being beaten by *The Army Game*: 'I know all the difficulties, but do hope that this sort of situation can be avoided in the future.' Sloppy scheduling seems to have been the evil for some time.

When the show returned with the *Ericson the Viking* episode for the start of the fourth series on Boxing Day 1958, its 8.7 million audience accounted for 23 per cent of the adult population. However, Hancock was watched by only 22 per cent of those capable of receiving both stations, as distinct from the 35 per cent who tuned into the game show, *Take Your Pick*, which overlapped the first half of *Hancock's Half Hour*, and the 41 per cent that watched *The Army Game*, which coincided with the second half. In the show Hancock even made a sly nod at the opposition. As he surveys his troops marshalled for the benefit of Sid's cameras, he moans, 'Look at 'em – fearless pagans from the frozen north. All you need is Bernard Bresslaw and you've got another *Army Game* here. I'm turning it in now.' Bresslaw had been the major star to emerge from the early success of the Granada Television services farce. Three weeks later Hancock was moved to 7.30, out of the firing line of the conscript comedy, only to find itself against the most popular soap opera of the day, *Emergency Ward Ten*. Hancock's figures remained consistent regardless. However, from the fourth show of the fifth series it was scheduled head to head with *The Army Game* in the 8.30 slot. ITV's stranglehold was tightened when from week six the start of the commercial show was edged forward by five minutes, while the commencement of another massive success, *Gun Law*, was brought forward to 8.55, five minutes before Hancock was due to finish. *The Army Game* already had the massive advantage of the mass audience built up by *Emergency Ward Ten* and *Take Your Pick* during the early evening. The sixth series saw the pattern replicated. For the last three episodes Hancock was shifted again to the hospital slot at 7.30. If this was in response to the Maschwitz memo, it seems a heedless move. According to the BBC's own figures Hancock dropped around 2 million viewers as a result.

By 1960 ITV was publishing the Top Ten based on its own TAM ratings. This prompted a comment from the 'In Vision' columnist in the *Stage* newspaper on 8 January 1959: 'It always seems strange to me why some of the BBC programmes never seem to get into the Top Ten. Whether you believe in ratings or not, it is most odd why at least one or two shows, which are obviously better than anything ITV puts on, never figure in the most popular programmes of the week.' He cited not only *Hancock's Half Hour* but also the successful sci-fi serial *Quatermass and the Pit*, as examples. Between 1957 and 1961 the Granada show never figured lower than sixth in the yearly Top Ten rated programmes prepared by TAM for ITV. No BBC shows appeared at all, although the evidence shows that while Hancock was on air he did have the power to divide the audience and keep the opposition out of the weekly Top Ten. He could derive additional solace from the fact that almost certainly the majority of those watching ITV would have been doing do so out of habit. In Hancock's favour was the appointment factor, subscribed to by people who would not otherwise have been watching at all, but made a note in their diaries not to miss his show on a Friday night. Even so, it must have been dispiriting that the programme planners at the BBC could not have been more flexible in their efforts. Everyone engaged on the rival show looked up to his talents. According to Alec Bregonzi, on the days when Hancock found himself matched against *Emergency Ward Ten* the *Army Game* cast would gather round to watch the Master before their own live transmission an hour later. In another irony, Bill Fraser, immortalised on the rival show as Sergeant Major Claude Snudge, had been a stalwart of several early episodes of the Hancock television programme, while one of the major writing forces behind the Granada show was Hancock's old friend Larry Stephens. Mario Fabrizi would become a regular for the last two series when the BBC show came to its end.

The pressure of ratings was one further element in the desire to keep standards high, expressed by Hancock in his rejection of several of the scripts Galton and Simpson offered him. An *Observer* profile in 1960 commented that his writers never gave him too long to read a script for fear he'd turn against it: 'At the start of a series he usually rejects one or two.' In radio, as we have seen, there was seldom time for this, but television with its need for a greater preparation period worked against it. Excluding *The Diplomat*, of the seven rejected episodes that linger in the writers' files it may be significant that three had already been adapted to camera scripts by Duncan Wood, namely *The ITA Quiz, The Letters* and *Gambling Hancock*. The others carry the titles *The Two Parties, The Girl Next Door, Do-It-Yourself Movies* and *Teenagers*. None of them are dated, so it is impossible at this late stage to establish a chronology, but on talking them through with Ray and Alan half a century later it is not difficult to reason why they were cast aside, and to sense that the decision was not always entirely that of the star.

They remember *The ITA Quiz* as probably falling foul of the quiz show scandals rampant on independent television around this period, although a contributing factor may have been Hancock himself, cast as the contestant, not appearing until page 8 and then never prominent until the action reverts to Railway Cuttings at page 26. The sponsors run the risk of bankruptcy if anyone wins the £164,000 prize and Sid as the quizmaster uses all his wiles to distract Hancock from his goal, resorting to filling the soundproof box with gas when everything else fails. Nothing daunted, Hancock produces a gas mask and soldiers on until, in a weak ending, he cannot spell the word, 'archaeology'. *The Letters* revolves around the return of correspondence inadvertently mislaid in a wartime sorting depot. The script would have been better suited to radio with its fantasy flashbacks triggered by the discovery first that Hancock had without his knowledge received admission into the officers' training school and then that he had just missed out on marrying into the aristocracy. Of greater concern to Hancock would have been the moment in the opening breakfast table sequence with Sid when the voice of a radio disc jockey announces the dedication of a record to 'Mrs Anthony Hancock'. The writers provide Hancock with his explanation: 'Well, they don't play records for men ... just because I don't wear slacks and a turban, that's no reason to cut me out.' In real life he expressed concern that people might read a homosexual connotation into his partnership with James, as he did with Kenneth Williams on the occasion of *The Alpine Holiday*. In the script for *The Italian Maid*, which *was* transmitted, he refuses to let Marla Landi, the actress playing the title role, do any of the work because she is so beautiful. According to Ray and Alan, even then he forced them to adapt a line addressed to Sid that went something like, 'I work my fingers to the bone and you don't appreciate a thing I do,' to convey the more basic reality that he was simply doing the housework because somebody had to.

Without question *The Girl Next Door* was discarded as too sentimental. The idea of a genuine, as distinct from caricatured, love interest cut against the grain of the image Hancock cultivated for his character, even if he would a few years later pursue the idea of properly falling in love in another television context. *Do-It-Yourself Movies* proved to be a more literal reworking of the radio episode, *The Sheikh*, with its stop-frame cinematography joke and may well have been rejected for fear of upsetting the BBC radio hierarchy; the less slavish *Ericson the Viking* was the result. *The Two Parties* was another radio retread, from *The Christmas Eve Party*, in which in Alan Ayckbourn-style two versions of Hancock's seasonal festivities are enacted for the benefit of the police, the raucous reality and the sedate smokescreen. *The Teenagers* would have presented a casting challenge, plunging Tony and Sid into youth culture in a way that was easier to achieve on radio with a show like *The Blackboard Jungle*. To have cast anything but actual teenagers for television would have been alien to realism, but it is unlikely that the comedy could have played off genuinely very young people. Any of the last four episodes could have been rejected by Duncan initially, not least because he did not advance them to camera script stage. As the producer he saw Alan's typed version before anyone else. Ray suggests that if Wood was unsure about any aspect he would not say anything to the writers. He'd send it to Tony with a note that said, 'See what you think.' With Hancock's insecurity, the very process was the cue for Tony to react disparagingly, saving Wood the embarrassment of himself having to reject something on technical or bureaucratic grounds in a way that might have rendered him weak or ineffectual in Ray and Alan's eyes. When Hancock did like a script – which was most of the time – he was overjoyed. When you take into account the vast number they wrote for him, the anger and disappointment they experienced on rejection is overshadowed by the quality of the rest. And when he was satisfied, he didn't interfere. According to Alan, he didn't tinker with dialogue or plotlines: 'He said his job was to act and our job was to write.' Ray adds that the only suggestion they ever heard from him was, 'I think we'd better move on.' He repeated the phrase several times during their association: 'He wouldn't be looking at us as he said it, always looking far off as if he was going somewhere.'

The outstanding casualty, one that *did* achieve camera script status, was the script labelled *Gambling Hancock*. Initially the focus falls on Sid's compulsion and Hancock's disgust. As the lad protests at yet another card game, Sid dismisses his pal, 'Oh, he's always the same ... he'll pass the song sheets round in a minute and get his tambourine out.' There follows an exceptionally funny sequence where Hancock *is* tempted to put his money into the game. He asks the whole table to turn away while he locates his nest egg. Having made sure they're not looking, he retrieves a key from under the wing of Polly, his stuffed eagle. He then unlocks the sideboard and takes out a box. He unlocks the box and takes out a lever. He then goes to the fireplace and dislodges a brick with the lever. This reveals a piece of paper. He goes over to the picture of Queen Victoria to reveal a wall safe. Reading the combination off the paper, he opens the safe. He reaches in and feels around. Nothing! Sid has beaten him to it. Hancock might have guessed. But there is no stopping him: 'Stop gambling? Me? I can't stop gambling. It's in my blood. I have to gamble. I can't stop myself.' Hancock takes his pal to a psychiatrist, identified in the script as John Le Mesurier. Eventually the consultant becomes more interested in Tony's neuroses, the tables turn and Hancock ends up with the addiction, losing 23 Railway Cuttings in the process. The script is funny, clever and well constructed, but was far too close for comfort in view of the real-life gambling habit of Hancock's friend and colleague, Sid James.

As an actor Sid was as adaptable as a Swiss Army knife, capable of instigating the plot or dissolving unselfishly into the background as the scripts dictated. When he had to register tedium visually, as in *The Set That Failed* – inspecting his fingernails, toying with a jigsaw puzzle, blowing imaginary dust off the table – he took disinterest to new levels of interest. Moreover, *Hancock's Half Hour* was seldom more compulsive than when a playful dynamism was at work between the pair. Hancock's look of crushing disdain was enough to put paid to most of the people who encumbered his progress through life, but, where Sid was concerned, there were twilight moments when his pal's fiddles were past worry and the camaraderie of the two men broke through on the screen without compromising the plot. In *The East Cheam Centenary* Sid's interest is aroused by Hancock's mention of the carnival lorry into which people can throw money for charity. Hancock is adamant: 'You are not driving it. It's your idea of paradise, isn't it? A load of loot and a getaway car, all in one.' Sid then threatens to stand on the corner with a megaphone shouting that Hancock's got hospital blankets on his bed, at which Tony's face bleeds from grimness to a shady attempt at innocence through which a smile seeps through. 'You wouldn't do that?' he says. One realises that beneath the surface of the plot they are playing a game, accomplices in a bigger joke defined by their friendly rivalry and their writers' preposterousness. It happens again in *The Economy Drive*. There is something approaching resignation when Hancock discovers that Sid had the telephone cut off before they went on holiday: 'You had it cut off? The one thing in the house you can leave on without it costing anything, you have cut off. *And* it costs money to have it put back on again.' At this point they have to turn away from one another for fear of corpsing. At times like these with Sid, Hancock was at his most engaging and most relaxed. In those heady days the prospect of a separation seemed unthinkable to their admirers, and yet at the time of recording *The East Cheam Centenary*, the penultimate show of the last series, Sid knew that he had only one show left to record with his friend.

Everyone will cherish their favourite episodes from the television series. Few show Hancock and Sid more equally balanced than *The Two Murderers* from the fifth season. In a stunning demonstration of comic misunderstanding the ever-susceptible Hancock presumes that Sid is intent on killing him when he sees him reading a book about perfect murders. Sid later overhears Hancock reading from the same book and supposes that his days are numbered also. Long before Galton and Simpson exploited the same device in *Steptoe and Son*, clever use is made of a split-screen technique whereby the interiors of both their bedrooms can be seen in one shot with the dividing wall between them. They enter and close their doors together. Sid heads straight for bed. Hancock, more warily, drags a blunderbuss from under the bed and sits facing the door at the ready. Sid, thinking Hancock is behaving strangely, then remembers he has forgotten to have his late-night salt beef sandwich. He gets out of bed and leaves the room. Hancock is agitated by the slamming door: 'He's off. He's on the move. He's searching for a weapon.' Apprehensively, he follows Sid to the kitchen where he peeps around the door to see him sharpening the bread knife: 'What a way to go – twelve and a half inches of cold Sheffield right across your tonsils!' Further ingenuity on the part of the writers is displayed at the breakfast table the next morning. The main part of the scene is played out in dumb show, with each performer providing a voice-over commentary on the actions of the other. Tony spots the way Sid cuts up his bacon: 'You can't use a knife like that and be normal.' Sid sees the shifty look in the other's eyes: 'He can't wait to see my lifeless body spread out all over the floor.' The incriminations continue to ricochet. 'Look at those hands – I can feel them squeezing the life out of me,' says Hancock. 'Just let him make one move and I'll have him,' retorts James. 'Go on then, one move and I'll have you,' echoes Hancock. By the end of the episode, the misunderstanding is exposed and there are declarations of trust all round, but not in sufficient time for them to cancel preventative measures already taken. Another day dawns and they go into breakfast in back-slapping mood, to discover the two heavies they have hired to taste their food seated at the table.

Galton and Simpson were never afraid to experiment with the imaginative device that could raise a routine episode onto another level. In *The Set That Failed* the two cohorts are so desperate in their craving to watch television they gatecrash a living room where a family they have never met before are so transfixed by the screen they blithely assume them to be two of their own. Hancock and Sid brilliantly merge into the wallpaper as the members of the household chatter amongst themselves – 'Dad, I got the sack today!' – and move around the room laying the table without once shifting their gaze from the television picture. The set becomes an electronic hearth in a manner that prefigured moments in *Till Death Us Do Part* and *The Royle Family* years later. It is silent comedy for a sound age, domestic comedy without the stultifying middle-class values. It also corresponds to the visual comedy of observation that Jacques Tati was making his own and to which Hancock would one day aspire. A scene in *The Economy Drive* where a hard-to-please Hancock plays an unintentional game of peek-a-boo with a waitress behind the criss-cross grid of serving hatches in a self-service restaurant carries a similar resonance. An earlier visual pun in the same episode has the authentic Tati signature. Amid the avalanche of bread that Sid has forgotten to cancel, Tony picks up a cottage loaf in one hand and a baguette in the other. 'What explanation do you have for this?' Hancock asks James. 'When's the Coronation?' cackles his sparring partner.

Hancock was on more conventional ground in *Twelve Angry Men*, which also emerged from the fifth series and was arguably the most effective single parody Galton and Simpson wrote for either medium. The pendulum of hypocrisy never swung more effectively in the cause of comedy than here. As foreman of the jury, Hancock embarks upon the challenge of persuading all the other jurors to change their guilty verdict in best Henry Fonda tradition. The tide turns when Sid cottons on to the fact that their daily expenses come to more than what he'd be earning outside. Fortuitously Tony's full-blown declaration to sway the others, which many would nominate as their favourite sweep of Hancock rhetoric, came about to a large extent as an afterthought. Duncan Wood remembered that at the first rehearsal Hancock was just getting into his stride when it seemed to stop suddenly. They rang the writers and asked whether they could write another minute and a half. Without that decision audiences might never have heard some of his most memorable lines:

> Take the case of doubting Thomas, who was sent to Coventry for looking through a keyhole at Lady Godiva. Can anybody prove he was looking at her? Can anybody prove it was he who shouted, 'Get your hair cut'? Of course not. This is sheer supposition. Does Magna Carta mean nothing to you? Did she die in vain – that brave Hungarian peasant girl who forced King John to sign the pledge at Runnymede and closed the boozers at half past ten? Is all this to be forgotten? My friends, it is not John Harrison Peabody who is on trial here today, but the fair name of British justice and I ask you to send that poor boy back to the loving arms of his poor white-haired old mother … a free man. I thank you.

All Hancock's pretensions – class, intellectual, moral – are wrapped up in those words. After this *tour de force* of mass persuasion it seems incidental, however typical, that Hancock, having pleaded on behalf of civic liberty, should waver in his own decision and swing back to a guilty verdict on the basis of protecting society. Half a century after the event there are people who cling to that memory as his finest screen moment. Others will make other choices. With help from writers of genius, a producer of stature and a craggy-faced screen partner to whom he was at once diametrically opposed and convivially aligned, no British television comedy performer has left more choices. And he still had one amazing series ahead of him, even if on the way he would make a decision that threatened to break the special bond he had created with the British public.

Chapter Nine

FACE TO FACE AND ABOUT-FACE

*'I no more got rid of Sid than
I got rid of myself.'*

When Roger Hancock was asked to identify the tipping point when his brother began the slide from conscientious professional who worked at each line of dialogue like a master craftsman to doomed obsessive set on a course of unhealthy introspection and self-destruction, he identified his 1960 appearance on the John Freeman television programme, *Face to Face*. Of the occasion he recalls, 'It was the biggest mistake he ever made. I think it all started from that really. He should never have done it. Tony was an intelligent man, but he was not an intellectual, and it gave him the impression that he was a thinker. He was very interested in where we'd all come from. He said, "You're not a bit interested in this," and I said, "No, I'm not. Just get on with the act." But he was carried away by John's intellect, thinking he was on the same plane. Self-analysis – that was his killer.' When he shifted that mind-set to his comedy the result was as disastrous as if the celebrated journalist had donned red nose and party hat to interview one of the loftier minds that comprised the staple fare of his programme. If only Hancock had taken heed of Chaplin's admission: 'I remain one and one thing only, and that is a clown. It places me on a far higher plane than any politician.' Barry

Humphries was even more down to earth when he said, 'There is no more terrible fate for a comedian than to be taken seriously.'

John Freeman's journalistic credentials were wrapped up in his links with the *New Statesman* magazine, which he went on to edit between 1961 and 1965. He had served as a junior minister under Clement Attlee in the Labour government elected in 1945, from which he resigned alongside Harold Wilson and Aneurin Bevan when Hugh Gaitskell, as Chancellor of the Exchequer, instigated prescription charges against the spirit of the National Health Service Act. He resigned from the Commons in 1955 and soon established himself as a political journalist. A distinguished later career embraced posts as High Commissioner in India between 1965 and 1968 and as Ambassador to the United States in Washington from 1969 until 1971. Adjectives like 'surgical' and 'incisive' were used to describe his interviewing style, which hid behind a veneer of relaxed charm. No extrovert seeker of the limelight himself, Freeman took self-effacement to paradoxical low-profile levels for a performer who must be regarded as a pioneer among the high-profile personality interviewers who now dominate the screen. With only the back of his head visible during the course of the interview, his approach allowed the viewer uninterrupted scrutiny of the subject. In this way the ambience of the show, with its sterile setting and concentrated lighting, conveyed something of the military intelligence chamber, something of a psychiatric session. The producer Hugh Burnett admitted years later that one of those involved in the behind-the-scenes research process had psychiatric qualifications, and there has been speculation that Freeman himself had been involved in military intelligence during the war. The interviewer himself acknowledged what he and Burnett were trying to achieve when he said, 'The camera was used almost as a secondary interrogator, capturing every flicker of an eyelid, every bead of sweat.' Playing a part in the process was the opening music from the Berlioz opera *Les Francs Juges*: no choice could have been more disarming. The programme came as close to revealing the person behind the mask of the public face as any show of its genre has ever achieved. If Hancock ever clamoured for close-ups, he had them here.

At normal times Hancock's attitude to interviews was distrustful. As a general rule he tended to be dismissive of the fourth estate, a necessary evil to be tolerated in the cause of public relations. To protect his privacy, his home was out of bounds to photographers. As he explained to the journalist Dee Remmington, 'There must be somewhere you can be absolutely private. I don't feel my private life is anyone's concern and that is why I don't like it photographed.' *Face to Face* fell into another category. In the late 1950s and early 1960s an invitation to be interviewed by Freeman outranked a knighthood. The programme was television's way of conferring its own Order of Merit on an occasional procession of major achievers in politics, philosophy, law and the arts. Hancock was the first popular entertainer to be so honoured in a roll call that had commenced with the judge Lord Birkett in February 1959 and then included among others Bertrand Russell, Dame Edith Sitwell, Carl Jung, Adlai Stevenson and King Hussein of Jordan at approximately monthly intervals. Aside from Hussein, Hancock was by far the youngest to have been invited to appear at that stage. Only the film director John Huston might be said to have represented mainstream show business so far. In the wake of the comedian came Henry Moore, Dr Hastings Banda and Augustus John. The total élite over the four years of the series amounted to as few as thirty-five notables, of whom Hancock was the twelfth. Whatever Tony thought of the matter, he had in Freddie Ross a publicity representative to whom he was becoming increasingly attached in his personal life. His inclusion would be perceived as a feather in both their caps and certainly more prestigious, say, than switching on the Oxford Street Christmas lights or appearing in the celebrity spot on *What's My Line?* It cannot be a coincidence that within five months of Hancock receiving the accolade, another of her clients would be sitting in the chair opposite Freeman. The racing driver Stirling Moss was the first of only two sports figures to be included in the series: the other was the footballer Danny Blanchflower. Hancock was the only comedian. When a slightly shortened version of the soundtrack of Freeman's interview with Hancock was issued as an LP in 1963, the interview with Stirling Moss was featured on the flip side. According to Joan Le Mesurier, Hancock was embarrassed to the end of his days that he had succumbed to Freeman's invitation, even though he liked to brag about it when he had had a lot to drink. Beryl Vertue confirms that it was wholly against type for him to let down the drawbridge on his private life in any way. He used to joke, 'Those pictures of comics in aprons in the kitchen doing the washing up have never appealed to me very much.' Had he realised he was signing a Faustian pact of a less trivial nature, he might have stayed away.

The imprimatur that the invitation placed upon his status was staggering, and one can imagine the scene that jubilant morning towards the end of 1959 when Hancock rushed into rehearsals at the Sulgrave Boys' Club to tell the news to Sid, Duncan and the rest of the gang. James was at his most back-slapping congratulatory. 'That's marvellous,' he declared to Hancock, 'but you won't do it, will you?' 'Of course not,' replied the comedian, before adding that he was simply overwhelmed just to be considered in the company of those Freeman had been interrogating through the year. But, if there existed an undertow of reality between the real Hancock and the social aspirant of Railway Cuttings, it would manifest itself before the day was out. Earlier that year in the radio episode called *The Waxwork* the lad had passed judgement on his projected inclusion in the entertainment section at Madame Tussaud's: 'Well, I don't think that's right … I'd thought I'd be in the "great men of our time" department. I'm not just a professional buffoon, you know.' By the time they had stopped for tea at the Boys' Club, Hancock was tackling Sid, 'What happens if he asks me about religion?' 'Well,' replied James, 'I wouldn't say you were an atheist because that might lose you a lot of customers.' 'Well, that's unlucky,' mused Hancock. 'I am an atheist and that's the way it is.' In his opinion *Face to Face* demanded a deeper truth than a chat with a fan magazine. Sid was far from certain: 'For God's sake, don't answer everything truthfully – you'll be right in it.' According to James, over the next few days Tony started to compile a list of questions he wanted Freeman to ask. A short while after the interview had been recorded on 28 January 1960 – for transmission between 9.30 and 10 o'clock on 7 February – he told his friend, 'You know, he didn't ask me one bloody question of the ones I'd put down.'

From a distance of almost half a century Freeman's technique *is* an object lesson of surgical probing beneath the guise of gentle persuasion, although his almost jocular opening question – 'Are you in a mood to come clean?' – tells us he is fully aware of the barrier of reserve and introspection he has to break through. Hancock, whose nerves are betrayed by the pursing of his lips, the puffing of his cheeks, and reliance on nicotine for the major part of the encounter, is focused upon being seen to tell the truth, in spite of James's advice, even if he cannot be drawn on certain matters. Today when television appears fixated on voyeurism and the trashy confessional for much of its product, it is hard to comprehend that in those days there existed doubt within the BBC top brass whether the recording should be shown at all. Although the answers to certain questions may not have fitted the general image of a 1950s' family entertainer, to the open-minded viewer Hancock would have come across as modest, self-critical and endearing, and certainly far from overbearing in the manner of his theatrical image. His stage persona – in so far as it relates to the real man – proved to be a subject of special interest to Freeman, as it is to this volume. At no point was Hancock's voice raised from conversational mode to anything approaching performance pitch.

It was suggested that some may have found his real-life intellectual pretensions and thirst for knowledge disconcerting, but, in fairness, the area went with the territory for the show. He confronted the religious question by shifting from atheism to agnosticism, admitting that he had no religion at that time. Brought up in the Church of England, he was keen to make it clear that he kept his religious options open: 'I'm deeply interested and shall we say I'm trying to find a faith, but I've had to throw away the initial faith that I was brought up in, and therefore am now starting again from scratch.' When pressed by Freeman whether there had been moments in his life when he had felt betrayed by God, he directs him to his later teen years without being specific in any way: 'I think I was fairly deeply Christian before that and it just failed. It was no longer believable.' When later in the conversation Hancock alluded to his elder brother, Colin, being killed during the war, an event which must surely have had some bearing on his decision, Freeman surprisingly did not pick him up on the matter. His relative naivety was also exposed when he referred to his subject's 'slightly unexpected names', without realising that 'Aloysius' and 'St John' were the creations of his scriptwriters.

Another sensitive area was that of children. When asked whether he would like to have them, the response was a direct 'No'. 'Why "no", I wonder?' countered Freeman. Hancock, more uncomfortable here than at any time in the interview, replied, 'I don't know. I think – I don't know, really.' When filming *The Punch and Judy Man* two years later, he admitted in an unguarded moment to the actress Sylvia Syms, 'I don't ever want children. I don't want the responsibility.' Perhaps he thought too much about the meaning behind life itself; perhaps he considered the matter from the child's point of view, acknowledging his own selfishness. The month before he died he told the Australian journalist Gareth Powell that in a moment of wickedness he once left his mother utterly confused when he announced, 'Just because you had nothing to do on a quiet day in September, here I am and I resent this very much. If there's nothing else to do you procreate a child. This is me. I'm suffering. If you planned it or thought about it – this I could understand.' George

Fairweather admitted that Tony confided to him that Cicely had become pregnant at an early stage of their relationship. Money was thin on the ground and he refused to let her proceed with the pregnancy. The abortion is verified by Cicely's sister, Doreen. Hancock attempted to rationalise the situation to his brother-in-law, Reggie, who would later become Air Marshal Sir Reginald Harland: 'He explained that he had left school with no educational qualification and that if and when audiences stopped laughing he had no means of getting any income to support the two of them.' With grim irony in the light of her father's profession, the surgical procedure – carried out clandestinely in those days – went horribly wrong and rendered Cicely unable to conceive. In spite of Syms's comments, Sir Reginald claims that Tony eventually changed his mind on the issue of children, but that when he did decide he wanted them it was no longer possible. He did once announce proudly to Syms and Philip Oakes that they were going to have a baby. 'Oh, Cicely's pregnant, is she?' Oakes asked excitedly. 'No,' replied Hancock. 'We've just decided we are going to have a baby.' It would not be the only time the writer encountered his friend's Walter Mitty streak.

The verdict must remain undecided on how effective a parent he would have been. Valerie James testifies to how nervous and uncomfortable he became in the presence of children, although the James's daughter Susan was a cherished exception. Joan Le Mesurier, whose relationship with Hancock would not begin until September 1966, maintains that he did want children of his own and was anxious to have a child by her. He even struck up a friendship with David, her son by her first husband Mark Eden, and discussed with Joan in the event of their own marriage the possibility of him carrying the Hancock name. When Joan acquiesced in principle, there were tears in his eyes. To this day David jokes about missing out on being 'Hancock's Half Heir'. He had a good rapport too with Syms's nephew, Nicholas Webb, who played the small boy in *The Punch and Judy Man*. When he overheard him saying to his aunt, 'Well, he didn't make me laugh,' Hancock knew he had found the right child for the part. They spent hours playing 'Flounder' together on the dressing-room floor. When Hancock entertained at Windsor Castle in the early 1950s, the Queen had enquired whether he had a family. 'Only that flippin' kid,' he said, turning to Archie Andrews in Peter Brough's arms beside him. Freeman tried desperately to gain some leverage from the early catchphrase, but with no success. Hancock insisted that far from representing some form of general antipathy to them, he loved 'other people's children'. The interview was at the half-way stage and this section had quite obviously been the most difficult for him. As Freeman went on to ask about Hancock's own childhood, his subject drew solace from the token glass of water at his side for the only time in the entire thirty minutes.

Only towards the end of the interview does Freeman become really insistent, when he asks whether after his first thirty-five years Hancock is happy or not. He responds by sidestepping: 'I have everything that anybody could want to make them happy, but ...' before Freeman reins him back in: 'I was going to say that the only happiness I can achieve would be to perfect the talent that I have, whatever it may be, however small it may be. That is the whole purpose of it, and that is the whole purpose of what I do.' The interview was unedited – many of the programmes were transmitted live – and may well in less persistent hands have ended there. Freeman senses that something appears to be troubling him about the world. Hancock continues in apparent honesty: 'I wouldn't expect happiness. I don't. I don't think it's possible. But I'm very fortunate to be able to work in something that I like ... and if such a time came that I found that I'd come to the end of what I could develop out of my own ability, limited however it may be, then I wouldn't want to do it any more.' At this point Freeman, while never forsaking his charm, becomes more unrelenting than at any previous point in their conversation:

FREEMAN: Tony Hancock, I wonder if you really get very much out of your
    triumphs. You've got cars that you don't drive; you've got health which
    you tell me is a bit ropy because you find …

HANCOCK: I didn't tell you that!

FREEMAN: … find it so difficult to learn your lines, you've got money that
    you can't really spend, you worry about your weight …

HANCOCK: I spend the money. I do. I enjoy it.

FREEMAN: Well, what I want to put to you as a final question is this. You
    could stop all this tomorrow if you wanted to. You're rich enough to
    coast along for the rest of your days. Now why …

HANCOCK: Money is of no account in this.

FREEMAN: Well, tell me why you go on, as a last answer.

HANCOCK: Because it absolutely fascinates me, because I love it and
    because it is my entire life.

Dennis Main Wilson came as close as anyone to summarising the
event: 'Freeman did a very good job trying to find out what made
Tony tick. Tony didn't know what made him tick either. So you
reached an impasse.' Hancock had already emphasised that his happiness was in his work. Why the host should tease any artist at the
peak of his powers about the need to carry on seems curious; it is
unlikely that he would have imposed upon John Osborne, Simone
Signoret or Albert Finney – all later subjects and similarly young
achievers in the arts – in a similar way. Perhaps Freeman thought
that the lowlier calling of the comedian could withstand a greater
flippancy. Perhaps he picked up on a sense of impending doom that
would have made a new life advisable. Not that Hancock understood
the route to any other destination than to an audience's laughter.
The general premise of the programme was enough to uphold Roger
Hancock's criticism of it; by pressing Tony at the end, Freeman was
pushing him even further towards self-questioning. Mix that with
self-identification with the great minds of the day and the cocktail
was likely to become hazardous.

Impertinent as Freeman may have seemed, his approach appears mild by today's standards. He was, though, widely criticised at the time and wrote to the *Daily Telegraph* in self-defence: 'I judged, I believe correctly, that more of Hancock's complex and fascinating personality would appear on the screen if he was kept at pretty full stretch. I hope viewers generally did not equate that with hostility. I am sure Hancock didn't.' In fact, the comedian and the diplomat-to-be, possibly united even further by the backlash, struck up a lasting friendship. In a 1963 radio interview Hancock described how he went to Freeman's home to view the transmission and stressed that he felt no embarrassment whatsoever: 'After all, we know that if you go on a programme like that, maybe some of the questions are going to be tough. Well, if so, don't go on the programme. They were tough, but good, and I was very surprised that there was this reaction and very disappointed for him, because he got the worst of the criticism.' His secretary, Lyn Took, recalls that Freeman and his wife Catherine would stay with the Hancocks at their Surrey home and when it was suggested to her that the interviewer, if only as a politician capable of playing a crowd, would have identified with the performer in Hancock, was keen to draw a distinction between them: 'John Freeman had quite a bit of the "aren't I lovely" about him, but Tony didn't have that, no, no, oh God, he didn't, no.' When Hancock's marriage to Cicely fell apart, Freeman granted Tony access to a family flat attached to his house near to Hampstead Heath. Hancock saw in his temporary landlord a helpful ally on the road to self-improvement and would defend him to the end. He stopped over in India to spend time with the Freemans *en route* to Australia on his final journey and in his last interview for *Chance* magazine allowed him to take centre stage: 'This man has such a fine mind ... and he was very good for me because he used to listen and then he'd say to me, "Some of your points are very good, but really you're talking like a student." Which is fair. I'm very fond of him ... he would make a great Prime Minister. He would indeed, without any question.'

There can be no question that the programme intensified Hancock's quest for some sort of meaning to life. His comparative lack of education became a theme of the interview, with Hancock pointing to H.G. Wells's *Outline of History* as a book that had given him a perspective on life: 'Viewing your own sort of ego and personality in terms of this vast time ... that really started me reading many other things.' Lyn Took remembers the bookshelves in the study of his Surrey home weighed down with volumes by Russell, Jung and all the other philosophers. On *Face to Face* he found himself sitting in the chair they had occupied. Here was a man who by his own jokey admission had read nothing except *Chicks' Own*, a children's comic, until he was thirty. His delusions of intellectual understanding were typified by one wall in the study that was dedicated to quotations from the likes of Kant, Hegel, Descartes and more, all jotted down in black crayon by Hancock and linked together in family-tree fashion, as if to make one definitive philosophical statement that would explain the riddle of the universe once and for all. Hancock attempted to explain it to Philip Purser: 'I'm trying to get a progression. You get some sort of evolutionary pattern which is highly connected with humour – the change-over from wearing things to keep warm to wearing things to look humorous. The evolution of the bowler hat ... just now I am interested in the Stone Age. They seemed to settle in communities and keep up with the Ogs next door, become conventional, like today.' Philip Oakes observed, 'He used to give the impression he was cramming constantly for some great philosophical argument. He wanted to be ready.'

As for the books, Oakes added that they were more handled than read, as though Hancock believed that the ideas they contained could be transmitted by osmosis rather than by actual study. Sid James recalled a visit to the intellectual section of Harrods book department where Hancock could not resist the biggest, thickest volumes what-ever their cost: 'Then he'd see something on acting written by some Russian name that not even Stanislavski's ever heard of, but he had to read this guy ... and then he'd start trying to improve my mind ... he'd get really mad at me – "For God's sake, learn a little" – and I'd say, "I know enough for what I need, Tony. I'm not going to be a professor ... is this going to improve my performance?" And he said, "It might. You never can tell. You might make a gesture this way instead of that way," and I said, "Why don't you go and tell Alec Guinness and leave me alone!"' Sid could – and did – laugh about it and, in truth, there was no harm in Hancock's aspirations to armchair academia. The danger came, as Roger Hancock saw, when the theorising became projected onto the comedy. It is an unspoken law that the more a comedian broods over his art, the more the nature of his comedy is likely to escape his understanding. Hancock would in time become its saddest casualty. He had a simpler explanation of the chart in his study for Philip Oakes: 'He used to say – with reference to comedy – "It's all there, from the first plip to the last plop," and it wasn't, of course.'

However one regards the experience of *Face to Face* from Hancock's point of view – confessional, ego-trip or unnecessary public relations exercise – the interview coincided not only with riding high on the back of his fifth television series, in which *The Economy Drive*, *Twelve Angry Men*, *The Train Journey* and *The Two Murderers* all tickled the funny bone of the nation, but also with an especially vulnerable time in his personal life, in itself enough to endorse Roger's stern reproof, 'He should never have done that programme.' On 17 November 1959, six days before the recording of the final show in the series, his stepfather, Robert Walker, had committed suicide from gas poisoning at the age of fifty-five. The cause of death was qualified by the phrase 'having taken his life while the balance of his mind was disturbed'. Unfounded allegations of Walker's philandering and the subsequent blackmail it triggered may have contributed to his decision. Walker and his wife had returned to Bournemouth after the war, where they embarked upon a series of tenancies of various pubs and hotels in the area. As news of his sexual misdemeanours filtered through to the brewery, they had been forced to move on several times. When the tragedy occurred, they had recently taken over the management of the Harbour Heights Hotel at nearby Sandbanks. In the spring of the same year the platonic distance so far maintained between Hancock and Freddie Ross had already teetered over into adultery. And if the comedian was not necessarily contemplating divorce from Cicely at this stage, he had begun to question the professional relationship that helped to define him in the eyes of the public, his partnership with Sid James. When Freeman questioned him on whether he saw the character in the Homburg hat and fur collar developing in any way, Hancock replied, 'Definitely. There are certain things I'd like to get away from now, really. They're difficult to talk about. And impossible to talk about, but gradually … you try and throw away the rubbish. I mean it accumulates all the time. You try and throw it away and come down to what is really your own personality.' He meant that Sid no longer fitted into his career plans, but with one further series of ten shows with James to complete under his BBC contract in the spring of 1960, public discretion was paramount. Eventually he would apply the same argument to Galton and Simpson, a point worthy of mention here if only because not once in the Freeman interview with its constant allusions to his scriptwriters were they mentioned by name.

It should never be forgotten that during the life of the radio show and its transition to television Galton and Simpson had been as influential as Tony, if not more so, in the decisions taken to distance 'the lad' from Andrée Melly, Bill Kerr and Hattie Jacques. Likewise Ray and Alan were themselves party to the James decision, which was being formulated at secret discussions between writers, producer and star around the very time the invitation to appear on *Face to Face* was made. No sooner had the last show in the fifth television series of *Hancock's Half Hour* been recorded on 23 November 1959 than Hancock called a formal meeting of the interested parties at his home. Sid was not included. The comedian was being courted heavily by the BBC to sign up again for another run of twenty shows to commence in the autumn of 1960. They might have done better by offering him the role of commentator at the forthcoming Rome Olympics. The proposition never received his consideration. He was rapidly losing trust in the East Cheam device. He reasoned to his producer, 'I've done everything in that room except be indecent in it. I've stood all over it. I've touched all parts of it. I've been photographed at all its angles. That room is a death cell.' His sights were set on a film career, but he stipulated that he would contemplate one further television series for the BBC on condition that he was seen to move away from the confines of the seedy suburban home and that Sid did not accompany him. The time had come to leave behind the Homburg hat and the coat with the astrakhan collar in their rickety, moth-infested wardrobe. Nor was Hancock averse to a step up the social or intellectual ladder, arguing, as he had done before, that to be seen to fall from a greater height would be funnier still. He was aiming for international recognition of some kind and argued that this would be easier to achieve within a less parochial setting. Galton and Simpson are on record that they could have gone on writing for the pair indefinitely, but have since admitted that the new dimension let new daylight into their thinking. They readily added their weight to his decision. Given the writers' separate importance to the BBC, Duncan Wood must have felt like a lackey, although even he could not have disagreed with Hancock's final argument, as expressed in a press interview three years later: 'It was going to get hackneyed ... I never wanted them to say, "It used to be good, now it's no good."'

Maybe Ray and Alan had seen it as inevitable. In their uncannily prescient way as far back as the end of the first radio series in 1955, they had written this exchange between the pair in an episode appropriately entitled *The End of the Series*:

SID: Hello, Hancock.
TONY: Hello, Sid.

SID: Good show tonight.

TONY: Yes, you did very well, Sid.

SID: Didn't I?

TONY: You got a lot of laughs, yes – they like you don't they?

SID: Mmm.

TONY: I don't think you're gonna to be in the next series.

Then it was meant as a joke, of course. In a later television episode, *Ericson the Viking*, Sid himself, contemplating his dodgy film enterprise, looks back with Hancock on the wisdom of change.

SID: I still think we did the right thing. It was time to do something
     different … you couldn't go on giving them the same thing year after
     year. It's only a matter of time before the public jellies to you. You
     couldn't build a career on *Hancock's Half Hour*, wearing a funny hat
     and a funny coat. It's not enough, kid.

TONY: Oh, that's me, is it? That's a complete assessment of my talents, is it?
     A funny hat, a funny coat, and *Hancock's Half Hour*. Thank you very
     much.

Another concern of Hancock was that the two of them were becoming as inseparable as Laurel and Hardy. The situation could not have been helped by Galton and Simpson giving him lines that conjured up echoes of Ollie's own comic petulance. In the episode *Lord Byron Lived Here* from the most recent television series Hancock turns to Sid as the fiasco of his crumbling abode gets out of hand and berates him with a version of Hardy's classic put-down: 'Another fine mess you got me in.' Away from the studio he found it irksome to find people shouting, 'Where's Sid?' as he walked down the street, trailing him like old boots behind a wedding car. According to Hugh Lloyd, similar cries greeted him when he went on stage to entertain the troops during a services tour of the Mediterranean in 1958. Stylistically Hancock and James were nothing like Laurel and

Hardy, let alone any of the stereotyped combinations of low comedian and straight man that had crowded the variety stage in its heyday. However, in another sense the couple from East Cheam *did* correspond to Stan and Ollie. For British audiences they represented the most popular comic association to come along since the little fellow from Lancashire and the big guy from Georgia hit the big time. Not even the soon-to-be-successful combination of Eric Morecambe and Ernie Wise hit the same note. Hancock and James were never billed as a conventional double act and Sid was always happy to take subsidiary billing; nevertheless the public affection extended to them both. In the case of the more traditional team, where equal billing was both traditional and *de rigueur*, there was always an imbalance of goodwill towards the one that wore the glasses. A neater analogy might be made with *The Two Ronnies* of later years, where Corbett, the stand-up comedian, and Barker, the character actor, came together, each helping the other in their contrasting discipline until a seamless whole was achieved. Sid and Tony could be said to have devised the process. Moreover, Hancock was well aware that James had his own successful film career when *Hancock's Half Hour* was not on air; Tony, forgetting his initial trade as a solo comedian, felt insecure when he had nothing else to turn to. In a similar way the BBC always seemed to find it easier to find individual projects for Barker than for Corbett in the close season of their mutual show.

From this viewpoint it must have been of some concern for Hancock that during the close season of his own show between the third and fourth series in 1958 ITV had given Sid a series of his own. *East End – West End* was a comedy drama written by Wolf Mankowitz, who in 1955 had provided the actor with one of his most memorable shady characters in the film version of his *A Kid for Two Farthings*. In an extension of his role as the diamond trader in that movie, Sid would play a street trader ducking and diving among London's Jewish community to keep out of gaol and still turn a near-to-honest profit to keep body and soul together. The BBC was disappointed by the move, explained by Sid in a letter to Tom Sloan dated 5 January 1958: 'Naturally I'm sorry too that I didn't have the chance to do the series for the BBC. Quite frankly I would have preferred to, but time was passing, I'm getting older and the money was *very* good!' He then goes on to confirm his continuing allegiance to the older show: 'Re "Hancock's Half Hour" I'd think I'd rather die than not be in it ... nobody knows better than I do that "Hancock's Half Hour" has done me the world of good.' The ITV series aired in February and March 1958 and was not renewed. Hancock was fully aware of his friend's career move. At a January reception where he was presented by Diana Dors with a 'Comedian of the Year' award on behalf of *Weekend* magazine, he happily gave a plug to Sid, who was also present. The event, covered by newsreel cameras for the cinema, gave the actor's core film public the chance to hear the lad himself joke about the matter: 'Don't forget Sidney James is starting his own series very shortly. I think it is a mistake, frankly – I don't think he'll get anywhere without me – when does it start?'

A similar vein of humour ran through a trailer recorded by them both in 1959 to help launch transmission of *Hancock's Half Hour* in Australia. After Hancock has set the scene at Railway Cuttings, he hands over to 'Mr Sidney James, my friend, agent, confidante, and owner'. Sid lowers the newspaper he's been reading and flashes his best grin at the colonial audience: 'Well, I hope you like the shows. As he told you, I'm his best friend – but if during the course of the series you find that you like me better than him, don't hesitate to write in and say so – because I'm after a show of me own.' Sid goes back to hide behind the newsprint for Hancock to make the ironic comment, 'As you will have guessed, his loyalty to me is one of the outstanding features of the series.' Eric Maschwitz, the BBC's Head of Light Entertainment and Sloan's boss, could well testify to that. In a letter dated 8 January 1959, with the recording of the fourth Hancock series in full swing, Maschwitz enquired of Sid's agent, Phyllis

Parnell, whether there was any possibility of her client being available for another situation comedy of his own in the summer of that year. By return Parnell confirmed Sid's interest but found herself stalling behind the uncertainty of his film commitments. However, two weeks later there had been a change of heart. In a further letter she pointed out that her client did not finish recording the current Hancock run until the end of March and alluded to the possibility that *Hancock's Half Hour* might reappear in the schedules (as it did) in the autumn: 'Sid does feel that with an added series in between, he may be outstaying his television welcome.' As she signed off her letter with the wish that the suggested programmes could be arranged for some future date, it is unlikely that either she or Sid could have contemplated the circumstances in which by the end of 1960 Sid was starring in his own series for BBC television.

I find it hard to believe that jealousy or spite played any part in Hancock's decision to liquidate his partnership with Sid James. The myth insists that Hancock's agenda was based on arrogance, but at that stage of his life the move represented part of a seemingly rational plan by a sensitive performer who was anxious to expand his horizons. A precedent had occurred in the late 1930s when one of his heroes, Will Hay, had stubbornly discontinued his trademark association with Moore Marriott and Graham Moffatt – the redoubtable Harbottle (the old one with the whiskers) and Albert (the young one with the moon face) of his most memorable films – when he broke away from Gainsborough Pictures. The risk of stagnation and repetition was invoked by Hay then. It would always concern Hancock, even if strangely he never applied the argument to his stage act. In the *Omnibus* television tribute to the comedian, Duncan Wood attempted to give his star's point of view as fairly as he could, while owning up to the challenge of phrasing it properly: 'He didn't say, "I don't want Sid any more," and he didn't really say, "I don't need Sid any more." It could have been anybody. He didn't want to be half of a double act and that was becoming a thing in his mind and he was

going to get rid of it, and did.' What Hancock overlooked was the possibility that, in Bill Kerr's words, 'Tony needed Sid more than Sid
needed Tony.'

If one accepts the professional rationale of his decision, one has
a greater difficulty with the way in which Hancock handled the
situation once the decision had been made. No one expects a top comedian to be an expert in man-management, but given the closeness
of the two men one might have hoped that the elementary courtesies
could have been observed. That they were not was more out of shy-
ness, embarrassment and social ineptitude than anything more sinister. Hancock should have talked the matter over first with his
friend. He *had* discussed his intentions with colleagues like Liz
Fraser and Warren Mitchell. The latter recalled how shocked and
sorrowful he was: 'You walk into something that seems to be perfection and you wanted it to go on being that way.' Eventually it was left
to others to break the news to Sid. Shortly after the summit meeting
at Hancock's Surrey house, James was summoned to a meeting at
the BBC. When he returned later to his wife, Valerie, at their Ealing
home he was close to tears: 'Tony doesn't want me in the show any
more. He wants to go it alone.' Valerie forgets at this remove who
dealt the blow. One presumes Maschwitz, Sloan, Wood or any combination of them. Galton and Simpson remember how distraught Sid
was at what he described as 'out-of-the-blue betrayal'. Even after –
or perhaps because of – his first flurry with television stardom at
Associated-Rediffusion, Sid remained more than content to play the
second banana roll. Of course, in declaring that preference he was
also absolving himself from ever having to tackle the sort of ruthless
decision Hancock now seemed to be making. As Galton has admitted,
'Hancock could be ruthless if need be, but I think anybody in that
position has to be – you've got to make unpleasant decisions at some
time in your life.'

There *is* an alternative version to what happened. It was spelled
out by James himself in a magnanimous interview he gave to the

Sunday Pictorial for 9 December 1962, where he states that Hancock had been giving him clues that he wanted to write *'finis'* to the show for some time: 'He dropped the odd remark like "We've really got to change the format" or "The viewers are going to get sick and tired of it." I didn't say anything. It was his show, but I knew what he meant.' He then tells of a drinking session one day after rehearsals, during which Hancock first mentioned to Sid a film he had been offered, which turned out to be *The Rebel*. 'I think maybe I ought to accept,' said Tony. 'I'm sorry, but there won't be a part for you in it.' James, who had been harbouring a feeling of gloom for the series, felt relieved. He had to admit he appeared in enough pictures on his own without Hancock. It was then that Tony announced they should split up for good, linked to the sentiment that Sid should be doing his own show: 'You've got a good public working for you now – the boys will write for you.' According to James, Hancock had made up his mind and, with an 'Okay, mate, and the best of luck' from Sid, they shook hands. The article is undoubtedly a public relations exercise to kill any 'nasty rumours' of acrimony between the two men: 'We never had the flaming row as some people suggested … when Tony broke the news to me he fair broke my heart along with it, but we parted good friends and we still are … the plain fact is that in this business you have to keep changing. After all you can't be a "Citizen James" all your life.' It would be part and parcel of James's practised profession-alism to go along with this version of events for the press – and doubt-less there was at least one late-night drinking session when the merits of the decision were discussed between them. But no cosy ver-sion contrived by the tabloids for public consumption can ever dispel the cold chill of disappointment the actor first felt after his earlier summons by the BBC hierarchy. Valerie emphasises, 'What hurt most is that it was the BBC who broke the news and not Tony him-self.' As far as the article is concerned, it says much for public inter-est in both performers that the matter was still worthy of headlines three years after it all happened.

In a tribute programme after Hancock's death James announced, 'I think he really was the greatest friend I ever had and very often Tony treated me like a father almost ... he used to lean on me quite a bit, which suited me because I felt that I put him at ease a lot.' These were not comments made in the sentiment of the moment. As Tony found refuge in the script and his inner thoughts, to many on the fringes of the radio and television shows Sid himself became perceived as the father-figure *manqué* of the whole enterprise, the one to consult for advice or friendship. In the wake of the death he continued to play the media with tact: 'I would have liked to have gone on for one more series – only one – and I was very upset naturally when he said that we've got to break it up now – we've got to make a clean cut and I said, "If that's the way it's got to be, that's the way it's got to be."' Sid had pleaded with Hancock to change his mind, but to no avail. According to Hugh Lloyd there was one moment during rehearsals for the last series when Sid bounced in with the news that they'd been made an offer to make four films together: 'Tony immediately showed disinterest. That really hurt Sid.' But James was not a man to indulge in bitterness and it says a great deal about him that their friendship continued: 'We were buddies, and we remained buddies, long after the so-called split-up.' Paradoxically, the depth of that friendship possibly made it more difficult for Hancock to treat James more graciously in the first place. Shared snooker sessions and holidays in the South of France where Hancock went around, according to Sid, 'generally unshaven in a loud Hawaiian shirt, blue trousers and dark glasses' continued for a while. When it came to work, the pair made a pact that they would never tell one another if they were going to be in the audience at each other's respective shows. Sid admitted, 'For him to see me in his audience would have thrown him. I reckon if I'd seen him in my audience, I would have felt it too. I loved that man and I missed him.' Even today Valerie James, with characteristic grace, harbours no grudge: 'I was very proud of both of them ... Sid was hurt, but accepted it ...

he'd have gone back at any time.' It is said that the two men only ever had one real row. James stuck on twelve as they were playing pontoon. Hancock questioned the legality of the move. Sid insisted it was allowed. Presumably Galton and Simpson were not present; the episode does not appear to surface in any of their scripts.

News of the split leaked from the BBC as Sid was filming the comedy *Watch Your Stern* with Hattie Jacques and several of the future *Carry On* regulars in Chatham dockyard at the beginning of 1960. For those in the know this cast a hazy mix of melancholy and speculation over the final series, but their on-screen performances still sparkled. Moira Lister had always seen their partnership as a 'marriage of opposites'. Sid's resilience and skill carried him through the difficult experience, which in terms of a real marriage would have been nothing but a meaningless charade. *The Poison Pen Letters*, the show in which his brilliantly crass cynicism would be pitted against Hancock's bombast and insecurity for the last time, was recorded on 29 April 1960. It is impossible not to sense a subtext to a plot in which Hancock is discovered to be writing hate mail to himself in his sleep and declared neurotic in the process. As Lister said to qualify her phrase, 'Because Sid was un-neurotic, he was able to cope with Tony's neurosis and was probably a very good balance for him, both in the studio and out of it.' In the episode Sid is shown as his real-life reassuring self: 'You see, boy, you've been over-working. You're all strung up. Your nerves are like violin strings, and secretly, underneath it all, you don't like the life you've been living, so your subconscious mind has revolted. I mean, you're like everybody else, really. *You* don't like you either … all you need is a bit of rest, a long break.' Hancock is puzzled that Sid hasn't been similarly affected. James explains the differences in his character: 'I'm stronger minded than you. I don't let these things affect me.' Sid then spots a poison pen letter addressed to himself and draws the conclusion that he's as crazy as Hancock. A stay in the country is called for and in a symbolic gesture for their final shot together they leave the parlour of 23 Railway Cuttings for the last time with their arms around each other. The script called for Tony to say, 'I don't think we'll be back for a few months.' On air he changes the final line to the more conclusive, 'I don't think we'll be back for months.' It is a poignant moment and it is painful to imagine what transpired between the two men behind the plywood walls of their old abode as the credits rolled. Hancock insisted on making an announcement at the end-of-series party that followed, an event invaded in festive mood by Eric Sykes and Bill Kerr, both equipped with flamenco guitars to enliven the proceedings. Kerr has recalled the speech as 'one of Hancock's saddest and most dramatic moments'; everyone already knew what he had to say. It had long been decided by Eric Maschwitz that at this event Hancock should be presented with the Light Entertainment Department's irreverent equivalent of the 'Oscar', an inscribed bronze ash bucket of the type that may still serve sentry duty by the lifts at Television Centre. On 19 April Maschwitz sent a memo to the appropriate party advising that Sidney James should receive the same accolade and that the bucket should carry 'the same inscription as that for Hancock himself'. Not one person watching that final episode could have disagreed.

Within weeks of Hancock's decision, Galton and Simpson had pledged their loyalty alongside that of the BBC in agreeing to write a series for Sid alone. *Citizen James* pursued the domestic Damon Runyon line of the earlier Wolf Mankowitz project and reunited him with Bill Kerr as his regular sidekick and Liz Fraser as the squeeze on his arm. According to Alan Simpson, 'It was exactly the way we had been writing up Sid for the Hancock shows. We took Sid away from Hancock so he could carry on working his get-rich-quick schemes.' The programme lost its way, however, after the first season, when Galton and Simpson had to leave to address other projects. Kerr and Fraser left too, and for the second and third series greater emphasis was placed on Sid's relationship with Sydney Tafler, another 'wide boy'. This was a little like pairing Laurel with

Costello or Abbott with Hardy. Duncan Wood had also handed over the production by now, which may explain a great deal. The idea of a comedy drama in the world of small-time criminality did not entirely click until *Minder* appeared on television screens in 1979, with George Cole immortalising the figure of Arthur Daley, another mercenary realist in an acquisitive society and a role that would have suited the more mature James to perfection. Sid then progressed to a more serious drama role for the BBC in *Taxi!* The role of a streetwise but conscientious London cabby was created for him by Ted, later Lord, Willis who had originated *Dixon of Dock Green*. It ran for two long series, but the mask of comedy still had James firmly in its sights. In whatever discipline, he had no need to worry for his future professionally. He would go on to become the lead figure of the *Carry On* films: those without him are like apple pie without the cloves, roast beef without the horseradish. He also became the indubitable star of a string of successful situation comedies for commercial television, of which *Bless This House*, which cast him as an unlikely but utterly believable family man, would run throughout the 1970s until his untimely death in 1976. Its total of sixty episodes beat the *Hancock's Half Hour* television tally by three.

James's perceived treatment at the hands of Hancock brought him considerable sympathy at the time, although his ongoing popularity had as much to do with the sustained quality of his work and his direct meat-and-two-potatoes appeal as with any residue of public sentiment. It is also unfair to suggest that Hancock might have been displeased by his friend's success. When he himself returned to ITV screens he commented in a *TV Times* article, 'People remarked on my breaking up with Sid James, but it is quite simple; you work in a show with somebody, but there is never any question of a hard and fast team and I liked having Sid in my shows very much. And then you move on to something else.' It is sometimes hard for the public, creature of habit that it is, to see things that way. The parallel of breaking up a family comes to mind. Ultimately James had understood. A recent biography suggests that Sid was not without a ruthless streak of his own where his more distant kith and kin were concerned. However, I am sure he possessed within himself a contradictory core of warmth and decency without which the British public and Hancock too would have rumbled him long ago. There is a sense in which Sid through his continuing success achieved – without malice – a last cackling laugh. In *The Bowmans*, one of the episodes of the solo series that Galton and Simpson subsequently wrote for Hancock, Tony played a popular character in a soap opera who receives his mortal come-uppance from producer and scriptwriters alike when his presence becomes intolerable. There is nothing whatsoever to suggest that 'Old Joshua Merryweather' – a parody of the Walter Gabriel character in *The Archers* – is based on Sid. However, the groundswell of public opinion that clamours for his return is not too far removed from the backing the press and the people gave to the most selfless 'straight man' that ever was.

In time Hancock would look back on the issue of parting from Sid as he contemplated his life story. He had said much of it before:

Sid saw nothing wrong with going on, but I don't think he ever felt quite the same way about the programme as I did. To him it was a job of work, a congenial one but a job of work which he took within his professional stride. To me it was a matter of personal involvement and I felt a progressive urge to call a halt before the public began saying it wasn't the show it *had* been. Or worse still, that it *was* the show it had been and we were going through the same old motions week after week ... I appreciated how people felt. Why bite the hand that was feeding us so well? Why not make the best of our good luck while we had it? But I could not look on it that way. I told them I was doing it for their own good as well as mine. 'Hancock's Half Hour' had gone on long enough. It had become an octopus and I wanted to free us all from it before it strangled us ... I must say it angered me to be asked why I had 'got rid' of Sidney James and

> before him people like Hattie Jacques and Kenneth Williams and
> Bill Kerr. You would have thought I had ruined their futures, but
> 'Hancock's Half Hour' was only a phase in their lives, a stepping
> stone to other things just as it was for me. I no more got rid of Sid
> than I got rid of myself.

Those last words contain a haunting poignancy.

Anyone keen to latch on to the *Face to Face* transmission for the slightest hint of personal trivia surrounding Hancock would have learned that he was now living in a large house in the country at Lingfield in Surrey. In this regard the programme also marked a watershed in his personal and domestic life. He had long voiced dreams of a status-symbol home, to which he could invite his cronies to symposia to discuss the ever intriguing matter of comedy. The Knightsbridge flat with its endless climb to the fifth floor hardly fitted the ideal. Bill Kerr made the observation that its interior resembled the sort of place you imagined him living in for the show, while Dennis Main Wilson once provided a fairly vivid inventory of the furniture and fittings: 'There was an old leather club armchair with the stuffing coming out, a few other odd chairs and a put-you-up settee. There was an underfelt on the floor but no carpet. There was a mark where someone had been sick. There were piles of fan letters behind the lavatory pan. I looked into the bedroom one Sunday and there was a *Sunday Pictorial* from the previous week still sticking out of the bedclothes.' Main Wilson omitted the two enormous poodles, Charlie and Mr Brown, encountered by Philip Oakes on his initial visit there. The writer described the first as a happy extrovert, the second as a nervous wreck which, Hancock insisted, saw ghosts. Oakes described the kitchen as 'a breeding ground for botulism' and also picked up on the fan mail that littered the lavatory floor, to the extent that one wonders to what use he put it.

Cicely, expert chef and chauffeuse combined, did not apply herself to housework with the same enthusiasm and was only too happy to go along with the slumming habits of her husband. The money accruing to him in ever larger amounts during the mid-1950s was perfect for expensive wines in elegant restaurants on European sojourns, but had little impact on the quality of their everyday life. Indeed for much of this time, in spite of his considerable earnings, he allowed his agent, Jack Adams, to keep him on a tight allowance of £20 a week spending money to curb his growing extravagance. Cicely soon learned to tolerate his eccentric ways. When in the early years of their marriage Hancock went off to Bournemouth for a variety engagement leaving her with little money, she seemed hardly fazed upon arrival at George Fairweather's hairdressing saloon a few hours and one train journey later. 'You know Tony,' she said to her husband's mentor, whom she was meeting for the first time. 'He's done it again. He just went off with a "Cheerio, ducks. See you Sunday."' They went off to find him together. In his dressing room at the Winter Gardens they discovered he had forgotten to bring any clean shorts or shirts with him. The ever-gallant George rushed home to replenish his friend's wardrobe, never to see his own clothes again. 'Cicely didn't have any hysterics about being left with no money like that,' commented Fairweather later. 'She was very placid, very easy.' Hancock once paid tribute to his wife's patience when he said, 'She is wonderfully understanding. When I'm working I must be a very difficult person to be with. I go at full stretch all the time and only notice her when she cooks me some food. We have an agreement to live like that when I'm working. We keep the fun till afterwards.'

The move to the semi-rural idyll of the pre-M25 outskirts of Greater London actually took place in November 1957, some two years before the *Face to Face* invitation. The solid mock-timbered five-bedroom house had been built in 1923 and was situated in one and a quarter acres of land two miles from Lingfield and just under one mile from the village of Blindley Heath. By the mid-1960s Hancock had disowned the country: 'It's not for me. I tried it once. The birds get up in the middle of the night and shout "Hello, hello, hello."

It's all right for them. They go back to kip afterwards, but I've had it. That's it. That's the night gone. The sound of the flowers opening keeps you awake after that.' For the moment, however, cows grazed nearby, racehorses trained, and the new residents seemed unperturbed by the council estate you could discern over the fence at the bottom of the garden. Hancock wasted no time in changing the house's original name of 'Val Fleury' to 'MacConkeys', after a doctor who had once lived there. They loved the stone unicorn on the roof and the *bas-relief* of the Marquis of Worcester over the front door. Hancock claimed it reminded him of Spike Milligan. The large white carpet that greeted visitors as soon as they entered the hall betrayed an elegance, however impracticable, to which their earlier home never aspired. Nevertheless, Philip Oakes, a connoisseur of fine furnishings, recalled a remarkable ragbag of a house containing nothing of period value at all: 'It had an extraordinary fireplace which was white with lots and lots of little coloured stones set into it in a totally random pattern – you thought a child might have had a go at it.'

A short stroll away the social life of the village revolved around the Red Barn country club and restaurant. The owner, Eileen Fryer, would, according to her daughter Lyn, become a confidante of Hancock bordering on mother-figure. He certainly discussed the decision to go on *Face to Face* with her. It was at Hancock's suggestion that Lyn, in her late teens and later to marry the comedy writer and broadcaster Barry Took, took over his secretarial work, when she was recovering from a sinus operation that had curtailed her previous employment with ABC Films at Golden Square in the West End. The new position gave her privileged access to the Hancock ménage. The families became close and Lyn vividly recalls the excitement when the Hancocks used to return from their holidays in France and their car swept into the Red Barn drive. On one occasion Tony could not contain his enthusiasm as he announced, 'Look, we've discovered this new craze.' 'It had been going on for years, of course,' remembers Lyn, 'but they'd just discovered it and we all had to play *boules* in the drive there and then.' She sighs with a half-chuckle as she transports herself back to what were – back then in the late 1950s when life had a less hurried agenda, even if your name was Hancock – obviously very happy times for them all: 'There'd be Cicely taking the game so seriously and my mother with her funny way of doing it and Tony laughing at the way she used to throw the ball.' The fun often continued in the bar of the Red Barn, more a converted living room than a conventional pub bar. 'It wasn't masses of drinking,' recalls Lyn. 'More about conversing and catching up with the world. He used to play darts too sometimes. He could be great company, oh yes. There were lots of laughs and lots of nonsense, my goodness, in that bar. He wasn't depressed all the time. When he got low, he was low, but they always arrived sparky and full of fun.'

When asked if she found Hancock and Cicely compatible, Lyn has no hesitation in answering 'Yes', emphasising how proud he was of his first wife, the fashion-plate model with the deep red hair, who looked as if she'd walked out of a Jaeger advertisement and represented the complete antithesis to his casual scarecrow look. In spite of statements he would make to Lyn at a later stage, she senses he never lost his love for Cicely, or his recognition of the stylish ideal she represented. The month after their divorce in 1965 he expressed his concern to the journalist Mike Tomkies that the emphasis in the younger generation was not on 'the delightful difference between the sexes' that it should be: 'I mean, going out with a woman wearing a pair of great boots, a pair of denims and a thick leather jacket – I don't know, it's not right, is it?' Lyn also testifies to his eccentric ways where money was concerned, his almost regal habit of travelling around with no cash on his person. The local Lingfield shopkeepers and publicans soon got around the inconvenience and the embarrassment by referring all bills to his accountant. Once when Cicely was in hospital Lyn had to accompany him on a shopping trip to buy food for the poodles: 'He didn't know what to get. He had no idea what he was supposed to be buying at all. He then wanted to call in to a specific pub. "It's all right," he said. "They know me here." And we had a drink and again he had no money to pay for it.' Her memories of the couple are suffused with affection: 'They were perfectly happy for me to be in their home, and that was nice. They were really relaxed and easy-going. There were always hugs – hugs and cuddles.'

The actress Annabelle Lee, who took part in five of Hancock's television shows between December 1958 and April 1960, recalled coming out of the rehearsal room and seeing Cicely waiting for him in her snazzy little sports car on the other side of the road: 'As he came out, she waved all happily at him and I thought, "Ah – isn't that nice." She looked so glamorous and he looked so happy. It all seemed so lovely. Then the marriage was over. You can't imagine what went wrong.' It was not until he moved to MacConkeys that Hancock's sexual liaison with Freddie Ross began, by her own admission in a hotel suite in Bond Street borrowed from one of her clients. Having initially discounted the idea of physical attraction in their relationship, in 1959 – some five years after she first represented him professionally – she succumbed to the inevitable and the irresistible: 'He knew everything about me and I knew everything about him. He was the one person I trusted enough to talk freely to.' As recently as 2006 she was insisting in a press interview, 'I absolutely did not pursue him.' Their professional connection would have provided ample cover as far as the media were concerned. It is impossible to pinpoint if and when Cicely first suspected that she did not have full claim on her husband's attentions. One certain fact is that the knowledge would not have lessened her own growing reliance on alcohol. The line she first adopted with friends was simplistic and self-deceptive: 'The more I drink, the less he does.' Tantalus and Florence Nightingale were never going to make easy bedfellows. Whatever the pressures of his work, it is likely that Hancock stepped up his own alcohol intake as a way of dealing both with the guilt of his affair and with the relentless strain of keeping it secret. And so a vicious circle gathered momentum. Valerie James, who admired Cicely considerably, claims she was simply terrified of losing him: 'I couldn't cope with all that drinking. Sid was a good drinker, but never to that extent. He tried to pull Tony back.' Bill Kerr has painted a desperate picture of a lovely lady running alongside her husband, trying desperately to keep up with him, but failing miserably. As Lyn Took shared with me her happy memories of the Hancock household, she stumbled to an emotional halt: 'Then over the years the drinking increased – I don't know where to go from there ...' In fact, it is very simple. In time life would spiral out of control for them both and they danced off the edge of the world that Lyn recalls so fondly. For the moment, however, Hancock still had glorious triumphs ahead, even if Sid James was Carrying On elsewhere.

Chapter Ten

'AND THEN THERE WERE THREE ...'

'I took one look at the script. It said something
about a race track attendant following the dogs
round with a dust pan. Sorry, that type of
humour just isn't me.'

For someone as talented and impressionable as Hancock, who had spent a large part of his informal education cosseted in the flea-pits and picture palaces of Bournemouth, it was inevitable that he should project his own fantasies as a performer onto the silver screen. His vision of cinematic stardom and the international recognition to come with it compromised any attempts by the BBC to sign him to a long-term contract, even though his first venture into the medium made little lasting impression on the industry. In the spring of 1954, at the time when he continued to consolidate his radio fame with *Star Bill*, he appeared in a low-budget minor feature entitled *Orders are Orders*. A service farce of the kind popular at a time when conscription impinged in some way on most people's lives, it had been adapted from an earlier stage play by Ian Hay and Anthony Armstrong entitled *Orders is Orders*. The impact of the film was underwhelming. Hancock was fond of telling how he summoned up the courage to take Cicely to the Astoria in Charing Cross Road to share his ordeal upon its release: 'I asked the girl at the box office, "Do you think we'll be able to get in?" She gave me a pitying look and said, "Get in? You can have the whole circle if you want it."' He dismissed his part as 'flashing on and off screen so fast, if you had stood up to let someone through you might have missed me altogether', as well as confessing that the plot made him confused and muddled: 'It made me so embarrassed that I had to go out before the end and hide in the cloakroom until everyone was gone.' This may have come as no surprise to the distributors, British Lion, who in their campaign brochure saw fit to outline the plot as follows: 'The story – as if it matters, with such a load of talent – is about a film unit entering an army barracks for the purpose of shooting scenes for a picture about invaders from Mars.' Sid James summed it up when he admitted, 'It was a bit of a stinker.'

Nominally the film starred Brian Reece – the actor and light comedian of *P.C. 49* radio fame – as the adjutant, alongside Margot Grahame as the token sex appeal, Raymond Huntley as the colonel and Sid himself as Ed Waggermeyer, a loquacious film producer with a less-than-convincing American accent. On this first outing together the screenplay allowed Hancock and James little opportunity to display the chemistry of future years. Indeed, they have little to do together, although much of the dynamic of the meagre plot is provided by the conflict between Sid trying to direct his movie while Tony tries to rehearse his band. Hancock is accorded the first close-up of the film in his role as Lieutenant Cartroad, the regimental bandmaster brought to despair as he attempts to achieve some kind of harmony among his unruly group of musicians. In the short space of six seconds he registers contempt (for his charges), smugness, coyness, disdain, earnestness, all in rhythm with the baton with which he is conducting a Sousa-style piece before uttering his first words, 'Yes, not bad. We haven't quite caught the poetry of it, have we? Never mind – break for an hour – band dismissed.' Sid's first acknowledgement of Hancock occurs when he looks through a window and sees him waving his baton from afar: 'Cartroad? Would that be the fat guy standing out there trying to keep the flies off?' Hancock's most effective scene is performed with Eric Sykes, who appears unbilled among the cast, although credited with providing additional dialogue. In effect Hancock on screen is an incarnation of his affected *Educating Archie* persona and this is presumably where Sykes's main contribution resided. The bandmaster provides Eric with individual tuition in the art of cymbal-bashing when he gets carried away: 'Didn't you feel it – the sunlight glistening on polished brass, the drawing of a sword at the famous battles of Balaclava, Mafeking, Waterloo, Crécy, Agincourt and to hell with Burgundy – all merged at the end in that one triumphant schluuump!' The scene confirms that Sykes's understanding of the humour that best suited his friend was embedded in this kind of posturing.

Although Hancock's film career would lie dormant for more than six years, the promise beams off the screen. Bob Hope once confided to the American interviewer Dick Cavett that the only advice given to him when he went into the movies was to 'act with your eyes'. Hancock's performance shows he already had a fair inkling of how to do just that, and according to *Picturegoer* magazine he 'annexed the comedy honours' on the film's release. That was no mean achievement when you consider that sharing a humble position in the credits was another radio man-of-the-moment, Peter Sellers, in what he described as his 'first decent screen role'. His bored batman, Private Goffin, was a clean-shaven precursor of Fred Kite, Sellers's shop-steward character from *I'm All Right, Jack*, crossed with his canny simpleton 'Bluebottle' type from *The Goon Show*. Sellers's role is underpinned by skilled understatement, while Hancock essayed the pompous bravura his early radio reputation expected. Many would disagree that Hancock walked away with flying colours. A tie, acknowledging their variant styles, would not be an unfair result. Soon, however, Sellers's film career would expand, while Hancock's, in spite of the initial promise, would stutter to a halt. As the ex-impressionist came to be identified with some of the most fantastical inhabitants of comedy's cinematic Wonderland – Pearly Gates, Clouseau, Strangelove, Fassbender, Sam the busker, Chance the gardener, Milligan's idea of

Queen Victoria and many more – so Hancock appropriated the more mundane devices of boredom and frustration in the cause of comedy and found himself locked into the media that arguably suited them better.

There were a few offers. He was asked to consider the role of a rotund bishop in *The Big Money*, a 1956 caper summed up in the trade literature as 'Crooked family's inept son steals counterfeit money from gang leader'. Hancock laughed at the twenty-year disparity in age between himself and the character. When the film at last emerged in December 1956, the part of the reverend gentleman was taken by actor and ballet star Robert Helpmann; Ian Carmichael played the token lead. Rank, the studio that dominated the British film industry at this time, thought it stood a better chance with a starring vehicle for the comedian. The director John Paddy Carstairs, who had guided Norman Wisdom's early cinematic success and would in time direct *The Big Money*, tempted him with the lead over veterans Stanley Holloway and A.E. Matthews in another low-life escapade set in the sphere of greyhound racing. Hancock was adamant that this again was not for him: 'I took one look at the script. It said something about a race track attendant following the dogs round with a dust pan. Sorry, that type of humour just isn't me.' The movie was released in February 1956 as *Jumping for Joy*, a title not exactly analogous to his performing style, but not with that of Frankie Howerd either, for whom it proved to be a popular success. In 1958 a move by Rank to persuade him to portray his idol, Sid Field, in a biopic fell by the wayside when the studio, according to Hancock, 'wanted to cut the money and put in a love interest'.

As an aspirant film star Hancock had initially to be content with appearing in the pages of *Film Fun*, the weekly children's comic that years before introduced this writer to the glorious two-dimensional world of Laurel and Hardy and Old Mother Riley, Frank Randle and Abbott and Costello. When eventually these names were discovered to be real flesh-and-blood performers, it was as if someone had waved a magic wand over the page. Perhaps, I wondered, they sneakily deserted their grainy paper home when one was away at school only to return to their inky confines under cover of the rival distraction provided by the *Dandy* or the *Beano*. Hancock was introduced as a weekly inside feature on 12 July 1958. In the issue dated 13 June 1959 the strip was extended to two pages, Hancock was joined by Sid James – heralded by a banner that read, 'assisted (more or less) by his old china' – and for the first time the location was specified as East Cheam. The couple were promoted to the front and back cover pages on 23 January 1960, where they remained until 7 January 1961, the date upon which they returned to the inside pages, eight months after the end of their association on television. Sid's inclusion would have further aggravated Hancock's feelings on the 'double act' issue, not least because traditionally the cover pages had for long been the special domain of Laurel and Hardy themselves. Nevertheless, with or without Sid, Hancock's inclusion in the comic represented a minor accolade in view of the fact that he had only one relatively insignificant, now-forgotten part in a movie to his name. He remained in the periodical until his strip was cancelled in September 1962, when the comic was merged with another and lost all sense of identity. Sid was discreetly removed in May 1961, with literally days to go before the start of Hancock's solo BBC television series. By that time Hancock's first starring vehicle in the cinema – without Sid – had been released. This was big news for the comic weekly. The issue of 25 March 1961 carried a photographic feature on *The Rebel* in addition to his regular comic strip elsewhere.

The eventual subject matter of the film that Hancock had dreamt about for years was foreshadowed in several episodes of his radio series, acknowledging paradoxically the cinematic nature of the earlier medium. The theme of Hancock as thwarted artist and intellectual had served Galton and Simpson well from the moment the comedian engaged in off-the-cuff conversation with Simpson himself on the subject near the start of the second series: 'What I wanted to tell you about was this barney I had with Alfred Munnings ... I'd painted a work of art entitled "Sunset over Sydney Harbour Bridge". D'you know what Munnings thought it was? "Fried Egg and Herring Bone".' By the fourth series the lad has progressed to sculpture: the episode called *Michelangelo 'Ancock* sees him enter a municipal competition to provide a 'new and original statue' for East Cheam's public park. At last, he exclaims, his LCC 'Plasticine' evening classes will begin to show a dividend. When Hattie Jacques in her Miss Pugh role complains that some of the bits he's chipped off look better than his abstract portrayal of an Olympic athlete, he assures her that the figure is not only a work of art, but a triumph of mathematical genius: 'Two tons of solid rock bending forward depicting the runner leaving the starting block balanced on his big toe ... Einstein couldn't have worked it out better!' When the show transferred to television, Hancock was depicted as a starving artist as early as the second episode, where he laments, 'Why is the public so slow to recognise genius?' while oblivious of painting over a stolen Rembrandt, which has been waylaid when an art theft by Sid goes wrong.

All of his pretensions to Bohemia fused in one spectacular flowering in the last radio series with the show entitled *The Poetry Society*, featuring the activities of the East Cheam Cultural Progressive Society. The episode broke new ground in having no incidental music, with the meeting of the group happening in real time throughout the transmission. Sid and Bill, who attend at Hancock's persuasion, are contemptuous from the beginning, but, in a sharp satire of the avant-garde, the experimental verse that Galton and Simpson give them to recite makes a greater impression than Hancock's. He ends up disowning the whole lot of them: 'I can't be bothered with them. I'll go down the coffee-house – there's bound to be another movement started up since yesterday. I'll start one of me own. How did that poem of Sid's go now? ... "Mauve world, green me, black him, purple her" ... that's it. That'll get 'em. A breakaway group

… the new intellectual movement to shake the world!' Hancock would go to Paris courtesy of the Associated British Picture Corporation to find it.

Shooting for *The Rebel* began at Elstree Studios in July 1960. At this moment there was no hint of his subsequent split from Galton and Simpson, and they had been attached to the project from its inception. As Hancock admitted, 'The trouble with British films and scriptwriters is that they can think of humour in only two ways – broad comedy or something stuffed with actors like *Whiskey Galore*.' The new film was not entirely exempt from either stricture, but with Ray and Alan, who understood his character as well as – if not better than – their own, the vehicle was prevented from the ignominy usually reserved for the cinematic débuts of most popular British comedians whose rightful place was on radio, television or the variety stage. Hancock was interviewed for radio by John Timpson on the set of the film. He was non-committal about tying himself down to any one medium. He obviously relished the slower pace of shooting two to three minutes of material a day, giving everyone more time to get things right, the cause for which he had battled unsuccessfully when at the BBC. When asked if he missed the audience, he replied in the negative: 'So much good comedy has been done on film and nobody ever missed it before.'

Significantly Hancock's own name was used throughout the film as it had been on radio and television, thus confirming the identification between the actor and his on-screen portrayal. For the first time in their association the writers found themselves discussing the subject matter with the star, a matter that still causes some resentment among them, in that he had never contributed a plot idea to the radio or television shows. In a moment of understanding, Simpson reasons that he wanted 'some say in his own destiny'. A week was spent hammering out the storyline and, at least, once it was set, he abided by it. There is always the proverbial first time for everything, but what really rankled with the pair was his insistence on a separate credit line that read 'based on an original story by Tony Hancock, Ray Galton and Alan Simpson'. Whoever had the original idea, it was psychologically astute to add in – or go along with – a dash of Gallic *je ne sais quoi*. In a press interview the year before, Simpson had said of France, 'There seems to be something about the atmosphere there that lets him relax – something freer in the air. He knows the country well, often talking with pride of the little *pension* where he can stay with full board for fifteen shillings a day.' Undoubtedly the lack of licensing laws helped. He once predicted to Freddie Ross that he would end his days as a vagrant, a fate that worried him not in the least provided he could be assured of a comfortable position over a warm air duct above the Parisian Métro with a copy of *Le Figaro* for cover and a bottle of wine for sustenance. The idea of the French capital as a cliché shorthand reference for a world of rebellion as represented by the artistic avant-garde was well known to him.

Within its first few minutes the film pays homage to two classics of recent film comedy. The scene where Hancock arrives on a deserted station platform and then beats the massed ranks of commuters on the opposite side to a seat on the train that comes into *their* platform by sneaking aboard from the wrong side through another train has a certain echo of the crowd control scene manipulated by Jacques Tati at the railway terminus at the beginning of *Monsieur Hulot's Holiday*. Then, having arrived at his desk within the premises of United International Transatlantic Consolidated Amalgamation Limited wearing the bowler-hatted, umbrella-carrying uniform of business conformity, he is submerged immediately in the serried ranks of identical desks that recede into apparent infinity, this time in obeisance to the similar scene at the opening of Billy Wilder's *The Apartment*. Driven to insanity by the endless monotony of office routine, he strikes out at his boss, played by John Le Mesurier, who has caught him sketching caricatures in his ledger. Forced to abandon his job as a teller and the prospect of a silver cigarette case in twenty-five years' time, he rushes home to don smock and beret and apply himself to the finer things of life. His top-floor flat is redolent of East Cheam in all its faded Victorian grandeur. It transpires that a less witch-like but no less wary Mrs Crevatte, in the more rounded guise of Irene Handl with a winning portrayal right down to the bra straps that dangle down her bare arms, is now his landlady. When she discovers the huge and preposterously ugly stone figure he is sculpting in her house, she is as unimpressed as Miss Pugh had been, not least to discover that Hancock's interpretation of 'Aphrodite at the Water Hole' is supposed to be a nude:

HANDL: Here you been having models up here? Have there been naked
women in my establishment?
TONY: Of course not. I can't afford thirty bob an hour. I did that from
memory. That is women as I see them.
HANDL: Oh, you poor man.

No sooner has she ordered him to leave than the weight of the statue sends it crashing through the floor, its own comment on the stultifying middle-class values he is determined to resist. He heads for Paris where his one genuine talent – for self-belief – stands him in good stead amid the arty Left Bank crowd: 'Anyway, so I said to Dali – "Salvador," I said ' Hancock is soon accidentally mistaken for the painter of several original canvases donated to him by Paul, a shy but genuinely talented fellow artist who, impressed by Hancock's innocent, child-like theories of art, has forsaken the Parisian ideal to return to England. The lad is soon fêted as the darling of the intelligentsia. Suspicion only raises its head when he is commissioned to sculpt an image of the sexy wife of a millionaire patron. Creatively he has only one figure within him, and Aphrodite manifests herself a second time. He heads back to London, where pressure is placed upon him to produce another exhibition. He begs Paul, played by the Canadian actor Paul Massie, to produce the canvases for him, but he has now changed his earlier style to the infantile daubing that characterises Hancock's own work. At the exhibition opening Paul's new *oeuvre* is acclaimed as the work of genius and Hancock decides to abandon all subterfuge. Pointing to the genuine artist, he refuses to leave the gallery without voicing his opinion to all the so-called trendy experts and moneyed hangers-on: 'You're all raving mad. None of you know what you're looking at. You wait till I'm dead. You'll see I was right.' He returns to his old lodgings to find solace in his chisel and granite with a more amenable Mrs Crevatte as his model. He asks her to show him 'the more primitive desires inherent in womanhood since time began'. 'Oh,' she succumbs, 'you wanna bit of leg.' We do not need to see the finished product to know that Aphrodite is about to make her third appearance.

Like Hancock, Galton and Simpson were on a learning curve in the new medium. They recall the producer, W.A. Whittaker, telling them to consider the jeopardy: 'By that he meant putting the character in trouble to see how he gets out of it.' In television they had only ever considered the comedy. The detailed plot that resulted still works best when it allows Hancock full rein to milk the artistic pretension of his character. When Handl takes exception to his painting of beetroot-coloured ducks in flight, his response is vintage Hancock: 'Well, they fly at a fair lick, those ducks. They're up, out of the water and away. You just have to whack on whatever you've got on your brush at the time!' He criticises Paul's paintings, which eventually establish *his* reputation, claiming the colours are the wrong shape: 'Look, the colours shouldn't end where the shapes end – they should send out a glow in the air ... an article will always suggest its own colour irrespective of the colour it's transmitting.' By that reasoning he sees Paul's dingy attic studio as indigo. His recipe for action painting in the Jackson Pollock style is first to pour paint onto the canvas and then to ride his bicycle and dance in Wellingtons over it. Hancock never allowed this sequence to degenerate into obvious slapstick, in spite of protestations from the director, Robert Day, for more 'involvement' on his part. According to Galton and Simpson this was the only time they ever saw him 'almost lose his rag' with a director. In the hands of the standard comedy repertory company of the British cinema of the time – Ian Carmichael, Leslie Phillips, James Robertson Justice *et al* – the film would have coasted along in mawkish fashion to an inevitable end. With Hancock at the helm any tendency to sentimentality was quashed and the film was vindicated as a valid vehicle for his distinctive style, in spite of the tendency to spiral off into slapstick chaos with the sequence set amid a fancy-dress ball on board a yacht where he has to extricate himself from the clutches of those who have called his bluff.

The existentialist party hosted by Dennis Price as a cut-price Salvador Dali figure provides one of the high points of the film. As Hancock expounds to a group of black-clothed, wan-faced interchangeable look-alikes why he had to escape from London – 'You have no idea how frustrating it is to work with people of no imagination. They all looked alike, they all dressed alike' – he is as impervious to the relative futility of his move as those he is talking to. The unintelligible free verse improvised by the actor John Wood could have come straight out of *The Poetry Society*, until Hancock volunteers an elusive last line, 'washing me feet in a glass of beer', that sends the long-haired poet into ecstasy. Even in such rarefied company Hancock was never far away from his vaudeville roots, a fact demonstrated by the moment when he finds a change of company in an Indian fakir balanced upside-down in a loincloth: 'I'd get you a drink, but I thought you might pour it up your nose.' His presence is the cue for Hancock to reminisce about a 'famous yogurt', who to prove the power of mind over matter was chained into a lead box and buried twelve feet below ground: 'He had no food, no water and no air and he stayed like that for six weeks. When they finally dug him out, to everyone's amazement he was stone dead. Of course, there were some sceptics who claimed it was a trick and he was dead when they already put him down.' He asks the yogi what he thinks, only to discover he's asleep.

The scene almost certainly had its roots in an incident from his past. In an interview in the *Radio Times* as early as March 1950 Hancock described an audition he attended at Walton Film Studios where they wanted an actor to stand on his head and recite poetry for a scene at a Chelsea party. He complied by standing on his head as requested. When asked by the casting director if he made a speciality of the upside-down lifestyle, he replied, 'Not really, I *can* work the other way up.' 'Hmm,' came the response, 'sorry, you're the wrong type.' Another nod to nostalgia was provided by the reappearance of his party-piece budgerigar costume. Desperate to escape his pursuers, he arrives at the airport with no time to lose. 'I want to fly to London,' he tells the bewildered ticket clerk. 'It's a long way to London, monsieur. You'd better wait for a plane.' One can almost imagine the whole film falling into place backwards from that one magnificent joke. Throughout, Hancock seems to be asking what the whole art world is if not a magnificent vaudeville of its own.

Although Galton and Simpson insist that the film was never conceived as an easy shot at the art establishment, rather a comment on Hancock buying into the dream of being an artist, it was construed as a valid comment on what constitutes art in the first place and the whole question of attribution. Interestingly the working title for the movie in its early stages was 'One Man's Meat'. It would be no less relevant today when unmade beds and medicine cabinets qualify for the tag as readily as old masters. In an absurdist real-life coda that Hancock would have loved, in 2002 Aphrodite and all his other works – destroyed automatically on the film's completion – were recreated for public exhibition by the London Institute of Pataphysics. The LIP – coincidentally evocative of Irene Handl's early admonition to Hancock, 'I don't want any lip' – is a fascinating group of British writers and artists dedicated to the pursuit of the 'inutilious', a word they prefer to the more prejudicial 'useless'. They emphasise that this was not an exercise in Hancock fan worship, rather 'an attempt to render a fictional body of work actual'. The paintings seen in the film were originally executed by Alistair Grant, an artist exhibiting in London in the 1960s. Forty years on, Hancock's ducks flew again in all their beetroot glory, while his child-like daubs of the Eiffel Tower and Sacré-Cœur, not to mention his old office doodles of John Le Mesurier, raised the question of how they might be regarded had they come from the brush or pen of Dali, Picasso or Van Gogh. Hancock's character felt a special empathy with the latter. As he gazes in his lodgings at a reproduction of the artist's self-portrait, he reflects on their early struggle: 'You went through it, didn't you, mate – made you cut your ear off – why do they persecute we great men?' Ironically the tragic curve of his own career would one day echo that of the artist, leaving behind a similarly complex conundrum of why he committed himself to his final irreversible act. It is a long way both in time and travel from the Sydney basement flat where Hancock took his life in 1968 to the wheat fields in France where Van Gogh shot himself in 1890, but there can be no question that the artistic anxiety they both experienced at varying times in their lives brought them closer together in a more haunting manner than the comic device in the film ever intended. Four years after Hancock's end, George Sanders, whose debonair insouciance contributed so much to the film, would commit suicide too, from an overdose of barbiturates in a Barcelona hotel room where he left a note complaining of boredom and wishing good luck to the rest of the world. The film had contained a line – delivered by an existentialist Nanette Newman – that came home to roost: 'Why kill time when you can kill yourself?'

The cast assembled to support Hancock represented a break from the more parochial traditions of British cinema at the time. George Sanders, the epitome of worldly sophistication, was an inspired, if expensive, choice as Sir Charles Brouard, the art critic and connoisseur who lionises Hancock. Dennis Price as the existentialist guru attempts the impossible in parodying Dali the master of self-parody: his half-moustache cultivated on only one side of his face is a neat living cartoon. Gregoire Aslan and Margit Saad as the patron and his wife added exoticism with their real-life continental backgrounds. Nanette Newman and Oliver Reed made early appearances. But the casting did not let the members of the Duncan Wood Repertory Company down. In addition to John Le Mesurier, Hugh Lloyd as another bored commuter in the early morning train that leads to nowhere, Liz Fraser as the waitress in the local coffee bar where Hancock demands coffee with no froth – 'I don't want to wash me clothes in it,' insists Tony – and Mario Fabrizi as her disgruntled manager, all had an opportunity to register on screen as well as to keep Hancock company off it. One person who was missing was Sid James. In view of recent events no one expected him to be there, although Galton and Simpson did push for him to feature in the briefest of cameos in the manner of those where Bing Crosby cropped up fleetingly in Bob Hope movies long after their co-starring series of 'Road' movies had finished its journey. One idea involved James surfacing from a swimming pool, showing, as he described it, 'his ugly mug above the water line', and disappearing again. Another had him cast as the aforementioned ticket clerk with the tag to the best gag in the movie. Sid was as cosy a part of British cinema tradition as the Pearl and Dean advertisements and would have been in his element. To Hancock this represented backward thinking, and a golden moment was lost. He explained to John Timpson that 'from a friendship and performance point of view' his absence did represent a blow, before taking refuge in his old argument that Sid had already appeared in countless films without him. James was gracious enough to attend the London première at the Plaza Cinema in Lower Regent Street on 2 March 1961, but then so did many others from Hancock's past. Hattie Jacques, Bill Kerr, Eric Sykes, even John Freeman joined fellow comics like Charlie Drake, Terry-Thomas, Ian Carmichael, Richard Hearne and Hylda Baker to wish the lad well. Newsreel footage of the reception at the event shows Sid lighting up the room with his smile without an apparent grudge in the world.

The film, which had already been shown at the Beirut Film Festival, received mostly disappointing reviews from the critics, although *The Times* hailed it as a 'gratifying success' and the trade paper *Variety* held out hope for Hancock internationally. While conceding that he would not find immediate stardom overseas, the review suggested that an American booking should deliver plenty of word-of-mouth support. Its main regret was that the title hardly suggested a comedy. When the opportunity to play in the US occurred later in October, that title had been changed to the dangerously arrogant – for a personality vehicle – *Call Me Genius*. For that to work at all, a prior understanding of Hancock's comic persona was essential. The star had not been consulted. To make matters worse, the change had not been made for the reason proffered by *Variety*. Hancock had been beaten to the title of *The Rebel* by a current series on American television dealing with the Civil War. A scathing review by Bosley Crowther in the *New York Times* was enough to dash all hopes of further transatlantic exploitation: 'Through it all, Mr Hancock stumbles vainly, giving a clumsy pretence of being funny ... and since he shares credit for the story, he must be charged with stumbling in that department too.' In a move worthy of a Galton and Simpson ending, Hancock, understandably upset by such harsh criticism, immediately left New York, where he had been attending the première, to drown his sorrows in absinthe among the bars and bistros of Paris. At a later time he pondered the problem: 'They weren't used to me like the folks back home. Here, we've grown up together. The British public knows when I'm taking the mickey and when I'm being serious. So when I was boosted as the big British comic, they came to the cinema, folded their arms and said, "Okay. Show us."' When he left England for New York he had seen *The Rebel* as an automatic passport to Hollywood. After one bad review, he might have been back in Sid's dodgy studio shooting movies with still-frame photography.

The film gave Hancock an opportunity to show that for the most part his timing could work in spite of the absence of an audience, although Barry Took felt that he seemed diminished by the big screen. Took meant that the close-ups that by now were second nature to him and his director in television, where he enjoyed such great intimacy with his audience, did not work in the same way in the cinema. The film's director, Robert Day, carried away by the combination of Technicolor, the Parisian background and the exoticism of much of the subject matter, never quite came to terms with how to capture that fleeting look that found laughs where not even Galton and Simpson had perceived them, a process Duncan Wood understood instinctively. And if Hancock's timing of a line may not have suffered, the lack of a continuous performance worked against the relaxed fluency of his best work for the small screen, however much he had argued to the contrary with the BBC hierarchy. Moreover, the television audience was now seeing him in colour for the first time, an experience that many would have found as disconcerting as attempts to colourise *Casablanca* and old Laurel and Hardy classics. Roger Lewis in his exhaustive biography of Peter Sellers makes the case that Hancock was made for television: 'The black and white gloom and blurry tuning were apt for the mood ... Hancock's old programmes appear made in the midst of foul weather which emanated from somewhere toxic inside him.' His second feature would compensate in black and white with a fair measure of literal on-screen thunder to match the moodiness within his character. But it was not a process upon which future movie stardom could rely, any more than what was by then happening within the inner man would be advantageous to his private life.

None of this prevented *The Rebel* from scoring a major success at the British box office, where upon release it established a circuit record for Associated British Cinemas in London and throughout the country, in many venues delivering a good week's business in a single day. It was the first of a three-picture deal for Hancock with the Associated British Picture Corporation, which had been announced in February 1960, although the details had been formulated by 1

July the previous year. The budget was set at £175,000, from which George Sanders would receive £10,000, twice as much as the star. The latter, however, did enjoy a percentage of the profits. For his first starring role in a feature film, the picture augured more promisingly for Hancock than most other British comedians had fared in their baptismal encounters with cinema stardom in the post-war period. Harry Secombe, Benny Hill, Dave King and Morecambe and Wise were all members of the new generation of television comics who floundered when they went into pictures. Later attempts to translate the brand leaders of situation comedy to celluloid – *Steptoe and Son*, *Dad's Army*, *Till Death* and more – always seemed to trail behind the parent product. As early as 1946 the industry even failed to transmute the golden glow of Sid Field to the big screen. Peter Sellers and Terry-Thomas both triumphed, but only after stuttering through a number of lower-profile roles. Only Norman Wisdom could claim instant success with a star cinematic début that outranked Hancock's. In 1953 his *Trouble in Store* broke house records almost everywhere it was shown during its first four weeks of release, a pattern he went on to sustain fairly regularly on an annual basis well into the mid-1960s.

Hancock was successful enough on his first outing to be able to rewrite his contract with ABPC, but the failure to register internationally – i.e. in America – in spite of all the efforts he made to purge the screenplay of needlessly British references and to set half of the movie in a romanticised ideal of a foreign country would weigh heavily on him until the end of his days. He would not give up the quest. 'I am aiming at a universal comedy that will transcend class and state barriers,' was a typical pronouncement from around this time. Jacques Tati continued to be the benchmark of everything he wanted to achieve, although one wonders if he ever realised how close he actually came to achieving this ambition, not in his film work, but on radio and television. Both comedians were at their most engaging when simply exploring the comic potential of being human. The phrase used by Denis Norden in his assessment of Hancock – 'echo of remembered laughter' – must apply equally to his Gallic *confrère*, as to few other comedians of recent years. To bask on a sandy beach, to play a game of tennis, to adjust a picture on a wall, to bump into plain glass, to sit in a traffic jam, to become ensnared by the remorseless gadgetry of modern life are all experiences – pleasant, tedious, painful – enhanced by the collective comic memory of the sublime French master. In this regard Hancock, in the final BBC television series still ahead of him, would soon reveal himself at his most Tatiesque. *The Rebel* also prefigured the six short shows of that series, with Hancock, cut off at the end by choice from the mad parade that accompanied his artistic odyssey, finally revealed as a man alone – on the assumption, that is, that Mrs Crevatte hardly passed muster for company.

The new series that Hancock had conceded to his BBC bosses when he cut his ties with Sid James did not reach television screens until May 1961 in the immediate wake of the general release of *The Rebel* and just over a year after he closed the door on East Cheam for the final time. In reality it had been placed on the back burner as a result of his film plans, but on 30 August 1960, with shooting on the feature drawing to a close, Eric Maschwitz raised the matter again by letter, invoking the success of a recent series of repeats under the banner *The Best of Hancock* in his cause and making the point that it would be unwise for Hancock to lose touch with his television audience. Maschwitz hoped that it might be possible for him to dovetail into his future film plans a limited number of appearances with any new format that he and his writers might have in mind, 'a view', he added, 'which I fancy your film company might share'. Six weeks later he had still received no reply and wrote again. Hancock's office telephoned to say that the film was not yet finished, but that Hancock would be in touch as soon as it was behind him. At last on 21 November an acquiescent comedian had lunch with Maschwitz and Tom Sloan and the seeds for the series were sewn; within days a draft contract for six shows was drawn up. This broke new ground in that for the first time in Sloan's experience the BBC Television Service was prepared to underwrite both repeats and transcription fees in overseas markets in order to achieve a guaranteed minimum financial return for the artist. If the offer of £1,750 per show was meant as a starting point for negotiation, it was not necessary. Beryl Vertue, now handling Hancock's affairs in tandem with Roger Hancock from the office of Associated London Scripts, wasted no time in accepting the terms, coupled with an auxiliary deal for Galton and Simpson. The Hancock figure comprised a basic fee of £1,000 a show, a guaranteed £500 for a repeat within twelve months of first transmission, and the sum of £250 for overseas distribution excluding the United States, where exploitation would be the subject of separate negotiation. The one bone of contention was a clause whereby the BBC held out for an option of up to a further thirteen programmes at the same fees to be made between October and March 1962. Hancock never had any intention of making an eighth series, although it was agreed that in the absence of an option, should the additional shows transpire he would expect no further remuneration.

The new series was called simply *Hancock* and ran at a short-ened duration of twenty-five minutes to allow for easier exploitation in overseas markets where commercial breaks might need to be inte-grated into the show. Galton and Simpson were under pain of death to eliminate all slang references that would be incomprehensible in foreign lands. They took away the props and the wardrobe, but oth-erwise his character remained substantially the same. Even the location retained the same initials. East Cheam became Earl's Court, a clever choice with its bohemian subculture and transient bedsitter population. Ray recalls it was full of young people from all parts of the world, and would become known as 'Kangaroo Valley' because of its large Australian population. It was a perfect setting for Hancock whose character was always trying to be 'young, hip and educated', constantly anxious to keep in step with what was going on in the big wide world. The usual noises were made about working with proper actors, but while Mario Fabrizi, Arthur Mullard and Johnny Vyvyan were not in evidence, a few of the old regulars – Hugh Lloyd, John Le Mesurier, Brian Oulton, Alec Bregonzi, Peggy Ann Clifford – happily were. In addition Jack Watling, Colin Gordon, Charles Lloyd Pack, Frank Thornton and above all Patrick Cargill freshened up the look of the old company, although Hancock's comment to Cargill seems slightly disingenuous given the quality of so many of the earlier established names: 'I'm used to working with comics who put on a doctor's white jacket or a postman's cap, but they're still a comic underneath; [when you're] working with actors you are the doctor, you are the postman. I'm able to rebound so much more because I've got real people there.'

The expectation for the new series was spine-tingling. The absence of Sid James provided its own litmus test, and far more so than in *The Rebel*, where, as Hancock had always maintained, the idea of their independence from each other had already been established in the multitude of films made by Sid on his own. The nation heaved a sigh of relief when he proved he could hold his own without James. The series would unquestionably produce some of Hancock's best work, but it should be stressed that the shows were not better or funnier because Sid was not there. Most people today would probably swear that he *was* in one or two. Moreover, few could disagree that, say, *The Blood Donor*, arguably the most memorable of the shows, might have been enhanced by his presence, with Sid's no-nonsense sidekick able to puncture the vainglory, pinpoint the cowardice of Hancock's donor to additional comic effect; or that *The Bowmans* might have gained piquancy if Sid had been standing by as Hancock's agent to fight his corner when he is sacked, only of course to make matters irredeemably worse for his client. However, irrespective of such speculation, when in 2005 the devotees within the Tony Hancock Appreciation Society exercised their right to vote for their favourite television episodes, as they had done with his radio programmes, all but one of the new series of six figured in the top ten, alongside *The Missing Page*, *The Economy Drive*, *Twelve Angry Men*, *Lord Byron Lived Here* and *The Train Journey*. This popularity accords with the bigger audiences Hancock achieved for the new season. The opening episode on 26 May 1961 was seen by an estimated 14.4 million viewers, the series achieving an average audience of 11.52 million. Friday night remained Hancock night, with his transmission time now fixed at eight o'clock. It may have helped that he was now scheduled against the softer opposition of the ITV current affairs programme, *This Week*, but any gains so achieved may have been offset by being transmitted during the lighter evenings of early summer. In the ten areas of the country where ITV provided an alternative, Hancock was invariably shown to be the most consistently watched BBC show. Nothing, however, could stop the double assault on the ratings exercised by *Bootsie and Snudge* and *The Army Game*, which alongside veteran shows like *Emergency Ward Ten* and *Take Your Pick* and a relative newcomer called *Coronation Street* dominated the combined national top ten to the exclusion of all BBC shows.

Pride of place in the appreciation society poll went to the second programme to be broadcast, a pastiche of *The Archers* radio soap opera entitled *The Bowmans*. The episode was not without its problems, the incompetence of the BBC Ticket Unit contriving to deliver into the audience no less than seventy children of an average age of eight years who reacted with the silence born of incomprehension throughout. In a memo to ensure it never happened again Duncan Wood explained that the cast was thrown completely and that only major retakes rescued the situation. As a result, he added, the show was not as good as it could have been. That does not prevent it from remaining one of Galton and Simpson's favourite shows. The storyline foreshadowed the more serious treatment of the same subject in Frank Marcus's play *The Killing of Sister George* by three years and, as we have seen, gave Hancock full scope to indulge his rustic yokel party turn, with a touch of Robert Newton as Long John Silver on the side, in the character of 'Old Joshua Merryweather'. After five years, by which time his persistent ad-libbing and dialogue tampering – 'I've got mangelwurzels in me garden, I've got mangelwurzels in me shed' – have strained the patience of his producer and fellow cast members to the point of zero tolerance, he is written out of the show. There is public outcry when he meets his end by falling into a threshing machine and for once Hancock gains the last laugh when he is reinstated in the cast as Joshua's twin brother, Ben. The irony of the episode is that within a few years Hancock could not prevent himself from falling into a threshing machine of his own making. In the interview he recorded for Alan Whicker the year before he died, the broadcaster tackled him on shrugging off his old East Cheam character and the constant remoulding that appeared to follow. Hancock replied, 'The British public is extremely loyal, but very against change. I mean, some of those serials that have been drearing [*sic*] on for years and years and years, you know – the dog gets killed and the nation goes into mourning. The loyalty is immense.' In his death scene, almost his last words as old Joshua were, 'Me last wish – I'd like me dear old dog to be buried alongside of me.' Hancock's public would have welcomed him back to East Cheam or Earl's Court any day, but he had no twin brother to repay its loyalty.

The third transmission was allocated to *The Radio Ham*, the programme that perfectly caught the obsessive nature of Hancock's character. Taking a hint from Bergson, Kenneth Tynan once argued that the person who sees life through the blinkers of a fixed idea is by definition comic. The argument applies as much to Jack Benny, whose wealth drives out all other considerations, as to Jacques Tati, whose myopic self-centredness is the key to his comic world. This episode confirms Hancock as one of that company. Having invested £500 in a spectacular array of short-wave radio equipment, he was now able to converse with like-minded people around the globe. As he contemplates the two new radio valves he has just unwrapped, the lad has never been happier: 'Ah, you little beauties. We'll soon have the watts throbbing through you, and your filaments glowing red hot, carrying the thoughts and words of mankind to the four corners of the world. Oh, there's nothing like a DS 19/87B. Look at you – a triumph of technological engineering – a work of art. They can keep their Mona Lisa. Give me the inside of a wireless set any day.' His new enthusiasm is not without its sacrifices. As he relieves himself of his headphones for a few seconds, he rubs his head tenderly: 'By golly, the old ears are hot under there – like a couple of braised lamb cutlets.' The world, he claims, is his oyster, although the focus of interest seems strangely limited. We sense that £500 is an expensive way of being able to play chess, cards and snakes and ladders one move at a time and to discover what the weather is doing where it least concerns you. Soon our thinking catches up with Hancock. His would-be-heroic side comes to the fore in a craving for excitement. He does not have to wait long before he picks up a Mayday distress signal from a sailor some 300 miles off the African coast. By the time he has dealt with a broken pencil, a lost wavelength, angry neighbours, a power cut and exploding valves, he discovers that his weather-obsessed contact in Japan – 'I bet there's not many people round here who know it's not raining in Tokyo' – has stolen all his glory by acting on the call himself. 'Well, that's my Duke of Edinburgh Medal up the spout,' he groans. 'Oh dear, what a life!' When another distress signal comes through from the Indian Ocean, he decides he's better off turning the dial to less dangerous zones. A Yugoslavian voice comes through loud and clear: 'Queen's Pawn to King's Rook Two. Checkmate, I believe.' At which point in an ultimate statement Hancock sweeps the chessmen to the floor and proceeds to pull out every plug in sight, while singing *sotto voce* through clenched teeth, 'When you come to the end of a perfect day!'

An equally frustrating day would be provided by the episode *The Lift*. It is intriguing that this show, the second to be recorded in the series, was demoted to fourth in transmission running order. The plan had been to record three weeks ahead of transmission, a procedure observed with the first episode. However, *The Bowmans*, which was recorded fourth down the line, was rushed forward to second place. Apart from the magnificent way in which that show milked Hancock's old impressions repertoire and actor-laddie aspirations, it was far less typical of the realistic situation Hancock and his writers had been working towards. The idea of being stuck in a lift at BBC Television Centre – or anywhere – resonates with glorious echoes of his disastrous train journey and that terrible Sunday afternoon at home. Perhaps in this respect it was considered too close in ambience to the opening show of the series, *The Bedsitter*, which we have still to consider. Or perhaps Galton and Simpson had fallen into the trap that would characterise much of his subsequent television work. Upon revisiting the episode after many years I question whether – before he has even entered the lift – Hancock has become not only obstreperous, but unnecessarily so. In commenting on his subsequent 1963 series for ATV, Ray Galton makes the fair observation that in their day the anger shown by the character required provocation to set it off: 'Provoked, he would turn, but he would never be angry with people until they kicked him.' Aside from the fact that they both have an eye for the same pretty girl, his comments to the young television producer played by Jack Watling don't quite ring true: 'Look, sonny, don't show off in front of the young lady. Don't push your luck. I may look a mug, but I know how to handle myself.' The clenched fist with its invitation to fisticuffs aggravates matters: 'See that. I don't usually muck about with amateurs, but I'm prepared to have a go.' It is the difference between being comically irksome, as he was on the train journey, and sheer unpleasantness, several uncomfortable leagues away from the 'Are you insinuating that I'm portly?' badinage with Hugh Lloyd's lift attendant later in the episode. Two weeks later when writing *The Bowmans* Galton and Simpson gave Hancock as old Joshua, fighting for his professional life, an apt line:

'It's the scriptwriters – they don't know what they're doing – they're making me far too unsympathetic. Last week I kicked the dog three times.' In *The Lift* he is saved by the intervention of a reverend gentleman. 'An ecclesiastical digit may be just what's required,' says Hancock. The episode then builds into one of his strongest, with Tony as the ninth person to step into a lift which will carry only eight. He refuses to leave and they get stuck between floors. The enforced incarceration gives him full opportunity to run the traditional gamut of wartime heroics, mock philosophising, charades and community singing. However, it cannot be overlooked that the estimated audience of 11 million viewers that watched *The Lift* dipped to 10.3 million for *The Blood Donor* the following week, before climbing back up slightly to 10.6 million for the final episode, *The Succession – Son and Heir*.

The quality of Galton and Simpson's writing for Hancock was marked by a depth and precision of detail, bordering on the poetic, which no one else ever captured. It was most in evidence in their greatest achievement, *The Blood Donor*. No sooner has Hancock confronted the nurse at the reception desk played by June Whitfield than he is in full flight: 'I've come in answer to your advert on the wall next to the Eagle Laundry in Pelham Road ... You must have seen it. There's a nurse pointing at you, a Red Cross lady actually, I believe, with a moustache and a beard – pencilled in, of course ... next to "Hands off Cuba", just above the cricket stumps.' Later in the waiting room he assesses his contribution to charity in an attempt to impress a fellow donor played by Frank Thornton. Hancock feels they should get a badge – 'nothing grand, a little enamelled thing' – when Thornton suggest he wants money. 'Don't be vulgar,' insists Hancock, bringing out his little black book. 'It's all down here in me diary. Congo relief – two and six. Self Denial Week – one and eight. Lifeboat Day – a tanner. Arab refugees – one and two. It's all down here – yes – yes – I do what I can. My conscience is clear. And when I'm finally called by the Great Architect and they say "What did you do?", I'll just bring me book out and I shall say, "Here you are, mate! Count that lot up!"' Before the pivotal consultation scene, it remains for Hancock to do his mock-heroic bit with Whitfield in the waiting room. He becomes apprehensive that something might be amiss in the surgery. As he explains, he's seen it all before, men built like oak trees keeling over like saplings in a hurricane at the sight of a needle. Not that needles bother him. 'I've got arms like pin-cushions,' he boasts. 'Yes, I reckon I've had a syringeful of everything that's going in my time.'

He is ushered in to meet Dr MacTaggart, whom he greets with a mixture of doggerel suggestive of a Hogmanay entertainment. Cargill, who gives as impressive a performance here as he had done as the curt radio producer in *The Bowmans*, asks him to sit down in a cultured English accent. Hancock apologises for lapsing into the vernacular, but the doctor assures him, 'We're not all Rob Roys.' Only Cargill himself could rival Hancock for superciliousness, and the dialogue that ensues remains the most quotable in the Hancock *oeuvre*:

DOCTOR: Hold your hand out, please. This won't hurt. You'll just feel a slight prick on the end of your thumb.

TONY: (*Surprised it's all over so soon*) Well, I'll bid you good day then. Thank you very much. Whenever you want any more, don't hesitate to get in touch with me.

DOCTOR: Where are you going?

TONY: To have my tea and biscuits.

DOCTOR: I thought you came here to give some of your blood.

TONY: Well, you've just had it.

DOCTOR: That's just a smear.

TONY: It may be a smear to you, mate, but it's life and death to some poor devil.

DOCTOR: No. I've just taken a small sample to test.

TONY: A sample? How much do you want then?

DOCTOR: Well a pint, of course.

TONY: A pint? Have you gone raving mad? You must be joking.

DOCTOR: A pint is a perfectly normal quantity to take.

TONY: You don't seriously expect me to believe that. I mean, I came in here
in all good faith to help me country. I don't mind giving a reasonable
amount, but a pint – that's very nearly an armful. I'm sorry. I'm not
walking around with an empty arm for anybody.

With those few unforgettable words – 'That's very nearly an armful'
– no actor had used indignation to such memorable comic effect since
Edith Evans with her infamous interpretation of 'a handbag?' had
made life impossible for all other actresses to follow in her footsteps
as Lady Bracknell.

Almost as noteworthy is the interlude in the recovery ward
where, to paraphrase the humorist Alan Coren, Hancock finds himself shallow in conversation with fellow donor Hugh Lloyd. This
sequence represents the culmination of all the platitudes Galton and
Simpson had strung together for the pair over the years. The health
clichés and trite expressions of well-being tumble forth, defining
conversation as what people use to fill the silences that hang
between them, far more so than as the straightforward conveyance
of meaning.

TONY: Yes, it's very funny stuff, blood.

HUGH: I don't know where we'd be without it.

TONY: That's true. That's very true. Where would we be without it? Yes, it's
very important, blood. It circulates right around the body, you know …

HUGH: … oh I see. Are you a doctor then?

TONY: Well no, not really. I never really bothered.

HUGH: Oh.

As with Pinter, it was all in what was left unsaid. Hancock, fortified
by the discovery that he belongs to a rare blood group – 'AB Negative,'

he announces with a smugness only he could relish – never relents his self-aggrandizing ways. 'I could have been a doctor,' he seems to be saying, 'but I had more important things to do in life.' Otherwise they might as well have been reading the mottoes from Christmas crackers. Nothing really matters until Lloyd has gone on his way and Hancock discovers he has walked off with his wine gums: 'Oh what's the use? If you can't trust blood donors, who can you trust?'

One of the most potent clichés of personal Hancock mythology is that *The Blood Donor* completely revolutionised his approach to learning lines. The record states that driving home around five o'clock in the morning after the recording of *The Bowmans* the week before, Cicely crashed their Mercedes sports car into a road barrier on Brixton Hill. She escaped with a gash to her forehead. Hancock's head went through the windscreen, as a result of which he suffered from concussion and double vision. He had been fast asleep when it happened. Neither had been wearing seat belts. They both went to hospital for treatment, but were able to go home a short while later. It is generally accepted among friends that her alcohol intake had been a contributory factor. Two days later at rehearsals for the next show it soon became apparent to Duncan Wood that Hancock, with his concentration and memory-span seemingly in tatters, was way behind in learning his lines. After consultation between producer and star, it was agreed the show could go ahead at the end of the week as planned with back-up from Autocue machines and cue cards, or 'idiot boards' as they were unkindly named. Although he was supportive of the comedian, the reliance on such devices did offend Wood's professional pride. He later conceded that Hancock's line of vision was askew and that he should have cancelled the recording. If with the benefit of hindsight you scrutinise the tape of *The Blood Donor* you can certainly detect his eye line veering slightly away from the character to whom he is talking in order to read his words from the machine. However, to the lay audience this, like a magician's secret wires, was not apparent on transmission. If Hancock's performance in all other respects did not appear to suffer, equal applause was deserved by Elizabeth Armstrong, the BBC make-up artist, who spent an hour before the recording working her own special magic to transform, in Wood's words, a panda with two of the biggest black eyes he'd ever seen back into the nation's comedy favourite.

The myth implies that Hancock had never resorted to memory aids in the past, and emphasises that once weaned on the principle now, he never bothered to learn his lines in the future. The latter is not true, although, as we shall see, he came to rely more and more on technology to the detriment of his performance. For his last BBC show, at Wood's insistence, he did make a genuine attempt to learn his lines as his performance reveals and the technology was used purely in a 'belt and braces' capacity. With regard to the proposition that he had never used prompting devices before *The Blood Donor*, if you study much of his soliloquising at the beginning of *The Radio Ham*, which had been recorded only two weeks earlier, he is quite obviously reading from cards. An even more blatant example occurred in *Football Pools*, the last episode of the previous series, where he fantasises about his triumphs at Wembley Stadium in 1939. This was recorded in the immediate aftermath of the suicide of his stepfather. It is understandable that in the circumstances with a tight transmission deadline and no shows in reserve he should resort to aid in this manner. Unfortunately the sequence is long and for Wood to accommodate the boards Hancock has to move over to the side of the set, where he ends up playing away from Sid, to whom he should be addressing his performance.

Although he preferred the weekly challenge of applying himself to a new script for television to the mechanised rote of repeating the same sketches over and over again in the theatre, learning lines had always been a strain and the cause of much personal anxiety. He evolved a method, not peculiar to himself within the acting profession, of recording everybody else's dialogue onto a tape machine and leaving gaps for his own. Most of Sunday would be spent hunched over his trusty reel-to-reel tape recorder talking to himself in this way. When Grundig heard, they cajoled him into endorsing a series of newspaper advertisements for them:

> Sitting with me feet on the mantelpiece mugging up the cues with the old Grundig, three hours to a tape, change it as often as I like, hear myself as real as I'm talking to you now; I could see what would happen. In next to no time there'd only be two names in steam radio. Mine and James Watt, who invented it ... there I'd stand in the studio, master of the situation, a radio script in one hand and a television script in the other, offering the less fortunate members of the cast a dip in me bag of jelly babies, flinging in a few lines of Gogol and that lot to give 'em a bit of cultural uplift. Nonchalant? Oh my word, yes. I'm twice the man on Grundig (and I may tell you there are people who'll say that isn't possible).

He once confessed to a journalist that their parrot did a wonderful impression of him working away on the tape recorder in 'a sort of low-pitched grunt'. Philip Oakes remembers the bird chipping in with irrelevant dialogue which threw Hancock completely. The creature did not remain in the household for long. According to Hugh Lloyd, this technique was enough to render Hancock word perfect at rehearsals the next day. But even this did not allay his fear: 'Until the recording started he was a trembling mass. Once he got a first laugh he was fine ... I never saw him forget anything. It was just the fear that he was going to.' Valerie James recalls the panic attacks in the dressing room before a show when the words would liquefy in his mouth and he'd stand over the washbasin in terror: 'My mouth is filling with water – I don't think I can say the lines.' Valerie, who never missed one of her husband's television recordings with Hancock, also remembers cue cards carrying the lines he feared he'd forget as a regular fixture on the set throughout Sid's association with the

show. Gerry Mill, now a director in his own right, was often responsible in a humbler capacity for this aspect of the production. He
explained the procedure to Richard Webber: 'There was a kind of pattern. He'd do two or three shows and would be word perfect; then,
perhaps the third or fourth show, he'd say, "Can you give me a cue
card for that line?" Then a couple of days later he'd ask, "Would you
do that other line?"' It ended with Mill putting the whole script on
cue cards. Lloyd recalled prompt notes all over the set. In one scene
Sid put his feet on the table less out of bad manners than to enable
Hancock to read the cues stuck to the soles.

I have purposely left for later consideration the first of the shows
in his last BBC series. It represents one of the major achievements
of the partnership between performer and writers, defining the
series to come and, in retrospect, capable of being seen alongside the
final show as one of two parts of a larger whole. At the time of writing Galton and Simpson had no idea that this would be the last television series they would write for Hancock, nor any inkling of the
tragedy that lay ahead for the comedian. Nonetheless the two
episodes together provide a fitting summation of their association.
Both shows underline the theme of isolation that came to define his
real life and provided the motif that runs through the other four
shows in different ways. As long as Sid was around, Hancock was
never wholly the outsider. Now, ostracised from his fellow actors,
cocooned in his Mayday world, turned against in a perilous situation, isolated from the herd by dint of blood and – if we include *The
Rebel* in the equation – left to his artistic devices, Hancock exists in
a world apart. The observation from *The Radio Ham* says as much:
'Friends from all over the world. None in this country, but all over the
world.' Not that he is inviting our sympathy. Only in the sense that
life would come to imitate art as he became more and more isolated
professionally does he require our understanding, if not our pity.
Among his most illustrious forebears, Chaplin, Keaton, Tati had all
made comic capital out of their detachment, but while the others

'Ancock's Angst, 1963.

In descending order: Sidney James, Tony, Bill Kerr and Kenneth Williams.

An early *Hancock's Half Hour* radio recording with Sid, Bill, Moira and Tony.

Hattie Jacques welcomed to the team by Tony and Sid.

Dennis Main Wilson, without whom …

23 Railway Cuttings, as the nation remembers it.

Iconic Hancock.

Looking up to Alan Simpson (left) and Ray Galton, also without whom...

With Kenneth Williams as Snide, on an early television show.

Tony at
rehearsals with
Sid and producer
Duncan Wood.

Sid: 'The greatest
friend I ever had.'

Being sketched by Feliks
Topolski for *Face to Face*.

The Blood Donor, with Patrick Cargill: 'It may be a smear to you, mate, but it's life and death to some poor devil.'

The world on his shoulders.

The Rebel: 'I want to fly to London.'

Learning his lines.

With Freddie on their wedding day, December 1965.

With Philip Oakes.

The Punch and Judy Man: 'You can't expect a performance when it's coming down like this.'

Tony with John Le Mesurier in the television episode *The Cruise*; Hattie hovers between them.

Joan Le Mesurier, at the time of her relationship with Tony.

Under pressure at ATV.

In Australia with Eddie Joffe (centre) and Hugh Stuckey.

As his friends remember him,
mid 1960s.

respectively used pathos, suspicion and reverie to deal with life's emptiness, Hancock remains shielded by a relentless antagonism. As he continually tells us, he finds the whole world raving mad anyway. In so far as humour works on the recognition principle, the fact that his comedy connected so well with that world suggests he may have been right.

The first episode almost seems to have come about in response to such a real-life outburst. If Hancock wanted to go it alone, the writers reasoned, they would take him at his word. The result was *The Bedsitter*. Ray and Alan took the script to Hancock in Shrewsbury where he was appearing for the week in variety, unsure how he would react to the idea of having to carry the full twenty-five minutes of a new script. They appreciated they were taking a risk, fully aware that with or without Sid James his success depended to a large degree on the reaction to and from other cast members. Fortunately he responded well to the idea, oblivious to any mickey-taking that was going on, preferring to read into the writers' ingenuity a massive ego-boost that he genuinely *could* go it alone. His performance proved to be a *tour de force*, at the time in his career so far when he needed it most. The speculation as to how well he would fare on television without James had been immense. Hancock was helped immeasurably by Duncan Wood's decision to use Alec Bregonzi as a stand-in during camera rehearsals, while he studied the television monitors over Wood's shoulder, making suggestions like, 'I think I can do something with my face there ... we can exploit that shot a bit more.' The result was twenty-five minutes in which nothing much happened at all. Here is Hancock on his sagging bed lifting his feet alternately heel to toe until the strain on his stomach muscles gives way – 'Getting old!' he exclaims; attempting to blow smoke rings and getting a burnt lip for his trouble; rummaging through a medicine cabinet for ointment only to discover rows of pre-NHS medicine, the white sediment as revolting as the murky liquid it has displaced, a nose-dropper with nothing to put in it and 'Oh, me nightlight … I've been looking for that!'; bemoaning the fact that the one chocolate left in the box is the marzipan; shaving: 'Ah, you can't beat the cold steel and the badger … razor blades – for men!'; reacting to the aftershave lotion: 'Fancy paying good money for stuff that hurts you!'; declaring that 'to waste one second of one's life is a betrayal of one's self' and then tuning in to a television Western in preference to Dr Bronowski. Amid this brilliant exposition of the minutiae of life's existence, what slight semblance of a plot does exist in the tenuous thread of telephone invitation to party from anonymous girl, his personal preening in preparation for the event, reversal of invitation when original partner does arrive, seems unnecessary, if not entirely irrelevant.

In another sense, however, this was the episode in which everything happened. Unintentionally Galton and Simpson provided Hancock with a kaleidoscopic overview of his life in microcosm. Here is the one-man *Face to Face* as he talks to himself in the looking glass; the genuflection to Peter Brough and Archie Andrews as he runs through the ventriloquial alphabet; the room not so far removed from the one he shared with John Beaver in nearby Barons Court; the regime at Durlston Court School in the medicine label that reads 'Master A. Hancock, Lower 4B'; the obsession with his feet; the impression of Maurice Chevalier, which was really an impression of George Fairweather impersonating the Frenchman; the pursuit of self-education in his determination to 'have a quick go at Bertrand Russell'; the passion for cricket, as he mimes Richie Benaud bowling from the pavilion end; the love of boats as he recalls flapping about in his Oxford bags on the towpath at Richmond. There could be no question that his new chunky-sweater intellectual look was exactly how Cicely and his closest friends most readily identified him; nor that 'Fred', the name of the previous tenant in whose place he is first invited to the party that never was, was his familiar name for Freddie Ross, his mistress. It is too much to suppose that his writers' crystal ball allowed them to see that this new resident of London's

Australian ghetto would spend his last days in a not dissimilar room in that very country, but here was the ultimate vindication of the theory Hancock had once expressed that great comedy could arise from 'frustration, misery, boredom, worry and insomnia'. In its own way the programme was as revealing as John Freeman's programme had ever been. The *Listener* went one step further when it said that 'no twenty-five minutes have more mercilessly or accurately pilloried the inner man in all of us'.

Hancock's attitude to the woman who stands him up is defiant: 'Eve has proffered the apple and Adam has slung it straight back.' The programme ends as it began, with Hancock adrift in an aimlessness of time. Bertrand Russell will have to wait for another day. 'It's all go, isn't it?' he says, as he settles back in an attempt to puff another smoke ring. For Hancock to have ended the episode anything but alone would have totally undermined the previous twenty-five minutes. It is significant that in the original script the show ends with a second phone call from the same girl inviting him to join her and Fred on their date. Hancock is adamant he wants nothing of it: 'What do you mean you feel sorry for me? I am not a poor little man. Now you listen to me, madam!' Any suggestion of sympathy or regret would have been anathema to the character. However, by the time of the last episode, *The Succession – Son and Heir*, he has conceded that the Hancock name will only be perpetuated by his tolerance of the opposite sex. He consults his little book of female acquaintances and, undecided between beauty, brains or breeding, settles on three possible contenders for marriage. In turn the floozie, the bluestocking and the debutante throw obstacles across the path of true romance, until in a hurried ending all three converge on his bedsitting room to accept his proposal at the same time. As they argue among themselves, Hancock grabs his suitcase and – in a neat touch that shows how well the writers understood their star – an unfinished bottle of wine and slyly makes his departure.

The last words Galton and Simpson unwittingly wrote for him were as final as they could have been without attracting sentiment:

'So exits the last of the Hancocks – good luck!' In the aftermath of subsequent events, the whole episode has an elegiac mood, as if the writers sensed that an end was on the horizon, while knowing not where. It is ironic that his early death and subsequent legend eventually forestalled the type of obscurity he imagined himself sliding into. In the opening scene he almost seamlessly picks up his conversation in the mirror from the first episode, but whereas first time around there was truculent buoyancy in his mood, now there is resigned wistfulness: 'What have you achieved? What *have* you achieved? ... You lost your chance, me old son. You've contributed absolutely nothing to this life. A waste of time you being here at all. No plaque for you in Westminster Abbey. The best you can expect is a few daffodils in a jam jar, a rough-hewn stone bearing the legend, "He came and he went," and in between – nothing! ... Nobody will ever know I existed. Nothing to leave behind me. Nothing to pass on. Nobody to mourn me. That's the bitterest blow of all.' He was only thirty-seven. It sounded funny at the time.

Elements of the loner had existed in his character from the beginning of his association with Galton and Simpson. To have become free of Bill and Hattie and Sid and all the others who had passed through his household had, for Hancock, not only signified a professional intention, but confirmed a comic advantage. It was perhaps inevitable that, set on such a course, he would become divorced from the writers who had seemingly become inseparable from him. Ray and Alan have admitted that the dream of naturalism and simplicity set out in Dennis Main Wilson's early manifesto for *Hancock's Half Hour* only really came to pass on a consistent basis in the last television series. Having achieved their goal, perhaps there was nowhere for the three of them to go without repeating themselves. Hancock could have had no idea how lonely life would really become when they set out on their divergent paths.

Chapter Eleven

MATTERS OF LOYALTY

*'Well, you go away and write some television
and I'll think about the film and we'll get
back together later.'*

According to correspondence addressed to the BBC, by June 1957
Hancock had decided not to renew his five-year agency agreement
with Kavanagh Associates. He may well have continued with them
had Galton and Simpson not by then established themselves within
a similar cooperative along the lines Ted Kavanagh had contemplated when he first entered management. The story has been told many
times of the office established up five flights of stairs above a green-
grocer's shop at 130 Uxbridge Road, Shepherd's Bush, by Eric Sykes
and Spike Milligan, with not a little help from Eric's agent, Stanley
Dale, known to all as 'Scruffy'. Dale had played an influential role in
establishing Frankie Howerd as a major star and as a character
could well have walked out of one of Howerd's rambling monologues.
He bore a close resemblance to Wilfrid Brambell and conducted most
of his business from the bedroom he shared with a formidable
Alsatian in the basement of a large house in Addison Road. Although
his physical appearance made it hard to imagine he had ever been in
the RAF, he had served as a flight lieutenant and won the DFC after
sitting on an incendiary shell that penetrated his plane. He lost a tes-
ticle in the process, and, according to Sykes, Milligan when he found

out took great delight in muttering, 'I hope he dropped it on Dresden.' Dale had already set up Frankie Howerd Scripts Limited for his client. Before long the two companies amalgamated to their mutual benefit. Eric has described the altruistic rationale behind the project: 'We would all do our own thing, but subscribe to a fund that would be there when one of us hit a fallow period. There were several rooms so we invited two young chaps who were just beginning to get the odd success to take one of them.' Following a meeting on 1 September 1954, Galton and Simpson agreed to join the combine that became known as Associated London Scripts when Companies House deemed Associated British Scripts too grandiose.

By January 1959 Hancock had authorised the BBC to make all future payments on his behalf to Stanley Dale at ALS. After a year, however, Dale left the organisation under a cloud, when it came to light that he had been funding private business ventures, such as skiffle contests and wrestling promotions, from money partly embezzled from his ALS colleagues. Fortunately by then the business responsibility for the cooperative had devolved effortlessly upon the shoulders of Beryl Vertue, an old school chum of Alan Simpson who had been recruited as secretary soon after he and Ray joined the team. Her level-headedness and organisational skills made her the perfect candidate to bring some sense of order into the lives and careers of the greatest combined creative force British comedy has ever known. When the contract for a series came to an end, Ray and Alan would simply bypass Dale and give her the nod 'to see if she could get some more work out of the BBC'. The informality matched the creative mood of the place and she became their, and eventually Hancock's, representative by default. Now Beryl recalls, 'I was the only one in the office who was not a writer. It was not until someone said to me, "How long have you been an agent?" that I realised I was one.' At the beginning of 1957 the firm left behind the pungent smells that wafted up from the fruit and vegetables at ground level and moved to the grander premises of Cumberland

House, an imposing red-brick mansion block on Kensington High Street two miles away. In time other writers of the moment like Johnny Speight, Terry Nation, John Antrobus and Brad Ashton would come on board. Towards the end of 1960, in an attempt to relieve the overworked ex-secretary, Roger Hancock, who had previously run his own talent agency, joined the company in a general managerial capacity principally at the behest of Galton and Simpson, following an interim period with Lou Berlin in a similar role. According to Beryl, 'You were never aware he was the boss. It was quite a casual organisation and you just got on with it. We were all so busy; you couldn't keep up with it all.' There is no truth in the supposition that Tony was responsible for bringing his brother into the company, and in the early days of Roger's tenure there was a strict stipulation from the elder brother that the younger should not handle his affairs. The company's move to the now legendary 9 Orme Court, where Spike Milligan retained his office until his death in 2002 and where Eric Sykes still follows his comedic muse, did not occur until the spring of 1961. By the end of the year the unimaginable had happened and Hancock's relationship with Galton, Simpson and Vertue had irrevocably changed.

The perceived wisdom behind their split is a continuing disagreement between Hancock and his writers over the screenplay for his second picture under the ABPC deal. His final BBC television series had been placed under threat because of their inability to reach a consensus on the matter, although fortuitously, by the middle of March, ABPC saw the sense of postponing their project in favour of the small-screen exposure they felt essential for Hancock's ongoing popularity. Beryl is convinced that when the time came he had conditioned himself into breaking with the writers, having made up his mind that having peaked together they were now limiting his horizons: 'He kept coming in and talking to me about the film script, almost willing himself not to like it.' It was a difficult situation for Vertue, caught in the middle and unsure of how much of this she should be passing on to her other two clients. Tom Sloan, in an internal memo ahead of the 1961 television series, had referred to Galton and Simpson as being in 'the writing doldrums', but only because of Hancock's cinematic uncertainties. The first film proposal, with the working title 'The Brothers', cast him as the layabout black sheep of a family, returning from South America to wreak havoc in turn on the more successful lives of his four brothers, ambassador, bishop, doctor and television executive respectively. The writers were a third of the way through the screenplay when Hancock phoned with misgivings that the idea was not international enough. He had not even seen what they had written, but they agreed to change direction. The second proposal, provisionally entitled 'Winter in the Sun', sent the comedian on a world cruise, a perfect premise with which to emulate the plotless but eventful ambience of Jacques Tati at his best, as well as having limitless international scope location-wise. The comic mileage to be provided by such familiar Hancock devices as a closed community, class consciousness and time to kill all augured well. A few weeks intervened before he phoned to express his doubts again. This time he was concerned that the picture was *too* similar to *Monsieur Hulot's Holiday*. And so another unread script was aborted as Hancock repeated his recurring mantra of admonishment: 'We can do better.' That the hard work put down so far had scarcely involved him at all seemed to pass him by.

For their third attempt the writers begged him to agree not to pass judgement until their screenplay was completed. His initial enthusiasm for the basic idea of 'The Day Off' was not misplaced, another Tati-style premise built around the vacuum of anonymous small-town life and the use and misuse of leisure. It is impossible to read the script today without seeing how effective a vehicle it could have been for him. Hancock begins the film cudgelled into consciousness by his elaborate triple alarm clock ritual and a dawn chorus of clinking milk bottles. On automatic pilot he drags himself through the daily drudgery of bathroom routine, throws on his bus conductor's uniform, breakfasts on the run on a cigarette and an apple, and dashes out of the front door. At this point his landlady asks him where he is going: 'But, Mr Hancock. It's Wednesday. It's your day off.' He stops dead at the garden gate and turns back slowly. 'Well, for crying out loud, why didn't you tell me it was Wednesday?' 'I've just told you.' 'I mean last night.' 'It wasn't Wednesday last night.' One easily pictures the glower on his face as he trudges back, snatches his copy of the *Ballroom Dancing Weekly* off the hall table, and returns to his room. From this point the day stretches ahead of him as he wanders aimlessly between barber's shop, supermarket, post office, menswear boutique, restaurant, cinema, park, bowling alley, *palais de danse*. Platitudes are spoken, silent gags are explored, fantasy sequences depict his innermost thoughts and *en passant* the script, in deference to the emotional undertow the cinema might require, provides him with what may have been a workable 'romantic' encounter. They meet in a café. He claims he's an important architect. She works as a shop assistant in 'Stella's Modes', but makes out she is an international model. They meet again by chance at the dance hall later. He walks her home to a luxury block of flats. A bus goes by and a driver friend waves. 'Had a good day off?' he enquires. 'Don't stay up too long. Early turn tomorrow.' Hancock's cover is blown and the couple part acrimoniously. Once he has gone, she hurries tearfully around the corner to the less than luxurious 'Clement Attlee House'. Hancock stays true to character: 'Stupid woman. Why don't they leave you alone? ... Tonight's the night, huh. The turning point it was going to be! A short haircut, a new hat, and I'm right back where I started. I don't know why I bother.' In the early hours of the morning he arrives back home with the street-cleaning truck. His landlady shouts out to ask if it's him. 'No, it's Jack the Ripper,' he shouts. At least there'll be another day off next week. The whole script flowers out of his initial discomfiture and pulls in its petals as the world shuts down for the night. Feasibly Frankie Howerd or another comedian could have made *The Rebel* work. 'The Day Off' could have been pulled off by Hancock alone. The opportunity never arose.

The principal day of reckoning as far as Beryl Vertue is concerned occurred some time in the early autumn of 1961. Emotion and disappointment have a tendency to distort recall, but almost half a century later Vertue recollects what happened with a focused clarity as if it were yesterday. It began with a summons one Sunday to the dingy brown and cream service flat that Hancock was renting within the White House Hotel along the Euston Road. The meeting was ostensibly to talk about the script for 'The Day Off'. Beryl remembers, 'There was no chit-chat. No talk about the weather. We had hardly sat down when he said to Alan and Ray, "I don't want you to do this and I don't really want you to write for me any more." He then turned to me and added, "And because you're so closely associated with the boys, I think it would be better if you didn't look after me any more. And so Roger will do it." We all sat there in a stunned silence and then we left, because there was nothing else to say.' Hancock looked embarrassed. The announcement must have been difficult for him, but he had at least faced up to the task and not taken refuge in the social cowardice inherent in his handling of the Sid James situation, even if the abruptness of his manner shows he still had a lot to learn in this area of personal relations. This time there was no BBC executive to hide behind. After a cursory goodbye, Ray, Alan and Beryl made their bewildered way downstairs where amid the echoing emerald green tiles of the deserted hotel pool they ordered a pot of tea for three: 'I thought I was going to cry and trying not to, but it wasn't anything to do with losing a client. It felt a bit like a bereavement. We were all so close. It was really sad.' As for Hancock she adds, 'There was not a hint of emotion. No "I'm sorry." The BBC was stunned and tried to talk him out of it, but he'd set his mind on it.' It was the first time she had seen even a trace of ruthlessness in his behaviour. With the tears stinging her eyes, the decaying grandeur of the surroundings was not lost on her. Had she compared notes with Phyllis Rounce, she might have considered herself well treated. Roger was still overall manager of ALS. He detached himself from the organisation as soon as the formalities were completed and took over the basement suite of offices for his own company. The writers, the agent and the younger brother were and have always remained friends.

Ray Galton supports the detail of this scenario, but finds himself in disagreement with his partner in so doing. In Alan's words: 'It's not so much that we disagree about what happened. What we disagree about is the chronological aspect.' Simpson sees Hancock's decision to leave Vertue and the matter of the script as two separate issues, a view strengthened by his memory that they were still working on the screenplay at the time of the meeting and continued to do so. For Simpson, the whole point of the White House meeting was to announce that he was detaching himself from Beryl. The separation between writers and artist came during a phone call shortly after that event, a conversation he remembers quite vividly, not least because by now Ray and Alan were both resigned to the outcome:

TONY: How are you then?

ALAN: All right.

TONY: Have you read the script?

ALAN: Yeh, we've read it. We wrote it.

TONY: Of course you did, yes.

ALAN: Well, what did you think of it?

TONY: Well, what do you think?

ALAN: Well, we like it.

TONY: Mm, yeh.

ALAN: You don't like it, do you?

TONY: It's not that. It's not that I don't like it, but it's not …

At this point Simpson had to emphasise to the sheepish Hancock that in no way could they go without payment for another six months writing screenplays on spec that were not going to reach the screen. They had financial obligations to themselves and their families. This let Hancock off the hook: 'Well, you go away and write some television and I'll think about the film and we'll get back together later.' There was no acrimony, only disappointment and uncertainty. The opportunity to collaborate on another movie never occurred. Hancock went scurrying back to an old idea of his which, according to Alan, had been rejected ahead of 'The Brothers', the story of a disillusioned Punch and Judy professor in a rain-sodden South Coast seaside resort. As the writers have slyly acknowledged, you couldn't get more international than that. Roger Hancock, while conceding that his brother did upset Beryl terribly, tends to side with Simpson and agrees that the main agenda of the meeting, at which he was present, was for Tony to announce his split from Beryl. The presence of Ray and Alan might have been intended to comfort her. It is unlikely that Hancock had any cause for actual complaint with Beryl herself. Valerie James adds an interesting footnote to the situation, recalling that her husband discussed the agent situation with Tony. There were indications that Hancock might have been considering the idea of Freddie Ross expanding her public relations brief to encompass all aspects of his management. Rather than see his friend centralise too much control in a single area, Sid, ever the pragmatist, encouraged Hancock to fall in behind Roger as a face-saving way out of the personal/professional dilemma.

Hancock's big mistake was less the decision to distance himself from his writers over one movie script, rather the assumption that they would always be there for him when the time came. Philip Oakes was always insistent that Hancock never intended the parting from Galton and Simpson to be final, a view endorsed by Roger Hancock. Simpson has never denied the callousness of the comedian's behaviour towards Vertue. But when the matter is discussed with them both, Galton emerges as the far less forgiving and, by his own admission, the more sensitive of the two. His own memory carries a cross for Beryl in a way that no one can begrudge either the writer or the agent. The only rational explanation to accommodate both viewpoints is that she was so shocked by her Draconian treatment at Hancock's hands that she displaced the sequence of events, the termination of the writers' involvement in the film project happening after her dismissal during the phone call that Alan describes. It is hard to believe that not long before – in fun – they had written the following lines for him: 'If it wasn't for me – the old breadwinner here – both you two would be in the workhouse – human derelicts both of you. I've carried you two long enough – this is the end of the line – the gravy train has just hit the buffers. You are now on your own. I do not need you any more.' The words had been addressed to Bill and Sid on the radio show, but they now carried a frisson their creators could never have envisaged. Within a year Hancock began to contemplate his next television series, this time for the independent network. The call came through to inquire if 'the boys' were available, which fate had decreed they were not. That is when the real slap in the face came. 'Well, never mind. We'll get somebody else,' was the reply. As if it could be that easy. As if the unstoppable inventiveness that had sustained him over the airwaves for the best part of a decade could be taken for granted in so cavalier a fashion.

In many ways the real separation had occurred with Hancock's apparent reluctance to do further television on a regular basis after the final BBC series. As he grabbed his suitcase and the token bottle of booze in his Earl's Court abode, he might already have been *en route* to his destiny in Australia. For Galton and Simpson, who might superficially have viewed themselves as the losers at the time, the future proved bright. They had always perceived themselves as the underdogs, patronisingly but affectionately referred to by all concerned as 'the boys', which relatively speaking in age terms they were. From being comedians' labourers they now enjoyed the boost of confidence to find themselves wanted entirely on their own merit. An unprecedented offer from the BBC to write their own series of ten unconnected half-hour comedies under the banner of *Comedy Playhouse* led by way of the fourth episode, *The Offer*, to the long-running series *Steptoe and Son*. They were no longer subsidiary to a star and could 'write down' to their hearts content, without fear of Hancock complaining either to Dennis Main Wilson or to Duncan Wood. Not many remember that an episode from the fifth radio series of *Hancock's Half Hour*, in which Sid assumed the role of a rag-and-bone man, had led the way. By the end of the show, which was entitled *The Junk Man*, Hancock too is plying the trade. 'Any old rags, bottles, or bones. Jam jars, sponges, firewood, washing machines,' he declaims in a hilarious strangulated cockney put on for the job. Essentially the new programme lifted the dynamic that had existed on air between Hancock and Sid onto the new emotional level of the father and son relationship. The comic collision between Wilfrid Brambell as Albert the Philistine groping for pickled onions in his bathwater and Harry H. Corbett as Harold the idealist gazing longingly at the stars was painful as well as funny. With Albert in constant fear that Harold would leave their junkyard home and Harold trapped in the prison of filial duty, so the writers discovered a new dramatic freedom and found they were able to tackle subjects that had not been possible before. Alan Simpson admits, 'You couldn't have a girl turn up on Hancock's doorstep who was eight months pregnant and claim that he's the father. Tony was a comedian and it doesn't work with comedians. You could make the young Steptoe a Socialist. The most Tony could be in those days was a Liberal or independent.' Audiences soon discovered that Albert and Harold needed each other. Hancock had already pronounced that he didn't need anyone. When he looked back on the whole affair in 1962, the success of the rag-and-bone men enabled him to spring to the defensive, but, of course, this was only in hindsight:

Again heads were reproachfully wagged when I went my own way to write my own script for 'The Punch and Judy Man' with my old friend Philip Oakes. You would have thought I had committed a major crime. How could I let these writers go – no, 'shed' them was the word – after all they had done for me? What did I think I was doing? The answer was that I was doing Alan and Ray the world of good by freeing them to spread their wings. They proved that well enough by writing some brilliant scripts for 'Comedy Playhouse' and out of that series grew their triumph with 'Steptoe and Son'.

When Beryl reassessed the situation in later years she was characteristically less concerned for herself than for Hancock and his writers. 'He could afford to abandon me,' she says, 'but I couldn't understand about Alan and Ray. They wrote for him so marvellously that when you heard the three of them talking together it was like a script in itself. They were him and he was them.' And possibly therein lay the problem. At times something almost telepathic would take over between them, to the extent that, as Simpson has observed, they could 'finish off each other's sentences'. But they not only had the measure of an idiomatically perfect Hancock. In many ways they knew him better than he knew himself. In an unnerving way they could have been watching his progress from the cradle, witnesses to events and insights into character they could never have seen. One recalls the young Hancock's defiance of public school, his acceptance of the potman's job as 'domestic manager', even the schoolboy preference for 'bread and *fromage*' to realise that the template for the persona they polished and defined was endemic in his earliest years. Starting off by writing for a voice – then purely a comic contrivance – they gradually brought the character into sharper, more natural focus. There can be little question that as they adapted many of Hancock's quirks and idiosyncrasies in the cause of comedy, these became blown up in the process, but Galton and Simpson have always taken pains to emphasise the elements of true-life

Hancock that they left alone. Alan distinguishes the 'quite sophisticated, well informed, intelligent person' he knew from the 'bombastic thickhead' they created, adding that much of this character was engrained in themselves as well. According to Galton, 'We took what we wanted and invented the rest, such as being very gullible and only half read, the sort of guy who reads all his information from the colour supplements,' or what passed for them at the time. Simpson admits that the famous incident from *The Bedsitter* where Hancock wrestles intellectually between Bertrand Russell and the dictionary was based on his own experience straight out of the sanatorium trying to comprehend the Penguin introduction to Kant and not being able to progress beyond the second or third page. Much of the 'punch up the bracket' patois that helped to define the world of East Cheam emanated more from the writers' South London milieu than from the slang of the comedian's RAF background, but, as Simpson acknowledges, 'Even if he didn't understand something, he was such a good performer, he could still get laughs with it.'

I am sure that one real-life episode that Dennis Main Wilson was fond of recounting catches the exact measure of the innocent swagger that made such an impression on Galton and Simpson. In the early years of Hancock's success his pride and joy was a converted pontoon grandly named *Shemara II*, in deference to the luxury yacht owned by Sir Bernard and Lady Docker, famous socialites of their day. Hancock had to admit that the vessel, which he kept on the towpath near Weybridge, was 'as low as you can get in the boat business'. It had seen better days. 'The decks are like blotting paper after a winter under water,' he admitted to reporters. One Easter Main Wilson and his girlfriend accepted an invitation to join Tony and Cicely on board: 'There was this wreck of an old hulk marooned on a mud bank – keeled over – moored at the back of somebody's garden – filthy and dirty … it *was* an old army pontoon that somebody had built a plywood cabin on with a roof. It looked like (it had) an old Austin Seven engine. Well I'd spent five years in the army in armoured cars and tanks and the gear box had been ripped and it only had third gear and reverse. We got the engine going and we actually managed to shove it out into the water and he'd even got the captain's cap with the mustard and cress all round – I can't tell you – hilarious – and we were having a ball with Tony up front doing the full master of the *Queen Mary* act. He's going "whoop whoop whoop" at the steering wheel and the people on the towpath are walking along faster than we were moving. It was enormous fun. He indulged in the fantasy.' Main Wilson was not present on a related occasion when Tony, all decked out in midnight-blue dinner jacket and suede shoes, found himself wading along the river bed after hauling to safety two men in difficulties in a canoe. 'What did you want to do that for?' enquired Cicely. 'Well, it wasn't for the sake of a cheap laugh,' replied Hancock.

Many were the moments based on real-life incidents. *The Threatening Letters* found its inspiration in an actual letter Tony brought to rehearsals. He reduced the cast to hysterics as he read out the contents: 'Dear Mr Hancock, I hate you, my wife hates you, and everybody down our street hates you. Why don't you give it up?' According to his writers, he had this mental picture of 'one whole street, both sides of the road, upstairs and downstairs, all united in their hatred of him'. In addition the letter came from Birmingham, his home town. 'It's probably the street where I was born,' he said. 'I do hope so.' One day Hancock bounced into the rehearsal room complaining that the milk supply at MacConkeys was under siege. A short while later the following sequence appeared in the *The Radio Ham*: 'Hello, the blue tits have been at my milk bottles again. Look at me gold top. Pecked to ribbons it is. They must have been like pneumatic drills, some of them. I will not have great feathered heads stuck in the top of my milk bottles, guzzling the cream.' His fear of flying, his superstition, his quest for knowledge, his token petulance and sheer bad luck were all turned into the stuff of laughter. The comedian Roy Hudd recalls being present at a drinking club for actors when Tony and Sid came in. Hancock proceeded to feed about £10 worth of sixpences into the fruit machine and didn't win once. He retired hurt to the bar and James took over, scooping the jackpot on the first go. As the noise of cascading coins enveloped his ears, Hancock didn't say a word. His face said it all.

Long before Hancock the professional became bored with the whole East Cheam concept, Ray and Alan latched onto a more pervasive ennui within the private man and turned it into comedy gold. Philip Oakes recalled that this manifested itself in a fascination for trivia. A regular column in the *Evening News* fed his interest. 'Rats build nest in mayor's top hat,' he pronounced to his friend one day. 'Mother of twins exhibits collection of lemonade bottles.' The East Cheam breakfast table became a perfect platform for such serendipity, the excuse to keep at bay the reality of another day. Much of his mock philosophising was constructed by Galton and Simpson upon the believe-it-or-not foundations of such a mentality: 'It's a funny thing, air. You can't see it, you can't touch it, you can't smell it, but it's there. It's just as well we've got it all around us. I mean supposing you had to carry your own supply around with you … you'd have to have something the size of the Albert Hall.' He goes on to reason that, at the rate we're all multiplying, the 'bloke with the biggest hooter' will survive. 'Well, you've got nothing to worry about,' says a fellow lift passenger. The television show where he had his nose remodelled struck a special chord with his mother: 'The family have got big noses and we've always been teased about them. It was even funnier to us when we saw the programme because we knew what was behind it.' If it wasn't the nose, it was the name. He never quite recovered from being announced as 'Mr Hitchcock' at that election night ball at Claridge's early in his career. Tiny Hitchcock, Tommy Hemlock, Toby Handcart were all sobriquets guaranteed to deflate his character on air over the years. In real life Beryl Vertue asserts that he detested being called 'Tone'. Its use was a sure-fire way for Galton and Simpson to inject a wrong note into an encounter with the opposite sex.

Hancock was well aware of the process. It was inevitable that during his *Face to Face* interview John Freeman should ask him how much of his on-screen persona corresponded to himself. After some initial blustering, he concedes that the character he plays is not one he puts on and off like a coat: 'It is greatly a part of me and part of everybody else that I see.' When pressed to be more specific about the things he dislikes in himself, Hancock admits to his own affectation as a prime trait for professional ridicule: 'I often find in a script things that I've said in all seriousness which they later write up in detail and absolutely which later turn out to be funny. If I've been angry or something like that. I look at this and I think, "Yes, that's very funny, unfortunately." It's something I've said at the time and been rather pompous about, and they've noticed this and written it down, and there it is.' So cleverly did the writers create his persona within his own image, it is no wonder he became confused. On the one hand, as he forged ahead independently of Galton and Simpson, he appeared at times like a man trying, in David Nathan's phrase, 'to lose his own shadow'; on the other he became committed to the process they had established. As late as November 1966, with new writers – John Muir and Eric Geen – now in attendance, he explained to the journalist Robert Ottaway the need for the writing to reflect his inner self: 'That's why writers have to spend a lot of time with me. I see Geen and Muir practically every day. We discuss what's going into the new series. But the important thing is that they should get to know as much as they possibly can about me. Delve underneath. Burrow into my psyche. Sort out the inner man. They have to know how I put things across in conversation before they can project the right sort of stuff for an audience.' Ray and Alan had devised the system. The invitation to join him for his ITV series in 1963 at least recognised that fact.

Philip Oakes acknowledged Hancock's own wonderful turn of phrase and suggested that he needed a Boswell to keep him constant company, without recognising that he and Ray and Alan fulfilled that very role. Friends and journalists were also witness to comments that never made it to the script stage, but leap off the page as if they had. There was the time a taxi driver advised him he didn't think much of his show on the box the night before. 'I don't like the way you're driving this taxi,' replied Hancock. When comedy actor and writer John Junkin shared with him a glimpse of his new passport photo, the comedian joked, 'Stone me, this man is wanted for assaulting a goat on Clapham Common.' There was the farewell line to the journalist at MacConkeys: 'Pick yourself some conkers on the way out. You'll have to find your own string, though.' And again the request for a headache pill at a showing of *The Longest Day*: 'Why, have you got a headache?' asked migraine-racked Freddie Ross. 'No,' retorted Hancock. 'Shell shock.' On another visit to the cinema to see *Lawrence of Arabia*, he made several visits to the concessions desk to recharge with supplies of Kia-Ora: after a while he turned to his companion and exclaimed, 'I don't know. I've had fourteen orange juices and they've only got to Damascus!' Oakes took great delight in Hancock's fascination with obscure English place names. One day they passed a signpost in Kent that pointed to the village of 'Throwley Forstal'. 'Small-part actor,' reasoned Hancock. 'Walks though French windows saying, "Tennis, anyone?"' If he detected a dirty mark on a glass, he would call the waiter, point to the blemish and say, 'Do you think you could go away and put some grease, some lipstick and a few more fingerprints round the edge and make a proper job of it?'

The sense of humour may have been oblique, but it *was* vibrant, a distinctive way of looking at the world. One yearns to hear all the *bons mots* that fell on deaf or inattentive ears, a catalogue of impromptu humour not even associated with performers like Bob Monkhouse and Ken Dodd, whose stage acts with their funny lines and observations might suggest otherwise. In the spirit of self-mockery that defined his character, Hancock could also tell wonderful stories against himself. He once mistook an errant shirt button for a

Dexedrine tablet he had pocketed to keep himself awake during a party thrown by impresario Jack Hylton. Having popped the pill in the early hours he became the life and soul of the event until sunrise. The next day he went to find the button that had come adrift when he was dressing the night before and discovered the tablet: 'I was a raving success on a swallowed shirt button,' he used to joke. 'God knows what I would have been like if I had swallowed the bleeding pill.' Of course, most of these lines are funny because Hancock is saying them. For their delivery he would adjust his more diffident natural speaking voice to the more affected register of performance mode. It did not alter the fact that the comic attitude was embedded within him, even if the edges between the private man and the public mask became further blurred as a result.

Maybe his own recognition of his way with a line beguiled him into thinking that he had more structured writing skills of his own. For Galton and Simpson the self-delusion would have been in character. On 23 November 1961, within weeks of his disagreement with them over the film script, he was announcing to readers of the Paul Tanfield column in the *Daily Mail* his decision that he could now do without scriptwriters: 'I'm writing me own stuff, mate. But it's a tiring racket, you know.' The article provided advance publicity for *The Punch and Judy Man* and the name of Philip Oakes was tucked away in the small print as his 'collaborator'. The last paragraph, however, tends to confirm Alan Simpson's version of recent events: 'From Galton and Simpson, I gather all this does not necessarily indicate a final break with Hancock. "We mean there have been no punch-ups or anything like that," they said. "But there are no plans for a future series for Hancock at the moment."' To give Oakes his due, he always stressed the importance of Hancock as a catalyst in what he did put on the page. Galton and Simpson had never admitted otherwise. In return, his interpretation – through emphasis and timing, gesture and expression – captured every tiny nuance of their scripts. As Beryl Vertue says of his performance, 'He gave so much.' In a questionnaire in *Picture Show* magazine during November 1960, when he was asked to name his closest friends in television, Hancock answered, 'My writers, Ray Galton and Alan Simpson.' The tide seemed to change so suddenly. Perhaps, if he had heeded the advice of Eric Sykes, events would have taken a different course: 'He used to come to me sometimes and say, "If I get another line from Ray and Alan like 'punch up the hooter' or something like that, I'll go mad," and I said to him, "Tony, it all gets laughs and all we're doing is trying to amuse people and a lot of people are amused." But he just passed it off.'

In distancing himself from 'the boys', Hancock lost the skills of two consummate story-tellers. However much they came to abjure plot for plot's sake, they were magicians when it came to conjuring up the narrative twist that set the stamp on one half hour after another. They were masters of the cyclical device whereby the end often mirrored the opening situation, so that when, for example, Hancock and Sid, in order to avoid the same passengers met on the outward journey by train, decide to return home by charabanc, it is fated that those same passengers should make the same decision and end up sharing the back seat with our heroes. Their stay in hospital, as a result of the dangerous false economies taken after a holiday abroad, itself triggers the same pile-up of stale bread, sour milk and dated newspapers that prompted their economy drive in the first place. When eventually freed from his night's imprisonment in the BBC Television Centre lift, Hancock returns in search of his lost season ticket and ends the show as desperately incarcerated as before. Their skill was such that – partly because you were laughing so much – you seldom saw the end coming. Even *The Blood Donor* was enhanced by the conclusion where Hancock gashes himself with a bread knife and is rushed to hospital to receive his own blood back. 'At least I know it's going to the right sort of person,' he says. 'Come on. Bang it in. I'm getting dizzy.' In *Sunday Afternoon at Home*, after the members of the household have chastised themselves for 'frittering away our lives like we've done today', the most telling line is

Hancock's valedictory, 'I'll see you next Sunday then.' There were occasions in radio when lack of a pay-off and pressure of delivery forced them to resort to the expediency of what Ray and Alan have described as 'everybody bashes Tony over the head with the script' endings, intended to cue laughter and signify the end of the programme. A variation was the 'talk-out' ending where there wasn't a punch line: 'I'm not having that – I tell you one thing – I've never heard anything so ridiculous – (*Cue music*).' At least that stayed in character.

The worth of Galton and Simpson was underlined when the BBC moved quickly to secure their services after the separation from Hancock. In effect this meant the end of Hancock's association with the Corporation, however hard the light entertainment hierarchy attempted to change his mind, reasoning not least that his American idol, Jack Benny, had sustained a career at the highest level of show business for thirty years with a not dissimilar characterisation – based on vanity, meanness, age, delusions of musical prowess and his interaction with a resident support team – that had remained constant throughout. Even Sid James gallantly interceded in an attempt to make his old colleague reconsider, but to no avail. The mood between Hancock and his old bosses had apparently been cordial. In a letter to Tom Sloan at the end of November 1961, Hancock wrote from a health farm near Godalming apologising for having to postpone a meeting with Sloan and his boss: 'They made a special arrangement for us to get in here for a week and I feel I must take advantage of it while I can. I would be only too pleased to exchange hot water and lemon for a full scale Maschwitz booze-up … perhaps we can meet sometime next week.' It is uncertain whether the meeting took place. Discussions about his television future continued with Roger Hancock, now fully representing his brother. The reality soon fell into place.

On 13 April 1962 Tom Sloan, now promoted to the position of Head of Light Entertainment, addressed a bleak memo to the

Controller of Programmes, Cecil Madden, in which he conceded that in his opinion everything possible had been done to keep the performer within the BBC's television fold. He reported that Hancock had made clear that the only way forward for himself in the medium involved a shift to the stop-start process of shooting that he had advocated two years before, but this time using film. He also expected to retain control of domestic and overseas rights. The Corporation, hedged in by bureaucratic and technical precedent, was not prepared to relinquish production control and refused to budge on either issue. Sloan, referring to Hancock as a 'moody perfectionist with a great interest in money and no sense of loyalty', added ominously that the star had obviously found an organisation which would grant him these privileges. In Hancock's defence Galton and Simpson, invoking phrases like 'sour grapes', stress that Sloan had missed the whole point of Hancock's objective, which was motivated by a desire for international recognition and not by cash. According to Galton, 'He wasn't any more interested in money than anyone else.' However, one line in his memo sounded a warning note. As Sloan listed the personnel who would no longer be by his side – Wood, Galton, Simpson, James – he added, 'The result could well be unfortunate.' The communication corresponded with a story in that day's *Daily Mirror* that ITV had captured Hancock in a deal worth £2,000 a show, at that point by far and away the biggest ever contract for a comedian in British television. The 'organisation' alluded to by Sloan was Lew Grade's Associated TeleVision Limited. His brother Bernard Delfont would be the intermediary producer. The BBC was stunned. On 17 April Ronnie Waldman, Hancock's early champion within the television service who was now elevated to General Manager of Television Enterprises, addressed an old pal's note to the comedian in which he expressed the view that in spite of the Corporation's stance in the video-versus-film debate, he thought they would at least have been given first refusal when Hancock finally decided to return to television, albeit down the filmic route.

Waldman, who had helped to nurse *Hancock's Half Hour* in its early television days added, 'Maybe I was wrong in feeling that I'd earned at least that!'

In the light of the restrictions it imposed upon itself, it is difficult to see what else the BBC could have done. It had attempted to make inroads into America on Hancock's behalf. CBS executives had viewed sample tele-recordings of *Hancock's Half Hour*, but a disappointed Ronnie Waldman found himself having to explain to Stanley Dale as early as February 1959 that nobody could understand the star: 'If people in New York are having difficulty in following him, what on earth is going to happen in the Middle West?' On the rebound, the BBC's US representatives went to the rival American channel NBC, which floated the possibility of a play starring Hancock that would help to familiarise the native television audience with the performer. Nothing more seems to have been said on the project. In March 1962, the month prior to Sloan's memo to Madden, another approach had been tried when the BBC managed to persuade NBC to screen a portmanteau package within their *International Showtime* strand. This shoehorned *The Blood Donor* in its entirety into a sixty-minute slot alongside an extract from the Eric Sykes classic where he gets his toe stuck in a bath tap and a Benny Hill sketch in which his Fred Scuttle character conducted an enquiry into television. Ironically, it was as a result of a not dissimilar exercise by Thames Television to showcase their wares in New York in 1976 that Benny Hill achieved the saturation coverage that made him a household name in America and beyond. Hancock would never have accepted the fact that the key to international recognition was to slog away in the same studio for almost ten years essentially reworking the same basic British music-hall format to the point where by default the sales team for the production company had enough programmes on the shelf to sell in the bulk that the American television schedulers required. *The Blood Donor* was sufficiently well received for the BBC to plan a full page advertisement in *Variety* offering the Americans more. In his letter of 17 April Waldman explained to Hancock that the ad had now been cancelled. In the notes that he subsequently compiled on his life, Hancock was suitably contrite on this point:

> I was genuinely sorry about that because Ronnie Waldman is one of the men I most admire at the BBC. Since the old 'Kaleidoscope' days he has done more than anyone else to create the whole pattern of BBC television comedy as we know it now. He has the real pioneer spirit and I wish a few more of his colleagues could be as sure of what they wanted.

Duncan Wood once intimated that a crafty side agenda to an arrangement with NBC involved the purchase of Hancock's television shows, not for transmission, but to gain access to the script rights. In this respect both Danny Thomas and Tony Randall were names floated as possible casting for the American 'Hancock'. The whole distinction between the comedian born out of his own personality and the actor who puts on his part like a coat is thrown into relief by the situation. By 1972 Galton and Simpson had replicated their *Steptoe and Son* success – potentially far less universal in appeal than Hancock – across the Atlantic where it was repackaged with different actors in the lead as *Sanford and Son*, in the process proving that as writers they *did* have something to offer in the international arena. In what would have been the ultimate irony for Hancock, the part of the elder Steptoe/Sanford figure had been offered first to Jack Benny. The veteran superstar loved the project, but considered himself too old: 'I couldn't guarantee I'd last the series.' When it reached American screens with the controversial black comedian Redd Foxx in the role, Hancock had been dead for four years. Benny would live for another two. The 'changed format' concept, which is now commonplace, was developed by Beryl Vertue. Other shows to undergo the treatment over the years included

Johnny Speight's *Till Death Us Do Part*, which became *All in the Family*, *Man about the House* by Johnnie Mortimer and Brian Cooke, reborn as *Three's Company*, Ricky Gervais's *The Office* and Simon Nye's *Men Behaving Badly*. The last was originated by Vertue herself out of her flourishing independent production company, Hartswood Films.

It is perhaps surprising that at the time of their greatest need the BBC lacked the vision to offer Hancock more stand-alone projects along the lines mooted by NBC. The rigid compartmentalisation among Corporation departments, not to mention the jealousy between them, may have stood in the way. Throughout his heady success of the late 1950s, the television establishment gave him only one opportunity to test himself away from the confines of East Cheam and Earl's Court. On 9 February 1958, in the period between the third and fourth series of *Hancock's Half Hour*, Hancock appeared in a recorded adaptation of Nikolai Gogol's *The Government Inspector* under the auspices of the drama department. In the immediate wake of his success Eric Maschwitz offered him the opportunity to play the lead in a modern version of Molière's *Le Bourgeois Gentilhomme*, but the idea was not pursued. Later in 1962 there was a half-hearted move to persuade him to appear in the N.F. Simpson play *The Form*. Hancock was not interested in that either, but there was no attempt at an offer that would capture the imagination or flatter the ego in a way that would have made the continuation of his comedy half hour seem less like house arrest, not even an accompanying subsidiary series that expanded on his talent in the way in which the BBC indulged Jimmy Edwards – a more versatile performer than his surface persona suggested – with *Faces of Jim* as an antidote to the vulgar rough-and-tumble of his hugely enjoyable schoolmaster burlesque, *Whack-O!*

Hancock had acquitted himself well enough with the Gogol play to point the way. Playing Hlestakov, the lowly copying clerk who takes advantage of the situation when the citizens of a small

Russian town mistake him for the more exalted rank of the play's title, he brought to the role an intelligence that had been missing from the all-singing, all-roistering big screen version that in 1949 featured Danny Kaye under the title of *The Inspector General*. Kaye relied on his usual repertoire of comic tics and knockabout tricks to bring the film to any sort of life, even resorting at one point to a song in celebration of hiccups. Hancock had no need to fall back on such desperate measures in an adaptation by Barry Thomas that played up to his subtler comedy strengths without in any way bastardising the original: 'Of course, I've written one or two trifles for the theatre. I've known all the great authors. Pushkin and I are great friends. Whenever I see him, I say, "Hello, Pushkin, old boy. How goes it?" and he shouts out, "Bearing up, old boy. Bearing up."' The producer and director, Alan Bromly, must have been confident he had the perfect casting when six weeks before he wrote to Hancock enclosing Gogol's own thoughts on the character: 'Hlestakov is not a professional fraud or a deliberate impostor. He forgets that he is lying and almost believes his own words. He unfolds himself. As his spirits rise he soars into flights of fancy … every one of us is, or has been, Hlestakov, but naturally we do not like to admit it. We mock at him inside other men's skins, but not in our own. I thought that one day an actor of many-sided talents would be grateful to me for uniting in one character such diverse motifs, and giving him the opportunity to display simultaneously the manifold facets of his art.' Bromly was doubtless sincere when a short time later he sent Hancock the script with a note expressing the sentiment that he couldn't think of anyone he would rather have in the role. He was not disappointed. The overall critical reaction was good, one writer describing Hancock's performance as 'funny, touching and original'. The play achieved an estimated audience of 9 million viewers, double that achieved for *Henry V* and *Amphitryon 38* in the same *World Theatre* Sunday evening slot. In later years Roy Dotrice, who had a humble part as a soldier in the production, recalled that on the afternoon prior to the recording the director announced two run-throughs, the first of which he wanted the cast to play flat out for comedy, and the second as serious drama: 'Naturally, with Tony leading the cast, the second run-through was by far the funnier.' In a strange quirk of fate the key part of the wily postmaster who intercepts the letter that uncovers Hlestakov's deception was played by Wilfrid Brambell.

Events caught up with Hancock in a controversial way on 1 June 1962 when the twelfth issue of the newly launched *Private Eye* magazine featured in its 'Aesop Revisited' series of cartoons the perceived tabloid version of what had been happening in his career. The sharp-etched pen of Willie Rushton depicted 'Tony Halfcock' in a cruel rendition of his life so far. One by one the funny-voice man, the straight man, the scriptwriters, the broadcaster – no disguising *their* names – are dropped, leaving T.H. commenting on an empty speech bubble: 'I'll think of something to put in there later.' In the end he disappears to evolve a new image for ITV, before deciding, 'I like God, but it's time for us to go our separate ways.' As if in some perverse version of the Stations of the Cross, the drawing in the final box reveals the comedian staring wistfully at an indeterminately attired statue of himself, beneath the moral: 'To Thine Own Self Be True.' Hancock was sufficiently wounded to consider issuing a writ against the magazine, but was deterred from so doing by the prospect of the even more damaging headlines that would result in more widely read publications. It is chilling to consider that this appeared six whole years before his death, but the stark reality was that the lion's share of his best work was now behind him.

In his desire to 'move on' and the search for international recognition Hancock's actions have often been misinterpreted. That does not lessen the anguish he caused those around him, but, as we have seen, much of what happened was the inevitable result of the editorial process. There was also within him an elemental need to prove himself, more out of guilt and conscience than envy, as his perceived reliance on other talents began to resemble a weakness in his own mind. The fear took hold that not to pull one's weight at all levels was to short-change or compromise the public. Hancock was, in fact, acting out a paradox. As more and more people laughed longer and louder at his shows and he ostensibly had less to justify, so the need to prove something deeper within himself took a tighter grip. I believe that jealousy *per se* never came into it: what he regarded as logic and shrewd professionalism were never absent from his reasoning, but sadly with each new decision his self-confidence ebbed away and his final goal was undermined. While I have no wish to sound melodramatic, his career became the child he never had, and he protected it – or so he thought – relentlessly. To the public, fed on the distortions of the media, it was easy to see this happening under the unfortunate guise of the pompous extrovert Anthony Aloysius St John Hancock, whom they knew so well, quite unaware that beneath that carapace was a serious, private, sometimes witty, ultimately inadequate man. Singularly Beryl Vertue is missing from the *Private Eye* comic strip, and she was the one treated most ruthlessly. It says something about the vulnerability of her one-time colleague that her words on the matter could be those of a saint: 'We were devoted to him and he dismissed the friendship of years in an effort to attain a height in his career which we could all have helped him to achieve out of friendship and regard.' Perhaps it was, though, fitting that when he came to make his next feature film he took as his subject the most self-sufficient dramatic spectacle of them all – the Punch and Judy Show.

Chapter Twelve

'THUMBS DOWN AND INTO THE CROCODILE PIT'

'Part of the art is to go on looking like melted butter
even though your nerves are screwed up to bursting.
I don't think folks realise how tough it is.'

On 22 January 1962, twelve weeks before the bombshell news of Hancock's forthcoming series for commercial television, the Associated British Picture Corporation made its own splash within the industry with a press release to announce that Hancock had formed his own production company, which would be responsible for producing a minimum of four films within a deal that superseded his previous contract with the Corporation, by which he was committed to make three films on a 'starring only basis'. It was a decisive move for ABPC, buoyant from the commercial success of *The Rebel*, and Galton and Simpson would have shared a moment of wry cynicism as they read in the trade journals that the first project under the new arrangement would be entitled *The Punch and Judy Man*. Hancock was specified as the writer of the original story, 'in collaboration with Philip Oakes'. The press release stipulated that the comedian would not appear on television until the film was completed. For ABPC to have signed over control of casting, music and the myriad other elements of movie-making was tantamount to saying that, if anything went wrong, Hancock and his associates at MacConkey Productions would have no one to blame but themselves. The response to the film upon its release in April 1963 was not helped by the disappointing reception accorded his series for ITV, which was recorded and transmitted between the intervening November and March. In the circumstances ABPC should have stipulated that its star stay away from the small screen until his seaside epic had had the opportunity to prove itself on its own terms.

Philip Oakes first met Hancock when he interviewed him in 1957 for *Books and Art* magazine. Highly respected in literary and journalistic circles as a poet and film critic, he would become best known for his novel *The God Botherers*, a tragicomedy on the interface between religion and the media, which was not published until the year after Hancock's death. When the Hancocks moved out of London, they discovered that Oakes lived about ten miles from Lingfield and their friendship gathered momentum. In Hancock's eyes, their association provided him with a certain intellectual imprimatur, although in Oakes's mind he was an odd choice for the role of Hancock's scriptwriter, having 'not yet been blooded in the ways of working with anyone remotely like him'. If the writer had heard a radio interview to promote *The Rebel*, given by Hancock to the BBC's *Radio Newsreel* in March 1961, he would have been clearer with regard to Hancock's aspirations. The anonymous interviewer asked Hancock about the frequency with which he played artists and intellectuals, which Tony acknowledged with a simple 'Yes'.

INTERVIEWER: Does this mean you'd like to be one?

TONY: Well actually I think I am deep down, you know. It's never been appreciated entirely, but I think it's there. I think I can safely say that. It's only a question of time.

INTERVIEWER: Before what?

TONY: Before it's recognised.

INTERVIEWER: What are you going to do when it's recognised?

TONY: I shall be away, shan't I? I mean that'll be it, won't it? About time too.

While Hancock teases his interrogator in his obliquely humorous way, it is impossible to listen to the sequence today without sensing the dream between the lines, namely that he truly did yearn for an intellectual destiny of the kind first intimated to him by the accolade of *Face to Face*.

The cultural aspirations that helped to forge his link with Oakes led Hancock to seek further collaboration at even more exalted levels. He wrote to Sir Arthur Bliss, then the Master of the Queen's Musick, inviting him to compose the score of the film. Bliss responded that he was an ardent admirer of the comedian, but in his early seventies too old for the task. According to Oakes, Hancock kept the letter in his pocket until it fell apart at the folds. Eventually he settled on his old double-act partner, Derek Scott, for the incidental music. More successful was the invitation extended to the celebrated photographer Henri Cartier-Bresson, who may have been persuaded that Hancock – not misleadingly – was a kind of British incarnation of Jacques Tati, to cover the shooting of the movie. 'It's like being photographed by Rembrandt,' Hancock rhapsodised to Oakes, but although the two men achieved a warm rapport the Frenchman was less than satisfied with his subject and abandoned the project early, allowing only two stills to be published. The agony that Hancock experienced on set was matched by that of the photographer through his viewfinder. 'What I was seeing was not the Hancock the world loved,' confessed the artist graciously. He did not appreciate then that one day despite its flaws the film would acquire the status of a minor classic.

That was a long way off from the wet autumn day in 1961 when the comedian introduced the poet to the story for the film that would take him closer to his career ideal: 'There's this Punch and Judy man, a genuine artist in his own way, with a marriage that's going wrong and a lot of bastards on the council out to nail him ...' 'It hardly seemed the international subject he had been seeking for so long,' recalled Oakes years later, echoing the view of the two writers whom he was in effect replacing. It is probable that at the time of their conversation the formal parting from Galton and Simpson had yet to occur, although in Oakes's published memoir of the comedian Beryl Vertue had already been dismissed and in the writer's words, the 'smoke was still thick over the land' when Hancock first telephoned him with the film proposition. By the end of their rainy day together the outline had taken firmer shape and, for Oakes, the idea appeared sound.

The full script took six weeks to write at a variety of locations embracing a hotel near the Arc de Triomphe in Paris, where Hancock retreated after the American failure of *The Rebel*; a suite that doubled as an office at the White House, his old stamping ground off the Euston Road; and at MacConkeys. In Paris, distraction was provided by Hancock's enthusiasm for pinball. More discerning than most, he insisted that the only machines worth playing were those that swept the ball into play with a plastic flipper. There may have been a hidden agenda to their quest. Oakes recalled searching for them in bars and bistros, 'all of which served a range of drinks which in the interests of science and connoisseurship Hancock felt duty bound to test. He especially liked a liqueur distilled from wild strawberries, but he was catholic in his tastes and most of the runners were given a fair sampling.' Their work room was well stocked with Pernod and it comes as no surprise to discover that after several days they were both suffering. Hancock put it down to the oysters. Oakes, more realistically, attributed their condition to liver poisoning. With little more than a dozen pages of substantially unusable script to show for their efforts, they returned home. Installed at the White House, Hancock soon discovered that he more than needed the discipline that someone like Oakes brought to the task. He later wrote, 'Wherever we worked, Philip had the same struggle to rouse me in the morning. There was he, brisk and wide awake, fingers itching to get at the typewriter, and there was I, stupid with sleep, trying first to force my eyes open and after that to stir my brain into action. But somehow he managed to drag some work out of me.'

It is still a matter of conjecture how much of the script beyond the basic idea is attributable to Hancock. In an interview for the *Sydney Morning Herald* on 16 June 1962, Oakes may have been generous: 'Reading the script now I find it hard to tell who wrote any given line in any given scene. Sometimes we could spark off several pages of dialogue by a minute's ad-libbing, a sort of mutual revving-up. At other times I would write a draft which he would later read for effect, amending it as we went along. There was also the time when Hancock came up with the perfect ending to a situation, which meant constructing the scene backwards.' Oakes may have been referring to the scene where the character he plays expresses his frustration by ramming a posy of artificial flowers into a china pig. The original idea was for the flowers to go in its snout, but then Hancock decided this was not strong enough: 'They have to go up its arse.' At great expense a specially designed pig was commissioned for the purpose. He would not have taken kindly to the fact that in recent releases for video and DVD the scene has been cut.

Hancock was his own worst critic regarding *The Rebel*. Some time before the reconstituted deal was announced, he hinted that things would need to change second time around: 'There were ideas I wanted to use, but other people said "No." When I saw it again six months afterwards, I knew I'd been right. Next time I'm going to have more control over my own ideas.' Once shooting for *The Punch and Judy Man* was complete, he set out his vision for the new project with almost evangelistic fervour in an article for the August 1962 issue of *Films and Filming* magazine: 'This is a film about people who are acceptable and real, as against *The Rebel* which was a fake thing, badly done in some ways from my point of view. I am not getting away from the *Hancock's Half Hour* kind of humour – you can't do that; instead you try to move on a bit. It is a question of coming down to the purity and simplicity of comedy. I know what it *should* look like. I don't say I can do it necessarily; but it's not fake any more.' He was referring particularly to his own role. He had never played a married man with full responsibilities before; nor, with the exception of *Orders are Orders* and the rare dramatic outing, had he portrayed someone whose name was other than Anthony Hancock. Philip Oakes took pains to stress that his character was aware of the consequences of his decisions, capable of genuine anguish, and prepared to take real action which was neither comic nor extreme. Unlike Anthony Aloysius, this Hancock has never been to East Cheam and has no illusions about life, although he does manage to deliver some classic lines that have the true ring of Galton and Simpson (and Hancock) about them. Whether he was passing judgement on the local hostelry: 'If he must water the beer, I do wish he wouldn't use sea water'; acting incredulous upon hearing that a darling of high society had to walk all of twenty yards when her airport bus broke down: 'What do you mean – actually putting one foot in front of the other? Isn't that marvellous? I am deeply moved'; or showing off his ballroom dancing prowess: 'Madame, have you ever experienced the rare delight of the Pinner left-hand-down, feather-reverse turn?' there was still something to please the diehard fans, although many would argue not enough.

Shooting began at Elstree Studios at the beginning of April 1962. The role of director was entrusted to Jeremy Summers, the son of the pioneer British film director Walter Summers, who had been prolific between the wars churning out everything from *The Return of Bulldog Drummond* to *McGlusky the Sea Rover*. There had been much talk of Hancock directing himself, but fortunately after much effort by ABPC and those closest to him he was dissuaded. By then it was too late to assign to the picture the heavyweight name his star profile could have attracted. A meeting was arranged and Hancock, after chatting to Summers for three quarters of an hour, responded to the 'extreme sensitivity' in the man. Probably what he really meant was that he sensed that the relative novice would be like putty in his hands. Although Summers had worked extensively in formula television detective series, he had not directed a feature film before; a credit as second unit director on Charlie Drake's execrable 1961 vehicle, *Petticoat Pirates*, might be perceived as his chief qualification for the comedy task in hand. The film would prove a rough baptism. According to John Le Mesurier, Summers 'was charming, inventive, technically sound, but had no idea how to handle Tony'. As David Nathan joked in all seriousness, it would have needed someone with the combined authority of John Huston, David Lean and Carol Reed to have controlled Hancock at this stage. Duncan Wood might have been useful too. Oakes summed up Summers as 'an inexperienced director who allowed Tony to bully him'.

Hancock played Wally Pinner, a Punch and Judy professor working the beach at the dismal resort town of Piltdown. His marriage to Delia, played by Sylvia Syms, the social climbing owner of a china shop catering to the souvenir trade, is poised precariously on the balance of childless intolerance. Although Wally and his *demi-monde* of fellow showmen are looked down upon as so much human flotsam by the mayor and town council, the mayoress begs Delia to ask her husband to give a special performance at a gala dinner to celebrate the resort's diamond jubilee. The fashionable socialite Lady Jane Caterham has agreed to switch on the illuminations on the night and Delia interprets this as her opportunity to gain entrée, however slight, to a world otherwise only glimpsed in the pages of the glossy magazines. The mayoress promises to introduce her to her idol, if she will deliver Wally to the proceedings. At first Pinner, representing traditional values against the synthetic airs and graces of the pompous small-town élite, refuses to play along, but after much soul-searching he changes his mind in an attempt to save his marriage, not least under moral pressure exerted by his friend, the sand sculptor, played by John Le Mesurier. This is the turning point of the film. As Oakes later indicated, 'What we wanted to show was how he reacted to a moment of crisis which affected his job, his marriage, his entire future. He was no hero, but he did not go under.' 'He just does the best he can,' said Hancock. 'That's all any of us can do.'

The gala ends in disaster as the banquet degenerates into a bun-fight played out with bread rolls, sparked by the least receptive audience Mr Punch has ever received. The sequence is as out of place in this film as some of Hancock's more philosophical musings would have been on the lips of Norman Wisdom. Wally's booth collapses in the *mêlée* and blocks the exit of the disgruntled Caterham, played with 'wicked witch' disdain by Barbara Murray. Throughout the evening it has become apparent to Delia that the promise made to her by the mayoress is as flimsy as the candy floss sold on the promenade. As her ladyship reaches for a soda siphon to take revenge on the puppeteer, Delia intervenes to protect her husband. The aristocratic slap she receives is a small price to pay for the excuse it gives her to land a stronger punch on the Caterham jaw. The following day, with her social aspirations in tatters, the Pinners make the decision to move on to another town. Although the film is non-committal, the marriage may be saved. ABPC were unsure about the ending, but Hancock and Oakes appear to have stood their ground. If one sets aside the gala slapstick sequence, which might have been more effective with better pacing from a more experienced director, the film impressively weaves its separate strands of snobbery, municipal corruption and decay, and – at a time when more people were holidaying in foreign climes – changing social mores. The name, 'Piltdown', stands as its own monument to the hypocrisy upon which the town is built, evoking echoes of the notorious 'Piltdown Man' hoax of 1912, when fragments of a human skull and the jawbone of an orangutan discovered in a gravel pit at Piltdown, a village with the same name in East Sussex, were passed off as the fossilised remains of an unknown form of early human. The hoax did not come to light until 1953 and would have been relatively fresh in the memory of the larger part of the cinema audience ten years later.

Permeating the film is a sense of nostalgic melancholy that obviously emanates from Hancock's childhood in Bournemouth. After three weeks at Elstree, Hancock had wanted to shoot the location scenes at his old adopted home town, but when the authorities stood in his way he opted for Bognor Regis, which is further east along the coast between Portsmouth and Worthing and the scene of his early summer season with *Flotsam's Follies*. It appealed to Hancock that an ailing King George V, in response to the suggestion that his favourite watering hole should be elevated from plain Bognor to the longer name in his honour, cursed, 'Bugger Bognor!' The King's private secretary deftly construed the classic obscenity as acquiescence. Irrespective of venue, Hancock set about recreating his childhood. The opportunistic beach photographer, the gypsy fortune teller swilling out her tea leaves in the gutter, and not least the sandman in his black beret and floppy bow tie, were all brought to life again: the last was especially affecting as he sculpted exquisite three-dimensional tableaux such as 'The Death of Nelson' and Millais' 'Bubbles' from sand, at the constant mercy of wind, rain, high tides, rough boys and peeing dogs. Portrayed by Mario Fabrizi, who at one point had been a street photographer in real life, Hattie Jacques and John Le Mesurier respectively, they must have exerted an even greater nostalgia for Hancock at this critical turning point in his career as he clung – some might say cynically – to some of his old team against the perceived spirit of his relationships with working colleagues at this time. A part was even found for Hugh Lloyd as the assistant of the Punch and Judy man who collaborates with him in his show, not a common occurrence. Punch professors, like stand-up comedians, are pretty much lone souls when it comes to performance. Hancock reserved affectionate mention for this select coterie in his *Films and Filming* article: 'Being brought up in a seaside town, you find these poor, underground entertainers who are absolutely honest. You may say they're finished. You may say what you like about the sandman, for instance, who makes his models in the sand. Every time I go to a seaside town, I find these underground people, maybe a Punch and Judy man, a dedicated man to his own trade, for what else can he do?' His identification with these people, who provided another manifestation of the independence of the old variety pros who coloured his childhood, helps one understand the compulsive need Hancock felt to make this film, in spite of all the claptrap about the international comedy marketplace.

Upon release the critical reaction was disappointing, not helped by the lack of confidence shown by ABPC in refusing to give the picture a West End première. Hancock's core audience found it hard to make the leap to the more muted, darker version of their hero, a burden from which the film would have been exempt if the more protean skills of a Sellers or Guinness had been applied to the lead role. However, not for the first time in Hancock's short cinematic career, *The Times* went some way to redressing the balance, drawing a parallel between the comedian and W.C. Fields and then emphasising the 'elusive, highly personal quality which derives almost entirely from Mr Hancock's presence', adding that the scenes between him and Syms were 'remarkably acute and genuinely sad as well as funny without mercifully ever straining after tear-behind-the-smile pathos'. Hancock, as he admitted to Alan Whicker in 1967, took consolation in the fact that *City Lights*, which he thought was 'the most exquisite full-length comedy I've ever seen', was originally panned by the critics: 'It was Chaplin's statement. I thought it was absolutely magnificent and I went to see it five times.' Time has been kinder to *The Punch and Judy Man* than the initial reaction would have led one to expect. Its intimate approach works well on the smaller television screen, where it remains most accessible, while the decision to shoot in black and white imparts a realism in keeping with the cinema at that time. An unsung hero of the project was the cinematographer Gilbert Taylor, who had developed the realistic use of monochrome in films such as *Woman in a Dressing Gown* and *Ice-Cold in Alex*. His future credits would include *A Hard Day's Night* and two disturbing psychological thrillers from the director Roman Polanski, *Repulsion* and *Cul-de-sac*. Taylor had also worked on *The Rebel* and he presumably agreed with Hancock's view on the matter:

'Colour slows down comedy. It is too peaceful. *The Rebel* had to be made in colour because of the paintings. Some films have to be made in black and white; look at the wonderful quality they got out of *Sweet Smell of Success*.'

Hancock developed an affection for *The Punch and Judy Man* that stayed with him to the end of his days, although there had been times when he wished to disown the project. Although there was no room for him in the movie, Sid James remained both a trusted friend and a reliable shoulder to cry on. After Hancock's death, James compared notes with Philip Oakes for a radio tribute, detailing the desperation Hancock expressed to him when it was all over: 'I would have liked to quit the film in the middle because I thought it was going to be a bad one and I couldn't. By that time we'd come too far ... when I'd finished the picture, I just wanted to go away to dig ditches, go anywhere, go to France, be a beachcomber, anything to get away from it. I couldn't stand seeing myself doing that again.' Philip Oakes found the film sad viewing, flashes of genuine brilliance intermingled with moments of truth in acting, but ultimately overshadowed by the promise of what might have been. Nor did he absolve himself from blame: 'The script and the direction should have been more positive, the laughs more frequent.' Hancock would have everyone in hysterics as he outlined situations to the cast and crew. When he went before the camera to bring them to life, the comedy crumbled to dust, as if the act of public exhibition had kindled a massive doubt, both in the material and in his ability to deliver it. Sylvia Syms is observant on how Hancock was intent on pursuing a policy of diminishing returns in this regard: 'The first time he did it, it would be marvellous. But he'd never leave it at that ... he'd make the director do it over and over again and you would see it die in front of you. It was almost as if Tony didn't want it to be good.' Surprisingly Syms is convinced the comedian missed his true *métier* as a director: 'His way of explaining an idea was brilliant, if only he could leave the actors and actresses to work the magic.' Hancock seemed to forget that in other areas of performance, namely his stage revues, repetition had worked against his best instincts. He appears a man torn between the relentless perfectionism of his idol Charlie Chaplin, who would polish the timing of himself and others through countless rehearsals both on and off camera, and the flair for the instinctive moment that he spoke about in his article for the BFI magazine, as if Syms and Oakes had been working on another film: 'There is a trend in films not to print the first take. I can understand this from the director's point of view. He thinks it can't be right, but it is … we have been going for first takes. It helps the comedy particularly. When you go for the second, you often find you are waiting around until number nine before it is right. And then something has been permanently lost.' This may explain the effectiveness of the scenes between Hancock and the boy, played by Nicholas Webb, where, according to Syms – his aunt in real life – they just went for it.

In casting Peter, the lonely child who wanders aimlessly around the resort without parental supervision, Hancock was in effect casting himself. The boy never seems to miss a performance of the show on the beach. 'You left the crocodile out!' is his opening gambit when Pinner, distracted by the shenanigans of the photographer, has deigned to conclude one performance early. They don't meet properly until later the same morning, when Wally spots the boy sheltering from the rain that is casting a pall over the resort: 'There's no point in hanging about, you know. You can't expect a performance when it's coming down like this. Well, can you? You'd better get off home then. All right, come on over here. Well, come on. I won't eat you.' Their coming together is curiously touching, but never allowed to spill over into sentimentality. When Wally offers Peter his bus fare home, the boy remonstrates that his mother says he shouldn't take money from strange men. 'But I'm not a strange man – you see me every day of the week – it's ridiculous!' barks Pinner. When Wally offers to escort him to the bus stop, the boy unobtrusively takes the man by the hand. We register embarrassment on the part of the puppeteer at the same time as we acknowledge that this is the closest we have come to discerning Hancock engaged in an expression of genuine affection. To shelter from the ever-worsening storm they take refuge in an ice-cream parlour.

Peter is on familiar ground and reels off his order by heart: 'I'll have a Piltdown Glory – two scoops of luscious vanilla, two scoops of flaky chocolate, succulent sliced bananas, juicy peach fingers in pure cane sugar, all swimming in super smooth butter-fat cream.' Wally and the ice cream man look at the boy in amazement, at which point he pipes up with 'Ooh, and a cherry!' Pinner, having already established there is no soup or tea in an establishment like this, is not to be outdone. 'The same,' he says to the man behind the counter, although the Hancock glower says so much more. The boy attacks his sundae first. A cagy Pinner watches and meticulously copies every move, as if initiated into some strange nursery ritual deprived him as a child. Not a word is said. In real life Hancock hated ice cream and after each take would wash his mouth out with vodka, adding an uneasy subtext to the suspicious glare of the ice cream man played with relish by Eddie Byrne, who silently challenges him to plunge to the final depths of the hideous rainbow dessert. The final *coup de grâce* comes when Peter tosses the cherry in the air and catches it in his mouth. All eyes descend on Wally as he attempts the same feat. He succeeds triumphantly, prompting from Peter a delighted, '*That's* the way to do it!' His childhood regained, Hancock beams in acquiescence as they leave the establishment. Without question he had shown some people, who thought they knew better, that he had the exact measure of the scene's comedy potential: 'When some people first read the script, they timed the ice cream eating sequence at one and a half minutes, but now it is over eight on the screen ... because they couldn't see what we were trying to do.'

For many the ice cream scene is the high point of the movie and maybe the nearest he came to emulating Jacques Tati in allowing the sunshine of comic observation to gleam on life's dull routine. The sensitivity shown by him towards the child is quite memorable. Possibly because it was evocative of choice moments between Chaplin and Jackie Coogan in *The Kid*, it was also Hancock's favourite scene, only matched for its silent eloquence by Philip Oakes's choice of the film's early morning opening, where we watch Wally getting dressed as he reacts with scorn to a housewives' record request programme followed by the daily sermon from some portentous radio parson. As the priest gives voice to an appalling parable, which makes no sense whatsoever, Hancock contemplates gloomily the miserable, wet day that looms ahead. In the old times we would have expected at least a 'Stone me!' or an 'Are you raving mad?' to have accompanied his reactions, but any comments here are confined to his explosive 'Good luck!' as he switches off the pop music that eventually assaults his ears. Throughout the opening scene his thoughts are loud and clear, albeit silent, and continue in this manner during the breakfast sequence that follows. Hancock runs the risk of conjuring up memories of radio breakfasts at 23 Railway Cuttings when a plastic toy aeroplane falls out of his Rice Krispies packet, but the trivial banter in which he might have once indulged has given place to the torturous silences of a marriage strained to breaking point. Every sound is magnified to the edge of intolerance. The rustling of newspaper, the stirring of tea, first the scraping, then the munching of toast achieve a decibel level of bedlam proportions as they hover in the air over the cosy domestic parlour like daggers over an escapologist. In time bickering masquerades as conversation and the mood of the film and its central relationship are brilliantly, if chillingly, established. Even Hancock admitted that some of the scenes between himself and Syms caused him 'a certain amount of jolt' when he watched them in the rushes, adding, 'We did all of these in the first week, which was rather embarrassing because people immediately expect a comic to be funny and I wasn't. I am slightly embarrassed to do straight acting, but I think it's all right. People outside think you should always be making people laugh.' Hancock knew full well that at this stage there was nothing or little in his life to laugh about.

Oakes acknowledged that the film marked a crisis in Hancock's personal life. In truth, the change – even simplification – of Hancock's character on screen had been paralleled by a deterioration in his conduct off. The writer detected a shift of emphasis at the press conference held at the Savoy to announce the film. Hancock seemed to overstep the mark in the number of assertions he made for his future career, including a casino and leisure complex in his name. 'What's got into you?' whispered Philip into his ear. 'Megalomania?' 'Just a touch,' admitted Hancock with a smile as he tapped the ash from his cigar. The on-set vodka provided a clue. Sid James had more contacts than most in the film industry and was kept informed: 'He so wanted the film to be the best thing he'd ever done in his life, but he was falling apart then, he was drinking too much, he was coming late on the set, he was trying to tell the director what to do.' Things were not helped at crucial times by the lack of moral support received from ABPC, as shown by its attempts to broaden the script – resisted – and its eventual mishandling of distribution. Making matters worse was the repressive atmosphere of a studio regime which kept an ominous black book in which were recorded each actor's time of arrival and the number of takes he took to complete a scene. Even a quick drink at lunchtime at the Red Lion across the road did not evade the eye of Big Brother. Hancock had been looking to escape what he had seen as the confinement of the BBC, but this must have made the other Corporation resemble some form of Shangri-la. Bognor itself did not provide much compensation. In his autobiography, *A Jobbing Actor*, John Le Mesurier described the underlying sadness they encountered in the resort, sensing that the location was well matched to the study of failure the film set out to be. In fairness it was early season, but one gets the drift regardless: 'The trippers had stayed away in swarms that year and the few brave regulars, who could not quite bear to break the habit of a lifetime, sat about in sad, usually damp, little groups reflecting on the irony of paying for a holiday that was best calculated to bring on a fit of depression.'

Hancock's choice of Punch – as distinct from the seaside generally – as a subject must have struck many as strange given his seeming antipathy towards puppets – *vide* Archie Andrews in an earlier life. Oakes recalled that he was terrified of the figures, not least the crocodile which represented a demon from the nether regions of hell. Most formidable of all was the swazzle, the little metal device incorporating a reed that Punch operators conceal in their mouth to distort their voice kazoo-fashion. Joe Hastings, a veteran Punch professor, was attached to the film as technical consultant and to operate the puppets in those scenes that did not need to show Hancock operating them. On the first day he turned to his pupil and said, 'Don't worry, Tony. Everybody swallows two or three of these when they start.' Hancock was a born hypochondriac and did not care at all for the idea of swallowing any foreign body unless it was alcohol or drug related. As shooting progressed, Punch was seen to be a malignant presence and got the blame for everything. 'The film's jinxed. *He* won't let it go right,' Hancock would fret, as he went to pour himself another drink. When Hastings died of lung cancer shortly after the completion of the picture Hancock felt confirmed in his convictions, although this did not prevent him sending a large floral arrangement in the form of the puppet to the poor man's funeral. Hastings's illness had been no secret to those on the set, and his welfare – or lack of it – cast a cloud of its own over the entire shoot. Hancock's irrational fears were even transposed onto the gift of a popular child's toy at the time, a coiled steel spring called a 'Slinky', which when positioned at the top of a flight of stairs would flip-flop down with a life of its own. It scared Hancock to such an extent that having failed to render it ineffective by brute force, he took it down to the beach one night and buried it in the sand. The gift had come from Pat Williams, a writer on occult matters. Hancock was susceptible, and it all made good copy.

No one proved a better witness to the changes in his old friend at this time than George Fairweather, treated by Hancock to a couple of days of filming on location and the opportunity of minor stardom as the heckler during the illuminations scene, even if he was given less than twelve hours' notice to get across from Bournemouth on his motorbike for the privilege. As the mayor introduces Lady Jane from the balcony, Fairweather is the one at the front of the crowd who bawls out, 'Haven't you pawned your chain yet, Arthur?' George found himself sharing a room with Hancock during his stay and they talked into the early hours. He wanted to know more about the film and asked where the laughs came. Hancock replied by trying to explain his idea of naturalistic comedy – a world apart from the variety theatres of basic Bournemouth – and that it was not supposed to be funny. When his friend predicted that it would then fail, Hancock answered, 'I don't care whether it does. I'm going to prove to them that I'm right.' 'You know your trouble,' said the veteran. 'You're trying to do a Chaplin.' The grin he received was the one Oakes had registered at the press conference. Given half the chance he would have made the tea and operated the clapperboard had it meant acquiring Chaplin's overall fingertip control of his product. In his autobiography, Chaplin referred to the personal difficulties he was under during the making of *City Lights*: 'I had worked myself into a neurotic state of wanting perfection.' For the screen icon the work process proved its own drug, but for Hancock, similarly beleaguered by artistic and emotional challenges, the answer came in a bottle. Sidi Scott, the wife of Derek, never forgot the long faces of her husband and Roger Hancock when they returned from viewing the first rough cut at Elstree, whereas the star remained full of bonhomie and forced humour: 'He just didn't want to say it could have been better ... the deed was done.'

Fairweather was quick to see how Hancock's increased alcohol intake had blurred his grasp of reality. Booze had won out over food in any claim on his friend's appetite, and George hadn't eaten since breakfast. As Tony attacked another bottle of vodka, Fairweather called room service with the unlikely announcement that Mr Hancock would like a large pot of coffee and some sandwiches. When the food arrived the old pro hid the bottle in his bedside cabinet and forced his pal to eat something. They reminisced until two in the morning and then fell asleep. At five thirty Fairweather was woken by the sound of Hancock's hand creeping from beneath the bed-clothes as if drawn to the bottle by some form of magnetic attraction. 'Put that back,' he yelled, as only a father figure could have dared. Tony pleaded he could not face the day without a drink, but did have the grace to admit that he felt better after the breakfast of black cof-fee and toast that George again insisted on ordering from room ser-vice. The star went one step further: 'I really wish I could have somebody like you around all the time, somebody to watch out for me and keep me off the bottle.' Fairweather took the suggestion serious-ly: 'If you pay me fifty quid a week and give me a few bit parts in your show, I'll look after you. I'd keep you off the drink all right.' According to George, they shook hands on the deal, but nothing more was ever said about the arrangement. A few months later, during the record-ing of the series for commercial television, Fairweather found him-self staying at MacConkeys for the night. 'Hancock had a bottle by his side all the time,' he observed. 'I said, "That will get you nowhere, you know." He said, "Well, it helps a bit." I said, "It won't help you in the long term. It's only temporary, you know."' Hancock countered with the observation that he was following in the footsteps of his idol, Sid Field, and that it had not done him any harm, which was not strictly accurate. After a similar night at MacConkeys discussing the music for the film, Derek Scott had to catch an early train to London. He was awoken at seven by Hancock, who placed a pint tankard of beer on his bedside table. Sidi recalled a day they spent on location. They were met by Tony and Cicely climbing out of the car clutching a crate of champagne: 'Goodness knows how much we did get through, but by the time lunchtime came I was nearly crying with a headache and then Tony said brightly, "Now, I think we'll go down to the pub."' He once joked away such indulgence to Sylvia Syms, 'Champagne is safe, sherry is the halfway house, and brandy is the end of the road – a touch of the infuriator.' As soon as he said it, those around him knew the day was lost.

Alongside the let-your-hair-down excesses of the social whirl, which Hancock presumed he had earned through his success, there was the darker side defined by his inability to meet the standards he set himself. Oakes said that he always knew when he had failed to deliver and refused to be philosophical about it: 'He just reached for the bottle, had a large drink, and then another large drink to top that, and then another drink to actually put the cap on it.' Hugh Lloyd recalled that on location he was disappointed if you went to bed before he did, still imbibing as he was at two o'clock in the morning. The next day they would gather for make-up at eight o'clock: 'He'd be there saying, "There's only one thing for it – vodka."' Nobody could stop him, and as the drinking eddied out of control he ran the risk of losing his greatest asset as a reaction comedian. It did not require great powers of observation to note that the expressions which once chased across his face with quicksilver mobility were being coarsened out of existence. The process was gradual and the storyline of *The Punch and Judy Man* may not have demanded much more than he adequately delivered, but if – heaven forbid – there had ever been a single valid argument why he did *not* need writers, it could only have been in the unique vocabulary of looks at his disposal. Philip Oakes put it succinctly: 'His instructions to the cameraman would be to stay focused on his face and if that face was frozen into some booze-induced concrete it rather missed the point of the joke.' It is disquieting to think that the virtuosity displayed in a sequence like that in *The Reunion Party*, where he tries to remember the name of an old service colleague, was fast becoming beyond him. It is even more uncomfortable to recall that in the lead up to that segment the wife of Hugh Lloyd's character pronounces, 'Drink is the refreshment of the devil.' Hancock answers, 'Yes, I suppose that's one way of looking at it. Yes, you've got a point there. A very valid one. I admire your strength. I couldn't do it myself.' All his friends feared that as his face became less pliable his timing would also suffer. Picking up on these things, Tony came increasingly to sense that his career was on the slide, a prophecy that became self-fulfilling. No scene from his entire career is more typical of his inner turmoil than when soaked to the skin he confronts the elements along the Bognor promenade. Oakes remembered how he would look the heavens squarely in the eye and see doom lurking behind the clouds. One day, as the thunder and lightning ricocheted around him, he mopped his brow and with indomitable spirit scowled at the god in whom he did not believe, 'Go on. Make it worse.' As he said to the boy in the film, 'You can't expect a performance when it's coming down like this.' In time gloom enshrouded everyone involved in the making of the movie and Mr Punch took all the blame. In a moment of weakness the loyal Philip Oakes likened the experience to 'surgery'.

For all Hancock may have been nostalgically probing his past through the seaside background, the Punch and Judy motif pro-nounced something disturbing about his present. When Hugh Lloyd as his assistant asks Wally whether he watches much television, he replies, 'No, too much violence. Very bad for the kids,' oblivious of the fact that at that moment in a separate world at arm's length above their heads Punch is raining blows on Judy with his stick for the delec-tation of an audience of youngsters. Not that Hancock had any kids, either in the screenplay or in real life. He must have been aware that the constant sniping and point-scoring in the marriage between Wally and Delia was reflected in the physical tug-of-war between Punch and Judy, even if the former never came to physical blows. Hancock was also highly sensitive to the fact that both scenarios reflected in their separate ways the more urgent crisis taking place in his own mar-riage. According to his co-writer, he knew 'without any equivocation at all' that the film was about him and Cicely, although failing to appreciate the separate analogy between himself and the puppeteer, another entertainer with the cards stacked against him and an uncertain future ahead. Hancock stressed in his *Films and Filming* article that audiences who didn't find life funny would not find the film funny either. He himself had so little to laugh about in his own personal life, the approach may have seemed doomed from the beginning. The ending between Wally and Delia remains inconclusive. As a husband, maybe he clung to an element of hope between himself and Cicely. As the originator of the film, he was adamant and non-committal at the same time: 'The idea is right; whether it comes off or not I don't know yet.' At least he deserved commendation for never once allowing the project to degenerate into the ghastly abyss of domestic sitcom.

As we have observed, the film was not a commercial success, and the other three pictures under the ABPC deal were never made. Hancock claimed to George Fairweather and to various interviewers that he lost £5,000 in the process. To understand his reasoning on the matter one needs to go back to the original deal for *The Rebel*. When this was restructured to accommodate MacConkey Productions, much was made of the fact that Hancock had no share of the profits from the first picture and that he was determined, as he saw matters, not to be short-changed in this way again. This was not strictly accurate. The deal entitled him to a guarantee of £5,000 and a share of net profits on a sliding scale of 17½ per cent rising to 25 per cent when they exceeded £100,000. It also stipulated the payment of a similar sum of £5,000 for the second picture, with the profit scale enhanced to 20 per cent rising to 27½ per cent on a similar basis. Figures are not available for the total profits achieved by *The Rebel*, but its wide commercial success in its country of origin suggests they must have been considerable, and certainly enough for Hancock and his brother Roger, now responsible for all details of his affairs, to feel sufficiently secure to take a flyer on foregoing a guarantee second time around in return for a higher profit share. At the time of renegotiation there was nothing to indicate in their minds that the film would enjoy anything other than the success of the first epic, or that as a result of Hancock's erratic behaviour it would go considerably over budget. Under the terms of the new arrangement Hancock and ABPC would each receive £15,000 from the net receipts after all production costs had been recovered. Hancock would then receive the next £15,000, when it became available, after which all profits were to be divided equally between the two parties in perpetuity. Without going into the finer mathematics, the difference to Hancock between the two pictures had they both reached a profit limit of £100,000 would have been £33,750. Had the brothers stayed as they were, they would have recouped £5,000 by way of guarantee, the figure Hancock claimed he lost, although technically he never owned the money in the first place. It is a gamble most of us would have taken. According to Roger Hancock the film made no money at all. Three years later in an interview Hancock owned up: 'Well, it didn't come off. And I lost a lot of money. Though I would have made a bomb if it had!'

As soon as he had finished the film in the summer of 1962 Hancock had to address the matter of his new television series. Today a top-rated name like David Jason can switch channels with impunity; in the early 1960s the whiff of treachery hung in the air. The project loomed ahead with the public expectation that surrounds the verdict of an infamous trial. If only lessons had been learned and applied from the film, it might have made a more positive impact. On *The Punch and Judy Man* Hancock had been given so-called 'artistic control'. In the opinion of Roger Hancock, this is where much of the trouble resided: 'It's a fatal thing. It goes to their heads, they can't think straight, and it's the least important thing because they're not going to make you do anything you don't want to do anyway.' Nevertheless the new series also came under the banner of MacConkey Productions with everything that implied. As far as ITV was concerned, artistic control was a pittance to pay for such a prestigious name on its marquee.

As a diversion from the briny breezes of Bognor, the Hancock brothers, together with the writer assigned to the series, Godfrey Harrison, paid a visit to the West Coast of America in the tax-deductible name of technical and artistic research. They were given access to the Desilu studio at Studio City to watch a recording of Lucille Ball in *The Lucy Show*, where they were impressed at first hand by the slickness of the multiple-shooting system which Hancock had tried to persuade the BBC to adopt towards the end of his association with the Corporation. This enables the final show to be intercut after the event from continuous footage taken from different angles, at this time usually three, thus precluding the margin for error that often occurred in the live direction of a show, where the director is at the mercy of the technician known as the vision mixer as he dictates the shots he requires from individual cameras. Roger acknowledges wistfully, 'The system left nothing to chance and cut down on rehearsal time. Lucy was doing a routine where she was bouncing off a trampoline, coming up to a window, delivering a line, going back down again and bouncing back up to deliver the next line. It was fabulous to watch and her timing was incredible. Every single nuance was caught on camera. But back home the unions still wouldn't play.' In later months Roger became secretly relieved that, with all else to contend with, Hancock ended up working essentially in the way he'd been used to all his life: 'It was enough just to get the scripts for that series without the complications of a new technique thrown in.' Meanwhile, his elder brother observed that the comedy legend had complete control of every aspect of the production. In his tentative memoirs Hancock expressed his admiration:

Lucille Ball was fifty-eight when I met her, but you would have taken her for thirty-three. Apart from looking beautiful and being so funny, she is a first class business brain, a woman who knows what she wants in a television show and insists on getting it. In the time I spent at the studios she was never off the set.

It was August 1962. For reasons that will become apparent before the end of this chapter, Hancock, while still in his thirties, was looking closer to fifty-eight.

Of the visit, Roger recalls, 'He wasn't worth tuppence over there – when he walked down the street nobody knew who he was.' This only sharpened his resolve to crack the American marketplace. In January 1963 Hancock beat the drum in the *TV Times* for his new series, which he explained as a progression from his previous television work: 'A development which takes you to a stage in which you can be in almost any situation at any time. Where the background is entirely negative and unidentifiable. Where you can become international in your humour. Like Chaplin. That's the ambition, anyway.' In his quest for advice on how to adapt to a world audience and with an eye to the American distribution that would ensue if he could, Hancock consulted arguably the next best source after Chaplin himself. Stan Laurel, deprived of a residual income that should have been rightly his from the exploitation of his work and image, was living out his days in modest retirement in a small apartment within the Oceana Hotel at Santa Monica. The Hancocks took advantage of their stay to make the pilgrimage. Bernard Delfont, a personal friend of Stan who in his early years as an impresario had given Laurel and Hardy a last lease of professional glory on their variety tours of the British Isles, would have made the contact. Upon the maestro's death in 1965 a tape recording of Hancock labelled 'A British Sunday' was discovered among his effects.

The poignancy of the encounter lingers with Roger Hancock to this day: 'I'm glad I met him, but wish I hadn't. It was so sad. He was very unhappy about life, but very nice. It had all gone. Unlike Chaplin he had never owned the negatives and you thought somebody like this ...' His words trail off in despair. The screen star had little advice for the young pretender from his homeland other than to 'cut out the slang'. In truth, neither Chaplin nor Laurel were intrinsically British when it came to applying their art to the screen, having been absorbed into the American culture from the very first day they entered the film studio gates. That they had succeeded universally was an acknowledgement of the pervasive influence of that culture rather than any secret formula tucked away in their bag of comic tricks. On the other hand, whether he liked it or not, Hancock's whole identity was wrapped up in his Englishness. One recalls the reply given to the British matinée idol Jack Buchanan when he enquired of a cinema manager how his musical *Good Night, Vienna* was doing in the South London suburb of Lewisham: 'Well, Mr Buchanan, about as well as *Good Night, Lewisham* would be doing in Vienna!'

When the MacConkey deal was made with Bernard Delfont, who presented the show as a package to the broadcaster, ATV, it stipulated not only that each programme be recorded simultaneously on Ampex videotape and as a 16 mm tele-recording, but that all tapes, prints and negatives should remain at all times the sole and absolute property of Hancock's company. The initial arrangement for six shows was increased to thirteen as 1962 progressed. MacConkey Productions were to receive £4,000 per episode in return for the comedian's services. In addition they were expected to commission all scripts at their expense, with ATV providing all production facilities and the cost of the supporting cast. Any profits down the line would be split fifty-fifty with Delfont. When the time came to commission the scripts, Hancock with his film behind him turned first, as we know, to Galton and Simpson, probably more as a reflex action than out of any careful consideration that their writing skills were perfectly attuned to the 'any situation at any time' ideal he set himself. According to Ray Galton, Tony went back to them cap in hand a second time, but Steptoe duty called. In any case, it is unlikely they would have accepted the challenge, having decided they rather liked the independence that came from writing for straight actors as distinct from comedians, who were far more likely to question the result of their labours. Philip Oakes was initially retained as script consultant, but became more and more frustrated as Hancock forged ahead commissioning scripts from other quarters without consultation with him. When the writer protested, Hancock barked back, 'What the bloody hell do you know about it? I'm the one with the money.' He eventually resigned when the comedian objected to the outline of a film by Oakes that might have become the next ABPC venture, had that deal prospered: the commercial success or failure of *The Punch and Judy Man* would not be discovered until after the end of the ITV series. Tentatively entitled 'The Courier', the new movie would have depicted Tony as the heir to a bankrupt travel company, desperately promoting out-of-season mystery trips around Britain, 'so that Hancock might find himself in Scunthorpe or Grimsby in mid-winter with a mixed coach-load of priests from the Vatican and oil millionaires from Texas'. Oakes thought it provided the springboard for some mordant observations on the British way of life; Hancock disagreed. It was the final straw. The writer, who was becoming ever more aware of the absolute inability of anybody to tie Tony down to some work plan, walked away.

The Hancocks turned in the unlikely direction of Ray Alan, the ventriloquist of 'Lord Charles' notoriety, who as Ray Whyberd had penned several scripts for the *Army Game* spin-off *Bootsie and Snudge*. Maybe in the combined Christian names of Galton and Simpson the brothers registered a subliminal flash of potential excellence. If so, Alan never gave them a proper chance to test their delusion. His initial suggestion of a plot that saw Hancock employed as an assistant in a department store, where he is challenged not to be rude to a single customer for a week as a means of paying off his outstanding account, held immediate promise for the star, and the script was written. Alan was invited back to MacConkeys to discuss other potential storylines. When he arrived, Hancock was interested only in discussing a rewrite of the first script. Ray recollects, 'He wanted me to cut out all the old "Hancockisms" that had made him the character we loved. He wanted to change his appearance, too, and become more smart and "with it".' As the ventriloquist railed against change by invoking the long-term branding of Laurel and Hardy, in much the same way as the BBC had used the example of Jack Benny, Hancock became thoughtful and reached for another bottle of alcoholic sustenance. Cicely agreed with the ventriloquist, but 'I knew then', remembers Alan, 'that I could never work with Tony and I left.'

The job eventually devolved to Godfrey Harrison, whose success with *A Life of Bliss* in both radio and television marked him out as a writer of shrewd observation, capable of being funny in the Galton and Simpson manner without recourse to jokes. It was also appropriate that he had written Hancock's earliest non-variety appearances for television, namely the 'Fools Rush In' segments for *Kaleidoscope* in 1951. Unfortunately his erratic methods of working outweighed his effectiveness, and the series was in danger of falling behind schedule unless additional writers were brought in. In the final tally Harrison was responsible for six of the total thirteen programmes and was effectively dismissed as the series came towards the halfway stage, while others were taken on board who were able to deliver to strict recording deadlines. Not only did Harrison struggle to produce scripts on time, when he did deliver they were over-long, necessitating a greater learning challenge for the star and extended hours in the editing suite by both Hancock and his director to reduce the show to its required duration, a situation that led to frayed nerves and bloodshot eyes for all concerned. Back-up came initially from Terry Nation, a young comedy writer who had already been approached by Hancock with the elusive challenge of writing new material for a short stage tour in the October prior to the start of recording on 4 November 1962; he would later become the creative genius behind the Daleks of *Doctor Who* renown. Richard Harris and Dennis Spooner were the last to join the Hancock team: Harris, without Spooner, progressed to considerable success as a playwright, most notably with *Outside Edge* and *Stepping Out*. It is no surprise that the series is uneven, with no consistent sense of style. Many of the episodes carry plots that are over-complicated, ironically at a time when Hancock, thanks to Galton and Simpson, seemed to have established the naturalistic sequence without excessive plot as his forte. Out of fairness to the co-opted writers they were working under intolerable pressure for a performer with whom they were not familiar and who was increasingly confused as to who he wanted to be himself. Even so, the episode where Hancock claimed to be a master carpenter and found himself at the dysfunctional end of a DIY wardrobe was puerile material unworthy of children's television and marked a nadir for the comedian, even though a pied piper of a comic like Richard Hearne as 'Mr Pastry' might have played it rather well. It is worth noting that in the absence of Galton and Simpson, a saving was automatically made on the writing front. Harrison was paid £500 an episode, Nation £400 and Harris and Spooner £375. For their last series together at the BBC in 1961, Ray and Alan had received a guaranteed total fee of £1,100 per programme.

Not unexpectedly much of the material proved to be a pastiche of Galton and Simpson. In two of Harrison's scripts, *The Eye Witness* and *The Memory Test*, the facial remembering gambit from *The Reunion Party* is brought into play and flags on both occasions. Harris and Spooner's *The Early Call* had been pre-empted plot-wise by the radio episode, *The Sleepless Night*, as well as by *The Bedsitter*, in that it attempted for the most part – right down to his recumbent attempts at blowing smoke rings – to be a solo *tour de force* by Hancock, for which his drinking now made him sadly ill-equipped. Episodes that carried the promise of genuine comic suspense in the manner of *The Poison Pen Letters*, like Harrison's MI5 escapade *The Man on the Corner* and his bank robbery driven *The Eye-witness*, demonstrably let the viewer down. However, it was not so much in the plotlines where the similarities niggled. The depth of language was missing, as if Ray and Alan's work had been translated into some obscure eastern European language and then translated back again. The cohesiveness too had gone, that binding quality born of character development and environment that prompted Denis Norden's 'novel' analogy in his assessment of their work for Hancock. At their best Ray and Alan would produce a line or a phrase that kindled the heart of the nation in its understanding of their utterly complex creation. One recalls the radio episode where the lad is bemoaning his old trade as a tram conductor: 'I couldn't master the punch … the old thumb nail looked like a castle battlement some nights,' and the moment in *The Blood Donor* where he praises the advances of medical science: 'I was glad to see the back of those leeches.' One searches the scripts of the ITV series in vain for such moments. The hollowness of Hancock's repeated assertion to Galton and Simpson, 'We can do better,' proved emptier still as the series demonstrated his relative lack of judgement in script matters, a situation aggravated by his drinking.

Alan Tarrant, a rising star within ATV, was assigned to produce and direct the series at the company's Elstree television studios. On paper his experience augured better than that of Jeremy Summers, with shows that included several episodes of ITV's sitcom success *The Larkins* and the experimental *The Strange World of Gurney Slade*, starring Anthony Newley, to his credit. But even Tarrant lacked that magic combination of discipline linked to editorial control that Duncan Wood was able to exercise so effortlessly. Maybe by this stage of Hancock's development, Wood would have found it harder to discipline his protégé. But, as Patrick Cargill had observed during his work with them at the BBC, Hancock 'used to like being disciplined'. Wood had never had any hesitation in telling the star to shape up when it was appropriate, and one senses that the deep level of respect between the two men would have been of some worth. He would certainly not have instigated the situation experienced by the actor Harry Towb when he worked on the new series: 'We did the read-through in the morning at about ten and just before eleven the director said, "Okay, you and you and you – the Red Lion." And we accompanied him and Hancock to the pub and Tony, God bless him, started off with large brandies and the incredible thing was it didn't seem to have an effect upon him at all.' It would not stay that way. Those around him soon came to realise the truth of Brendan Behan's observation on himself, that one drink was too many and a thousand not enough.

The decline in Hancock's performance as the series progresses is painful to watch. The deterioration in his facial reactions – best described as a visual slurring – becomes ever more apparent and, as Roger Wilmut has indicated, it is difficult to accept that the second half of the series *is* of the same series. Although Hancock is never drunk on camera, the voice drags, the bags droop beneath his eyes and all the worst signals that were apparent in *The Punch and Judy Man* appear magnified. The ease has drained from the face which once put a nation most at ease. Tarrant would soon prove that he lacked Duncan Wood's empathy with Hancock's mastery of the reaction shot, and matters were not helped when in a moment of madness or stupor or both the star allowed a hairdresser to cut his hair with almost skinhead brutality. He arrived at the studio as if about to audition for the part of Magwitch in *Great Expectations*. 'What have you done?' asked Alan Tarrant in horror. 'I asked for a short back and sides,' replied the sheepish Hancock. The new look played havoc with continuity, and all the while Hancock was placing greater reliance on autocue and idiot boards.

Paula Burdon, who worked on the series as Alan Tarrant's PA, recalls the moment the autocue machine came into rehearsals as the moment of final defeat in this regard, although recollecting the help she gave a less-than-on-top-form Hancock by listening to him learning his lines during the early part of the series. Her happy memories of the gentlemanly courtesy he extended to her at this time were only overshadowed by the disappointment of the finished project. This coincides with Roger Wilmut's assertion that he did learn the early scripts properly – it is hard to detect a slavish distraction in his eye line during the early shows – and that only when the pressures became too great did he take refuge in the teleprompter, although the late delivery of material from Harrison would have been sufficient excuse for cue cards in the early stages. Duncan Wood may have regretted his moment of leniency towards the end of the final BBC series, but he would never have tolerated a situation where Hancock did not learn his lines in normal circumstances. Warren Mitchell summed up the curse of the cue cards in a radio programme on the comedian: 'When he went to ATV they spent their rehearsals drinking champagne and they said, "Don't worry about learning it, Tony." That was the big mistake he made, listening to their blandishments.' There is reason to believe that Tarrant did remonstrate with Hancock on the matter, but the performer insisted that nobody could tell and, besides, the likes of Bob Hope and Jack Benny would never appear on television without support of this kind. He never considered the hidden skill the two American masters displayed when they did resort to teleprompter or card. One journalist joked that he took the easy way out because he knew that some of the lines were not worth learning. It was said that when Hancock completed the series, there were more autocue machines on the studio floor than cameras. That may have been meant as a joke as well. The moment his job became – as Hancock surmised – easier, life became more difficult. The naturalness of his performance suffered and his career became ever more vulnerable, irrespective of the even more frightening complications for his health. In the words of Alan Simpson, 'Now he could drink and not worry about anything,' when in fact there had never been more to worry about, in both his personal and professional lives.

The disorientation Hancock – overwhelmed by production responsibilities with which he never had to contend at the BBC and cast adrift in a vicious circle where more and more drink battled with less and less sleep – must have felt is summed up by one marvellous line from *The Radio Ham*: 'I wonder if a longitude's any good without a latitude.' On one occasion Tarrant went into Hancock's dressing room and found him banging his head against the wall. When he questioned the comedian, he was told he was trying to make himself relax. It was a long way from the self-confident boast he made in the *Radio Times* at the start of his latest radio series five years earlier: 'Can't miss, really. I've got everything – good supporting cast, producer, scriptwriters!' Curiously the new supporting cast was very good indeed, going one step further in the direction of quality acting talent than the BBC had done. Mario Fabrizi popped up only once, a few months prior to his untimely death which Hancock put down to the baleful influence of Mr Punch, but comedy regulars like Johnny Vyvyan and, sadly, Hugh Lloyd were nowhere to be seen. Distinguished names of the quality of Denholm Elliott, Martita Hunt, Kenneth Griffith, Peter Vaughan, Dennis Price, Edward Chapman, James Villiers and Geoffrey Keen supplanted the regulars from the Duncan Wood Repertory Company. Patrick Cargill and John Le Mesurier returned on merit alone. This quality was carried over into the scenic design. Many of the shows began with Hancock as the perpetual looker-on standing at a street corner in the symbolic vantage point of Everyman before, in the words of the pre-publicity, 'going out of his way to offer help – usually to people who did not want his assistance'. No expense was spared to make the thoroughfare as extensive and realistic as possible, right down to the real paving stones to achieve the correct sound of people walking by. Alas, it failed to make the shows any funnier. The total budget for the series was ballyhooed at £300,000, which, according to the publicity, also granted Hancock his long-held wish that the programmes would be shot in short takes filming-style. In fact the early recordings were shot in the conventional manner of his BBC work, scene by scene with a live studio audience, although they enjoyed the luxury of two days of camera rehearsal in studio. As the series progressed and the pressures for Hancock intensified the system was modified.

After the fifth taping, the recording was broken down into two or three separate sessions spread over the two days and the edited show was played back to an audience at a later date when laughter was dubbed on, not an ideal situation when, as sometimes happens, an incoming line crosses over laughter that has still to die away.

The original plan to commence recording on a weekly basis two months before transmission with a well-earned two-week break for Christmas gives no indication of the panic that descended upon the series. Tarrant, with persuasion from Roger Hancock, had the sense to juggle the transmission order to advantage, although that in itself must remain subjective. This resulted in Ray Alan's script, *The Assistant* – with changes by Nation to assuage Hancock's fears – going out first, although it was recorded seventh in line. Ray Alan had agreed on condition he was credited merely with the storyline: he reasoned, 'I simply did not want to be involved with what I believed to be a disaster.' Harrison's *The Eye-witness*, in which Hancock witnesses a bank robbery and helps – or hinders – the police in their investigation, was recorded first and transmitted second. This kind of zigzagging continued until the end of the run. Matters would have been helped if the transmission pattern had been split into two shorter runs, with time for everyone to recharge and regroup in the interim, but in view of the advance publicity given to the run of thirteen, this may have been interpreted by press and public alike as an admission of defeat. Almost certainly the BBC would have been more flexible in the face of his problems, even if it could not have persuaded him to modify the demands of his ego as Hancock persisted in his attempt to be all things to all men.

The new series appropriated the straightforward title of *Hancock* from the Corporation. Although he had been absent from the small screen for eighteen months, the new title sequence must have triggered culture shock in many of those accustomed to the jaunty pomposity of the old Wally Stott opening that had identified Hancock for the better part of the previous decade. Derek Scott, already under contract to ATV, again enjoyed the patronage of his old partner, contributing a sprightly hippety-hop signature tune that was more in keeping with the times than the man. It was made to work through some agile juxtaposition of footage of Hancock on a traffic island aimlessly acknowledging the traffic in Jacques Tati fashion and at the last moment ducking out of the way of his own surname as the title graphic careers in from the right of screen. In the first transmission the homage to Tati continues when Hancock, in a brilliant piece of physical comedy, holds up his coat to a department store window to protect the modesty of a mannequin that is being disrobed. Without realising the window is under repair, he falls head-first through the glassless aperture and ends up on the pavement in a compromising position with a headless torso in a state of *déshabillé*. Once employed by the store, he is put to work in the packing department where he gets caught up in an impassioned reminiscence by a colleague – played by Kenneth Griffith at his stirring best – of how the Welsh peasantry stood out against the English in the dark days of the depression. By the end Hancock has become more Welsh than the Welsh. More visual comedy occurs as he battles with a roll of Sellotape while wrapping a vase and then has to apply similar skills to packaging a rubber dinghy which gradually inflates as he attempts to fit it into a small box, a problem he solves by attacking the boat with a pair of scissors. He finishes by throwing in a lifebelt: 'Compliments of the management – they're gonna need that!' He is transferred to the toy department where he is told to replace Mario Fabrizi as the children's favourite, Uncle Bunny. Hancock acknowledges that he looks ludicrous in his sub-Disney costume: 'I look like Nanook of the North.' Before long he enters into an altercation with a child: when her doll goes 'Mama', he adds, 'And you can belt up as well.' Script-wise the episode is flawed because the issue of whether he pays off his debt to the store, the reason he was employed in the first place, is never acknowledged. One wonders how many of the strictures would be relevant, had the old BBC production machinery been in place with Hancock nearer the peak of his powers. One guesses that even the old signature tune and the absence of a commercial break might have conditioned the audience into thinking it was watching something more akin to the old Hancock.

Hancock must have greeted the first transmission on 3 January 1963 with all the foreboding his alter ego voiced to Sid in a parallel situation years before in *Ericson the Viking*: 'Tonight my career will be in ruins, shattered beyond recognition, lying at me feet a tangled mess of childish hopes and dreams.' When James interjects that they'll make 'a lot of loot', Tony adds, 'I wouldn't be so sure. You have to see what the viewers think ... personally I think it's going to be thumbs down and into the crocodile pit.' It did not help matters that the BBC, by a quirk of fate as much as from spite, had scheduled the new series of *Steptoe and Son* on the same evening in the 8 o'clock slot, immediately prior to Hancock's transmission at 8.30. *The Times* appeared to give Hancock the benefit of the doubt: 'If Messrs Simpson and Galton do not need him, he does not need them and the main result of their separation would seem to be the totally pleasurable one of giving twice the amount of enjoyment in a single evening.' Not all the reviews were as charitable. Critically the lowest point was reached half way through the run when the reviewer for the *Birmingham Evening Despatch*, a newspaper that had always been well disposed towards its local son, found himself confessing, 'Last week I did something I never thought I'd do – I switched off a Hancock programme half way through ... tonight's chapter is called *The Reporter*. Oh dear.' In fact, with unconscious irony, the Terry Nation script reveals Hancock as a theatre critic who is complimented on his choice of adjectives in reviewing the latest play: 'banal, conventional, routine, stereotyped, hackneyed, dull, insipid, weary, flat, stale, humdrum and monotonous'. 'Yes, well, I didn't want to be too hard on it,' remarks Hancock. It must have made awkward viewing for him too.

In *Punch*, Bernard Hollowood, an enthusiastic champion at the beginning of the series, was not the only writer to revise his opinion: 'I was hopelessly wrong a few weeks ago when I suggested that the new *Hancock*, shorn of the services of Galton and Simpson, would still make the grade. It has now deteriorated so badly that viewing has become a chore … in the old Hancock, idiotic conceit masked a fair amount of bewildered common sense and shrewdness; in Mark II, idiocy is all, a shambles of meaningless tomfoolery. And not funny.' 'The critics seem to resent the fact that I want to progress,' reacted Hancock. To many he had certainly proved different, but only in so far as he was now the victim of a mediocre script as distinct from the beneficiary of a good one. The critical reaction can be measured against the remark made by Derek Hill in the winter 1961 edition of the television magazine *Contrast*, in the aftermath of Hancock's last BBC success: 'Occasionally a television series wins a kind of exemption from criticism. Once a programme is accepted as being one of the best, comment is confined to a verbal salute and an indication that the latest instalment was better than, up to or not quite as good as the usual standard. The standard itself goes unquestioned. Tony Hancock is the only comedian to have earned himself this kind of critical dispensation.' Those days were now behind him. In a television interview on *Late Night Line-up* with Michael Dean in October 1965, a mellowed Hancock, who the month before had admitted in *Planet* magazine that the scripts for the ATV series had not been as good as for his BBC shows, faced up to the difficulty of maintaining standards, admitting that the worst criticism he had ever received was not from the press – 'There's no malice. They have a right to say what they feel' – but from a newspaper seller, a great fan from whom he used to pick up his papers in the morning: 'He was so enthusiastic about everything all the time and he just gave me the papers and took the money and looked at me and said, "What happened last night then?" I knew that nobody could have been more for me than him and if he didn't like it, then things had collapsed.' Partway through the ATV series, Wilfrid Lawson, that inveterate drinker among actors, had joined the cast in the occasional role of an argumentative newspaper seller always happy to pick a quarrel with Hancock. The irony would not have been lost on the star during the interview, unless the occurrence had actually inspired the character in the first place.

Meanwhile the TAM ratings told their own tale. By the beginning of 1963 the ITV network was complete throughout the British Isles. In the first week *Hancock* secured an audience in 7,755,000 homes, which placed it third in the national top twenty programmes and won Hancock arguably his biggest television audience to date. The top two places were taken by the Monday and Wednesday episodes of *Coronation Street*. By the second transmission almost a third of that audience had fallen away to 5,544,000, plunging the show to eighteenth in the table. By the third week it had dropped out of the top twenty altogether, while in an amazing reversal of fortune *Steptoe and Son*, which had begun in twelfth position, had worked its way up to the third place which *Hancock* had started out by occupying, albeit with a slightly lower figure of 7,152,000 homes. It maintained that position for the next three weeks, before securing second place with a resounding figure of 8,794,000 homes with its final show. When *Steptoe and Son* came off air during February, Eric Sykes continued to perform strongly for the BBC, while *Hancock* floundered, banished totally from the top twenty. To save face, he found an excuse for the poor audiences in a fault with the power supply caused in certain areas by bad weather conditions. He explained to the *Daily Express*, 'I really believe the viewers hadn't the chance. All they could see was a postage-stamp-sized Hancock and so they switched off. There is nothing, absolutely nothing wrong with my new series. Within a few weeks everything will be all right.' But not even a return to full voltage could improve his performance or restore his on-screen persona to the more likeable image of his heyday. As Alan Simpson remarked of the characterisation, 'To be nasty after you have been rejected is reasonable; to be nasty before you have been rejected is gratuitous.' Ray and Alan had proved that pomposity need not embrace unpleasantness. Surliness was a different matter. That they unconsciously broke their own rule towards the end of their association, as we have seen, does not negate their argument. There was also a sense in which Hancock had appeared a 'nicer' person when Sid James was around, always on hand to bring him down to size. The star of the ATV series was no longer a person you necessarily wanted to invite into your home, not least because his enjoyment in his own performance was now largely absent, the rapid downturn in ratings casting an even darker shadow over the remaining recordings. In real life, though, for all his worries he maintained a degree of grace. When he bumped into Galton and Simpson at Orme Court one day, he commented, 'Saw your show, last night – very good.'

For all the faults, however, almost every programme has a redeeming moment, a comic highlight for his staunchest fans to enjoy. The execrable *The Craftsman* contains a visual sequence in the best tradition of his stage act when, ignorant of the correct terminology of the tools he requires, he resorts to mime to imitate the function of plane, spanner, chisel and screwdriver for the man behind the counter in the DIY shop. In Harrison's *The Politician* one longs for Patricia Hayes to play the woman in the crowd who harangues Hancock for insulting an older man. 'You ought to be horsewhipped,' she remonstrates. 'Well, that dates *you* for a start,' says Hancock. Possibly my favourite moment in the entire series occurs in the final show, *The Escort*. Harris and Spooner depict Hancock, incongruously attired in top hat and tails, in professional attendance on his brash Australian date in a transport caff in Stepney. The owner comes over to Hancock's table and slams down his plate of beans in front of him. Hancock looks at him wearily: 'And what am I supposed to eat it with?' 'I thought you was a magician,' comes the reply. Hancock's look of derision as he takes the knife and fork offered him is worth the price of admission for the entire thirteen shows. The moment is almost matched in what follows when Tony asks an Irish navvy, played by Harry Towb, 'to pass the condiments'. 'I'd be delighted to, if I knew what they was,' says the labourer. Eventually he bombards Hancock with salt, pepper, ketchup, vinegar, salad cream and more. 'I want to eat it, not suffocate it,' explains the comedian. Alas, both gems would have been funnier had Hancock's features been more mobile and Duncan Wood been directing to catch the close-ups properly.

The Godfrey Harrison episode entitled *The Girl* was a credible attempt to put Hancock into a genuine romantic situation, a scenario turned down not so long before in Galton and Simpson's working of *The Day Off*. Since the relative failure of the girlfriends in his early radio shows, Hancock had always resisted the idea of a woman falling in love with a 'buffoon' like himself, or vice versa, unless she too was a caricature. The change of attitude indicates how he saw his own character developing. He begins the episode standing on his street corner. An attractive nurse, played by Judith Stott, stumbles into him when the heel of her shoe breaks. His attempt to mend it fails and she rushes off leaving Hancock infatuated as never before. The flower seller, whom he tends to ignore, gives him some advice: 'You know what you ought to do if you want to see her again? Buy some of my lucky heather.' Hancock is unimpressed – 'Oh, shut up' – and goes home to try to forget, but love songs on the radio and a hospital drama on television stand in his way: 'I don't know what's got into me. Is she any different from other girls? Yes, she's different altogether. Hair the colour of corn, soft brown eyes … there's definitely something wrong with me. I'm sick!' With his head in a spin and stars in his eyes he makes for the local hospital to be encountered by an unsympathetic doctor played by Dennis Price. 'I'm looking for a nurse,' explains Hancock. 'Don't you think we should find out what's wrong with you first?' reasons Price. 'I just want to speak to her for a moment,' adds the star. 'This is a hospital, not a social club,' says

Price. One wishes the pair had worked more often together. Is it wishful thinking to suppose that Hancock might have made an effective Wooster to Price's near-definitive Jeeves? Soon the potential lovers meet over tea and cakes. A phone call is promised. Eventually the girl has to admit to Hancock that she is engaged. We then discover that his attitude to the opposite sex has not changed substantially since the Galton and Simpson days. 'I'll think of you every time I put my shoes on,' says the nurse as she leaves. 'Thank you very much indeed!' says Hancock with just the right ring of contempt. He looks up at the sign nearby. It reads 'Casualty'. 'That's me all right,' mutters Hancock. He returns to the street corner, the scene of their first encounter, when another girl bumps into him and damages her shoe. He immediately buttonholes a suitable passing male and acts as matchmaker. As they examine the broken heel, Hancock points to the flower seller: 'If I were you I should buy some of her lucky heather … you're probably going to need it.'

Much of what Hancock had learned about revue comedy was channelled into one scene in Harrison's *Shooting Star*, where he tries to act out a part for the film cameras at a screen test. In many ways the sequence is more immediately suggestive of other comedians: Tommy Cooper instantly springs to mind again with his esteemed 'Hats' routine, where the lines of his recitation get hopelessly out of sync with the pieces of headgear that should illustrate them. Cooper's finesse in the routine was born of countless performances. Hancock and his fellow actors, including Denholm Elliott as the director, achieve as near to a precision performance as the once-only demands of a television recording could hope to achieve. The film, for which Hancock auditions, is supposed to be a gritty docudrama. Hancock plays the bullying working-class husband returning home to his stoic wife, played by Frances Rowe. 'Stop staring at me or you'll get what's coming to you,' is his repeated refrain as his actions keep lagging behind his lines and his props – bottle of beer, glass, newspaper, her handbag, cigarette, flat cap, a knife as weapon

– are never in the right place when the words demand. As she struggles to help him, their lines get desperately muddled, Hancock not helped by the clapperboard that sets him on edge every time it cracks into action like a lion-tamer's whip. There is a hilarious moment when he literally does forget the extremely complicated sequence and turns to cue card or teleprompter, 'Where were we? Start again, eh? Right!' Had he made less point of the lapse, no one would have known, but it shows his vaudeville training and the fun he makes of the slip-up allows him to bond more closely with the audience. The show was only the second to be recorded. No one involved could have guessed that the sequence would foreshadow the genuine difficulties with learning his lines that were still to come, any more than they had cause to blink an eye at the drinking motif that is given as the cause of the husband's loutish behaviour. Near the beginning the character turns to Rowe to explain himself: 'Yes, I've been drinking …' There is a pause, where the director misses a much needed close-up, before Hancock continues, '… and it seems to have affected my memory.' By the end of the series, reality had again overtaken the stuff of comedy. The programme does contain one *conscious* joke against himself that assures us that for all his worries Hancock did retain a personal sense of humour. Soliloquising on the possibility of film stardom, he turns to a mirror and asks himself, 'Tell me, Mr Hancock, has fame meant any difference to you?' 'No, I don't think so, Mr Freeman,' he replies in an affected voice. 'Just made me more conceited, that's all.' One can almost hear Philip Oakes in the background, 'A touch of megalomania, eh?'

Another episode that reflected reality in a candid manner, this time after the event, was Terry Nation's *The Night Out*. A better title might have been *The Morning After*. After a bibulous night on the town, Hancock wakes up sprawled across a sofa in a hotel bridal suite. The ghastly sight of his haggard face and waking eyes would not have required much acting at this late stage in the series, an image redeemed in the name of humour only by the miniature party hat on elastic with which he finds himself precariously crowned. Hung over and grotesque, he teeters on the brink of consciousness. Eventually the possibility that the girl asleep in the bedroom may be his wife is dispelled by the arrival of her husband, played by Derek Nimmo, who begins to educate his guest in the details of the night before. It transpires that after they met up at a night club Hancock became the life and soul of the party: 'Remember that dance you did with my wife? Had us all in stitches, you know.' Tony, who can't recall a thing, is apologetic: 'Lucky you came in … I didn't offend anybody, did I? … I do know I can be a bit of a wag when I'm on the milk stout.' 'You sure I didn't offend anybody?' becomes the refrain of this show as the cast from the night club cabaret emerge from the other rooms. Hancock hardly ever acted drunk on screen – a tradition in which his heroes Jimmy James and Sid Field were acknowledged masters – and there is no suggestion that, however heavily he had been drinking in real life, he is at all intoxicated on this recording – or any other. In retrospect, however, the episode is unsettling, with Nation drawing on his experiences on the road with Hancock the previous October, when he assumed the role of a 'hundred pounds a week babysitter' to look after Tony, after most of the new material he had written for his stage show fell by the wayside. The version described by David Nathan has Hancock returning from Liverpool to London on the night sleeper with Nation, co-star Matt Monro and Tony's road manager Glyn Jones. Their spirits were high and the wine flowed. In the morning the writer called on Hancock in his compartment to discover the comatose comedian lying naked on the bunk. An agitated Jones was struggling to pull his socks on and as Hancock prised his eyes open to the world he joked, 'Glyn is trying to give me a fitting for a sock.' As they paraded down the platform at Euston, Hancock kept asking, 'Are you sure I didn't offend anybody last night? I sometimes wander out into the corridors stark naked.'

A more startling, expanded version of the tale depicts Hancock disgracing himself by compromising Monro sexually on the journey.

It is corroborated by a later admission from Nation that in the middle of the night he was drawn by the sound of an argument to Monro's compartment, where he discovered the singer distressed and Hancock cowering naked in the corner. The incident was hushed up and it was agreed that nothing further should be said on the matter. Nation's account is not substantiated with regard to date or source. It seems unlikely that the writer, who died in 1997, would run the risk of compromising his own standing and friendship with Hancock by embarrassing him with a reminder of the second, more salacious version of events, had it taken place, even if it was now a closed book among the four men. According to Nathan, when a few months later Hancock confronted the echo of the incident in Nation's script, he apparently grinned and announced, 'You bastard!' Galton and Simpson had been there before. Again, it says much for Hancock's sense of humour *in extremis* that he allowed the script to go ahead as written. Of course, if the incident had occurred, he may well by now have blocked it from his mind. Years later, when Kenneth Williams's diaries were published, the entry for 24 April 1972 proved revealing. Williams has been filming on location with Sid James, who 'talked at length about Hancock and said ... that Matt Monro told him he'd waken up one night to find Hancock going down on him for the fellatio, and that Matt had "given him a right-hander" ... of course one wonders how much of this is factual and how much gossip put together from disjointed accounts'. If the incident did occur, it may cast more light on a state of mind disturbed under the influence of alcohol than on his sexual preferences.

When Roger Hancock is asked to recall his memories of the ATV series he holds his head in his hands as if still nursing the anguish. 'There were no happy moments, no,' is his subdued response. 'And also it wasn't very good. The public are not idiots. They were right.' The closing credit for MacConkey Productions featured a comic coat of arms depicting an Aladdin's lamp and the motto, *'Optimus Butyrus Erat.'* Translated from the Latin the words mean, 'It was the best butter.' Today Roger's sense of humour allows him to concede, 'It ended up the worst margarine!' Both he and Alan Tarrant found themselves in a 'no-win' situation: 'Alan used to say to me, "Okay?" and I'd say "Okay" because by that stage there was nothing more we could do. Tarrant was effectively employed by our company, although he had his masters at ATV. He's looking after their side of it, but we had artistic control, so he's caught in the middle of any decisions.' When challenged to say how Duncan Wood would have handled the disaster, Roger is candid about a man whom he respects and who, shortly before his death in 1997, edited together a not discreditable compilation of the better moments of the ATV series: 'He wouldn't have done it. It's as simple as that. The series was an absolute night-mare. It got worse towards the end when the scripts really were dreadful and I think Tony was drinking virtually twenty-four hours a day. And it never got better. It just went on and on and on.' The younger Hancock might have been led to expect the worst from their trip to America to watch the Lucille Ball project. Roger is fearlessly honest, admitting it was not merely the vodka that caused him con-cern: 'He'd wake up at one thirty in the morning and take three or four Tuinal tablets. So many times he was totally out of it. On the Los Angeles trip we stayed at the Beverly Hills Hotel and he trashed the room the night before. He must have knocked himself out because he had a terrible black eye and we spent hours applying make-up try-ing to make him look all right. The combination of vodka and Tuinal really did it. That shows how bad he was getting.' Roger recalls that in the end his brother was in no fit state to meet the first lady of American comedy, although as we know Tony claims otherwise. It is not difficult to see how he may have been confused on the issue. Meanwhile, as Lucy continued to convulse her audiences in the Desilu studio, another *grande dame* of entertainment was making the headlines. While the Hancock brothers were in America, on 5 August 1962, Marilyn Monroe died from an apparent drugs over-dose.

Alan Tarrant appears to have got on well with Hancock, even if he found his behaviour perplexing: 'He was a very interesting chap when he was relaxing. I remember him talking about philosophy and he gave a sort of Cockney version of various philosophies, which was hilariously funny. And he was like the character he played in a strange sort of way. He was a nervous man and he told me that once, when he was having a big dinner with Harry Secombe after a show, he said to Harry, "You know – we should be at the NAAFI now." He could not get over the fact that he had got so far so fast.' Whatever his status on the production, Tarrant, no doubt inspired by his innate humility, was loyal enough to stick his head above the parapet after the poor reception accorded the series, contributing a letter to the *TV Times* by way of an *apologia* for the comedian. The banner headline proclaimed, 'How do you stand in the great Hancock controversy? One man who stands at the eye of the storm has his say here.' Tarrant invoked Hancock's old argument about boredom with his character: 'My problem was to ensure that Hancock was kept on his toes – experimentally – and that you would continue to think he was funny … if you laugh I am happy. If you don't, then there is a way out; possibly it involves me jumping off Waterloo Bridge.' It was an unfortunate choice of words.

Recording for the series came to an end on 15 February, after which Hancock had to fulfil a week's commitment to an advertising campaign for the British Railways Board. Roger Hancock is convinced that with that behind him the best antidote for his brother would have been to have gone on the road immediately, kept out of mischief in the provincial theatres that still held a nostalgic hold on him. Instead, complaining of exhaustion – not an unfair diagnosis, however much alcohol contributed to his condition – he took refuge in Paris as if on automatic pilot. There an alleged incident when he insulted some guests at the same hotel was dealt with discreetly by the management, saving Tony from a night in a French police cell. Within a week he was back in England. Late in 1962 he had committed to appear as guest of honour at an Australian television awards ceremony scheduled sometime during the second half of March 1963. On 15 March the British press announced that he had cancelled the trip on doctor's orders and entered St George's Nursing Home in London suffering from viral pneumonia.

For Hancock the previous twelve months had embraced major challenges in film and television. They had been made more difficult by being played out against the backdrop of his failing marriage. When the comedian described the atmosphere of Wally Pinner's marriage to Philip Oakes as one of 'mutual hatred', the writer was in no doubt that the comedian was referring to his own. In his article for *Films and Filming* Hancock was obviously speaking with the voice of experience: 'When marriage gets scratchy and when after some years you know the other's weaknesses, you also know how to go for them. This works from both sides. One sees so many times that marriage as a relationship doesn't work. People keep up the illusion and know how hard to hit each other (in the subtlest possible way) and become expert in tearing each other apart.' Against his wishes, Cicely would visit her husband in his dressing room and on the set of both the film and his television shows. His attitude was born out of professionalism and his need for concentration as much as anything personal. Often the proceedings would be disrupted by the bitter quarrelling between them.

By now the Hancocks had advanced from the converted-pontoon stage of nautical ownership and were the proud owners of a thirty-five foot converted Breton fishing boat moored at Antibes. It was originally called *Fredericka*; Tony wasted no time in rechristening it *Wokki*, after his pet name for Cicely. He once explained to Joan Le Mesurier that the name dated back to the day she had worn a tight-fitting black-and-yellow striped sweater that reminded him of a wasp. On a calm day the vessel could just manage one and a half knots and was best advised not to drift too far from shore. Upon emerging from the nursing home, Hancock invited Terry Nation and his wife, Kate, to spend a holiday with them. 'You don't mind if we all sleep in the same cabin, do you?' were their host's first words as they stepped aboard: the second cabin was doubling as a sail locker. For the next three weeks, in impossibly cramped conditions they observed a constant cat-and-mouse game played out around them in the name of matrimony. The Nations might have been the invisible supporting cast in a *Topper* novel by Thorne Smith, so unperturbed were the Hancocks by their presence. One night as they lay on their bunks a book fell off a shelf, waking Cicely. She thought Hancock had hit her and rounded on him in return. The Hancocks continued to take it out on one another while the Nations pretended to be out to the world. When the real culprit was found the next morning, it carried the title *The Dawn of Civilisation* on its spine. History doesn't record whether Hancock asked his fellow passengers, 'I didn't offend anyone last night, did I?'

Oakes had sensed the real tension developing between them on the occasion Hancock, overcoming his superstition regarding the colour green, bought his wife a peace offering of an emerald ring: 'It was beautiful, but Cicely was convinced it meant ill fortune. She had Irish blood and saw the devil more readily than most people. Hancock, of course, was deeply superstitious and that made life worse and they actually fought and it was dreadful really. There wasn't much joy and happiness going on privately for him.' Someone with a privileged view of the state of their marriage during this time was Hancock's secretary Lyn Took, whose step-father, a manufacturing jeweller by profession in Hatton Garden, had crafted the ring for the comedian for an alleged sum of £1,000. Her mother, Eileen Fryer, would often come to its rescue at those volatile moments when it became a missile of domestic warfare at the Red Barn. Eventually Tony asked her to make arrangements with her husband for the ring to be changed to a single stone diamond. Lyn, who was close to both members of the relationship, is anxious to downplay some of the more sensationalist reporting that has attached to the marriage in recent years, finding it hard to accept the 'vicious beatings' he is alleged to have inflicted on her: 'A push, a shove, but vicious beatings, no, no. I'm really sorry, no … they would have rows and disagreements, but there was also lots of laughter and fun. They would be excited about things together. They always had plenty of things to say, but anger never turned to violence. The drinking was always more noticeable in Cicely than in him.' She even concedes that in the event of a physical *contretemps* Hancock was more likely to come off the worse as a result of Cicely's advanced judo skills, first cultivated to deter the unwanted suitors her earlier career as a model had tended to attract. Her brother-in-law, Sir Reginald Harland, testifies that she did once sustain a broken arm as a result of such a tussle with her husband and that she became progressively scared of the effect alcohol had on him, irrespective of the love she always harboured for him.

Cicely had reasoned with her own mother, 'What goes down my throat does not go down his,' while Roger Hancock points out the competitive element in their relationship: 'The drink was the only way she could keep up with him. They'd drink at least a bottle of vodka at night and when they came to stay with us we'd always find an empty vodka bottle in the morning.' Terry and Kate Nation had witnessed the real-life *Days of Wine and Roses* scenario at first hand in the South of France. One night Ciccly was in no fit state to drive them back from a restaurant. As she slumped over the wheel, Hancock bullied her awake: 'Do your job. I do mine. It doesn't matter how I feel – I've got to go on. Now do your job – drive the bloody car and get me home.' None of the others could drive. Somehow Cicely, manhandled into alertness by her husband, reached the boat without incident. Back in England Hancock began to stay overnight in town with greater frequency, a situation that may have enhanced his relationship with Freddie Ross, but was also its own indication of his wife's increased unreliability as his trusty chauffeuse. On one such occasion she seriously broke her leg falling over one of their dogs while attempting to cut a lettuce in the garden. The extreme likelihood is that not for the first or last time alcohol played a part in the accident. Lyn sensed an unease in the marriage when it needed some persuasion for Hancock – who *did* have an aversion to hospitals – to agree to let her take him to see his wife: 'She was in a very bad way, very tearful in a ward of her own, and he went off around the wards signing autographs, which was not like him at all, because he didn't put himself forward like that. She was desperately upset and he said, "I've brought you a book by Bertrand Russell."' As he spouted off about the philosopher, Lyn lost her patience, and when the nurse came in took him to one side. Her words carry passion when she repeats them today: 'What do you think you're doing, for goodness' sake? She doesn't want that – she doesn't want that anyway – what she wants is you – time with you and some sympathy. You're being very unfair. Come on!' Lyn left him for half an hour. 'I hope he behaved himself, but I doubt it,' she says with a chuckle of resignation. She may have remembered his admission from one of his mating forays on the radio show: 'Half a page of Bertrand Russell and they're putty in my hands.'

More poignantly Lyn recalls the occasion later that same day in 1963 when in the study at Blindley Heath Hancock confided to her that his marriage was all but over. Having confronted him with the strange, unkind behaviour he had shown at the hospital, she plucked up the courage to ask her employer and friend, 'Do you love Cicely?' 'And that,' says Lyn, 'is when he said, "No, I don't. I don't love her any more." But he didn't say, "No, I don't – I've met somebody else and I'm in love with somebody else," which is the natural thing to say if it happens to be true. It was just that he'd lost the feeling.' Lyn describes his manner in the discussion that followed as neither apologetic nor high-handed: 'He was like he always was with me – no anger, no irritation, answering me straight, accepting what I had to say.' It cannot be stressed enough that this was how most people found him when sober, the side that genuinely belied the screen persona. However, there can be no question that as his wife drank more she became physically less attractive to him, not because at this stage she had lost her looks, but simply because hypocritically he found drunkenness in a woman abhorrent. The days were far distant when they would lie in bed giggling, reading passages of A.A. Milne to each other, fantasising themselves into the stories. Cicely became Wol after the wise old owl; Hancock saw himself as Pooh, rotund and put-upon, although he reserved his softest spot for Eeyore, the perfect tragic hero, confronting his reflection in the stream – 'Pathetic. That's what it is. Pathetic.' – and interminably sad about the last thistle being sat upon before he could enjoy it. He particularly liked the story where Eeyore has lost his house in the snow and has to explain his discomfiture to Christopher Robin: 'In fact … quite-between-ourselves-and-don't-tell-anybody, it's Cold.' The actress Damaris Hayman, his friend and companion from later years, who also shared his enthusiasm for the Pooh *oeuvre*, is equally adamant that he would never have physically harmed Cicely. When it is suggested to Hayman that in *The Punch and Judy Man* he may have been alert to similarities between Mr Punch's behaviour and his own towards both Cicely and Freddie, she leaps to a qualified defence: 'No, not Cicely – he would never have knocked Cicely about.'

As 1963 progressed, it became an open secret within the profession that for increasingly long spells Hancock was sleeping over with Freddie Ross at her central London flat in Dorset Square. He eventually moved in on a permanent basis and even today Lyn Took finds it difficult to believe that he made the decision to leave Cicely to live with another woman: 'He would never have struck me like that.' She had not even heard of Ross until the publicist arrived at the Red Barn announcing herself as a friend of Tony's during Cicely's hospitalisation. According to Philip Oakes, during the filming of *The Punch and Judy Man* it was Freddie who made sure that he regularly phoned home to Cicely. An expert organiser, she began to arrange his domestic life along the lines of his professional regimen. Sally

Mordant, an associate of Ross in her public relations business, observed that she tried to give Hancock the kind of home he never had with Cicely: 'He said it was like living in *Emergency Ward Ten*, because as he flicked ash into an ashtray she would remove it and clean it. She thought that if she gave him the security of a well-run home, that if she organised him like an office, it would give him an anchorage.' It is never wise to expect, let alone demand, that someone who works in the theatre will be through the bathroom and out of their dressing-gown by midday. In later years he commiserated with Joan Le Mesurier on the change in lifestyle: 'He said that when they'd eaten she would immediately clear the table and start washing up and he'd say, "Sit down, for God's sake – just sit down and talk." But she was more intent on keeping everything clean and tidy – him included.' Visitors to his dressing room were treated with similar efficiency, as Joan and her second husband John Le Mesurier discovered when they went to visit him backstage at the Talk of the Town, long before Tony had established an emotional attachment to Joan: 'She was not welcoming and very defensive, wanting us to leave very quickly.' In his published diaries Kenneth Williams in another backstage situation referred to her even more disparagingly as 'That Freddie Ross ... after all he's said about her in the past!' But as Freddie explained matter-of-factly to David Nathan, 'I had to open an office at nine o'clock in the morning. Tony thought that everything should revolve round him. I was trying to run a business as well.' A close friend of the comedian summed it up for me from Tony's point of view: 'She scared him in the end. She was too domineering and too possessive.' The one consolation – for them both – had come in the boot of the car that finally brought Hancock to her for the supposed duration. His complete set of the *Encyclopaedia Britannica* represented a safe haven all of its own for the troubled star, an erudite ball and chain of his own devising.

When one listens to people who were close to the comedian, it is hard to believe that the same depth of emotion existed between

Hancock and Ross as there had once flourished between Hancock and Romanis. In a BBC television documentary as late as 2005, Sidi Scott recalled, 'To me she was always the agent, always in command. She was extremely good company, but I would take a step back from her as a personal friend whereas I would have gone forward to Cicely – they were chalk and cheese.' Tony was married to Cicely for almost fifteen years. His marriage to Freddie in December 1965 lasted two and a half years, during which they lived together for little more than seven months. As we shall discover, it was ironic that as his first divorce was being processed in the summer of 1965 he was already living through the early stages of the break-up with Ross, to whom he was not yet married. Throughout this time his wife-to-be continued to look after his public relations interests. Another of her clients was the Steptoe actor Harry H. Corbett. It is curious that at a time of great public vulnerability for Hancock she masterminded a double-page article in the *Daily Mirror* featuring the two performers. With Steptoe riding high and Hancock languishing in the ratings, the two stars are pictured side by side in a major article in the issue for 8 February 1963. Their very positioning casts Hancock as the loser, with Corbett given pole position on the left-hand side of the photograph. The accompanying headlines spell out the comparative statistics of Corbett's triumph and Hancock's downfall. It is surprising how similar the men look with their striped knitwear, slouched shoulders and earnest expressions. The accompanying discussion, conducted by the journalist Donald Zec, reads as an attempt by Corbett to upstage – albeit jokily – Hancock with *his* mock philosophising. It is left to Hancock to utter the few words that make any serious contribution to the piece: 'There are no fixed ingredients for talent. You can't bake it like a cake. Part of the art is to go on looking like melted butter even though your nerves are screwed up to bursting. I don't think folks realise how tough it is.' His words were sincere, but Hancock did not deserve the otherwise negative exposure.

Chapter Thirteen

'THE LIMBO IS CALLING ...'

'I want to stand there as I am. No props.
No pretence. No defence. And say,
"There it is – here I am."'

The sorry reception accorded his commercial television series signified that Hancock's career was in free fall, a plight which the release
of his second major film did nothing to arrest. It is indicative, however, of the accrued goodwill of his BBC years that from now until the
end of his life the British public never withdrew its interest in his
exploits, any more than his dedicated fan base withdrew its affection.
No comedian ever had an audience more on his side, always on hand
in the hope of recapturing the halcyon hilarity of days gone by as it
willed him to succeed. The sympathy he aroused was like that for a
pet unable to find its way back home, however hard it tries. One visu-
alises him in the guise of one of Thurber's doleful dogs, licking his
wounds with one eye askance at the increased momentum not only in
the careers of Galton and Simpson, but also of Sid James, as the actor
forged ahead as an undisputed star on the back of the *Carry On* saga
and television opportunities galore. As the 1960s progressed,
Hancock, plagued by personal problems and professional doubt,
formed part of a curious trinity with Edith Piaf and Judy Garland,
whose concluding performances were also played out in the public
scrutiny of the new tabloid-and-telly era. No one could ever doubt the

determination they wore on their breast like campaign medals. Hancock too refused to believe he was finished, but in his case the challenge of laughter made the spotlight even more exacting.

For Hancock the next five years came to resemble a shabby patchwork quilt of bookings, stitched together sporadically with no sense of rhyme, reason or progression. To make matters more disconcerting his career seemed to be played out at two levels, the stark reality of the one contrasting with the more fanciful Walter Mitty dream world of the other. When it did seem as if he were about to recapture former glories, projects dispersed in the air with the evanescence of an aerosol spray. It seems contradictory, therefore, to state that apart from the occasional poorly attended week in variety his first secure booking after the ATV series was an eight-week run topping the bill at the London Palladium. However, any traditional prestige attached to that engagement was somewhat dented by the way in which it came about. In July 1963 Hancock backed out of a six-week cabaret season at the Talk of the Town theatre restaurant – formerly the London Hippodrome – booked under the aegis of impresario Bernard Delfont by his loyal lieutenant Billy Marsh. Last-minute fears that he could not adapt to the cabaret situation, which positioned him with an audience on three sides, occasioned the decision. A few days later on 5 August Marsh was in his office when a telephone call advised him that Arthur Haynes, the star of the Palladium's recently opened summer revue, *Swing Along*, for which he was also responsible, had just collapsed with cardiac arrest. Such news travels fast in show business circles. Within minutes of hearing, the remorseful Hancock was on the phone to the agent volunteering to step into the breach: 'You in trouble? … All right, if you want me I'll go in.' The courage of his gesture cannot be underestimated, bruised as he was from critical knocks on two fronts.

At that moment the élite of British stage comedy – represented by the likes of Dodd, Cooper and Forsyth – was comprehensively deployed on summer season duty around the coastal resorts and Marsh had few, if any, options at the level required to compensate for Haynes's marquee appeal. The following evening Tony took refuge in his tried-and-tested stage routine and showed that it could still deliver the laughs. All thoughts of having to live up to the image of a 'new' Hancock were happily put on hold for the time it would take for Haynes to recover. Tony was an unlikely substitute. In the later years of Hancock's BBC success, ATV had been developing Arthur Haynes as commercial television's own Hancock figure with some considerable success. After many years as staunch comic support on Charlie Chester's radio show, *Stand Easy*, Haynes, with his pawky, belligerent humour and inspired gift for comic mime, found his Galton and Simpson in Johnny Speight. He provided a sound reason to watch ITV on a Saturday evening until his early death at the age of fifty-two in 1966. During Hancock's recent fall from the TAM top twenty, Haynes had more than held his own in the chart in those weeks when they were both appearing on the same channel. Nicholas Parsons, Haynes's straight man, recalls that Hancock was in a low state during the Palladium run, remembering him seated at the end of the settee in his dressing room in a kind of Buddha-like position: 'He seemed desperately sorry for himself, like a child who feels misunderstood and is desperately trying to attract attention. And there was nothing I could do to cheer him up.' Tony's friend Alan Freeman, the record producer and not the disc jockey, went to his dressing room on the opening night to discover him looking 'as white as a sheet'. 'Thank God for a friendly face,' mused Hancock as he despatched Alan to the auditorium. 'I want at least one person in the audience laughing.' Billy Marsh, however, always testified to the professionalism of the man and recalled the banter that took place as the deal was swiftly settled between them – a straightforward guarantee of £1,000 a week against 12½ per cent of the gross. At the time Marsh also represented a famous singing star, who in his contracts insisted on his name being billed in big blue letters and a large blue Cadillac in attendance at the stage door. As he went to leave Billy's office, Hancock joked, 'And don't forget – I want to be billed in blue.' 'Yes, on a blue background,' said Marsh without looking up from his desk. A scowl of joy floated across Hancock's face. He seemed thrilled to be back in the good-humoured cut and thrust of the variety world.

The Palladium season gave Hancock the opportunity to recover some ground with the press. 'I am going through a period of readjustment,' he announced. 'At thirty-nine I've still got big ambitions. I am anxious to sell myself in America as a television star.' It says much for what he still meant to the BBC even after the disappointment of the ATV series that on 8 July Tom Sloan had written to Hancock to inquire if there was any chance of his returning to the Corporation. One senses that Hancock's refusal to pursue the overture was bred more out of the embarrassment of his recent failure than disinterest. In June 1965, two years later, the press was announcing that within hours of his opening in cabaret at the Talk of the Town – he eventually succumbed – he was being asked to return to the BBC in a new television series following a series of repeats of his old shows due to air in the autumn. Hancock was quoted that he would like the series to be handled by his old writers. When asked to comment, they explained they could not make a commitment because they were so heavily booked. The lack of any corroboration for the project within the appropriate files in the BBC archives suggests that the comedian was clutching at straws, quite as he appears to have been when he talked about his supposed involvement with American television. In October of the same year he announced to the *Glasgow Sunday Mail* that after a three-week cabaret season at the Chevron Hilton in Sydney the following month, he was going to Los Angeles to make a pilot film for an American television company. Around the same time he reiterated the same claim to Michael Dean on *Late Night Line-up*. When Dean raised a discreet eyebrow at the news, Hancock invoked the power of the Beatles as his new passport to transatlantic acceptability: 'The four boys went over there and all of a sudden there has been a tremendous breakthrough for English people – I never thought I would ever ride along in Hollywood listening to "Mrs Brown, You've Got a Lovely Daughter".' No such pilot was ever made. It was all so much pie in the sky, symptomatic of the psychiatric imbalance from which Roger Hancock asserts his brother was now suffering, like the claim he made to Gay Byrne on the television show *Open House* in December the previous year, repeated in an interview for *Photoplay* magazine the following March, that he had just signed a television contract that would keep him in the USA for seven years: 'We're trying to make international comedy and that naturally must include national comedy and I don't quite know when I have to go.' The *Photoplay* article added that the shows would be delivered in series of thirty-nine episodes at a time, set against a backdrop of various American cities, one of which would be Chicago. 'Everyone has the idea that Chicago is a big, draughty unfriendly place,' explained Hancock, 'whereas in fact it's not that at all. I would bring this contrast between what people think and what the facts are into the show – in comic fashion.' 'He probably thought,' says Roger, 'that if I talk about it long enough, it will happen. It was a total figment of the imagination.' By the time he was interviewed by Robert Ottaway in *Nova* magazine in November 1966, the fantasy had embraced an offer to play Nero in an American television serial planned to run five years. He did admit he had turned that down.

In February 1964 the idea that he might play the part of Elwood Dowd in a British remake of the invisible-rabbit epic *Harvey* had fallen apart, depriving fans the opportunity of seeing him play alongside Margaret Rutherford, the *grande dame* of British film comedy. Later a disappointed comedian would explain, 'They couldn't seem to get the script right, and in the end, with everyone saying it was too close to the Jimmy Stewart original, the whole thing was shelved completely.' At the time his own impatience added considerably to the decision. However, there appeared to be more prestigious consolation at hand. Since the ATV series much of Roger's time had been taken up pursuing the suggestion of the major starring role in the film of Eugene Ionesco's absurdist play *Rhinoceros*. The production company behind the venture was Woodfall Films, formed by John Osborne with Tony Richardson to put his *Look Back in Anger* on the screen and numbering *A Taste of Honey* and *Tom Jones* among its recent successes. Hancock was inspired casting for the role originated by Olivier on the London stage, one that could tentatively bring him the international recognition he craved, as well as stature as an actor: 'Next thing,' joked Hancock, 'it'll be a touch of burnt cork and Othello.' He would play the part of Bérenger, a humble clerk in an unnamed European city, who defines himself as the last member of the human race while his fellow humans submit to metamorphosing into rhinos, creatures symbolic of contented anonymity and insensitive conformism. He alone is incapable of making the transition. Roger accompanied the film's director Alexander (Sandy) Mackendrick, whose *Sweet Smell of Success* had once made such an impression on Hancock, to New York, where they persuaded the great Zero Mostel to play the second lead, the one character who is seen physically to *become* a rhinoceros in the play, following his success in the Broadway version. When Roger gave his brother the good news on his return, Tony turned on him with contempt and bewilderment: 'What *are* you talking about?' Roger reasons that he had thrown out the idea because it was too intellectual: 'It's what he *thought* he should be doing, but when it came down to it he'd rather be in variety. So much for acquiring the class he was obviously seeking. We'd done a deal. They'd paid us money. He knew all about it. But it was the drink and it was the final straw as far as I was concerned. I sacked him!'

There may be other reasons why Hancock had second thoughts about the picture. Oscar Lewenstein, one of the film's producers, claimed Hancock had become impatient with both the script process and the complications of devising a convincing beast in an age before animatronics and CGI techniques. In a final letter of persuasion to the star after the two brothers went their separate ways, Lewenstein insisted candidly that he should only accept the role if he was going to do so of his own free will. In a face-saving operation, doubts were settled and contracts were signed, but the film was never made. Lewenstein subsequently paid Hancock the compliment, 'Olivier had to *play* the part, but Hancock was Bérenger to the life – an aggressive man but nonetheless more human than any of the others. Hancock would have been the right survivor for the human race.' In Mackendrick he certainly had the right director of distinction and sensitivity. With Ealing comedies like *Whiskey Galore* and *The Ladykillers* behind him, he had exactly the kind of talent that could have turned around *The Rebel* and *The Punch and Judy Man*. Maybe Tony feared the competition on screen from Mostel – potentially a scene-stealer of Kenneth Williams magnitude; maybe his judgement was affected by the occasional drying-out sessions that saw him disappearing into nursing homes with increased regularity; maybe he was scared of his identification through alcohol with the character. At one point Bérenger says in the play, 'I'm conscious of my body all the time, as if it were made of lead ... I can't seem to get used to myself. I don't even know if I *am* me. Then as soon as I take a drink, the lead slips away and I recognise myself. I become me again.' Roger remains convinced that the cause was deep-rooted psychologically. As he attempted to explain the tight corner they were in with Woodfall, Tony was unrelenting. 'Well, I don't remember anything. I don't remember anything about it at all.' In fact, in recent months he had seldom given an interview without bragging about the part! And besides, he had already incongruously mooted to Roger the possibility of suing the producers for moneys owed to them under their option on Tony's services. At this stage Roger became certain that his brother's brain was going: 'Sandy was a very, very successful director ... it was like rejecting us both ... "You're out of your minds. You don't know what you're talking about," Tony went on ... we'd had enough.' Somewhere in his head was a place where the information had become detached from reality.

In the spring of 1964 the brothers parted company. The surviving sibling adds, 'It was a sad end to what had been a pretty good relationship up until the ATV experience. And I'm glad I did it because I really learned so much from him in different ways – how to deal with people and how not to deal with them. I don't think I ever saw him again.' Any contact appears to have been restricted to 'a few tempestuous phone calls', but by now his behaviour had teetered over the brink. Roger had seen the assumed brain damage reveal itself in strange ways: 'He'd check himself into a clinic and take himself out after a couple of days. He'd come and see us and then go off to Paris for two days. Then he'd come back to us and say, "I need an overcoat. Can you go to Simpsons in Piccadilly and get me an overcoat?" I'd get him the overcoat and he'd be off back to Paris.' If it had not been for real, it might have been scripted by Ionesco. In time the circumstances became more desperate. 'Once when he had a flat just off Bond Street,' recalls Roger, 'it took me about an hour to persuade him to get up off the floor, put on a coat and come with me to the drying-out clinic in Surrey. Fortunately my doctor was meeting us and we got him there together. At times like that, when he did sober up, he wouldn't remember anything or wouldn't want to remember.' Just before the split he did undergo voluntary treatment within the psychiatric unit of the Charing Cross Hospital. He did not stay long. Roger remembers a call from the psychiatrist saying, 'You've no idea what he's like. He's chained himself to the railings at Primrose Hill.' The only solution Roger could volunteer was work, preferably on the road, but opportunities for that were fast drying up. And the less he worked, the more time he worried and the worse he became. It was nothing for the Hancocks to receive calls in the middle of the night demanding room service: they were not meant as a joke. Seven weeks after Hancock's death, their mother wrote to Eddie Joffe, his Australian producer, 'Thank God I have Roger, although it is a great grief to me to know that these two brothers were not friends.' Roger went on to concentrate on his highly successful theatrical and literary agency, handling the affairs of clients as varied as Bruce Forsyth, Barry Cryer and important writers like Sid Green and Dick Hills, Terry Nation, David Renwick and John Sullivan. Hancock followed his instinct and invited himself into the illustrious comedy line-up of Norman Wisdom, Morecambe and Wise, and Harry Worth under the care of Billy Marsh within the Bernard Delfont office.

Marsh was a tolerant, kind man, whose word was always his bond and whose editorial instinct for his performers was invariably correct. He was also arguably the most respected individual in his profession on the variety side. In joining him Hancock was firmly setting the variety agenda for much of his future work: he would never again work in the situation comedy format in this country. The respect between the two men never deteriorated throughout the turmoil of Hancock's later years. Michael Grade, who learned much about the business as an apprentice at Billy's side in his uncle's agency, recalls, 'However low or incapacitated he was, Tony never let us down. If he agreed to an engagement, he would pitch up as arranged, whatever state he was in and, like a child, seek reassurance, asking plaintively, "I haven't let you down, have I, Billy?"' The transition was smooth, with Marsh characteristically refusing to take any commission on existing deals; after Hancock's death he similarly refused to take a share of outstanding residuals. Billy's influence behind the scenes of the top variety show, *Sunday Night at the London Palladium*, ensured for one night only Hancock's high-profile return to television as the top of the bill on 15 November 1964. Once again he had to endure the old tedious comments about the familiarity of much of his material, a criticism never levelled against the likes of Dickie Henderson, Tommy Cooper or Bruce Forsyth. All that survives of the appearance is an audio tape. The reception and the laughter speak for themselves, although it is said that Hancock's out-of-condition appearance worked against him in a way that history does not record, although he did have the sense to introduce the *Gaumont British Newsreel* with the words, 'and now, if I can still breathe …' The magician John Wade recalls working for Harry Secombe at the Grosvenor House in Park Lane that evening and never forgetting how a whole gaggle of comics, including Arthur Askey, Kenneth Horne, Michael Bentine, Sid James and Harry himself, paused at the bar to hoist their glasses to wish 'the lad' luck at the appropriate time. No one ever wished him less than well and for the first time in his life he topped the ratings.

The only other booking of significance that year was a cameo role in *Those Magnificent Men in Their Flying Machines*, one of those ill-advised attempts to prove that there are more stars on screen than in the heavens: in truth, the true stars proved to be the brilliantly diverse aerial contraptions of the second part of the title. An international success, the film, based on the London-to-Paris air race of 1910, brought Hancock's name before American cinemagoers, but few in Texas, Kansas or Ohio would have taken the time to register who he was amid more familiar faces like Sarah Miles, James Fox, Robert Morley, Terry-Thomas and their own Red Skelton. Cast as Harry Popperwell, a scatterbrained inventor, he almost never made the shoot. Just before filming began in July he sustained a Pott's fracture in his ankle: 'Named after Sir Percival Pott, 1765,' he relished telling people. 'Very painful.' The circumstances of the injury have remained a mystery, but his first wife always maintained he was drunk at the time. Hancock was expecting to withdraw, but the British director, Ken Annakin, was so anxious to have him as part of his comedy constellation that he wrote his plaster cast into the plot as well. Hancock's devoted fans had to wait for thirty minutes until he appeared in the first of his two short sequences, flapping his arms in an attempt to impart flight to his machine. When asked if it will fly, he is adamant: 'Of course it will fly. What do you think it'll do – lay an egg?' When it crashes, he becomes philosophical: 'Oh well, we all make mistakes.' Later he is discovered in another machine, ostensibly sitting the wrong way round. When an official played by Robert Morley questions this, he responds, 'Do you take me for an idiot? ... it's an idea I had in the bath when sitting with my back to the taps ... you see, the wind resistance on the tail is less than it would be on the wing ... I shall most likely be in Paris before any of this lot have even got to Calais.' He ends up *en route* to Scotland. Advance publicity claimed that a new scene had been written to explain Hancock's predicament. If so, it appears not to have made the final cut. His performance fails to display much enthusiasm, although the observation that it was enhanced by his discomfort is probably true. He was paid £1,000 a day for the task, with a guarantee of three days' work, but it must have irked that however diplomatically the producers juggled his name into a supposedly significant final title credit, he was billed lower than significant rivals on the domestic comedy front like Eric Sykes and Benny Hill.

1965 started ominously when Hancock's second stepfather died on 15 January. Hancock had always claimed he sensed an aura of death in the man's company. His mother had married Harry Sennett, a retired Chief Executive Officer within the Ministry of Pensions, on 7 September 1960, three days after her seventieth birthday and ten months after the suicide of her second husband. In spite of protestations from Cicely, Hancock had refused to attend the ceremony at Poole Register Office, sending a telegram and pleading as his excuse that he did not wish to involve her in possible publicity. Legend has it that he sent the couple a canteen of cutlery instead; it had always been a family joke that whenever anyone got married in their circle Lily was the first to oblige with the knives and forks. In 1963 the couple emigrated to Durban in South Africa, where Sennett fell seriously ill, necessitating their return after a couple of years. He was diagnosed at the London Clinic with haemochromatosis, a little-known disorder that produces excessive deposits of iron in the liver and pancreas. Towards the end of his illness his mother and her spiritualist medium, Bill, persuaded her son to participate in the laying-on of hands. On visits to Bournemouth Tony was urged to place his palms on his stepfather's chest. Freddie later said, 'His mother's blind faith in Tony was rather moving in a way. She wanted to believe that he had this gift of healing.' Hancock was not averse to the suggestion that he might have some kind of healing power – he often attempted to cure Freddie's migraines by touching her forehead – but came away from Bournemouth dejected and exhausted. He made no attempt to attend the funeral. Within days of the death he was in New York attempting to interest television companies in his old recordings, before moving on to Los Angeles to audition for an unlikely patron, Walt Disney. The trip, arranged at the last minute, also conveniently spared him the mortification of having to visit Freddie, who was undergoing surgery in hospital.

There appears to have been nothing of significance in his professional calendar between then and the day in April when he received the call to tell him that Disney had offered him the role of a barnstorming actor-manager braving the perils of the Californian Gold Rush in *The Adventures of Bullwhip Griffin*, a film version of Sid Fleischman's children's novel, *By the Great Horn Spoon!* Although Hancock claimed he accepted the role without reading the script, on paper the part seemed custom-built, with touches of his old self and W.C. Fields intertwined, the kind Robert Newton would have walked through in his sleep a dozen years earlier. The industry is notorious for the short notice it can give performers, and Hancock, about to enter a health farm at Bexhill for a week, had no more than four days to pack his bags for Hollywood to take third billing in the picture alongside Roddy McDowall and Suzanne Pleshette. The promise of greater things to come rather than actual prestige must have been the motivating factor. Alas, the lights-cameras-action urgency of the telephone call was not matched by the reception that greeted him. He would not be the only British entertainer to discover the hollow lethargic reality of Los Angeles. A lonely Hancock was a vulnerable one, a nervous one even more so. Whatever his state of mind, he must have realised that there was no way the Americans were not going to try to make him funny on *their* terms, whatever that might entail. Stranded on permanent stand-by within the cosseted isolation of the Beverly Wilshire Hotel, Hancock would sit at the pool in his jacket and tie beneath a parasol struggling to learn his lines – there would be no artificial aids to memory this time – as sexy, sun-tanned bodies jostled around him. He found distraction in champagne – 'less fattening than vodka' – and the cursory charms of the British wife of a distinguished Canadian film actor staying at the same hotel, although it has never been established that their relationship was other than platonic; her marriage was dissolved two years later.

Every day Hancock would telephone Freddie Ross. Gradually she detected the strains of alcohol in his delivery. When she was connected to the actor's room in an attempt to talk to Hancock, she was told in no uncertain terms, 'It's common knowledge. He seems to be in love with my wife. Now, I have a job to do, so please get off the line.' He too had lines to learn. The wife later admitted that she felt sorry for Tony: 'He was totally lost and he was the sort of man you can't help caring about.' It is a refrain we shall hear again. Admitting that he did become intense about her, she added, 'But then, I think he would have got intense about the flowers in the foyer if they had waved at him.' There had been a 'couple of drunken scenes'. With a week to go before shooting began, Freddie flew out to join Hancock in Los Angeles. He met her at the airport half an hour late looking, in David Nathan's words, 'unshaven, red-eyed and crumpled'. Freddie instilled some order and domesticity into his life and valiantly helped him keep away from the booze. Her care did nothing to prevent the events of 27 May, when in the early afternoon Hancock collapsed on the set, most probably from heat prostration. The temperature had shot up some twenty-five degrees during the lunch period, not the ideal conditions in which to be wrapped up in the heavy coat and cape of an old-time thespian under the searing studio lights. At Freddie's insistence, he was admitted to hospital where he underwent two days of tests including painful lumbar punctures. It was proved that he had remained sober over the shooting period and his health was given the all clear. The insurance that Disney, with some possible difficulty, had taken out on him at the outset of the project could stay in place. However, before the report came through his role had been recast.

It is impossible to imagine a more demoralising letdown to his aspirations. Hancock's hopes of ever becoming an international star appear to have crumpled from that moment. In his brother's opinion, they simply threw him out at the first excuse. Subsequent comments made by the British-born star, Roddy McDowall, who senses Hancock was a man 'weighted by some obscure responsibility', substantiate the theory, together with the discovery that Hancock's replacement, Harry Guardino, had been lined up for the role within a week of Tony's arrival in Hollywood. According to another cast member, Hermione Baddeley, 'As soon as they realised what state he was in, the rumours started to fly … Disney was quite openly waiting for Tony to make a mistake. The only person who didn't know was Tony.' He had committed the unpardonable sin of allowing his insecurity to show within the brash nirvana of Tinseltown, a place where everyone is insecure, but has no wish to be reminded of the fact. Reports surfaced that he had been argumentative on the set, questioning the quality of his lines and defeated by the comic Shakespearian dialogue. Moreover, whatever rumours were circulating about his private life in the hotel before Freddie joined him from England, the Disney studio with its family image was the *one* studio in Hollywood that had to keep the merest sniff of scandal at bay. The film was later released to considerable acclaim as a family movie, the *Motion Picture Herald* noting that each character served to create 'a make-believe atmosphere in the fine tradition of Disney pictures', a state of play that must have made things even more soul-destroying for Hancock.

In June 1965 Hancock provided the British press with his own brave-face version of events: 'I just went spark out. I think it was the result of the pressures of three years of trouble and frustration. But half an hour later I was perfectly all right. I was thoroughly examined by a doctor who said, "There is nothing wrong with you" ... the amazing thing is that when I came round after blacking out I felt a different person. Everything seemed to have dropped from me.' He may have been sober at the time, but a line from W.C. Fields seems apt in the circumstances: 'We are sitting at the crossroads between art and nature, trying to figure out where delirium tremens leaves off and Hollywood begins.' Tony and Freddie fled to New York, while the money men thrashed out some form of settlement for wrongful dismissal. But all Hancock wanted was to escape to Paris. He checked out of the hotel without Ross, leaving her ticket at reception. She caught up with him at the airport. The dialogue that ensued was made for Punch and Judy: 'Haven't you forgotten something?' 'What?' 'Me, for instance.' From Paris they moved on to Cannes, where with amazing serendipity they bumped into Bernard Delfont, who was puzzled his client was not in Los Angeles fulfilling the contract his colleague Billy Marsh had negotiated for him. Perhaps understanding his brother's idea of what constituted the best therapy for himself, Hancock suggested to Delfont that he was now ready to play the Talk of the Town. There was nothing else in his date book. On 28 June, one month and a day after collapsing in Hollywood, Hancock opened at the theatre restaurant for a short season in the star cabaret spot that followed the resident revue, *Fatal Fascination*. It was never easy for Delfont and Marsh to book such venues. As his brother says, 'If you have to choose between the Bachelors – a popular close harmony act of the day outside of the pop mainstream – and Tony Hancock, you're going to go with Tony Hancock.' The business was only adequate, the comedian achieving on average about £500 a week while he was there, half the potential for the room.

For six weeks Hancock delivered his act 'as known'. The comedy writer Brad Ashton popped in on the opening night. The following morning he intercepted a phone call from the star to someone in the

ALS office and told him he'd been in the night before. 'I didn't hear any laughs,' complained Hancock. 'I died the death, didn't I?' Brad disagreed. He had been with two American guests, who found him very funny indeed. 'Why didn't you come round? You've cheered me up,' said Hancock. He was able to be more objective about the experience when he was interviewed by the magazine *London Life* in September the following year: 'The Talk of the Town – that's an ideal audience. It's fast, tough and close to you. It's likely to heckle, and that's good ... it's participation. It's a return to music hall, isn't it? It used to be cloth caps and cheese sandwiches. Now it's smoked salmon and charcoal grey suits. One wants to get away from the artificial barrier between the player and the audience.' Two years before, when his nerve went and Joan Turner replaced him at the venue, he had dropped in to pay his respects one evening. As they left in the early hours Hancock suddenly excused himself. Turner saw him grope his way onto the stage in semi-darkness where he began to flex his feet on the floor beneath him. 'I am just getting the feel of the stage, because I *shall* come here,' he explained. He carried on, talking to himself, 'Yes, I think I could do it.' Later in the year on *Late Night Line-up* he was telling Michael Dean that he found it much more satisfying than playing a variety theatre. Being able to see the eyes of the audience had something to do with it. Sadly it was too late to be of any avail.

One night during the run Dennis Main Wilson was working late on a camera script in his office at Television Centre when he received a phone call from an old acquaintance, the stage door keeper at the Talk of the Town: 'The boy's on, sir ... and he's making an arse of himself ... can you come down?' Hancock had been drinking heavily and was in an agitated condition. The management considered calling a doctor, until someone suggested the idea of contacting Main Wilson. Dennis shot along to the theatre: 'He was just coming off and I didn't barge in. I said, "Just let him know I'm here."' He waited and waited and then two uniformed attendants from the front of house came down and had him ejected. 'He wouldn't see me,' said Main Wilson. 'My wife and I tried to figure that one out for ages. We loved him and we think that he didn't want me to see him in the state he was.' The last time he had spoken to the comedian he had picked up the phone to hear inconsolable grief: 'Do you know Mario's died?' He was referring to Fabrizi. There would be one further occasion. 'I know seven different ways of playing Lear,' said the distant drunken voice, before the phone hung up.

It was during the Talk of the Town season that the possibility of working with Sid James raised its head again. An American producer had sent Sid a film script written for the two of them. It must have had potential if the actor was prepared to subject himself to the prospect of further humiliation by the comedian. When Sid and his wife Valerie had paid a visit to the Hancocks on holiday in Antibes in the summer of 1962, Tony had been briefly enthusiastic about the idea of a reunion. Valerie recalls, 'We came away very happy. Tony, for all he had said in the past, was equally keen on them starting again.' Two weeks later her husband received a curt note from Hancock, in which he revoked the thought of reviving the partnership, adding 'and that is my final word on the subject'. Now three years later, in Hancock's dressing room, they talked positively about the new project until dawn. 'I saw him away through the empty West End streets with a promise he'd join me that afternoon and we'd go and talk turkey with the producer,' recalled Sid. 'I felt that blasted early Sunday morning was like a new birth.' The meeting went ahead. The following day came a letter to say he'd had second thoughts and that it would be a backward step to work with Sid again. 'It was unbelievable,' commented James. 'He just didn't want to know when the real chance for us to get back together came up.' They *would* work together one more time, when later in the year Alan Freeman reconvened the old team to record two vintage episodes of the television series – *The Reunion Party* and *The Missing Page* – to issue as a long-playing record. Graham Stark was co-opted to the cast of the former and recalls how unkempt he looked: 'It was all very embarrassing and *he* found it embarrassing. He couldn't do it. He couldn't time!' If proof were needed, Galton and Simpson recollect both half-hour episodes overrunning by about ten minutes. The writers went along to the editing suite to help Freeman salvage the project, eliminating fluffs, shaving away dead time, and rectifying disproportionate audience laughter that had been prompted by Hancock's looks and not the lines themselves. Freeman later admitted that much of the problem had been down to the star's drinking, but confessed, 'I couldn't stop him or we would have lost everything.' The exercise marked the last straw for Sid. Totally disenchanted with his old friend's lack of professionalism, James vowed never to work with him again.

The recording session was a commercial decision brought about by the announcement by the BBC that from October 1965 it was going to repeat twenty-six classic episodes of the television show, in effect the final two series of *Hancock's Half Hour* and the very last series without Sid James. The decision was financially attractive for Hancock, even if the continual exposure of that part of his career which he was attempting to consign to history did play on his neuroses. Although they were scheduled against the Wednesday edition of *Coronation Street*, the repeats achieved a remarkable average audience of around 9 million viewers. Suddenly it was Hancock season again, helped by his cult inclusion in Jack Jackson's Saturday lunchtime radio show, *Record Roundabout*. Like Kenny Everett at a later time, Jackson was more than a disc jockey, possessed of a shrewd comic touch for editing music and comedy tracks in an original way to create an entertainment that made for compulsive listening. The gradual accumulation of Hancock radio and television programmes on record down the years had provided the former bandleader with an archive of 'Hancockisms' that enabled the comedian, to his great delight, to have what seemed to be an unofficial starring role in the show. In January 1963 the *Radio Times* wrote, 'If *Record Roundabout* has a hero – other than its creator – it is the intrepid Tony Hancock, the Don Quixote of East Cheam ... he has to do battle with such formidable windmills as Steptoe and Son, Shelley Berman, Robb Wilton, Bob Newhart, the Goons, the Rag Traders, etc ... and, of course, Jack himself. Even extraneous pianos seem to gang up on Hancock, but the lad's curt reply of "Oh, shut up!" proves to be effective against all adversaries.' To add to all this exposure, there were for the first time Hancock's appearances *between* the programmes on the other channel, advising the nation of the advantages of eating eggs.

The potential financial gains of the advertising industry to a high-profile public face had been brought home to Hancock by an earlier contract negotiated for him by his brother. This provided his services for a press campaign in which he was cast as the voice of public concern in an attempt to sugar-coat the bitterness left by the ruthless cuts made in the cause of supposed efficiency by Dr Beeching, the Chairman of the Railways Board. Hancock appeared in a series of eight advertisements, which were subsequently issued in booklet form as *The Truth about the Railways – The Hancock Report*. His grumblings ranged over the usual cause of complaint – late trains, dirty carriages, weather-exposed stations. Here he pronounces on cuts to the service:

> That Beeching! Look what he's done now – removed my favourite train from the service. 29 after midnight, and very cosy too – the 'fall abouts' special, we used to call it – only one passenger per carriage, so you could really put your feet up and make yourself at home. 'You can cut what trains you like, but you can't cut *mine*,' I said to Beeching. 'I've heard that before, matey,' he says, 'but we ain't running a private chauffeur service, not even to please *you*.' I'll sort him out good and proper, one of these days, see if I don't.

Following each grouse came the British Rail point of view, in this case the official spin on the inefficiency of empty trains and the waste of manpower. To have been a total Hancock triumph it needed him to respond to official comments like 'The few people affected may have to use other forms of transport or travel earlier,' but that would have somewhat defeated the purpose. The project proved that pastiche Galton and Simpson could be effective, although the copywriter, David Gillies, went uncredited. Ray and Alan were asked to comment and with tongue in cheek declared, 'We have hereby been done out of a job.' Hancock received £10,000 for the week-long shoot with photographer Terence Donovan that took place the week after he completed the ATV series in February 1963. It remains a point of pride for Roger Hancock that not only did the deal take only five seconds to conclude, but that he was able to secure a fee commensurate with half of Beeching's annual salary. There were complaints from snooty officials at public enquiries that Hancock's presence undermined the whole seriousness of the issue, but his fans were smiling, as they had done several years earlier when their hero had allowed his image to be attached to advertisements for Grundig tape recorders – a tool of his trade – and 'Telesurance': 'Tony Hancock says, "Has *your* tube gone again?"' It would only be a matter of time before he appeared in a television commercial.

The opportunity came in August 1965 when he made a series of commercials for the Egg Marketing Board for screening the following spring. At the time they presented the brightest glimmer of this later period that he might still be able to bounce back to his old form. It was easy to forget, however, that the television commercial with its short duration was the one visual medium where his short attention span did not matter. The BBC Hancock had always made out that he was against the genre. 'Fancy him doing adverts,' he sneered of a rival in the radio show *The Impersonator*. 'I wouldn't go on an advert. It takes away all your dignity.' Away from the microphone, he later explained his real-life quandary, unable to endorse a product he didn't believe in: 'I wouldn't have done it for corsets, or for that toothpaste that gives you the ring of confidence, or a smelly mouth, or whatever it is. But eggs, they're different. Nourishing. Wholesome. Don't melt in your hands. So I took the plunge.' He also had to concede that the money made a difference, allowing him the 'independence which allows me to do what I want'. Official figures are not to hand, but Roger Hancock estimates he received £6,000 for the first six and that he made a similar amount for another half dozen at a later date. With his long-established series for Schweppes tonic water, Benny Hill had already shown the way, declaring it was easier making money through advertising than by appearing on stage, which he detested. The egg campaign, in which the novelist Fay Weldon played an important creative role, revolved around the slogan, 'Happiness is egg-shaped,' about to replace 'Go to work on an egg' as the rallying call to a high-protein diet. As an advertising copywriter she also coined the slogan 'Vodka gets you drunker quicker'. She once explained, 'It just seemed ... to be obvious that people who wanted to get drunk fast needed to know this.' It was never used, but its appropriateness to Hancock's troubles has a ring of black humour that he might have appreciated.

Weldon's memory of Hancock is that he hated making the commercials: 'He felt it was a great come-down, he didn't want to do them and did them as a kind of mockery. I sat in the studio listening to him moaning and complaining, so we just wrote what he wanted.' From the beginning he even refused to say the slogan itself. The director, Kenneth Carter, who had directed Hancock in his very first television series for Associated-Rediffusion in 1956, explained the consequences that could involve Hancock in litigation if he did not proceed. With the comedian digging his heels in even further, Carter asked if he would be happy for someone else to say the words for him to react to them. Hancock's attitude changed immediately, especially when the director suggested Patricia Hayes in her old Mrs Crevatte character. Hayes, who found herself on camera with less than a day's notice, later admitted, 'His instinct was right, because it was much funnier for me to lean into the camera and say, "Happiness is egg-shaped," and for him to say, "Get a bit of glamour in, they said. Dear, oh dear, oh dear!"' When she repeats the line, Hancock adds, 'Oh, shut up! Let me get on with me breakfast. And where are me soldiers? You know I can't eat – oh!' He sees them on the plate and tucks straight in, transported back to idyllic boyhood starts to the day. The idea to incorporate the fingers of toast was his. Hayes joined him in most of the short sketches. The basic scripts for the commercials, if not the slogan, were the work of experienced comedy writer Dave Freeman, for many years writing partner to Benny Hill. Galton and Simpson, who were not involved, must have been reminded of an earlier exchange at Railway Cuttings. 'What a misery that woman is,' moaned Tony. 'She's positively Bolshevik at times.' 'So what,' protests Sid. 'She does a marvellous egg.'

As Hancock involved himself with the advertising campaign, Ray and Alan were busy with a new stage project, collaborating with Leslie Bricusse – co-composer of one of his favourite songs, 'What Kind of Fool Am I?' – on a musical adaptation of the play *Noah* by the French dramatist André Obey. In this the title character is portrayed as a contemporary farmer who hears voices urging him to build a boat and becomes an irascible partner in God's plan to save the earth. The part had been played on stage in London by John Gielgud in 1935. The writers were not adapting it with Hancock in mind – more possibly for Harry Secombe, who had enjoyed a major success with the musical *Pickwick* – but as soon as Bricusse saw their script he remarked, 'Well, you realise what you've done? This is perfect Hancock.' The producers of the ill-fated *Rhinoceros* had already perceived him as the ideal last survivor of the human race. That view was endorsed again in this new context by the producer, Bernard Delfont, who ran the agency that looked after the performer. The writers had little option but to allow Hancock to read their words, not expecting him to be as enthusiastic as he was. He joked that chatting to God would be a cut above Sid James: 'Can you imagine that face looking at you from a stained-glass window?'

You've chosen me? To build a what? You're joking. I can't even build a five bar gate. Well, if you help, yes ... there's nowhere to launch it, of course. You haven't thought of that, have you? My pond's not big enough. Rain? What rain? It hasn't rained round her for four months, you ought to know that. They've been praying every day. You haven't taken the slightest bit of notice of them. The vicar's lost a lot of face. How much rain were you thinking of? It's going to take a lot of water to float one of them. That much? Oh. A deluge. I see. What, just round here? All *over!* Do what? Not everybody. All except me and the family. Don't you think that's being a bit vindictive? No, no. I'm not trying to tell you your job.

The nearest he'd been to a flood on stage before had been in his old lighthouse sketch with Jimmy Edwards. From that experience Galton and Simpson knew of his aversion to long runs. They also knew that with its elaborate special effects the production for this show was budgeted at £100,000 and would need to run for at least twelve months to recoup its costs. These factors did not even take into account the complications of the star's alcohol addiction and learning difficulties. As far as the comedian was concerned, the practicalities were disregarded and the project assumed a spurious reality in his mind, another prospect to cling to in interviews when talk of repeats and commercials carried little interest. Hancock went on about having singing lessons – 'I'm not particularly melodious, but I've got a sense of pitch, which helps' – but the on-stage flood shimmered into a mirage. In the accustomed manner, the more he talked about it, the less likely it was to happen. A lunch for Ray and Alan with Tony was arranged at a restaurant in Kensington Church Street on 20 August 1965, to incorporate a photo-call with the *Daily Express* to publicise the project. Tony did not arrive until three o'clock. 'Been a long time,' he said to the writers, adding with a touch of sarcasm, 'Had anything good on telly lately?' In truth, the comedian was paralytic, as were the two companions he brought in tow, his actor buddy Wilfrid Lawson and *Noah* set designer Sean Kenny. Eventually the producer lost confidence and the rights to the play lapsed, although Tony clung to the idea until the end of his life.

Hancock was late for the lunch because he had been discussing another dream project with his drinking accomplices. In view of Galton and Simpson's justifiable reservations over his casting as Noah, the thought of him in a major Shakespearean role seems plainly laughable. He always stressed he had no wish to play Hamlet, but there were other options. Had they both been at a more reliable stage of their careers, the idea of Wilfrid Lawson as Lear and Hancock as the Fool could have made history; the secondary proposal – surely alcoholically induced – that they might switch roles on alternate nights is asinine. Hancock expanded on the concept to Barry Took, by which time Richard Burton's name had been added to the equation on a 'perm-any-two-from-three' basis, whereby Lawson would play the Fool to Burton's king, then Hancock the fool to Lawson's monarch, and so on and so on ... At another time Nicol Williamson's name was invoked in the context. The project was building into a drinkers' convention, from which Trevor Howard could not have been far distant. No right-minded angel was going to back such a venture. When the concept is mentioned to Roger Hancock today, he blames John Freeman and gives a resigned chuckle. However, theatre director Peter Hall, who *could* see him as Dogberry in *Much Ado About Nothing*, has pointed out that – Hancock's *folie de grandeur* aside – it is unlikely that he fully understood the part of the Fool: 'I don't think he'd enjoy playing the fool in *Lear* because it designably has a fool who is unfunny, and the convention is to see if a fool that finds nothing amusing will amuse us.' One has to look to Hancock's own words and the perspective provided them by his own tragedy to see the vulnerability that a skilled director like Hall may have instilled into his performance as the monarch: 'I want to stand there as I am. No props. No pretence. No defence. And say, "There it is – here I am."' Hancock was simply talking about the business of being a comedian, but the image of Lear exposed on the blasted heath was not far away.

He would work with Lawson – fleetingly – one last time, on a film adaptation of *The Wrong Box*, the novel by Robert Louis Stevenson and Lloyd Osbourne, a macabre comedy of presumed deaths, switched corpses and juggled coffins centred around a tontine, a sinister form of lottery in which twenty parents each contribute £1,000 into a kitty for their children, the last survivor to draw the cash. The director, Bryan Forbes, marshalled Ralph Richardson, John Mills, Michael Caine, Cicely Courtneidge, Peter Sellers, Irene Handl, Peter Cook and Dudley Moore – in their first substantial film roles – and his wife Nanette Newman to the cause. Hancock, who shared equal cameo billing with Sellers, appears in the last twenty minutes of the picture as a Victorian detective investigating a body stuffed in a barrel, who finds himself unravelling the considerable complications of the plot after an obligatory chase involving one corpse, three hearses, all the key characters and the tontine banknotes. In his autobiography, *Notes for a Life*, Forbes states that Hancock told him, 'You're the only director who ever told me I wasn't being funny. Most of them were afraid, they always felt I knew best and, you see, I never knew. I've always wanted to be told, and now I've left it too late.' If he was being rational, one presumes he was talking about his work for the cinema. Whatever Forbes said to him on set, it was not an effective performance. He plods around with a forced expression that suggests he may be about to lay an ostrich egg. He later admitted to Damaris Hayman that he was miscast. Certainly the fast-cutting slapstick style gave him little scope for extended facial reaction. Had he been serious about applying the philosophy of 'no props – no pretence – no defence' on camera he would have done well to study Richardson's performance, but it was Hancock's last appearance for the cinema and the time had gone. The film ends with him falling ignominiously into an open grave. Shot in the late summer of 1965, it would not be released until May of the following year. The *Monthly Film Bulletin* recorded the lost opportunity: 'Tony Hancock arouses expectations as a detective snooping in the background, but appears and disappears literally without being given anything to do.'

Repeats aside, 1965 saw Hancock score his greatest impact with the general public with a stray appearance on Eamonn Andrews' Sunday night talk show in October. He chatted about *Noah* and how, when he looked up to the heavens and asked God, 'But where am I going to get the wood?' timber would cascade down from the flies, oblivious of the fact that the idea had been worked in an entirely different context by Jimmy Jewel and Ben Warriss in their traditional double act for many years. Sean Kenny had worked things out so that the wood would miss Hancock, although the comedian was worried that Kenny might 'get him with the water'. He also delivered his observations on *Come Dancing*, his favourite programme, sending up 'the boys in their white gloves' – 'he's a sheet-metal worker, you know' – from 'the Ada Unsworth Formation Dancing Team from Slough' in a highly original version of the military two-step. Subsequently he was invited to become a member. Unsworth announced to the press, 'He's welcome to the weekly sessions at the Community Centre, but if he does go along he'll have to be one of the boys and wear the white gloves.' The consensus was that Hancock was back on form. He would have loved the review that said he had rescued a show that until he came on 'had been as soggy as a damp dish cloth' and went on to suggest that in the context of his recent below-par appearances perhaps 'all he needs is his scope to be himself'. Talents as diverse as Peter Ustinov, Billy Connolly and even Kenneth Williams have over the years shown that the chat show chair is a perfect platform for their individual skills, but it is unlikely that he could have matched them for true improvisational genius, however much he aspired to. When he met John Osborne in the early days of the *Rhinoceros* project, the playwright was left with the feeling that the comedian resented writers: 'The mere act of writing implied to him an assault on any spontaneity.' They spent much of the time swapping limericks together.

Buoyed along by his reception on the talk show, Hancock was now of the opinion that the days of the half-hour comedy were numbered: 'It's the Andy Williams and the Eamonn Andrews kind of show that is going to pinch the peak places on the telly. Bags of gags, bags of guests. You know what I mean.' He might have added, 'There it is – here I am!' and within a few months ABC Television, the company responsible for the Andrews show, had obliged. It might not have done so had they observed his erratic cabaret performances the following month at the Chevron Hilton in Sydney. One night Ed Doolan was in the audience. 'I begged him to be brilliant and he wasn't,' explains the broadcaster. 'I came away so disappointed, it was as if the man had personally let me down.' Hancock began 1966 with a short and dispiriting variety tour of Scottish theatres, an unusual affair where he shared top of the bill with Billy Cotton and his Band. They opened in Dundee on St Valentine's Day, and snow fell all week. 'Cold!' explained Hancock. 'We had to run from the dressing room to the stage to get some heat from the footlights.' At one point Hancock threatened to withdraw from the tour, but Billy Marsh politely but firmly explained that if he did so he would be abandoning his career. At least he was back on a stage, the focus for the proposed television project. When it occurred, it would be played out in the full glare of headline scrutiny, with all the gory fascination of a blood-spattered attraction on the other side of the motorway reservation. Since Hancock moved in with Freddie Ross in 1963, his domestic life had been on a collision course with his professional one. The crash was bound to be catastrophic. It is hard not to surmise that their relationship was doomed from the start.

Freddie Ross, in accord with Lyn Took, has always insisted that Hancock was not a violent man, not even a 'fighting drunk', but that the cruelty and abuse she incurred at his hands was always the result of her acting as a self-imposed barrier between him and his drinking. 'Sober, Tony wouldn't have hurt a fly, but he was a very strong person, very determined,' she explained to the *Independent on Sunday* in September 1991. 'That is a very different thing from being systematically beaten up.' Whatever, she suffered knockout blows, a broken nose, a pierced eardrum, an attempt at strangulation, and bruises galore for her troubles: the latter forced her to favour long-sleeve fashions for much of their time together. Inevitably her professional life incurred additional strain: 'Most of the stress came from trying to keep it out of the papers and protecting his fantastic talent and career.' She had always believed in him, a credo consummated when on his birthday in Hollywood in 1965 she presented him with cufflinks engraved with the words, 'If I had a talent like yours' on one, 'I'd be proud, not worried' on the other, the first words she had ever addressed to him. Her brother Leonard Ross, a solicitor by profession, became caught up in the ambivalence Tony created in people. He told David Nathan, 'Overall, the balance of his character was in his favour. When he was sober there was no one like him. He was generous and kind ... I know he treated Freddie very badly, but I felt this was an enormous clash of temperament rather than cruelty on his side or misunderstanding on hers. Over the years she had succeeded in bringing him round from time to time and I think she felt she could do more for him by living with him. I always doubted whether this would be the case.'

It did not help that in her attempts to steer Tony to sobriety she resorted to drastic measures of her own. She made at least five attempts on her life without understanding that in the distorted mind of the alcoholic such extreme gestures are unlikely to receive a rational response and may spur the drinker on to greater excesses as he distances himself from the hateful reality of the threat. Matters were not helped by an early incident when Freddie took an extended overdose of laxative tablets, under the mistaken impression they were pills of a more lethal kind. The next day Hancock felt fine, while she was confined to the bathroom. They laughed at the time, but it further undermined the extent to which he would take her subsequent actions seriously. As her business colleague Sally Mordant said, 'Freddie could not do anything less than the big gesture. Everything was for an Oscar.' Her own words underline this assessment: 'I thought in my twisted mind I could bring him to his senses ... I thought my death, which wouldn't harm a lot of people, would make him realise what a wonderful talent he had and was wasting.' In December 1964 Hancock gashed open his head on the edge of a glass and wrought-iron dressing table during one drunken fall and was admitted again to the Holloway Sanatorium in Virginia Water on a course of alcohol aversion therapy. Freddie booked into a hotel to be near him and proceeded to the clinic. She discovered a quivering, gibbering wreck anxious to hold her hand and stroke her hair: 'He was just like a baby. That's why you never had the hardness to turn your back on him.' She would not be the last member of her sex to be affected by him in this way. The impending divorce from Cicely, which cited his adultery with Freddie Ross, was announced on 6 July 1965, during the Talk of the Town season. The judge exercised his discretion in respect of Cicely's own adultery with an unknown party, stating that the lapse had been short-lived and that it should not stand in the way of the divorce, before adding, 'She admitted it to her husband and he forgave her.' It has been suggested that 6 July was the date Dennis Main Wilson received the sudden telephone call to go to Hancock's aid, but there appears to be no corroboration for this.

There was a frustrated attempt by the new couple to get married in Honolulu in November on the return from Hancock's Sydney cabaret trip, during which Cicely's divorce became absolute. Their intentions fell foul of legislation that required blood tests and descended into amazingly familiar comic territory after Hancock's patience gave out after twenty minutes in the queue: 'I came here in good faith to give 'em a spoonful of the best British blood. If they don't want it – the best of luck. I'm going!' Freddie followed. They married almost as soon as they returned to London on 2 December 1965 at

Marylebone Register Office, a ceremony that Leonard Ross regarded as a mere formality, since they had already packed into their time together enough incident for one marriage. When Hancock tried to pay the registration fee with a pound note, the staff had no change and Freddie reached into her handbag to oblige: he owed her the money until the day he died. She ensured that the event was covered by the press and news cameras. Freddie's car was delayed. As Hancock waited for his bride, he quipped, 'Well after all, it's the sort of thing that only happens eight or nine times in your life – I think she must be here.' Pictures were issued of them staring jokily into each other's eyes. Hancock had insisted on vetting her costume the day before, but had not seen the fur hat she wore for the occasion. He dismissed it with the comment, 'You look like a Grenadier Guard.'

The role Freddie saw for herself as her husband's saviour was not helped by being the new Mrs Hancock. 'Our marriage broke up our friendship,' she has said. To her brother, it could be said to have broken up their 'marriage'. In 1996 she confessed that it got off to a terrible start: 'In the rush to get married, I forgot to have my passport changed from Ross to Hancock. He thought I'd deliberately "forgotten" because I didn't like the name and so he didn't talk to me the whole way over to Ireland, where we were having our honeymoon.' Months later she discovered that the orange juice that sustained him at Dublin's Gresham Hotel had been heavily laced with vodka. The 'untouched' vodka bottle in the mini-bar became a source of pride with her husband: Freddie had no idea he was replenishing it with water after each sneaky swig. They returned to live in a furnished flat overlooking the Edgware Road. Within ten days there was a flaming row and Hancock went to find solace with Cicely at MacConkeys. According to Cicely's sister, Doreen, on the very day he married Freddie he had called his first wife and asked her to take him back.

Hancock had recently cultivated a friendship with the writer Len Costa, who was summoned to the house with the call, 'We are going to write.' The men shared a twin-bedded room and, according to Costa, 'Tony and Cicely were friendly – nothing more.' The next day the divorced couple began to jostle in a half-joking sort of way. Presumably fuelled by alcohol, the skirmish got out of hand and Cicely again used her judo skills on Hancock, smashing a small side table in the process. When things escalated Cicely phoned the police: 'It all got too much.' It was eventually dismissed as a domestic tiff and Hancock was delivered back to Freddie in time for Christmas. The greatest gift he could bestow upon either her or himself was to accept the nature of his condition as a confirmed alcoholic. He voluntarily admitted himself into a Hampstead nursing home and his new wife spent her first New Year with her husband 'on the floor of a hospital holding him while he had terrible shakes from trying to dry out'. He was no stranger to drying-out clinics, but this was the closest he had come to facing up to the nature of his disease, although David Nathan wrote, 'He only stayed for two weeks. He would never admit that he was an alcoholic. He always thought that one little drink wouldn't do him any harm.' Of course, the most innocent sip is enough to poison the system all over again. The aversion therapy consisted of injection-induced vomiting after a choice of drink. Hancock built up such a strong resistance to the cure he was able to wash away the aftertaste with more drink. To all intents and purposes, he might have been washing away the taste of the ice cream in *The Punch and Judy Man*.

The marriage buffeted along, adrift on a sea of booze, but for Hancock the ocean was never deep enough. Being in denial only exacerbated the problem. Roger Wilmut has propounded the theory that in addition to his growing self-doubt, the car accident returning home from the recording of *The Bowmans* in 1961 may have had a significant bearing on his subsequent behaviour. Dr William Cleverly, Hancock's physician, confirmed that Hancock's alcohol intake increased considerably after the event. This may have been linked to the fact that irrespective of his line-learning challenge,

Hancock now had a greater opportunity to sit back and relax than at any time in his intensive radio and television career. Indeed the pressures of having constantly to deliver a standard to the BBC were behind him. On the other hand, although Hancock's injuries were not serious, he had been confronted with his own – and Cicely's – mortality. To paraphrase a line from *Days of Wine and Roses*, there comes a time in the life of every alcoholic when the bottle becomes God and Hancock was beholden. In the words of Jack Lemmon's character, anything worth having must be worth suffering for. The paradox of the situation has always been that while alcohol with its *'carpe diem'* message is symbolic of enjoying the present, it also represents the catalyst for misery and decline. Alas, he never found his way to Alcoholics Anonymous and his brother swears that he never had the willpower for that to have been an alternative, if he had. In the opinion of Joan Le Mesurier, this was never an option: 'Because he was such a shy man he could never have stood up in a crowd of strangers and said, "I am an alcoholic." Besides with his celebrity he would have been considered a pariah.' Freddie claims there *was* a period of four and a half months in their relationship when he kept off the booze, even though 'the strain was horrendous'. This must have been during the first half of 1966. However, in Cleverly's view, Hancock crossed the line of total dependency about two years after the road accident, namely somewhere between the ATV series and his Palladium season. His psychotic behaviour with its increased mood swings went a long way to explaining the inconsistency of so many things, from his unpredictability as a performer to anomalies like the *Rhinoceros* débâcle.

Freddie Hancock's last suicide bid defined the end of their marriage. They were now living at William Mews in Knightsbridge, and as he prepared to leave to record his show in Blackpool on 9 July 1966 Hancock grabbed a second bottle of champagne. Freddie, as she had done many times before, tried to stop him, only to be pushed aside. In retaliation she reached for a bottle of barbiturates. As she started to guzzle them, he bade her goodbye and went for his car. He had a show to do. Apparently, his parting words were, 'Take enough this time. Make a good job of it, because I shan't be calling an ambulance.' She was later discovered by the daily help amid the debris of overturned furniture and rushed to the Middlesex Hospital. She remained unconscious for three days. When she was discharged, she went to live at her parents' home. By Christmas she was working as a casting director on a new series for ITV. The star was Harry H. Corbett.

Hancock later confided to Damaris Hayman that he was convinced that all Freddie's suicide attempts were staged because of the regularity with which she seemed to be rescued in the nick of time: 'He said he got sick of getting calls of SOS and going to hospitals where she'd be pumped out.' A psychiatrist had once informed his wife that she was not the suicidal type. Hancock may have sensed the expert opinion, but that does not diminish the potential danger of the situation, with which the comedian was emotionally unable to cope. He also confessed to a close associate that he resented the way 'she tried to manipulate him where she wanted him'. Another recalls him 'spitting fire about her'. An antipathy of sorts had existed as far back as the writing of *The Punch and Judy Man*, when after a quarrel she threatened suicide and locked herself in the bathroom at the White House. Philip Oakes remembered there were razor blades inside. 'What if she used one to slash her wrists?' asked the writer. 'Let's hope she does a good job,' replied Hancock. In marriage, his feelings escalated into recriminations of disloyalty and infidelity. In fairness to Freddie, he may have misconstrued her genuine concern, but with time her attempts to rehabilitate him became as delusional as his own to achieve international recognition. Freddie herself has conceded, 'When you love, you can love too much sometimes ... I'm not the perfect person: I may have made some mistakes in trying to save Tony from drink.' When the doctor at the Holloway Sanatorium first announced that Tony was a chronic alcoholic, he told her, 'If you were my daughter I would turn you round, show you the door and beg you to keep walking.'

Hancock and Ross first met at Blackpool, so there was a bitter irony in the decision by ABC Television to feature the comedian as the star host of their prestige ITV Sunday evening variety series from the resort. The show marked a return to his variety roots, but the announcement that he was stepping into the compère's role was met with some scepticism. He was no Bruce Forsyth or Bob Monkhouse and theoretically the last man you would have picked for the task. An earlier television episode of *Hancock's Half Hour* – expanded to *Hancock's Forty-three Minutes* for Christmas transmission in 1957 – in which he essayed a similar role had not been judged a success. Eight and a half years later the gloriously irreverent concept of taking the sycophancy out of the hackneyed task of the master of ceremonies suggested a refreshingly new approach: 'Well, we've got a right lot of old rubbish here for you tonight.' It had been three years since he had been on the screen in a new show of his own, but on the strength of the egg commercials and his BBC repeats he had become more visible than he had been for a considerable time. There is no denying he still had the magic of a star, even if one writer wrote that he looked uncertain and that it was only by great effort of will that he seemed to stop himself from disintegrating. Hancock was particularly touched when at the end of the series Peter Black, an early champion of his radio days, compared him in the *Daily Mail* to the late Gilbert Harding as seeming 'to be living out a badgered and baffled section of his life in public ... the watchful distrust and sense of looming catastrophe are projected with great technical skills'. Hancock certainly cultivated a furtive air: only he could have guessed at the real catastrophe ahead, possibly relating to Harding's ignominious end, dead at fifty-three in a gutter outside Broadcasting House. George Fairweather was allowed a privileged glimpse into how he really felt when he made a visit to the series. Hancock insisted on taking him to see a 'friend' in the Blackpool

Tower zoo. It turned out to be a large long-haired sloth. 'He's the only one who knows exactly how I feel,' explained Tony, 'hanging on for grim death and trying not to fall off.' In a similar spirit at an earlier time he would take Philip Oakes on visits to see the solitary gorilla named Guy at the zoo in Regent's Park. Their encounters confirmed his own sense of being caged, even if the bars had been of his own making. One day the creature caught a sparrow in its massive hand and then released it without a feather being out of place. Tears ran down Hancock's cheeks as he said, 'It's too painful to watch. He shouldn't be alone like that.' They never returned.

For the new venture ABC provided him with two fresh young writers, John Muir and Eric Geen. Hancock joked that they sounded like a ventriloquial act, before describing them as 'English, fast and sardonic'. They had begun as a comedy double act and moved on to writing for Tommy Cooper. For Hancock they adapted old material – like the Crooner and Shakespeare sketches – and came up with new. From the beginning the comedian was deliciously self-mocking, in a way that only enhanced the gladiatorial aspect of the spectacle: 'It has been some years since I graced the small screen ... and since then one or two things have happened. First there was the war ... then the general strike ... but I am pleased to note that the legend of Hancock lives on, perpetuated by BBC repeats and Jack Jackson's record show. And if I hear *The Blood Donor* again I'll smash the set.' On the first show he genuinely forgot the name of one act he was introducing, but segued into finger-snapping *The Reunion Party* mode to cover the lapse. The shows were recorded 'technically live' at eight thirty at the ABC Theatre for transmission that same evening at five minutes past ten. There was no leeway for editing except in the most extreme emergency. Any idea of stop and start again was entirely out of the question. It became harder as the series progressed. John Muir explains that writing the monologues was difficult: 'Hancock haranguing imbeciles within the scope of a sketch worked fine, but when it came to haranguing the audience, it worked against him.'

For the sketches he was provided with an unusual and effective foil in John Junkin, who played 'Evelyn', a general theatre factotum who was bolshie and precious at the same time. One memorable sequence parodied the 'Yes – No' gong interlude from the quiz show *Take Your Pick*. Junkin loses and then suggests he has a go at Hancock:

TONY: You want to have a go at me? The Brain of Britain 1938. Times
    crossword – three minutes. All right. Have a go. I don't mind.
EVELYN: Ready.
TONY: Yes.
EVELYN: (*Strikes gong*) You've lost!
TONY: I didn't know you'd started, you idiot.

The first transmission went to the very top of the ratings, being seen in 7,450,000 homes. The show never left the TAM top ten, and Hancock would secure the top slot on two further occasions. ABC Television records reveal that he was paid £1,250 per show.

Freddie's latest suicide attempt coincided with the fourth show during the weekend of 9 and 10 July. Hancock did not hear of her condition until later on the Saturday when he arrived at the Adelphi Hotel in Liverpool, where he always stayed. 'Why did this have to happen now?' he queried, when told by a member of the ABC production team. He looked so ghastly someone offered him a whisky, which he waved away. For the next hour he sat staring at the wall, muttering to himself, 'I must still do the show.' In his act he had always dismissed the idea of 'the show must go on' as 'a load of old rubbish'. The following morning the tabloid headlines screamed, 'Hancock's Wife in Coma'. That night he went on stage. It is said that Hancock refused to communicate with the doctors. The pills Freddie had taken had been largely prescribed for him and it would have helped her cause if they had known exactly what they were. He did not return to London until the Tuesday. He visited his wife in hospital as she was beginning to revive. By her own account he swore at her and left the ward. Callous as his behaviour now appears, it is possible to see the situation from Hancock's point of view: Freddie had set precedents, and the middle of a series was no time for such distractions. The laxatives episode had a lot to answer for. And besides, when she had gone through the routine before, it always seemed that there were friends at hand to rally her round.

The following Sunday he staggered through his performance like a zombie, ever more reliant on cue cards in the wings and the orchestra pit. On the same day the *News of the World* published an exclusive interview in which he attempted to explain his feelings to Weston Taylor: 'I hope this doesn't sound brutal, but after what has happened in the past week, that is it as far as my marriage is concerned. It's over. It's finished.' It was scarcely seven months old. Hancock continued, 'Of course, I know I can be difficult and awkward at times. We've had our problems. And I suppose the blame could be shared on a fifty-fifty basis. But my wife can do this to me only once so far as hurting me is concerned.' Taylor argued that he must surely still be suffering from the shock of his wife's illness: 'I urged him to try to change his mind, but he said "No" slowly and deliberately.' Regarding his appearance the previous week, the comedian added, 'I wouldn't have gone on if my wife had been in any danger, but the doctor assured me she was recovering gradually, so what else could I do? I was afraid, I tell you, but angry also ... when transmission time came I honestly didn't know what day it was ... this is where I had to show myself to be a true performer ... that was the greatest test of my life.' John Muir was present at the Taylor interview, which took place at the Talk of the Town in London where the Blackpool show was rehearsed, and recalls the journalist as 'a nice man and a real fan': 'Tony turned very nasty on him – swore at him – the guy was next to tears – shattered – it was a horrible moment.' In the same way he also saw Hancock reduce Stan Gibbons, an ex-wrestler and close friend who often acted as part-time road manager and general factotum for him, to tears when the comedian turned on him: 'You think you're fucking tough – you fucking wrestler, you – I don't think you're fucking tough at all.' According to Muir, the Jekyll and Hyde effect that alcohol distilled in his system produced 'a very nasty flip to him sometimes. He never did it to us, but he did it to lots of other people, and he loved the idea that this guy had been a wrestler.'

Taylor's interview contained no mention of the fact that on the day of Hancock's 'greatest test' his first wife, Cicely, had also been rushed to Redhill General Hospital. According to the *Evening News* for 11 June she was suffering from an alleged attack of gastroenteritis. For the sixth show Hancock was demonstrably too ill to appear and was admitted to a nursing home with 'nervous exhaustion'. At the last moment Dave Allen assumed the role of compère. When he returned the following week – for the only show in the series that survives – he looked disoriented, his hair plastered down as if he had just walked through the shower, his gaunt face at odds with his sub-Hitchcock potbelly. With help from his writers, however, he soon established the right note: 'Sorry about last week – must have been a spot of sunstroke or something.' Maybe for therapy he went into his old hunchback impression. For a few magnificent moments he distorted his features into a grotesque Miró-like image that reminded variety fans of old times. But there could be no disputing the sense of melancholy that hung over the whole show, which he closed with another well-tried piece of business when he thanked all those involved with the series, getting carried away by Churchillian rhetoric, before announcing, 'Well, there will now be a two-minute silence for my ovation.' It doesn't quite arrive and Hancock has to pick himself up quickly: 'as I say goodbye to *The Blackpool Show*, which (he lowers his voice for effect) will hereon be known as *The Blackpool Incident*. Goodbye.' The ovation came at the end. It had already been announced that the eighth and final show would be presented by Bruce Forsyth. On the same day, in the understatement of his career, Hancock had told the *Sunday Times*, 'Life is not as good as it should be.'

His tenuous state of mind throughout the series was later revealed by John Junkin. At one point in a routine for the third show John had to unscrew an electric light bulb from the footlights. When the actor strained a cartilage, the director, Mark Stuart, happily agreed that he could unfasten one of the bulbs attached to the side of the proscenium arch instead. Hancock would not agree to the change: 'I've learned it with him kneeling down there. If he's not kneeling down there I won't remember the words. If we don't do it like that I can't do it.' As Junkin explained, 'It wasn't temperament and it wasn't "I'm a big star", it was total, total, total insecurity.' They reverted to the original plan and John suffered for his art as planned: 'And Tony never said "How are you?" – not because he was an unpleasant man, but because all his focus was on "Tony Hancock" getting through that particular show and everything else was peripheral.' Frankie Howerd, who was the principal guest during the sensitive weekend of 9 and 10 July, also remembered his mental fragility. Hancock had been anxious to revive an old routine with Howerd as his stooge. Frankie sensed intuitively it would not work and a compromise was reached whereby he reverted to a solo patter routine and they would exchange a few lines at the end of the show. As Hancock joined him for the finale, Howerd, in best mocking mode, teased, 'Ah – here comes Batman.' He fully expected Tony to respond with 'All right, Robin,' getting a big laugh in the process. As Frankie explained in his autobiography, *On the Way I Lost It*, 'You could hardly think of two characters less like Batman and Robin than Tony Hancock and Frankie Howerd. But he didn't rise to the bait and I learnt later that he was terribly upset about me calling him Batman: such was the sensitivity of his mental condition he associated the name with "batty" or "batty-man".' Howerd was truly shaken. For all his own anxieties, he was a kind and considerate man and had never intended to cause his old colleague distress.

We shall never know the exact reason for Cicely's hospitalisation on 10 July 1966; whether, in fact, the news of Freddie and her concern for Hancock pushed her over the edge drinking-wise. For all the formality of their divorce, the tie between the couple had never been completely severed. When Hancock and Freddie were licking their wounds in Cannes after the *Bullwhip Griffin* fiasco, Tony telephoned Cicely to join him. Ross looked on as the former model comforted her estranged husband and the pair took solace in drink together. Freddie described the routine: 'I kept on losing him … it was like living on a volcano that was about to erupt any second. He was burning himself up. The slightest thing would topple him over.' For the public relations consultant there had been times when his return to MacConkeys had paid dividends. After he moved in with Ross in early 1963, it still made good copy for press interviews to be conducted in the semi-rural surrounds of supposed domestic bliss. He would not publicly admit that his marriage to Cicely was over until November 1964. Hancock booked the Maharajah Suite of the Mayfair Hotel to announce his 'engagement' to Ross. When the few friends and relations had left, she asked him why he seemed depressed. 'I'm going back to Cicely,' he shrugged. After the Blackpool tragedy none of the friends who held him in true affection would have been surprised to learn that they had effected a reconciliation. Indeed five weeks after the Blackpool run, Cicely, composed and sober in a Bournemouth hotel, pleaded with him to return permanently. But by then a third woman had begun to write herself into the Hancock story as indelibly as Cicely Romanis and Freddie Ross.

Chapter Fourteen

'... YOUR STAR WILL BE FALLING'

'Ring your dad and find out if there's a vacancy
for a crane driver in Ramsgate. I'm going to
be out of a job by tomorrow.'

Joan Le Mesurier would become the key witness to the final months Hancock spent in the country of his birth. During that time she would fall in love with him and endure cruelties and indignities bred in the pit of alcoholic despair. She first met him in the early days, on a visit to MacConkeys with her future husband, John, at that time on the threshold of his divorce from Hattie Jacques. Tony played the engaging host from the moment they stepped through the door, engulfing Joan in a great bear hug. He showed her round the garden, introduced her to the poodles, Charlie and Mr Brown, and ended up rolling on the floor in laughter when she made him laugh. After shove-halfpenny at the Red Barn and dinner of planked steak, they were invited to stay the night and in the morning Joan unobtrusively tidied up the mess in the kitchen bequeathed by Cicely's *cordon bleu* triumphs of the day before. Tony, sensing kindness rather than strict regimentation, was touched by the gesture. In later years John inadvertently prepared her for the worst. He would return from visiting Tony in remedial clinics with tears in his eyes as he explained, 'He was sitting dejectedly in the garden trying to make a fucking coffee table in order to please his therapist.' Le Mesurier, twelve years his senior, was one of Hancock's oldest and closest friends, and the warmth and charity he continued to display towards him as the comedian played havoc with all their lives runs like a redeeming golden thread throughout the story. The trio met again on a back-stage visit after Tony had ostensibly left Cicely. Hancock, looking grey and bloated, must have resembled a reject from the zoo as he sat there in his fluffy white towelling robe, his hands shaking. Joan remembers her words: 'Well, if this is what show business does, I'd rather be a lavatory attendant.' He responded with a rueful laugh.

Freddie Hancock has always been at pains to suggest that in spite of the misleading impression conveyed by the 2005 television documentary, *The Unknown Hancock*, the emotional involvement between Hancock and Joan did not happen until after her final sui-cide bid and thus had no influence on it. *Dear John*, the memoir in which Joan chronicles her marriage to the actor, and Le Mesurier's own autobiography, *A Jobbing Actor*, both substantiate this. Joan re-entered Tony's life six months after her marriage to John, by which time Hancock, at his most suggestible, had succumbed to the chal-lenge of a solo concert at the Royal Festival Hall scheduled for 22 September 1966. One Sunday evening in mid-August, John answered a distress call from his friend and immediately left their home in Barons Court to rescue him from the desolation of his Knightsbridge flat, from which he had removed all traces of Freddie, leaving little more than what appeared to be a single upright chair, a bed and a mound of empty bottles. Tony stayed with the Le Mesuriers for more than a week. On the second Monday of that stay John left early to go the film studios. According to Joan, later that morning Hancock, in a rare flash of self-honesty, admitted to her, 'Do you know that I'm an alcoholic?' At Billy Marsh's suggestion, he had agreed to go into a nursing home in Highgate to dry out immediate-ly prior to a week in variety at the Bournemouth Winter Gardens commencing on 5 September, booked to enable him to run in new material for the Royal Festival Hall event. Joan agreed to go with

him in the car to the clinic. Upon arrival they were shown into a waiting area where they were brought tea and biscuits. Hancock insisted she stay until he was settled. Looking into her eyes, he said, 'How
romantic, our first meal alone together.' They might have just donated blood. By the end of the relationship they had both spilled plenty.

The Saturday before Tony's Bournemouth opening, John left to
join a film location in Paris. By the time he returned from France two
weeks later, Tony and Joan had, in her own words, fallen in love: 'I
had left my husband, our home and my reason behind ... people do
fall when they love that intensely. They fall under a spell where there
is no reality or sense.' Joan recalls the lack of self-esteem with which
Hancock confronted the affair: 'I'm John's best friend and I'm in love
with his wife ... I didn't intend this to happen.' The resolve with
which he was anxious to face John with the situation took her by surprise. Joan was anxious to break the news to her husband by herself
and did so upon his return. After a tearful night, she left for the
Mayfair Hotel where Tony had again installed himself in the
Maharajah Suite: 'It was during the time I was in transit and Tony
had been up all night in such a state because I hadn't been able to
phone him and tell him anything and he phoned John. When I came
through the door he was in tears. He was still on the phone to John
and the first thing he said was, "You've got to go back to Johnny. I
can't bear it – you've got to go back to him," and he gave me the phone
to speak to John and he was really so upset and distraught about it.'
No more, of course, than Le Mesurier, whose trademark air of wounded helplessness had been put to the reality test. He later gallantly
attempted to rationalise his wife's behaviour by saying, 'I think she
felt, rightly or wrongly, that Tony needed her more than I did, that
she could be a steadying influence on him – even that she might
eventually stop him drinking.' Of course, she had fallen for the modest, shy, humorous man who desperately wanted to be liked; she had
yet to see the darker side riddled by moods of self-loathing that now
invariably ended in drunken violence and abuse. As for Hancock, 'If

only he'd come over and hit me, or call me a bastard, or behave badly, I could accept it more easily,' he'd puzzle. Perhaps he underestimated the love John had for him too.

Hancock's state of mind at this time may be measured by his behaviour to another loyal friend, George Fairweather. The week before he was due to return to Bournemouth, he sent a message to the veteran entertainer, now running a hairdressing establishment in Westover Road, opposite the Pavilion Theatre, to tell him to drop everything the following week in favour of a golfing break together. George, with some sacrifice to his business, dutifully adjusted his working schedule and ensured he was at the Winter Gardens between the first and second house on the opening night to progress the arrangement. He asked to be announced, but was told a few minutes later that the star was too busy to see him. Fairweather understandably snapped, 'Tell him if it wasn't for me, he wouldn't be in the top position he is now.' John Muir recalls Hancock's road manager, Glyn Jones, pleading with him: 'You've got to see him – the guy loves you.' 'Nah,' Tony replied in the flat, clipped voice, which meant his decision was final. Jones came out and made the excuse that the star was busy with his writers. Hancock made no effort to make contact with Fairweather for the duration of his stay in the town. They would meet one more time. Several months later a bedraggled comedian dropped by the salon on a visit to his mother. 'You know what you can do, don't you?' berated the barber. Hancock cited his high-profile troubles as an excuse. George had heard most of it before, and showing the comedian his own unpaid bills pointed him to the door. Hancock, however, insisted he had come as a customer and installed himself in a chair. It was the first time he had used Fairweather's services. By the end of the visit Hancock had also spent twenty-five minutes on the phone and inveigled George to lend him a spare toupee to play a joke on a friend. Fairweather never saw payment for the haircut or the telephone call or the return of the toupee, but joked about being scalped by Hancock for the rest of his days.

Before we address the imminent challenge facing Hancock at the Royal Festival Hall, it will be instructive to learn a little of the background of Glyn Jones. Described by Roger Hancock as a Liverpudlian-American, he was an elegant, silver-haired man employed by the Bernard Delfont organisation, who played a large part in the running of the Talk of the Town theatre restaurant. However, he could always be contractually guaranteed to be seconded to the comedian when Tony went on the road. As Roger notes of his brother's unlikely decision to step into the Palladium at such short notice in 1963, 'He knew he'd have Glyn Jones to look after him and if Glyn was going to be there, he'd feel safe.' Minder, mother hen, best friend, booze-withholder and ego-feeder, he had played the same role to some of the top Hollywood names when they toured Europe in the early 1950s. Johnnie Ray, Nat King Cole and Frank Sinatra all came within his remit. With the latter he learned how to deal with perfection. According to Roger, when Sinatra and Ava Gardner arrived from Italy at the Caledonian Hotel in Edinburgh with a new set of crocodile-skin suitcases, the doorman took the luggage inside, leaving a briefcase stranded on the rain-spattered pavement. The singer took one look at the solitary bag and said, 'That's no good, Glyn. You'll have to go back to Rome and get another one.' And he did. Hancock had a Sinatra fixation, clinging to the example of his 1953 comeback in *From Here to Eternity* as proof of the importance of resilience over talent. In October 1965 he explained to Michael Dean, 'He was flat on the floor and really begged for this part and was paid – by his terms now – peanuts: but now, the Empire!' For Hancock, the Sinatra hat, the flow of booze, the open-top blue Cadillac all fed his image, however out of place the latter looked on Blackpool promenade. The example kept his hopes alive. The fascination also extended, by proxy, to Sammy Davis Junior.

It cannot have escaped the ears of Hancock's more acute fans that some time in the early 1960s he adopted the entertainer's signature tune, 'Mister Wonderful', as his own. The main reason he booked himself into the Maharajah Suite at the Mayfair Hotel on portentous occasions was because it was where, back then, Sammy stayed in town. To be given the chance to step onto the platform of an international concert hall like these idols only completed the self-flattery. In his eyes he envisaged the concrete shell on the South Bank of the Thames as the equivalent of what Carnegie Hall had been to Judy Garland, the crowning moment in a career of highs and lows that would silence all detractors. He commissioned a new script from Muir and Geen and clung to it like a lifeline. 'The best thing ever written for me,' he declared as he carried it everywhere rolled up like a newspaper in the weeks leading up to the performance. The writers question whether he ever read beyond the opening page. They were worried whether he was capable of learning it, if he had. Joan secretly prayed that if the event fulfilled his expectations he might call halt on his theatrical career. Hancock certainly talked of 'going out with a bang and not a whimper' and of going to live in Ramsgate – Joan's home base – 'for the fishing'. 'Why Ramsgate?' queried a reporter. 'None of your fucking business,' he replied in his best Noël Coward voice. Joan says, 'I so desperately wanted his swan-song to be a triumph that every day I would urge him to rehearse so that he would be word-perfect.' He decided he would follow the example of Sinatra and Davis by rehearsing at night. John Muir recalls, 'He said, "It's no problem. You just reverse your day." So we're given a time of two a.m. at the Prince of Wales Theatre. We get there. We wait till about three. Next day there's a message from Tony: "Sorry, but I overslept!" The following day we did rehearse in the middle of the night – what passed for a rehearsal, but what it amounted to was Tony standing centre-stage pronouncing, "This theatre's a bastard – this theatre's a bastard – come and get me baby – I'm gonna battle this theatre – I'm not gonna let it beat me – this fucking theatre is not gonna fucking beat me!"' When he got a chance to speak, Muir pointed out to Hancock that when the day came he was not going to be playing this theatre: 'Why don't we just get on with it?' But

Hancock persisted with the self-abuse. By now Cicely had arrived, looking as if she was about to topple over at any time. 'She seemed to be having trouble walking in a straight line. She was absolutely wiped out by drink,' recalls John. 'He was still seeing a lot of her at this point. He never fell out of love with her.' Her presence undoubtedly made Hancock appear relatively self-controlled in his own eyes. The fact that in a sedated condition he was often given leave of absence from the Highgate nursing home to attend such rehearsals makes the whole scenario all the more bizarre.

'The Lad Himself Will Entertain You', proclaimed the advertisements for the forthcoming challenge. Hancock's reluctance to grasp his new material sent him scurrying in other directions. Three days before the event he called Kenneth Williams three times on the *Carry On* lot suggesting they recreate the *Test Pilot* sketch from the radio show. He received the snooty comeuppance one might expect. Williams refused to speak to him and channelled the calls through his agent. 'The sheer impertinence of this man is phenomenal ... I'd rather leave the business than work with such a Philistine nit,' wrote Williams in his diary. June Whitfield was more amenable, agreeing to the indignity of delivering her lines as the nurse from their *Blood Donor* sequence from the wings. No easier method has ever been devised for the reading of idiot boards. His performance was recorded by BBC Television and can therefore be reassessed today. From his first entrance he appears desperate and sluggish, a performing seal trapped in the shiny skin of his Sinatra suit, a homunculus humbled by the vast space. At least Muir and Geen recognised the opening line as theirs: 'Good evening – I don't think I've ever seen such an ornate garage.' He surveys the gallery, 'Good evening to you in the big dipper,' then turns and sees there are people in the choir seats at the back of the platform and comments, 'Always bothers me a bit when the audience is behind you. Seems to bring in a strange sort of person. In any case, I don't like these places where there's no smoking and coughing and Tchaikovsky in the interval. Still, since they pulled down the Metropolitan Edgware Road, I suppose there's nowhere else to go, is there?' The coughing reference referred to the sign in the auditorium that stated, 'Patrons are respectfully reminded that in an auditorium possessing such sensitive acoustical properties, unstifled coughing can mar the enjoyment of the whole audience.' You wouldn't have found that at the Met.

Hancock was on stage for an hour, the jazz singer Marion Montgomery having contributed the first half of the programme to a troubled reception when the sound system let her down. It would be his last major theatrical appearance in this country and maybe from the rapturous reception he received the audience sensed it. Once again he paid comic obeisance to his ersatz Rat Pack roots with one of his favourite lines: 'Yes, I'm one of the clan. There's me, Frank Sinatra, Shirley MacLaine, Elsie and Doris Waters, Sandy MacPherson. We're always at it, to coin a phrase.' Half way through the proceedings he asked for a bourbon on the rocks and then after an immaculately timed pause added in candid self-mockery, 'Whatever that might be.' A new Shakespearian segment was sad and confused, not helped by a lacklustre straight man, Joe Ritchie, a mate of Glyn Jones conscripted at short notice to play fool to his Lear, or was it Lear to his fool? Wilfrid Lawson may have found it funny, but is unlikely to have seen it: he died five days before the television transmission. Otherwise, the retrospective of his tried – detractors said 'tired' – and tested material was inevitable. The old routines and familiar lines swirled around him like some nostalgic alphabet soup – the impressions, the crooner, the newsreel mime. The fans had been willing him to succeed from the beginning and in one sense he did not let them down. He later admitted to the *Observer*, 'I decided that if I'd got fifteen minutes in and hadn't got anywhere I'd make this terrible speech – no, I can't possibly repeat it, it was *terrible* – and that would be the finish of a career.' The blurb in the *Radio Times* attempted to beat the drum: 'Disaster has always been a strong feature of the comedy style of Tony Hancock. Social disgrace, penury, damage to person and property, violent abuse are all familiar props. Of late, Hancock's life has shown a distressing tendency to imitate his art.' It concluded, 'Nothing in his whole astonishing career could have been further from disaster.' However misleading the spin, it encouraged no more than 2 per cent of the viewing audience from tuning in at five past nine on Saturday 15 October on the fledgling BBC2. For all his talent he came over on the small screen as a distant relation of his past self, a juggler of old clichés diminished by the death of hope and originality inside the promise of what might have been. It was his last television appearance for the broadcaster whose identity he had helped to define.

Joan had taken him to the South Bank earlier on the big day. His parting words had been, 'Ring your dad and find out if there's a vacancy for a crane driver in Ramsgate. I'm going to be out of a job by tomorrow.' At that moment she would happily have settled for that. Later she watched the proceedings with Hancock's mother from the back of the top level of the auditorium to prevent the possibility of eye-lines colliding. She was shaking with nerves, as Hancock had been two nights before when she thought he was about to suffer a heart attack. Joan describes it as 'pure terror'. Lily reassured her. 'He's going to be fine. If you had been through this as many times as I have, you wouldn't worry.' Afterwards she unceremoniously yanked her lover – 'grey, sweating and trapped' – from under the surge of celebrities spilling out of his dressing room. The following day they swapped the opulence of the Maharajah Suite for a shabby first-floor flat in a tumbledown mansion on Ramsgate seafront. After a short time they moved into a modern four-bedroom bungalow with a garden which ran down to the cliff at nearby Broadstairs. It was called 'Coq d'Or' and vaunted a weather-vane in the shape of a cockerel on the roof. Budgerigars notwithstanding, Hancock was superstitious about birds, but was prepared to forgo the anxiety. No doubt the existence of a built-in bar in the living room, complete with wine-racks and optics, made amends. In such a space, her – and maybe his – domestic dream was over before it began.

Whatever the parallels between their relationship and Hancock's two previous commitments, there was one dramatic difference: Joan had a nine-year-old son, David, by her first marriage to the early *Coronation Street* actor Mark Eden. Any plans she had for living a settled existence with the comedian had to take this apparent 'complication' into account. The first time they met, Hancock lavished on the child the extent of his experience of children, namely the less than imaginative gift of a football and a visit to an ice cream parlour where, as life mirrored art once more, hideous coloured concoctions in long tapering glasses were consumed in 'Piltdown Glory' style. However, the image of the childless comedian waiting at the school gates with the local Ramsgate mums doesn't quite ring true. For all Joan might declare she wanted *his* child, she had to acknowledge the child that still lurked within her lover himself, as well as the rivalry for her attentions that he manifested at his most vulnerable, even though in Tony's more lucid moments the two guys struck a happy note together and David appeared devoted to him, seeing in Hancock a much younger, more desirable partner for his mother than John Le Mesurier. But as she says, 'Tony knew David was the biggest love of my life by far.' The highs and lows of their life together have been chronicled in vivid, sometimes searing detail by Joan in her account of their relationship, *Lady Don't Fall Backwards*.

The book presents an uncomfortable mosaic of alcoholism at its ugliest, but a sequence where Tony turns angry on the child for taking exception to the escargots he has ordered for lunch may well be the most unsettling in its explicit, bloody, vomit-strewn pages. 'What do you mean, "Yuk?"' he rages. 'You ungrateful little bastard. These are delicious. Go on, eat one.' With that he grabs the child by the chin and attempts to force one down his throat. Her child in tears, Joan protests, 'Leave him alone.' Hancock just adds callousness to cruelty, as he grabs his chin again: 'There's not a tear in the little bastard's eye. Look at him, mother's little darling.' The incident underlined why his childless condition may have remained a blessing. The dancer Mikhail Baryshnikov once referred to a suggestion that performing artists should not have children: 'I agree and disagree; we are very selfish animals. Stanislavski said that art needs sacrifice: yes, but the sacrifice falls on the shoulders of spouses, lovers, everybody around.' That is never more so than when the selfishness is suffused with 80 per cent proof. Joan simply took reassurance from her son. 'I know he loves you,' he would say to his mother with a knowing if disturbing sensitivity.

Life and love became compromised in a web of deceit as Tony pursued the clandestine route to alcoholic sustenance. 'I'm just popping out for a bit to join the library,' he explained. 'At seven thirty in the evening?' she enquired to an empty room. One endeavour to distance her lover from the bottle led to a violent attempt by Hancock to smash an iron coffee table through a window. They ended up on the floor together, Hancock's badly cut hand trapped beneath the table. The pain brought him to his senses and he murmured, 'I do love these quiet after-dinner chats.' But the full horror of his condition could never be redeemed by any amount of humour. Hancock's drinking spiralled increasingly out of control. Within a few weeks of bungalow-living, he had drunk himself into a coma, which necessitated having to be rushed back to the clinic in Highgate for the drying-out to start all over again. His psychiatrist advised that his wife's suicide attempts had done her husband irreparable damage. A cocktail of deep sedation, vitamin injections and electric shock therapy was prescribed, but everyone knew it would be meaningless without the one ingredient Hancock could only himself provide, willpower. Joan made a vow to the psychiatrist that she would warn Tony she would leave him if he had another drink. 'You've got to make him think he has lost you,' she was told. In time Hancock's struggle to keep the booze at bay became as great a test of willpower for her as for him.

She found the promise impossible to keep. She also overlooked a rival for her attentions that she had not considered, namely the lure of the spotlight, linked as it was to the need to earn a living, if, that is, there remained anyone interested in his services. It might have surprised people who saw him come round from electric shock therapy that he might ever work again. According to Joan, 'He didn't know who I was or where he was. He just lay there looking like a vegetable, staring at me with empty eyes.' But eventually his health returned and he became sufficiently well to accept an invitation to appear as a guest with Harry Secombe in his series, *Secombe and Friends*, for ATV on 13 November 1966. Reunion with his old chum would have been as good as any therapy on offer at that time. He reprised the budgerigar routine, with the life-affirming Goon donning feathers to join him in his cage. 'Oh no, not again,' moaned Hancock. 'As soon as you start looking moody, they think you need a mate. Well, I only hope they've had a good look this time. I had a lot of trouble with the last fellow.' The material, adapted by Jimmy Grafton from Galton and Simpson's original, was more risqué than one might have expected from Hancock, but he acquitted himself well. Maybe living with the easy-going, fun-loving Joan had broadened his mind.

The Secombe experience bolstered his confidence for a two-week trip to Hong Kong to appear in cabaret at the Mandarin Hotel in December. The engagement was a marked improvement on his Royal Festival Hall performance. Peter Goodwright, the impressionist who was booked to follow him in, managed to catch a few of his later shows, which were received with great acclaim: 'There was no hint of any inner turmoil when he was "on stage" and he gave a masterly performance.' Needless to say, Glyn Jones was in attendance. Hancock later expressed his opinion of the place to the writer Michael Wale: 'Oh, it was all right for me, sitting in one of those clubs with a boy to pick up your cigarette if you dropped it. The poverty there is appalling. There's all these people living in rabbit hutches, all on top of each other, and there slap bang in the middle of the place is a neatly manicured cricket pitch. Typical. I wonder if Red China watches the score through binoculars.' The most famous outcome of his visit to the colony was the enormous teddy bear he purchased there on impulse. 'What,' asks his brother, 'is a man with all his marbles doing buying an eight foot high teddy bear that he then takes on a flight back to England booked as a separate ticket?' Whatever that cost, he also had to pay an additional £50 in duty. When they arrived home a label was found attached to the bear that read 'Made in England'. The discovery sent Hancock into a fit of giggles. Moreover, it turned out to be a product of Chad Valley toys, the company chaired by radio comedian Kenneth Horne, who would happily have presented the same model to his colleague as a gift. Upon its return to England, the mascot sat on the floor of the sitting room in his barely furnished London flat, where visitors later testified that its legs made awfully comfortable seats. For Hancock and Joan it became a living presence and in time acquired a violin under its chin. 'He was playing "The Flight of the Bumble Bee" all bloody night long,' Tony would explain. In John Osborne's *Look Back in Anger* Alison attempts to justify the cuddly animal syndrome in Jimmy Porter and herself when she says, 'It was the one way of escaping from everything ... a silly symphony for people who couldn't bear the pain of being human beings any longer.' Later Jimmy lays bare his apprehension: 'There are cruel steel traps lying about everywhere just waiting for rather mad, slightly satanic, and very timid little animals.' 'Oh poor, poor bears!' says Alison as the play ends. The traps ahead in Hancock's life were never more relentless than they turned out to be during the weeks ahead, when he would reveal himself as mad, satanic and timid by turns.

Realising that life could not be centred upon Broadstairs, Hancock and Joan gave up the bungalow, and when the lease expired on the Knightsbridge apartment in December they moved to a service flat in Dolphin Square. It was seen as a holding measure while another flat of their liking was readied as a more permanent home, conveniently ten minutes' walk from Barons Court, where John still lived. The forthcoming festive season, however, entailed a return to old ways. Joan was intent on a normal family Christmas at Ramsgate with her parents, her son and John, to whom she was still married. Tony was supposedly destined for Bournemouth to stay with Lily. In Joan's absence he fell in with a resident couple, who were hard drinkers, at Dolphin Square and walked backwards fast. In the immediate wake of the holiday Joan saw herself quickly installed in her own words as Tony's 'nurse, gaoler and bodyguard'. The new drugs administered to Hancock affected his sanity and about the only redeeming aspect of his imminent behaviour was its sheer absurdity. Sometimes he imagined they were on a plane, calling air traffic control on the telephone to divert them to Paris or summoning a bottle of Dom Perignon to the front cabin. Joan would oblige with a tonic water laced with ginger. 'It was,' she says, 'like humouring a large St Bernard dog.' Matters became horrendously serious on the fourth night – New Year's Eve – when Joan woke up in the middle of the night to find Tony standing at the foot of the bed supported by two hall porters: 'He was giggling like a naughty schoolboy, stark naked except for a jockstrap, which was on back to front, and a green candlewick bedspread.' While Joan enjoyed a dreamless sleep, he had escaped to the downstairs restaurant and the risk of public ignominy. Hancock had his own version of what happened. He had been shopping for a shawl for Lily, then put it on and gone for a drink: 'I heard a woman scream, and when I looked down, someone had cut the end of my jockstrap. Luckily the boys got me out before there was a nasty scene.' The next day, after seeming to recover, he suffered a liver attack. The words of the specialist cut like a scalpel: 'If you don't stop drinking, you will be dead in less than three months.'

On 18 January 1967 Hancock signed his last will and testament leaving everything to his mother. He and Joan had now moved into the awaiting apartment at 22 Abbot's House, St Mary Abbots Terrace, tucked in behind Kensington High Street at the Olympia end. Over the next three days he recorded three television interviews, one with Alan Whicker for a documentary on the business of being a stand-up comedian within his *Whicker's World* series, and two consecutive editions of *The Frost Programme* with David Frost. None appear to have survived; the first interview was omitted from the final cut when Whicker's director, David Rea, decided it slowed down the pace of the documentary. The quick return to Frost's show was triggered by a member of the viewing public volunteering the details of a sentimental ballad which Hancock recalled his father singing. Fortunately, Whicker maintained a transcript of his conversation which he was able to publish in *Within Whicker's World*, the book he published on his ground-breaking series. Hancock went through his usual platitudes about truth in comedy, before the journalist and broadcaster asked him how his career had been affected by the publicity attracted by his recent problems: 'I don't think it's affected at all. In any case, very few people go through life without something of this sort.' Whicker then confronted Hancock with the cutting phrase applied to him by Robert Ottaway in his *Nova* magazine profile the previous November, 'the master of the self-inflicted wound':

TONY: No, it's not a bad phrase; whether it's accurate or not is another thing. I think if you're trying to achieve as much perfection as you can ... then you're going to go through certain experiences – not always particularly pleasant – or I don't think you'd be able to give whatever is necessary.

WHICKER: You've had a fairly tortured time of it?

TONY: Who hasn't? There's a certain sensitivity demanded if you're going to make anything in this business ... but it makes one a little more vulnerable possibly. That's something you have to accept.

WHICKER: I'm wondering how this kind of torment, such as it is, is affecting your work.

TONY: It's helped. For one thing, you have a deeper understanding of other people's problems – and that's all comedy is really about. I don't regret it, but I wouldn't want to go through it again. I do the very best I can – nothing is worse than to come off and disappoint them. That's awful, because you can't blame anybody but yourself.

WHICKER: I'm sure I'm typical of all the people who watch you, and if you're not doing well, I'm broken up …

TONY: May I ask *you* a question? Don't you think sometimes perhaps you ask for a little more than there is to offer?

WHICKER: Of course – we always want more.

TONY: Yes, and I'm trying to give more, you know, so we're mutually dissatisfied.

Whicker never doubted the sincerity of the comedian, whom he found an agreeable if unhappy man, but it is not easy to reconcile the extremes of Hancock's behaviour during the last two years of his life with the experiences of the ordinary people who comprised his core audience.

In moments of introspection he would tuck himself away in his study at Abbot's House and apply himself to his last grandiose scheme, a screenplay entitled 'The Link'. 'It's a comedy about religion,' he explained. 'It looks at the silly little foibles and pokes a bit of fun.' When questioned whether some might not find it offensive, he replied, 'Now you mention it, there will probably be so many people who think it's controversial that it'll never be made.' He had his excuse. It was subtitled 'Anyone for Tennis?' People, Joan included, have joked that he never got past the title page. That is not true. Among his few remaining papers reside two relevant sheets of typescript. They reveal the semi-incoherent state of his thinking, but suggest an anxiety to delve more deeply into the moment he lost his faith during the war years, the issue he sidestepped so cautiously with John Freeman. All grammatical mistakes and punctuation errors are transcribed from the original.

The first page is dated 16 September 1967 and is headed 'The Link':

A general description of the British Isles as already written establish the boy about to go into the forces including the priest use the Chamberlain speech – see him leave and the first two or three days in the forces which start to change him and then the troopship. He goes to Italy – we must cut back to the English scene throughout establishing the constant change – his awakening to the false scene of the Catholic religion – the weeping Virgin – Lichfield Cathedral – the church of Assisi – St Peter's – the collapse of Imperial Power which we keep cutting back to throughout and the estrangement of the three generations for which he is the symbol and why it is therefore called 'The Link'. He then returns and there is the scene with the priest when he is completely disillusioned and the last scene in the pub when they laugh at him and we end up with any more for tennis.

The second page, undated, builds upon the first:

There are three things to keep in mind ... he is a young man from a farming community who is taken away during the war and here there are a few points ... here we have to establish his religious attempts, using the various churches ... and his gradual realisation of his own lack of knowledge ... this is eventually why he is able to move against the other people when he returns, though really unsure. Also we use the quick cutaway ... there must be a big scene when he tries to explain between the two sides what his points really are ... he should be vulnerable and searching but in a brainwashed sort of way. At the end of the film when he dies we go through a backward evolutionary spot ... on the Nietzschean principle ... that any clown can knock him off the main line of thinking also including the idea of the television cut for big gags ... music is vitally important ... the graduation of the churches is particularly important because it shows the process of development inherent in this particular man. A good scene would be to show him in an intellectual conversation with someone highly informed which could go any way.

His disillusion with war, with religion, and with the hypocrisy whereby they fed each other were doubtless sincere, but hardly the stuff by which his credibility as a comedian would be restored.

That Cicely still cared for Tony was shown by the phone calls she made to Joan. 'If you go to Paris,' she told her, 'be careful, because he always drinks a lot there. And don't let him go near the brandy. He turns into a killer on the stuff.' Joan would discover this for herself during an impulse visit sprung upon her one weekend in the spring when she found herself plunged into a living nightmare with a 'black, evil stranger' whom she did not recognise. As Hancock's drinking and self-doubt degenerated jealously into a torrent of verbal and physical abuse, she too lost control. At this point her account assumes the tone of a dime novel: 'Suddenly I wanted to kill him. My fingernails seemed to grow into claws and I vaguely remember running at him, wanting to tear him to shreds, to tear that evil look off his face ... and that is what I did.' Having discovered a strength she did not know she had, she brought Hancock to his senses. Plans were made for a fast return home. Dark glasses were duly purchased at the airport to disguise his black eye and her swollen eyelids. On the flight home, she turned to him and said, 'You look like Wallace Beery.' The film star was old enough to have become a new addition to his impressions routine. They laughed all the way back to England, where administering to his delirium tremens soon became an established part of domestic routine as Joan measured out the daily allowance of two ounces of alcohol permitted by his 'tapering-off cure'. At night he would fight the barbiturates and stagger around the flat trying to find her secret source. It was a long time since

Hancock and James had appeared in one television half hour as improbable babysitters and Sid – not Tony – had homed in instinctively on the booze supply in the strange house. 'I can always find it,' he joked. Suddenly the memory wasn't funny any more, nor the shining echoes of Jimmy James and Sid Field teetering with all their skill into some prop cardboard lamppost on the variety stage. Hancock made the best effort he could. Unlikely as it may sound, he had a television series to record.

Only an inverted form of loyalty and the dedicated persuasion of Billy Marsh could have induced ABC Television to give him another chance after the events of the previous summer. *Hancock's* pitched Tony at the shallowest end of television light entertainment, cast as an unbelievable nightclub proprietor who sees himself as the 'fulcrum' – 'It *is* a word' – of the swinging London scene, moodily introducing a string of middle-of-the-road musical guests when not engaged in a series of sketches limited in theme by the surroundings. Everything about the concept was wrong, as Virginia Ironside indicated in the *Daily Mail*: 'Night clubs, dinner jackets ... these are not for him. He doesn't look right. He's a baggy-cardigan man, an egg-stained tie man, a loser trying to better himself, not a successful nightclub owner making a mess of the wine list and the gambling table.' In a reminder of his very first television series, June Whitfield provided her usual solid support as the hat-check girl, in spite of the strain his condition placed upon everybody. As she recalls, 'We never knew whether he'd arrive on time ... when the first question on everybody's lips when the star of the show comes into the studio is "Is he all right?" it's not very good, is it?' According to Joan, for the first few weeks Hancock managed the best he could to stay sober, but not for long. Roger Allan, the art director on the series, remembers, 'It soon became obvious that he had lost control ... he forgot his lines, his timing had gone and he was very violent. His driver and keeper was always one step behind him with a bottle and a glass: by that time he was on a bottle and a half of brandy a day.' Allan recalls one sketch in which a surly youth came into the club and started playing a fruit machine. Hancock was scripted to pick an argument with the 'yob' and throw him out. It was supposed to be funny, but when the moment came Hancock went berserk: 'He beat the actor to the floor and pushed the fruit machine over the balcony.' One of the most harrowing moments occurred behind the scenes when the *Dad's Army* actor Bill Pertwee, booked to provide the studio warm-ups for the show, found his wife and himself having a drink with Hancock in the pub next to the studios at Teddington. Bill recollects, 'All of a sudden he started thumping the table and shouting at her, "Get him out of the business. It'll kill him. Get him out of it!"' Mrs Pertwee started shaking and the proprietor indicated that Hancock should leave.

The scripts for the series were again provided by Muir and Geen: according to Billy Marsh, Hancock was convinced they could in time assume the position of excellence long ago vacated by Galton and Simpson. Sadly, they never had the opportunity to prove themselves in situation comedy for the comedian, reduced as they were here to the sketch format. Muir recalls the moment it dawned on them that Tony was looking for a succession of sketches in the mould of his hero, Sid Field, and claims that much of the material was written with Field in mind. There can be no question that it would have been more effective in his hands or, more realistically, in those of a Howerd or a Secombe, where expectation would have been less demanding and peak performance could have been assured. Matters were not helped by arguments between the star and the director, Mark Stuart. 'I'm in a two-shot all the time,' Hancock complained. 'The camera should be on the face.' Stuart explained to the writers, 'The problem is his face is so terrible.' Nevertheless he caved in to Hancock's wishes. It was a serious error of judgement. The decision was made to screen a completed show at the ABC offices in Hanover Square. At the end there was a strained silence. Hancock broke the ice. 'I look like a fucking frog,' he groaned. But not any old frog, one from whose face all expression had been drained. He might have been wearing a mask. In Muir's opinion Hancock was beginning not only to see the reality of his situation, but also to talk about it. For one read-through he appeared very, very sober and calmly declared, 'This is about the best piece of material I've ever had written for me. If I fuck it up, it's my fault.' In effect he was saying, 'I can't blame anybody but myself.' Again it was too late.

The series, which was recorded during April and May, received a chequered transmission pattern, the various regions that comprised the ITV network shuffling the transmission time of the show to suit their own whim. In the Southern Television area, for example, the first three episodes went out at seven o'clock on Friday evening from 16 June 1967, while the final three were shunted back to ten thirty. Some regions switched transmission to Tuesday, while six others, including London and Granada in the North, appear to have deferred airing the show until later in the summer. Mercifully only the merest fragments survive on video, but enough to fill the pit of one's stomach with the sour unease that comes from watching the Marx Brothers in the dire *Love Happy* or those sad twilight talkies where Buster Keaton was pitifully upstaged by Jimmy Durante. Audiences switched off or over in their millions and without the support of the full network the series stands as a trite and pathetic end to Hancock's television career in this country. There was no question that he was now a liability and not an asset. A review in the *Guardian*, while recalling his past glories, was sadly prophetic: 'It is hard to see why he should continue in this particular form of suicide.'

In the middle of June he was booked for a week at the Batley Variety Club. This engagement was an unmitigated disaster. Carl Gresham, who was press officer at the venue, remembers the occasion: 'He was my hero, so on the first night to see him walk on stage to a standing ovation and thirty-five minutes later – he should have done an hour – walk off to the sound of his own feet, muttering something about "Mrs Hathaway's Cottage", just wasn't a nice feeling.' As the week progressed, in order to save face for the comedian, it was agreed that he'd go down with a throat infection on the Thursday night. Within a month he was flying off on a five-day tour – with quizmaster Hughie Green of all people – to entertain the British troops in Aden, a few months short of independence. In 1958 he had gone on a more extensive tour of duty to entertain the forces in the Mediterranean. This became the inspiration for the radio episode, *The Foreign Legion*, and Sid's line from that show ricochets across the years: 'Well, you might as well go – nobody wants to know you over here exactly.' In the Middle East their hotel came under fire and the company were accorded the protection of armed guards. At least Hancock rose to the occasion with some topical and untypical material, reeling out a list of countries where the army had taken over the government and adding, 'Now you know why Harold Wilson has kept you here for so long.' He also told a joke about a priest who exclaimed, 'It's a miracle!' when the customs men discovered his bottle of holy water was gin. On 22 July a *Daily Express* writer who accompanied the trip reported that just two hours after Hancock visited gun positions in Aden's 'trigger-tense' Crater district, a British soldier was shot dead. The military had balked at Hancock's decision to enter the area to chat to the men who had been unable to see any of the shows staged in the heavily guarded camps. Eventually, with only hours to go before the flight home, the high command relented and he spent an hour signing autographs and admiring tattoos. 'They're blinking art galleries,' he joked. According to Green, Hancock had been drunk when he boarded the plane in England and he was drunk when they landed back in England. The day after his return he checked into a London clinic. It was reported that he was 'ill with nervous exhaustion after visiting Aden'.

As Hancock staggered from one setback to another, Joan's fortitude finally gave way. In the late summer of 1967 the comedian went missing for four days, the second such occurrence in recent weeks. He arrived back at the flat, drawn, derelict and disgusting. Joan recognised the demon beneath the surface: 'He kept grabbing me and mouthing obscenities.' The hypocrisy of the six dozen long-stemmed red roses that preceded him only made matters worse. She rushed to the bedroom where on impulse she swallowed a handful of his sleeping pills. When amid her self-induced haze Hancock later attempted to impose himself on her, she swallowed the rest. That Joan survived is thanks to Tony's housekeeper, who found her early the next morning and summoned a doctor. Hancock was unconscious in the next room. They were taken away in separate ambulances. There was another futile attempt at reconciliation, but a watershed came when they went to see Burton and Taylor in the film *Who's Afraid of Virginia Woolf?* The tale of marital antagonism and desperate drinking seems a strange choice in the circumstances, and by the end of the evening Joan had barricaded herself in the study as Tony acted out an alarming real-life version of what they had just seen. Days later he announced that he did not want to sleep with her that night and coldly declared, 'I think you should go right away from me for your own good, because there's some part of me that is capable of harming you, even killing you.' For once he sounded sober. Joan went to live with her cousin before returning to John. As far as her mild-mannered husband was concerned, she had simply been 'AWOL'.

One consolation to emerge from his last television series was the close relationship he forged with the actress Damaris Hayman. She has always denied that this was anything but platonic, but her presence in his life during his final months in England displays a soul mate who was certainly attuned to his medical and intellectual, if not his sexual, needs. It is not necessary to spend long in her presence to feel the care and affection she harboured for him. She first encountered Hancock in a sketch in which he played a gypsy fiddler and she had to gaze at him and say, 'Play some gypsy music – something you used to play around the campfire.' Their friendship was kindled soon after. Maybe the knack they shared of appearing to come across as older than their actual age played a part: 'We just clicked – electric currents, I suppose. He had a dread of being left alone. I used to get calls in the middle of the night to come round and I used to read to him.' Hancock was worried that he was losing his eyesight; Damaris is convinced that all he needed was new glasses. She took great pride in interesting him in 'proper' philosophy: 'He liked Bertrand Russell and I thought that a mistake. My mother had known Russell as a young man and never thought highly of him at all, rushing around Cambridge looking like the Mad Hatter. So I read Plato to him and did, in fact, make a tape of *The Apologia* for him to take to Australia on his last trip. It obviously didn't have the soothing effect one might have hoped it would.' She did go along with Hancock's suggestion that at his advanced age Russell should have a personalised underfloor-heated flagstone reserved for him in Trafalgar Square, since he seemed to spend so much time there at sit-downs for the CND. In lighter moments Damaris reprised for him the exploits of Eeyore and Winnie the Pooh, this time with the Hong Kong teddy in earshot. Together they went to see another Burton/Taylor epic, *The Taming of the Shrew*, and spent the night dissecting every single line of the performance. According to Hayman Tony would 'talk the hind leg off a field full of donkeys'. When he allowed her to, they would embark upon long cross-talk sessions, which she claims stood her in good stead a few years later during her successful working relationship with Les Dawson. She also discovered his penchant for 'directoire knickers', a childhood echo of sexual initiation by a chambermaid in his parents' hotel:'I think early precocious fumblings had involved getting up the elastic of the knickers. And he liked stockings and suspenders and he didn't like tights – which at the time quite a lot of men did.' On another occasion the actress observed that he loved the whole débutante scene, although, she added, 'You were expected to take her home in a taxi and he would have been labelled "not safe in taxis" almost immediately.'

The relationship does not appear to have suffered from physical abuse. Damaris admits to having been knocked over once by

Hancock, but claims it was an accident when he was not in control of his actions. With a cabaret trip to Australia beckoning at the beginning of October, she took him to the Priory at Roehampton for the drying-out process. There she found herself discussing her feelings for him with one of the doctors. She was told, 'I think you have been sent to him as a lifeline – whether he can take it or not is the question,' but she knew instinctively that by now he was beyond lifelines. That afternoon he released himself from the clinic; she later discovered he had taken refuge in the basement flat of the concierge. Damaris provides as vivid an account of the comedian's anguish from *his* point of view as anyone: 'The curious thing was that he'd got to the stage when he had to have the brandy, but he didn't like it … he used to say that the craving for a drink was like tigers clawing his back. He didn't like it all that much, but it sent away the tigers.' Bérenger in Ionesco's *Rhinoceros* had hinted as much when he said, 'I don't like the taste of alcohol much. And yet if I don't drink, I'm done for; it's as if I'm frightened, and so I drink not to be frightened any longer.' Hancock's drinking also subjected him to strange dreams, which he took to be real. One morning he announced to Damaris that he'd been talking to General de Gaulle: 'And he thought he really had, and it must have been a dream.' His liver may have been shot to pieces, but he had a physically strong body – 'stripped, he was a solid corpse', is how she describes him – and, whatever the doctors warned, he carried on with life as if there were still a million tomorrows. Damaris reasons, 'If you think you'll die soon anyway, you wouldn't bother to commit suicide. He certainly had an invincible streak. He had got away with it for so long.'

By now there was no room left in his affections for his second wife, whose divorce proceedings against him were about to go through the courts. The day after the Royal Festival Hall concert he had consigned her engraved cufflinks to the care of a maid, adding, 'Give those to your husband. They might give him a bit of confidence.' On 9 June 1967 the *Evening Standard* reported that Freddie

Hancock was seeking leave to present a petition for divorce against him within three years of the start of their marriage. In those days it was customary to wait three years from the wedding date before proceeding. 'We mustn't let the bitch win,' he'd confide to Joan, but for Cicely he maintained a constant concern, even if he was not always in the best condition to help her. Since her book was published, Joan has admitted that on the two times Hancock went running from her he went to stay with his first wife. On one occasion he arrived back at the door of the flat looking every bit like a music-hall drunk. 'You'd be proud of me if you knew what I've been doing,' he slurred. 'What was that, Tony?' 'I've been helping a sick friend,' he replied. He meant Cicely, now as hopelessly alcoholic as he was. Presumably they drifted together and apart again on a wave of 'River Ouse' – Tony's favourite rhyming slang – and drowned their mutual sorrows amid whatever comfort they could extend to each other. Joan insists, 'He never said anything unkind about her; he said a lot of unkind things about Freddie.' At times tears would well up in his eyes as he described his first wife's condition, with greater anxiety for her than for himself. In candid moments he confessed something approaching guilt to Damaris: 'He felt he had been instrumental in destroying her, because she thought if she drank with him it would check his drinking ... it couldn't and it doesn't ... it fed his remorse.' One afternoon – although it is unclear whether it was before or after his 1967 visit to Australia – he arrived at the Red Barn in Blindley Heath with Cicely, who had now moved from MacConkeys to a cottage at South Godstone. During that visit he told Eileen Fryer that he intended to go back to her. It is not difficult to imagine, not least if at that time he was estranged from Joan.

In the months following the recording of the ABC series, Hancock's public image was at its most vulnerable. Even in the heady 1960s alcoholism was still considered shameful and degrading, something not talked about by 'nice' people. For Hancock, merely to walk outside ran the risk of stepping into a snake pit of opprobrium, but the press appear to have stayed loyal; in today's tabloid climate each rush to hospital would be accompanied by banner headlines. When in 1955 Sid James and Bill Kerr acted alongside Tony in the radio episode, *The Chef That Died of Shame*, chronicling the rise and fall of a pie-stall cook who reaches the highest achievements of *haute cuisine* before plummeting to the gutter through drink, neither they nor Galton and Simpson could or would have foreseen the reality it portended for the years ahead. Thrown by success, the title character becomes conceited, neglects his wife, and fails to return home for four days at a time, sustained by alcohol and little else. His wife, played by Andrée Melly, provides an uneasy indication of times to come:

ANDRÉE: I've done everything I can. I've even threatened him. Last week I
    told him if he didn't stop drinking I'd put my head in the gas oven. He
    was very polite about it.
BILL: What did he do?
ANDRÉE: He held the door open for me.

Broke, broken and suicidal, the chef treads a downward path that was then in reality as distant an option for comedy's glittering prizewinner as the role of prime minister or the captaincy of England. Then one day in the summer of 1967 Bill encountered Tony in the streets of Mayfair looking lonely and desolate, 'as though he didn't have two bob in the world'. He urged Kerr to join him for a Turkish bath in Jermyn Street, but the actor had a show to perform. Hancock urged him to come back later in the evening. 'We can have a yarn,' he seemed to plead. Bill never made it and regrets it now, but at least he got to speak to his old colleague. Sid James was not so lucky. Driving down London's Piccadilly around the same time he spotted the dishevelled figure of Hancock stranded on a traffic island: 'He was really full of liquor that day, swaying around. Cab drivers were pointing at him. It was highly dangerous.' Sid parked the car as quickly as

he could, but by the time he returned to the scene Hancock had disappeared. It was the last time he saw him. His regret was even more
rueful: 'I wish to God I had been able to catch him that day – it's the
little things that can change people's lives.' The circumstances were
particularly poignant in that Sid had only just recovered from a
heart attack. While he was in hospital, his wife Valerie received a
telephone call. There were no introductions. Hancock simply mumbled, 'How is he?' After a startled, 'It's you,' Valerie added, 'He will be
fine.' Tony said, 'Give him my love,' and quietly put the phone down.
Sid's face lit up in the hospital when he was told. Forty years later
Valerie acknowledges the effort it had taken for Tony to make that
call.

Allegations that around this time Hancock also came to frequent gay drinking establishments in London's Soho have been
impossible to corroborate, although with a chuckle his brother, a
happily married man for many years, adds that he and many another heterosexual have frequented such bars. However, the question of
Hancock's potential bisexuality has to be addressed. Irrespective of
the embarrassment with Matt Monro on the night train from
Liverpool and an anonymous gay liaison he is alleged to have had
while serving in the RAF, John Muir recalls that on one occasion
when the comedian was staying at his home he did make a serious
attempt to get into bed with him: 'It was really quite hair-raising. I'm
not into men and he probably was drunk, but he was still aware of
what he was doing.' Michael Wale, the co-writer on his Australian
series, also sensed a disquieting frisson of attraction from the comedian towards him, although no direct overture was ever made. One
close friend from service days was the homosexual Rex Jameson,
alias that comedy doyenne, Mrs Shufflewick. His biographer, Patrick
Newley, while certain there was no emotional attachment at any
time between the two performers, asserts that they remained close
pals for many years and regards it as highly probable that he could
have introduced Tony to the 'discreet' gay pub and club scene at this

time. With regard to the RAF allegation, Newley adds that the Gang Show provided the perfect environment for a liaison, 'given the general "camping about" that was deemed acceptable within the Gang Show units – and highly unacceptable within a normal fighting unit!' It is now no secret that Ralph Reader, the power behind the Gang Show, within both the RAF and the Boy Scout Movement, was himself homosexual. Today the irony of one of the many lyrics he wrote for the show shrieks out: 'Stepping out, stepping out, we're about to go *gay*, say goodbye to the sighs and the yawning, never getting home till the morning's dawning ...' To the public at large the word 'gay' then had a different connotation.

Close friends of both sexes laugh with ridicule when the matter is raised in Hancock's name. Roger Hancock has no doubt, 'It was the birds he was after. And he'd got this wonderful line. They all felt sorry for him and thought they could cure him – he'd got it made.' The view is endorsed by his RAF chum Graham Stark; so much so that had he been in the navy he would have lived up to the boast he once made from his East Cheam sitting room: 'I can't deny me own reputation. "First-down-the-plank Hancock", they called me. A string of broken hearts from Melbourne Mary to Scapa Flo.' Roger says he can recall around twenty women scattered all over the country, including a postmistress from Harrogate, who at various times all thought they had first claim on his attentions, adding that the main difficulty in arranging his memorial service was making sure they were all deployed in different parts of the church. Neither Damaris Hayman nor Joan Le Mesurier is prepared to believe for one second that Hancock had a homosexual other life. Damaris jokes quite healthily about the chorus girls who threw themselves at him at Blackpool, while his appeal to the maternal instinct permeates everything Joan says about him. 'Poor darling' is a phrase she uses today as if it happened yesterday. Equally her memoir is testimony to his carnal appetites: 'His intensity and demands for sex frightened us both slightly and we tried to cut down a bit. "I'm going to draw an imaginary line down the middle of this bed, over which no tits, arses or willies must stray," he said. But it didn't work, and I was no help at all – I found him irresistible.' Writing in his diary in 1972 when the Matt Monro rumour spread, Kenneth Williams said, 'I'd never heard that Hancock was interested in homosexuality. Sid said, "It got so that he'd try *anything* ..."' Maybe Sid was right. The probability must be that his sexual appetite – whatever its persuasion – fell in line with the addictive streak in his character. But another insight may be provided by the comedienne Joan Turner, who one evening discovered Tony leaning over a bollard in Shepherd Market. She jumped out of her cab and asked him what he was doing there. 'Looking for someone to have a drink with,' was his reply. To Philip Oakes, he was as contemptuous of Judy Garland's homosexual following as he was passionate about her. 'She doesn't need that lot,' he said, 'but she needs somebody. We all do.' Sometimes loneliness has a lot to answer for.

At the end of September he went off to Australia sober and looking fitter than he had done for some time, having managed to pull himself through an exhaustive treatment process that caused him allegedly to shed some 32 lb. He opened at the Dendy Cinema in Middle Brighton on the outskirts of Melbourne on 4 October. It was a curious booking, with the television favourite from London performing the first half of a shared presentation that closed with a feature film, a throwback to the old days of Cine-Variety, a format that never really took off in England. The contract stipulated an engagement of three weeks. On Tuesday 10 October he also recorded an appearance for the television show, *Something Special – Nancye*, hosted by the presenter Nancye Hayes. Although it would not be transmitted until June the following year, twelve days before he died, it revealed that with his familiar material he was still capable of delivering something approaching a polished performance that was measurably superior to his swan-song at the Royal Festival Hall. At a reception after the show it is alleged that a miscreant, well aware of Hancock's condition, laced his tomato juice with vodka. This opened the floodgates to dependency once again, and the results were catastrophic. Anxious not to disappoint the audience at the Dendy that night, he insisted on going on stage. There he fell over several times and at one point found himself in the auditorium. He clambered back on all fours. The audience began to catcall and he asked for a spotlight to be shone on a heckler. Bedlam ensued and after an ugly encounter with the theatre manager the star was escorted off stage. His performance had lasted twenty minutes. Later Hancock claimed he was suffering from the after-effects of cholera injections. He also added that he'd had only two beers all day. Vodka or beer, the outcome would have been the same. The following night he bounced back with, 'as I was about to say before I fell off the stage ...' and he was a hero again. In a curious twist Hancock was dining later that night at a restaurant when he heard that Matt Monro, who was performing in cabaret at another restaurant for the same management, had been taken ill. He jumped into a taxi and stepped into the breach. The comedian was reported as saying, 'In a way I'm glad it happened, because I've cleared the slate.' Eddie Joffe, his producer in Australia, has a theory that Hancock's trouble of the previous day had begun on a binge with Monro, although it is hard to see how there could have been time for that between the television recording and his show early in the evening. The following Sunday he gave a free performance for those who had been in the audience the night of the débâcle, wiping the slate clean again. After finishing the Dendy season on 22 October he flew to Hobart, Tasmania, to fulfil a week's cabaret engagement at Hadley's Hotel, before returning to London. This time he brought back no teddy bears, rather a contract to return the following year to make 'a television series of up to thirty-nine episodes'. It stipulated that he would receive the modest sum of A$1,000 for each complete episode, enhanced by the promise of 25 per cent of net income from the sale of the series outside Australia. Billy Marsh had not been consulted on the matter.

On his return from Australia, Hancock was welcomed back on to *The Eamonn Andrews Show* on Sunday 19 November. The programme trailer earlier in the day announced a 'mystery guest' and Joan, watching in Ramsgate, shared with her son a premonition that it would be Tony. David owned up that he had heard his grandparents discussing a phone call from Hancock the day before: 'And they told him you were back with John and to leave you alone.' Joan watched the show with trepidation and was overjoyed to see Hancock looking surprisingly fit and on terrific form. She was unaware that Hancock had been assigned a male nurse to look after him in the run-up to the transmission. He took one look at him, kicked him out, and asked Damaris to stay with him that weekend to keep him off the brandy, which she did. She also ensured he was well fed, enlisting the vital help of 'meals on wheels' to deliver a proper Sunday lunch: 'He ate the roast beef and Yorkshire pudding, but left the apple pie.' Later that evening on the show he reminisced with fellow guest Jimmy Edwards about their old lighthouse sketch, talked about the impending Australian series, and traded good-natured banter about audiences. Jimmy dismissed American audiences for laughing at anything.

TONY: What else do we want in this game? People to laugh at anything –
    that's what we want.
JIMMY: We don't want people to laugh at anything.
TONY: We don't want to be intellectuals like you.

Confronted with the lines alone, most people would have assigned them in reverse. The next morning Joan returned to London, having made contact with Hancock from a call box. He met her at the station with a trademark hug. From that moment Joan began to live her biggest lie, promising Tony that she would spend as much time with him as she could, but that John must never know. It was inevitable that during this period she would discover the existence of Damaris.

Outright he explained that on a trip to Bournemouth he had taken a woman with him for company. He insisted she was just a friend. Joan concedes that when the initial jealousy had faded it was a relief to know that 'he wasn't alone at night half drugged and falling about or drunk and depressed'.

Suddenly it was Christmas again. Joan went back to Ramsgate for a family celebration, taking her secret with her. Tony went to Bournemouth with a broken rib, incurred from a fall in his flat. He promptly went down with pneumonia and was admitted to a nursing home. At that point he summoned Damaris to come and spend the lonely days with him. They ushered in his last New Year watching Will Hay in *Oh, Mr Porter!* on a juddering television screen which she had to thump into stability. Damaris claims he could always be bounced out of depression by certain lines from the film. She would play Harbottle to Hancock's Hay: 'Every night, when the moon gives light, the miller's ghost is seen. As he walks the track with a sack on his back and ...' 'His ear-hole painted green!' piped in Tony. Harbottle's explanation for Albert's eccentricity – 'He plays with the pixies' – always tickled him. They returned to London, where he was offered a quick return onto the Andrews show. Damaris was prevailed upon once again. Another guest was to be Jacqueline Susann, promoting her blockbuster novel, *Valley of the Dolls*. On the Friday Tony was sent an advance copy to read for comment during the programme. He asked Hayman to read it for him and then to provide him with a synopsis. Her ability to speed-read helped, although it must have proved a disconcerting read. The book proved to be a thinly disguised *roman à clef* of Hollywood life, one of whose characters, with her own self-destructive alcoholism and drug dependency, is a thinly disguised version of Judy Garland. Inevitably Eamonn asked the comedian to contribute his views on the pressures of show business. Hancock, who admitted to being in America at the time of Marilyn Monroe's death in 1962, replied, 'There is one American psychiatrist who described a live television show as – in terms of shock

– the equivalent of a car crash. There was one American comedian who used to go straight into a nursing home for a couple of days after he finished [a show] because of the pressure.' It is painful to consider that these words were the last he uttered on British television. In the enforced jollity of the studio, it went over the heads of everyone that he was also talking about himself.

A short while later Lily came to stay at the flat at St Mary Abbots Terrace. One morning in the early hours, looking like a ghost from a Will Hay film himself, he walked into his mother's room to make the boast that he'd just downed a bottle of brandy in five minutes. At which point he passed out. When he came round the doctor asked him if he wanted to die. He said, 'Yes.' The act was the nearest he had come to a single decisive flirtation with death. Joan has described it as a game of Russian roulette. Called to the scene by Lily, she stood by as Tony, pumped to the eyeballs with vitamin injections, pulled through one more time. She claims that from that day she never saw him drink again, but, of course, her time in his company was curtailed out of her superficial loyalty to John. Hancock had his mind set on Australia, however much she might attempt to persuade him otherwise. April arrived and their parting at Victoria was perfunctory as he stopped halfway across the station concourse to announce, 'I'm leaving you here.' A kiss, a hug and he was gone. He took with him her promise that if he stayed dry for a year she would leave John again and marry him. He flew off for Australia on a wing and a prayer. The words would have had meaning for him. He might have been his brother Colin embarking upon another bombing raid. Maybe it was destined he would never come back.

Chapter Fifteen

'TOO MANY TIMES'

'Maybe I should have kept the props.
After all, Chaplin never really abandoned his cane.'

Hancock had become well nigh unemployable at home. He'd been there once before, but not in reality – in the television show where Sid playing his agent was reduced to booking him into a tacky night club on the Costa Brava:

TONY: Whether they want me or not, I'm an artiste. Oh, fame, fame, thou inconstant nymph! What a pathetic figure I must cast?
SID: Yes.
TONY: A fading star unwanted by a public who once acclaimed him.

Australia was a long way to go for confirmation of his talent, but his pride never deserted him. 'My best is yet to come,' he bragged to the media ahead of his departure. He had scarcely been more vulnerable. His Australian engagement had not been endorsed by the Bernard Delfont management, as a result of which he did not have the redoubtable Glyn Jones in attendance. Had Billy Marsh done the deal, his client would never have travelled alone, his only company, as Damaris Hayman has observed, 'a Gladstone bag full of enough pills to kill him several times over' and an empty promise that he could invite some guests out from England to appear on the series at a later stage. They shared a happy time compiling a short list that featured, in addition to Damaris herself, June Whitfield and Hugh Lloyd. It soon became obvious to Hayman that this was not going to happen, but 'he wanted to believe it, so he believed it'.

There was a poignancy attached to the way Hancock said his goodbyes. The night before departure he rang Eric Sykes to see if they could have dinner together. Eric recalls, 'I was in Weybridge at the time and I said, "No, Tony. It's eight o'clock. I'll have dinner with you tomorrow night." He said, "You can't tomorrow, because I won't be here." I often wonder if maybe I'd made the effort – but I don't wonder too much, because it would have made no difference.' Early the following morning he surprised Alan Simpson with a call from the airport: 'When I come back the three of us are going to do the greatest thing that's ever been done. We're going to knock their eyes out.' Alan replied, 'Good luck, Tony. Give us a ring on your return.' They were the last times he spoke to the two men who – together with Ray Galton – had done so much to mould his success from a creative standpoint. Terry-Thomas was another old friend from his past to whom Hancock went out of his way to say goodbye in person before leaving British shores. There would be a further farewell when he stopped over in Delhi to stay with John Freeman – now installed as the High Commissioner to India – and his wife Catherine on the outward journey. Her recollection of that visit is that Hancock was in a lowly state and drinking heavily. He had effectively already broken his promise to Joan Le Mesurier.

At the time the Australian project did not appear such a bad idea. It marked a return to situation comedy, the genre in which he was always most comfortable, as well as to the East Cheam persona complete with Homburg hat and astrakhan-collared coat. With the blessing of Galton and Simpson, this breakthrough was achieved by Michael Wale, the London-based writer, co-opted to the series to capture the correct turn of phrase in Hancock's dialogue. When Wale raised the issue over copious cups of tepid Nescafé on an introductory visit to St Mary Abbots Terrace, the star admitted that he had been mistaken in abandoning the character. 'I had to do something new. I had to progress. But looking back on it now I think it was a case of throwing the baby away with the bath water,' he agreed. 'Maybe I should have kept the props. After all, Chaplin never really abandoned his cane.' 'The lad himself' was all set to portray an immigrant down under, arriving on a £10 assisted passage with Polly the stuffed eagle under one arm and his cherished portrait of Queen Victoria under the other. In the BBC television episode *The Emigrant* he had already considered the prospect, but had to make his position clear to the emigration officer: 'You want me *and* ten pounds. You want jam on it, don't you? ... I shall take my custom elsewhere.'

On paper Australia provided him with the perfect foil, signifying, as Wale noted, 'a head-on collision between the insularity of the British and the extrovert, muscle-flexing masculinity of the world's most booming nation'. The expectation for the series was established early as he leant against the rail of the ship and reflected, 'Of course, we Hancocks always have been a seafaring race. If it hadn't been a question of time, I'd have sailed across single-handed. But life's too short to fit everything in. It's all right for Sir Francis Chichester, but I've got too much on me plate. I've got to help build a new country. After all Captain Cook didn't arrive single handed, did he? ... I wonder if Matilda's still waltzing around with that kangaroo.' Whatever Wale's precise contribution to the script, the importance of his persuasion cannot be overstated. Producer Eddie Joffe confirms that it was a precondition of Hancock's involvement long before he became attached to the enterprise himself that the comedian take the accoutrements of East Cheam with him: the Australians were still enjoying repeats of his old BBC shows and the lack of continuity if suddenly a 'new' Hancock appeared would have put the new venture at risk. This, however, was never written into his actual contract. Had Wale not cemented the change in Hancock's mind, subsequent events might have proved very different. Even so, those who commissioned the series in Sydney, insulated from what had been happening in Melbourne the previous October, must have received a shock when they saw the drastic physical change in the man from his BBC heyday.

According to head writer Hugh Stuckey, the immediate plan was to make an initial thirteen episodes of the ominously titled *Hancock Down Under* for ATN7, an Australian equivalent of ITV, or Channel 7 as it was known. Subsequent options to make up the maximum commitment of thirty-nine shows would be exercised in further instalments if the series was deemed successful. On the technical side, it appeared that Hancock had at last acquired the facilities he had been dreaming of for so long. The episodes would be shot on 35 mm colour stock using the E-CAM system, making them technically acceptable for showing on a global basis. Unfortunately, since he had seen it in operation on the Lucille Ball show in Hollywood, the system – through an attempt to economise on the use of film stock – had been refined from one whereby the complete action was shot continuously on three separate cameras to what amounted to little more than a film version of the old video process: as the director chose his shots from the control gallery, so only one camera filmed at a time. It did not help that Eddie Joffe, brought from England through the good graces of Phyllis Rounce, had not used the system before, or that no one in his crew was completely *au fait* with the equipment. At a key stage in the proceedings bureaucratic short-sightedness prevented Eddie from bringing in a relatively inexpensive recording device that would at least have shown him the results of cutting between cameras as he went along and not until after the footage had been developed and edited. This blatant display of false economy necessitated frequent retakes. Inevitably, Hancock continued to give his best performance on the first take. After that his energy and interest faded away and mediocrity set in. He did enjoy what he perceived to be the consolation of recording discontinuously in short sequences without a studio audience.

Joffe says that Hancock was insistent on working with a British director and, ever hopeful, first invited Duncan Wood to join him. When Wood declined, the executive producer, John Collins, made contact with Sydney agent Jack Neary to help him in his quest. Neary happened to be the Australian representative of International Artistes, which is how Phyllis Rounce entered the final chapter of the Hancock story. Her client Eddie Joffe was working for Grampian Television in Aberdeen at the time. A South African by birth, he had arrived in Great Britain at a young age in 1957, in time both to have worshipped Hancock during his glory days and to have witnessed his troubled times. When he asked Rounce what he would be letting himself in for, she replied that if he could rise to the challenge of restoring Tony to his rightful place at the top of his profession, the public, the world of show business and Hancock himself would all be indebted to him. Eddie, now a respected documentary film maker, is realistic enough to accept that he was probably the last person in a long line to be asked. When he first met his idol, he was taken aback: 'He was forty-three years old, but when he came to the door he looked sixty-five. He had grown into a *Spitting Image* version of himself.' Notwithstanding, Joffe took an immediate liking to the man. 'He became like an old, old friend to me,' explains the director. 'We had no fights. We had arguments. He and I made an agreement that if we had anything to say to one another, we'd go to the dressing room to discuss it.' A number of people had forewarned him of the temperament Hancock might display on the set, a myth that proved unfounded. Eddie recalls a committed professional, who demanded the best from everyone around him, craving the perfection that had eluded him after *Hancock's Half Hour*, even though that expectation of himself became undermined by his dependency. Forty years later he remembers their association and the events that overtook them both with an emotion that is touching and sincere.

The seeds of the series were propagated rapidly during the Dendy Cinema season. In order to keep Hancock occupied during the day, John Collins, executive producer for the Willard King Organisation which was promoting the live event, brought him together with Stuckey, one of the pioneer writers on Australian television, who lived in Melbourne and also happened to be under contract to Collins. By the time Hancock returned to London a sample script was on the table, sufficient to have enabled Collins to clinch a deal with Channel 7. In the spring of 1968 Joffe had other commitments that prevented him going out to Australia ahead of or with Hancock. Tony went out by himself in early March, his first destination Melbourne, where he rekindled his bond with Stuckey. The writer has said, 'He had the capacity to trust only one person at a time – at this time I just happened to be that person.' He soon slipped happily into the Stuckeys' domestic routine and appeared not to be drinking, *apart from* the occasional beer. After two weeks Hancock's resistance to alcohol had given way completely. When it was time for them to move on to Sydney together, Hancock was in tears. At the airport he threw his arms around Shirley, Hugh's wife, and pleaded, 'Please don't make me go. Please stop them. Please stop them.' Stuckey soon found himself sucked into the role that Ross and Le Mesurier knew only too well. As he kept the comedian company into the early hours and the booze at bay as best he could, he became worried by an additional hazard. Hancock had fallen into the habit of falling asleep with a lighted cigarette in his hand. The consequences could have been unspeakable. In his concern, Hugh began to get the full measure of the man: 'Whatever that magic quality is that gets to audiences, was in him. He was so vulnerable, you just had to do something.' Collins also felt vulnerable, anxious that the word of Hancock's worsening condition should be kept from the studio bosses. An ominous note had been sounded at the press conference upon

Tony's arrival at Melbourne. When he was asked the name of the series, he answered, *Marie*. Eddie concedes that Hancock was being mischievous with the media, but it is difficult not to associate the behaviour with his condition. Had he been completely sober he would surely have grasped the opportunity to pontificate on his visit as another step in his grand agenda for achieving universality in comedy.

Michael Wale considers that Hancock was brought out far too early – Joffe did not arrive until 9 April – and inevitably his alcoholic intake increased in direct proportion to his boredom, something which somewhat contrived visits to cricket matches, agricultural shows and Sydney's Chinaman's Beach did little to alleviate. At the beach he risked undoing the buttons of his cardigan as a concession to the temperature; when it was suggested he might roll up his flannels and paddle on the edge, he was taken aback: 'You must all be stark raving mad. And for God's sake, don't go in the water. It's shark-infested.' He once flinched when a large seagull swooped down onto the sand. 'What on earth's that?' he asked Wale. 'I thought it was an eagle. You never know over here. They've got spiders, you know, that can kill a man in four minutes.' Eddie was always amazed how quickly Hancock could switch from being the best company in the world to a minion in thrall to the bottle, but the full reality did not sink home until the week of the first recording, which the director had already insisted should be treated as a pilot exercise given the uncertainties inherent both technically and star-wise in the situation. The gradual effect on his performance that week would prove demoralising for the entire crew. The first read-through took place on Easter Monday, 15 April 1968, with Tony contributing a *tour de force* that was in Joffe's words 'the best Hancock performance anyone had yet seen'. Even if one allows for the hyperbole of such a sentence, Hancock's flamboyance and enthusiasm suggested he had at least found a way back into enjoying his performance, contributing a spark long absent on British television. Regrettably he felt his success called for a celebration. Soon the champagne that had bubbled within his personality took a more literal form. The following day he arrived at rehearsals the worse for wear and it quickly became apparent that the slide had begun. Clare Richardson, Joffe's PA, wrote home to England, 'By the end of the week, rehearsals were just a dreary, sitting-about drag, while the director sat and talked and cajoled Hancock into a few slurred lines of the script.'

In his memoir, *Hancock's Last Stand*, Joffe vividly chronicled the gallant attempts he made during that week to keep Hancock this side of dignity, sobriety and professionalism. In his innocence, however, he made the basic error of thinking he could modify his alcohol intake, when he should have been slamming the drawbridge shut on the tiniest droplet, a Herculean task way beyond the call of duty. The comedian managed to stagger through the first day of recording with some self-respect. The second day, which was dedicated completely to his solo sequences, saw him in a deplorable state. By now Joffe could guess the routine: 'He had taken his usual morning "hair of the dog" steadier, then washed down some pills with another drink, after which he'd popped a tranquilliser to counteract the drink, then a stimulant or two with a slug of vodka to counteract the tranquilliser.' In other words, the snake was swallowing its tail, no longer immune to its own venom. The theme – and title – of the pilot show was *Sleepless Night*, a familiar theme for his humour. One sequence brought sad disbelief to every member of the crew. According to the plot, his insomnia is exacerbated by a persistent drip, the outcome of which is that he has to stem the full flow of water from a faulty tap with a finger of one hand, while reaching – with pre-calculated difficulty – for the telephone that is only just within reach with the other. He manages to phone the emergency services. When he gets through, the voice asks, 'Fire, ambulance or police?' Tony had to reply, 'Fire, but have the ambulance standing by.' The task defeated him completely. Hancock would either forget to lift the receiver or to dial the number before speaking. The few times he *was* coordinated, he would dredge out of his subconscious some line from a long-distant show that had no relevance to the scene he was recording. Things deteriorated when a stray bird found its way into the upper reaches of the lighting rig. The studio was brought to a standstill as the creature's persistent chirping played havoc with the sound system and, while the members of the crew spent an entire hour playing their Sylvester to its Tweetie Pie, a haunted Hancock allowed his superstition about birds to intrude upon what little lucidity he had left and retreated to his dressing room for an early lunch of pills and vodka. When the scene was resumed in the afternoon, the star was no longer of this world. 'He had no idea where he was or even who he was,' recalls the director. 'Despite the safety net of the cue cards, the opiates and alcohol had disconnected his batteries and blitzed his brain.' Eddie remains bewildered by it all to this day: 'He just couldn't do it. He couldn't do it for his life. We must have gone to thirteen takes.'

Joffe had no option but to summon Geoff Healy, Head of Production for Channel 7, to see for himself. Healy begged Eddie to complete the day's schedule, but, as the director explained, things were out of his control. Everything depended upon the star's condition. Another sequence that afternoon required Hancock to take a shower. He is so tired he drifts out of the bedroom in his pyjamas, the shower is heard, and then he returns, still in his pyjamas, soaked to the skin. Bedraggled and defeated, he was directed through the scene like a puppet, almost oblivious to the repeated drenchings he was suffering in the name of art. The day took its toll on Clare Richardson, who wrote, 'I left the studio and drove home, too weary and bewildered myself to weep either for the swallow or the man.' The shower sequence stands revealed as the perfect metaphor for his physical state, a joke on insomnia turned tragic reminder of the reality of his plight. One recalls those puzzle pictures which alternate between two entirely different visual interpretations: one moment the frail wisp of a girl, the next an ugly, chin-probing hag; sometimes a candlestick in silhouette, at others two profiles immobile in confrontation. It seems to be saying, Who needs masks for comedy *and* tragedy, when one will suffice for both?

The bad omens put out by Hancock's condition had already had one desirable effect in that John Collins was no longer attached to the production, ATN7 having bought out Hancock's contract, which had been held by the Willard King office. This meant that the power to dismiss the comedian now devolved to the broadcaster. There had been little rapport between Hancock and Collins, described by Joffe as 'a short, aggressive wheeler-dealer' not noted for his sensitivity. From the moment things started to go wrong, Tony offloaded the blame onto the Australian, whom he regarded as a con man who had tricked him into making the series under false pretences, as well as the scapegoat for all his troubles. Joffe, who would take over the producer's role in addition to his directorial responsibilities, now found himself advising his superiors that Hancock appeared incapable of completing the series and recommended they abort the production. Discussions were held regarding a possible replacement with Harry H. Corbett as the most obvious choice, but he declined. Milo O'Shea was also considered. No one quite had the courage to tell Tony how terrible the pilot had been. Indecision hung in the air until Monday 29 April when Eddie was summoned into the presence of Rupert Henderson, the Channel 7 Chairman. His description of the man – courteous, slight in build, and just one clothes size this side of elegant – suggests an echo of Billy Marsh. Hancock was never in greater need of the tolerance Marsh would have shown him at such a sensitive time, although it was not immediately forthcoming from the executive. After Eddie had provided him with his version of events, Henderson shot from the hip: 'Fire him.' The director insisted this was not his responsibility and Henderson agreed to wield the axe himself at noon the following day. In the interim Hancock was advised wishfully by Eddie that the only way to save the series would be for him to offer to take the cure. The comedian begged, 'I can't do it, Ed. I've been through this before. It's agony.' The next day Henderson relented and Hancock agreed to enter the Cavell House Private Hospital at Rose Bay at Channel 7's expense without delay. In his compassion, the Chairman was more abrupt than Billy Marsh would ever have been: 'One more drink, mate, and you're on the first bloody plane back to Blighty.' The whole fearsome round of tapering-off measures, drugs and delirium tremens began all over again. There is no truth to reports that Hancock resisted the tapering-off process and proceeded straight to the cold turkey treatment. He spent his forty-fourth birthday in hospital. When he emerged he had shed pounds and looked much older. Like Henderson's, his clothes hung a little too loosely on his frame. He had been in the clinic for three weeks.

A condition of his release was that Tony should not live alone. As a short-term measure he lodged at the home of the Channel 7 company doctor and his family in the suburb of Killara, before moving into a self-contained four-roomed garden flat with views over Royal Sydney Golf Course in the lower level of a large double-storey house set on a hill at 98 Birriga Road, within the upmarket Bellevue Hill area of the city, not far from Bondi Beach. Hancock helped to find the property himself in the company of Myrtle Joffe, Eddie's wife of the time, who by now had come out to join her husband with their three children. It seemed an ideal arrangement for them to live above Tony, with their company and domestic ambience at hand whenever he needed them, without disturbing his privacy at other times. Everyone was willing him to succeed. Both Joffe and Wale testify that henceforth he remained on the wagon until the night he died. He began to learn his lines again, reverting to his old tape-recorder technique, with cue cards standing by only for the psychological boost they gave. With outspoken honesty, Hancock admitted to Wale what nobody needed telling: 'If I don't complete this series, I've had it. I know that.' But he had not lost his sense of humour, once phoning Wale to announce, 'I'm ringing from a pub.' There was an anxious pause before he continued, 'Well, it's the only place where you can have both a telephone call and a pee.' Somehow he found time within his Australian schedule to record local commercials for Ilford film and Cadbury's Nut Milk chocolate. His attitude must have been that if, many miles from home, Steptoe and Son could advertise Ajax cleaner and Warren Mitchell, as Alf Garnett, Heinz soup, why not! He was also clear-minded enough to express certain misgivings to Michael Wale: he was unhappy with the camera system – he had no way of knowing which camera was shooting him, as he would have done in television with lights on the cameras – and at last came to admit that he found recording without an audience difficult. He observed to one Australian magazine, 'Funny though – canned applause sounds like the Hollywood Bowl gone completely mad and genuine applause sounds like three old people tittering at the back of a hall.' He also pined for the camaraderie of the old Duncan Wood days, a golden tradition from which Joffe had been excluded.

The scripts again provided variations of early Galton and Simpson with some clumsy attempts at Jacques Tati thrown in, although when they met in later years Ray and Alan did have the grace to say to Hugh Stuckey, 'We saw all your scripts. They were good. But you wrote for the Tony Hancock we wrote for; by the time he got to you, he wasn't that Tony any more.' Whatever the challenges Stuckey and Wale faced, they would have been no less for Ray and Alan had the trio ever reconvened. Michael Wale was particularly fond of a sequence where a lonely Hancock, unresponsive to the Antipodean sporting ideal, is poised betwixt the two cultures:

> It's the mind, not muscles, that really matters in this world. Socrates, Plato, Aristotle – they didn't play for the All Blacks. We're cast in the same mould. The only difference between us really is that they wore a sheet and I wear a dressing gown. They had no trouble making friends. They always had an eager group of students at their feet as they read out their latest theories. Yes, that's

what I need – my own discussion group. I can see it now, 'The
Hancock Set'. Perhaps a few of my works hand printed. A forum of
prose and poetry. I'll ask round Patrick White, Sid Nolan. In fact,
the whole of Australian culture. That's the best of being intelligent.
You can learn from your mistakes ...

He goes to call a literary society for advice, only to discover that they
have all gone to the football.

Three episodes were completed. When they were edited together into a complete package after his death, those words were – bar
the phone call – the last he spoke as a performer. When a short while
later Roger Hancock viewed the finished product, he immediately
reached for the phone: 'I called Lew Grade and I called Tom Sloan. I
said, "I've just seen this show and I'm ringing to ask you please don't
buy it." And Tom agreed not to and Lew said, "As far as I'm concerned,
it's grave robbery – we won't have anything to do with it."' *The Tony
Hancock Special* – a total misnomer if ever there was – was transmitted in Australia in a ninety-minute slot on 25 January 1972.
Released on video many years later, it makes painful viewing today,
irrespective of the poor technical quality of the picture, which is possibly due to the use of an unauthorised cutting copy. There are odd
flickers of the old Hancock magic, but he does not genuinely sparkle
at any stage. His timing is compromised by the dubbed laughter syndrome. His voice lacks energy. His face seems frozen. An expression
of infinite sadness lingers in the eyes. Nevertheless, Jim Oswin, the
Managing Director of Channel 7, was already thinking about exer-
cising the option for the second run of thirteen.

Hugh Stuckey retains a clear memory of the chain of events. The
rushes for the first three episodes were viewed to favourable reaction
on Monday 24 June, and Hugh recalls fondly, 'I sat next to Hancock at
the screening. He grabbed my leg in sheer enthusiasm and said to me
sotto voce, "I've still got it!"' Everything, of course, has to be seen in the
relative context of his earlier failure. He would never be the old

Hancock again, and no one was fully expecting a permanent cure, but nobody wanted to be reminded of that now. Hugh says, 'There were only brief glimpses of the old Hancock, but it was encouraging to see him on a high.' For Tony things *were* looking up and to have led him to believe otherwise would have been self-defeating. Following the screening, an encouraged Hancock returned to rehearsals for the fourth show, while back in his office Oswin, in the company of several other senior executives, commissioned Stuckey to write the second batch of thirteen episodes. At such an early stage in the first run, it is unlikely that Hancock had even begun to consider the options for further shows. It has been suggested that, had he been aware of the option renewal, the news might have averted his tragedy. But Stuckey is insistent, 'Tony certainly knew that there were an initial thirteen episodes commissioned ... and nearly all of them written ... but I don't know if he knew about the second series. The concept of Tony's knowledge of planned scripts or lack thereof played no part whatsoever in his decision to take his life. The real reason for the suicide was personal. Totally personal.' Of all his colleagues down under, nobody knew him better at a personal level than Stuckey.

Hancock was making a determined effort professionally and health-wise. At about four o'clock on the afternoon of 24 June he returned by taxi to Birriga Road, having declined an invitation to go out to dinner with the Joffes that evening, intending to work at his tape recorder on his lines. He spent an hour or so enjoying a cup of coffee with Myrtle Joffe and making some phone calls before going down to his own apartment. At around 8.30 he knocked on the Joffes' door, ostensibly to return a jar of coffee he had borrowed earlier. Their babysitter, Mary Flod, explained that the Joffes were out with friends. Hancock uttered something about remembering and excused himself, 'I've got to go now.' At seven thirty the next morning, 25 June, Myrtle Joffe gave Hancock his customary wake-up call by banging with a shoe on the floor. Two further attempts failed to bring a response, and at eight fifteen she sent their daughter, Lynn, down to investigate. When the child failed to get an answer at the door, Myrtle followed in her tracks down the steps that extended around the outside of the house. She soon sensed what had happened: 'As I came round the corner I was aware of an aura of death.' She quickly dragged her husband out of bed. Eddie remembers the heat that engulfed him like smog the moment he entered Hancock's room. It was midwinter in Australia and two large industrial electric heaters – on loan from the studios – had been left on at full pelt all night. Then the chill of reality gripped him as he discerned the half-clad body on the bed. Hoping against hope, he attempted to shake Hancock back to life, but the vivid blue eyes staring up at the ceiling told their own story. A cigarette had burned to ash in his left hand; a ballpoint pen clung to the other. An empty flat half-bottle of vodka was at his side. A macabre rainbow of pills and pill bottles lay scattered around. He had used the back of the last two pages of his script for the next show to write two messages in his wiry oblique hand. The first one read:

Dear Eddie

This is quite rational. Please give my love to my mother, but there was nothing left to do. Things seemed to go too wrong too many times.

Tony

The other went:

Ed –

Please send my mother this. I am sorry to cause her any more grief as she has already had enough – but please pass on this message to her – that the soul is indestructible & therefore Bill, who means nothing to you will understand.

Please send her my love as deeply as possible …

The writing gradually loses stability and one struggles in vain to make sense of the last four indecipherable lines that testify to Tony's final moments of consciousness. Eddie does not give the impression of being an overtly sentimental man, but even today tears come to his eyes as he relives the trauma of that morning: 'I just sat on the bed and wept – I could have been there any amount of time – two minutes – ten minutes – being with a dead person – not knowing what to do. Then I phoned his mother: "There's been an accident." There was a pause before she said anything: "He's dead, isn't he?"' In time the official finding would stipulate, 'Died from the effects of poisoning by amylo-barbitone, self-administered whilst affected by alcohol and whilst in a state of severe mental depression.'

In the immediate aftermath of the event nothing was more unsettling than the obscene theatricality of the photograph of his death bed beamed around the world like some prurient peepshow. The Sydney media had a habit of monitoring police calls, and one photographer beat the emergency services to the chase by a whisker. Michael Wale stresses how much Tony, 'a gentle, retiring person at all times', would have hated that intrusion. The insensitivity of much of the subsequent headline coverage was typified by the Sunday tabloid which incorporated a clip from *The Rebel* in its television advertising campaign: 'You're all raving mad. None of you know what you're looking at. You wait till I'm dead. You'll see I was right.' Long ago the essayist Leigh Hunt had written, 'The death of a comic artist is felt more than that of a tragedian. He has sympathised more with us in our everyday feelings, and has given us more amusement … it seems a hard thing upon the comic actor to quench his airiness and vivacity – to stop him in his happy career – to make us think of him, on the sudden, with solemnity – and to miss him for ever … it is something like losing a merry child.' There were times in both his personal and professional life when Hancock might not have been the merriest kid on the block, but his comic legacy had been founded upon a happy and star-struck, if self-sufficient, childhood and that fact alone made the grief for family and close friends no less disturbing. At the inquest on 4 September 1968 the coroner gave his own view: 'Looking at the background and the worries that beset him, one can only admire his fortitude in carrying on his work and giving pleasure and enjoyment to others when he was beset with problems in his own private life ... suicide is not a disease, a crime, or a sin, but a symptom of many different problems, ranging from chronic mental illness to an impulsive solution, or occasionally a more planned solution to a crisis in an individual's life.'

But why? What specific crisis? If things *had* gone wrong *too many times*, what was the final eventuality that sent the whole pile of misfortune tumbling catastrophically to the ground? Or did there descend upon him one apocalyptic flash of insight? The realisation that the glittering prizes of his earlier years had corroded to rust and would be impossible to replace with an inferior version? The brutal fact that for all his talent his personal failings were holding him back from conquering the world? The truth that the comic who denounced pathos was in danger of becoming nothing but pathetic? A Hancock without pride was like an Einstein without genius. And, as he had said to John Freeman, '... if such a time came that I found that I'd come to the end of what I could develop out of my own limited ability ... then I wouldn't want to do it any more'. In *The Drowned and the Saved* the Italian writer and Holocaust survivor Primo Levi, who would later take his own life, indicates that suicide 'allows for a nebula of explanations'. Certainly in Hancock's case, any attempt to rationalise what did happen entails wading through a myriad of evidential details *en route* to a conclusion which in the circumstances has to remain speculative. However, if the process is capable of bringing into focus a potential truth it should be grasped.

Aside from his general malaise at being so far from home, there were several matters that would have given him further cause for depression at this time. He was living under the shadow of a libel action for a statement he had made about the Bernard Delfont

agency in his interview to Gareth Powell for the Australian magazine *Chance*:

> The great Delfont Organisation consists entirely of failed perform-
> ers. Billy Marsh, who is Chairman, was an impressionist for one
> year with Carroll Levis. Keith Devon, who is the next to him, was a
> very bad comic who used to quote a gag of Max Miller's – 'Mr
> Drummer, would you give me a touch of the wire brush. Not too
> much, because I might get to like it.' The brothers are marvellous.
> Bernie, I'll come back to him later. Lew was the Charleston
> Champion of 1928. Leslie didn't do it at all. Glyn Jones was with
> *Casey's Court*.

In fact, he never returned to the subject of Bernie, but there can be
no way that Hancock, carried away by the flippancy of his remarks
as comedians so often are, intended any malice by his words. Indeed,
the accusation of failure was a long-standing joke in show business
circles that applied to many agents and managers, but particularly
to Delfont, another dancer, and his brother Lew Grade, who arguably
with their brother Leslie Grade represented the three most powerful men in British entertainment. When Hancock received notification of the libel threat at the end of May, it specified that his
allegations were defamatory to Michael Sullivan and Sydney Grace,
two other executives within the vast Delfont–Grade empire, whom
he had not mentioned by name. The letter stipulated that the accusation had caused damage to their reputations and demanded an
apology, reserving all rights against Hancock. It was one more thing
to worry about.

On 18 June the Alan Whicker documentary on comedy, bereft of
his contribution, received a repeat transmission in Great Britain. In
his book on his series, Whicker writes, 'I could imagine his rueful,
gloomy acceptance of that last failure, the shrug of those overbur-
dened shoulders at his final dismissal ... *had he ever known about it*.'

The italics are mine. The programme was first transmitted on 20 May 1967 when Hancock was at his lowest London ebb with the disaster of the series *Hancock's* falling around his ears. After recording the interview he had received an official letter from the producer to thank him for his participation, stating that 'it should make an interesting sequence in our programme'. There is no evidence in BBC files that he was formally told he had not made it to the final cut and it remains conceivable that he did not find out until a phone conversation with someone at home at this time disclosed the information. Maybe a rueful shrug was optimistic thinking on his interviewer's part. The title of the Whicker episode carried its own irony: 'If they don't like you, you're dead.' To have discovered that he was now the face on the cutting-room floor would have been yet another reason to be downcast.

Eddie Joffe still retains the $1.67 receipt from the Bottle Department at the Hotel Bondi for the half-bottle of vodka that contributed to Hancock's fate. Astonishingly it bears the date of 25 June, the day on which his body was discovered at breakfast time. The hotel's Bottle Shop stays open to midnight 'for client convenience'. The assumption has to be that in an age before computers did such things automatically, the following day's date had been pre-set on the till in advance. The slip carries no specific time of purchase. The natural supposition is that Tony bought the bottle later in the evening. The hip-pocket option suggests the covertness of his action: a full bottle would have been harder to conceal either on his person or in his rooms. No other bottles were discovered in his apartment other than pill bottles. The walk from Birriga Road to the hotel on Campbell Parade is just over half a mile. But we do not know whether Hancock returned from the hotel intent in a moment of weakness on throwing abstemious caution to the wind or with more drastic intent. He knew full well that the former option was tantamount to killing his career anyway. Henderson's threat to pack him off home on the first available plane would have hammered through his brain on the very first slug and the pills would have provided their own *coup de grâce* in delayed retaliation. Suicide could have been committed with the pills alone, but then who would have deprived him of one final gulp as oblivion set in? Joan Le Mesurier thinks, 'He bought the vodka not to get drunk, but to wash down the pills with the thought "If I'm going to go, I might as well do it with vodka rather than water."' One smiles at the thought of a perverse frugality descending upon him as he realised he would not need a full bottle for the task.

One fact that has not been emphasised in previous accounts is that between settling into Birriga Road a few weeks earlier and the time of his death Hancock had no telephone access in his apartment. Alone in his own space he had no contact with the outside world, able to pick up the phone to his mother, his friends or his lovers as the whim took him. Eddie Joffe states that they had been advised by the telephone company that he would have to wait 'a few weeks' for the service; this meant privileged treatment, since the normal waiting time could be several months. Unable to receive early morning alarm calls, he had opted for the more primitive form of reveille provided by Myrtle Joffe knocking with her shoe overhead. Throughout his time in Australia the telephone had been his lifeline to England. In the preliminary period in Melbourne alone he had clocked up calls to his mother, his mistress and his lawyer to the equivalent of A$1,800, more than £800. In order to make calls from Birriga Road, he had to resort to the Joffes' phone in the main part of the house. On his last day these had been confined to the hour or so he spent with Myrtle Joffe after returning from the studio in the late afternoon. Hancock made no further calls from the Joffes' phone during the period the babysitter was installed in his friends' absence upstairs.

In the press, the greatest speculation inevitably centred upon his supposed unhappiness at the news that on Friday 21 June Freddie had been granted a decree nisi from her husband. When they had gone house-hunting together Hancock had shared his feelings about the matter with Myrtle Joffe: 'He talked a lot about his impending divorce, and he seemed sad about the breakdown of this relationship, but he was not suicidal. He was quite pragmatic about it. I think he felt the breakdown was inevitable.' With greater candour he admitted to her husband that 'he had fallen out of love [with Freddie] in less time than it had taken him to bed her in the first place'. Eddie adds, 'He couldn't stand her. Nor could he explain why he'd married her. He claimed she'd married him for business purposes to enable her to bask in his reflected glory.' He cannot have been upset by the fact that the customary three-year separation period ahead of divorce had been waived on the grounds claimed by Freddie of her 'extreme hardship'. That released him technically from her clutches all the sooner. The matter of the financial settlement would loom, but that was a *sine qua non* of the situation. The amount of £700 per annum in alimony had already been agreed on 29 January 1968 pending hearing of the divorce proceedings and does not seem an excessive amount to pay for an earner of Hancock's capability. The divorce was granted on the grounds of Hancock's adultery with an unspecified woman. The natural conclusion must be that he was now free to marry Le Mesurier at whatever time they could reconcile the matter of his alcoholism and her standing with her current husband. When Eddie Joffe asked Joan why she had not come out to Australia with Tony, she offered the excuse that his solicitors had advised they stay apart to prevent her being cited as co-respondent. Nevertheless, although she was not named in the judge's ruling, she was named in Freddie's petition, having been shadowed by a private detective. But in Hancock's eyes the possibility of getting back together again with Joan had begun to recede into the distance.

During their separation both had derived consolation from John Donne's words, 'More than kisses, letters mingle souls.' In addition to the phone calls sneaked at prearranged times, Hancock wrote regularly and lovingly to Joan from the moment he arrived in Australia. For secrecy's sake the letters were addressed to a Post Office box number, but as his health and professional problems worsened, calls became more difficult and his letters less frequent. Matters were then complicated by an Australian postal strike. Joan concludes that when her last few letters failed to arrive he jumped to the conclusion that their relationship was over. Joan is also convinced that this was confirmed in his mind when he read or had drawn to his attention a front-page article that appeared in the *Sunday Express* naming her as the other woman in the divorce case. Her name had been leaked, and two reporters delivered themselves to her doorstep. She admits that she should have slammed the door shut, but caved in to their questions. When they tackled her on her alleged affair with the comedian she claims she replied, not without some honesty, 'I had a very brief fling a long time ago – it's all over now – I'm back with my husband,' which as far as John and her parents were concerned she was. It is easy to gain the impression from Joan's book and from talking to her that the story appeared in the paper over his last weekend. This is not the case. The piece, headlined 'Mrs Tony Hancock Names Wife of Actor', appeared on the front page of the *Sunday Express* on 12 May – coincidentally his birthday – while he was still at Cavell House, six weeks before the divorce was granted. The article is not at all as hurtful to Tony as Joan remembers it to be. In it she is quoted as follows:

> I really must not talk about it until I have seen my solicitor. I have not seen Tony for a long time. As far as I know he is still in Australia doing a television series. I had no warning at all this was going to happen. I was served papers quite suddenly out of the blue. It is all terribly embarrassing as I am still living with my husband.

The article contains no denial of the relationship whatsoever. Tony would have seen it or been told about it, but it was noncommittal and unlikely to have swayed him to take the view that Le Mesurier no longer harboured feelings for him.

At the end of his life Joan received two last letters from Tony on the same day. Neither was dated. In the first, which was delivered to her box number, he wrote, 'What else is there to say but this? All will be well, just hold on to the fact that we will be together in time.' In the second, obviously written at a later date, enclosed with a letter addressed to Joan's parents, he wrote, 'I loved you more than I thought possible, but now I realise that you never shared that feeling. I now relinquish you to your own life and will forget you in time. You admonished me many times about wasting my life. Now I say the same to you. I shall not brood over you. In a few weeks our relationship will be dead, cold and unremembered.' The letter to her parents, Fred and Ellie Malin, apologised for any distress he had caused in their lives and announced that he would have no further contact with their daughter. It seems one of the worst excesses of fate that he should have concluded that their relationship was over as a direct result of a union dispute. When were postal services ever reliable? But who would have given less consideration to such relative trivialities than Tony Hancock? He was obviously convinced somehow that she had abandoned him. On the other hand it may have been the sheer irrationality of the man that changed his attitude towards her.

According to Joan's version of events, upon reading his second letter during his last weekend she realised she had to make contact with Tony. Matters were complicated by her being in Ramsgate without privacy from her family, so she waited until her return to London on the Sunday, where she contacted the studios, the only number she had. Sunday evening in England meant Monday morning in Sydney and, although no one knew it then, time was running out fast. He may have received a message that Joan had called. She was told he was in rehearsal, which he was. Among the calls he made from the Joffe home early that Monday evening was one to his mother. Two weeks after her son's death – on a cruise ship in the vicinity of Naples – Lily wrote to Eddie Joffe to thank him for his condolences and explained how her son had called her early that evening – morning in England – to tell her of his new address and to announce he would be having his own phone installed, at which point he could phone her more often. Six weeks later she wrote to Eddie again, this time mentioning that 'when he phoned me he seemed so happy'. That seems at odds with the major drift of the conversation that Joan claims Lily had with her son, conveyed to her by her own mother, Ellie Malin. It emerges that Tony had just tried to call Joan, but had been unable to reach her. He seemed anxious to speak to her to make up. 'She will come back to me, won't she?' he had asked his mother. 'Of course, she will,' Lily said. He asked her to make contact with Joan's mother as part of a roundabout way of getting Joan to call him. She complied with the request, only to be told by Ellie Malin in Ramsgate that the Hancock chapter of Joan's life was closed and, wrongly, that Joan was in Rome with John. This message was conveyed back to him by Lily. He may have rung her back for the information. One has to ask why the apparent change in his feelings towards Joan should happen at this point.

However, Hugh Stuckey is convinced that this scenario was not the key factor in precipitating his decision. The writer insists that throughout his time in Australia, right up until that last day, Hancock had 'hung on to some romantic vision of his first wife'. He suggests that the comedian's final call that evening was a plea to Cicely to take him back: 'She refused. That was the moment.' The refusal to get back together is verified by her sister, Doreen. Away from the convolutions of the Le Mesurier scenario, this last spoken encounter has a welcome and obvious simplicity. But I do not believe it was simply a matter of Cicely's rejection; in her likely alcoholic state she was probably too confused to provide Tony with a rational answer. As Damaris Hayman has said, 'He felt he had been instrumental in destroying her.' In his current sobriety he may have sensed this more painfully than at any time before, and the guilt came flooding back. In his attempt to solve the conundrum of suicide, Primo Levi offered as one explanation the idea that 'suicide is born from a feeling of guilt that no punishment has attenuated'. Hancock had no need to feel guilty over Joan and in his own eyes no need to feel guilty over Freddie. Cicely was the exception, and in a moment of dark despair he exercised the need to punish himself. A call from Hancock to his first wife at this time is alluded to by Wilmut, while in an interview for the *People* newspaper the second Sunday after his death Cicely revealed that Hancock had been seeing her about once a week after the split with Freddie: 'We would talk about the old times and he asked me three times if I would marry him again … I told him to wait until the divorce [from Freddie] came through.' She was wearing his diamond ring and said, 'I loved Tony – and I think he still loved me.' In the same edition of the newspaper his last chauffeur, Gerry Gray, revealed how Hancock had been subsidising her own drying-out treatments: 'He used to try to raise her spirits up when she was feeling low. He used to stick his jaw out and tell her, "You've got to fight it."' Their continued closeness was also confirmed by their mutual friend Stan Gibbons, who was around when Hancock proposed just before his departure overseas. Upon her death in January 1969 he told the *Sun*, 'She told Tony she wanted to be absolutely sure first that he was ready to marry again. But Cicely told me later it was her dearest wish to be reunited with him and she never recovered from his death.' The divorce was now a reality. A conversation was in order. Somehow a last unfulfilled dream turned to dust as they spoke. Whatever her emotional state at the time and whatever she said later, maybe Cicely saw the impossibility of their situation. Maybe Hancock saw it too.

There are so many imponderables. Why did he bother to return the jar of coffee? If he was expecting to see the Joffes, did he have one last phone call in mind? The babysitter remembered how sad and disappointed he looked. Possibly the disappointment of not finding Eddie and Myrtle at home cued the walk to the hotel, where presumably he would have been able to make further calls. Eddie Joffe conjectured that Hancock's attempt to find them upstairs may have been to solicit help with his tape recorder. When his body was discovered, the tape had spooled right off the machine. With no one to help him over a possible technical hitch, he then opted out of life in fear that his subsequent inability to learn his lines for the following day would have suggested he was drinking again. It seems a flimsy reason in the context of the larger 'nebula of explanations'. It is far more likely that the machine was running when he died and that the tape spooled off afterwards. Eddie even wondered if Tony had left a message on the tape. No words of relevance were ever found.

The mention of 'Bill' in his second note inevitably raised the matter of Hancock's religious beliefs. It may have been no more than a consoling gesture to his mother without deep spiritual significance. However, in spite of the scepticism Tony shared with Joan about the worst ectoplasmic excesses of the sham spiritualist trade, she recalls occasions when he used to imagine he was in spiritual touch with his deceased brother and address her as if he were Colin: 'And he was saying, "You know, he always was a trouble, always a trial, but I know he loves you." I don't know whether he was faking it, but the tears were falling down. He was talking to me as if Colin were talking through him. And at other times his father too. "Look after him," his dad would say. "He's a good man. He needs help."' Joan does admit he had been drinking heavily. All those close to him in Australia – Eddie, Hugh, Michael Wale – as well as his surviving brother refuse to countenance claims that he consulted a medium a few days before his death. George Fairweather may have had a different view. At the time Hancock received notification of his inclusion in the Royal Variety Performance in 1952, he expressed sadness to his friend that his father would not be there to see him on the big night. George, a religious man, replied, 'Don't you think he will be?' to which Tony responded, 'Oh don't give me that rubbish. The only spirits come out of bottles.' Nothing more was said on the matter. A few weeks after Hancock died, Fairweather received a letter. There was no address, no full signature. In it the sender explained that he had been sitting in meditation when he heard what was clearly Hancock's voice coming through. It said, 'I thought the only spirits came out of bottles and I am one now ... tell anyone I love that I'm not blotted out and will see them all again one day.' The writer, who identified himself or herself as 'K R – a believer', asked for the message to be passed on to anyone who might derive comfort from it, but that it should not be used for publicity purposes. George assured me that he had never told anyone about their conversation in 1952, adding 'It shook me rigid when I kept looking at it.'

At the risk of courting 'Auld Lang Syne' sentimentality, one notes several instances that took on the guise of intimations of mortality upon his death. A few days earlier he had written out of the blue to Max Bygraves to thank him for the advice he had given him when he played the London Palladium. On that last day, Spike Milligan was surprised to receive a call. Hancock appeared to be in a jubilant mood about the Australian project, confirming Stuckey's opinion that what happened later was not out of professional considerations: 'He said, "It's wonderful here – I've got a great series coming up – you must see it."' That day also saw Phyllis Rounce passing through Sydney with her client Rolf Harris. Hancock had pleaded with her on the telephone to meet up with him at an earlier stage of Rolf's tour, but the logistics stood in the way. On that last day again she tried to make telephone contact, but failed. Rolf remembers flying with her from Sydney to Vancouver as the news of his death came through: 'She was distraught. To be so close and not to have been able to do anything must have been awful.' The view was echoed by John Freeman: 'When I read of his death I was absolutely aghast. I was extremely surprised and left with a feeling of very great guilt that I who had at least had some opportunity perhaps to spot this a little bit ahead had not done so. I was surprised. Many of my friends are unhappy, but not very many kill themselves.'

For all the resilience and determination he had shown in his professional life, most of those (his family excepted) who had known him longest – Fairweather, Sykes, Milligan, Simpson, Vertue, Oakes, James, Kerr – were not unduly surprised when he decided to call it quits with life. Ray Galton was more resigned than most: 'I expected to see it every day when I opened a newspaper – every day for years – I really did. I couldn't imagine him tolerating such an existence, being from up here to down there. He was a proud man.' His old agent Stanley Dale recalled that after the inquest on Hancock's stepfather, who took his own life in 1959, he confided to him, 'That will happen to me one day.' Fellow comedian Charlie Drake recalled that two years earlier after a drinking session with Hancock he turned to him and asked, 'What do you feel about committing suicide?' Drake replied, 'What do you mean, together?' Hancock said, 'Yes.' 'I'll have another drink first,' joked Charlie. 'We've done it all, haven't we?' reasoned Hancock. Drake insisted Tony was serious: 'He wanted out of the game. He was totally lonely, even with people.' The incident occurred as early as December 1957, after they had recorded the *Pantomania* show together. Hancock was only thirty-three, Drake a year younger; one thinks of the two old tramps in *Waiting for Godot*, regretting they have missed the chance: 'We should have thought of it when the world was young ... hand in hand from the top of the Eiffel Tower, among the first.' He had often discussed the subject with Damaris Hayman and according to the actress knew perfectly well that it didn't get you anywhere, 'which was why I was so distraught when he actually died, because I wondered and wondered if there was anything I could have done, anything I could have said which would have stayed with him and stopped it, but there wasn't. It was just despair, like the Giant Despair in *The Pilgrim's Progress* who attempts to get the travellers to commit suicide.' But this traveller had no key in his possession to extract himself from the dungeon of Doubting Castle to the Delectable Mountains on the other side. According to his mother, his doctor in England said that he was never suicidal, otherwise he would not have entrusted him with so many sleeping tablets. But what else would he have said?

The shock was much greater to those who were part of his latest routine. Hugh Stuckey was always convinced that Hancock's end would come accidentally one day when he set fire to himself in bed, while Eddie Joffe is adamant that 'there had been nothing about Tony's behaviour at any time to suggest to me or anyone else working with him in Australia that suicide was remotely possible'. One night he discussed the subject with Myrtle Joffe, but only in general terms. Leaning on the mantelpiece he slipped into his Long John Silver impression and chortled, 'Aaahh, Jim lad, them's what threaten never does it!' According to Myrtle, 'Suicide certainly wasn't anywhere on the horizon, and there was no indication that he might even be thinking of it. His whole demeanour had improved.' Back in England he had voiced a similar sentiment to Joan: 'He'd mentioned the number of attempts Freddie had made and we'd be walking along the cliff at Broadstairs and he'd always be picking places for her to jump off. "She wouldn't get it wrong if she jumped off here," he'd say. He added, "If ever I wanted to do that, I'd get it right. I'd do it once. You don't *try* to kill yourself. If you want to kill yourself you do it."' He lived up to his word.

Back in Barons Court Joan was awakened in the early hours by her husband with the news. Her anger at Tony for taking what she saw as a coward's way out was soon transferred to John for being the one who survived. Little did she realise in her demented state that his grief was as great as hers: 'There was almost a sense in which we shared him in a way – shared the affection we had for him. When Tony was under sedation in various nursing homes, I would go to see John to talk to him about it and he could not have been more sympathetic and understanding. He was completely on Tony's side in some funny way. He loved him. He really loved him.' One can only begin to guess at the true tensions and undercurrents of the triangle they represented. On one occasion when she had popped in to see John on some domestic matter, he begged to go back to see Tony with her: 'I said, "He'll be terribly embarrassed because he's so ashamed," but I took a chance. And they were both so polite and sat there and talked. Tony was mortified, ashamed really of what he'd done, and when John left he said, "Why did you do that?" and I said, "He wanted to see you. He misses you."'

Suicide is not an obvious subject for comedy, but it is perhaps inevitable that like so much else in Hancock's life it should have been reflected in his work. As a boy he may well have been introduced to the concept in his favourite film, Chaplin's *City Lights*. The idea of throwing oneself into the deep – an attempt thwarted by Charlie, when the millionaire jumps – recurred, courtesy of Eric Sykes, in Hancock's first television series, when as a frustrated orchestral conductor he threatened to hurl himself off the Thames Embankment. The idea came up again years later in *The Rebel* when his aspiring artist is agonising about past failures: 'I've had my moments of doubt, wondering whether I've got anything to offer. I've stood on Westminster Bridge looking down at the dark, swirling waters. I jumped once.' 'What happened?' asks a colleague. 'I woke up in a barge full of wood on my way to Southend.' Galton and Simpson brought comedy to bathos again in the television episode, *The Tycoon*, where the lad is poised to jump from a great height: 'I've made up me mind. All the talking in the world won't stop me. Anyhow, I've thought it over and decided this way is best for everybody … well I mean what's the point of carrying on in the circumstances? I mean look at it from my point of view – there's nothing left for me to live for, is there? No, there's no more to be said.' For a brief second Sid turns aside from his paper: 'Oh, come in and put the kettle on.' 'Oh, all right,' says Tony. He no longer has the guts to go through with it. That is the one detail his writers did not subconsciously predict. One watches the television episode where he nurses a cold and is struck by the sheer morbidity of it. No comedian could have made a *Half Hour* script dedicated to the ending of his life as funny as Hancock could have done. As the drama critic Eric Bentley commented, Samuel Beckett was able to rid himself of his despair, if only temporarily, by expressing it in his work. Hancock embodied the irony that as the prime purveyor of despair in comedy he failed to get the process to work as a form of catharsis for himself.

Whatever single personal factor caused Hancock to teeter over the brink, his demise was no less attributable to the headlong rush to self-destruction, for which his career provided its own template. Had his career still been flourishing, it might well have provided the mattress to cushion the fall of any private disappointment. For all the outward professional optimism he displayed to Hugh Stuckey in the Channel 7 viewing theatre, he must have seen that reality was catching up with him. Roger Hancock is convinced that whatever personal issues were involved, his brother's decision was not divorced from work considerations: 'Nothing is cut and dried. The most important thing in his life was his work and he *must* have known it was all going terribly wrong. We'll never know. My instinct is that he did it instinctively at that moment.' Hancock was not the first to be destroyed by the demands of his profession, the inexorable job of coaxing laughter from an anonymous audience that may by turns be inscrutable, belligerent, bloody-minded and itself drunk. Within the British variety tradition, where Hancock won his spurs, the roll call embraces music-hall veteran Mark – 'I Do Like to be Beside the Seaside' – Sheridan; eccentric comedian T.E. Dunville; the wittiest of magicians, Peter Waring; and Hancock's fellow tutor at the *Educating Archie* academy, Robert Moreton. Dan Leno, Marie Lloyd, Tommy Handley, Sid Field – all at one time among the nation's favourites – may not have administered their own demise, but had lives shortened by the pressures of fame. The previous year, Jerry Desmonde, straight man to Field, had taken a lethal combination of alcohol and sleeping tablets, a fact that would not have escaped Hancock's attention.

One has to confront the cliché question. If the demands of the profession are so high, why do it? No one better summed up the vocation of the comedian than Bob Monkhouse, when, speaking from experience, he said, 'The need to hear laughter and know that you are the cause of it, that's a delight to almost every child. The desire to repeat that experience *ad infinitum* is the driving force behind the comedian's ambition, notwithstanding the risks of rejection and failure.' Driven by the need to seek an unattainable perfection and too frail to carry the burden of a talent he never properly understood, Hancock tried and tried to refine his career until his own resilience and the inner resources that might have seen him through snapped. His perfectionism became addictive and legendary in turn, but he never accepted that the precision one might demand from a brain surgeon was not a prerequisite of his own calling. Duncan Wood said, 'He never knew when he was at his peak. He always thought there was one step more to be taken, and this is where you had to step in as a director and say, "That's it … there isn't any more to be got out of this script."' According to Valerie James, Hancock gave himself little time to enjoy his success: 'After a recording he never allowed himself to remain elated for long, before he started to worry about the following week's show.' In 1962 he himself admitted, 'I have been called the Great Worrier – nothing I have yet done has been good enough for me. After every performance there is an inquest – a post-mortem on what went wrong – and it is usually about two hours before I can relax again.' Moreover, as Galton and Simpson distilled his real-life thoughts and foibles into the most expansively idiosyncratic of recent British comic heroes, there must have been times when he felt cheated out of his real identity. When he went on the run from that character, he was in effect running from himself. However amusing he could be in private life, as a performer he was totally dependent on a script. Had he been his own best scribe, like Milligan, John Cleese or Barry Humphries, this story may well have had a different ending. Eric Sykes had done his best to offer advice: 'I used to say, "Don't try to analyse it. Humour is unfathomable. It either happens or it doesn't." Unfortunately, he took it so seriously that he tried to make comedy add up like a column of figures, but it is not an exact thing.' The American humorist Robert Benchley once wrote, 'All laughter is merely a compensatory reflex to take the place of sneezing,' but Hancock would never have seen the joke.

On the cold grey morning of Friday 28 June, the day he should have been recording the fourth episode of his series, 150 mourners – mainly admirers and television colleagues – gathered at St Martin's Church in Killara to pay their respects. The reading was taken from Chapter 13 of St Paul's First Epistle to the Corinthians: 'For now we see through a glass, darkly; but then face to face. Now I know in part; but then shall I know even as also I am known.' They were pertinent words for a man who had tried to explain to John Freeman that for himself comedy represented a distorted mirror in which could be seen our true selves and not least those human characteristics one despised, even feared. In his address Jim Oswin, the Managing Director of Channel 7, declared:

> He had a modesty and humility that made him particularly vulner-
> able. All of us need love. Fortunately many of us are able to cope
> with this need in times of stress because of an inbuilt confidence in
> ourselves – but Tony lacked this ability. He could not love himself.
> Modesty and humility made him more dependent than most of us
> on the love of other people. The wonderful thing was that everybody
> did love him – instantly. He was one of the quiet small band who
> have the ability to inspire laughter – surely the most attractive and
> rarest quality of all.

His body was cremated that weekend. On Thursday 18 July his mother and brother led the mourners at a memorial service at St Martin in the Fields, Trafalgar Square. Cicely and Freddie were both present. The Le Mesuriers did not attend. It was a low-key affair by show business standards. John Freeman read the lesson and the Reverend Lord Soper gave an address in which he said the obvious things, but with none of the insight into character that Oswin had displayed.

On 1 July his remains were brought back to London by the humorist and cartoonist Willie Rushton. Hancock would have loved the idea that Willie carried his urn in an Air France bag. At the beginning of his decline, Rushton had penned the *Private Eye* cartoon that had caused him so much grief. That was forgotten when a few days before the tragedy the pair enjoyed a convivial evening at a Sydney restaurant, united by their shared passion for cricket. When Rushton, who was travelling economy, told the air crew he was returning with Tony's ashes, they insisted they should travel first class, on an unoccupied seat just behind the pilot's cabin. The night he died Michael Wale had been lying awake listening to England skittling out Australia at Lords and thinking that Hancock also would be tuned into his transistor sharing his relish at the triumph. Although Australia drew level with England that series, there was something singularly appropriate to Roger, Willie, Michael and all lovers of the game that *his* 'Ashes' should be returning in this way. They were eventually interred alongside the boundary wall in the grounds of Saint Dunstan's Church, Cranford Park, near to his brother's home, where his mother's remains joined him before the end of the following year.

According to probate published on 10 December 1968, Hancock left an estate of £32,559 gross, £18,702 net, of which duty payable was £3,156. Even for those days it appears a modest amount by superstar standards. Eddie Joffe estimates that in the time since he had known Joan intimately he had endured no less than sixteen detoxification attempts. When he was not lining the pockets of psychiatrists and the other members of the drying-out profession, the legal fees attendant upon two divorce cases, his generous support of his mother and his addiction to international telephone calls all drained his resources. His mother inherited his entire estate, which included the income from future residuals, which one day with ever more sophisticated mechanical reproduction methods would prove considerable. Cicely, who would die before affairs were settled, does not appear to have made any claim on the estate, but Freddie Ross, who technically remained Mrs Hancock since no decree absolute had yet been granted, brought an action in the High Court in which she sought 'reasonable provision' for herself. The hearing was delayed from November 1969 until February 1970, after Lily herself passed away on 8 November, leaving her son Roger as her sole beneficiary and likewise the sole beneficiary of his brother's estate in turn. In words that must have stung from the other side of the grave, Mr Justice Buckley indicated that Hancock owed his wife 'a moral obligation of a very high order' because of the disruption the marriage had caused to her business, social and domestic life. Freddie was awarded £11,500, £5,000 less than her counsel had suggested to the court. It has been suggested that, having left his estate to his mother in his will, Hancock timed his suicide to ensure that his assets accrued to her rather than get swallowed up in a divorce settlement. As we have seen, an arrangement for alimony had been settled in advance. Since the death of her third husband, Lily had come to rely more and more on her elder son. On her death she left an estate of £7,896 gross, £7,273 net.

He died at the age of forty-four, the time in life when Will Hay was just about to make the first of his twenty films. He had completed his best work by the time he was thirty-eight, the age at which Sid Field broke into the big time of the West End and one year younger than Jacques Tati when he began to commit his first masterpiece, *Jour de Fête*, to celluloid. The one redeeming feature of his tragedy is the stark reality that he most probably did not have long to live anyhow. According to Eddie Joffe, he was beginning to have problems with his bodily functions. As the director went through the comedian's belongings he discovered a small airline bag packed full of pills of every size and colour: 'Barbiturates, benzodiazepines, Antabuse, sodium amytal, you name it.' He'd once joked to Hugh

Stuckey, 'There isn't a doctor in the world who'd refuse a prescription from Tony Hancock.' Eddie also draws attention to a research study published by the medical profession in 1997, which stated that the more often a person has dried out and then relapsed, the more likely he is to have incurred brain damage. But Roger Hancock had sensed the worst long ago, even if he had not known specifically that brain cells destroyed by excessive drinking cannot be replaced. As the American poet Gerald Locklin once wrote, 'What's cirrhosis of the liver but suicide on the instalment plan?' When in October 1965 Michael Dean asked Hancock whether he had a major regret about his life or career, he took a sip from his cigarette W.H. Auden-style and replied, 'I don't think so – not at all – no. I think you just – it's like life – you play it by ear and you have no choice anyway.' Choice was a line crossed long ago. He could have stopped, but in Locklin's words:

> *... you don't stop, you don't stop*
> *for the same reason that you started in*
> *the first place, because without it you'd be*
> *insane or the quicker kind of dead.*

Locklin had probably never heard of Tony Hancock. His poem is entitled, 'judy garland is dead'. It amounts to the same. Amazingly she would survive him by a year. Quite simply, they had both used themselves up. As Philip Oakes admitted, we had all taken him for granted: 'We said "genius" and left it at that,' ignoring what it took beneath the surface to keep us enthralled. Eddie Joffe has never recovered from the shock of that June morning. There is nothing he could have done to change things, but that does not lighten the load he still bears: 'He killed himself in *my* home. That's been with me for forty years. To me he was an idol. I'm not ashamed of the fact that I loved the man.' All those who worshipped Tony Hancock can take comfort from the courage he must have mustered at that final moment when in death all his hopes and expectations came crashing against the realities of life. As Woody Allen said, 'It's not that I'm afraid to die. I just don't want to be there when it happens.' Hancock chose not to avoid the fact.

Chapter Sixteen

'WHAT WAS HE *REALLY* LIKE?'

'To read some of the things that have been written about me, you would take me for a near suicide. But if I give the impression of being morose, it is only because I am so deeply absorbed in my work.'

There can be no single answer. The question will reverberate as long as celebrity thrives, the one admission by a star-struck public that on the other side of appearances a more honest reality lies. The question is even more intricate in the case of Tony Hancock, given the extent to which his true self overlapped the image that defined him at the peak of his success. The sculptor Antony Gormley was generalising when he said, 'Our faces belong more to others than they do to ourselves,' but no comedian ever felt the weight of that ownership more heavily than Hancock, or ran faster to escape it when he thought he could. The single characteristic we all share is that we are all far more complex than we are willing to acknowledge. This was reflected in Hancock's on-screen persona more vividly than in those of his comedy contemporaries and must account for a large part of his comic appeal. Meanwhile in private Hancock embodied as many contradictions and inconsistencies as the next person. He could be moody and morose, remote and introspective. He could also be magnanimous and endearing, receptive to humour and as funny offstage as on, qualities which won him continuing loyalty among the majority of those who found themselves divorced from playing a key role in his career.

Some were privileged to see the varying sides to his character in quick succession, like Angela Ince, writing in *London Life* magazine: 'When he is bored or disinterested he switches off his eyes – they go blank and grey and solid and there is nobody there. Then he lights up again and he is suddenly a blue-eyed schoolboy who has just bowled Garry Sobers out, or an executive making a phone call, or a boxer flooring an opponent.' Michael Grade too observed the contrast: 'Just occasionally, the mist would clear and it was as though a bright light had gone on inside him; he would radiate charm, wit and ebullience.' For Damaris Hayman there was the vast gulf between 'the sheer fun that he could be when he was happy and the desperate desire to help him that one had when he wasn't'. Allowances always had to be made for his preoccupation with work. He owned up to this himself when with black humour he contemplated his achievements in 1962:

Somehow I seem to have acquired the reputation of being an acute melancholic. In fact, to read some of the things that have been written about me, you would take me for a near suicide. But if I give the impression of being morose, it is only because I am so deeply absorbed in my work. Once I concentrate on the job in hand, I am lost to the world.

Hayman noted the distance he would keep at rehearsals, but perfectly understood why: 'At lunch breaks Tony would retreat into his own foreign country. One didn't go and chat to him, but it was nothing personal. One would be in a pub and Tony would buy you a drink, but he wouldn't come down and consume it with you. It was sent over.' Bill Kerr equally understood when, in referring to his moods, he said, 'I like to think of him as one of the saddest and happiest men I've ever met. When he was on top there was nobody like him in the world, and when he was down you just understood.' For all his faults and venialities – and certainly in the period before alcohol exerted its ugly hold on his behaviour – he had a quality that seems to have made it impossible for people to dislike him.

Galton and Simpson relax with beaming smiles as they recall the laughter they shared together and refuse to admit that the man they knew was morose at all. According to Ray, 'You couldn't ask for a greater audience. At the first read-through if Tony found something funny he'd be rolling on the floor. It would be good for us because we had driven to the studio anxious whether he'd like it at all.' He attempts the Hancock laugh, not as loud as Bill's, as dirty as Sid's or as camp as Williams's, but a deep infectious chortle as he hugs himself into a ball of contentment, 'Oh dear, oh dear, oh dear.' Beryl Vertue provides a privileged snapshot of the man on holiday in the South of France playing poker for matchsticks in a favourite café: 'It was one of those rare occasions I remember being hysterical with laughter, he was so funny. Ray was doing particularly well and had a lot of matches. Tony didn't have any. He would look at Ray and in a very posh voice would say, "Mr Galton, I wonder if you could see your way clear to financing a little project." It was a happy time. I remember it with great fondness.' Hugh Lloyd remembered equally jolly times when Hancock would visit him at home to play 'Pick Up Sticks', a game requiring the steadiest of hands as you attempt to separate individual sticks from a haphazard pile without disturbing the rest: 'How he could ever do it with his hands I do not know, but he used to absolutely love trying to do it.' Lloyd also recollected the habit he had when enjoying himself of flinging his head back and laughing: 'Once during rehearsals for *The Reunion Party* he laughed so much he threw his head back and disappeared off the end of the backless sofa, much to Duncan Wood's consternation.'

Research for a volume of this kind provides its own anthology of what made its subject laugh. A stray line could tickle him into paroxysms of mirth, whether from a Will Hay movie or from a respected rival. In *The Wrong Box* Peter Sellers played a dubious and decrepit doctor destroyed by drink: 'I wasn't always as you see me now. In the old days the sick and the groggy would come to me from miles around.' For days afterwards Hancock went around clutching his sides at the thought: 'Oh dear, the sick and the groggy.' When he discovered that Snoopy, his favourite cartoon character, was suffering from 'rejection-slip shock', having had his book sent back to him, he went into a similar obsession with the new phrase. He loved to quote Arthur Miller's reply when asked if he was going to attend Marilyn Monroe's funeral: 'Why? Will she be there?' At a similar level of life and death, Derek Scott recalled the epitaph they both chuckled over long after it became known to them: 'Here lies the body of William Barker, spent his life as a billiards marker – he's gone to the long rest.' Away from words, he also responded to the absurdity to be found in life itself. Ray Galton recalls the occasion he found himself nudging Alan and Tony to take a peep at a fellow standing behind them in a pub. Ray remembers, 'He was wearing a big turtleneck sweater right up to his chin and he had a hole cut in it out of which came this big tie. Tony looked and spilled his drink. He had to leave the pub. He was in hysterics.' In a not dissimilar vein, Cicely told Philip Oakes of the time they were entertained to tea by the Lord Mayor of Blackpool, who was immensely proud of his cocked hat with all its plumes. He said, 'Look, I'll just try it on for you,' and started striding up and down the room. The Hancocks sat there and duly said all the correct things until the Lady Mayoress chirped in with, 'Aye, but he does look a bloody fool when it rains.' At which point Tony, hardly able to restrain his laughter, hurriedly made excuses to leave.

His sense of mischief revealed itself in an early habit he shared with Larry Stephens and Spike Milligan of frequenting a particular café in Chalk Farm, purely for the pleasure of hearing himself say, 'We'd like three boiled rice with three raspberry jams, please.' Once ordered, the desserts were disregarded. The fun had been had. The trouble Hancock would take in order to achieve a comic effect was recalled by Patrick Cargill, in the aftermath of their decision to meet up with one another on their overlapping holidays in the South of

France. The arrangement was made some months in advance. Cargill arrived at a very elegant rendezvous to be greeted by Cicely without Hancock. A drink or two later the actor heard a familiar voice and looked up to see Tony advancing towards them: 'There he was – dressed in a pair of sandals, grey flannel trousers rolled up to the knee, a white shirt, braces and a belt with a knotted handkerchief on his head. For somebody to remember to do a gag like that some three months after was just wonderful. He was a marvellous man.' Only the bucket and spade were missing. Michael Wale recalls how Hancock's love for trivia could carry him away, with hilarious results. While in India he discovered a surgeon who had experimented in drilling holes in the tops of people's heads. Hancock explained, 'When he'd bored the hole he'd put a cork in it. Then whenever the person was feeling depressed and wanted a bit of a lift all he had to do was pull the cork out for a few moments and he'd feel fantastic … the only snag with the operation is that you always have to wear a hat.' Serious so far, Hancock then collapsed into a fit of giggles. The surgical procedure known as trepanning had been known since Neolithic times; for Hancock it represented a half-truth crying out for comic exaggeration. Even in the extremes of alcohol-fuelled marital discord, his comedian's instinct was never disconnected completely. As Freddie poured a bottle of brandy over him in disgust, he retorted, 'Usually I take a spot of soda with it.' A few years later when he tried to mollify Joan with a bouquet of roses, she laid into him with the flowers until they disintegrated. To all intents and purposes it might have been the same joke, cleverly reworked: 'Stone me. I'm glad I didn't try to win you over with a bottle of champagne.'

His love of laughter extended to the open support of many of his contemporaries, a not too common trait in the front-line battle of comedy for a nation's affections. As Joan Le Mesurier has remarked, 'He was always so generous in his praise of other performers and so hard on himself.' On *The Laughtermakers* radio tribute to himself in 1956, Hancock lavished praise on Frankie Howerd, 'a great natural

comic clown – it's his wonderful observation that makes you laugh';
on Al Read, 'there you get marvellous turn of phrase – my normal
reaction on hearing him is "Why didn't I think of that first?" He covers every type of humour. There's no barrier of class or intelligence';
and most notably Peter Ustinov, 'to my mind he is the greatest we
have in Britain by far – his radio programme, *In All Directions*, was
the nearest thing to perfection I've ever heard on air'. He admired the
ease with which Ustinov could conjure up all of mankind with a word
and a gesture and still remain a wholly private person throughout.
In this way the aspirations of the younger Hancock stood defined by
the achievements of others. Like Ustinov, who once described himself as the perennial wallflower, Hancock hated the whole idea of
being the centre of attention in a pub or at a party. Patrick Cargill
remembered how he was content to sit back and listen to the anecdotes of others: 'And all this time his eyes would be wandering
around and you could see he was observing various characters ... and
probably just by observing somebody adding another fraction to the
character he'd created.' He discussed his Tati-like obsession with
human behaviour with Joan Le Mesurier: 'He was a great listener
and used to hang on to every word. If I'd been down the road and seen
something really funny, he'd want to know all about it and his little
eyes would light up. He used to say, "It's people that are funny, not
me."'

Philip Oakes admitted how much of Hancock's life was spent in
searching for the perfect anecdote Ustinov-style that he could stow
away 'until its perspectives had somehow become rooted in his own
experience ... only then would he bring it out, not just as a funny story, but as an illustration of his own point of view; a peephole through
which he saw the world'. Very often his own take on a subject was far
funnier than the raw material, *vide* the subject of trepanning.
Memories from old variety days, of absurdist speciality acts and theatrical landladies from hell, always an excuse for a good time among
pros, fell into this category. One of his favourite stories concerned the

day he returned to his digs with a fresh chicken and presented it to the landlady with the query, 'Would you cut this up, mince it and boil it for four hours.' 'Oh yes, Mr Hancock,' cringed the woman. 'Yes,' muttered Hancock as he snatched back the bird. 'I thought you bloody well would.' Another echo of music-hall lore was provided by Sir Ralph Richardson, who introduced Hancock to his party *pièce de résistance*, an impersonation of Little Tich, the diminutive comedian whose acrobatic dance in his elongated boots provided one of the defining images of the traditional genre. Hancock would explain that he was going to leave the room and once outside knock on the door. When he did so, everyone was to ask, 'Who's there?' To which Hancock would reply, 'Little Tich,' and everybody had to shout, 'Come in, Little Tich.' When the door was opened Hancock was no longer there, or at least not at full height. He was now on his knees in homage to the tiny superstar. When he worked the routine on Eddie Joffe and his writers in his Sydney hotel room he had just emerged from the shower with a towel around his waist. By the time he walked back into the room on his knees the towel had been lost and for one night only Little Tich appeared naked as the day he was born. Hancock had a special empathy with Richardson, another giant of his profession who had been slated by the critics, and would tell the tale of how somebody overheard the actor in the wings ruminating on the situation: 'I had a little talent once. But I think I've lost it. I think I'll put an advertisement in *The Times* to say, "A little talent lost. If found, please return to Ralph Richardson."'

Meanwhile, the reverence Hancock showed for his own comic heroes remained passionate, extending at times to evangelistic defence. When on *Open House* in 1964 Gay Byrne asked him to name his 'favourite man of comedy', he replied without hesitation, 'without a doubt at the moment – Jack Benny'. After an uncomfortable pause, Byrne rather patronisingly referred to the choice as 'rather unusual – I didn't expect you to say that'. Tony's somewhat curt, 'Why not?' said everything. When Byrne suggests Benny might be regarded as 'sort of *passé*', Hancock's incredulity cannot be contained, although his response remained dignified, in keeping with the man they were discussing: 'This man is a *great* comedian. They are rare.' The moment set an uneasy tone for what remained of the interview, but Hancock had made his point. If Jack Benny with all his technique, his gift for characterisation, his star quality and his humanity did not qualify, then the lad from East Cheam or Earl's Court or wherever was a non-starter. In the interview he gave to *Chance* magazine in Australia a short while before his death, he was asked more specifically to nominate the giant of English comedy during his formative years between the wars. He remained loyal to Max Miller, the man who first defined for him the concept of a true comic identity: 'To come on and say, "Good evening, I'm a commercial traveller and I'm ready for bed," is not a bad opening line. This was a very kind man. He was very much underwritten. He did charity privately, which was never known. And so he died. And everybody said he was very mean. He wasn't, though. He was terribly funny ... the greatest front-cloth comic we've ever had.'

For Hancock money was never an end in itself – except for the freedom it gave him to do what he wanted in his career, in other words the ability to say 'No' to projects in which he had no interest. He seldom carried cash on his person and proved an incorrigible borrower, invariably owing money to every member of the crew from the producer all the way down to the floor assistant, although, as Philip Oakes noted, this did not stop anyone from being prepared to go the extra mile on any Hancock project. Not long after he arrived in England from Australia, Rolf Harris landed a small role in a *Hancock's Half Hour* television show. He remembers a flustered Hancock arriving late at rehearsals, 'larger than life, with his overcoat draped over his shoulders like a cape'. 'Can somebody lend me ten bob to fix up this taxi?' asked Tony. 'Sure,' said the obliging young performer, as he proffered the requisite note. Hancock took it without a word. 'That's the last you'll see of that,' said Sid James out of the side of his mouth. Alec Bregonzi waited three years before the star paid him £3 in expenses incurred when he performed in the budgerigar sketch for the 1958 Royal Variety Performance. Bregonzi would have been happy to waive the sum for the 'honour'; Rolf never saw his 10s. again. Bill Cotton, who often subsidised Hancock's lunch to the tune of 5s. in the BBC canteen, commented, 'I don't think he was mean in the traditional sense. I just think he was forgetful. There were other more important things on his mind.' According to Stanley Dale, 'He would walk two miles in the rain to save a twopenny bus fare, but this was the man who would never pass a busker in the street without slipping him a pound.' Likewise, with a sneaky regard for anyone who could outwit the system, he could never resist a con man with the chutzpah to break through every last reserve of thrift and prudence. He once walked out of a West End hairdressing salon clutching an elaborate ivory hairbrush for which he had no need. It cost him £12. Tony declared the sales pitch had been worth every penny. John Muir agrees with Cotton that Hancock was far from mean *per se*, and could in fact be an especially generous host both at home and in restaurants: 'In my experience, he never let you pay for anything, unlike, say, Tommy Cooper who was chronically mean.' There were times when he simply loathed the physical act of parting from his earnings, as if it were tantamount to cancelling out the time and toil invested during his earlier years to acquire his wealth in the first place. Roger Hancock remembers how difficult it was to get his brother to sign a cheque in the early Adelphi days, when he looked after his accounts for him: 'You had to pick your moment and that moment might come over a period of five or six days before you could say, "Oh, could you sign this – just get this out of the way," because he'd go, "No, I don't want to sign it now."' Like so many comedians who came through hard times as part of their graduation process he lived in fear of penury. Seeing Stan Laurel almost on his uppers in America only reinforced the dread. 'And he doesn't get a penny for any of the repeats,' agonised Hancock. 'There he is, poor bugger; another genius who got screwed.'

After his death Cicely Hancock announced of her late ex-husband, 'He supported me entirely since we parted. There was never any haggling over money between us. Tony was never one for agreements and contracts and things like that. If he made a promise he always kept it. He was always more than generous with his money.' Much of that generosity was kept from public gaze and even went unknown to the beneficiary. In the early 1950s Clive Dunn was about to present a concert party for the summer season in Southwold when Tony approached him with the request that he take on his brother, Roger, who wasn't long out of school, as an assistant stage manager. Clive put the matter to the theatre management, only to discover there were no surplus funds available, at which point Tony said, 'Don't worry. I'll give you the money, but don't tell Roger.' Hancock paid the £12 a week to the management, and only in recent years has Roger discovered his brother's kindness. 'I'm glad Clive didn't tell me at the time,' he says. 'The reason he did it was to find out if I was really that serious about it – that was the underlying thing, and that was lovely, I thought.' A different kind of generosity by stealth was exercised towards Warren Mitchell, on the occasion the actor covered for Hancock when he forgot his lines on live television; as a result Warren acquired his first substantial press coverage, a half-page article in the *Daily Mirror* heralding 'television's new bearded comedian'. Mitchell recalls, 'It wasn't until months later that someone at the BBC said, "That was nice of Tony, wasn't it?" When I asked what he meant, the guy told me that Hancock had come down to the office and said it was about time that I got a bit of publicity because I was doing so well in the show.' He was also capable of acts of considerable thoughtfulness on sheer impulse, as when he discovered a nearby hospital lacked the funds to purchase a cine-projector for the children's ward and decided immediately to donate his own, throwing in a personal gift for each child in the ward as well. After his death a doctor, who was one of his closest friends, revealed that at Christmas at the height of his fame Hancock would ask him for a list of disadvantaged people and would call on them with food parcels which he made up himself. Many of them, not having television, would have had no idea who he was.

After his marriage to Freddie fell apart, Hancock employed Mary Jacobs as his daily help and housekeeper. Mary, a kindly soul in her early seventies who would sleep at the flat when he'd had too much to drink to be left alone, described him as 'the most wonderful man in the world – he was so kind and good, I won't hear a word against him'. When her mother died she begged to be excused from her duties for the day to travel by Green Line coach to Tonbridge to arrange the funeral. Hancock told her to sit down and have a cup of tea while he made a phone call. She recalled, 'About half an hour later he said, "Come on, Mary. It's ready." I said, "What?" and he said, "Go downstairs and see." I went down and there was this beautiful car good enough for a queen and this chauffeur came up to me in a proper uniform. I had the car all day and it never cost me a penny. I shall never forget it. When I showed him the letter from the police telling me about my mother, he put his arm round me and cried on my shoulder.' Gerry Gray, his own chauffeur in those later years, recalled how he sent his wife two dozen red roses to cheer her up when she had a stomach upset. 'He would always try to be considerate,' remembered Gray. 'He'd tell me if he didn't want me for three or four hours. He had some very, very good points until he got on to the bottle … that was why I stuck with him.' A glimpse of the compassionate Hancock was also seen by Lyn Took when she lost a baby in the spring of 1967: 'He wanted to come to see me, although I remember telling my mother, "I hope he doesn't." I didn't want to see anybody then except Barry and my mother. On the other hand it was good to be reminded that he cared, that he had that soft side.'

He may well have mellowed over the years. In the early 1950s, after meeting a group of members of the Archie Andrews fan club,

Peter Brough thanked him: 'It was nice of you to be so patient with that little boy. He really loved meeting you.' Hancock was not so sure: 'Before, I was an idol to him. Now I'm just an ordinary bloke.' In those days Hancock, oblivious of the impression the variety stars of the 1930s had made in person on *him* as a boy, had his sights set on a stardom that was by definition out of reach to mere mortals. Fifteen years later on his flight to Hong Kong he was confronted by a seven-year-old boy intent on introducing him to his closest friend. 'My teddy bear's called Tony,' he said. 'In that case,' responded Hancock, 'we had better make it official,' as he took his pen and wrote a signed message on the bear's vest. As they disembarked, Hancock asked the boy, 'Is your bear really called Tony?' 'No, but he is now,' came the reply. From grudging behaviour to spontaneous gesture, Hancock probably never connected the two incidents. It cannot be argued that in the eyes of two small boys his kindness – far from 'ordinary' – probably raised him to heroic status on a line with the gods. Freddie Hancock says it was an incident involving older fans, who insisted on addressing him as 'Tone', that triggered the one time she saw him lose his temper. Lyn Took recalls his aversion to the practice, but reminds us that he was capable of laughing at himself at the same time: 'I remember joking with him on one occasion, "Oh, come on, Tone." He absolutely hated "Tone" and I did it to needle him. And because I was joking and because I was young, he thought "That's OK." And every time I said it, we would both laugh. He never minded. He took it as a joke. He never got angry or upset about it. It was fun. It was all right.'

Steve Martin has written with some dismay about the expectation of having to live in public the figure he represented onstage, haunted by a 'freakish celebrity aura' and the syndrome whereby every conversation degenerates into an autograph request for some distant relative. Hancock had been there before him, feeling like public property whenever he heard his name hailed 'like a taxi'. One day he was crossing Kensington Gore with Bill Kerr and

Kenneth Williams when a bus drew up in his path and the driver jumped out yelling, 'Tony, hoy, Tony.' The traffic was brought to a standstill as he bombarded the comedian with bonhomie: 'You're great, mate. You're great. I'm going to shake your hand. You've given me more laughs than anybody else.' As Hancock protested above the sound of honking motor horns, the burly guy got hold of him and hoisted him into the driver's seat. When other people saw who it was, anger turned to delight and they emerged from their cars to shake his hand too. Eventually the three comics extricated themselves from the embarrassment and reached the sanctuary of Hancock's flat, where Williams admitted he was impressed by the adoration Hancock inspired in people. 'Yes,' said Hancock. 'But it's the money that worries me. Look at the vast sums they're paying me and think what that bus driver gets.' His brother stresses that he was a shy man and that any kind of recognition was greeted with difficulty. Hancock glossed over the matter with Gay Byrne on *Open House* in 1964, making the right noises about the inevitable consequences of achieving fame, though drawing the line at fans who ask for your signature on bare flesh. Oakes revealed that he had a particular dread of being spiked 'like a pickled onion at a cocktail party'. Parties represented a particular *bête noire* when people approached him 'to do funny things'. In those circumstances, he admitted to Byrne, he had a particular riposte that always did the trick: 'I say, "Ooh, excuse me. I'm terribly sorry. I have a bad leg. I hurt it in a crash." So it's easy.' With a limp he would hobble away into the night.

Away from the cameras and the footlights Hancock flaunted none of the flamboyancy of show business, denouncing the jargon and eschewing the company of the phoneys that proliferate in the industry. And when he did make an effort to play the publicity game, he often got it wrong, as on the occasion he and Sid were invited to a West End première of a cowboy movie with the request that they arrive suitably attired. Hancock went to great efforts to acquire authentic costumes, only for the couple to arrive at the cinema a week early to the disbelief of the regular filmgoers. All his friends emphasise there was nothing big time in his attitude at all. It is so easy to imagine every single move he made offstage, every merest thing he said, being overlaid with the pomposity and bumptiousness that were writ so large within his comedy character. Phyllis Rounce stressed, 'He wasn't big-headed at all, ever. Difficult, but not big-headed. But only as difficult as you'd expect an artist to be to get it right. He never got a big head because he was always fearful for his success, frightened the audience might not laugh.' He was happiest when he could dress down and loved to cultivate a look half way between untidy and raffish. Philip Oakes remembered, 'He borrowed a sweater of mine which was cashmere and beautiful and cost a fortune and he wore it once and it was as if a camel had inhabited it – I couldn't wear it ever again.' The raffishness extended to his eating and drinking habits: 'He fancied himself as a wine expert. He wasn't particularly an expert, but he was an enthusiast and liked a particularly robust red wine called Échézeaux, which he said you'll never forget because it sounds like a sneeze.'

In the manner of his *Rebel* characterisation, the tendency to cultivate untidiness connected to his intellectual leanings. However, the interest he cultivated in the philosophers should not overshadow his admiration for a wider range of authors that embraced the archaeologist Leonard Cottrell – Hancock once said that in another life he would have chosen to have been an archaeologist or geologist, 'a job where you can trace things back to their origins' – and the great North American humorists, who formed a substantial part of a one-off forty-minute radio programme he made for Christmas Day transmission in 1964, his last substantial contribution to the medium. Apart from introducing some favourite gramophone recordings and interviewing – perhaps under pressure from his public relations representative – the racing driver Stirling Moss, he read from Stephen Leacock's digression on 'Winter Pastimes', with specific reference during the season for party games to his invention of 'Indoor Football' or 'Football without a Ball':

> In this game any number of players, from fifteen to thirty, seat themselves in a heap on any one player, usually the player next to the dealer. They then challenge him to get up, while one player stands with a stop-watch in his hand and counts forty seconds. Should the first player fail to rise before forty seconds are counted, the player with the watch declares him suffocated.

He also narrated the same author's 'The Conjuror's Revenge', in which the prestidigitator gains his comeuppance on the know-it-all 'Quick Man' in the audience, who pipes up with an explanation after every miracle:

> Ladies and gentlemen, you will observe that I have, with this gentleman's permission, broken his watch, burnt his collar, smashed his spectacles, and danced on his hat. If he will give me the further permission to paint green stripes on his overcoat, or to tie his suspenders in a knot, I shall be delighted to entertain you. If not, the performance is at an end.

James Thurber was represented by 'The Unicorn in the Garden'. Triumphant males were rarities in Thurber's world, but in this fable the husband, who espies a unicorn eating roses, is consigned to the police and a psychiatrist by his disbelieving wife:

> 'Did you tell your wife you saw a unicorn?' asked the police. 'Of course not,' said the husband. 'The unicorn is a mythical beast.' 'That's all we wanted to know,' said the psychiatrist. 'Take her away. I'm sorry, sir, but your wife is as crazy as a jay bird.' So they took her away, cursing and screaming, and shut her up in an institution. The husband lived happily ever after.

Throughout the forty minutes he makes no attempt to slip into the pompous, aggressive character that found a home on the airwaves during the previous decade. On the one hand the programme is totally engaging, in that it reveals that the man himself has won the right to our company and vice versa; on the other it is disappointing in that the readings cry out for some form of dramatisation with Tony at their core. The conjuror sketch shrieks for enactment by Hancock and Kenneth Williams in his Snide character; the Thurber interlude shows there would have been no better person to enact the trials and tribulations of the Thurber male than Hancock himself. The difference is all in the projection. In the manner of *Face to Face*, the recording is further evidence of the disparity between his stage persona and his quieter, more modest self. One recalls Harry Secombe's words, 'I found him gentle and self-mocking.'

With musical contributions from Carmen McRae, Count Basie, Caterina Valente, Judy Garland and alto saxophonist Johnny Hodges playing with Duke Ellington, *'Ancock's Anthology* acted as counterpoint to his selection of eight gramophone records for *Desert Island Discs* seven years earlier on 5 August 1957. Only Judy Garland with 'The Man That Got Away' and, from France, Mouloudji, singing his 'Un jour tu verras' from the film *Secrets d'Alcove* figured in both selections. Most significant alongside his choice of Rossini ('The Thieving Magpie'), Franck ('Symphonic Variations'), Sibelius ('The Swan of Tuonela'), and flamenco guitar music from Pepe de Almeria ('Soleares') were 'Migraine Melody' from David Rose and his Orchestra and 'Gloomy Sunday' from Artie Shaw and his Band. He dedicated the first to 'anyone who has ever been to a very good party and this, shall we say, is the following morning'. The second was more contentious. Written in 1933 and made popular many years later by Billie Holliday, it had been dubbed the 'Hungarian suicide song' in the United States after unsubstantiated rumours that it had inspired many suicides, although it is fact that its composer, Rezsö Seress, took his own life by jumping out of a window, hauntingly in the same year that Hancock took his own. Presenter Roy Plomley was not known for questioning the choices of his guests, but on this occasion was moved to state, 'Well, it's all a matter of taste – I don't honestly think I'd have that among my own eight Desert Island Discs.' 'No?' 'I find it a bit gloomy.' 'Ah, well,' sighed Hancock. This was eight months before the idea of a gloomy Sunday had taken on comic significance within Hancock's radio canon. In spite of the absence of electricity on the island, Hancock chose a television set as his luxury. The choice of a book did not then apply. Significantly, unless one includes 'Gloomy Sunday', true jazz was not acknowledged until the *'Ancock's Anthology* show. As he once confided to John Le Mesurier, 'You have got to have suffered to appreciate jazz.' Fortunately he did have a happier streak of musical appreciation. Philip Oakes tells us that he also liked brass bands and male voice choirs and Rimsky-Korsakov, while Damaris Hayman vouches for the fact that in his latter years nothing was more guaranteed to lift his spirits than Noël Coward singing his rousing saga of 'Uncle Harry', the story of a would-be missionary who falls from grace on a South Sea isle where there were enough sensual distractions to render television sets obsolete.

His friends might have expressed surprise at Hancock's ability to operate a gramophone in the first place. He was hopelessly inept with all mechanical contrivances, which to those who knew him intimately made sequences like that provided by *The Radio Ham* all the funnier. Of course, his ineptitude as a driver became legendary. Valerie James recalls the momentous day he was driving through Hyde Park, stopped the car and, recognising he was a danger to himself and others, walked away: 'He found the nearest telephone, called Cicely to collect it, and never drove again.' Electric razors had the same bewildering effect on him as gearboxes and steering wheels. When they were working on the script of *The Punch and Judy Man* together, Philip Oakes came to the repair of just one of several that had given up working on Hancock. 'I had a look and pressed a button,' recalled the writer. 'It sprang open and six months' compressed hair flew out. He'd never thought of cleaning it.' Once when he was staying in the Maharajah Suite at the Mayfair Hotel, John Muir and Eric Geen arrived at the door to discover the comedian in his dressing gown distraught in pitch darkness. 'When you think of all the flippin' money I'm paying for this suite and the lights don't even work,' moaned Hancock. Muir made contact with the hotel switchboard to get somebody sent up to fix things. In a short while an electrician arrived, walked in, flicked the switch on the wall and the lights came on again. As the poor man left, Hancock was heard to mutter, 'All right, but don't let it happen again.'

Eddie Joffe has a wonderful vision of Hancock as a Victorian transposed magically to the technological age. His inability in real life to cope with car doors and lifts was such that he always seemed to exit into advancing traffic or to proceed in the wrong direction from the sliding doors. His fear of flying probably owed as much to a lack of any understanding of aeronautics as to his fanciful theory that the commanding Dan Dare figure of a captain who patrolled the aisle prior to take-off was speedily substituted by an inferior mortal the moment he entered the flight deck, so that he could quickly move on to perform the same ritual in the next plane in line for take-off. Dave Mills, the drummer with The Temperance Seven jazz band, recalls sharing a flight with Tony from Spain around the time he made the egg commercials. They had to change planes at Orly, but Hancock was in such a paranoid state he refused to get on board again for the second leg to London. While the rest of the band went ahead, Mills stayed to look after the man he'd admired since childhood. Eventually, with the help of BEA officials, he managed to get him on board the next flight, but Hancock was little short of delirious, protesting, 'We're not going to crash, are we? I can't swim.' Dave insists that in no way was this put on for comic effect. When they were back at Heathrow, a becalmed Hancock insisted that his chauffeur drive Dave all the way home to Southend.

In Hancock the qualities of modesty and humility that Jim Oswin drew attention to in his funeral address are the easiest to overlook, precisely because they were not part of his theatrical persona. As Philip Oakes has said, 'He had no side, no snobbery about him whatsoever.' In tribute to his friend, Frankie Howerd added, 'You're never touched by a phoney. That's what made Tony so great … even his tragedies were real. He was lost in an emotional jungle. He couldn't get out.' When Hancock was resident at the Adelphi Theatre, a supposed retired army major used to haunt backstage with a special line in whisky, then generally in short supply. You could take the standard Johnny Walker Black Label at £5 a bottle on the black market, or the more exotic Night Rider at £8. Hancock found the latter vile, but urged all self-proclaimed experts to subscribe. He reasoned that if they bought it without trusting their taste buds, they deserved to be bilked. He detested the hypocrisy of the counterfeit liquor connoisseur as much as he loathed airs and graces of any kind. It is demonstrably not true that television can easily spot a phoney – the airwaves are polluted by them – but viewers have always reserved a special place for the individual capable of rising above that mire where so-called celebrities grow rampant like bindweed. The ravages of alcohol could never erode the genuineness of the man and for this reason his public never gave up on willing him to succeed. In the same way, however infuriating and intolerable and exasperating he could be, he kept his key friends to the end. George Fairweather summed him up better than most: 'He only had to say, "You know me!" He was a lovable character. You couldn't be cross with him. You really couldn't. He was like a child in so many ways. He was a great, great chap with a lovely sense of humour. I loved him.' To which Damaris Hayman adds her own footnote: 'If he liked you, you could do nothing wrong. If he didn't, God help you.' To quote Frankie Howerd one last time, 'There wasn't a speck of phoniness in his whole body.'

Epilogue

'FUNNY AND SAD'

'I've been criticised quite a lot because I try to move on.
And the British public, though very loyal in many ways,
are very resilient to change. But comedy is such a fascinating
art that you cannot stay static and just collect the cheque.'

How, one wonders, would Hancock regard the continuing interest in his work and the affection that persists towards him some forty years after his death? The laughter aside, his one great legacy is an enduring suspicion of the world, a point of view of even greater value today when Orwell's fast-approaching worst fears are the stuff of television ratings and the anonymity of communication and commerce is encouraged by the e-culture. When in 1962 the journalist Ray Nunn questioned him on the matter of what he might want to leave behind after his death, he replied, 'To look for immortality? Yes, I suppose almost everybody does ... but I see myself as a small speck on this spinning world. Who cares what I leave behind? Life for me never gets anything less than more interesting as every day passes. That is all I care about.' Better that he should have been incredulous of his position in history in the first place than that he should have dismissed its reality as shallow and insincere, a paper moon in a flimsy Barnum and Bailey world.

The tragedy of the Hancock story did not end with his own demise. On 11 January 1969 Cicely Janet Elspeth Hancock died at the age of thirty-eight following a fall down the stairs at her South

Godstone cottage. Her two beloved poodles were by her side. Heart failure – maybe literally a broken heart – and chronic alcoholism were given as the cause of death on the death certificate. The inquest revealed she had sustained the latter condition for four years. The net value of her estate amounted to £9,657. On 8 November that same year Lucie Lilian Sennett died of cervical cancer at the age of seventy-nine. The last years of her life had been additionally saddened by the death of her prospective fourth husband. For others in the story there was a happier outcome. After several years Hancock's second wife established a demand for her public relations skills in New York, where she still resides. In 2002 Freddie Ross Hancock was awarded the MBE in recognition of her services to 'UK–US cultural understanding'. Joan Le Mesurier lived in contentment with her husband, John, until he died in 1983 and flourishes still in her elegant, beloved Ramsgate home. Sid James, like all the other familiar faces who supported him in his heyday, went on to show that he did not need Hancock and confirmed his own stature as a comedy icon, best measured by his inclusion as the only professional funny man among the fifty faces chosen to define the essence of Britain in the Self Portrait Zone of the Millennium Dome. Only Sid, as a South African, could have pulled that one off, but no one argued. Few performers of any kind have ever achieved a greater feel-good factor with their public. Sadly he died eight years after Hancock, at the tragically early age of sixty-two, after collapsing on stage on 26 April before a first-night audience at Sunderland's Empire Theatre. Today the only survivors of the resident radio teams are Andrée Melly and Bill Kerr. Dennis Main Wilson and Duncan Wood, arguably the two best producers a British comedian ever had, died within ten days of each other in January 1997. George Fairweather closed the doors of his hairdressing salon opposite the Pavilion Theatre on 31 December 1985 and would share his memories of Hancock for another fourteen years until his death in 1999. Philip Oakes succumbed to a heart attack on 18 December 2005, having written on a Christmas card,

'May your Christmas be full of friends and booze and no shocks.' Hancock would have loved the irony.

Ray Galton and Alan Simpson continue to enjoy the fruits of a career that flourished beyond Hancock into Steptoe and points beyond, epitomised by performers who appreciated their work for both television and the cinema as diverse as Frankie Howerd, Les Dawson, Leonard Rossiter, Peter Sellers and Lionel Jeffries. An attempt to rework their Hancock scripts with Arthur Lowe and James Beck from *Dad's Army* as Hancock and Sid respectively was forestalled by Beck's death in 1973. A later attempt in the 1990s featuring Paul Merton in the role of his hero proved less than successful, the casting overlooking the acting skills of Hancock and the extra dimension he brought to the words. Nevertheless, Merton's efforts were affectionate and sincere, as was shown in the re-enactment of *The Bedsitter*, where the observant viewer might have spotted a Homburg hat and an astrakhan-collared coat hanging inconspicuously on a coat stand in a corner by the door. Many years before in the *Laughtermakers* programme, Alan had said, 'A script written for Tony would be virtually useless for any other comic. A gag comic could get laughs from a script written for another gag comic, but Tony's material is completely individual. He has a definite style of his own.' Notwithstanding, over the years Ray and Alan's written Hancock legacy has undergone successful translation for France, Germany and particularly Norway, where the Hancock character, known as Fleksnes, is applauded for being so in tune with the Scandinavian spirit, as proved by its success throughout Denmark and the whole Scandinavian peninsula.

Watching at home during his twilight years, Hancock would spare no invective for comedians whom he claimed stole his mannerisms, of whom the chief offender was perceived to be the bullying and unsympathetic Terry Scott, who co-starred in *Hugh and I* with Hugh Lloyd, a partner who was far too good for him and looked upon by Hancock as one of his own. In later life, however, Tony learned to take inverted pride in the fact that had it not been for him *Steptoe and Son* would not have existed. Far beyond that, the combined influence of Galton, Simpson and Hancock on British television comedy has proved incalculable, extending the boundaries of popular comedy series to embrace actors as well as comedians. With the support of their producers, they brought to British screens a naturalistic style and narrative strength that proved a standard bearer for, in chronological order, shows as diverse as *Till Death Us Do Part*, *Porridge*, *Rising Damp*, *Fawlty Towers*, *Yes Minister*, *Only Fools and Horses*, *One Foot in the Grave* and *Knowing Me, Knowing You … With Alan Partridge*. All focused upon mavericks of self-delusion and exaggerated behaviour set against the conformist background of society with Hancock as their patron saint. Graham Stark speaks for many when he says, 'It's hard to watch television comedy today – a lot of nose picking and jokes about condoms. But to have a wonderful fruity sort of Dickensian man like Tony Hancock appear? Well, there aren't any. When you see stuff today you realise just how amazing he was.'

Of course there are exceptions. Forty years on, Hancock's closest heir apparent within British comedy would appear to be Ricky Gervais, specifically in his creation of David Brent, the self-important branch manager in *The Office*, whose foibles in Slough are derided in the way that Hancock's once were in East Cheam, right down to the habit of performing hackneyed impersonations whenever the mood takes him. It is not difficult to imagine Brent donating blood, attempting to respond to a Mayday signal or getting up the nose of those suffering alongside him in a trapped lift, irrespective of the *faux*-documentary style in which the programme was shot. It is significant that Gervais pulled the ejector cord on this initial success after only two series and a couple of specials, in order to reinvent himself in the character of Andy Millman in the similarly successful *Extras*. Set in the self-deluding world of the film and television industry, at times it comes even closer to the Hancock spirit as it explores themes of desperation, frustration and fame. In his lifetime

Hancock achieved two Comedian of the Year awards within the television industry. Success as a comedian came later to Gervais, who today at the age of forty-seven can boast three Golden Globes, two Emmies and seven Bafta awards, all won in the last seven years. At a time when the international media marketplace is thoroughly understood, Gervais, whose contribution to his own scripts is acknowledged by a writing credit, has been hailed as both a celebrity and a success in America, where both series have been shown and *The Office* has been reworked in a local version.

One can only surmise what Hancock, whose gift for characterisation has a depth that Gervais can only aspire to, might have achieved with a clear head and with greater flexibility on both his part and that of the BBC, had the media climate of fifty years ago allowed him to discuss other creative options in addition to *Hancock's Half Hour*. One also wonders whether his East Cheam character would have proved as restrictive had it been given a name that was not Hancock's own; and had Hancock himself been granted the ability to compartmentalise his talent in the manner of, say, David Jason or Ronnie Barker. Either side of the law he would have made a quirky Inspector Frost and an intriguing Norman Fletcher. Sadly nobody thought laterally enough. There was so much he could have done. He would have been an effective Rumpole of the Bailey, a natural for the Theatre of the Absurd, not to mention a magnificently mediocre Archie Rice. John Osborne wrote that he was inspired to write *The Entertainer* after watching the 'awesome banality' of a variety impersonator at the Chelsea Palace performing an impression of Charles Laughton as Quasimodo that was 'bad, direct and immediate'. Hancock pulled off that trick every night he stepped on a stage, but deliberately so. His only problem with the Osborne play would have been learning the lines. There would have been no cue cards or tele-prompters at the Old Vic.

As for the quintessential Hancock, had he been able to surmount his health problems and emerge with his original talent intact,

Spike Milligan had it all worked out long before he died. The opening shot would show Hancock leaving the labour exchange in his Homburg hat and astrakhan-collared coat. He arrives at Galton and Simpson's office and rings the bell: 'Just thought I'd give you lads another chance. Let bygones be bygones. All this *Steptoe and Son* stuff – there's nothing in it.' With Hancock's gift for self-mockery, it could have worked, had his personal pride allowed. Seven years on from his last solo series would have been the optimum time for some form of comeback. Frankie Howerd's career had dipped over a similar time span and then come bouncing back with a vengeance. Eric Sykes's situation comedy featuring himself and Hattie Jacques benefited from being rested for a similar period. Even *Steptoe and Son* resurfaced recharged after a slightly shorter gap. Ray Galton and Alan Simpson may have been daunted by the prospect, but concede that had Hancock been in the same mental and physical condition he was in at his peak, he would still have been the 'top man'. Ironically with *Steptoe and Son* in hiatus, the BBC may well have welcomed the return and, according to Valerie James, had even intimated as much to Sid, who regardless of his own star status would have gone back to partner his old friend with no prompting at all. But it was not to be.

Although Hancock faltered the moment he let Galton and Simpson slip through his clutches, he should, in fairness, elicit some admiration for wanting to expand his horizons creatively. The actor Kenneth Griffith, who had provided him with memorable support in one of the better episodes from the ATV series, equated what he perceived as Hancock's courage and spirit of adventure with the decision by Picasso to move from his blue to rose, or his African to Cubist period: 'There was this refusal to accept that what he had achieved was the very best. He would not stay still. He wanted to go on creating and perhaps now and again he created something that wasn't quite as good, but he had the will, the indestructible will to create.' Hancock saw the premise of continuity for continuity's sake as a false god as far as his professional life was concerned. As he tried to explain to David Frost in 1967, in an echo of the interview he had given to Alan Whicker the same day, 'I've been criticised quite a lot because I try to move on. And the British public, though very loyal in many ways, are very resilient to change. But comedy is such a fascinating art that you cannot stay static and just collect the cheque.' But what his public expected had little to do with art or ambition. It simply demanded a readiness to be seen over and over again in the same situations wearing the same mask. Part of the symbolism of the theatrical term 'star' is that the heavenly kind do on the face of it remain unchanging.

It was also valid that admiring them as he did Hancock should wish to follow the path to international acceptance achieved by W.C. Fields, Jack Benny, Jacques Tati, Laurel and Hardy and Chaplin. He shares with Charlie the distinct honour of being the only British comedian who remains instantly identifiable in any context from his surname alone, perhaps because no performer of the British television era has come closer to achieving Chaplin's grasp of the human condition in the cause of comedy. Both learned and polished their technique and cultivated their versatility in the rough and tumble of variety entertainment where the cornerstone of their act was to guy the industry that sustained them: long before Hancock had parodied the standard fare of the tired impressionist and the concert party entertainer, Charlie, under the aegis of the impresario Fred Karno, had been the featured performer in a sketch based on a run-down music-hall show called *Mumming Birds*. Similarly, long before television gave 'captive audience' a new meaning for Hancock, Chaplin's fame was built upon that very phrase, as week after week his regular public assembled in their local movie palaces to see the numerous short films he made before he progressed to features. It has been reported that Hancock detested Chaplin for his pathos. On the contrary, he admired him for his attitude towards it: 'I get mad when I hear people talk about Chaplin's pathos. Why, he fights like a tiger and doesn't scruple to kick a tramp in the stomach.' Hancock loved to recall the scene in *City Lights* when Charlie is in the Rolls Royce, gets out of the car, does just that to the tramp, picks up his cigar butt and drives off: 'Nowadays you would probably be advised not to do it. Only the great could get away with it.' Chaplin understood that pathos worked best when it was underpinned by irreverence, and Hancock may have received his first lesson in the technique when as a boy he watched the early scene in which the blind flower-seller unknowingly douses Charlie with water. The romance of the situation and the slapstick are totally dependent upon each other for their mutual impact. That Hancock had this capability was shown in the episode of *The Reunion Party*, where he attempts to recapture the magic of his youth and fails, confronted by the pale shadows that are his service colleagues of twenty years before. But then there was never a time when the definitive Hancock was not desperately trying to hold onto a belief system upon which the sun was slowly setting.

Paradoxically, while Hancock's stature diminished in the fading years of his life, it has recovered to full strength since his death. His legacy – untainted by the *déjà vu* of nostalgia and out of all proportion to the short time in which it was built – lives on as if it happened only yesterday, principally in the episodes of his radio and television series that have survived and through that 'echo of remembered laughter' that extends away from mere situations into the attitudes and vocal inflections that Hancock brought to being Hancock. As recently as 2007 reruns of his egg commercials were banned for breaching healthy eating guidelines more than forty years after they were made, testimony both to his own reputation and the glaring need for a Hancock to tilt at the windmills of modern frustration. If he were with us today he would be battling with jargon-speak, the internet, the sexual revolution, reality television (while fancying himself on it), recycling (with Sid insisting the planet is doomed anyway), not to mention the food warnings that confront us daily in the press. Concerned for his carbon footprint and the decline of the BBC, he might well consider standing for No. 10, with Sid as his spin doctor, as well as in charge of party funding and the honours system.

Asked in 1966 what he would do if he were offered an official award in the honours list, Hancock replied, 'Refuse it. I don't want to be rewarded. I'm a practising comedian. I'm in it and I love it. I want to make the people laugh, and as long as that happens, that's enough reward.' He would surely have wrapped up in those last two words the remark of the Queen Mother when, according to Valerie James, she confided to Tony and Sid, 'You are so popular in our house, we all stop in when *Hancock's Half Hour* comes on.' Since his death a controversial statue has been installed in his native Birmingham, while in 2002 a poll to coincide with the launch of BBC7, the digital radio channel specialising in archive comedy and drama, placed him in first position as Britain's funniest man. There is a danger, however, that statues to funny men and the polls that categorise them may be in danger of overkill to the point of trivialising those who truly deserve them. Recognising the rebel in himself, he may have got the greatest satisfaction from being included in a re-creation for *The Times* of the Peter Blake cover design for *Sgt Pepper's Lonely Hearts Club Band* to mark the record album's fortieth anniversary in 2007. It is puzzling why he never made it to the original. Max Miller, Tommy Handley, W.C. Fields and Laurel and Hardy, of course, did. In a similar vein legends from different cultures have immortalised him. Pete Doherty, the troubled lead singer of Babyshambles, who was born more than a decade after Hancock's death, is among them. *Up the Bracket*, the title of the début album of his former band, The Libertines, derives from Hancock 'I'll fetch you a punch up the bracket' vernacular. Just before the comedian's death, J.B. Priestley published his novel, *London End*, featuring a paranoid funny man by the name of Lon Bracton, self-confessedly modelled on Hancock. Tony would have taken greater delight in the 1975 fantasy novella for children by his friend, the Dalek creator, Terry Nation. *Rebecca's World* features another alter ego for the comedian, the character of Mr Grisby, 'who has the most painful feet in the universe ... he wasn't very cheerful, but at least he was friendly'.

As we approach the end of our story, we should pause to remind ourselves that the tragedy that befell Tony Hancock clouded the last few years of a twenty-one-year career, during the larger part of which he enjoyed fame as a household name in the country of his birth. Moreover, right up until the final curtain he never surrendered the fight, never wrote himself off, however desperate some of the steps he took may have appeared. At a time when the word 'genius' is hawked around with indiscriminate abandon, one treads carefully for fear of tainting Hancock with such banality. However, it would be disingenuous to offer that as an excuse to forgo in this context the words applied by Max Beerbohm to Dan Leno, the comedian who started the whole personality cult of the funny man: 'Only mediocrity can be trusted to be always at its best. Genius must always have lapses proportionate to its triumphs.' Hancock fully understood that you cannot have real comedy without a sense of sadness. He implied to John Freeman that it came with the job description: 'I think [the world] consists of two things, both funny and sad, which seem to me to be the two basic ingredients of good comedy.' He frequently declared that comedy was pain, and was happy to suffer for his art. As we know, every night on stage he tolerated the indignity of being stamped hard on the foot in his 'Crooner' routine. He used to say, 'A little stamp doesn't get the right effect. They've got to see me really suffer before they laugh.' No comedian more vividly expressed a sense of life's futility in his work: in some ways his whole career represented a Galton and Simpson episode, the refusal to admit to his own failure writ large. Ultimately he was Humpty Dumpty, continually pushing himself off an ever-growing wall of self-aggrandisement for our amusement until reality caught up with the artifice, the laughter dispersed and there was nobody around to pick up the pieces, let alone mend them. To have grown up with him is to have acquired a guardian angel for one's own pain and disgruntlement, one's doubts and despair. Certainly with Hancock hovering over one's shoulder, the world becomes an easier place in which to navigate the trials of modern living. We all want to curse the car park attendant or the person in the ticket office, the pompous bureaucrat or the spineless politician. His indignation is our indignation shared, and in that sense he represents every single one of us. A positive force for life, he'll endure as long as blood is given.

Of all the interviews I conducted for this book the one with Graham Stark was especially affecting. The gleam in the eyes of this comedy stalwart is as bright as ever, although his mobility is not all it should be. Having said my farewell, I was a few paces down his drive when I heard him zimmering after me, calling me back. Over one final handshake he was concerned to make one last point clear: 'Please realise that for all his faults Hancock was not an arsehole. A lot of them were, but Tony was just a very sad man.' One day George Fairweather found his friend feeling low: 'He wanted pity and all that. I said, "You, a star, wanting pity from me, a semi-pro! Rubbish! You ought to go and see a psychiatrist," and he said, "I have." "Honestly?" "Yes, I went to the best in Harley Street." I said, "What did he say?" He said, "After an hour with you, Mr Hancock, I'm going to see *my* bloody psychiatrist!"' That was Hancock. Funny and sad. Sad and funny. Eeyore to the end.

INDEX